D0912175

THE TASK OF OLD TESTAMENT THEOLOGY

The Task of Old Testament Theology

Substance, Method, and Cases

Essays by

Rolf P. Knierim

William B. Eerdmans Publishing Company
Grand Rapids, Michigan / Cambridge, U.K.

© 1995 Wm. B. Eerdmans Publishing Co.
255 Jefferson Ave. S.E., Grand Rapids, Michigan 49503 /
P.O. Box 163, Cambridge CB3 9PU U.K.
All rights reserved

Printed in the United States of America

00 99 98 97 96 95   7 6 5 4 3 2 1

Library of Congress Cataloging-in-Publication Data

Knierim, Rolf P., 1928-
The task of Old Testament theology: essays / by Rolf P. Knierim.
p.   cm.
Includes bibliographical references (p.).
ISBN 0-8028-0715-1 (paper: alk. paper)
1. Bible. O. T. — Theology. I. Title.
BS1192.5.K538   1995
230 — dc20   95-20781
CIP

To

Hildegard

Contents

Foreword

This book is about biblical thinking. It is for biblical scholars and everyone alike who reads the Bible. Normally and inevitably, we have been preoccupied with the meaning of the ancient texts for us today. However, biblical thinking is first of all concerned with the understanding of the relationship of the biblical texts within the total Bible itself. This relationship is not self-evident. It has always required and continues to require an understanding on behalf of the Bible itself which we ourselves must bring to the Bible through the process of our own thinking.

In 1955, my first year as an associate pastor in Germany, I published a reflection in the monthly newsletter for the congregation entitled "Biblisches Denken" (biblical thinking). It was written to laypeople who, by years of religious education, by biblical preaching and study in church, and by daily reading of the Bible in their homes, had a considerable knowledge of the biblical texts. Because the Bible was the compass for their lives, their need for understanding its texts in the context of the entire Bible was all too obvious.

Little did I fathom at the time that the task of biblical thinking was to become the mainstay of my professional life for the following decades until today. And although I inevitably have had to be involved in the scholarly side of the task — even more modestly confined to the understanding of the Jewish Bible, the Christian Old Testament — I have never believed that biblical thinking is reserved only for the scholars.

The year 1955 was for me highlighted by the conclusion of my formal theological studies, the beginning of my parish ministry six weeks later, and between these two events by Hildegard's and my wedding. Twenty years earlier, after Easter 1935, the two of us had as first and second graders attended the same school class. Particularly, we had daily — and pretty exclusively — been walking home together after school. This book is singularly dedicated to Hildegard. To begin listing the reasons for this dedication would be futile. It would only marginalize its totality, which comes from the heart.

Claremont, California
Easter 1995

ROLF P. KNIERIM

Introduction: On the Essays in This Volume

A. The essays for this volume were selected because of their overall focus on the method for, and their use of case studies in, Old Testament theology. Other essays already published or on file which do not exemplify the task of Old Testament theology, or exemplify it less, were excluded from the collection.

Although the juxtaposition of essays in this volume represents the format of an anthology, and although the individual essays are the result of often-necessary attention to specific subjects in the process of my work during more than twenty-five years, the collection reflects an overall focus more than a random one, just as the nature of work in the essays themselves is — or is intended to be — more than incidental or eclectic methodologically.

It is clear to me that the conceptual relationship among the essays is, while on occasion explicitly stated or implicitly apparent, not yet programmatically defined. This could be done, but it would require a still additional essay. This operative deficit may influence the reader to become part of the heuristic systematizing process by interpreting the kinds of relationship her/himself.

I am also aware that the titles and foci of the essays approach the task from various possible angles, such as from exegesis of a text or a key word or a cluster of words or its concept, or from a topical angle, or toward substantive conceptualization, especially toward the conceptualization of the diversity of discussed subjects. Indeed, the variety of approaches, procedurally or substantively, points to the principle of openness in approach to the task as long as the task itself is pursued.

It is just this openness in approach that enables us to apply Old Testament theological interpretation to any subject relevant within the Old Testament's horizon. As long as it is based on the coherent conceptualization of the task, it represents a decisive advantage, not only because it precludes one dogmatized and stifling approach but also because it is freed from the stranglehold of questions that predetermine what may or may not be discussed and that even predetermine the answers. Lastly, the criterion for any of the published works on Old Testament theology is whether or not it meets the conditions for the theological task proper in Old Testament interpretation and not, at least not so much, whether it addresses some subjects while missing others, or whether it says it all at once.

B. Some of the essays were originally published elsewhere, some in English, some in German, some in Portuguese. The essays on "Food, Land, and Justice," on "Hope in the Old Testament," on "The Spirituality of the Old Testament," on "I. Exegesis of Psalm 19" in the first part of "On the Theology of Psalm 19," "On the Contours of Old Testament and Biblical Hamartiology," on "A Posteriori Explorations," and "On Gabler" are herewith published for the first time.

The first three essays, "The Task of Old Testament Theology," "Responses to 'The Task of Old Testament Theology,'" and "On the Task of Old Testament Theology," belong together. Together they demonstrate the inevitable and heuristic process of the ongoing discussion, and especially the invaluable contribution by critical colleagues not only to the advancement of the discussion in dialogical discourse but also to any individual's — certainly my own — world of thought.

Most of the previously published essays have undergone clarifications, substantive as well as stylistic in nature. If there is something like a "canonic" edition, it exists in their presently published form. Especially the four essays subsumed under "The Interpretation of the Old Testament" have since their original publication in Portuguese received some significant expansions.

C. I wish to express my sincere appreciation to a number of senior Old Testament Ph.D. students who as my research associates provided significant and competent support in the process toward the publication of this book. Early on, Randy Merritt and Michael Phelps helped editorially. Brenda Hahn and Mignon Jacobs, assisted by Sandra Hawk, initiated the system of the indexes, a task completed by Mignon Jacobs and David Palmer; and David Palmer outdid himself reading the galleys with me. Naturally, all responsibility rests with me.

Last but not least, I remain as always greatly indebted to the Institute for Antiquity and Christianity and the Claremont Graduate School for providing decisive institutional support.

Abbreviations

I. Miscellaneous Abbreviations and Symbols

BCE	before common era
CE	common era
Dtr	Deuteronomistic source
Fest.	*Festschrift*
hiph.	hiphil
J	Yahwistic source
LXX	Septuagint
MT	Masoretic Text
P	Priestly source
pi.	piel
RP	Redactor of Priestly source

II. Publications

AB	Anchor Bible
AnBib	Analecta biblica
AT	American Translation
ATANT	Abhandlungen zur Theologie des Alten und Neuen Testaments
BETL	Bibliotheca ephemeridum theologicarum lovaniensium
BFCT	Beiträge zur Förderung christlicher Theologie
BGBE	Beiträge zur Geschichte der biblischen Exegese
BHT	Beiträge zur historischen Theologie
Bib	*Biblica*
BKAT	Biblischer Kommentar: Altes Testament

ABBREVIATIONS

BWANT	Beiträge zur Wissenschaft vom Alten und Neuen Testament
BZAW	Beihefte zur *Zeitschrift für die alttestamentliche Wissenschaft*
EOTH	C. Westermann (ed.), *Essays on Old Testament Hermeneutics* (Richmond: John Knox, 1963)
ETL	*Ephemerides theologicae lovanienses*
EvT	*Evangelische Theologie*
FAT	Forschungen zum Alten Testament
FOTL	The Forms of the Old Testament Literature
FRLANT	Forschungen zur Religion und Literatur des Alten und Neuen Testaments
HAT	Handbuch zum Alten Testament
HBT	*Horizons in Biblical Theology*
IDB	G. A. Buttrick (ed.), *Interpreter's Dictionary of the Bible*
IDBSup	*Supplementary Volume to IDB*
JSOTSup	Journal for the Study of Old Testament — Supplement Series
NFT	New Frontiers in Theology
NRSV	*New Revised Standard Version*
OBT	Overtures to Biblical Theology
OTL	Old Testament Library
RGG[2,3]	*Die Religion in Geschichte und Gegenwart,* 2d ed., 3rd ed.
SBLDS	Society of Biblical Literature Dissertation Series
SBT	Studies in Biblical Theology
SJT	*Scottish Journal of Theology*
TDNT	G. Kittel and G. Friedrich (eds.), *Theological Dictionary of the New Testament*
TDOT	G. J. Botterweck, H. Ringgren, and H.-J. Fabry (eds.), *Theological Dictionary of the Old Testament*
THAT	E. Jenni and C. Westermann (eds.), *Theologisches Handwörterbuch zum Alten Testament*
ThB	Theologische Bücherei
TLZ	*Theologische Literaturzeitung*
TRE	*Theologische Realenzykopädie*
TWAT	G. J. Botterweck and H. Ringgren (eds.), *Theologisches Wörterbuch zum Alten Testament*
TZ	*Theologische Zeitschrift*
VTSup	Vetus Testamentum, Supplements
WBC	Word Biblical Commentary
WMANT	Wissenschaftliche Monographien zum Alten und Neuen Testament
ZAW	*Zeitschrift für die alttestamentliche Wissenschaft*
ZTK	*Zeitschrift für Theologie und Kirche*

The Task of Old Testament Theology

I. The Problem

A. The Old Testament contains a plurality of theologies. This fact is well established exegetically. It represents the theological problem of the Old Testament, and the discipline of Old Testament theology is constituted by the task of addressing this problem.[1] The theological problem of the Old Testament does not arise from the

1. Our focus on the Old Testament in its own right, while not exclusive, is legitimate. Its legitimacy does not depend on whether the Old Testament should be read together with the New Testament, or whether it should be read by itself before being read with the New Testament. This question should not be determined by an either/or. As long as both testaments are read together eventually, the question of where to start the process of reading is of secondary importance.

However, the claim that the Old Testament is theologically significant only when it is read in light of the New Testament, or of Christ, has imperialistic implications and is theologically counterproductive: it is imperialistic because it censures the Old Testament's theological validity by external criteria; and it is counterproductive because the theological significance of Christ or the New Testament, in as much as the Old Testament has something to do with them, cannot be substantiated with reference to the Old Testament's theological insignificance.

The legitimate focus on the Old Testament in its own right depends on some mutually supportive reasons. *First,* this corpus is claimed by the Jewish as well as by the Christian tradition. The two claims conflict, and an arbitrating third party is not present. It should be clear, at least for Christians, that an interpretation of their Old Testament must be mindful of that dissensus and, therefore, rest on the Old Testament itself and not on their New Testament or on an a priori combination of both. Such a combination of both testaments on the well-meant assumption by some Christians that Christianity is essentially Jewish because Jesus was a Jew does not stand up to scrutiny. Jews will not recognize any Jewishness in Christianity on the ground of Jesus' Jewishness, and rightly so. And for Christians, the condition and ground for the election of all humans into God's kingdom and salvation is not based on the Jewishness of Jesus. Salvation may have come from or through a Jew, but it is not Jewish in nature. Christians

separate existence of its particular theologies. It arises from their coexistence. The coexistence of these theologies in the Old Testament demands the interpretation of their relationship or correspondence, a task that is more than and different from the interpretation of each of them in its own right, which is done in historical exegesis — if exegesis does its work. While generating this central theological problem and demand, the Old Testament itself offers no direct approach or answer to it.

B. In the history of the discipline of Old Testament or biblical theology, the ever-increasing awareness of the plurality of theologies, as well as the danger of the Old Testament's theological disintegration and atomization implied in that plurality, has been met with attempts to identify holistic dimensions or perspectives which pervade all the Old Testament scriptures, messages, or theologies, or which embrace or undergird them. In fact, one of the primary postulates for the task of Old Testament theology has been that the Old Testament must be understood as a whole. The implication seems universal that as soon as a holistic dimension can

---

owe Jews a great debt indeed, and for more than one reason, but Christianity is not essentially Jewish.

The recognition that Jews are not Christians, and that by far most Christians are not Jews, has nothing to do with racism. It amounts to a mutual recognition of difference. However, the Christian designation of the Jewish Bible as their Old Testament must not mean "passed away, inferior, invalidated, abolished." It can only mean antecedence to the New Testament historically, even as this antecedence is not the basis for determining the relationship of the two testaments.

Secondly, the Christian tradition has distinguished, in essence, between two testaments in its Bible. Their relationship has been subject to varying and often controversial interpretations. However, each interpretation has always claimed to be legitimate, and not a usurpation or imperialization of one testament by the other. This claim must be taken seriously. The proper way for the Christian tradition to submit to its standards is to recognize the Old Testament in its own right before its relationship with the New Testament is determined.

Thirdly, there are, in a substantive sense, not only continuity and congruency connecting both testaments, but also discontinuity and incongruency separating them. The questions remain open, and indeed undecided, as to which of the testaments interprets which and in such interpretation what is the role of continuity or discontinuity, or whether either of the two testaments should be the basis for the interpretation of the other. This open situation suggests that the case not be prejudged in advance, and that each testament be understood as a whole in its distinctiveness before both are compared.

It is true that the title "Old Testament" presupposes the "New Testament" and, hence, the Christian Bible. This fact does not mean, however, that the Old Testament cannot be interpreted in its own right. It only means that the relationship of the two testaments must also be determined. Under discussion is whether this relationship is to be determined prior to and as the basis for, or after and on the basis of, their independent interpretation.

Likewise, nothing is said against the need for a biblical theology. Emphasized is only that the approach to it must be based on a genuine comparison of the theologies of the two testaments for which the independent interpretation of each is at least as viable a starting point as their correlated interpretation from the outset.

be discerned the plurality of theologies in the Old Testament can be regarded as an enriching phenomenon rather than as a critical problem because the whole by definition represents nothing other than the semantic homogeneity of the plurality.

This implication is indefensible.[2] For example, the fact that a plurality of theologies is held together or even generated by a holistic reality says *eo ipso* nothing about the kinds of their relationship, i.e., whether they agree or disagree, and says even less about the degree to which certain theologies are related. What is under discussion can be exemplified by the two types of holistic reality that have played the dominant role in the recent discussion: tradition history and the canon.

1. Ancient Israel's theological tradition history, certainly a type of holistic reality, generated the plurality of Yahweh-theologies. Yet the same holistic process did not clarify whether and how the theologies generated by it correspond to one another. It did not clarify the nature of the theological plurality even as it created that plurality. It is one thing to affirm all the Old Testament's theologies as the outgrowth of the tradition history of Israel's Yahweh-faith. It is quite different to ask how they are related among themselves. The question raised in the latter is not at all resolved by what is affirmed in the former; nor is the answer to this question of the relatedness of the different theologies a negligible issue. As long as the nature of the plurality, i.e., the relationship of the many theologies among one another, did not become self-evident through the historical process, the unavoidable result was that the dynamic process of tradition history generated the problem of the relationship of these theologies even as it generated their plurality. It generated the plurality of theologies as a central theological problem, and ever more so as new generations continued extending the process.

2. The study of the understanding of the holistic dimension or perspective in the history of our discipline is fascinating. The book by H.-J. Kraus, *Die Biblische Theologie: Ihre Geschichte und Problematik* (Neukirchen-Vluyn: Neukirchener, 1970), offers a convenient point of entry, among others. Attempts have been made to define the whole in terms of a thematic-theological unity pervading the texts themselves. Essentially, they have turned out to be unsuccessful. Again, the whole is seen as something in addition to or different from the texts, yet something that embraces or undergirds the texts, and of which the texts, messages, or theologies are a part: a common ontology such as a dynamic Yahweh-word-reality; an evolutionary or universal-historical process, or a process of some other sort; Israel's common theological, credo-oriented tradition history; the history of Israel's living faith-community; Israel's common affirmation of the oneness and exclusivity of Yahweh; the canon of scriptures; and so on. Occasionally, it is asserted that the whole as a postulate for Old Testament theology must consist of the sum total of exegesis. Such an understanding of the whole is obviously deficient. The sum total of exegesis demonstrates the plurality of theologies, and hence, the theological problem. This problem cannot be answered by an exegetical summary, no matter how complete.

The review of the history of this issue and of current literature shows that we urgently need a critical scrutiny of the assumptions and definitions of the notion of the whole which are in use, as well as a valid theory of it. The same is true for the widespread uncritical use of the notion of plurality and pluralism, and finally for the relationship between holistic and pluralistic reality.

Thus, the entirety of this process of tradition history is essentially pluralistic. The whole process is not the answer to the problem arising from the plurality of ancient Israel's theologies because it is itself the primary reason for that problem. The holistic dimension of Israel's tradition history, therefore, offers no basis for solving the problem arising from the plurality of the Old Testament's theologies. It partakes in that problem and is itself in need of theological clarification from a different type of theological vantage point.

2. The canon has finalized the problem. In the process of canonization, authoritative theological traditions from many generations and diverse settings were condensed into close juxtaposition on the same synchronic level. In the canon, they have come together face to face — so to say — in conference, and their canonic situation, if it means anything, authoritatively demands the clarification of their relationship. The question of whether or not the various theological positions in the Old Testament are substantively or semantically in agreement, and if they are, of how they appear to be related or can become related, becomes the key problem precisely because of the legitimate and simultaneous canonic coexistence of these theological positions. In generating this problem without resolving it, the canon itself calls for the discernment of a theological criterion for the purpose of its own proper theological understanding.[3]

C. The holistic dimensions that pervade or encompass the plurality of the Old Testament's theologies do not resolve the problem of the relationship of those theologies or, for that matter, of the nature of the Old Testament's theological pluralism. The discussion must focus on the Old Testament's pluralism itself. This pluralism represents a fundamental problem precisely because it reveals *eo ipso*

3. For the history of the major problems of Old Testament theology, of biblical theology, and of the canon which is presupposed in this paper, see among others, R. C. Dentan, *Preface to Old Testament Theology,* rev. ed. (New York: Seabury, 1963); R. E. Clements, *One Hundred Years of Old Testament Interpretation* (Philadelphia: Westminster, 1976); G. Hasel, *Old Testament Theology: Basic Issues in the Current Debate,* 4th ed. (Grand Rapids: Eerdmans, 1991); B. S. Childs, *Biblical Theology in Crisis* (Philadelphia: Westminster, 1970); H.-J. Kraus, *Die Biblische Theologie: Ihre Geschichte und Problematik* (Neukirchen-Vluyn: Neukirchener, 1970); K. Haacker and others, *Biblische Theologie heute: Einführung-Beispiele-Kontroversen,* Biblisch-Theologische Studien 1 (Neukirchen-Vluyn: Neukirchener, 1977); Henning Graf Reventlow, *Hauptprobleme der alttestamentlichen Theologie im 20. Jahrhundert* (Darmstadt: Wissenschaftliche Buchgesellschaft, 1982); and most recently, the important work by S. J. DeVries, *The Achievements of Biblical Religion: A Prolegomenon to Old Testament Theology* (Lanham, MD: University Press of America, 1983). Cf. also the essays by B. S. Childs, J. D. G. Dunn, G. F. Hasel, and W. Zimmerli in *Horizons in Biblical Theology* 4/1 (1982). This essay cannot endeavor to document all the aspects that have played a role in the history of the discipline. Such documentation is available in the literature just listed and elsewhere. Nor can I afford to document all the positions in the past and current discussion with which I agree and from which I differ. The informed reader will no doubt know where the agreements and the differences are.

nothing about the kinds and degrees in which the many theologies correspond to each other, and because this pluralism may represent a chaotic reality just as much as a harmonious one. The Old Testament's pluralism may mean either that the various theologies are mutually inclusive, compatible, and homogeneous, or that they are mutually exclusive, incompatible, and heterogeneous. They may be subservient or dominant to one another, compete against each other, or coexist in mutual isolation from one another. The theological pluralism of the Old Testament is in principle an ambiguous phenomenon which may be either meaningful and justifiable or meaningless and unjustifiable.[4] Its theological identity and validity are not constituted by the fact of its existence. The fact of its existence is itself subject to theological scrutiny, identification, and validation. Such scrutiny, identification, and validation can only take place through the examination of the relationship or correspondence of the individual theologies within this theological pluralism. This examination must concentrate on the semantic aspect of their relationship and, therefore, must involve above all the comparison of their contents. It must focus on the substantive issues addressed in the theologies contained in Israel's tradition history and in the canon, rather than on that tradition history or the canon as the substantive issue. Finally, it must ask what the issue *("die Sache")* is all about in the comparison of the many issues *("im Vergleich der Sachen")*.

I wonder what would have happened in Jerusalem around 612 BCE had an encounter taken place between the deuteronomic theologians, the Jehovist, the priestly temple theologians, sages, and Jeremiah, Zephaniah, Nahum, and Habakkuk; or a hundred years later, around 515 BCE, how a theological encounter would have looked with all of those just mentioned present, but now also with the addition of Ezekiel and his school, the deuteronomistic school, Deutero- and Trito-Isaiah and their disciples, and Haggai and Zechariah as well. Unfortunately, we are only left with their juxtaposition in the canon but not with any discussion about their relationship, neither their own discussion nor a discussion by those who juxtaposed them canonically. At this point the theological problem of their plurality appears. If we accept their coexistence at face value without asking how they relate to one another, we neglect the possibility of essential theological ambiguity or heteronomy in their pluralism. In effect, they would then be theologically valid because they exist as part of the tradition, and not because of what they say. The fact of their being part of tradition would guarantee their right to exist regardless of their theological identity, and their right to exist would prove that they are right. Differences in substance, in kind and degree, would be irrelevant and negligible. Such a

4. The classic example in the Bible is Paul's discussion with the Corinthians. This discussion involves two mutually exclusive kinds of pluralism. The pluralism of the Corinthians, a Christian congregation, was chaotic and self-destructive. Paul's own understanding of plurality reflects the orderly relationship of the members in the body subordinate to its head. On the basis of his understanding of proper plurality, Paul rejected the pluralism of the Corinthians.

pragmatic and traditionalistic understanding of pluralism allows as much for the relativization and devaluation of what is important as for the overvaluation of or even the monopolization by what is less or not important. Ultimately, it is capable of neutralizing substantive theological distinctions and of establishing indifference or arbitrariness as the highest value. Then, the preponderance of the interpreter's subjectivity would replace her/his submission to priorities that can be discerned in the Old Testament itself. It is time for us to demythologize pluralism.

As soon as we recognize that the Old Testament's theological pluralism is itself under theological scrutiny, we will be forced to ask whether these theologies are semantically compatible or not, and what the criteria are under which they can be legitimately related to one another. The Old Testament has not solved this task for us. It is not its own theology. But it has posed the problem for us, and we must clarify it or we will not know how to read the Old Testament theologically.

D. The theological problem of the Old Testament's pluralism comes into focus even more when we look at it from the point of theological substance. All theologies in the Old Testament are united in affirming Yahweh as the one and only God. Yet at the same time, their explications of this affirmation vary or differ. These varying or differing explications of the oneness and exclusivity of Yahweh reach to the heart of the theological problem of the Old Testament, especially as they coexist in the canon.

It is true that Yahweh has acted and spoken in many ways and that humans, especially his people, can approach and witness to Yahweh in many ways. However, this affirmation fails to address the real problem, namely, whether the various and diverse explications of Yahweh self-evidently reflect the oneness of Yahweh in the richness of his manifestations, or whether they reflect many and different Yahwehs and, in effect, reflect the witnesses to different gods in the Old Testament. Let there be many ways to God! But how do we know that they all lead to the same God, and not to many gods? We have no problem with the pluralism of the Old Testament's mono-Yahwism or monotheism; but we have a fundamental problem with the evidence for monotheism in the Old Testament's theological pluralism. Because of this pluralism, the affirmed monotheism is no longer self-evident. It can only become evident if we can show that the pluralism itself has a monotheistic structure. As long as this problem is not clarified we do not know whether the structure of the Old Testament's theological pluralism is monotheistic and in accord with the affirmation of the oneness of Yahweh, or whether it is polytheistic. Ultimately, we cannot know what the Old Testament means when affirming Yahweh.[5]

5. To those for whom this analysis appears unnecessarily abstract and pessimistic, I should like to point out that it keeps just as much of an eye on the controversial understanding of the God of the Old Testament throughout the entire history of the Church (from Marcion via the Reformers up to Harnack, Bultmann, et al.) as it does on theoretical arguments and, above all, on

For the examination of the monotheistic structure of the Old Testament's theological pluralism the question of how the individual theologies relate or correspond to one another becomes all the more important. In fact, it appears to be the only way by which to substantiate theologically the Old Testament's claim to monotheism. Once again, and now for the theological reason proper, the task before us is the examination of the correspondence or relationship of the Old Testament's theologies themselves. Under discussion is the substantive or semantic structure of the Old Testament's pluralism, as well as its theological identity and validity. This is the task of Old Testament theology because it reflects the Old Testament's central problem. For such an examination, we need the proper criteria. These criteria have to be drawn from within the Old Testament itself. Their discernment and definition are the task of the methodology of or the prolegomena to Old Testament theology.

II. The Criteria

Our discussion so far points out that we need to determine a basis from which to conceptualize the Old Testament's theology. This basis apparently must be found in the comparison of the Old Testament's theologies themselves. For such a process we need guidelines.

A. Inadequate Criteria. Before discussing the guidelines proper, I will list some notions that are inadequate as a basis because they provide no access to solving the theological problem posed by the plurality of theologies in the Old Testament. These include:

1. The notion of Yahweh's oneness and exclusivity, or of the Old Testament's mono-Yahwism. This notion does not explain the nature of Yahwism's pluralism. In fact, its own intelligibility depends on the evidence of the monotheistic structure of Yahwism's theological pluralism. However, the very fact of the affirmation of Yahweh's oneness demands that the theological pluralism be explained, justified, and validated as nothing less than the explication of the one and the same Yahweh.

2. The personalistic structure of religiosity found in the Old Testament, its I-Thou existential encounter theology. Apart from the fact that many texts project no such encounter structure, the explications of this structure of religiosity are potentially just as theologically heteronomous as any other form of theological pluralism.

---

the problems posed by the actual comparison of many of the Old Testament's own theologies. By analogy, we must ask whether the understanding of Christ as expressed in diverse theological interpretations triggered by the New Testament is at times so controversial among Christians, today as throughout history, that they reflect a polytheistic more than a monotheistic Christology or Christianity.

3. The notion of Yahweh's presence. Undoubtedly also very important, it is fundamentally pluralistic, and hence in need of a theological criterion by which the fundamentality of this presence and the interrelationship of its various modes can be discerned. The presence itself does not offer such a criterion. Other gods are present, as well, directly or indirectly, in revealed or hidden fashion, and elusively.

4. The notion of kerygma, or word of God in forms of human proclamation. This is not a sufficient criterion upon which to base an Old Testament theology. Not only is the Old Testament literature not all kerygmatic, technically speaking, but the kerygmata, also, partake in the theological pluralism and its problem.

5. Conversely, the notion of the history of the living faith-community behind the Old Testament's theologies provides no adequate basis for an Old Testament theology. Undoubtedly, the Old Testament reflects that history. Unfortunately, the intensity as well as the continuity of Israel's faith in Yahweh also generated the pluralistic understandings of Yahweh. No heretic has ever been impious. Neither has piety ever guaranteed that the manifold ways of understanding are God's and not just those of the pious soul, nor has it agreed on how these ways are related to one another.

6. The same is true for all other models in which tradition-history may be conceived, be it in the dialectic of word and action, of revelation and faith, in dynamic vitality in which past, present, and future converge and keep moving forward, etc.

7. Notions such as revelation, inspiration, word of God, and spirituality are not sufficient criteria for establishing Old Testament or biblical theology. We all affirm that the entire Old Testament is revealed, word of God, inspired. The more we affirm it, the more we intensify the problem because what is revealed, inspired, and word of God is the Old Testament's theological pluralism. We intensify both the unclarity concerning the inter-relationship of its revealed theologies and the possibility of a polytheistic understanding of revelation.

8. I finally must emphasize what has often been said, that the substantive plurality of the Old Testament's theologies renders it impossible for us to understand it in terms of unity under a singular theme identifiable everywhere. The covenant motif is the example *par excellence.* Its theological problem is not so much that the Old Testament does not everywhere talk about covenant or in terms of covenant, even as one may presuppose the covenant-community everywhere behind the texts. Its problem is the fact that the covenant-community and its texts speak of a sequence of various covenants which raises the problem of their remaining validity and of their relationship to each other. This problem is not solved by the Old Testament, but indeed represents the theological question which it poses. Similar things can be said about concepts such as messianism, prophecy and fulfillment, forgiveness, salvation, torah, law, etc.

B. Adequate Criteria. In order to determine the relationship among the Old

Testament's theologies we must be able to discern theologically legitimate priorities. We must ask which theology or theological aspect or notion governs others, and which is relative to, dependent on, or governed by others. Ultimately, we must ask whether there is one aspect that dominates all others, is therefore fundamental, and must be understood as the criterion for the validity of all others.

Such relating of theological aspects according to priorities is often done in the Old Testament itself. In fact, it is deeply rooted in Israel's understanding of reality and history and in its ontology and sociology. The same is especially true for the composition of text units. Anyone who has ever studied the relationship of parts in the semantic structure of a text unit has been confronted with this basic phenomenon. Also, the search for priorities in such relationships should surprise no one. Wherever and whenever the Bible was and is read, priorities have been at work, whether accounted for or not. The problem is the grounds on which they are chosen, not that they are at work. The grounds or criteria according to which we define priorities is therefore the question that demands attention.[6]

1. The criteria for discerning the theologically legitimate priorities must obviously be found in primarily substantive aspects. They depend on what is said, and not equally as much on how, where, when, or how often something is said. It is irrelevant in the canonic convention of the Old Testament's theological tradition history and form sociology whether a decisive theological argument was made more or less often than others; whether it was made by a historian drawing from the past, a prophet looking toward the future, a priest, a sage, or a layperson; or whether it was made by a man or a woman. It is equally irrelevant whether an argument was made early or late in the history of Israel's faith, or at its "axis-time." Why should any of these different types of Yahweh's servants or their time have per se a greater validity than any other? Also, why should any generic form of language — narrative, instructing, legal, prophetic, proverbial, hymnic, complaining, poetic, prosaic — have an a priori theological priority over the others? Why should the "telling of the story" (which covers only part of the Old Testament language anyway) be theologically more or less important than language speaking

6. These questions and problems clearly set the task of Old Testament theology apart from the task of Old Testament exegesis. They are not germane to the methodological repertoire of historical exegesis. They establish Old Testament theology as a necessary discipline in its own right. It presupposes exegesis, but its task is, strictly speaking, not to provide a sum total of exegesis, something like an appendix to an exegetical commentary. Nor do works in which theological notions are merely juxtaposed, as in a theological dictionary, deserve the name "Theology." Nor must Old Testament theology have to recount the history of the Old Testament's theologies as is done in a history of Israelite religion or even of Israelite literature. Old Testament theology must systematize the theological traditions of the Old Testament. A good eye-opener in this respect, at least for theological students, is to ask how the chapters in one or several available Old Testament theologies are related to one another as parts of a systematic whole.

in systematic concepts? Every exegete knows that the Old Testament also speaks conceptually in terms of doctrine. Moreover, the exegesis of every text shows that form of expression and conceptual understanding are intrinsically interrelated semantically, and that one form of its expression can be transformed into others. We must look for criteria that reflect the heart of the theological substance.[7]

2. We must focus on those criteria by which priorities among the theological arguments themselves can be distinguished.

a. The Old Testament's theologies are expressions of Israel's Yahweh-spirituality. In their center stands Israel's experience of its encounter with Yahweh, and its affirmation of his oneness and exclusivity. This spirituality pervades the entire Old Testament and its tradition history. This spirituality finds its particular expressions in Israel's knowledge of Yahweh's initial and ongoing revelations, in its remembrance and worship of Yahweh, and in its exclusive commitment to Yahweh. This spirituality reflects an anthropology in which a community experiences itself as structured theocentrically and monotheistically, and not anthropocentrically or polydynamistically. Invariably, Old Testament theology from the outset must focus on the central aspect of Israel's experience of Yahweh's oneness and exclusivity if it wants to address its proper subject.

However, this aspect represents only the presupposition for the problem which Old Testament theology must address. In fact, it creates the theological problem. For when affirming Yahweh's oneness and exclusivity, the Old Testament speaks neither about a lone Yahweh in splendid isolation nor solely about the encounter between Yahweh and Israel. Yahweh relates in many ways to many realms of reality, and vice versa. The manifoldness of these relationships between Yahweh and reality, and of the types of these relationships, actually constitutes the particular question by which the interpretation of the plurality of the Old Testament's theologies, i.e., their relationship to each another, is guided. As long as these questions are not clarified, the nature of Israel's entire Yahweh-spirituality remains ambivalent. These questions also reveal that the criteria for understanding Yahweh are not found in Israel's Yahweh-centrism, mono-Yahwism, or monotheism, but that the criteria for the theological integrity and validity of Yahweh-centrism, Israel's mono-Yahwism or monotheism, are to be found in those aspects which show the extent and the modes of Yahweh's relationship to reality.

b. The Old Testament, strictly speaking, does not speak about Yahweh. It speaks about the relationship between Yahweh/God and reality. The interpretation of this aspect represents the basic substantive task of Old Testament theology. More

7. This statement does not mean that the socio-historical data are theologically irrelevant. They indeed express in an endless variety of ways that theology is a concrete witness which is always related to actual reality. However, neither a witness nor its concreteness is a sufficient criterion for true knowledge of Yahweh. They are themselves subject to scrutiny with respect to whether their actualizations reflect what must be said in the context of Yahweh's total dominion.

specifically, Old Testament theology must interpret the relationship between Yahweh/God and reality with respect to the Old Testament's affirmation of Yahweh's oneness and exclusivity.

In view of this task, two questions are constitutive. First, *how* are Yahweh and reality seen as related, and *how* are the various modes of this relationship related one to another? And secondly, *with whom* and *with what* is Yahweh related, and especially, how are the various realms with whom and with which Yahweh is related, related among one another? The first question refers to qualitative notions in relationship while the second question refers to relationship's quantitative notion or to its extent.

1) The qualitative modalities of Yahweh's relationship to reality are reflected in words or word fields and concepts such as creation, sustenance, election, liberation, covenant, law, justice, righteousness, peace, atonement, forgiveness, judgment, mercy, and so on. We find these aspects everywhere in their respective Hebrew word fields, and in smaller and larger text units.

With regard to the plurality of these aspects, Old Testament theology must explain how Yahweh through them relates to reality, and how reality through them responds to Yahweh. It must explain, so to say, Yahweh's ethos toward reality and reality's ethos toward Yahweh — obviously in this order.

But Old Testament theology especially must explain how these modes are related to one another. Once these questions are asked it becomes clear that Old Testament theology has more to do than juxtapose essays on biblical words or concepts or on biblical books in nice isolation from one another, as in Bible dictionaries, commentaries, Old Testament introductions, or histories of Israelite religion, or as in our libraries where Barth, Bultmann, Calvin, and Cobb stand peacefully side by side.

It is known, for example, that in many parts of the Old Testament, the relationship between liberation and commandment is understood to have a distinct and irreversible order. What seems to be less well known but quite clear in the Old Testament is the kind of relationship between liberation and justice. Both notions are different and must not be used interchangeably. They are related to one another in a distinct way in which liberation is neither the beginning nor the end of a process. It is always release from injustice, and it points toward the restoration or establishment of justice. It is itself an act of, and part of a process of, justice. The theology of liberation is not an independent theology in the Old Testament. It is a subchapter of a dominant theology in the service of which it stands: the theology of justice and righteousness.

This is not the place for examining the qualitative kinds and degrees of relationship between Yahweh and reality, and their relationship to one another. However, it is the place for emphasizing that herein lies the task of the Old Testament theologian, and that this task can be undertaken. In its pursuit we will discover semantic relationships and a semantic hierarchy in which priorities exist, in which theologies identify and validate each other in their respective place and function in relation to others, and in which ultimately appear those aspects which show what the relationship between Yahweh and reality is first, last, and always about.[8] It is true that God spoke of old to the ancestors of the early Christians "in many and various ways" (Heb 1:1). In fact, he not only spoke "by the prophets," he also acted. But much more is at stake. The "many and various ways" do not mean that every way has the same place and function in the order of things, and that every theologian or preacher can pick and choose or prioritize at will, at the neglect of true biblical priorities. He/she may not invert the biblical order of priorities and justify a pseudo-religion with reference to the pluralism attested to in the Bible. Heb 1:1 cannot be the basis for conceptualizing an Old Testament, New Testament, or biblical theology, or for understanding every part of the Bible to be on equal footing with every other part.

2) The quantitative aspect involves the extent or the realms of reality to which Yahweh is related, and the modes of their relationship to one another. In the Old Testament, there are three essential realms: the cosmic and natural world; corporate human existence, including Israel's; and individual human existence. In our terminology: cosmos and nature, history and society, and existentiality. Again, Old Testament theology must interpret how Yahweh is related to each of these realms, and vice versa. Especially, it must interpret how these realms are related to one another as they are related to Yahweh.

It is clear, for example, that in the Old Testament the cosmic and natural world and human history are related, just as Yahweh and history are related. The question we must ask is which of the two relationships is more fundamental, and thus, the basis for the other, i.e., which depends on which. For this type of question, the two-hundred-year-long history of our discipline finds us ill-prepared because that history has been preoccupied with the primary ontological and epistemological category of history, while cosmology and nature have fallen by the wayside. Ironically, the history of philosophy throughout the millennia has been amazingly in touch with the problem of cosmology and nature, and with what we have come to call natural science. By contrast, the history of biblical theology has virtually lost contact with natural science, an unjustifiable situation with respect to both the evidence in the Old Testament and our current situation. The question involves not only the aspect of the cosmos proper, but also the aspect of our earth and its natural life, which is bound to and dependent on the cosmic order, and which includes the provision of fertility, water, and food for the sustenance of the living. When has anyone bothered to include in an Old Testament theology a — massive! — chapter on a subject as trivial as a theology of food? Why should any theologian seriously take into account G. Dalman's monumental work *Arbeit und Sitte in*

8. In the New Testament (1 Corinthians 13), Paul knows of a "better" way and of the ultimate criterion.

Palästina[9] when doing theology? Is the provision by Yahweh of food for all the product of historical existence on which cosmos and nature depend, or is it primarily the product of the earth's cosmic-natural vitality, without which human history, including salvation history, and the believer's existence would cease to exist within less than a year? Which of these realms is the basis for which? Which depends on which, and which is independent of which, even as each is related to Yahweh in its own way? Certainly, history is seen as the peak, the goal, and the purpose of the creation of the world. But this does not mean that human history or existence is ever perceived as having nothing to do with the order of creation, or that the order of creation is not perceived as the criterion for the truth of history, even for the truth of the history of God's people.

Furthermore, Yahweh is not the God of creation because he is the God of the humans or of human history. He is the God of the humans and of human history because he is the God of creation.[10] For the Old Testament, just as for the New Testament, the most universal aspect of Yahweh's dominion is not human history. It is the creation and sustenance of the world. This aspect is at the same time the most fundamental because creation does not depend on history or existence, but history and existence depend on and are measured against creation.

Similar questions will have to be raised with regard to the relationship of humanity's and Israel's corporate existence, not only under the perspective of history, as is usually the case, but also under the perspective of their relatedness in the order of creation. Which of Yahweh's relationships to any of these realms is more fundamental and therefore has priority over which? The answers to these questions will also shed light on the problem of a particularistic or universalistic understanding of Yahweh as God.

As for human existence, is it, according to the Old Testament, isolated from the order of creation and from history, or is it dependent on and constituted by them? In the Old Testament's understanding of Yahweh's relationship to various realms of reality, where is the place and function of human existence in the totality of Yahweh's dominion?

c. I have argued that the interpretation of the relationship between Yahweh and reality involves two basic aspects: the qualitative and the quantitative. If we now ask which of these two aspects ultimately controls the other, we will realize that the quantitative aspect of the relationship between Yahweh and the totality of reality governs all the qualitative aspects just as it governs those quantitative aspects

9. G. Dalman, *Arbeit und Sitte in Palästina,* 7 vols. (Gütersloh: C. Bertelsmann, 1928-42).

10. Psalm 8 sees it well: humans stand on top of the pyramid of the order of creation, and just as they pray to Yahweh, they understand themselves as part of, and in the context of, the order of creation. It is in this context and on this basis, and not without them, that their historical existence can unfold and hopefully remain at the top of the pyramid onto which they have been placed.

concerning the less inclusive realms of Yahweh's dominion. The reason for this conclusion should be fairly obvious. Every exegete knows that the qualitative notions of justice, righteousness, liberation, peace, etc., are found in the relationship between Yahweh and every known realm of reality. Justice, peace, and/or liberation can involve the cosmic order, Israel's life, or the individual's life. They could be perceived universalistically, particularistically, or individualistically. On what ground, however, are we to decide in any qualitative relationship between Yahweh and various realms of reality how these realms are related to one another and which realm has priority over which? For example, are justice and righteousness in Israel revealed and required because they reflect Yahweh's relationship to the totality of his creation and of humanity, or because they stand for nothing but Yahweh's relationship to his elect regardless of his relationship to the rest of the world? Which realm of Yahweh's relationship to reality in justice and righteousness constitutes the ground and norm for which? Clearly, justice is indispensable, but the criterion for its theological validity and for its protection from perversion and manipulation is the relationship in justice between Yahweh and the total dimension of his dominion. To this realm, justice among the elect is accountable, otherwise it is not accountable to Yahweh in the totality of his dominion; toward this realm, it must be transparent; and by this realm, it is always transcended even as its actualization among the elect is socio-historically contingent.

1) The heuristic comparison of the modes and of the realms in which Yahweh and reality appear to be related shows that the aspect of the most universal extent of Yahweh's dominion represents the most fundamental theological criterion and, hence, the most fundamental theological priority. If Yahweh is not, in principle and before everything else, the God of all reality, he cannot be the one and only God because he is not God universal. Yahweh may be Israel's God in oneness and exclusivity, but if he is not Israel's God because he is first of all God of all reality and of all humanity, he is a nationalistic deity or an individualistic idol, one among others, actually a no-god. Without the critical notion of universality, the affirmation of Yahweh's oneness and exclusivity does not substantiate the affirmation of his true deity. This affirmation is substantiated only when Yahweh is perceived as the God of universal reality. The notion of universal reality, which is basically reflected in the notions of Yahweh's creation of and dominion over heaven and earth, is therefore the criterion for the Old Testament's affirmation of Yahweh as the universal God, and for his true deity. It is the only persuasive argument for the significance of monotheism.

2) The notions of Yahweh's universality and of universal reality complement each other. Universality is their common denominator. This horizon represents the most fundamental of all theological aspects in the Old Testament. It is most fundamental because it constitutes at the same time the ultimate criterion both for Yahweh's deity and for the dimension of his dominion. No other theological notion can compete with it. In fact, all others are relative to it. They receive their validity

from it. Moreover, Yahweh's relationship to universal reality as expressed in the theology of creation, in the final analysis, can be discerned as what is at issue in the Old Testament. In this horizon, human history, Israel's election, and individual existence receive their meaning because they all are part of and have their place and function in Yahweh's dominion of his world.[11] This horizon is not the only one in the Old Testament, but it is foundational to and the criterion for all others.

3) Finally, when the universal horizon of the relationship between Yahweh and reality is coordinated with the semantic hierarchy of the modes of relationship in these realms, the basic vantage point for the concept of Old Testament theology emerges. I have already suggested that the notions of justice and righteousness seem to be governing the other qualitative notions, and that they represent the most fundamental of the modes in which the universality of Yahweh's relationship with reality is perceived.[12] It also seems that the other modes are either gradationally relative to or elaborations of it. However, that may be in detail the ultimate concern discernible in the Old Testament, and hence, the ultimate vantage point from which to coordinate its theologies toward *the universal dominion of Yahweh in justice and righteousness.* This dominion is expressed time and again directly in the categories of cosmic nature, human history and existence, and most fundamentally in the theology of creation. Its interpretation represents the fundamental task of Old Testament theology. All other kinds and degrees of relationship between Yahweh and reality, both qualitative and quantitative, as well as their own correlations, are subservient to this dominion. They are not insignificant and must not be ignored, yet their place in the whole and, hence, the degree of their theological validity can be understood only to the extent to which they reflect implementations or manifestations of Yahweh's universal dominion in justice and righteousness. For such an understanding, it is not necessary that each of the Old Testament's theologies speaks of nothing other than universality and justice and righteousness. However, it is necessary to interpret how a qualitative notion relates to others, what the horizon of its extent is in a given text, and whether or not it can be understood as a case or paradigm for Yahweh's universal dominion and its fundamental nature.[13]

11. Jonah said it: "I am a Hebrew; and I fear Yahweh, the God of heaven, who made the sea and the dry land" (1:9).

12. Cf. H. H. Schmid, *Gerechtigkeit als Weltordnung,* BHT 40 (Tübingen: Mohr, 1968). This systematic conclusion is quite independent of the controversy over the historical origins of the concept of justice whether from the ancient Near Eastern cosmogonies or from the tradition of the ethos of clan solidarity. For the importance of the notion of justice and/or righteousness in connection with the universal dominion of God in the New Testament as well, cf., among others, Matt 6:33; Rom 1:17; 2 Pet 3:13. (Cf. Lloyd Gaston, "Abraham and the Righteousness of God," *Horizons in Biblical Theology* 2 [1980]: 39-68.)

13. E.g., the theology of Israel's relationship to the nations in the promised land in Deuteronomy raises questions as to how this theology corresponds with other theologies concerning the same issue, how it corresponds with the Old Testament's theologies of peace, and whether or not it can be considered a paradigm for Yahweh's universal justice and righteousness attested

C. The Twofold Task. I must now attempt to formulate summarily the task of Old Testament theology. This task is twofold.

1. Old Testament theology must first of all examine the semantic structure of the relationship between Yahweh and his world. In this pursuit, it must distinguish between Yahweh's relationship to the world and the world's relationship to Yahweh. Furthermore, it must distinguish between the quantitative extension and the qualitative nature of that relationship. Specifically, it must clarify, on the one hand, the order in which the quantitative components are set in relationship to each other and, on the other hand, the order in which the qualitative components are set in relationship to each other. Above all, it must identify those components which are fundamental and, thus, to which all others are accountable. In this paper they are assumed to be the theology of creation and dominion of the world (the most universal quantitative aspect) and the theology of justice and righteousness (the most fundamental qualitative aspect).

This first task is systematic in nature. It is guided by systematic questions which arise from the theological pluralism of the Old Testament. It draws its approach and its conclusions from substantive aspects, and avails itself of all the Old Testament scriptures regardless of their tradition-historical, generic, or canonical order. Its execution would have to fill the first, and programmatic, volume of an Old Testament theology. It is concerned not with one topic, a uniting theme, but with the criteria by which to relate all themes or *theologoumena* under theologically valid priorities.

2. Based on the understanding of the systematic relatedness of the Old Testament's theologies, Old Testament theology, secondly, must assess the individually exegeted messages, kerygmata, and/or theologies in the Old Testament in light of the semantic structure of the relationship between Yahweh and reality.[14]

The approach to this task can follow the tradition-historical development as far as we know it, or the canonic order of the books, or a systematic order as found in many publications. The choice between these approaches is relative. As long as the individual theologies are subject to confrontation with criteria that are decisive for all, neither a tradition-historical nor a canonical nor a thematic approach can, in principle, claim priority over the others.

---

to in other theological strata in the Old Testament. The interpretation of this issue is complex. Its task is very different from the exegesis of the deuteronomic theology. Cf. the essay "Israel and the Nations in the Land of Palestine in the Old Testament" in this volume.

14. This assessment involves a theological critique of the individual theologies in light of those theological criteria from the Old Testament that are foundational and represent its priorities. To those who say that such critique is illegitimate, I can only answer that such critique is part of the biblical tradition itself, and that it has always been part of the history of biblical interpretation either practiced programmatically or de facto without a single exception by anyone who has ever read the Bible. The question is what our criteria for a theological reading of the Bible are, and not whether a critical assessment of its theologies is legitimate. The alternative to such assessment amounts to the abandonment of any theologically accountable reading of the Scriptures.

The second task is important. For it is here in the texts that the meaning of it all becomes a matter of actual debate. The texts are not the criterion for their own validity. But without them, Yahweh's relationship to reality would remain speechless and removed from human experience. Less pressing is the ideal of an exhaustive completeness requiring the inclusion of all exegetical details ever discovered. The chances for such completeness become more and more remote every day. Moreover, such completeness is not mandatory for the validity of the program.

Conclusion

A. This is not the place for suggesting the actual outline of an Old Testament theology based on the criteria just discussed. Instead, I want to mention a number of points that highlight the different implications of the proposal presented here.

B. The need to discern kinds and degrees of quantitative and qualitative relationships among the Old Testament's theologies, by asking which embraces or governs which, amounts to the recognition of an order of semantic priorities in which the place and function, and therefore the validity, of theological notions or messages can be determined.

Likewise, the need to discern the most fundamental theological aspect (Yahweh's universal dominion in justice and righteousness — the aspect which expresses what talking about Yahweh and reality, Yahweh and Israel, Yahweh and people is ultimately all about) indeed amounts to the recognition of a theological aspect that is normative for all others. It amounts to the discernment of a canon in and for the canon.

C. Once these two principal heuristic guidelines for reading the Old Testament are identified, some differences come into focus.

1. Old Testament theology is not concerned with finding a unifying topic that replaces all others. Instead, it is concerned with criteria by which the various theologies can be correlated in terms of theological priorities, including the ultimate priority governing all others. The need for the process of working out these priorities remains, even if some of the substantive assumptions referred to in this paper should have to be updated or revised.

2. Old Testament theology is not conceptually based on traditionally assumed methodological antinomies such as concept versus story, idea versus text, theology versus message, kerygma versus reflection. None of these categories substantiates per se the theological validity of what is said; nor are there any texts, small or large, that reflect the surface structure or the story line only, and not also a conceptual depth structure. An Old Testament theology based on such antinomies

overlooks the fact that all of these categories represent modes of transformation in the interaction between language and meaning. But neither these modes nor the constant process of which they are a part constitutes theological validity per se. Old Testament theology must be based on the theological argument itself. It must be theology in the strict sense of the word.

3. Categories such as the Word of God, revelation, Yahweh's presence, inspiration, etc., provide no basis for solving the theological problem of the Old Testament. They have their place in the interpretation of Israel's theological anthropology, of Israel's knowledge of Yahweh, or of its theological spirituality, all of which are themselves subject to substantive theological criteria.

4. The function of the Old Testament theologian is neither descriptive nor confessional. It is systematic. In one way or another, Old Testament theology must be a systematic theology of the Old Testament, or an Old Testament theology in the singular is impossible. Under theological priorities discerned from within the Old Testament, it systematizes the plurality of theologies analyzed by exegesis, summarily described in the conclusions of or appendices to exegetical works, and provides the criteria for the accountability of what ought to be confessed. It is the indispensable and distinct relay station between exegesis and systematic theology or hermeneutics. In this place, the Old Testament theologian has to stand on the Old Testament's behalf. This task differs from the task of systematic theology or biblical hermeneutic because its criteria and agenda are intrinsic to and drawn from the Old Testament. It does not have to be unsystematic because dogmatic theology is systematic. The category "systematic" ought not to be reserved for systematic theology alone.

5. The conceptual basis for the systematic theology of the Old Testament is neither the view of the evolution or the continuity either of a central or several important motif(s) or of the believing community nor the prevalence of one setting or genre over others. The basis is the content of the decisive theological arguments themselves regardless of where, when, how, and by whom they are expressed. The criteria for the theological validity of any continuity or discontinuity, including the theological validity of the history of the believing community, are located in the arguments themselves, both in their relationship to one another and in light of Yahweh's universal dominion in justice and righteousness. They also represent the locus of the criteria for the validity of the forms and settings of these messages, theologies, ideas, concepts, motifs, stories, and kerygmata.

6. Such an Old Testament theology takes into account the extent to which the socio-historically contingent theologies in the Old Testament have potential for universalization in the horizon of Yahweh's universal dominion. This marks its point of critical difference from methods of theological interpretation such as allegory, typology, spiritualization, and midrash, or from methods of interpretation based on the assumption of the multilevel nature or of the multivalency of the Scriptures or of passages thereof. None of these methods as such guarantees that

the semantic potential of a text is examined in light of the theological criterion of Yahweh's universal dominion and its priorities. Moreover, the establishment of this criterion does not depend on any of these methods, nor, for that matter, on the method of historical exegesis. As soon as this criterion becomes the basic method for theological interpretation, and as soon as texts are read in light of it, the alternatives between the various methods of interpretation become relative. In fact, none of them is either valid or invalid by virtue of its methodological idiosyncrasy. Rather, the validity or invalidity of each depends on whether, in light of Yahweh's universal dominion and its priorities, it reveals either the potential of a text to point to that dominion or its resistance to that potential.

7. Also, the fact of the history of the ongoing validity and effectivity of texts *("der Wirkungsgeschichte von Texten"),* including the effectivity of Old Testament texts in the New Testament, provides no theological vantage point for an Old Testament theology. No one denies this fact. Yet this ongoing vitality and effectivity, this ever-new adaptation, reinterpretation, and new interpretation of texts, proves only the dynamic self-perpetuation of an institution in ever new facets — nothing more, nothing less. It does not demonstrate per se why any of its arguments is legitimate. For them to be considered legitimate by virtue of the fact that they are part of the process, especially of the process of the faith community, is not good enough. Every history of such ongoing vitality and effectivity is itself inescapably accountable to theological criteria that verify its legitimacy. Indeed, none should be recognized theologically until it has stood the test under the criterion of Yahweh's universal dominion in justice and righteousness, along with its subsequent priorities. We have every reason to emphasize this point. There are too many vital and effective *Wirkungsgeschichten* around that have little if anything to do with the Bible's central perception of God's dominion.[15]

8. The same is true also for the so-called charismatic or pneumatic element in interpretation. Charismatic or pneumatic interpretation can be pluralistically heteronomous. It can be true or false. Therefore, it must be guided and controlled by theologically legitimate criteria. Whenever it is so guided, such interpretation, indeed every particular interpretation so guided, becomes a legitimate charismatic or pneumatic event. This type of charismatic event gives interpretation its freedom. In fact, it represents the most authentic type of interpretation.

9. The type of theological interpretation proposed for the Old Testament can also be proposed for the religions of the ancient Near East. Ancient Israel's Yahweh-theology is part of the view of reality in the ancient Near East. It is a religious phenomenon. It is not theological whereas their views of reality are only religious.

15. For an example of the continuity of the vitality and effectivity of a stratum of biblical texts from ancient Israel to our times, basically sustained by the history of the believing community, and for the ambiguous quality of such a vitality, see the book by J. Ebach, *Das Erbe der Gewalt: eine biblische Realität und ihre Wirkungsgeschichte* (Gütersloh: Gerd Mohn, 1980).

Nor are their views nontheological because theology is reserved for Israel or Christianity. The religiosities of the ancient Near East and Israel developed theologies, all of which belong to the phenomenon and history of human religion. The theological task within this total religious environment would be to examine each theological system in its own right, and subsequently to compare the systems critically. Such a process would go a long way in demonstrating not only what they have in common and where they are different, but also where they complement and validate each other and where they do not.

10. The task of Old Testament theology as defined in this paper should also be to provide a fresh basis for examining the relationship of the two testaments of the Christian Bible, including the role of Jesus Christ in this relationship. I no longer believe that this relationship can be sufficiently explained on the basis of patterns such as Old and New, continuity in whatever form, promise and fulfillment in whatever form, one or more Old Testament aspects ending up in the New Testament, quotations of Old Testament passages in the New, etc. Nor is the thesis sufficient that the Old Testament must be interpreted from Christ, or Christ from the Old Testament. What is true is that both the Old and the New Testament, including Christ, must be interpreted in view of what can be discerned in either testament and in the Jewish tradition as God's universal dominion over his world, and the world's response to this dominion, and the priorities subsequent to this aspect. Such a vantage point may also offer a basis for a fresh review of the relationship between the Jewish and the Christian communities. We are dealing with the problem of the horizon in view of which not only the varying but also the conflicting traditions in the Old and New Testaments and in the Jewish-Christian relationship can be sifted and amalgamated.

11. Finally, Old Testament theological interpretation does not presuppose the production of comprehensive volumes. It need not always say it all to be legitimate, but what it says must rest on a foundation that is applicable to all. Likewise, it can be applied to the interpretation of texts or traditions or corpora or themes. It can be thematic or homiletical. Just as much as the selection of the point of access to the material can be variable and circumstantial, so can the choice of approach. Here is freedom for true plurality and flexibility. Decisive for any of these approaches is the interpretation of the chosen subject in its transparence in light of Yahweh's universal dominion, and the interpretation of its place, function, and the validity which it possesses in light of the discernible theological priorities. With these criteria in mind, I envision a thriving pluralism of teaching and preaching and, last but not least, of a specific genre of expertly executed theological essays, monographs, and dissertations.

Responses to "The Task of Old Testament Theology"

I. The Limited Task of Old Testament Theology

Walter Harrelson

The field of biblical studies has needed this lucid, ground-clearing essay for many years. It arrives at a time which may be propitious indeed, for many are ready and indeed eager to consider the fresh start that the author proposes. When one observes how Professor Knierim cuts through the plethora of perspectives, approaches, and notions, illuminating all of them as he orders and systematizes the materials of the field, one can only be deeply grateful for the clarity and the fresh perspectives that are provided.

This is a programmatic essay in the best sense of that term. It indicates our lack and need; it offers a few germinal theses and supports them with brief but weighty arguments; it shows what is wrong with alternative approaches; it gives clues for the wiser application of the approach laid out; it makes clear how such an approach avoids parochial or narrow perspectives; it claims for biblical studies some philosophical and theological undertakings that have been too long pushed off onto our colleagues; it is elegant and esthetically appealing and persuasive as well as closely reasoned; and it is sensitively put, avoiding all unnecessary or cheap polemics. I find the paper to have served the purposes for which it was sought, and to have been written magnificently.

My comments will be brief and limited to two points of some weight and one of perhaps minor interest and importance. The first concerns the author's understanding of Old Testament theology, an understanding which I share but which I believe needs to be identified very clearly for what it is and is not. Otherwise, the mode of argument in the paper may well not carry the weight and persuasive power that it can be claimed to have. The second is concerned with the way in which creation seems to dominate the discussion as the author deals with Yahweh's universal dominion. And the last, little point has to do with the use of the term "Yahweh."

The existence of many theologies in the Hebrew Bible constitutes the problem of Old Testament theology, Professor Knierim argues (pages 1-7). What is wrong with a rich pluralism, a lush variety, a many-faceted picture of the relation of God to the world, to Israel, to the individual? What demands the relating of these, the ordering of them into some hierarchy, the discovery of what is central and what is subordinate? One thinks of Gerhard von Rad's reply to the criticism of Walther Eichrodt. One can of course look finally for central and dominant perspectives in the theological outlooks of the traditions of Israel, but must one have a single, controlling concept or form of relation between God and the world, Israel, the individual in order to have an Old Testament theology as such?

Yes, says Knierim, if one intends to fulfill what is the actual, specific, indispensable task of Old Testament theology, or, for that matter, to fulfill the actual theological task of interpreting the religious literature and heritage of any community. Why? Because theology by definition has to do with the systematic ordering of thought, it involves comparison and contrast, the relating of this understanding or practice to that one, and the critical evaluation of life, thought, and ethos in light of the claims made within the tradition as to the truth and the fundamental meaning of it all. Old Testament theology is systematic, because it is Old Testament *theology.* The demand then for some qualitative and quantitative modalities of the relation of Yahweh to reality that will show themselves to be central, all-inclusive, and capable of being shown, by critical thought, to be central and all-inclusive *derives from this understanding of theology as a systematic endeavor.* It would not suffice just to describe what empirically seems to be some dominant perspective and then to call one's theology descriptive. It would not suffice to relate the several theologies to some other theological outlook and to show how nicely they correspond with that other outlook, for one must *systematize the variety* before one has done the theological task.

I think, therefore, that we need to underscore the point that our author's paper is describing and outlining a very concrete and specific task for Old Testament theology, or for any theology of a given body of literature, life, and tradition, and thus might have entitled his paper "The Limited Task of Old Testament Theology." All the other tasks of biblical scholarship have their weight and their place. But there should not be confusion: when we speak of Old Testament theology we are talking about the systematic and critical evaluation of the relation of the deity to the cosmos, to the community, to its individual members, as this relation is portrayed in the community's surviving materials available to the theologian.

My second point has to do with the dominance of the notion of creation in the author's sketching of the dominion of Yahweh over the cosmos. I like the emphasis upon creation very much and think it right for the biblical scholar to be summoned to join forces much more heartily with colleagues in the natural sciences than has been the case for decades. Knierim also makes it clear that he is speaking of Yahweh's universal dominion over the cosmos as a continuing reality. But he gives little if any attention to the eschatological perspectives of Old Testament thought, those found in cultic texts, in the prophetic literature especially, and in apocalyptically leaning or apocalyptic texts. This lack is regrettable, I believe, for such attention offers a way to relate the qualitative and the quantitative modalities of Yahweh's relation to the cosmos, in my judgment.

Qualitatively, we learn that Yahweh relates to the cosmos in justice and righteousness (the two terms are not identical, and need to be identified as to their precise meanings or fields of meaning), and quantitatively, we are reminded that Yahweh's relation is to the totality of the creation. That is right and is of fundamental importance for the new perspectives opened up by this immensely important paper. But we need to bear in mind that it is a *theological* judgment that Yahweh relates to the entire cosmos and that Yahweh does so in justice and righteousness.

Now the truth of the theological affirmations of the Old Testament is not established by historical existence, neither Israel's nor any other people's nor all people's. Nor is the truth of the affirmations established by the theological program as outlined by our author. That theological program gives us more, however, than a description of what the Israelites of biblical times thought about Yahweh's relation to the whole of the cosmos in justice and righteousness. It offers to us their view of how that relation in reality obtained: Yahweh's dominion over the cosmos in justice and righteousness was their central affirmation of faith, was that to which the community's thought inevitably led, whether or not all or most or many of the members of the community recognized this to be the case.

Now the Old Testament makes abundantly clear that Yahweh's dominion was recognized to be a hollow mockery for many, a cruel joke to some, and a banality of superficial religiosity to others. For this reason, I would like to see the author give more attention than he has in the present paper to the pictures of the Last Day, when Yahweh will be disclosed publicly, unmistakably, and enduringly, as exercising dominion over the cosmos in justice and righteousness. This forward dimension to biblical religion and thought helps, I think, to relate the qualitative and the quantitative dimensions or modalities of Yahweh's relation to the cosmos. It also makes clear that there are new elements in this dominion of Yahweh: it is not a matter of a return to the primordial "justice" of the creation; it is a matter of the consummation of Yahweh's "life" with the totality of the cosmos, a "life" marked by as yet to be discovered dimensions of justice and righteousness.

The term "Yahweh-spirituality" sets my teeth on edge and was the cause for me initially to ask whether the retention of the personal name for the deity is appropriate in this paper. As for "Yahweh-spirituality," could one not simply say "religious devotion to God"? But as to the name itself, is it not the case that the continued use of the personal name might well be an anachronism? I am confident that at least by the late seventh or early sixth century, if not earlier, this personal name had become the name for "the one who exercised dominion over the cosmos," and thus meant "the LORD." Our perpetuating the name Yahweh not only gives unnecessary offense to some religious sensibilities; it may also be misleading in terms of the history of Israelite religious development and in terms of Old Testament theology. Of course, our use of the name intends to maintain precisely the sense of personal being and of intimacy, between people and the deity. But who is to say that the term "the LORD" does not do so equally well? And in an effort to lay out the task of Old Testament *theology,* why not use that other term — God?

II. Is Old Testament Theology Equal to Its Task? A Response to a Paper by Rolf P. Knierim

W. Sibley Towner

Even the most ingenuous reader of the Old Testament is confronted by the fact that it contains not one but many pictures of God and God's relationship with the world, just as the New Testament contains not one but many portraits of the Christ. Anyone who tries to persuade this reader that this pluralism is more apparent than real is doing this reader a disservice. Professor Knierim puts it plainly in his very first sentence: "The Old Testament contains a plurality of theologies."

Holistic approaches of various kinds in fact do the ordinary reader the disservice described above because their goal is finally to dissolve the multiple theological outlooks into dimensions of a central theological structure around which the whole Old Testament is organized. Speaking extremely precisely, Knierim argues that a holistic approach will discern in "the plurality of theologies in the Old Testament . . . an enriching phenomenon rather than . . . a critical problem because the whole by definition represents nothing other than the semantic homogeneity of the plurality" (I.B). And that, says he, is bad because it is wrong.

Rather than denying the multiplicity of Old Testament theologies, Knierim proposes to make a virtue out of necessity. A plurality of theologies is both to be expected and to be affirmed. Such diversity arose over many ages of reflection by many writers using many genres and operating at many levels of sophistication in the face of many and diverse historical situations. This being the case, it is inevitable that every proposed organizational rubric — be it a concept or a process — finally gets relativized. Far from providing the unity which von Rad thought it would, tradition history only demonstrates the constant complexification and amplification of older themes, leaving them at the end more plural, not less. Covenant proves to be a concept with so many faces that it can hardly serve as a single organizing principle. Let us reframe this problem as an advantage, proposes Knierim. Accepting and maintaining the incredible richness of the text, let us simply ask it to organize itself around its own skeleton, namely, the hierarchy of priorities intrinsic within it.

Setting out through the lush thickets of *theologoumena* of the Old Testament in search of those which are intrinsically of higher priority than others, Knierim identifies two paths along which to move. One of these paths can be called "modes" (i.e., qualitative aspects of Yahweh's relationship with the world); the other is "realms" (i.e., three quantitative aspects of Yahweh's relationship with the world — cosmic, national, and personal). These paths seem to lead directly to the top theological priorities. In the category of the *realm* of Yahweh's work in the world, the theological claim intrinsic to and of first priority in the Old Testament itself is the universal realm, expressed in creation theology. In the area of *modes* or qualitative aspects of Yahweh's relationship with the world, justice and righteousness emerge as the primary expressions of that relationship and thus the top priority categories around which to organize other theological material. Thus is the program set. All that remains is to discover the hierarchy of priorities within the text and exegetically to confront individual passages with these central and decisive theological criteria.

I personally applaud this demanding undertaking, and hope that Rolf Knierim succeeds in implementing it. We will all be better off for the effort.

Before beginning, however, three issues or questions raised by this program piece may require further exploration.

(1) Knierim proposes as his central organizing rubric for an Old Testament theology based upon theological priorities intrinsic to the text the theme, "the universal dominion of Yahweh in justice and righteousness" (II.B.2.c.3). Justice and righteousness are the *modes* of Yahweh's relationship to the world and the *realm* of that relationship is universal. The question is: Why aren't these categories subject to relativization just as all the other ones which scholars and critics have proposed are subject to relativization? Do not justice and righteousness mean quite startlingly different things in different contexts? Speaking of these modes, Knierim admits in effect that they can be relativized. In a footnote, he observes that the "theology of Israel's relationship to the nations in the promised land in Deuteronomy raises questions as to how this theology corresponds with other theologies concerning the same issue, . . . and whether or not it can be considered a paradigm for Yahweh's universal justice and righteousness attested to in other theological strata in the Old Testament" (II.B.2.c.3, note 13). It seems to me that justice, while admittedly always relational in its character, can be spoken of in ways as richly diverse as, let us say, those in which covenant or salvation is described.

As to the most fundamental theological claim about the *realm* of Yahweh's relationship to the world, namely, that it is universal and related to creation itself, perhaps this theological theme is not subject to relativization simply because one cannot imagine any more universes than one. To speak about reality as a whole in a relative or pluralistic way would be to speak the absurdity which my old biology teacher once spoke on our final exam: "Describe the universe and give two examples." But even here one senses that the universal hegemony of Yahweh can at least be imaged in radically different ways. Remaining simply on the cosmic level, the universal praise of God by sea monsters and deeps, mountains and hills, kings and maidens of which Psalm 148 speaks seems to be a very different kind of acknowledgment of the fundamental conviction that Yahweh is king of the cosmos, than that, e.g., of Eccl 3:1-9, which speaks of inexorable laws and rhythms in the universe which are not even directly related to Yahweh's goodness and grace but which work cosmically and inevitably on their own.

So much then for my first question: How can theological priorities even of the first rank avoid being relativized when taken over by the whole sweep of the Old Testament?

(2) The second problem area which Knierim's proposal discloses but skirts has to do with his own primary issue of unity and diversity. Consider these sentences (II.B.2.c.3): All other kinds and degrees of relationship between Yahweh and reality, both qualitative and quantitative, as well as their own correlations, are subservient "to this [universal] dominion [of Yahweh in justice and righteousness]. . . . The degree of their theological validity can be understood only to the extent to which they reflect implementations or manifestations of Yahweh's universal dominion in justice and righteousness. . . . It is not necessary that each of the Old Testament's theologies speaks of nothing other than universality and justice and righteousness. However, it is necessary to interpret how a qualitative notion relates to others, what the horizon of its extent is in a given text, and whether or not it can be understood as a case or paradigm for Yahweh's universal dominion and its fundamental nature."

If I understand these remarks correctly, the theological validity of the religious truth claim of any passage of the Old Testament will rise in direct proportion to the degree to which it reflects the most fundamental teaching about the realm and mode of Yahweh's relationship with the world. Presumably a teaching which diverges widely from this central motif, and cannot "be understood as a case or paradigm for Yahweh's universal dominion and its fundamental nature," will be regarded as of inferior significance, or perhaps even as misleading and detrimental to sound theological work with the Old Testament. But precisely because of the multiplicity of Old Testament theologies with which Knierim begins his realistic appraisal of the situation, will certain texts inevitably not relate themselves to the central priorities? Will there not be theologies in the Old Testament which simply go in other directions? Isn't that the very meaning of pluralism? Or is Knierim really going to argue that every lower-priority way of speaking about the relationship of Yahweh to the world is merely a less successful way of raising the very themes which the top-priority theological assertions make crystal clear, namely, that Yahweh has universal dominion in justice and righteousness.

If that is Knierim's intention, then my second question can be put crisply: If all *theologoumena* can finally be subsumed at least to some extent under the central priorities, then has not Knierim succumbed to the old bugaboo of a holistic biblical theology?

(3) The third and to me most important issue this essay poses has to do with the problem of subjectivity. Let me lead up to my actual question gradually.

Subjectivity is, of course, what modern biblical theologies seek above all to avoid. So does Knierim, and yet — granting that this is a programmatic essay and not his final word — it appears to me that he never does say why the text requires that creation and the universal perspective must be regarded as the most fundamental theological criteria for talking about Yahweh's quantitative relationship to the world. Once he says it is "assumed" that this is the case (p. 16). As far as justice and righteousness are concerned, this mode of Yahweh's relationship to the world is even more clearly simply asserted, e.g., these notions "seem to be governing the other qualitative notions. . . . It also seems that the other modes are either gradationally relative to or elaborations of [this mode]" (II.B.2.c.3). What is it within Scripture itself that drives us to identify universal sovereignty as the *realm* of Yahweh's relationship to the world and justice and righteousness as the *modes?* Is it frequency of occurrence of these words and their semantic equivalents? Is it because one can assert that any kind of right relationship whatever requires balance and freedom from perversion (i.e., justice)? Is it the placement of the issue of the universal lordship of Yahweh on page 1 of the Bible that literally gives it priority? Is it the constant inner-biblical transformation of these themes?

In short, it seems to me that Knierim has not yet fully presented the evidence (upon which he himself insists) that these particular "criteria and agenda are intrinsic to and drawn from the Old Testament" (page 18). One therefore senses that the categories of universal rulership and justice and righteousness are selected as central partly for subjective reasons, because Knierim wants to select them as central.

A great deal is at stake here. In Knierim's ambitious vision, every theological use of the Bible should be held accountable to the intrinsic theological criteria that verify its legitimacy (page 19). Once the primary theological claims of Scripture itself are set forth on an objective basis, history of interpretation and *Wirkungsgeschichte* alike will have to bow the knee to these normative priorities. Whoever gets to say what they are becomes the judge and divider over all theology.

Of course, one could say that this has always been the case. Luther identified Hab 2:4 and its New Testament transformations in Rom 1:17 and elsewhere as the central thrust of the Bible, and judged everything by the teaching that "the righteous shall live by his faith." Calvin did something similar with the sovereignty of God; Barth did something similar with his emphasis on the scriptural centrality of

Christology; and even Tillich did something similar with his stress on ontology, though he did not spend much time appealing to Scripture. In such company, our colleague would need not apologize for allowing a certain subjectivity to enter the picture. Nor do I fault him for it; I simply hear in his proposal the unmistakable voice of a twentieth-century person deeply concerned with the deteriorating ecosystem, the threat of cosmic disaster at human hands, and the specter of increasing injustice as the gap between the poor and the rich widens.

This leads, then, to my third and final question of the Knierim proposal: What is wrong with allowing subjectivity a little play in selecting among theological themes intrinsic to the Scripture itself those which *for our time* must become organizing principles of the first order? Why not readily add to the interpretative rubric, "I will try to be objective as long as I can," its twin, "I will try to be objective as soon as I can"? I think such a move is not only admissible but necessary. Using the diachronic and synchronic distinction employed by Paul Hanson in his book *Dynamic Transcendence* (Philadelphia: Fortress, 1978), let me suggest that even in an enterprise in which objectivity is urgent, as it is for biblical theology, the diachronic experience of the peoples of God with the text itself develops a certain normativeness over the centuries. Let me also openly affirm that in the rich synchronic encounter between the text and the interpreters of our own times, those themes which have to be central for our time will emerge from among the several candidates which Scripture itself puts forward. And there may well be several candidates, for even in a single generation Scripture discloses different emphases intrinsic to itself to different interpreters — to male and female interpreters, to interpreters living in different parts of the world, to poor interpreters and rich ones.

I close with words of great appreciation and encouragement for the enterprise which Professor Knierim has set before himself. To describe in a systematic way the theology of the Old Testament based upon priorities intrinsic to the Scripture is a task the difficulty of which is amply exceeded by the value of its accomplishment.

III. A Response to "The Task of Old Testament Theology"

Roland E. Murphy

The problem Professor Rolf Knierim has addressed in his thoughtful paper is this: What is the task of Old Testament theology in the face of the theological pluralism, or "theologies," found within the Old Testament itself? He raises the specter of choosing between one Yahweh or many if we do not solve the problem of theological pluralism (I.D).

His solution is described both abstractly and concretely. The task of Old Testament theology is to interpret "the relationship between Yahweh/God and reality" in its quantitative and qualitative aspects: *how* are Yahweh and reality related, and *with whom/what is* Yahweh related (II.B.2.b). This involves the determination of all these relationships to each other, a systematization. Knierim's rather abstract program is made concrete by the affirmation of "the criterion": the universal dominion of Yahweh in justice and righteousness. This is the principle which guides systematization, and it cuts across the three essential realms to which the Lord is related: the natural world, human corporate existence (including that of Israel), and individual human existence.

Although this criterion is stated, it is neither proved nor illustrated. Working out the principle remains the agenda for a future Old Testament theology which Professor Knierim is well equipped to write. For the moment he has limited himself to stating the task and proposing the principle according to which the task is to be carried out. It is important to emphasize that this principle is proposed as a means of correlating biblical data that seem to be disparate, of arriving at an Old Testament theology that overcomes biblical pluralism without destroying it.

I do not think it would be fair to judge the criterion until it is put to work. Its real test will come in correlating the complex relationships between Yahweh and reality. While that test remains in the offing, let me express some agreements and disagreements — with due apologies to Gerhard von Rad, a kind of *"Offene Fragen"* (Open Questions).

On the positive side, Knierim has put his finger on a central aspect of the Bible: there is a plurality of theologies in the Old Testament. He has resolved to relate them in order to achieve a conceptual unity. Moreover, he has effectively shown the inadequacy of various criteria for unification that have been proposed in the past, such as covenant, etc. (II.A.1-8). I am particularly impressed with his recognition of the centrality of the doctrine of creation [II.B.2.c.2)]: "Yahweh's relationship to universal reality as expressed in the theology of creation, in the final analysis, can be discerned as what is at issue in the Old Testament."[1] Finally, I think that Professor Knierim's criterion ensures that his biblical theology is more than a history of religion; it is a *fides quaerens intellectum,* as all theology must be.[2]

1. Such an appreciation is also to be found in his earlier study, "Cosmos and History in Israel's Theology," *HBT* 3 (1981): 59-123. This article also indicates the direction which his thought has taken in the present paper. See p. 181 in the present volume, where he speaks of "the discernment of the theological system within the totality of the theological aspects that emerged in Israel's history. Only if we discern an identifiable systemic coherence in the Old Testament theologies are we entitled to speak of an Old Testament theology in the singular."

2. On this see R. de Vaux, "Peut-on écrire une 'Theologie de l'Ancien Testament'?" in *Bible et Orient* (Paris: du Cerf, 1967), 59-71.

Still on the positive side, I would address some questions to Professor Knierim. First, how did he arrive at his criterion? It strikes me as a reasonably broad category under which a fair amount of theology must be organized. But how did it emerge? In this connection I wonder if "in justice and righteousness" (במשפט ובצדקה) (or whatever likely combination of the appropriate roots) is not somewhat redundant. Some may consider that an unholy thought, for a biblical redundancy is not to be tampered with. But holiness and systematization (which is to be guided by the criterion) are two different things. One cannot really question the Lord's universal dominion; his power and will are surely dominant in biblical thought. But perhaps I am already asking how the criterion will be applied — how the "righteousness and justice" (why not "kindness and fidelity"?) will correlate with their apparent absence (Job, Qohelet?). Secondly, I don't think I understand the significance of the word "semantic," which is used liberally in the paper. It is used several times with "priorities" (III.B) and with "structure" (II.C.1 and 2). Sometimes "semantic(ally)" is used outright, as in II.B.1: "the exegesis of every text shows that forms of expression and conceptual understanding are intrinsically interrelated semantically, and that one form of its expression can be transformed into others."

My basic difficulty with the paper goes to the heart of Knierim's enterprise, and it has to do with systematization. He describes his biblical theology as systematic (III.C.4) and standing between exegesis and systematic theology, but differing from the latter "because its criteria and agenda are intrinsic to and drawn from the Old Testament." But the fact remains that the systematization is done by postbiblical persons, faithful to the Bible to be sure, but imposing upon it a unity that is necessarily extrinsic. While the criterion, as Professor Knierim rightly says, is derived from the Bible, its *use* is foreign to the Bible itself. Israel never made use of such a criterion. It may be a help to us as a means of unifying disparate data, but so are the criteria which have been judged insufficient in II.A.

The systematization of biblical theology calls for elaboration.[3] Ultimately it derives from "systematic" theology as this has developed in the Christian world. The drive to systematize can be traced back through the medieval period to the Greco-Roman *ratio*. But can it be applied to the biblical encounter of Israel with Yahweh, which occurred over several centuries of variegated history? Systematic theology professes to work with Scripture, tradition, and human experience. Scripture provides insights or building blocks for the edifice. Philosophical concepts of

3. On method in biblical theology, see A. Descamps, "Réflexions sur la Méthode en Théologie Biblique," in *Sacra Pagina,* vol. 1, ed. J. Coppens, et al., 2 vols., BETL 12-13 (Gembloux: J. Duculot, 1959), 132-57, and the considerations of K. Stendahl and A. Dulles, "Method in the Study of Biblical Theology," in *The Bible in Modern Scholarship,* ed. J. P. Hyatt (Nashville: Abingdon, 1965), 196-216. Cf. also J. van der Ploeg, "Une 'Théologie de l'Ancien Testament' est-elle possible?" *ETL* 38 (1962): 417-34; and David Kelsey, *The Uses of Scripture in Recent Theology* (Philadelphia: Fortress, 1975).

diverse origins expand the biblical data by shaping the understanding of the Bible and providing extended levels of meaning that are presumably in harmony with the Bible, while going beyond biblical categories. Systematization is then born in a postbiblical era of changing cultures and worldviews.

I am not saying that systematization of biblical thought is the same as systematic theology. But the same drive for unity is at work in both cases. Is it possible to speak of systematization *within* the Old Testament? Certainly not of the global sort projected by Professor Knierim's paper. Perhaps one may point to an embryonic systematization. For example, the attribution of the book of Psalms to David (with "appropriate" settings as indicated in Psalm 51, etc.) is a genuinely biblical systematization. Similarly, the attribution of wisdom to Solomon (Proverbs, Ecclesiastes, Wisdom of Solomon, and perhaps the Song of Songs?) is another attempt, as modest as that of the Davidic psalter. The Chronicler is an example of one who systematizes Israel's history, *suo modo,* for the postexilic community. Within the area of wisdom Gerald Sheppard has pointed out what might be called a kind of systematization, as wisdom attempts to interpret Torah.[4] But all this is not what we consider systematization at the service of a unified biblical theology. Indeed, these examples help us to understand what we are doing when we do biblical theology. We are creating a synthesis which the Bible never created and which cannot hope to be an adequate conceptual expression of Old Testament theology. The synthesis will be helpful, beyond doubt, but it will never be adequate.

A striking example of Israel's indifference to systematization lies in the affirmation of Yahweh's universal dominion, a cornerstone of Professor Knierim's criterion. The Bible pays little attention to what we call secondary causality. Everything, good and evil, comes from the hand of God. On the other hand, the responsibility of human beings (what we call free will) is affirmed with equal emphasis. No effort is made to harmonize these differing points of view. Again, it is systematic theology, in the postbiblical period, that has attempted to offer solutions.

A biblical theology that aspires to be systematic goes counter to the ongoing development within the Bible. The most one can do is recognize what might be called systems or, better, biblical categories of thought, which are in themselves diverse and were never conceived or recorded from the vantage point of systematization. This is not to deny continuities within the Old Testament. But the discontinuities are too severe to be included in a logical system. In systematization a guiding idea, which is never used as a guide within the Old Testament, is imposed upon the material in order to arrive at "biblical theology" as a unitary concept. Such a move is intrinsically related to our cultural drive for system.

Judaism has underscored this aspect by its marked indifference to the "the-

4. Cf. Gerald Sheppard, *Wisdom as a Hermeneutical Construct,* BZAW 151 (Berlin: de Gruyter, 1980).

ology" of the TaNaK.[5] In this respect the thirteen points drawn up by Moses Maimonides are instructive.[6] He outlines a theology of Judaism based on certain key points in the Bible, while going beyond it (e.g., that the Torah is unchangeable). In a similar way Christians have constructed a theology based on the Bible, systematic theology.

Thus far, I have claimed that Old Testament theology cannot be systematized. What am I left with? Answer: biblical theologies which are not capable of ultimate systematization but which provide various insights for the postbiblical person to exploit. Does this lead to the affirmation that several different Gods or Yahwehs are affirmed in the Hebrew Bible? I don't think so. I don't think that the unitary *concept* which mesmerizes the modern held that same attraction for the ancient. For this reason the various attempts of H. D. Preuss to exclude the wisdom literature from Old Testament theology are doomed to failure.[7] The question whether there were many Yahwehs or one Yahweh (I.D) for the Israelite is *our* question, conceived in our logic, not the question of ancient Israel.

In conclusion, I suppose that I would say that I doubt if Rolf Knierim's program will work, or at least that I do not think it is a tragedy if this or any other systematization of the Old Testament fails. One can live comfortably with the several theologies of the Old Testament without the need of any hierarchical systematization of its pluralism.

5. A striking exception is M. H. Goshen-Gottstein, who has written of the "gap" in "Jewish Biblical Theology," in "Christianity, Judaism, and Modern Bible Study," in *Congress Volume, Edinburgh, 1974,* VTSup 28 (Leiden: Brill, 1975), 69-88, esp. 87. See now his "Jewish Biblical Theology and the Study of Biblical Religion," *Tarbiz* 50 (1980/81): 37-64, in which he invites Jewish scholars to become involved in Jewish biblical theology.

6. Cf. Alexander Altmann, "Articles of Faith," *Encyclopedia Judaica,* 3 (New York: Macmillan, 1971), 654-60, esp. 655.

7. Cf. H. D. Preuss, "Erwägungen zum theologischen Ort alttestamentlicher Weisheitsliteratur," *EvT* 30 (1970): 393-417; "Alttestamentliche Weisheit in christlicher Theologie?" in *Questions Disputées d'Ancien Testament,* ed. C. Brekelmans, BETL 33 (Leuven: Leuven University Press, 1974), 165-81.

On the Task of Old Testament Theology: A Response to W. Harrelson, S. Towner, and R. E. Murphy

Introduction

Regardless of agreement or disagreement, or of the need for clarification of what is said, or for the further discussion of the subject, I am deeply obliged to my colleagues for their engaging critiques of my paper. They serve me very well, as well as our mutual understanding of the task.

I will respond to Professors Harrelson and Towner first because their arguments seem to address more or less confined, though important, questions, but not the basic assumptions of my paper. Professor Murphy's response, however, primarily represents a critique of just those basic assumptions, and I suspect that with his own assumptions he is by no means alone. An answer to that critique requires, therefore, a probing into the background of the way many of us have come to see the problems and, thus, a more extensive treatment. It is obvious that, whatever happens after this discussion among those of us presently involved, by no means will everything be said.

I. W. Harrelson

Professor Harrelson raises two issues of "some weight," as well as two queries more peripheral to this methodological discussion.

A. In his first point, Harrelson suggests that I might better have entitled my paper "The Limited Task of Old Testament Theology." While affirming systematization, he interprets my paper, if I see correctly, as saying that "it would not suffice just to describe what empirically seems to be some dominant perspective and then to call one's theology descriptive. It would not suffice to relate the several theologies to some other theological outlook and to show how nicely they correspond with that other outlook, for one must systematize the variety before one has done the theological task." A bit later he affirms that "all the other tasks of biblical scholarship have their weight and their place."

Harrelson addresses the indeed important question of the relationship between the systematizing role of Old Testament theology and its other proposed tasks, such as empirical description or the relating of several theologies to some other theological outlook. This question involves a number of aspects.

1. One of them concerns the nature of the system in distinction from the nature of the theological task. System or systematization may be an a priori postulate, the logical, necessary precondition for the theological task. In this case, it is not a part of the theological task itself. Rather it is, formally and substantively, a nontheological, extrinsic criterion to which the theological task is subjected, whereas the nature of the task itself is not necessarily systematic. However, systematization may also be understood as the consequence of the analysis of the problem, and as the explication of the definition of the theological task. In this case, it represents the conceptualization of the nature of the theological task itself. It is intrinsic to that task because it serves it and is subject to its agenda. It is not the criterion for the theological task, but the theological task is its criterion. I reject the former understanding, and advocate the latter. It must be clear that both a systematic presentation of the theologically relevant relationships and its application to all the Old Testament texts for the sake of their theological evaluation (however that application may be ordered systematically, cf. the second paragraph of II.C.2. in my paper) belong to the nature of the theological task. But I realize that I give cause to confusion (by creating a tension between what an analysis of the thrust of my entire argument might show and what I say) when saying in II.C.1. that "this first task is systematic in nature," while giving the impression in II.C.2. that the approaches available for the assessment of the exegeted messages (traditio-historical, canonic, or "systematic" = thematic) are nonsystematic, or even independent of the "first" part of the task. *Mea culpa!*

2. Another aspect concerns the order of execution of the program. Here, too, I admit to unclarity. In the sections II.C.1. and 2. just referred to, I speak of the "first" and the "second" task, and of the "first volume," thereby indicating that the second volume will consist of the second task. As they stand, these statements speak in terms of the sequential order in doing Old Testament theology as a matter of principle. They should instead speak in terms of logical order (how students of the Bible distrust *logic!*), i.e., of which is presupposed by which in the determination

of the relationship of the two modes of interpretation: the relating, comparing, and evaluating of theological notions on the one hand, and the theological critique of the individual texts or messages on the other. The two modes of interpretation differ, but neither can do without the other. Also, it should be clear that the first-mentioned mode of interpretation already presupposes the sum total of exegetical work without which the theological notions could be neither known nor related. As far as I can see, however, our understanding of the kinds and degrees of relationship of theological notions discerned through exegesis presupposes their critical comparison, whereas the theological critique of texts and messages inevitably presupposes our systematic understanding of the relationship of theological notions. Our understanding of relationships does not depend on our theological critique of texts, but this critique depends on our understanding of theologically relevant relationships. I may arrive at a cycle in theological interpretation: exegesis — determination of relationships — theological critique of texts. The nature of this cycle is essentially logical, a view which is different from the question of the sequence of its application. That question is secondary. The point of entry into the cycle may vary and be subject to practicality, although it seems that, wherever we enter it, the fact remains the same that the one mode of interpretation presupposes the other. In this sense, my reference to the "first volume" cannot be based on the priority of sequence. It can only be based on what seems to me a more practical application of the principal relationship of the two modes of interpretation. But both are understood as parts of the theological task.

3. A third aspect concerns the relationship of the theological and the descriptive-empirical tasks. To this point, I answer that my contention of the insufficiency of the "descriptive" approach is not based on the call for prior systematization. Rather, it is based on the assumption that the method of describing the theological notions addresses neither the question of their relationship nor of their theological validity. However, the fact that description provides no sufficient basis for the definition of the theological task does not mean that it is not part of that task. On the contrary, historical exegesis is just as descriptive as our histories of Israel and our introductions to the Old Testament literature. Neither the discussion of the relationship of theological notions nor the theological critique of the texts themselves is possible without the clear description of these notions and of the texts. The descriptive task is indispensable for the theological task, but it is not identical with it. It is subject to its own set of questions, which does not include the theological task as formulated here. On the contrary, the theological task includes the descriptive task, and hence, is more inclusive.

4. Harrelson assumes that I demand "a single, controlling concept or form of relation between God and the world, Israel, the individual in order to have an Old Testament theology as such." I am not positive that this statement clearly expresses what I mean. The Old Testament has not established a single, controlling concept or form of that relation. It offers us many forms and concepts without

explicitly defining which controls all others. That definition is a matter of interpretation, even as it must point to evidence from the Old Testament.

Perhaps Harrelson means what I would prefer to express as a single, controlling *question* of relation between God and the world, Israel, and the individual, and a single, controlling *method* for answering that question. The *question* of God's relation to reality is single and controlling because it is derived from and embraces all the Old Testament texts in all their forms, concepts, aspects, and questions. But it neither excludes nor invalidates the other questions which are raised by and about the Old Testament. The *method* of relating and comparing the various forms and concepts of God's relation to reality is single because it is consistent. It is controlling because it is itself constituted and controlled by the question. Just as the question is accountable to the Old Testament, so the method is accountable to the question. But neither is proposed because of a preconceived notion of Old Testament theology which "by definition has to do with the systematic ordering of thought." No preconceived notion of Old Testament theology provides the condition for the imposition of question and method on the Old Testament, but both question and method arising from the Old Testament provide the conditions for Old Testament theology.

1.-4. Whether or not the task described here is "limited" depends on whether it is inclusive of other tasks, or whether other theological tasks are excluded from this description. This remains to be seen.

B. I agree with Harrelson's reference to the importance of eschatology. He might have added apocalypticism. The fact that neither is mentioned in my essay is purely coincidental. Except for the notion of creation (including new creation), which had to be mentioned because it represents — in my opinion — the most universal theological notion of the Old Testament, my references to any other theological notion are merely illustrative in this methodological paper. Eschatology did not have to be chosen, but it certainly plays its role in any Old Testament theology. More important methodologically is the fact that it, too, is subject to theological evaluation.

Harrelson is also correct in saying that the truth of my program is not established by the fact of its existence or — God forbid! — that I say it. It will be valid if it represents a better saying. That is all that we can strive for.

C. I use the term "Yahweh-spirituality" because it describes most adequately the nature of the Old Testament scriptures as documents whose authors were inspired by Yahweh. It is more direct and specific than the expression "religious devotion to God."

A similar — and in no way scholarly-mechanical — intent lies behind my usage of the word "Yahweh." I am familiar with the forms and shifts in the Old Testament's usage of words for the deity. But the Old Testament knows that the word for the name has a meaning different from the words for titles such as lord or king, or from a generic word such as God. Its words for the deity are only secondarily interchangeable. A statement such as "God, or the Lord, is Yahweh" is different from the statement "Yahweh is God, or the Lord." The Old Testament uses the word "Yahweh" for good and primary reasons. Our reasons for avoiding it programmatically come from a secondary tradition with reasons that cannot be considered absolute. While resisting pressure to submit unequivocally to those reasons, I do not intend to be irreverent.

II. W. S. Towner

A. Professor Towner's comment on the relativization of theological categories, such as justice and righteousness, or of different ways of envisioning the universal hegemony is perfectly in order. For the sake of brevity, I refer to my discussion of this matter in my response to Professor Murphy. Only one thing may be said at this point: the fact that these notions must be seen in relativity to one another also means that the kinds and degrees of such relativity must be determined. In such a pursuit, priorities can be discerned. Moreover, even within the category of Yahweh's universal hegemony, the "radically different ways" of imagination in the Old Testament can be compared and prioritized, or seen as complementary. Methodologically, I see no problem with this.

B. On the issue of subjectivity, Towner contends that I "never" say "why the text requires that creation and the universal perspective must be regarded as the most fundamental theological criteria. . . ." This statement surprises me, for I think that I have argued that point in several ways, and I hesitate to repeat. That criterion is the most fundamental because it is inclusive of all other aspects, and because the aspect of the universality of reality is intrinsic to the understanding of the universality of God as God, and not as a particularistic half-god.

As for subjectivity itself, I am aware that there is no such thing as absolute objectivity. We even substitute a word such as intersubjectivity for the word "objectivity." In any objective statement, our subjectivity is always involved. At stake is not our subjective involvement, but whether or not we demonstrate that the criteria we define are based either on our own preferences and predilections, or on the preferences and predilections in the subject itself which we discuss. I also realize that no such demonstration is absolute, and that we may at best discern the better among several possibilities. Such a process is possible. In such a model, the question is not whether we achieve absolute objectivity, but to what extent our subjectivity is objectified. It should become clear that our subjectivity is controlled by the issue under discussion, and not by our own assumptions. We represent that issue and are its servants, not its lords. Furthermore, none of us speaks alone. And finally, it is clear that authority rests with the better saying, and not with any person.

In this sense, I believe in "objective basis." And if, under the argument of theological validity, "history of interpretation and *Wirkungsgeschichte*" appear unable to be the ground of their own validity, so be it. The Old Testament knew that argument long ago. I would like to reformulate Towner's statement that "whoever gets to say what they [the priorities] are becomes the judge and divider of all theology" (which de facto always happens in everyone's own theology!) in this way: whichever normative priorities that can be identified become the judges over theology, regardless of who identifies them, be they one or many. The judge over theology is the normativeness of the better theological argument. Furthermore, the authority or legitimacy of anyone who adjudges is subordinate to and derived from that argument. More we do not have, and less is not good enough.

Towner hears in my proposal "the unmistakable voice of a twentieth-century person deeply concerned with the deteriorating ecosystem, the threat of cosmic disaster at human hands, and the specter of increasing injustice as the gap between the poor and the rich widens." Quite frankly, all these concerns are indeed very much on my mind, and I do not mind at all when anyone perceives in my statements the congruency of the Old Testament's and our concerns. However, I would be gravely mistaken if my personal or our contemporary concerns (or concerns of some of us), or even a dialogically negotiated concern-consensus between us and the Old Testament, were the basis for determining the concerns of the Old Testament and for defining the task of its theology. If that theology is not defined on the basis of the Old Testament's own agenda, regardless of our own concerns and regardless of the complementarity of its agenda and ours, it is not worth its name.

As soon as we ask the legitimate question of its meaning "for our time," we are no longer dealing with Old Testament theology but with Old Testament hermeneutic. This discipline is subject to quite a different set of questions which indeed involves the explicit, critical dialogue between the Old Testament and our own time, including our subjective experience and, also, its own relativity. In this discipline, we certainly allow "subjectivity a little play in selecting among theological themes intrinsic to the Scriptures." Many rabbis and preachers do that every Sabbath and Sunday. Quite legitimately, it happens all the time.

Even so, Towner's description of that hermeneutical process following P. Hanson's *Dynamic Transcendence* is problematic. No one has anything against "themes central for our time" which emerge from the rich encounter between the texts and the interpreters (to whatever extent that is the case), or against different emphases in a single generation. Furthermore, no one should dispute the fact that this encounter "develops" certain norms, and that themes "emerge." But do we not also have to contend with the massive fact, all around and within us, that in the same generation norms develop and themes and emphases emerge which are not only richly different but radically contradictory, if not exclusive of one another, and that these stand in direct confrontation, and not just in isolated juxtaposition? Should we accept each of these contradictions and exclusions, or perhaps their dialectical relationship in thesis and antithesis, as revealed truth simply for what they are, and on the ground that they "emerged" and "developed" in the feuding parties' encounter with the Scriptures? Should we forget asking which of them is valid and which is not, or which is more valid than the other? (The assumption of a dialectic relationship requires the synthesis, anyway.) If not, on what ground can we discern that one theme, emphasis, or norm emerging from the encounter between us and the Scriptures is valid and the other invalid, or more valid than the other?

Furthermore, even if we assume that a theme is critically transformed in the encounter (to whatever extent that happens!), on what ground can we discern the validity of the transformation? Does not the fact of dynamic transcendence, this "emerging" and "developing" of themes, also allow for mutual reinforcement through the encounter of invalid (or less valid) themes, norms, and emphases, as well as for a de facto conspiracy on false themes between us and the Scriptures? Does the fact of this process demonstrate validity? The history of biblical interpretation should make us very alert! Or, are we to plead for the autonomy of this process which carries its validity in itself and is not (as is everything else) in need of theological validation? What, then, is the criterion for the theological validity of the dynamic and of the transcending? If they, or their process, are not valid by virtue of what they are, or by the fact that they happen, what is it that makes them valid or invalid, or more or less valid?

It seems that these questions can only be answered if we discern criteria by which the process of dynamic transcendence itself can be evaluated. Although it is clear that in biblical hermeneutic, just as in any other, the needs of the interpreters play a legitimate role, the process of evaluation not only applies to the themes and emphases emerging from the dialogue between us and the Scriptures; it also applies to our *selection* of the themes, both ours and theirs. We need to be aware that even as we are selective, our need and our subjectivity, or intersubjectivity, are not the self-evident ground of theological values.

Finally, it may not be possible for any one person to succeed at implementing the full extent of this program, especially not for those among us who are becoming the older generation. In my own experience, the program has already generated the dynamic of constantly new learning for which there is no end in sight. Many observations on texts are preliminary and qualified by "it seems." It is more important that many, and by no means scholars only, try their minds and hands on it, and that it can be applied in the interpretation of individual texts canonically, traditio-historically, and thematically, in confined studies, as well as in large tomes.

III. R. E. Murphy

Professor Murphy submits three critical objections.

A. The first is concerned with my reference to the hendiadys justice and righteousness as the superior qualitative notion of the Old Testament.

1. It is known that each qualitative notion in the Old Testament refers to a plurality of quantitative horizons, such as the individual, family, tribe, nation, humanity, and world. This fact is also true for justice and righteousness and for either of the two words alone. It is the result of the variety of ancient Israel's societal settings and of its tradition history. This pluralism must not be ignored, for sociological and historical reasons as well as for theological ones. This affirmation specifically requires our necessary attention to the concrete situations to which particular notions are applied in our texts. The texts for the most part do not discuss notions in the abstract.

Nevertheless, their concreteness by no means is evidence for the absence of conceptual notions. Certainly, we should not expect a particular text to address all the horizons of a notion with which it is concretely preoccupied. But does this mean that a notion was generated by a situation and remained confined to it, or does it mean that a transient notion was applied to a situation because it was applicable to many situations? And how should we read our lexica? How should we understand the relationship of the various horizons documented for a notion in our lexica? Is "justice and righteousness" constitutive for the world, for humanity, for the group, and for the individual because it is constitutive for the individual, the צדיק, or is it constitutive for any of these realms because it is constitutive for the more, and ultimately, the most inclusive ones? Moreover, is God's justice and righteousness constitutive for the world because it is constitutive for Israel, or is it constitutive for Israel because it is constitutive universally? Are we prohibited from raising these questions because the texts, in their concretizing nature, often do not raise them? Can we even understand a concrete text without raising these questions? Does the absence of conceptual explicitness mean that ideas of such relationships were nonexistent or nowhere presupposed? If we were prohibited from raising these questions, would we not have to conclude that the Old Testament advocates a plurality of justices and righteousnesses which have in principle nothing to do with one another? Would the Old Testament endorse such an exegesis, simply on the ground that the Old Testament itself often does not interrelate these various aspects of this issue?

2. Murphy asks how " 'righteousness and justice' (why not 'kindness and fidelity') will correlate with their apparent absence (Job, Qohelet?)." This query involves two questions: the relationship of "justice and righteousness" to other qualitative notions, and its absence in certain texts.

a. There is indeed little research about which of the different qualitative notions (justice, righteousness, or both, fidelity, kindness, love, mercy, goodness, etc.) is more inclusive than others, or most inclusive, and which are relative to others, and how various notions are, and are to be, related to one another.

1) First, I will deal with the obvious. Qualitatively, the Old Testament speaks about positive and negative notions, about justice and injustice, righteousness and sin, liberation and oppression, etc. All these texts and their language presuppose a value system, changing or shifting at times, in which values are understood in opposition to one another or as mutually exclusive, and without which neither a positive nor a negative value could be expressed. It is the semantic matrix of the texts. The fact that this value system is nowhere the subject of an explicit systematic treatise means neither that it did not exist, nor that we can ignore it if we want to understand any text. The opposites are systematically related to one another. We must interpret that systematic relationship or we will not have a full picture either of justice, righteousness, liberation, or of injustice, sin, oppression. Such interpretation of the systemic relationship intrinsic to our texts, I call systematization. I do not know how to avoid such systematization, or why it should be wrong, unless I am compelled merely to recite the texts and to give up interpreting and understanding them.

2) As for the positive qualitative notions, a question must be forced into the open that for too long has been on the sideline: How are these notions related to one another? How are justice and liberation related, as well as migration and settlement, justice and holiness, justice and mercy, justice and peace, blessing and liberation, etc.? As for the relationship between justice and judgment, is judgment an act of justice or of injustice? Does justice include or exclude judgment? What is the relationship between judgment and grace, and how is justice related to both? Which of these notions, when compared with any other in any of the Old Testament's theologies, is seen as foundational to and more inclusive than the others, and which is relative to or dependent on the others? Further, when comparing different understandings in the Old Testament, which of them has the better argument? Should this obvious quest for their critical comparison be disallowed because the Old Testament has neglected to pose and solve it for us universally? All these questions, and more, arise from the Old Testament materials. In fact, they are quite frequently, explicitly, and programmatically addressed in the Old Testament itself.

The only difference is that I propose to expand this process to the entirety of the Old Testament. Such an activity is not foreign to the spirit of the Old Testament. Furthermore, it is not impossible. It will significantly lead beyond what we have seen so far, even in our exegesis of individual texts. Only in the process will we learn where its limits are, vis-à-vis speculation. It may be, e.g., that certain qualitative notions are, and must be, related in tandem, in a sort of *Bedeutungsfeld,* a field of truly complementary notions in which neither dominates the other, in a true and not artificial "both-and" relationship. But such results must be found out.

b. As for the most foundational notion, which at the same time is related to

Yahweh's universality, Murphy asks, "Why not kindness and fidelity?" A perfectly legitimate question. In response, I would point to the deuteronomic theology and say that Yahweh's treatment of the Canaanites is not exactly an example for the universality of Yahweh's kindness. Whether it documents the universality of Yahweh's justice is a different question. In Deuteronomy itself and elsewhere, it is understood in that way. But I doubt that the Old Testament unanimously shares this understanding.

More important is the witness of the book of Jonah! That writer relates the notion of God's mercy for Nineveh to the creator God. The question arises whether God's mercy is, for this writer, totally unrelated to God's justice, or whether it is understood as the ultimate essence of justice itself. In either case (alternatives to these two options aside), the foundational qualitative notion related to God's universality would appear to be mercy which either replaces or qualifies justice. This interpretation is reinforced by the book's criticism of the prophet Jonah's own particularistic view of God's mercy, and of his anger about God's apparent injustice in being merciful universally. The book is, therefore, emphatic in pointing out that the criterion for God's justice is the universality of his mercy and nothing less.

In the Old Testament, we may find texts in which the order of relationship of these two notions is opposite to the one found in the book of Jonah. The comparison of such opposing orders would then mean that the Old Testament canon and tradition history have left us with an unresolved theological problem, and a legitimate one at that. We may decide to take cognizance of this problem and leave it at that. To me, the better way seems to be, while describing the situation, to interpret the opposing theologies in critical comparison and to find the better answer. That answer will no doubt be a critical one, and it will be an answer that is our own — which is nothing new in the history of good interpretation. But such critical comparison guarantees that, for the sake of Old Testament theology, we also include the Old Testament's theological problems, and not only the description of its answers.

However, should the relationship of the universality of God's mercy to God's justice as portrayed in the book of Jonah be uncontested in the rest of the Old Testament, the case could be made that ultimately the most foundational qualitative notions related to God's universality (Israel's God Yahweh) are kindness and mercy because they are the criterion for and the foundation of Yahweh's justice and righteousness. Then the book of Jonah would represent a remarkable step forward in redefining the priority, given the place of justice in the ancient Near Eastern concept of world order. Moreover, it would have already provided an answer for the question in New Testament theology, namely, of the relationship between the universality of the kingdom of God and its righteousness, and *agapē* as the ultimate reality of the new world.

Should this interpretation of the theology of the book of Jonah be sustainable, Murphy's question "Why not kindness and fidelity?" would, with some change of notion, point to a qualitative criterion that is indeed superior to the criterion of justice and righteousness advocated in my essay. What matters here is not whether this or that specific interpretation is for the moment correct. What matters is the test case, methodologically, which shows that the different notions can and must be related, and that answers can be found.

Furthermore, the "apparent absence" of a theological topos in one or more of the Old Testament's theologies is irrelevant because the validity of a topos, any topos, is independent of its presence in all texts and at all times. Of all the notions found in the Old Testament literature, it is possible that none is found everywhere. This fact, however, makes it neither illegitimate nor impossible to relate the theology of a text in which a certain notion is not used to that notion used elsewhere, or to relate its own notion to the same notion elsewhere. As for Murphy's assumption that justice and righteousness are apparently absent in Job, among others, I am at a loss. I have always assumed that the book of Job deals above all with that problem.

c. Murphy might have referred to another important case in point: the relationship between justice and peace in the Old Testament. How are the two notions related? On this issue, compare the instructive discussion between H. W. Wolff and W. Pannenberg in *EvT* 44 (1984): 280-97.

d. In the context of Murphy's affirmation of "the Lord's universal dominion," he refers to the dominance of "his power and will" in biblical thought perhaps as a possible alternative to justice and righteousness. But power and will are dynamistic categories. They can be destructive or constructive. They can be, and are, related to war but also to peace, to particularistic or universalistic aspects. They can reflect justice or injustice. Their nature entirely depends on the qualifier. They do not represent a superior qualitative notion. This statement does not even account for the thought that the notion of God's powerlessness is superior to that of his power because it reflects the criterion even for his power. A hermeneutical aside: we have every reason today to know better what we say when relating the notions of power and will to God. In our religious communities, there continues to prevail a deep-seated collective presumption reinforced, if not generated, by parts of the Bible that strong power and will (politically, militarily, and economically) are the true and self-evident signs of God's blessing presence, and that for God the power of and will toward war is just as good as, if not better than, the power of and will toward peace. Jer 9:23-24 and Psalm 33, among others, already had better sayings.

B. Murphy's second query concerns my usage of the word "semantic." For the time being, I prefer passing on this issue. For some twenty-five years, we have experienced an intensive discussion on semantics in general and on biblical semantics specifically. We even have a periodical, namely, *Semeia*.

C. Murphy's most vehement objection concerns what I have called "systematization." He rejects the idea that the theological pluralism of the Old Testament is a theological problem and claims that "Old Testament theology cannot be systematized." He doubts that the program will work and affirms that "one can live comfortably with the several theologies of the Old Testament without the need of any hierarchical systematization of its pluralism." With this judgment, he accepts the first sentence of my paper as sufficient and renders the rest in principle as useless. His position cannot be defined in terms of *"Offene Fragen."* It is a set answer. Murphy underscores his position by several bibliographical references which show that this specific debate affects basic assumptions held in Old Testament scholarship in general, and not only the two of us.

1. Murphy rejects the idea that pluralism is a problem. However, I doubt that he has realized what I believe to be the seriousness of my analysis. At least, I find no significant substantive critique of my parts I.C. and D. in his response. As long as this analysis is not invalidated, Murphy's own affirmation of the theologically unproblematic nature of pluralism remains unsubstantiated. His rejection of "systematization" provides no substitute for the substantiation of his own affirmation.

2. Which brings us to the subject of "systematization."

a. Every one of some sixty Old Testament theologies published in this century represents a systematic approach in one way or another. The mere juxtaposition of topoi in many of them does not at all mean that these works do not rest upon an explicit or implicit systematic conceptualization, or that the treatment of each topos is not in itself systematic. What is true for our century has been true for the entire history of biblical interpretation. The difference between the pre-Gabler and the post-Gabler eras of biblical interpretation is not that the former was systematic, whereas the latter has been unsystematic.

b. There is no preacher whose plurality of biblical sermons, if it is to make any sense, is not guided by her/his awareness that the essence of one sermon must not contradict and/or invalidate the essence of another. Such an awareness involves a constant systematizing effort. This effort is not artificial, regardless of whether its criteria are drawn from biblical or extrabiblical perspectives. It is unavoidable because the alternatives to it would be chaotic.

c. What, then, is the problem with "systematization"?

1) First of all, we must look at our choices of words.

a) I have been using words such as "system," "systemic," "systematize," "relationship," "relating," "correlation," "correspondence," "(critical) comparison," and "hierarchy."

b) Murphy's description of my paper claims that I want to relate, to systematize, to synthesize, to unify, and to harmonize.

a) and b) It is clear that in both cases words (perhaps more or less accurately describing what is meant) are used in the context of word fields that control their meaning. It is also clear that Murphy's word field is, in part, different from my own. This difference affects our understandings of systematization. I chose those words which I felt most accurately reflected my meaning. I avoided words such as "unity" or "unifying," and even "synthesis," because of the discredited systems proposed in the past to which the word "unity" was tied, systems that I do not want to resurrect. I find it especially hard to see that I am anywhere attempting to "harmonize." In fact, I have the exact opposite in mind.

However, Murphy's critique causes me to admit that systematization involves synthesis and, in a sense, unification. The question is, then, not whether we systematize, synthesize, or unify, but what the nature of these activities is. This is the point where words come into play, such as "relationship," "correspondence," and "comparison," but also "contrast" and "opposition," even "hierarchy," and with them the substantive aspects.

2) Murphy says that systematization is done "by postbiblical persons," "born in a postbiblical era of changing cultures and worldviews," and "intrinsically related to our cultural drive for a system," a "logical system," and that it derives from "systematic theology" developed in the Christian world, the roots of which lie in the medieval period and ultimately in the Greco-Roman *ratio.* He speaks of Israel's indifference to systematization, and says that "its use is foreign to the Bible itself. Israel never made use of such a criterion." He further states that systematization imposes "a unity that is necessarily extrinsic" to the Bible; represents "the same drive for unity" that is at work in systematic theology; imposes "a guiding idea which is never used as a guide within the Old Testament . . . in order to arrive at a 'biblical theology' as a unitary concept"; and is "at the service of a unified biblical theology." In short, "Old Testament theology cannot be systematized."

a) None of these arguments is new. Of all of them, only one (more meant than expressed in Murphy's response) is partially correct; namely, the fact that the final juxtaposition of all the Old Testament books is not presented to us in the form of a systematic treatise. Any attempt to systematize their relationship exceeds in formal respects what the final composers of the tripartite TaNaK themselves did. Such exceeding would take place, as far as I can discern from Murphy's statements, in three areas: unification of all the biblical books; systematic-logical abstraction from their direct, situation-related language and perspectives (as in the Greek philosophical systems and their descendants); and transition from the plurality of generic forms of expression *eis allo genos,* namely, to the one form of systematizing language, i.e., the area of the transformation of generic language.

This exceeding must be disallowed because it is foreign to the activities of the biblical writers and to the spirit of the Scriptures, and is, perhaps by implication, a racist or chauvinistic or imperialistic imposition — the original sin in biblical interpretation. Murphy says that "it cannot be done." What he means is that it must not be done, because it surely can be done. If I see correctly, the bottom line of Murphy's argument, his methodological a priori and sine qua non, is that Old Testament theology must only do what the Old Testament writers did, but never what they did not themselves do. Under this assumption, it is ultimately irrelevant how systematization is understood, and how important the distinctions among different types of systematization are. No form of systematization is legitimate because the biblical Scriptures are not systematized.

b) For the moment, I want to postpone the question whether or not, and to what extent, the final composers of the TaNaK were indifferent to systematization, to logical systems, to guiding ideas, etc. Instead, I want to discuss Murphy's contention that, apart from "embryonic systematization," systematizing activity is essentially absent in the Old Testament and apparently alien to the Hebrew mentality. This judgment, widespread as it seems to be, is in my opinion outright wrong. In fact, systematizing activity pervades the entire biblical literature. It can be observed throughout its tradition history. This activity is highly developed, astonishingly sophisticated and logical, and anything but embryonic. Its nature is not determined by the form of abstract theoretical treatises. It is at work in all the genres of the Old Testament literature.

(1) The Hebrew language itself is clearly logical and systemic, and it is employed that way in the texts. The structures of the texts themselves, both small and large, reveal in their absolute majority logically and hierarchically organized systematizations of manifold aspects under guiding ideas.[1] The legal corpora in the Covenant Book, in Deuteronomy, and in the Holiness Code, just as, e.g., the Code of Hammurabi, represent for the most part, if not in their entirety, eminently systematized collections of laws and blocks of laws. Indeed, Herrmann has called Deuteronomy the first attempt in Israel to present a systematic theology. The historical works of the Old Testament (**J**, **P**, **Dtr**, **R**$^{\mathbf{P}}$, Chronicles) represent unifying systematizations of history in terms of arrangement and of guiding theological ideas. The priestly instructions for the building of the tabernacle are highly systematized. The same is true for the clearly systematized instructions for the execution of the sacrificial rituals, instructions that reflect the systemic nature of the procedures themselves. These instructions show, perhaps unlike anything else in the Old Testament, the congruency of language and setting. The same is also true for Ezekiel's blueprint for the Second Temple.

In some instances, the aspects vary under which systematization took place. Obvious examples are the books of Psalms, Proverbs, and Job. The book of Psalms appears to consist of five books, whereas the sequence of the individual psalms is more or less coincidental, probably for good reasons (cf. our hymnbooks). The organization of the speeches in Job is primarily interested in the system of speech cycles and less in the progress of thought. That interest may reveal an emphasis on a paradigm for the just and fair order of a debate in which each voice, but first the seniors and second the junior, has an equal right to be heard regardless of

1. Compare the published and forthcoming volumes of the commentary series The Forms of the Old Testament Literature (FOTL).

whether or not its position is right or wrong. The absence of systematization in some regard in these and other books or texts, however, does not mean that systematization is altogether foreign to them.

(2) Similar things can be said for the book of Proverbs and the prophetic literature as a whole. Of special importance, however, is the fact that larger corpora comprising disparate genres and substantive aspects are composed under the dictate of unifying guiding ideas. They are forms of systematic unification of pluralities and diversities. These forms must be accounted for, or these corpora cannot be understood. The systematizing activity may be explicitly expressed on the surface of these corpora, especially in programmatic introductions or conclusions, as in Gen 12:1-3; Exod 3:7-9; 19:4-6; 25:2-9; many passages in Deuteronomy; in Psalm 1; or Prov 1:1-7. The number of examples is endless. These statements have a systematizing function. They serve as direct hermeneutical guidelines for a unifying understanding of what otherwise may appear to the reader as a bewildering diversity.

But the systematizing activity is also at work underneath the surface of the text corpora. This is certainly true for the prophetic books for the systems of which preconceived systematic theological notions are responsible, such as Israel and the nations, judgment-salvation-restoration, or eschatology, and their relationship to one another.

This systematizing activity beneath the surface of the texts is especially at work in the transition of conceptual theological notions from one genre of expression to another, or in the transformation of genres. The Exodus tradition is the standard paradigm. This well-known phenomenon shows that transition or transformation in forms of expression was nothing alien to the ancient Israelites; that the same conceptual notion could be expressed in many genres used contingently and not limited to specifically Israelite genres; and that it functioned as the systematic unifier which made the plurality of its expressions possible in the first place.

The fact that the ancient Israelites have not left us with a methodological treatise on this subject means neither that doing so would have been foreign to them (we do not even know whether or not they did do it anyway), nor that the activity of systematization did not exist and was never at work. To have denied themselves in principle systematic reflection on their own systematizing activities while at the same time practicing them would have amounted to an eminent case of self-contradiction. I am not prepared for such an interpretation. On the contrary, I prefer to interpret the relationship between the unifying subsurface conceptuality and the plurality of surface texts as a hermeneutical system in which the conceptual unifier, while controlling the expressions, allows for their flexibility because of different concrete settings, situations, and needs. These settings, situations, and needs constitute the legitimate causes for the appropriation of specific forms of language. The absence of explicit treatises on conceptual activities in the subsurface of texts means only — if at all — the absence of a particular need for such treatises. It does not mean that they would be disallowed should such a need arise. Neither does it mean that something which is at work in the subsurface of the text, especially a conceptual notion, may not be made explicit beyond what the writers themselves made explicit — at least not if what we make explicit is intrinsic, and demonstrably not extrinsic, to the hermeneutical system in which the writers operated. In view of this, the difference between their and our modus operandi is relative.

(3) The matter of generic transformation of text compositions guided by systematic-theological perspectives increasingly becomes a factor in our interpretation, especially in the wake of redaction-historical studies. It now appears that the book of Isaiah in its entirety was composed as "an exhortation for re-establishing and maintaining the Jewish community in Jerusalem in the fifth century B.C.E."[2] This exhortation employs doctrinal categories, such as judgment and grace, for the composition. Prophecy became Torah. Thus, the book of Isaiah owes its composition to a drive for systematization guided by doctrine.

(4) Also, the claim that the Old Testament does not hierarchize or even relate traditions reflects at best our untrained eyes in this respect, but not the facts. Once we begin to direct our attention to this question, we shall discover more cases than can be accommodated in a tome, let alone an essay of this size. Therefore, I will not exemplify this matter at this time.

(5) However, much more is at stake. When Murphy claims that systematization is foreign to the Old Testament, then the only legitimate form of interpretation would be to recite or to re-narrate the texts, to tell the story, or at most, to exegete them. Systematizing statements *about* the theologies of **J**, **P**, **Dtr**, the psalms, the prophets, and all the others would be illegitimate because none of these books or texts is given to us in the form of such statements. We speak of the plurality of the Old Testament's theologies. In fact, none of these "theologies" exists in the Old Testament. They exist only in the forms of our own systematizing conceptualizations, in transformations in form. These "theologies" are our forms, not theirs. In Murphy's sense we are left not only with no unified theology of the Old Testament, but without any theology of it at all. His contention would invalidate all our biblical theological literature that is anything more than exegetical.

Also, most of the genre definitions in form criticism are our own. Murphy's own "better-saying" is not a definition expressed in the texts. It is his own systematizing definition of a sentence in which two facts are precisely related comparatively and qualified hierarchically. In fact, this systematization involves a good degree of abstraction. I fully support it. And I do not believe that the method of our own genre definitions is illegitimate. In addition, when Murphy affirms that "everything, good and evil, comes from the hand of the Lord," he makes an eminently systematic statement, and an abstract one at that.

2. M. Sweeney, "Isaiah 1–4 and the Post-Exilic Understanding of the Isaianic Tradition" (diss., Claremont Graduate School, 1983); published in abbreviated form under the same title in BZAW 171 (Berlin/New York: Walter de Gruyter, 1988).

(6) Murphy asks whether systematization can be "applied to the biblical encounter of Israel with Yahweh, over several centuries of variegated history." The answer is yes. Already the historical works in the Old Testament have done that, and so have the prophets. Especially, I do not see why the systematization of this encounter — which certainly must be accounted for — must be expressed only in the forms found in Israel's history writing or in the prophetic speeches, and not also in the form of systematic statements.

(7) Murphy's reference to the Greco-Roman-Christian drive for systematization, believed to be foreign to the Old Testament, also deserves scrutiny. It involves a problem situation far more extensive than is generally recognized, namely, of our phenomenology of the Hebrew and the Greek mentalities. I no longer believe that the Hebrews were descriptive, intuitive, and peripatetic, in contrast to the Greco-Romans who were abstract, rational, and systematic: the aesthetic Hebrews versus the intellectual Greco-Romans!

The similarities and differences must be defined along different lines. They may be found in the explicitness of thematic treatises among the Greeks, as compared with their implicitness (nevertheless intrinsic) among the Hebrews, and in a higher attention to abstraction among the Greeks than among the Hebrews. These similarities and differences may also be found, in part, in the greater comprehensiveness of the Greco-Roman-Christian tradition, e.g., the law codes from Solon on, as compared with the more selective Hebrew law corpora. However these differences may be defined, it is methodologically questionable to establish them on the basis of explicit unifying rational systems, and then to conclude that the Hebrews had nothing to do with systematic unification. The ability to unify systematically does not depend on a specific form of system, because a specific form of system is only one of many kinds of systematization. It is questionable that the comparison of forms of systematization provides a proper access to the comparison of the Greeks and Hebrews. Apparently, this comparison must rest on a more fundamental phenomenological interpretation of the mentality of the two traditions which would have to include all the forms of their expressions. It would have to notice that the Greeks did not write only abstract treatises. They also wrote systematized histories,[3] as well as poetry. Our evaluation of the Greco-Roman-Christian drive for systematization rests too one-sidedly upon our attention to explicitly systematic treatments while ignoring the tremendous variety of different genres in the Greco-Roman-Christian tradition. In addition, it ignores the fact that systematization, unification, logic, and *ratio* are not only employed, either among the Greeks or among the Hebrews, where one speaks or writes for the sake of a system. That the Hebrews, whose writings we possess in the Old Testament, did not write for the sake of systems (which is only a half-truth anyway), proves neither that

3. Cf. the excellent book by John Van Seters, *In Search of History* (New Haven: Yale University Press, 1983).

they could not have done so or that it was not done in writings which we do not possess, nor that writing for the sake of a system, i.e., the Greco-Roman-Christian drive, is in principle extrinsic to the Hebrew mentality.

The Hebrew thought pattern of *Tatsphäredenken,* their dynamistic understanding of reality, may have been different in kind or degree from the understanding of reality prevalent among Greeks (which Greeks?). But it was certainly not unsystematic, whether they expressed it in an abstract treatise or not. It represents an understanding of causality, widely presupposed in the Old Testament, contested but ultimately not disproved by Job, and without which many texts simply cannot be understood. This thought pattern involves the perception of a universal dynamic unity-process which did not have to be unified by anyone.

This process was perceived as systemically coherent, inherently logical, and causal. The bipartite prophetic judgment speeches, expressing the reason for and the announcement of judgment, rest on the assumption of the logical coherence of cause and consequence, a coherence over which Yahweh is the guardian. The analogy to these speeches is found in those laws in the law corpora that substantively, and to a great extent even syntactically, express the causal coherence of case and consequence. The same assumption generated the formulation of numerous proverbs. Moreover, innumerable texts from Genesis 1 on show that the whole creation was perceived as a systemic unity. Furthermore, many texts reflect this perception in their unifying structure. Ultimately, a perception of the unity of reality and its expression in many forms was inevitable for the Hebrews because it corresponded to their belief in creation as order, or as orderly process, and not as chaos.

Thirty years ago, Thorleif Boman said in his valuable book *Hebrew Thought Compared with Greek*[4] that the Greeks were logicians, the Hebrews psychologists. The Greeks seek the objective truth of being, the Hebrews personal certainty about the laws of life, history, and morals. Greek thinking is synthetic-architectonic; Israelite thinking is analytical and deep-scrutinizing. I submit that this judgment is subject to revision in many respects, just as much as our comparisons between Israel and the ancient Near Eastern cultures have been subject to revision. Our comparison seems to be influenced much more by our own history of interpretation than substantiated by the evidence and by an updated method of cultural anthropology.

We should read Herder once again. Herder's position is not simplistic. He knew that the Mosaic laws were wonderfully thought through *("wunderbar durchdacht"),* and not the work of a moment. He also knew that the more ancient Greek poetry, not only the poems but the entire Narrating Muse *("die erzählende Muse"),* embodied all of genuine human wisdom — not as well as Hebrew poetry but still

4. Thorleif Boman, *Hebrew Thought Compared with Greek,* trans. J. L. Moreau (Philadelphia: Westminster, 1960).

genuinely authentically. However, with the rise of writings, the sciences, and philosophy, poetry lost out to prose, and the resulting philosophical dialogues and systems could not have the same immediacy, power, and authenticity as poetry once had. Now one was removed from the ancient, original, innocent *simplicitas*. For Herder, the basis for comparing the Greeks and Hebrews was not the different forms of expression or kinds of activity, not even the difference between poetry and philosophy. The basis was the different mentalities, the poetic versus the philosophical *spirit* incarnate in the different forms and activities: genuine, authentic, original intuition versus dry, if not decadent, rationalism. The philosopher was in a "foreign land." Herder's comparison, and his evaluation of *ratio,* system, and logic as inauthentic and foreign, rested on his own philosophical assumptions rooted in the cultural anthropology of romanticism.

What he did not know was that poetic intuition was by far not the only element at work in the mentality of the Hebrew literature; and that systematization, logic, and *ratio* were very much intrinsic to the Hebrew mind, and not only embryonically. They were even at work in the systematized generic structures of his beloved Hebrew poetry. This post-Herder evidence forces us to reconceptualize not only our understanding of the Hebrew mind, but also the criteria of the philosophy of romanticism for determining authenticity or foreignness. The usage of the word "foreign" in our comparison of the Old Testament and the Greco-Roman-Christian tradition does not refer to the description of differences alone. It represents a qualitative judgment about mutually exclusive mentalities. The scrutiny and reconceptualization of the background for this judgment will make the judgment itself obsolete.

(8) Finally, Murphy contends that "the discontinuities are too severe to be included in a logical system." I do not see why they cannot be included. Are we to say that the interpretation of these well-known discontinuities has to be irrational or illogical, even if the discontinuities at times appear to be devoid of sense and logic? Should we not attempt to penetrate to the point that explains why some discontinuities are devoid of logic while others are quite logical? And if discontinuities in historical development represent characteristics opposite to those of continuity, since when can the interpretation of such factors not be part of a logical system? Can a logical system explain only continuities? Is there any alternative to systemic logic in the interpretation of historical development, continuity or discontinuity, as long as it is an interpretation?

Perhaps Murphy assumes that for the purpose of logic I am driving for a system abstracted from the Old Testament texts, homogenized or harmonized. I have nothing of that well-known fallacy in mind. I seek to discern the theological criteria by which even the Old Testament tradition history can be theologically evaluated. Such evaluation constitutes the essence of the theological task. It has to be more than the description either of the sociological or traditio-historical realities, or of the texts themselves, because the texts were not written for that purpose, and above all, because the Old Testament understands Yahweh not as the describer of his world but as its evaluator. For his evaluating judgments Yahweh has criteria, logical criteria. They are reflected in Israel's testimonies, and also pertain to the history of these testimonies. We need to know these logical criteria, or we will not know how to read the Old Testament according to the will of Yahweh. Such knowledge will also remind us that the Scriptures are not Yahweh, and that they, too, are subject to Yahweh's evaluation. Moreover, as long as God has not personally revealed his opinion about them in the eschaton, we can only search for the better criteria discernible in the Scriptures themselves for evaluating the Scriptures and their historical development.

Without injecting substantive perspectives from the New Testament into the discussion, I think that Paul, or a redactor, utilized a good methodology for truth -finding when saying in comparison with things discussed previously, "And I will show you a still more excellent way" (1 Cor 12:31); and when, even then, defining this way as "the greatest" among the more than one "more excellent" ways (1 Cor 13:13). This is a typically hierarchical argument. The criteria for such evaluation are not self-evident, neither in the Old nor in the New Testament. For their discernment, we need arguments. I do not see why the use of logic, which is by definition systematic, should be suspect.

Moreover, the reference to the discontinuities is not relevant to this methodological discussion as long as it does not raise the question of their theological validity. Severe or not, they are theologically neither valid nor invalid on the basis of their continuity or discontinuity. The criteria for their evaluation must be discerned. That theological discernment of the validity of history, continuity, and/or discontinuity, as well as of everything else, involves a systematic relating of theological notions, e.g., of the relationship of creation and history, of justice and peace, of mercy and peace, or of judgment and grace.

(1)-(8) One may say that I see systematizing, (cor)relating, unifying, prioritizing, hierarchizing, and contradicting occurring everywhere in the Old Testament. Indeed I do. What I neither see nor propose is harmonizing, at least not in the sense that the plurality of theological notions is replaced by one notion; that one notion is expected to be found everywhere; that it is imposed on others without the recognition of their own place and validity; that all notions mean the same; and that contradictions are excluded and differences overlooked. The book of Job certainly criticizes theological positions held to be canonical elsewhere in the Old Testament. So do the book of Jonah and others.

As for hierarchy, it means the higher validity of some statements as compared with others, and not the dictate of any person who is in authority or, perhaps, closer to the cult or to the directness of revelatory experience. This statement is especially important for many biblical books because the question as to what extent we owe their existence more to societal power structures than to the better arguments is at least a matter of debate.

As for systematic unification, I continue to believe that the Old Testament's central affirmation of the oneness of Yahweh and the oneness of his world provides a substantial theological reason for reconstructing the pictures of that oneness in its diversity, and for comparing the Old Testament with it.

c) All of this leaves us with the fact that, in spite of all that has been said, the TaNaK is not presented to us in the form of a unifying theological system. It is not a systematic theology. Never mind that its composers systematized it by giving it a tripartite structure with a hierarchically understood validity. Even so, this fact is not insignificant in view of Murphy's statement that "a biblical theology that aspires to be systematic goes counter to the ongoing development in the Bible." This "ongoing development" is entirely the result of our critical and highly systematized reconstruction. It is our own picture of the TaNaK, not its self-portrait. Its historical books narrate history, but nowhere do they present themselves as the history of the ongoing development of their history writing.

If we reject systematization with reference to the unsystematic nature of the TaNaK while arguing for the ongoing development in the Bible, we commit a twofold fallacy. First, while rejecting systematization altogether we nevertheless systematize, namely, in the ongoing development of the Bible. Second, while reconstructing this ongoing development, we ourselves act in distinct contrast to what the composers of the TaNaK did. At any rate, the self-portrait of the TaNaK is much closer to a systematized understanding of the hierarchical validity of the major components of its tradition than to a systematized understanding of the ongoing development of that tradition.

But the case must be advanced on still different grounds. The contention that systematization of the Old Testament is invalid can only be upheld if no systematization of any one of its books is legitimate, and if no systematic treatment of any subject for which evidence exists in any of these books is legitimate. Such a methodological maxim would be radical in the extreme, and indeed new. I do not believe that we are prepared to endorse it. Until that happens, I must conclude that our systematization of all the biblical books is just as legitimate as that of any one of them, or of any of its subjects found in some or in all of them. The difference between the systematic treatment of individual books or subjects and of the entire TaNaK is a matter of extent and degree, but not a matter of principle. And a larger extent is better than a narrower one.

Conclusion

I would like to think that theology in general is a particular genre of systematic endeavor concerned with the theological nature of its issues, and that Old Testament theology is a subgenre of that endeavor because it focuses on the theological nature of the Old Testament Scriptures. This genre must be distinguished from history of theology or of Old Testament theology and religion. These two genres are not the same. For example, a treatment of the history of the works of Luther, who never wrote a systematic theology, is generically different from a systematic treatment of Luther's theology drawn from these works even as it takes this history and the specific forms, functions, and occasions of these works into account, and, hopefully, reserves for itself a chapter about a theological critique of this history which is derived from criteria appearing within it. Such a systematization is not only possible and legitimate, it is necessary. Its execution is not triggered by a drive for systematization born out of the idiosyncratic mentality of an epoch — to which Luther at least would not belong. It is necessary if one wants to understand and to evaluate not only the various but also the sometimes differing and conflicting statements in Luther's theology, and above all their roots. It serves neither the drive of an epoch nor its own ends, but only the appropriate understanding of its confronted subject.

There is nothing wrong with a history of Old Testament theology and religion as long as we do not overlook that such a history is the result of our own construction just as much as a systematic theology of the Old Testament is. The Old Testament itself is neither such a history or theology. Therefore, if our own reconstructions are foreign, both constructions are foreign. However, in any reconstruction of the history of the ongoing development of Israel's theology, as soon as the question is raised as to what validates that history, including its own understanding of validity, namely, the question of whether or not and why that history and its understanding among the Israelites is valid, the genre of systematic theology (in our case, systematic theology of the history of the Old Testament's theologies) is a legitimate, if not necessary, genre. This genre embraces both the history writings in the Old Testament and the rest of its books because all of them belong to that history.

It is clear that the Old Testament is not its own theology. If we reject an Old Testament theology in the singular, the only alternative left to us is not (here I must update my formulations from the first sentence of my original paper) a plurality of theologies, but a variety of theologically oriented narratives, laws, prophecies, proverbs, etc. What is wrong with doing theology *as* narrative, hymn, prayer, and innumerable other forms of actual human language? Why not do theology *as* form criticism? Indeed, this actualized theological language is very important in any theology and must be accounted for. It belongs to the chapter on theological anthropology, i.e., Israel's experience of Yahweh's presence and Israel's response to it.

However, the reference to these different genres of expression, to theology *as . . .* , focuses at best on the theological significance of forms only. But it does not consider the substantive content expressed in these forms at all. Are we to say that their contents, let alone the assumptions beneath the texts, are theologically irrelevant? Furthermore, are we to say that it is irrelevant whether these contents expressed in all the genres and the assumptions underlying them agree, complement, or contradict each other? These questions are not addressed, let alone answered, in a program of theology *as* narrative, prophecy, hymn, etc. As soon as we address them, any "theology *as* . . ." is necessarily transcended by the actually controlling function of the focus on *what* is said over against *how* it is said. In the theological enterprise, a "theology *as* . . ." will have its legitimate place. But it is neither a substitute for nor an alternative to a systematizing Old Testament theology.

Above all, no "theology *as* . . ." represents the basis for recognizing its own validity. This is true for both the forms and the contents of such theologies. While it is true that theological validity includes concrete forms of expression, it is not true that such forms constitute the criterion for theological validity. A Yahweh-hymn is not theologically valid because it is a Yahweh-hymn. Prayer can be invalid because its form, its setting, and its content can be horribly abused (cf. Jer 7:1-15 and Isa 1:10-17). In addition, while it is true that theological validity always includes content and substantive aspects, it is not true that content and substance as such constitute the criteria for theological validity. The content and substance of all "theologies *as* . . ." are themselves subject to validating evidence. Any hymn can praise God for godless reasons, and any prayer can pray against God's will.

Why is the insistence on theological validity in Old Testament theology, as in any theology, so important? It is because it reaches to the heart of the Old Testament's understanding of the nature of God, an understanding without which the Old Testament cannot be adequately interpreted at all. This understanding knows that God-Yahweh is not only the creator and redeemer of the world and of Israel but that he is also the sole judge of Israel's history and pluralistic society (including their history of faith and theology) and of the forms and contents of their theological expression as well. They are not all valid because of what they say, how they say it, and what they are. Nor may any of these positions ever have hoped to be exempt from the inescapable evaluation by and verdict of Yahweh, regardless of whether this verdict entails disapproval or approval. The Old Testament knows that to say Yahweh-God means to be aware of the confrontation with the question of the validity of everything that exists, and also the validity of Israel's own witnesses and piety, even at its best. Thus, Israel experienced the sovereignty of Yahweh in its midst. No Old Testament theology, however conceptualized, is worth its name unless it accounts for this fundamental fact.

Therefore, Old Testament theology must explain how and why the diverse forms and contents of the Old Testament's witnesses along with the history of their ongoing development (besides other aspects, including the canon), as seen by Israel or by us, are theologically valid. Moreover, this discipline distinguishes itself from the history of Israel's theology and from any "theology *as* . . . ," while at the same time applying its evaluative criteria to them all. It is distinct because it raises questions which are intrinsic to the very nature of the Old Testament, but which are not raised in other types of endeavor. This type of explanation is inevitably systematic. Its systematic nature is developed and governed by its subject, just as any other method is.

To reiterate, this explanation is certainly necessary for each kind of text and for each theological notion. Above all it is necessary in view of the many and differently oriented Old Testament traditions. In view of this necessity, I have attempted to propose a methodology for such explanation because the Old Testament's pluralism itself offers no answer to the problem its existence raises. Murphy's rejection of a "system" leaves him, as he admits, with the fact stated at the beginning of my paper and with the reliance on the status quo in current interpretation. However, Murphy's position does not represent an acknowledgment of the problem raised by this fact, let alone a suggestion for an alternative answer. Is this a comfortable situation?

The Interpretation of the Old Testament[1]

INTRODUCTION TO THE LECTURE SERIES

It is a great honor for me to have been invited to give the lectures at your 1989 Semana Wesleyana. Your invitation has provided me with the opportunity to be in South America for the first time. I regret that I speak no Portuguese, and already would like to thank my translators at this time for the superhuman task of making understandable for you the difficult arguments that I am going to present about the Bible.

I am aware that I am in no position to inform you about your situation in Brazil or in South America. For many years I have tried to read and hear about the situation in the so-called Third World. But you live in that situation, and know it through constant, direct personal experience. In this regard, I must listen to you and learn from you. For this reason alone, my lectures are not designed to discuss either primarily or directly your own experience. They focus instead on our reading of the Bible. I hope that we all have in common the task of understanding the Bible as a basic element of our ministry, and that my lectures convey, however indirectly, the relevance of biblical theology for your own situation as well as my personal interest in and commitment to your situation. My focus on the Bible rather than on your situation ought not to be understood as retreat from your concerns or as passivity on my part in regard to them.

Since I do not know to what extent each of you is equally informed about

1. This essay is based on the lectures I was honored to give at the United Methodist seminary in São Paulo, Brazil, on the occasion of its Semana Wesleyana in May 1989. The printed text represents some revisions, but at times also, and in part significant, expansions of the lectures given. I have sought to preserve the style of the oral presentation.

the development of biblical studies in recent decades, I may say things with which some of you are more familiar and some of you are less. In view of my own uncertainty about the extent of your personal acquaintance with biblical studies, I have opted to reflect with you on the basis of the current international standard in biblical interpretation, a standard that specifically includes the important contributions of South American theologians, without which no discussion of the Bible can any longer be regarded as sufficient. By aspiring to this standard, I hope to remind you of the best in your own state of biblical interpretation.

My lectures are not meant to be a review of the current state of biblical studies. Such reviews are recorded in many other publications. The lectures focus instead on my own opinions regarding both the problems facing biblical interpretation and the direction this interpretation ought to take. The four lectures are interdependent and ought to be considered together. I shall speak first about the difference between the tasks of exegesis, biblical theology, and biblical hermeneutic; then about the method of Old Testament theology; thirdly, about the topic of justice in Old Testament theology; and finally, about the method of biblical theology, or about the Old Testament, the New Testament, (comma!) and Jesus Christ.

FIRST LECTURE: BIBLICAL EXEGESIS, THEOLOGY, AND HERMENEUTIC

Introduction

My choice of topic indicates that in biblical interpretation I differentiate between exegesis, theology, and hermeneutic. When consulting publications on the Old Testament, the New Testament, or the entire Bible, one observes that this threefold subdivision does not have a highly visible place in the method of biblical interpretation — if it has any place at all. In my first lecture, I will give you the reasons for this differentiation.

One widespread mode of interpretation is based on the distinction between *exegesis on the one hand, and theology and hermeneutic combined on the other hand.* This distinction rests on considered assumptions in philosophical or theological hermeneutic; but it is also the result of a long development which began with the emancipation of biblical studies from church dogmatics. Martin Luther's *sola scriptura* represents the roots of this development and the powerful incentive for it. In 1787, 202 years ago, 250 years after Luther, and four years before John

Wesley's death, Johann Philipp Gabler drew the final conclusions.[2] He proclaimed the need for a biblical theology independent of the doctrine of the church. What emerged was the discipline of a systematic biblical theology vis-à-vis dogmatics. This *biblical* discipline was followed by the separation of the theologies of the Old and the New Testament. (John Wesley was not affected by this development. His sermons and writings show the close interdependence of the Bible and church doctrine, despite the fact that he was called the man of one book. He, the Anglican priest, already had the articles of faith in his mind before he began to understand the Bible.)

The emancipation of biblical theology from church doctrine and its autonomy directed the focus toward biblical studies themselves. This focus generated another development, now *within* biblical studies, namely, the rise, especially during the last hundred years, of historical-critical exegesis. With its ever-increasing focus on individual texts, results of historical-critical exegesis came to be characterized by the recognition of the historical distance between the world of the texts and ourselves (what we call the experience of distantiation) and the recognition of the diversity of the texts themselves (what we call the experience of diversification). These experiences signaled the emergence of biblical exegesis vis-à-vis biblical theology, and in effect the emancipation of exegesis now even from biblical theology itself. It is ironic that the emancipatory impetus of biblical theology, away from its dependence on church doctrine, has led to the replacement of biblical theology as the foundation of biblical studies by exegesis, and to its own disintegration under the onslaught of the atomization of exegetical results. Today, we have a flood of diverse exegetical results but no consensus on the definition of biblical theology.

We are equally uncertain about the distinction between biblical theology and hermeneutic. While some draw a distinction, others do not, sometimes by design and sometimes by default.

Most recently, movements have emerged which in effect amount to a linkage between the exegesis of biblical texts and biblical hermeneutic. They can be found in the disciplines of structuralism, structural linguistics, cultural anthropology, and the new literary criticism. In addition, the direct linkage between a biblical text and our contemporary situation can certainly be found — however reflected or unreflected — in countless publications and sermons.

I am aware of the hermeneutical circle in which exegesis, theology, and hermeneutic are inseparably conjoined. However, their inseparability does not mean that they ought not to be distinguished from each other. Each involves a set of

2. J. P. Gabler, "De justo discrimine theologiae biblicae et dogmaticae regundisque recte ultriusque finibus," in *Kleinere Theologische Schriften,* vol. 2 (Ulm, 1831), 179-98; cf. J. Sandys-Wunsch and L. Eldredge, "J. P. Gabler and the Distinction between Biblical and Dogmatic Theology: Translation, Commentary, and Discussion of His Originality," *SJT* 33 (1980): 133-58.

requirements and questions which is different from the questions and requirements involved in the others. *What, then, is the respective distinctiveness of exegesis, theology, and hermeneutic? How are these three related?*

I. Exegesis

It is the task of exegesis to interpret the biblical texts in their own right, on their own terms, apart from us, by way of conscious distantiation. Exegesis focuses on each individual text, be it small or large, and includes attention to its literary context, to its tradition, and to extratextual factors such as anthropology, sociology, history, ontology, epistemology, etc.

The available exegetical methods are well known. They are philology, text criticism, literary criticism, form criticism, rhetorical criticism, tradition and transmission history, and redaction criticism. It is important to note that the sequence of these methods reflects the sequence of their historical emergence, but not necessarily the sequence of their application in actual exegetical work. Depending on the text, which at any rate controls the methods, the sequence of applied methods may vary. However, the application of a number of exegetical methods does not yet represent an exegetical methodology.

Individually and combined, the methods listed above have had weaknesses, and exegesis reveals itself as having a fundamental deficit. The explicit categorizations of the methods do not cover the full extent of necessary exegetical work. Moreover, exegesis as such provides no criteria for the verification of the validity of a text.

Let me comment first on the methodological weakness. Exegetical methods are analytical and synthetic tools for the description of textual, i.e., linguistic, literary phenomena. Problematic in their classical definitions is the fact that they refer predominantly to the formal aspects of texts, while reference to the content of texts is sometimes not explicit. And even where it is explicit, the place and importance of content are not sufficiently defined. It is a fact, however, that all texts say something. They express a subject matter in each element of their reality addressed by the exegetical methods. The neglect of these substantive statements, or their underrepresentation, in exegesis is certainly a major methodological error. The exegetical methodology must be designed so that in each exegetical step both the formal aspects of a text and a text's substantive statements are given equal consideration, separately, as well as in their constant interaction. Indeed, one should be ready to raise the question as to which of the two factors governs the other at any given time, and why.

Furthermore, since the substantive statements of the biblical texts are basically theological, the theology of a text belongs to its exegesis from the outset and throughout each of the subsequent steps. If the text is theological in nature, exegesis is for that reason theological. Theological exegesis is not a separate method in addition to the other methods, or an appendix to them. It is not rooted in the theological interest of the exegete, but in the nature of the text. We are not to theologize a text. We are to exegete its theology.

This methodological weakness has been significantly alleviated by the advances achieved through structural linguistics. This discipline has especially highlighted the fact that a text represents above all the totality of a linguistic, semantic system. The principal task of exegesis is, therefore, to interpret this system as a whole, and not only one of its aspects. Fundamentally, this interpretation takes place by means of the identification of all parts, aspects, and statements within a text, the determination of their relationship, and the definition of the whole arising from these two steps.

This task requires more than some of us were taught. We have been taught that exegesis makes intelligible what is explicit in a text. However, the semantic system of a text includes more than what is explicit on its surface. It also includes what is inexplicit underneath its surface but nonetheless at work in it. It includes presuppositions, concerns, concepts, and intentions. Indeed, these elements are the reasons why the texts were produced in the first place, as well as the reasons for what the texts say and how they say it. The underlying concerns represent the blueprints for the texts, and the unwritten commentaries to the blueprints. They control the texts.

As long as exegesis focuses only on the surface expressions of the texts, it may be able to describe the obvious, but it will not achieve what is ultimately necessary: to explain *why* the obvious is said, so that we may *understand.* It will not be able to define the meaning of a text. Difficult as it is, exegesis must not only describe what a text says; it must also attempt to reconstruct the presuppositions on which it rests. Such reconstruction must start from and be controlled by the signals provided by the text itself. It is inevitably hypothetical. Even so, the requirement for such reconstruction supersedes the tentativeness of its hypothetical nature. To be sure, a hypothesis is only a theoretical model, a scholarly construction and proposition, rather than a conclusive proof. It may be in need of revision or even replacement by a more appropriate one. However, since we need to understand the presuppositions that constitute the basis for the very existence of the texts, although not made explicit in the texts themselves, we must reconstruct them hypothetically, however tentatively and provisionally. A necessary hypothesis is better than none at all. The inclusion in the exegetical process of a text's infra- and possibly extralinguistic life leads, if not to the solution of all problems, significantly beyond much in the present state of exegetical affairs. In my fourth lecture, I shall apply this principle more thoroughly to the exegesis of the relationship between an explicit text and its inexplicit concept, and to an explanation of the exegetical consequences for the interpretation of Old Testament and biblical theology and of biblical hermeneutic. Already at this juncture, however, an example may illustrate what is meant by the conscious reconstruction of presuppositions or concepts that are not expressed but nevertheless operative in a text.

Rather than aiming at completeness, the exemplification will focus on a few selected points in Lev 1:2aβ-3. Here I am intentionally quoting the *Revised Standard Version,* a standard translation of the Bible, which says: "When any man of you brings an offering to the LORD, you shall bring your offering of cattle from the herd or from the flock. If his offering is a burnt offering from the herd, he shall offer a male without blemish; he shall offer it at the door of the tent of meeting, that he may be accepted before the LORD."

The problem of the relationship between what this text says and what it presupposes already begins with the translation. Quite apart from the fact that the English translation could in some instances render the Hebrew statements accurately (at least more so), the expression of the Hebrew text itself is at times ambiguous. Such ambiguity points to the possibility that it presupposes only one meaning, rather than more than one meaning at the same time. Yet even where the Hebrew expression is unmistakable, one clearly observes that it rests directly on known presuppositions which it assumes to be known by its readers, or else the text could not be understood, let alone applied.[3]

First, when speaking of "any man" in verse 2aβ, the English translation is ambiguous because it may refer, according to the traditional usage of the word (as in "mankind"), either to any person, male or female, or to a male person only. This ambiguity in the translation can be removed by a clear rendering of the Hebrew

3. For the purpose of substantive clarification, I am using the words "ambiguous/ambiguity," "ambivalent/ambivalence," and "multivalent/multivalency" distinctively for the sake of exegetical work. These words refer to different textual phenomena. Because all language is multivalent, a claim to a text's multivalency is a truism. Since multivalency does not mean equivalency, however, the kinds and degrees of "valency" in a text must be discerned by distinguishing each valency from the others. The discernment of a text's value system is necessary because valency must be identifiable or it is not valency. Especially necessary is the distinction between a text's own value system and interpretations drawn from aspects or elements of it under the influence of the interpreter's subjective interests. Inasmuch as a text's multivalent system is *homogeneous,* its different valencies reflect and are controlled by a basic criterion. The reference to multivalency requires these distinctions. It means that the many valencies must be identified, that their qualitative differences are relevant, and that the adoption of any of them is not the interpreter's subjective prerogative exclusive of the text's own criteria.

By comparison, I take the words "ambivalent/ambivalence" to refer to an appearance of a text's multivalency in which distinctions between kinds and degrees of valency cannot be identified or, if identifiable, cannot be evaluated, or in which kinds of valency conflict. These words refer to unclarity regarding the aspect of or claim to valency. Finally, I reserve the words "ambiguous/ambiguity" for texts or statements that in effect are not clearly expressed, and are therefore equivocal, whether they involve the question of valency or not. With these latter words so clarified, we may be able to discern whether they reflect one or more meanings in a given text. They may then also offer a basis for the evaluation of the aspects of multivalency or of ambivalence.

word אדם, which is, particularly in the priestly texts, used for humankind in general including both female and male. However, the removal of this ambiguity in translation does not solve the problem that the usage of the Hebrew word itself is ambivalent in this context. When one reads in the following that such a person may have to sacrifice a male ox or steer, it is an open question whether the text presupposes that such a sacrifice (and the ritual prescribed for it in vv. 3-9) can or may be executed by a woman as well as by a man. The Hebrew word itself is ambivalent because it does not clarify that question while nonetheless speaking about a man or a woman. This ambivalence can only be resolved through further exegetical work. Exegesis will have to confront the possible tension between what the word אדם says, i.e., its lexical meaning, and what it means in this context, i.e., its contextual meaning. Only after such exegetical work can one truly decide whether this word is in its lexical meaning bivalent, i.e., multivalent, or univalent, and whether or not a genuine tension between a clearly multivalent lexical expression and a possibly presupposed univalent meaning has in effect created a multivalent text, which in turn lends itself to a reconceptualized adaptation of its original meaning by later interpreters, now of the text of the writers rather than of what the writers meant to say.

Second, when our translation speaks in verse 2 about "bringing" an offering and says in verse 3, "he shall offer" a male, it is again ambiguous. To "bring" something does not necessarily mean to "offer" it, and something offered does not necessarily have to be brought. Depending on the meaning of either of the English words, the translation may express and presuppose quite different things. It may be that there is no ambiguity since each expression may be appropriate in its immediate sentence. However, the suspicion of ambiguity arises because two different English words render the same Hebrew word, קרב, hiph, "to bring near." Does the Hebrew word refer in both verses to literally bringing something near, from one place to another? Or does it refer to offering something regardless of how this happens? Or does it refer to both, whereby one either dominates or merely complements the other? Or does it refer to one aspect in one statement and to the other in the next? Each of these possibilities has significant consequences for our understanding of the text. It seems that the ambiguous translation of the same Hebrew word is caused by unclarity regarding the different semantic possibilities of the word itself, and that this word is used ambiguously because of its presupposed multivalent (not ambivalent) meaning. Again, both the meaning of the Hebrew word and its proper translation are in need of clarification through exegetical work.

Third, the *Revised Standard Version* translation of the conclusion of verse 3, "that he may be accepted before the LORD," is also ambiguous. The Hebrew says, "for favor to him before Yahweh" or "in his favor. . . ." The Hebrew phrase says not that "he" is accepted, but that *his offering* is counted in his favor. Nor does it speak about "acceptance." The Hebrew says "to his favor." While implying acceptance, it emphasizes *favorable* acceptance. One may have to accept something grudgingly, although one does not like it. Or one may like something and therefore accept it. The latter, which has considerable consequences for our discernment of what the text presupposes, is unambiguously expressed by the Hebrew text. By contrast, the translation "to accept" emphasizes a subordinate connotation, thereby missing the major notion of the text.

On the issue of the relationship between the explicit text and its inexplicit presuppositions, we need to distinguish between presuppositions that are directly operative in the text, i.e., presuppositions the text implies must be known for the understanding and adoption of what it says, and presuppositions that are in the text indirectly because they reflect assumptions (whether known by everyone or not) which underlie many or all texts but do not belong to the particular subject addressed by the text.

Just one example from Lev 1:3 must suffice, the statement "he shall offer [or bring] a male without blemish" (v. 3aβ). This is what the text requires when someone brings a burnt offering from the herd, i.e., cattle, rather than from the flock of sheep and goats. The ox or steer must be "male, complete" — so states the Hebrew, which does not say "without blemish." The text also says that such an animal is "his (her?)" offering, which must be taken to mean his property, whether by purchase or, more likely, from his own herd. What it does not say but inevitably presupposes is that he/she must select this kind of animal from his/her herd in which there are cows as well as oxen and incomplete as well as complete oxen. To select his exemplar, however, he must know the criteria for distinguishing male and female, which should be easy, and complete and incomplete, which may be more complicated. The knowledge of these criteria is certainly presupposed, and this inexplicit presupposition is directly operative in the text. Even more specifically, the sequence in which the text lists the two words is not coincidental. The word "male" stands before the word "complete." When selecting his sacrificial exemplar, the offerer scarcely looks for a "complete" animal first. If he did, he might find a "complete" female and then have to pass it up because it is not male. If, instead, he focuses first on the males, he will have to pass up only those that are "incomplete," but not a "complete" exemplar because it is not male. It is, therefore, most probably not coincidental that the Hebrew text says, with an intended comma between the two words, "male, complete," rather than "a complete male." In choosing this phrasing, the text apparently presupposes and reflects the sequence of steps in which such animals are selected.

What has been said about verse 3aβ shows that this prescription involves more than what it says. It involves direct presuppositions about the need and even the process for the selection of a sacrificial exemplar, and about the offerer's knowledge of the criteria for its selection. Were these presuppositions not operative in the text, the offerer could not even start to bring his animal "to the opening of the tent of meeting." Without them, the sacrifice of the animal is impossible. Of course, the text focuses on what it says, and the questions are inevitable as to why it says what it says and why it does not express what it presupposes. The answer to these questions must be found. However, the exegesis of both what the text says and what the text presupposes does more than only help us to discern more clearly the interest of the explicit text, i.e., to understand what it says rather than merely to restate it. It will especially enable us to reconstruct the conceptuality undergirding the text's own statements, without which it could not say what it says. Not everything in a text's and in our own understanding of a situation is put into words and texts. Much of what is understood affects and controls our words and texts. The fact that inexplicit presuppositions and concepts must be distinguished from explicit statements and that their exegesis is related to the need for the exegesis of the text's own statements does not mean that they are, therefore, irrelevant. Indeed, they are so relevant that the texts are, in terms of substance, relative to their conceptual presuppositions.

There are also presuppositions in our text which are not directly operative in it, at least not in the sense that knowledge of them would be necessary for the understanding of the text and for the performance prescribed by it. Thus, while the offerer must know the difference between a male and a female, a complete and an incomplete animal, he/she may know, but does not have to know, *why* the animal is subject to these conditions. The offerer is capable of executing the prescribed ritual and its direct presuppositions without knowing the answer to that question. The *why* question is not unimportant or illegitimate, and we are interested in it as well, but it belongs to presuppositions, or to a level of preunderstanding, which are not the subject of the text's discussion. It aims at explaining something the text is not engaged in explaining, neither in its statements nor in its presuppositions for them. It does not belong to the text's agenda. Whatever the answers to this *why* question may be, and wherever they may be found, e.g., in a gender- or economy- or purity-oriented worldview, they belong to the explanation of the more or less conceptualized presuppositions of all texts, but not to the text's own agenda.[4]

Of much greater consequence than the methodological imperfections in exegesis is a fundamental deficit of exegesis itself, which cannot be solved by any exegetical method. This deficit is created by the fact that intrinsic to the biblical texts is their claim to truth which they present to their readers for acceptance. This intrinsic element of the textual reality confronts exegesis with an insoluble dilemma. Exegesis must acknowledge the presence of this intrinsic element by recognizing this claim to truth. However, since what is being claimed is truth, exegesis would have to evaluate and verify that claim, precisely because the text asks for such verification by presupposing its own truth. Semantically, a text may

4. For a more thorough discussion of this issue, and of the chosen example, see my separate publication *Text and Concept in Leviticus 1:1-9: A Case in Exegetical Method,* FAT 2 (Tübingen: J. C. B. Mohr, 1992).

be completely consistent and particularly meaningful, but its validity or truth does not consist in its semantic coherence or in its meaningfulness. If that were so, many words of the prophets would have been rejected on the basis of their semantic properties, regardless of their truth (or lack thereof). The truth of a text depends on criteria which validate it, and not on the text itself, not even on its systemic-semantic integrity. Such criteria are extraneous to the text. They represent a supra-textual factor.[5]

In their claim to truth, the biblical texts themselves indicate that they are true not because they are texts and not because of what or how they speak, but that they are texts and speak because they stand on truth. This self-understanding of the texts themselves is the reason why the biblical texts are not God, but at best God's word. Our expression "Word of God" means that it is God and God's truth that constitutes the truth of his words, and not the truth of the word that constitutes the truth of God. The texts point to God, rather than to their own linguisticality, as the ground of their truth. While exegesis must acknowledge a text's claim to truth, it cannot verify the truth of a text because no text or word or statement is true on the basis of what it claims or says or means. Thus, exegesis reaches the limit of what it can achieve precisely at the point where everything the text says and is, is at stake. At this point, exegesis must state that the text calls for more than what exegesis, by virtue of its own limitations, can deliver.

II. Biblical Theology

Biblical theology is to be distinguished from both exegesis and biblical hermeneutic because an encounter with an individual text in isolation from all others is not a sufficient basis for its *biblical* truth, and because the *biblical* truth of a text, when discerned, does not automatically and unilaterally reveal its truth for our present reality or, if you will, the truth of the presence of God in our own reality. Accordingly, a method of biblical interpretation that is based on the individual texts alone is at best a method for the exegesis of their intratextual theology and hermeneutic, in isolation from their biblical validity and from their hermeneutical validity for our reality. It is neither a method for establishing the biblical truth of a text nor a method for the discernment of its truth for us today. Therefore, what must be clarified is, on the one hand, the relationship between the exegesis of biblical texts

5. By *supratextual* I mean the conceptual umbrella over all texts but not outside or beyond them. By contrast, I take *intratextual* to refer to the conceptual totality within an individual text, including its surface; *infratextual* to refer to the subterranean/subsurface world of a text or texts; and *intertextual* to refer to the relationship of texts, including their systems, as, e.g., observed through tradition and transmission history or redaction criticism.

and biblical theology, and, on the other hand, the relationship between the biblical validity of the texts and their hermeneutical validity, i.e., their validity in the encounter with the totality of our present reality. In this section I will discuss the problem of biblical theology, before moving on to the problem of biblical hermeneutic in the next section.

I have emphasized that the biblical texts are, above all else, theological texts. They focus on the relationship between God and the world. Furthermore, I acknowledge that in their focus they claim truth and validity. Whatever a text contains in terms of information and presupposition, perceived theologically it represents a claim to truth.

However, in the Bible we are not confronted with an individual biblical text in isolation from all others, but with all the texts at the same time. We are, therefore, confronted with the theologies of every text in the biblical canon, rather than with the theology of only one text, biblical source, or book. This fact constitutes the basis for the theological problem of the canon and, in addition to the deficit of exegesis, the second reason for the need for biblical theology. The sum total of exegesis of the biblical texts has irreversibly demonstrated a considerable plurality and diversity of theological positions in and among the canonic texts. Because of this fact, no text considered in isolation from the others self-evidently assures us of its truth or of the degree of its truth. I am addressing the well-known problem of the "canon within the canon." Indeed, everyone has always operated with "a canon within the canon," in whatever form, on whatever priorities, and whether intentional or accidental. While such prioritization pervades the entire history of biblical interpretation and even the Bible itself, the movement of historical-critical exegesis has finalized the problem of the validity of all texts because of its definitive uncovering of their theological pluralism and diversity. Indeed, by uncovering that pluralism and diversity, historical-critical exegesis has disclosed the texts' own mutual self-relativization much more than it has relativized their claim to validity and truth. The theological self-relativization of the biblical texts challenges the credibility of the Bible much more than does the historical distance between the Bible and ourselves.

If the problem of Old Testament, New Testament, and biblical theology, and not only the problem of the theologies of individual texts, could be solved merely by bridging the cultural and historical distance between the texts and ourselves, the task would be relatively easy. It is predominantly and universally approached by decontextualization and recontextualization on the basis of analogy, and where necessary by deconstruction and reconstruction or deconceptualization and reconceptualization. In a general hermeneutic, these methods are certainly fundamental, indispensable, and indeed universally practiced.

However, the methods of bridging the cultural and historical distance do not yet take into account the difference between the interpretation of an individual text and the determination of its validity in the context of all other texts that exist together with it in the biblical canon and tradition history. They may (and often do) address nothing more than the analogy of an individual text or text group and a specific modern condition, both of which are taken in isolation from all other cases of similar bipolar analogy.

The problem of the theological validity of an individual text arises not only from its distance from our time; it arises, first of all, from the unresolved relationship between its own claim to truth and the multiple truth claims of all these texts with which it coexists. This problem cannot be short-circuited by relating an individual text to our current situation. This practice may be called intratextual hermeneutic, but it is not biblical hermeneutic, no matter how widespread it is. It accounts not only for the rich complementarity but also for the frustrating incompatibility of diverse hermeneutical interpretations of the Bible in modern theology and church life.

In summary, the truth and validity of individual biblical texts cannot be discerned only through their meaning for us today. Their truth and validity must, first of all, be discerned by means of their comparison with other biblical texts. This necessity constitutes the task of Old Testament, New Testament, and biblical theology in distinction from and in addition to the task of exegeting the theology of each text. It cannot be said clearly enough: Old Testament, New Testament, and biblical theology must provide the criteria, discerned from within the Bible, by which the truth and validity of each text can be established. While these spheres of theology are still concerned with the validity of each text, they proceed to establish that validity by comparison with the theologies of all other texts, and not by identifying a text's theology in isolation.

Here, then, is the final irony: the exegesis of the texts, which was expected to uncover the Bible's own coherent theology, has uncovered the opposite instead. The Bible contains diverse theologies; it is not a theology. The diversity of theologies within the Bible is the fundamental problem of and obstacle to a self-explanatory biblical theology. Without a biblical theology, however, we will not know how to evaluate the individual biblical texts. We, therefore, need what neither the Bible nor exegesis can do for us. In order to recognize the truth of the biblical texts, we need to conceptualize biblical theology ourselves, a task the Bible and our exegesis of it have generated but left undone. The discipline of biblical theology presupposes exegesis, but is neither a part of exegesis nor an appendix to it. It is in principle a discipline in its own right, generated by a distinct set of questions, and to be conceptualized accordingly. Its foundational questions are: What constitutes the truth of the biblical texts, and by what criteria can we discern what constitutes their truth? This task is neither confessional nor descriptive. It is rational. The methodology for this task must provide the criteria for the theological evaluation of the biblical texts, and its execution must implement that methodology.

Biblical theology must also be distinguished from biblical hermeneutic, and not only from biblical exegesis. It does not address the question of the relevance of the Bible for us today, as does hermeneutic. It merely confronts the sum total of the biblical texts and establishes the validity of those texts before their truth claims can legitimately confront us today. The truth of a *particular* text for us depends on more than that text alone, i.e., its *biblical* truth, just as the truth of a particular current situation depends on more than that situation alone. Because exegesis by itself cannot establish the truth of a text, the encounter between a particular text and a particular current situation, which are analogous and comparable, takes place within the encounter of the two truth systems, the Bible's and our own. The counterpart to biblical hermeneutic is biblical theology, and not biblical exegesis. Without biblical theology, the recognition of the truth and validity of the whole Bible for us today is without foundation. This is the reason why the demise of past concepts and the current disarray in matters of biblical theology are so disquieting.

III. Biblical Hermeneutic

In distinction to hermeneutics of other bodies of literature or tradition, the subject of biblical hermeneutic is the Bible. Biblical hermeneutic mediates the encounter between the foci of biblical texts and of comparable situations in our present reality. However, since this encounter involves not only the two sets of data representing two specific positions encountering or confronting each other but also their mutual truth claims, biblical hermeneutic involves more than the encounter of a text and a comparable situation today. I have already argued that the theological validity of a biblical text can only be discerned within biblical theology, and not in isolation from it. Analogously, I am now arguing, along with others who have said the same, that the meaning of a specific situation today, and especially its truth, can only be discerned within the complex web of relations which characterizes the totality of our own reality, of which each situation is but a part.

The task of biblical hermeneutic is, therefore, twofold. While inevitably presupposing the exegesis of both biblical texts and comparable current situations, biblical hermeneutic involves the encounter between, on the one hand, the validity of the texts within the entire biblical theology and, on the other hand, the validity of today's situations within the totality of our own reality. In this twofold encounter scenario, biblical theology, together with exegesis, is the representative of the world of the Bible which confronts our world and its many and equally diverse situations. Ultimately, biblical hermeneutic involves the encounter of two systems of meanings and their respective claims to truth. In this encounter, each speaks independently to the other; neither is the only one that speaks; and it is only through the comparison of the two systems, facilitated by their encounter, that the criteria appear for what is fundamental, guiding, and authoritative, and thus, for orientation, values, truth, and ethos today, and specifically for the authority of the biblical texts themselves for us.

The range of hermeneutical aspects is vast, and the literature on those aspects endless. Most importantly, we must distinguish between hermeneutic as method, on the one hand, and as actual interpretation of texts (as, for example, in preaching), on the other. At this time, I am focusing on method. Methodologically, we must distinguish between description and evaluation. When compared with the mainstream of the current hermeneutical discussion, this distinction involves a shift in the definition of the problem. The title of Gadamer's book *Truth and Method* is a case in point.[6] The problem does not lie in the relationship between truth and method, but the problem is one of method itself and lies in the relationship between reality and truth, between description and evaluation, and in the function of method for the clarification of this relationship.

The prevalent hermeneutical discussion in theology, philosophy, structuralism, structural linguistics, and new literary criticism, among others, demonstrates that the methodological focus has been increasingly preoccupied with the correct *description* of the system of the conceptual basis (such as ontology, epistemology, history, and sociology) and with the *description* of the system of the mechanisms of the hermeneutical process (such as way, vehicle, locus, instrumentalities, contextualization, transformation, resignification, refiguration, and so on). These concerns are indispensable to a hermeneutical methodology, and their achievements are indeed impressive. However, hermeneutical methodology has not equally, if at all, developed the criteria for the evaluation of the truth claims of the biblical texts and of our own time.

It is, therefore, not surprising that Gadamer establishes no criteria for the discernment of truth. His "fusion of horizons" is a fact, but scarcely a criterion for truth. Moreover, according to Lynn Poland, Paul Ricoeur suggests that the appropriation of the meaning of a text requires "a process of interpretation" of the text's semantic totality, but that "the question of truth at this level . . . lies beyond the task of interpretation . . . in the province of philosophical thought."[7] Indeed, Ricoeur's work has demonstrated that the meaning of a text does not necessarily constitute its truth. He has advanced to its conceivable limits the description of the system by which the meaning of texts as language may be experienced, but he has not developed a method for the discernment of the truth and validity of a biblical text, or of language itself for that matter. His work contains a number of indicators, but they are not developed into a methodology. Such a method, however, is indis-

6. *Truth and Method,* trans. J. Weinscheimer and D. G. Marshall, 2d ed. (New York: Crossroad, 1990).

7. Lynn Poland, *Literary Criticism and Biblical Hermeneutics: A Critique of Formalist Approaches,* American Academy of Religion, Academy Series 48 (Chico, CA: Scholars Press, 1985), 178.

pensable precisely because claim to truth is intrinsic to the biblical texts. A hermeneutical method that excludes this claim is insufficient because it fails to appreciate this claim as the texts' own urgent contribution to the totality of the hermeneutical deliberation.

The decisive question for biblical hermeneutic is, therefore, what kind of method can be established by which the truth of a biblical text for us today may be discerned, experienced, and confronted with our own truth claims of today. Such a method must certainly include the phenomenon of the text with regard to both its form and its content in all their conceptual and mechanical aspects. But it will have to go beyond these factors and ask why any of them is true and valid. It will have to define the relationship between formal and substantive aspects and to establish which of them represents the foundation from which to develop the criteria for what is true for us.

Furthermore, since the biblical truth claims are theological in nature and rest on theological assumptions peculiar/germane to the Bible, and not likewise to literature in general, biblical hermeneutic must respond to what is germane/peculiar to the Bible. It belongs to the province of theological thought. The fact that it must address its theological subject with a philosophically or rationally controlled methodology does not deprive it of its nature as a theological discipline.

SECOND LECTURE: THE METHOD OF OLD TESTAMENT THEOLOGY

I. The Shape of the Problem and of Its Solution

In the first lecture, I argued that the claim to theological truth and validity represents the distinctive concern and presupposition of all biblical literature, especially when considered canonically, and that neither the exegesis of individual texts nor their correlation with analogous current situations provides a sufficient ground for verifying that claim. This deficit is intensified by the fact that the claim of each text is relativized through the canon itself due to the coexistence of theological diversity within all texts in the canon. This exegetical and canonic situation demands biblical theology. The methodological task of biblical theology is to establish the criteria by which the truth claims of the biblical texts may be evaluated.

The methodology for the establishment of these criteria must satisfy two conditions: it must develop the criteria from the biblical materials themselves rather than from outside them — the substantive condition; and it must be a heuristic device through which the evaluation of the biblical texts can proceed — the procedural condition. Since the principal obstacle to the discernment of validity is the self-relativization of the biblical texts through their theological diversity, the device for their evaluation must be developed so as to overcome this obstacle. It is precisely at this juncture, the self-relativization of the biblical texts, where the answer must and can be found for the discernment of their validity. More specifically, the truth and validity of the biblical texts can be discerned *through* their relativization! The very process that leads to their relativization will be the vehicle for reestablishing their validity and truth.

This proposal should not be surprising. It does not require that we do something that has never been done before. It has always been done. The entire principle of "the canon within the canon" rests on the prioritization of some aspects and, therefore, the relativization of others. Even under the most literalistic understanding of the Bible as "the Word of God," all biblical "words" are never considered equally valid. Some are more important; others are less important. In addition, within each "word," i.e., text, something is more important, while something else is less important. The degree of importance results from the fact that the texts, just as the elements within them, are relative to each other. Such relativity does not mean irrelevance. However, it does mean that we should not strive for a truth that is absolute. The Bible, because of its knowledge of God, knew, long before modern science and philosophy established it, that there is no knowledge of absolute truth and that no knowledge of God is absolute. This insight must be a fundamental theological assertion (cf. 1 Cor 13:8-12).

Relativization means, therefore, that we adopt as a methodology what the Bible itself suggests; that is, that we relate its many and diverse theologies which are themselves already related, as they are at least juxtaposed in the single canon. The canon is the cause for this necessity. Whoever relates, however, must inevitably compare. It is through comparison that we gain the criteria for prioritizing and subordinating. In the process, we are enabled to discern and to affirm the degrees of validity and truth. This process is rational and can account for its results.

This methodology serves two objectives: it provides the basis for our evaluation of the truth claims of the biblical texts, and it aims at the inclusion of all biblical texts. *Biblical theology is not concerned with the description of the theology of each biblical text but with the basis for their evaluation. The former belongs to the task of exegesis, whereas the latter can only be achieved through the comparison of a text's theology with the theologies of the other texts.*

II. The Relationship of the Two Testaments

The task of biblical theology is the same for the Old Testament and for the New, and for both together. The difference between the theologies of the Old and New

Testaments does not, therefore, lie in the methodological approach. It lies in the various ways in which the two testaments are distinguished. While a united biblical theology should not be assumed to be ultimately elusive, a separate focus on the theology of each testament is required so that, before any biblical theology is proposed, each testament receives the right to its own case without interference from the other.

The requirement for beginning with two separate theologies is based on three special reasons. First, the Jewish community possesses the TaNaK, along with its own subsequent body of authoritative interpretations, but no New Testament. In this community, the TaNaK represents the beginning of a trajectory which differs from its trajectory into the Christian community. The reality of these divided trajectories cannot be ignored, and the Christian claim to the sole rightful possession of the Jewish Bible is historically unverifiable and, for that reason alone, nothing more than a claim based on a presupposed Christian faith not shared by Jews, and inherently anti-Jewish.

Secondly, the adoption of the Jewish Bible by the early Christian community was inevitable because it had no alternative for demonstrating its theological legitimacy. However, at least since the adoption of the New Testament canon, the original Christian necessity for authenticating its existence through the Jewish Bible no longer existed. Indeed, the basis for Christian authentication from then on shifted to the New Testament, while the Old Testament, for that final reason, became the problem, and continues to be the problem to this day (as if there were no problem with an isolated New Testament). The replacement of the Old Testament by the New as the source for Christian authentication has led to its effective subordination, if not to the disqualification of much of it, already within the Christian Bible itself. We affirm the whole Bible of both the Old and the New Testaments as the one word of God, but consider the word of God in the Old Testament as dependent on and (to be) adjudicated by the word of God in the New Testament — which is another case of the inferiorization of the Jewish religion.

Thirdly, the tradition of Old Testament theologies by Christian scholars demonstrates that New Testament influences constantly flow in one way or another into the evaluation of the Old Testament, and even into the description of its theologies, even at the exegetical level, despite the often explicit assertion by scholars that the Old Testament must have the right to speak for itself. The violation of explicit assertion is often evident, and equally often suspected. The suspicion already arises with the title "Theology of the *Old* Testament," but also with the fact that Jewish theology has not equally developed a theology of the TaNaK. The absence of such a theology in the Jewish tradition makes it appear as if its systematic construction were a specifically Christian necessity and mode of conceptualization, inherited perhaps from the Greco-Roman and medieval tradition of conceptual thought assumed to be alien to Hebrew thought. But apart from the fact that Hebrew thinking was never nonconceptual, the need for the conceptualization of the Hebrew

Bible arises neither from a medieval or modern mode of thinking nor from the fact of the Christian Old Testament. It arises from the problem of the theological diversity within the Hebrew Bible itself (just as such a problem would arise from any other equally diverse body of literature) and from the inevitable discussion about it, even in the Jewish community. The need for such conceptualization shows that it is equally inevitable for all, and not a cultural idiosyncrasy of Greeks or Romans, medievals or moderns, Jews or Christians.

On these grounds I now turn to the Old Testament.

III. The Problem of Criteria

What are the criteria which emerge from the comparison of the theologies of the texts and which can serve as a basis for their evaluation? Once this question is raised, many unsuitable notions must be set aside.

A. Deconstruction of Unsuitable Criteria

1. All notions or factors that refer to the unity of the Old Testament are unsuitable for this purpose because they do not address the diversity within that unity. Such notions are the reason for the problem rather than the ground for the answer.

The search for unifying aspects or common denominators has been widespread in the history of Old Testament studies. This search is legitimate, and notions in regard to which the Old Testament is united are indeed evident. Many of them represent demonstrable, empirical, or at least defensible conceptual data, such as Yahwism, monotheism, words and/or acts of God, God's universality, fear and knowledge of God/Yahweh, covenant, communion, community, and solidarity — as well as canon or scripture or literature. The same may be said for notions such as revelation or inspiration. The discernment of such unifying notions is not discredited because one or the other notion claimed by interpreters remains controversial, e.g., as in the case of Eichrodt's famous Old Testament theology for which the unifying notion is "covenant."[8] Nor is it discredited by the fact that a combination of several such notions itself poses the problem of their own relationship, namely, which of them is/are more fundamental and which is/are less. This problem alone has as yet received no comprehensive attention by biblical scholars, despite more or less subjective suggestions.

For example, the Old Testament speaks of both God and Yahweh, in addition

8. W. Eichrodt, *Theology of the Old Testament,* trans. J. A. Baker; 2 vols. (Philadelphia: Westminster, 1961).

to other words for the deity. Both words reflect, at least in the end, the matrix of Israel's monotheism in which the Old Testament writings are unified. These writings are Yahwistic and monotheistic literature. However, although Yahweh and God are perceived as one and the same, each word denotes something different. "Yahweh" refers to the identity of a specific God, whereas "God" refers to the deity of Yahweh. Which of these two notions is constitutive for the other in the Old Testament, even as they represent a unifying factor?

This example already indicates that despite everything that can be said in favor of the Old Testament's unity, the search for unifying notions is fundamentally misdirected inasmuch as it is prompted by the hope that the theological problem of the Old Testament can be solved by finding a unifying concept. The fact is irrefutable that within each conceivable unifying umbrella there exists theological pluralism and diversity, a chorus of not only different but also differing voices. These differences exist despite their unifying umbrellas, just as they exist in the Jewish and Christian traditions and in those of other religions as well. With regard to this theological pluralism and diversity, the question arises if and how the many voices complement each other, or if, on the contrary, they contradict one another, how such contradictions may be evaluated.

This question is especially acute with regard to claims of truth and validity made by or afforded to each of these theological positions in the canon. Since each position rests on the same unifying presuppositions, those presuppositions function merely as the basis and incentive for mutual dialogue among the positions or for the dispute brought about by their diversity, rather than as criteria for our adjudication of dialogue and dispute. Unifying presuppositions have not actually resolved the problem of pluralism and diversity within the Old Testament itself.

The notion of the word of God may serve as another example. The theological problem of this notion lies not so much in the fact that the Old Testament also explicitly refers to mere human words, nor in the question as to what extent references to God's speaking should be considered as both divine and human word. It lies in the fact that, even if all Old Testament words were/are perceived as word of God, this word is pluralistic and diverse. The same is true for the unifying notions of revelation, inspiration, and faith, as well as for other similar notions.

It is, therefore, necessary in our pursuit of Old Testament theology to shift the focus of study from the search for unifying notions to the direct comparison of the Old Testament's various theologies. In this way, the degrees of their validity may be recognized, and ultimately the unity of the diversity may be established as a system of relationships.

2. A specific factor perceived as unifying is the Old Testament's tradition and transmission history. It, too, is an unsuitable criterion for the evaluation of the theologies of texts through comparison with others. I am referring to the continuity or discontinuity of trajectories, to the interdependence of language and event as or in process, or the process of either of the two alone, to the dynamic nature of this

process and its vitality, to the dialectic of projection and adaptation, to transformation, resignification, and de- and recontextualization, to the production of meaning, and to more of the same. The same is true for any particular stage in the tradition or transmission history of the biblical texts, be it original, secondary, or part of the extant text, or for any method of transmission, oral or written, methodical or free. As in any other history, all these evidently existing factors belong primarily to the mechanisms of the general historical process in which continuities and discontinuities intersect. Indeed, they represent unifying influences. But do any of these factors, including their meaning and even the totality of their process, reveal as such that what happened and was said, in part or *in toto,* was and is valid? Since when is the totality of a historical process self-evidently true by virtue of being a process and/or a totality, even a dynamic one? Is not history full of processes which were evidently untrue and contested even in their own time and unmasked by posterity? Since when is tradition true by virtue of being tradition or time-honored, or transmission true by virtue of being transmission? All these factors belong to ancient Israel's phenomenology and history of religion, but none represents a criterion for what is true and valid.

What has just been said also applies to any more or less encompassing corpus of scriptures and traditions which are outside the Old Testament or the Christian Bible and may be under comparison. The extent of any corpus may, and does, vary, and each variation depends on specific reasons. However, the method for the comparison of all indicators must be equally applicable to any chosen corpus, be it narrow or wide.

3. Also unsuitable are the *instruments* through which and the *settings* in which the texts were spoken, written, and transmitted — instruments such as the forms, genres, or rhetorical or literary devices which occur in the Old Testament, the artistic interpenetration of their forms and contents, and the integrity of systemic totalities of texts; or settings and their respective representatives, such as storytellers, historians, lawgivers, homileticians, prophets, psalmists, and sages. These instruments and settings are important for exegesis and the sociology of religion because they reveal the life of the texts through many forms of communication and in various societal settings. They show the omnipresence of Yahwism in Israel's society. They are also important theologically in the sense that theological truth and validity are indeed involved in the real affairs of life rather than being retreats into abstractions, and in the sense that, because reality is pluralistic, they are inevitably and legitimately pluralistic rather than uniform and unilocal. However, they do not reveal why any one of them or its meaning is theologically valid.

A priest, prophet, sage, psalmist, historian, or lawgiver is not valid by virtue of having that function. Nor is any of his/her statements true by virtue of the authority of his/her office. What he/she is or says depends on substantive criteria which themselves validate, relativize, or invalidate what he/she says and is. Nor can we say that the word of a prophet is more important than the word of a priest or sage because it is a prophet who speaks. The same is true for any societal group or for any individual.

We must also admit that no genre of oral or written expression is theologically valid simply by virtue of being a genre. A hymn may praise Yahweh for true, relative, or false reasons. The same is true for a lament, proverbially expressed, as in Jer 31:29. The super- or macrogenre of narrative has gained particularly prominent attention in Old Testament interpretation, often with the assumption of its intrinsic theological relevance. Narrative language most directly reflects the processes of actions, events, and history. This understanding of narrative is certainly relevant. However, narrative is not the only form in which the Hebrews expressed their perception of reality. Other forms speak about what is, not only about what happens. Moreover, narrative, just as any linguistic (and extralinguistic) expression, always includes interpretation, which may be circumspect and true, but may be partial, self-serving, or outright incorrect or untrue. It does not, therefore, reveal as such which of its inherent possibilities are actualized. It is by itself no more evidence for truth and validity than any other genre. The criteria for the truth and validity of the narratives in the Old Testament must be found in what they say, not in the fact that they narrate. These criteria apply even to the events themselves, not only to the narratives about them. No history is true by virtue of the fact that it happens. All historical events or developments are factual. But their factuality does not constitute their truth and legitimacy. History consists not only of truth, justice, and what is good. It is also full of untruth, injustice, and outright criminality.

What has been said about narrative also applies to the much acclaimed supergenre of oral rhetoric, which throughout the total history of humanity, including Israel and Christianity, has occupied a central place in running the affairs of humanity. Even preachers, just as rhetoricians in antiquity, must be trained in the art of rhetoric. However indispensable and beneficial it has been and is, rhetoric is a value-neutral instrument which has always stood and continues to stand in the service of ideologies, right or wrong, and all too often in the service of outright demagoguery, of tricks, lies, and the manipulation and seduction of people. Rhetoric as such is no criterion for truth and validity.

The search for the criteria for truth and validity helps to clarify the distinction between Old Testament sociology and theology. In this search, what matters is the argument in comparison with other arguments (short of any absolute or ultimate argument), and not societal forces. It is the better saying that counts. In ancient times, just as in modern times, groups, nations, and the masses of humanity were used by and had to contend with those in control of the power mechanisms, who were usually in the minority. The Old Testament knows that power is no proof of truth, whether in the hands of minorities or of majorities. One of its prominent concerns is the tension between the powerless righteous and the powerful unrighteous (e.g., in the story of Saul and David, in the fate of the prophets, especially of the suffering servant, and in many psalms and proverbs). Nor does the truth automatically lie in the hands of either majorities or minorities. "Do not side with the majority for evil, and do not distort the evidence in a dispute by favoring the majority" (Exod 23:2).[9] An individual or a minority, even in a modern democracy, may speak the truth more than her/his society, even in the society's own better interest. But just as often he/she can be wrong and society right.

4. In view of the universally acknowledged pluralism of the theologies in the Bible, it must be said that any methodology for a biblical theology that does not provide the tools for evaluating that pluralism is insufficient. For example, a proposal which states that the Old Testament itself provides checks and balances, confirms only the obvious. It affirms the long-standing Reformation principle that Scripture is its own interpreter. This principle is to be understood in the sense that we ourselves make the Bible interpret itself because that is what to a large extent it does not do on its own, and where it does, it does so from one standpoint without accounting for others. Unless that proposal identifies the criteria for the validity of those checks and balances, it remains a truism. A similar truism is the reference to the multivalency of a text or to the theological pluralism in the Bible, and to the inherent adaptability of texts for recontextualization and resignification. The multivalency of a text, or of all texts together, means that each element in the system of a text, down to its last word, is meaningful; but it does not mean that each element is equally meaningful such that recontextualization and resignification could be at liberty to take off into every imaginable direction simply because they start from a biblical text. The texts' own prioritizing value systems resist such arbitrariness. That such liberties are and were taken, even within the biblical transmission history itself, is a well-known fact. However, this does not mean that these liberties are valid because they have been and are taken — even by the believing community, and are, therefore, beyond evaluation. The chronistic work represents a resignification of the deuteronomistic work. Whether it is, therefore, more or less valid, or whether both works are equally valid or equally relative either in their canonic coexistence or in the time for which the chronistic work was written (the third century BCE), remain open questions which are not answered with reference to the resignification of one by the other. All texts are multivalent, but not all texts are equivalent. This irrefutable fact alone demands criteria for the discernment of higher and lower degrees of validity, precisely because of the text's, or the texts', insistence of "valency"! Such criteria must be worked out. They do not come automatically.

B. Constructive Criteria

1. I take it for granted that the Old Testament speaks, directly or indirectly, about God's relationship to his world and the world's relationship to God, and about the

9. Translation by B. Childs, *The Book of Exodus,* OTL (Philadelphia: Westminster, 1974).

place and role of humans in these relationships. The notion of the relationship between God and the entire world represents the most inclusive horizon of both God and world. In this horizon, the Old Testament texts make their truth claim. They claim that God-Yahweh's truth revealed to Israel is true for the entire world. Therefore, in view of this horizon and its notion, constructive criteria must be established which will enable us to compare the theologies of the individual texts with each other and thereby to evaluate their validity.

Assuming that the notion of the relationship between God and world is the most inclusive horizon in the Old Testament, I conclude that this notion represents the basic criterion for the process by which the theological validity of all aspects of the Old Testament may be evaluated. This process requires the programmatic recognition, consideration, and comparison of all aspects, regardless of whether or not, or to what extent, an individual is in a position to carry out the program in full. Only one factor in the notion of the relationship between God and world needs to remain in focus; namely, that the aspect of the total world is for the understanding of God just as constitutive as the aspect of God is for the understanding of the total world.

The notion of universal inclusiveness does not at all invalidate specific, particular, or unique situations, whether they are characterized historically, sociologically, existentially, or otherwise, and especially if they (as is very often the case in the texts) do not explicitly address the issue of the universal horizon of the relationship between God and world. Universality and particularity are not mutually exclusive. Nor may "universality" function as an abstraction from the reality of particular situations. The emphasis of South American theologians, for example, on the indigenousness of the conditions in South America and on indigenous South American theology is a case in point. It is legitimate because other indigenous theological movements such as African American, feminist, African, Asian, and Native American are generally acknowledged, and rightfully so. Such theologies not only take special conditions as their point of departure; they also respond to, focus on, serve, and are designed for those conditions specifically. Not only the historical and sociological but also the theological study of the Bible affirms such foci. South American and other indigenous theologies are also legitimate as correlatives to and correctives of the traditional white male Western theologies which are historically just as indigenous as all others. Any program of centralization, be it cultic, theological, or administrative, even in the Bible (Deuteronomy!), must confront the question of how it responds to indigenousness.

However, the white male Western theologies have already shown that indigenousness alone is not a sufficient criterion for truth and validity, not even for its own situation, let alone for the situations of others. A bumper sticker in the United States says: "Private property is a divine right." This maxim can be traced to biblical sources, and claims to be Christian. It certainly reflects much of the indigenous American ideology. Whether or not, or to what extent, it is true depends on criteria by which indigenousness itself is judged.

It should be clear at the outset that nothing can claim validity by virtue of being indigenous, if it functions to exploit and oppress other groups. I would also argue that indigenousness, for all its rightful position, must answer the question of whether that which claims validity by virtue of being indigenous does so exclusively, i.e., regardless of comparable conditions elsewhere, or inclusively, i.e., because its own condition also belongs to comparable conditions everywhere. In the former case, indigenous theology would be, or would tend to be, particularistic. It would not only forfeit any relevance for others; it would also be in danger of becoming enslaved to the imperfections of its own cultural and historical particularities — unless one assumes that there is an indigenous culture without any imperfections or "original sin." In the latter case, indigenous theology would not only be a universally contextualizable paradigm; its validity would also be evident because its particular focus would be nothing but a necessary application of what under comparable conditions is true for all.

A specific example for this argument is the practice, noticeably in South America, of reading the Bible for the poor. For obvious reasons this focus must be supported, and has precedents in the history of Christianity. However, this focus cannot be isolated from its context. The Bible should also be read for the rich, even in South America, and with regard to both their own wealth and the plight of the poor, and certainly not only to justify their wealth — a shameful and obscene practice. Furthermore, in view of the painful history of the function of the Bible as an instrument in the hands of the powerful for the perpetuation and legitimation of poverty, care must be taken that the Bible, read for the poor and by the poor (and laypersons in general), does not continue to function as "opiate for the masses," the religiously sanctioned drug for the masses, freely given to them as the surrogate for their liberation from poverty, rather than functioning as the entitlement to liberation from all types of human enslavement, including their poverty. The Bible must be read for the poor specifically because its God is the God of all equally, and because the poor are in reality not treated equally.

2. What, then, are the criteria generated by this most inclusive horizon?

a. The criteria must, first of all, account for the Old Testament's fundamental awareness of the difference between God-Yahweh and the world. God-Yahweh is not the world, nor is the world God-Yahweh. This fundamental distinction calls attention to the notion of the divinity of God-Yahweh on the one hand, to the notion of the world on the other hand, and especially to the relationship between the two notions, because neither is unrelated to the other. Therefore, what does Israel's understanding of God-Yahweh mean for its understanding of the world, and what does its understanding of the world mean for its understanding of God-Yahweh? And what is Israel's understanding of the relationship between God-Yahweh and the world? Especially, is Israel's understanding always the same? If not, on what grounds are we *to evaluate the order of priorities* according to which the different articulations of the divinity of God-Yahweh, as well as of the identity of Yahweh-God, of the world, and of the relationship between God and world, can be explained? Since the Old Testament considers neither the world without God nor God without the world, the evaluation of the order of priorities must be focused, from the outset, on the relationship between God and the world.

b. Continuing in this direction, a first question centers on the relationship among the divine attributes in God-Yahweh's relationship to the world. The two attributes of God's lordship and justice may serve as a case in point. God is as much said to be Lord as he is said to be just. These two attributes should complement each other. Whether or not they do, and how, needs to be analyzed, explained, and evaluated. Is God-Yahweh the Lord because he is just, or is he just because he is the Lord? If God is Lord because he is just, God's lordship is determined, legitimated, and controlled by his justice. Thus, God's lordship is relative to the criterion that only a God who is just and not a tyrant is entitled to be Lord. If God is just because he is Lord, God's justice depends on his lordship, and is relative to his authority. Justice is, therefore, what the Lord determines regardless of any other notion of justice. Indeed, this Lord may be a tyrant, or an otherwise unjust god. Do all the texts rest on and express the same assumptions?

Similar questions will have to be raised about the relationships among divine attributes and activities such as holiness, mercifulness, forgiveness, liberation, love, patience, anger, judgment, omnipotence, etc. The book of Jonah addresses the tension between Yahweh's judgment against and mercy for Nineveh. Involved in both cases is the question of justice. Written by a sage, the book not only narrates a humorous story and entertains at the expense of the theological positions of the prophet Jonah, but also exposes his outright disobedience and questionable actions. Underneath its narrative surface, it deals with a serious conceptual problem, namely, the tension between the opposites of the justice of judgment and the justice of mercy. Both judgment and mercy are recognized as just. Justice is not only their common denominator but also the criterion for the legitimacy of each. However, when compared, especially in application to an actual situation which makes the neglect of either impossible, the two principles of justice collide, and the question arises as to which of them has priority in their relationship. This question is inevitable, even as one must account for the fact that the penitence of the Ninevites, their return from evil, is the condition for Yahweh's turning from his judgment, a condition Jonah would not accept when it was met by the Ninevites. According to the writer, Yahweh's mercy is the greater justice because Yahweh is the sustainer of all life, even of animals and plants, and therefore even more so of those humans who are neither Yahweh worshippers nor Israelites. It is greater because his loyalty to his creation supersedes the justice of its destruction.

The juxtaposed descriptions in biblical lexica of the various attributes and activities of Yahweh are necessary, but they do not fulfill the requirements of Old Testament theology because they do not address the question of the relationship of these notions. These descriptions only offer the necessary data from which the evaluation of such theological notions or texts, which happens through their comparison, must proceed.

c. The attributes and activities of Yahweh just referred to have one thing in common: they all deal with qualifications. They are qualifiers which correspond to the qualifying side of the biblical language, and it is important that they not be understood in abstraction. They express dispositions which function in God-Yahweh's relationship to and presence in the world. This, in turn, brings into focus the aspects of worldly space and time in which God and world are related. In Israel's polytheistic environment, different gods belong in various degrees to different spaces, times, and functions. For ancient Israel's monotheism, it is self-evident that a god who is God of the total world in space and time and of all else within space and time is a god of all. Its perception of the divinity of God rests on three indispensable conditions: God's own universality, the universality of the one world, and God's universal presence in the total world. Further, it is with respect to God's universal presence in the total world that questions arise regarding the relationships among the realms and times of the world in which God is present, i.e., regarding the relationships between the cosmos, the earth, the lands of the earth, Israel's land, and all places; between all living things, humanity, Israel's community, and individuals; and also between the past, the present, and the future of all these realms. Here I am discussing the quantifiers.

Just like any other land or country, Brazil is neither alone on the globe or in the cosmos nor the sole globe or cosmos. The first chapter in the Bible already focuses on the two basic quantifiers of space and time. Notice that it speaks not only about the time and, implicitly, the age of the world, but just as much about its space. Contrary to some interpretations in which the cosmology is set aside as a theologically irrelevant and discardable shell, Genesis 1 and similar texts explicitly qualify these cosmological quantifiers as theologically important: they are "good," and the whole is "very good."

Of similar theological importance is, for example, the relationship between all humans and each individual. The Old Testament speaks about corporate humanity as well as about individuals. It recognizes individuality. It does not consider these two categories mutually exclusive. Its anthropology and sociology are neither collectivistic nor individualistic. In what we call "corporate humanity," both the individual and the group — however inclusive — belong together in a balanced relationship. Individuals are members of corporate humanity, and humanity is not constituted by the statistical count of, or the social contract made by, independent individuals. Yet, the individuality of persons is already recognized by the fact that they are given a personal name at birth. Theologically, Yahweh cares for the individual because he cares for all, and not regardless of his care for all. Attention to individuals is attested in the laws, in the complaint psalms of the individual, in the proverbs, and indeed throughout the Old Testament. It exists because of the perception of corporate humanity, not in spite of it.

Which of these quantifiers have theological priority over which, and which are relative to which? And how autonomously or heteronomously are they considered in the various Old Testament texts? Once these questions are answered we will be in a better position to determine the greater or lesser theological validity of the texts.

d. However, neither the qualifiers nor the quantifiers can be considered in isolation from each other. The relationship between God's mercy and universality may be a case in point. As long as we speak only about God's mercy, a qualifier, we have not yet said whether in quantitative respects it is perceived universalistically or particularistically. Moreover, as long as we speak only quantitatively about God's universality, we have not yet said whether it functions qualitatively as mercy for Israel and at the same time as judgment against the nations, a particularistic kind of mercy, or whether God's mercy for Israel is a universalistic paradigm of God's universal mercy. The fact that the texts focus predominantly on Israel is natural. It represents legitimate attention to Israel's particular situation. Whether or not this perspective is grounded in a particular*istic* or a universal*istic conceptuality* is a question not at all answered with reference to its particularity.[10] God-Yahweh's universality may be seen to be in the service of his covenant people, or God's covenant with Israel may be seen as a paradigm of his relationship to humanity and the world. Both are mutually exclusive. They directly affect the nature of God's divinity. Moreover, their clarification will enable us to discern the theological validity or relativity of the texts.

e. The problem of the relationship between particular and universal perspectives cannot be solved with reference to the well-known increasing universalization of originally particular witnesses through the process of decontextualization and recontextualization. Such universalization through de- and recontextualizations, basic hermeneutical realities in any historical development, presupposes trajectories of systemically identical paradigms which make not only possible but also legitimate the transition and transformation from one context into another. The de- and recontextualization from a particular horizon into a universal horizon, for example, presupposes an actually universalistic paradigm already at work in the particular perspective and, thus, a potential that encourages rather than resists universalization. If a paradigm is particularistic, it can only be de- and recontextualized particularistically in a systemically consistent traditio-historical trajectory. However, the shift from a particularistic paradigm to a universalistic paradigm, or vice versa,

10. Here and elsewhere, I distinguish terminologically between universal*ism*/universal*istic* and particular*ism*/particular*istic* on the one hand, and between univers*ality*/univers*al* and particu*larity*/particul*ar* on the other. A particular or a universal situation or condition may presuppose a particularistic or a universalistic concept. The particular may be either inclusivistic or exclusivistic, just as the universal may serve either particularistic or universalistic objectives.

involves more than de- and re*context*ualization. It represents a transition *eis allo genos,* i.e., a de- and re*concept*ualization into a different or even opposite paradigm! Such a reconceptualization is possible, but it presupposes specific and critical reasons and decisions for the abandonment of one paradigm and the acceptance of another. Otherwise, such a transition will not happen because generally tradition prevails. A reconceptualization represents a substantive criticism of a paradigm and its tradition. It represents a break with tradition, not the continuity of tradition as in de- and recontextualization.

De- and re*concept*ualization, and therefore a break with tradition, may be necessary. But its necessity is itself subject to criteria for theological validity, just as it would not arise without such criteria in the first place. It is not valid because it is necessary or happens. It may be necessary for valid reasons which are themselves subject to validation. Neither loyalty nor opposition to tradition, and neither the commitment nor the resistance to novelty or change, is as such a sufficient criterion for theological validity. The religio-historical phenomena of continuity and discontinuity that can be observed in ancient Israel's tradition and transmission history are theologically irrelevant. They only point to the question of the criteria on which their own validity depends. Once those criteria are discerned, either continuity with tradition or the break with it will be acknowledged where due.

The difference between de- and recontextualization and de- and reconceptualization (or de- and reconstruction) becomes particularly acute in modern biblical hermeneutic, the dialogical application of the Bible for us today. For our understanding of this important difference, frequently used words such as reinterpretation, resignification, and transformation are no longer useful because they blur the difference rather than indicate it. There is enough in the Old Testament that lends itself to de- and recontextualization, even in the context of the New Testament. But the inevitability of de- and reconceptualization or of de- and reconstruction seems to be much greater than has traditionally been recognized. The feminist rejection of patriarchally based theology is only one case in point. Other cases include those traditions in the Old Testament that represent Israel's ethnocentric covenant concepts: the theologies of the symbiosis of God and nation or of Yahwistic and national identity, and of outright militant intolerance and destructive aggressiveness against anything and everyone within and without Israel which is culturally and cultically different; the theological justification of war, especially in the name and for the sake of theological orthodoxy; and the "ban" on defeated enemies and their properties. Some other cases are the prosecution of and even death for violators of cultic or confessional taboos; the conquest of the land of others in the name of the monotheistic divine mandate; the final, irreversible societal elimination of sinners, i.e., their "being cut off"; the rigid self-separation of the righteous from the unrighteous, rejecting the common bond of all humans and splitting even the corporate society itself.

The same principle applies to the biblical view of ecology, currently receiving much attention. Whatever the word "subdue" in "subdue the earth" in Gen 1:28

means specifically, humans are considered to be at the top of the pyramid of creation (cf. Psalms 8; 104) and to have dominion over the earth and the animals (cf. also Gen 9:1-6), while the world is considered to have been created for humans — if not also for the institution of cultic holiness in Israel. Even when one acknowledges that human dominion refers only to the right to secure food for life and to the control of the animals, the fact still remains that in those traditions the world is created for the sake of humans. Whether or not the world has any value without or besides that purpose, as can be seen in other traditions, is an unaddressed question which implies two different conceptualities and opens the potential for human dominion over a nonvaluable world based on the distinction between what is valuable, i.e., humans, and what is not, i.e., the world. The actualization of this potential through the history of civilization and its isolation from alternative options in the horizon of a biblical theology constitute the heart of the current ecological crisis and problem.

It should be noted that the New Testament is not exempt from the methodological problems of de- and recontextualization and de- and reconceptualization. Nor do the questions and proposals raised reveal new facts. They only make explicit what in one way or another has always been done. They urge us to account, critically and self-critically, not only for the biblical concepts and their influence throughout our history but also for our own conceptual presuppositions and ideologies.

f. Finally, Old Testament theology must discern the truth or untruth of the world's response to God's presence in the space and time of the world, and especially of its direct response to God in personal encounter. This involves the response by cosmos and earth, and by humanity, Israel, and persons, and the validity of each in relation to the others. Israel's or an individual's own response to God may be very direct and personal, but without regard to God's interest in his world. The same may be true for the response to received communal blessings, in which whether or not all receive the same blessings is irrelevant. Again, Israel's legitimate response to its own received blessings (and judgments) raises the question of whether these responses are based on the understanding of the covenant as a preferential status vis-à-vis humanity, or of Israel's paradigmatic status for humanity. The former would — without reconceptualization — be irrelevant for humanity, whereas Israel's vocation to be a light for the nations would have its validity in the latter.

a.-f. It is not important in the context of this paper that all aspects are listed and all criteria identified. Some aspects may need adjustment and further development. Nor is the question important of how much must and can be done, and by whom. Important is the direction in which we are moving in reestablishing the discipline of, at least, Old Testament, if not biblical, theology. None of us can do this work alone. Many of us are called to promote it into the future, as long as we all have a future.

THIRD LECTURE: JUSTICE IN OLD TESTAMENT THEOLOGY

Introduction

For the reasons given in my second lecture, I am confining the discussion of my subject in this lecture to the Old Testament. On the basis of the first two lectures, the task of "Justice in Old Testament Theology" can be immediately defined: it must establish the validity of the many theologies of justice in the Old Testament and of the many texts concerned with it.

I. The Problem with the Evidence

We already encounter the problem when we ask what justice is. A good English lexicon offers several definitions. Any one of them may be operative in our minds when we read an English Bible. The situation is the same in any other modern language. Whether any modern definition reflects what the Hebrew, Greek, or Latin Bibles mean by "justice" is a perfectly open question. Our understanding of justice is hidden in the diversity of its conceptualizations and expressions. The same is true for the Hebrew Bible.

A. The Words and the Word Field for Justice in the Hebrew Bible

1. The main word for justice, משׁפט, refers in various contexts to a legal case or lawsuit, legal claim, decision by arbitration, legal decision, or case law. The verb from which the noun is derived refers to a similar diversity of activities. As in other cases, the variety in the usage of the same word shows that the meaning of the word is complex, but also that its complexity is a major problem. Its meaning may be embedded in an inclusive preunderstanding or common conceptual denominator which makes the choice of the same word for a variety of aspects possible, but it may also be the result of diverse or even conflicting preunderstandings, or of differing concepts. Whichever of these possibilities is the case is not known a priori. It must be established through the comparison of exegetical results. Only one phenomenon is common to all aspects: the issue of justice as a focus and a concern.

2. What has just been said is also true for the variety of words that belong to the word field of justice. The most important words belonging to this cluster

are: צדקה/צדק, "righteousness"; אמונה, "steadfastness"; אמת, "faithfulness"; חסד, "kindness"; מישרים and מישור, "uprightness"; שלום, "sufficiency, peace"; חק, "statute"; מצוה, "commandment, ordinance"; תורה, "instruction"; מוסר, "correction, warning"; תם, "completeness." These words alone amount to some 3,800 references. They refer to aspects other than justice specifically, but at the same time reveal aspects implicit in justice itself. Again, it is an open question whether this word field points to an all-inclusive, homogeneous worldview in which all aspects are complementary and operate meaningfully, or whether it points to heterogeneous preunderstandings or concepts which conflict in their canonic juxtaposition.

3. The word field opposite justice reinforces this picture. The word field for sin, which is closely related to and overlaps that of injustice, amounts to some forty Hebrew words.[11]

B. Texts and their Preunderstandings

What has been said about the lexical findings is also true for the Old Testament *texts* in which the words for justice are used. These texts refer to many facets of justice. In diverse ways, they actualize one or more understandings of justice which they presuppose but never define, at least not fully. That such preunderstandings exist is very clear from the various semantic fields within which the texts function. It is even clearer in those texts that address the subject of justice without ever using the central terminology for it, as, e.g., the book of Jonah.

In both types of texts, there is an interdependence of specific aspects expressed in the texts and a conceptual preunderstanding of justice underneath their surface, a preunderstanding without which the texts and what they say would have no coherence. The fact that a preunderstanding is not abstractly defined does not mean that it does not exist and is not operative in the texts. The absence of definitions of justice does not mean that the Hebrews could not think conceptually. They could and did. The evidence is overwhelming.

An interpretation of justice in the Old Testament must, therefore, not only pay attention to the variety of actualized aspects in the texts; it must also attempt to reconstruct the conceptual presuppositions on which those actualizations or applications depend. Indeed, these presuppositions represent the bases for the truth claims of the actual texts. They are conceptual and systemic, and represent the level within which the variety of the theological concepts of justice appears.

11. R. Knierim, *Die Hauptbegriffe für Sünde im Alten Testament* (Gütersloh: G. Mohn, 1965), and "On the Contours of Old Testament and Biblical Hamartiology," pages 414-65 in this volume.

C. The Actualizations of Justice in the Old Testament

The concern for justice pervades the entire Old Testament. It is found in the historical, legal, prophetic, and wisdom literature, and in the psalms as well. It is found throughout the entire history of the Old Testament literature. It is by no means the property of the prophets alone. The prophets did not invent it, nor were they the first or the last to address it.

Accordingly, justice is at issue in many genres of Old Testament literature. The concern for it is not confined to any particular genre. In turn, the genres point to the settings of Israel's societal life, none of which could afford to neglect the fundamental importance of justice. The evidence for these facts is easily available in the Old Testament itself, and is presented in the commentaries and lexica.

The evidence shows that the concern for justice was one, if not the central, factor by which ancient Israel's multifaceted societal life was united throughout its historical changes. This unity was decisively reinforced as well as molded by Israel's Yahwistic formation of monotheism in which the concern for justice was even more fundamental.

However, the great diversity within this unity of concern and focus deserves special attention. It shows that no sphere of Israel's life was exempt from the concern for justice, and Yahweh was known to be at work in all its spheres. The texts, which reflect the actualizations of this concern, document the ongoing dynamic of this penetration. Whatever the problem is with this evidence, the all-pervasive concern for justice indicates that the Old Testament has laid down a basic criterion against which everything it says must be evaluated. The Old Testament submits itself to this criterion. This means, however, that its own *concern for* justice becomes the motivation for the interpretation of its own *concepts of* justice. *It is at this juncture that the problem of the Old Testament theology of justice arises.* For at this juncture it becomes clear that what the texts say, how they say it, when and where and by whom it is said, are not criteria for validity simply because these texts exist. They point beyond themselves to their concern for justice as the criterion for their truth claims and to the comparison of these concepts for the sake of their evaluation. They are not the criteria themselves.

What has been said thus far indicates that the treatment of this or any other subject in the horizon of the entire Old Testament involves more than the exegesis of individual texts, the lexicographical definitions of terminology, the orderly juxtaposition of various semantic aspects in lexica, or the description of the history of the words and concepts. It differs from all these types of work because it involves the comparison of all exegetical data, including their conceptualities, and the discussion of their validity in their relationship. This task makes the other just-mentioned tasks by no means superfluous. On the contrary, it makes them mandatory.

II. The Conceptualization of the Evidence

A. Various Aspects of Justice in the Horizon of the Old Testament

We must turn to some of the various aspects of justice on which the Old Testament texts rest or which they express. The following list is by no means complete. It does not and cannot in such a paper aim at discussing all the data. It aims at laying out a range of aspects that is sufficient for encountering the problem, for charting the way to approach it, and for discussing the criteria for the validity of the various aspects of justice in the horizon of the Old Testament.

1. Life in Justice as the Cause of Well-Being

Based on a dynamistic worldview, many texts express or presuppose a direct empirical link between a person's just behavior and her/his successful life. "It is well with those who deal generously and lend, who conduct their affairs with justice" (Ps 112:5). Or, "Tell the innocent how fortunate they are, for they shall eat the fruit of their labors" (Isa 3:10). On the other hand, the idolaters "sow the wind, and they shall reap the whirlwind" (Hos 8:7). In such texts, just attitudes and behavior are the condition for and cause of success and well-being, and well-being is an organic outgrowth of just behavior. Without just behavior, there is no success. Just behavior generates success. The "doing well" of a person is the extension and return of her/his "doing good." Through being a benefactor, a person becomes the beneficiary of her/his own good actions. Not only the doing of justice, but the link itself of cause and effect is perceived as the manifestation of justice in reality. Reality itself, a dynamic organic process, is just. The link of cause and effect can be — and has been — the motive for doing good in order to harvest well-being (which has nothing to do with salvation or being saved!), where the purpose of doing justice is to secure one's own benefit rather than doing justice regardless of the consequences. This linkage can be — and continues to be — the reason for concluding that both good fortune and misfortune must have their respective root causes in a just and unjust lifestyle, which is the argument of Job's friends, and which may or may not actually be the case.

This dynamistic ontology, with its strong impetus for the moral distinction between good and evil and for personal responsibility — be it for self-serving or altruistic purposes — is also the conceptual matrix of texts in which Yahweh himself guarantees the link of cause and effect, as, e.g., in Psalm 1, where those members of the covenant community which has been given the "law of Yahweh," who do no evil but "delight" in this law and "meditate day and night," are "like trees planted by streams of water, which yield their fruit in its season, and their leaves do not wither. In all that they do, they prosper" — "for the LORD watches over the way of the righteous. . . ."

The fact that in this and many similar texts Yahweh himself is considered at least as the protector ("the LORD watches over the way of the righteous"), if not as the creator, of the link of cause and effect reflects the important and well-known difference between the natural and theological expression of this worldview. The two types of expression complement one another, but they have different empirical roots. The observation of the link of cause and effect did not originate in Israel's experience and knowledge of Yahweh. It was — and is — one element of the property of human experience and wisdom internationally, and it has been claimed to express a principle of reality that is universally just. Apart from and before its connection with a specific theology, an assertion such as Ps 112:5 could be said anywhere. The theologization of this dynamistic worldview, expressed in texts such as Psalm 1, shows basically that Yahweh and the world are seen as related, and yet at the same time that Yahweh is neither the world nor is the world divine or Yahweh. Specifically, it shows that this link of cause and effect is not so much considered to be true because it is confirmed or even created by Yahweh, as Yahweh is considered to confirm or even to have created it because it is true. It shows that Yahweh, rather than being himself the principle of universal reality, is committed to that substantive and empirically verifiable principle of universal justice.

Excursus. This type of view of just reality, including its theologized form as expressed in Psalm 1 and similar texts, is portrayed according to a unidirectional development: from doing the right or wrong thing as the cause or condition to inheriting from it well-being or evil, respectively, as the effect or consequence; from being a benefactor or malefactor to being overtaken by the beneficial or malefic consequences. However, this view does not have as its logical complement another statement saying that a person who has received well-being is therefore obligated to do good. It only says that the ethical obligation is the condition for a naturally and organically evolving result, or that such an outcome is the organic effect caused by a person's own responsible stance. The other statement would and could (but in this context does not) say that an initially received state or process of well-being implies the ethical obligation to do good. In the first case, an ethical or unethical attitude releases the evolution of its consequences, a good or bad end, whereas in the second case it is the reaction or response to a received beginning, good or bad.

It is sometimes claimed that Psalm 1, a paradigm text in the discussion about these two views, does not reflect the type of view of just reality referred to above. For example, in his commentary H.-J. Kraus points out that the word "Torah" means instruction in the sense of the gracious revelation of the will of God or the gracious instruction which includes the narratives about (salvation) history, and must therefore not be understood in the sense of law. Torah means the living address from God, the refreshing and gladdening power which radiates light and brightness. It is God's life-giving and salvific gift which brings enjoyment and happiness and has nothing to do with "Jewish nomism" and "the 'Pharisee' with his utmost rigoristic obedience to the Law."[12] As if the Pharisees were not delighted in the law!

Kraus's argument against "nomism" misses the point. No one should dispute that the Torah is understood as the gracious, life-giving, gladdening gift of God. We should even add that it is the expression of Yahweh's covenant, which is itself a gracious gift, and that as such it is based on the history of Yahweh's salvific acts. But for all these presuppositions, Psalm 1 does not speak about the salvific nature of the Torah. Already on the basis of syntax, the Torah is the object of a person's activity, not the subject that generates and determines a person's destiny. For all its goodness, the psalm does not say: "How good is the Torah." It says: "Happy are those." It praises the righteous who, by virtue of their incessant study of Yahweh's Torah, yield — metaphorically — their fruit at its proper time, do not wither, and are successful in everything they do — and all this in contrast to the sinners who are vanquished because of their neglect of the Torah. Psalm 1 focuses on the dynamic connection of a person's response to and incessant study of the Torah with the natural outgrowth from that response and study for that person. It does not focus on the connection between the life-giving Torah and its effect on persons. Inasmuch as the latter connection plays a role in Psalm 1, the psalm speaks about the Torah's life-giving effect only for those persons who are committed to it. That commitment is the exclusive condition for the effect of their success. Without that commitment, the Torah has, if any (certainly in the deuteronomic-deuteronomistic tradition), the opposite effect, namely, vanquishing.

The conceptuality of Psalm 1 is perfectly homogeneous. While its substantive and metaphoric statements complement one another and therefore interpenetrate, both rest on and express the consistent dynamic process from the cause, a person's attitude toward the Torah, to its inevitable effect. Because of that effect, the righteous is at the outset of the psalm called "fortunate."

Due to the consistency of the same kind of evolution from a person's own behavior toward its fulfillment in that person's life, the courses of the righteous and sinners run toward their opposite respective results. Moreover, because of this same conceptuality of dynamic coherence, the two parties can be contrasted. In its own particular course, each party is involved in the total process. It inherits what it does. Whichever kind of life it lives, it inherits its effect, whereby one may accentuate that the righteous do not live like sinners because they study the Torah, whereas sinners live like sinners because they do not study the Torah. Of course, the contrast of the two parties means neither that the psalm is expressed in the form of a doctrine about two ways nor that its specific focus on the praise of the righteous

12. H.-J. Kraus, *Psalms 1–59,* trans. Hilton Oswald (Minneapolis: Augsburg, 1988).

must exclude the use of a reference to sinners as a reinforcement of the praise of the righteous.

The two parties are strictly separated. The ground for their separate destinies lies in and begins with their opposite reactions to the God-given, life-giving Torah, through which Yahweh's salvific actions and covenant are mediated to Israel and which is itself the same gift of God for all Israel before Israel is split into two separate parties. The ground for that split is not the nature of the Torah itself but the opposite responses of individuals to it. If the Torah itself were the ground or cause for the split, it would itself create not only success but also failure. It would generate destruction as well as life and ultimately even be responsible for the opposite responses to it, both of sinners and of the righteous. But just as the righteous are not considered successful because of the nature of the Torah, so sinners are not considered vanquished by its nature. Each party inherits its opposite status through its own response to the same life-giving Torah.

Sinners are not Gentiles. Together with the righteous, they are members of the same covenant community. But neither this community nor its Torah is considered to be the cause for their sinful ways. Since the Torah generates life rather than death as well as life, why should it not keep sinners from their ways just as it generates the way of the righteous? The two parties are separated within the same covenant community, and the cause for their separation is not that community but their opposite response to its offer of life for all. Therefore, just as sinners are vanquished by their own response to the community's Torah, so the righteous are rewarded by their own response. Moreover, inasmuch as their opposite attitudes separate individuals, built into their separation is the impetus for a development in which the covenant community is no longer constituted and identified by the same nature of the Torah for all its individual members but by individual loyalty to the Torah. This conceptual shift from the salvific Torah and its community to the individual's reaction to the Torah as the condition for the individual's final outcome not only means that this final well-being is not generated by the Torah itself. It also means that the Torah community, in which the righteous are separated from sinners by virtue of their response to the Torah, is a community of the righteous alone, and that it is their own loyalty to the Torah that makes them righteous, not the gift of the Torah. Gerstenberger is precisely on target when saying in the concluding sentence of his exegesis of this psalm: "Concentration on the Torah and dissociation from nonbelievers were absolute prerequisites for *survival*" (emphasis mine).[13]

Whether this conceptuality is called "nomistic" or not, it highlights the worldview according to which justice organically unfolds as the consistent outcome of a person's actions and attitudes, her/his own way of life. This outcome is all the more consistent in that the actions and attitudes may be responses to preconditions

13. E. Gerstenberger, *Psalms, Part I: With an Introduction to Cultic Poetry,* FOTL 14 (Grand Rapids: Eerdmans, 1988), 44.

that are neither neutral nor ambivalent but salvific or blessed. The matrix of this worldview is one of the patterns of common human experience. It is found in the international ancient wisdom tradition and represents a distinct understanding of reality as a normal, empirically verifiable process through which justice is disclosed and which is itself just.

Of course, it is the entirety of this coherent and consistent process that stands for justice. In its entirety, the return of evil to the evildoer is just, even though the total process is one of evil and even though the initial evil act is unjust. Only when an initial act is good does the justice of a process of goodness coincide with the justice of its initial act. The two opposite types of process, the evil and the good one, reflect the same principle or concept of justice, because each process manifests the same coherence and consistency. Because of this identical principle, two different statements such as "the malefactor reaps evil" and "the benefactor reaps benefits" are complementary, and it is relative whether under a narrow perspective only one or the other is stated or whether both are expressed together under a comprehensive perspective.

However, the separation of the just process of goodness from the just process of evil shows that the fact of the same kind of justice in both processes and the fact of opposite types of process rest on different criteria. Since the dynamic, coherent, and consistent process is the same for both its good and evil types, the criterion for the justice of either type rests on the consistency of its dynamic. Its justice is intrinsic to that consistency. However, the criterion for the just separation of the good from the evil process cannot be that of the same consistency in both processes. It must instead rest on the opposites of good and evil themselves, opposites perceived as ontic and discerned through the comparison of experiences. This comparison generates not only the awareness of qualities such as good and evil, but also of their opposition, rather than merely of the relative (let alone equal) degree of their relationship. The criterion for the just separation of the good from the evil process is intrinsic to the qualitative separation of good and evil. Thus, while the justice of the dynamic process lies in its consistency, the justice of the consistently separate processes of good and evil lies in the mutual exclusivity of good and evil.

Through its adaptation by Israel's Yahwism, this wisdom ontology of justice was theologized. This theologization not only means that Yahweh is considered as confirming and protecting the consistency or stability of the same dynamic process. It also means that Yahweh adopts and confirms the morality of its separate types. Rather than being himself the moral source for that separation, Yahweh identifies with and confirms that source. The theologized form of this concept of justice is in both respects rooted in the human awareness that reality itself inheres in and reveals the justice of the moral separation of good and evil just as it inheres in and reveals the same consistency of each of its separate courses.

On the other hand, it is well known that this concept of justice is contested in the Old Testament, on the level of its natural as well as its theologized empiricism. The books of Ecclesiastes and Job are two cases in point. It must be especially noted that Yahweh is not everywhere considered as merely confirming this principle of justice, let alone as being unconditionally subject to it. Yahweh influences the process in various ways, thereby asserting not only his lordship but also additional and more inclusive criteria of justice (see below). Nevertheless, the cause-and-effect concept of justice must be acknowledged because, on the one hand, it is massively documented throughout the Old Testament in juxtaposition to its variations and contestations, and because, on the other hand, it is not invalidated through the equal or superior validity of alterations or alternatives. Indeed, since this concept and its direct expression in cause-effect language are so elementary and pervasive, the expressions of all other aspects, be they alterations of it or conceptual alternatives to it, will have to be evaluated in comparison with it.

2. *Justice as Liberation of Israel's Poor from Oppression*

The prophet says: "Cease to do evil, learn to do good; seek justice, rescue the oppressed, defend the orphan, plead for the widow" (Isa 1:16b, 17). This message of the prophet is not genuinely prophetic. While its form of direct address in the imperative and its focus on acts of justice may at first glance suggest a prophetic origin, the message is conceptually, and most likely traditio-historically, rooted entirely in the worldview of the dynamic connection of cause and effect. It applies that worldview with reference to particular foci. Not even its kind of application is specifically prophetic. All of its elements are found in the nonprophetic literature, e.g., in the book of Proverbs.

With few exceptions, the language in Prov 10–22:16; 26–31 is descriptive. It describes in varying forms reality as it is, especially the positive and negative aspects of reality. These descriptions speak in the third person about persons, and sometimes portray only their positive or negative actions and sometimes the connection between their actions and the effects thereof. However, the book of Proverbs also contains prescriptive language. This language addresses a person directly in the second person. Especially with regard to negative aspects, at times it admonishes only that a person not do something (as in Prov 22:22, 24, 26, 28; 23:3, 4, 6, 9, 10, 13, 31; 24:1, 17, 19, 28, 29; 25:6; 27:1; 30:10; 31:3), and at other times it instructs a person not to do one thing but to do another (as in Prov 1:15; 3:3, 7, 21; 4:14f., 24-27; 9:8; 19:18; 20:13, 22; 23:17, 22, 23; 24:21; 25:8f.; 26:4f.). In either case, it sometimes focuses on the actions alone and at other times it refers both to an action and to its consequence.

It is well known that different types of expression, for instance, of description and prescription, of both positive and negative aspects, and of the connection of act and consequence as well as of acts alone, are rooted in the same, rather than in different, worldviews. A comparison of these types shows that their common denominator is the view of cause and effect, of an act and its consequences. This is directly expressed in statements about both an act and its consequences, whereas the descriptive and prescriptive forms, the qualifying positive and negative aspects, and the focus on actions alone represent for particular reasons the various articulations of the same worldview. Because of this common denominator, the various types of expression are complementary, and their relationship can be discerned. Thus, the language prescribing ethical action or behavior appears to be rooted in the experience of reality and the language describing that experience. The language of the description or prescription and of the difference between negative and positive aspects is rooted in the experience of that qualitative difference in reality. Furthermore, the reference to an act alone rather than to the act and its consequence focuses on the importance of that act for its consequence rather than on a systematized statement of both.

For example, Prov 20:4: "The lazy person does not plow in season; harvest comes, and there is nothing to be found," describes cause and effect according to a negative aspect. By comparison, Prov 6:6, 8-10: "Go to the ant, you lazybones; consider its ways, and be wise. . . . it prepares its food in summer, and gathers its sustenance in harvest. How long will you lie there, O lazybones? When will you arise from your sleep? A little sleep, a little slumber, a little folding of the hands to rest, and poverty will come upon you like a robber, and want, like an armed warrior," describes cause and predicted effect for both positive and negative aspects, couched in the style of personal address, and is both descriptive and exhortatory-prescriptive. Again by comparison, Prov 26:13-16: "The lazy person says, 'There is a lion in the road! There is a lion in the streets!' As a door turns on its hinges, so does a lazy person in bed. The lazy person buries a hand in the dish, and is too tired to bring it back to the mouth. The lazy person is wiser in self-esteem than seven who can answer discreetly," describes the negative acts and attitudes but without any direct address or prescriptive exhortation and without any reference to their effects. These three passages, and others about the lazy person, are conceptually complementary.

This worldview and its expressions are also the matrix for the prophetic message quoted above. All aspects expressed in Isa 1:16b and 17 are found in the wisdom literature. Not coincidentally, its specific concern regarding oppression is directly expressed in an admonition such as: "Do not rob the poor because they are poor, or crush the afflicted at the gate" (Prov 22:22). The prophetic demand for the liberation of the poor from oppression is adopted directly from the general social ethos. This ethos is not genuinely prophetic. The prophets agreed with it, and fought against its corruption and for its restoration. Even in this passage where Isaiah focuses only on the necessary actions rather than also on the consequences (which the context does), he adopts the foci already present in the general ethos, because it is the action where the problem lies and because it is the action that must and can still be changed.

The fact that verses 16b and 17 are part of a Yahweh speech (Isa 1:10-17) means that the general ethical command to do good and the admonition to cease to do evil have been appropriated by Yahweh himself and that the text's specific concern for the active liberation of the poor from oppression has become the major thrust of Yahweh's message for the very existence and survival of his own covenant community. The emphasis on these acts of liberation, or Micah's emphasis on the "doing of justice" (Mic 6:8b), reflects the particular concern for the continuing existence of that community and, therefore, a particularly vital aspect in the Old Testament's theology of justice. Indeed, Isaiah, Amos, Micah, Jeremiah, and others consider the doing of justice with specific attention to help for the oppressed, poor, orphans, widows, and aliens in Israel as the condition for the ongoing existence of Israel's community as a whole. They all make it clear that corporate Israel has no right to (and will not) survive without the actions that fulfill this condition. For them, this condition has deteriorated so much that the fatal consequences are already almost inevitable and that Amos can say, "Seek good and not evil, that you may live. . . . Hate evil and love good, and establish justice in the gate; it may be that the LORD, the God of hosts, will be gracious to the remnant of Joseph" (Amos 5:14-15).

The reason for this intensification of the demand for action in support of the disenfranchised in the prophetic theology of justice must certainly be found in the presupposed concepts of Yahweh's historical election of Israel and of his covenant with Israel as a community. Nevertheless, in this aspect of justice as well, neither the salvific election nor the covenant has changed the basic pattern according to which Israel will receive what it does. Instead, the presupposition of election and covenant, salvation history itself, has reinforced the pattern of cause and effect and made their connection even more indissoluble. This presupposition has intensified the responsibility for ethical action and the specific focus on the disenfranchised. Just as in the general ethos the outcome of the individual's life depends on his/her actions, so does Israel's outcome depend even more on its actions. In either case, the actions make the outcome predictable. Whatever the visionary component is in the prophetic appearance, inasmuch as it involves the analysis of actions, the prophecy of the consequences is prediction. The communicative function of their claim to the validity of their predictions, including their claim to speak on behalf of Yahweh, rests on the rationality of the dynamistic worldview shared by friend and foe. In this worldview, personal existence and the movements of history are subject to the same principle.

3. Justice as Divine Liberation of Elected Israel from Oppression by Others and as Yahweh's and Israel's Oppression of Others

This theology of justice is found especially in Exodus-Joshua, and in analogous texts in the Old Testament. Included in it are the traditions in Exodus and Numbers about the defeat of those nations who resist Israel's campaign march into the promised land. This concept states that Israel's oppression of the Canaanite nations and Israel's liberation from Egyptian oppression are equally just. It justifies, and this in the name of Yahweh, both liberation of and oppression by the same people. The obvious problem of two mutually exclusive concepts of justice is assumed in the Old Testament to be resolved by reference to the concept of Israel's election as Yahweh's people. On this basis, justice is what serves Israel's election by and covenant with Yahweh, rather than and regardless of a principle of justice that is the same for all nations.

Excursus. It is well known that the Old Testament offers an additional rationale for the justification of the dispossession or subjugation of the Canaanites by Israel. The conquest of the promised land and the dispossession of its nations are justified because of the idolatry of these nations, their sins, abominations, and wickedness.

Indeed, in the Old Testament the sinful polytheistic identity of the nations is a decisive reason for Yahweh's judgment against them. Inasmuch as the Canaanites are a part of the polytheistic world, they are for this reason included in the theology of judgment against the nations. This theology has its roots in Israel's monotheism, which by definition represents the opposite of polytheism and in which, in view of exclusivist conceptuality, the notion of judgment against polytheism is intrinsic. One must recognize that Israel's Yahwistic religion had in its own time the right to its distinctiveness, and from its monotheistic vantage point also the right to speak about the sins of the nations, especially since Israel did not fail to confess its own sins.

Nevertheless, this right, and even the indisputable validity of the concept of monotheism, does not mean that either the rejection of polytheism or the judgment against the polytheistic nations implies by definition the denial of their right to exist and to possess their lands and, therefore, the program for their annihilation and dispossession. As far as their sins of polytheism are concerned (and regardless of other sins such as, e.g., brutal warfare), the legitimacy of that polytheism is denied. Even when the nations lose their existence and land, they lose them as a consequence of their sins just as Israel does, but not apart from that consequence and not because they have no right to exist and to possess their land. It is their sinful polytheism that is unjust and the reason for judgment, not their existence and land, even when they lose both for that reason. By no means does the Old Testament uniformly say that loss of existence and land is always, let alone necessarily, the consequence of the sins of the nations.

The destruction and dispossession of the Canaanites by Israel in the name of Yahweh is certainly connected with the reference to their sins. It may seem that this judgment is nothing more than another of those cases in which nations lose their existence and land as the consequence of their sins. They are destroyed because they have defiled the land (Lev 18:24-30; 20:23f.) (which land? every land?) by their wickedness and abominations (Deut 9:4b, 5b; 12:2f.; 18:12; etc.). But in light of different arguments, this reason given for the Canaanites' destruction and dispossession is traditio-historically, and especially substantively, a secondary, derivative rationalization.

On general grounds attested in the Old Testament, the right of Israel to distinctiveness did not inevitably include the demand for the destruction of the other, culturally different nations. If the reference to the sins of the Canaanites were meant to be a self-sufficient argument for the justice of their oppression, the texts would have to state that each nation on earth which commits idolatry must be destroyed and dispossessed, or that Abraham should have dispossessed Ur instead of leaving it and that the plagues over Egypt should have functioned for Israel's conquest of rather than its departure from Egypt. Except for the apocalyptic-eschatological vision of a new world epoch, the destruction of historical nations on account of their polytheism is neither in principle required nor generally attested in the Old Testament.

The true reasons for the destruction of the Canaanites and their polytheism are very clearly documented. The first and most basic is Yahweh's promise to give this particular land to the patriarchs. In the book of Genesis (from Gen 12:1, 7 on), the sins of the Canaanites play no role as a reason for that promise. If they did, it would make no sense anyway. Israel will receive the land because Yahweh promised it to the patriarchs, and neither the fact that the land of Canaan is the property of the Canaanites nor their polytheism has anything to do with that promise. Yahweh gives a promise in favor of Israel, not against the Canaanites, and even their destruction is not considered in that promise. Their destruction and dispossession is not even an inevitable consequence of the fulfillment of the promise. It is, rather, the consequence of the threat to Israel's own identity and existence in the promised land which the Canaanites' polytheism represents.

When the texts speak about the sins of the nations as the reason for their destruction, it is not because the nations are sinful as such, but because the sins, specifically of the Canaanites, are a temptation, a snare, to Israel's election, monotheism, and loyalty to Yahweh (cf. Exod 23:28-33; 34:11-16; Num 33:50-55; Deut 7:1-5, 16, 25; 8:17-20; 12:29-31; Josh 23:13; Judg 2:1-3; etc.). The texts speak about the Canaanites specifically and about the necessity of their destruction not because of their polytheism but because of the danger of that polytheism to Israel. They do not presuppose a principle of justice according to which sinful nations must be destroyed. They consider the dispossession of the Canaanites as just because Israel will lose the right to its land if it is tempted to be disloyal to Yahweh by following other gods. The reference to the sins of the Canaanites as the reason for their destruction is not a rationale for justice independent of the theology of Israel's exclusive election. It depends on and serves that theology. For the sake of Israel's election, the responsibility for Israel's temptation is laid squarely on the Canaanites. For this reason, they themselves are responsible for their doom, not

Israel, who executes it. They are condemned to losing their existence and land not because they are sinfully polytheistic but because of the temptation their existence presents to Israel's monotheistic allegiance. They are responsible for the injustice and, hence, for the reason for the justice of the judgment, whereas Israel's own responsibility for preserving its integrity in the face of this basically nonaggressive temptation plays no role in this concept. Their disappearance is necessary so that Israel may live free from temptation.

It is not coincidental that this understanding of justice exclusively reflects the Israelite perspective and interest. It considers neither the possible tolerance of Israel's distinctiveness by the Canaanites, the Canaanites' own ethos of loyalty to their religious traditions for which the Old Testament shows almost total contempt, nor any recognition at all of the complaints by the Canaanites over their pronounced or factual destruction or subjugation, as if such complaints should not be assumed. Last but not least, it differs sharply from the Old Testament's own conceptual sociological-theological claim, according to which Yahweh judges justly, by defending all who are oppressed and by evaluating (!) — or commanding to evaluate — the claims of both parties in court rather than siding with one party only.

This exclusivistic theology is most explicit in the deuteronomic-deuteronomistic literature. Its roots are evidently much older. These roots provided the justification for Israel's demarcation from the Canaanites and also for its claim to the sole possession of their land in the first place. But the statement about the idolatry of the nations in the land as the legitimate reason for their dispossession is not yet explained with reference to these roots alone. Its specific origin lies in Israel's reaction against the temptation which Canaanite polytheism represented for the permanence of its possession of the land. This permanence depended on Israel's permanent loyalty to Yahweh alone. To this permanence, the sins of the Canaanite nations provided a permanently dangerous presence. Instead of seeking the resistance to this temptation in the strength of Israel's own Yahwistic traditions and identity, the deuteronomic theologians justified the dispossession of the Canaanites through the need for the removal of the temptation itself, and therefore, through the rationale for the cause of that temptation, the idolatry of the nations.

When one compares this conceptuality of the theology of justice with those previously discussed, it is clear that the concept of justice based on the worldview of the consistent connection of act and consequence, which applies universally, has been enveloped, relativized, and even superseded by the principle of the exclusive covenant between Yahweh and Israel, which is itself rooted in the concept of Israel's election from among all nations. In this paradigmatic shift, which is reinforced by the concept of monotheism, the criterion for justice is no longer the separation of good and evil in the dynamic process of act and consequence. Instead, it is the guarantee of Israel's separation from the polytheistic nations in the land that determines what is good and what is evil, and their respectively separate processes. To be sure, neither Israel's election nor even its separation in the land had to be understood as the legitimation of the oppression of the Canaanites. They could have been — but were not in this theology — understood as the paradigm for the equal right of all nations to equal justice, for the same liberation of all other oppressed nations, and certainly for Israel's own abstention from the oppression of other nations. The monotheistically shaped concept of Israel's election from among the nations necessarily involves the fundamental aspect of the relationship between Israel and the nations. Israel as a concept is impossible without that aspect. Intrinsic to that aspect, however, is international justice as the manifestation of the justice of the one God of and for one world. In this respect, the question is inevitable as to whether the elect witness to the same justice for all nations, or whether all nations are subject to — and victims of — a justice exclusively reserved for the elect.

4. Justice as Judgment against the Nations for Their Oppression of and Aggression against Israel

This aspect of the Old Testament portrays Yahweh as the universal God who is involved in political and especially military events in the defense of Israel against the aggression of foreign nations. The subject is highly prominent, and its prominence attests not only to the precarious historical conditions under which Israel always existed but also to the tension between the strategies of the historical empires and those of Yahweh which lie at the heart of the course and meaning of human history. The variety of its formal and substantive aspects has its ground in different reactions to specific historical experiences and in different theological traditions such as, most prominently, the Exodus and Zion-David traditions and their settings. This variety continues to be a subject of study. One question, however, affects each of the various articulations of this topic: does the God of all nations protect every other nation just as he protects Israel against aggression, or does he only protect his people and not the other nations likewise? Whatever a modern theology has to say on the issue of war, it is clear that the Old Testament is only very infrequently critical of warfare. It legitimizes war. Indeed, Yahweh's own warfare is a manifestation of his justice in history. In whatever way the Old Testament's theologies of war may be evaluated, the question of justice in warfare depends very much on whether the operative principle of justice is the same for all or reserved for one against all.

The topic of judgment against the nations in defense of Israel is theologized throughout almost the entire Old Testament. The topic is found, for example, in Exod 7:1-5; 17:8-15; Num 33:3; Deut 32:34-43; Judg 6–8; 1 Sam 20:16; 2 Sam 5:17-25; 8; 22:47-49 // Ps 18:46-48; 2 Kings 18–20 // Isa 36–39; Psalms 2; 46:7, 10 (*NRSV* 46:6, 9); 48:5-9 (*NRSV* 48:4-8); 59; Isa 10:5-19; 29:6; 34:8; 47; 63:1-6; Jer 30:18-21; 46–51; Ezek 25–32; Nahum.

5. Justice through the Ethos and Law of the Liberated

This variation emphasizes the kind of consequences that follow from the experience of initial liberation or blessing: the obligatory ethical and legal requirements. It says that the justice received in liberation or blessing must be activated through ethos and law in the ongoing life of the liberated or blessed. In it, justice received is justice to be done. Its movement from being a beneficiary to becoming a benefactor is opposite to the movement discussed in example 1 ("Life in Justice as the Cause of Well-Being"). Ethos and law are the conscious, responsible, active ethical decisions for which the experiences of liberation or blessing are the ground and reason. Ethos and law are not understood as the natural outgrowth of an already received divine causal activity. They do not presuppose that the divine action flows organically into human nature. They presuppose that the divine activity, having provided the condition for life in justice, is subsequently at work in a transformed way: through ethical and legal guidelines, through various modes of their communication, and through the mobilization and activation of human responsibility and obedience. The Decalogue in Exodus 20, along with its introduction, is the best-known and most direct expression of this understanding of justice.[14]

6. Justice as Divine Judgment against Israel for Apostasy and Oppression

This aspect pervades the Pentateuch from the book of Exodus on, and the historical and prophetic books and many psalms as well. It is so prominent that specific references are unnecessary. What should be recognized is that the justice of divine judgment over Israel was acknowledged by Israel itself, and by no means only in the voices of some prophetic outsiders or after their prophecies had come true. To be sure, not all Israelites were at any time able and willing to admit to their own injustice and to the divine judgment on it. Indeed, at times precious few did. But both the broad attention to this factor in the variety of the texts and the increasing inclusion of it in Israel's review of its past history as a learning mechanism for present and future generations represent a major chapter in the total system of Israel's theology. They point to the paradigmatic and exceptional ability of this society to confront, rather than to repress, the dark sides of its existence and history and, ultimately, to be open in its encounter with God, and because of this encounter to be open to the revision of its concepts of justice, even of divine justice. The painful acceptance of the inglorious side of its history is one of the most difficult, if not impossible, challenges for any nation, and at the same time the only true sign for its claim to integrity, justice, and truth.

14. See also the laws in Exod 12:1-36, in the entire Sinai pericope, Exodus 19–Num 10:10, and more within Numbers 15–36, and the parenesis of the laws in Deuteronomy with reference to Israel's liberation from Egypt.

7. *Justice as Political Liberation through Divine Forgiveness of Sins*

The Old Testament speaks about Israel's restoration from foreign military and political subjection through the divine forgiveness of its sins. In contrast to the initial liberation from Egypt, which does not depend on this aspect, the notion of restoration through divine forgiveness presupposes the alternating fortunes of Israel's ongoing history in the land, understands calamity as Yahweh's judgment for its sin, and expresses the liberation from calamity as the historical effect of Yahweh's forgiveness. It is variously expressed in narratives or poetry which speak of the experience of forgiveness-liberation, such as Judg 2:16; 6–8; 1 Sam 7:1-14; Ps 85:1-3; in intercessory petitions, such as 1 Kgs 8:33-34; and in prophetic announcements of it, such as Isa 40:1-2; 44:21-28. The texts, especially in the deuteronomistic theology, clearly indicate that restoration as the consequence of forgiveness is understood as an ever recurring possibility, so long as Israel repents and returns to Yahweh.

In terms of experience, hope, and promise, the notion is, therefore, a basic assumption in the theology of Israel's unending political history. As a notion of justice, it is characterized not only by the general assumption of the fulfillment of divine justice in the course of human history, but especially by the belief that in this course the divine justice of forgiveness in principle outweighs the divine justice of momentary or periodic judgment. But again, the question remains open as to whether Israel's experience rests on an understanding of universally equal justice or of an exception reserved only for Yahweh's covenant people. There is also the question of how this experience of justice is related to the experience of empirically unverifiable justice.

8. *Divine Justice Equally for Israel and the Nations*

"Say among the nations, 'The LORD is king! The world is firmly established; it shall never be moved. He will judge the peoples with equity. . . . He will judge the world with righteousness, and the peoples with his truth' " (Ps 96:10, 13b). "The LORD is king! Let the earth rejoice; let the many coastlands be glad! Clouds and thick darkness are all around him; righteousness and justice are the foundation of his throne. . . . The heavens proclaim his righteousness; and all the peoples behold his glory" (Ps 97:1f., 6; cf. Psalms 82; 98; 99).

These and similar texts speak about Yahweh who reigns over the nations by dispensing justice with "righteousness" and "his truth." The language of these texts, notably of Psalm 82, portrays Yahweh as the God of universal justice who adjudicates among the nations according to the principle of equal justice rather than of preferred nationalities. Specifically, the terminology for "judging" means rendering judgment after evaluating conflicting arguments. However, it is, at least, not impossible that these texts express more than they mean. The possible ambivalence between their expression and their meaning surfaces in the question of whether these statements of universal justice are meant to relativize other statements based on Yahweh's relationship with Israel or to be relativized by those statements. The question is important for the clarification of the theology of justice in these texts. While it is left open for the time being, it should be noted that their language lends itself not only to prompting the question but also to conveying an understanding that challenges a concept of justice which is in favor of Israel and against the nations.

9. Justice as Both War and Peace

With but very few exceptions, the tumult of warfare and of warriors and their weaponry resounds throughout the books of the Old Testament. Yahweh himself, the "man of battle" (Exod 15:3, author's translation) who "trains" the warrior's "hands for war" and "[his] fingers for battle" (Ps 144:1), is constantly practicing war in Israel's and humanity's history, including history's eschatological and apocalyptic dimensions and notwithstanding the announcements of a new epoch in which "He makes wars cease to the end of the earth; he breaks the bow, and shatters the spear; he burns the shields with fire" (Ps 46:10 [*NRSV* 46:9]), and in which the nations "shall beat their swords into plowshares, and their spears into pruning hooks; nation shall not lift up sword against nation, neither shall they learn war any more" (Isa 2:4 // Mic 4:3; cf. Hos 2:20 [*NRSV* 2:18]). Not even for Yahweh is there an exception to "a time for every matter under heaven: . . . a time for war, and a time for peace" (Eccl 3:1, 8b).

The Old Testament considers Yahweh's wars, and many of Israel's as well, as executions of justice. The song of Deborah praises the "צדקות יהוה," "the righteous acts of Yahweh" (Judg 5:11). The same is true for some wars of other nations, notably those serving Yahweh's judgment over Israel. A survey of the total evidence shows, perhaps contrary to well-meaning opinion, that war is much more documented as justified than it is criticized. Nevertheless, war is also criticized, especially campaigns of total annihilation, the strategies of which contradict Yahweh's own plans in warfare, as in Isa 10:5-19; Amos 1:3f. The psalmist prays: "Trample under foot those who lust after tribute; scatter the peoples who delight in war" (Ps 68:31b [*NRSV* 68:30b]; cf. Ps 76:6 [*NRSV* 76:5]). Micah criticizes the prophets who "declare war against those who put nothing into their mouths" (Mic 3:5b). Even more basically, Ps 33:16f. affirms: "A king is not saved by his great army; a warrior is not delivered by his great strength. The war horse is a vain hope for victory, and by its great might it cannot save." Jer 9:22f. (*NRSV* 9:23f.) at least subordinates war to justice in principle: in the humans' praise of values, the praise of the knowledge of (that) Yahweh who delights in and practices steadfast love, justice, and righteousness in the earth, it denies the validity of the praise of their own wisdom by the wise, of their own (military) might by the warriors, and of their own wealth by the rich. The God of Jer 9:22f. (*NRSV* 9:23f.) is a God of loyalty, justice, and righteousness in the world, and not a god of human wisdom, might, and wealth. The rejection of the injustice of human might does not exclude in this text the implicit notion of war as a means of divine justice. At the very least, however, it subjects even Yahweh's war to his practice of justice, the criterion for which is independent of, supersedes, and opposes the praise of might. Even so, war is, for this God, ultimately the opposite of what he loves and practices.

The Old Testament speaks not only about the inevitability of war in human history. It also speaks about war in qualitative terms, from its justice at one extreme to its injustice at the other. Its qualifying perspectives become particularly clear when it contrasts war with peace or with Israel's rest from its enemies. The statement in Eccl 3:8b can scarcely mean that war is as good or as just as peace. It is always, at least, worse or less just than peace. Even the justice of Yahweh's own wars is less valid than the justice of Yahweh's gift of peace or rest (cf. Josh 21:44; 22:4; 23:1; 2 Sam 7:1, 11; 1 Kings 5:18 [*NRSV* 5:4]; etc.). In the relationship of the two, war appears to be just or unjust while true peace (rather than treacherous peace, which is a special problem) is always just, and more just than just war.

In an Old Testament theology of justice, the evaluation of the relationship of these qualifiers is therefore necessary. Such evaluation involves more than the exegetical recognition of a text's assertion of the validity of its statement about war or peace, and more than the simplistic reference to the text's theological pluralism. It requires the validation of any text's claim to validity through comparison with the claims of other texts. This requirement is generated but not fulfilled by the Old Testament. Without the procedure of such validation, the theology of any one text can appear as valid or as invalid as the theology of any other, and the result is in principle the equal justification of any textually documented condition for war or peace, either with reference to the claimed legitimacy of unique and particular conditions or, worse, on the ground of a blatantly subjectivistic and opportunistic abuse of biblical texts. However, with a procedure of validation, the validity of each text is relative to the claim of validity in other texts, and the presumption of the equal validity of all texts becomes just as impossible as the opportunistic selection of any text. And wars, even Yahweh's wars, represent, if not injustice altogether, at best a degree of subordinate justice. They are never legitimate in themselves either as means or as ends, especially when compared with their opposite, the justice of peace or the peace of justice.

The validity of war as an instrument of justice in human history is relative at best. This relativity is reinforced by the Old Testament's statements about the peaceful order of the world in its creation and in the coming of the new, eschatological aeon. These statements provide the vantage point for the distinction between the Old Testament's theologies of warfare and the place of warfare in Old Testament theology; the latter in the framework of justice in Old Testament theology is under consideration here. Just as the theology of creation in principle disqualifies any world of or with war, so does the eschatological vision of a world without war. But more than the theology of creation, the eschatological vision of a new world of peace implies a problem which must be addressed.

The Old Testament's, indeed the Bible's, eschatological visions have become at least relative in the sense that they are inextricably linked to the conditions and events of their times and in the sense that they expected the new aeon to arrive as the replacement of those times. However, they certainly did not expect it to be in the distant future indefinitely. One can observe that the eschatological vision was recontextualized throughout ancient Israel's history. One may also debate whether or not such recontextualization remains indefinitely called for on the ground that the vision is declared valid for all times, and whether the vision of a future new aeon loses its validity because its recontextualization was not meant to go on indefinitely and should not. So much is clear: the vision has become postponed indefinitely. Such postponement undermines the claim that a future new aeon is the decisive criterion for the disqualification of the history of the ongoing world, including war in history.

However, when it is reconceptualized, the eschatological vision of a new world of peace remains decisive for the evaluation of war in history. Regardless of whether or not its major notion of a future aeon will materialize, already implied in this eschatological notion is the connotation or presupposition that, ultimately, peace is valid whereas war is invalid. In terms of ultimacy, the eschatological notion is reconceptualized in the sense that it is but one aspect by which to express the validity of peace and the invalidity of war. This aspect is rooted in the historicality of the eschatological vision, and is consistent with such a historical perspective. Yet rather than being the criterion for ultimacy, its historicality is subject to the criterion of ultimacy. It only shows that ultimacy is not abstracted from, or unrelated to, history. But whereas ultimacy itself does not depend on a particular kind of eschatological future, it is the ever-present criterion for the truth or untruth of history, of its past, of its present, and of whatever is its future. As such, it is the ground for an inevitable ethos of just history against perverted history and, hence, of peace against war. This criterion is ultimately based on the theology of creation. Intrinsic to this theology is the irreducible claim that the true meaning of creation is actualized in history by peace, not by war. This claim is not invalidated by the ongoing fact of wars. On the contrary, it is the judgment over all wars.

What has been said primarily for methodological reasons also relativizes the often explicit claim or implicit assumption of an intrinsic theological validity of unique, particular historical or existential situations. The uniqueness of such situations is a fact, and the historical exegesis of the biblical texts irreversibly points out this universally recognized fact. However, the necessary recognition of particularities, circumstances, contingencies, indigenousnesses, and even uniquenesses is not identical with the evaluation of the validity of any of them. No fact, typical or unique, is valid because it is a fact. If it were, Jeremiah and Hananiah would not have had to fight over the validity of their conflicting claims (cf. Jeremiah 27f.). This statement has nothing to do with a retreat from the Old Testament's important attention to the realities of this world into a sphere of abstract theory. On the contrary, it takes that attention seriously, including the Old Testament's own focus on evaluating those realities. Inasmuch as a particular situation is real, its validity is relative. It is subject to the possibility of and to comparison with alternatives, just as a text about war or peace is subject to such comparison in the horizon of a theology of justice.

10. Social Justice in a Stratified Society

The entire Old Testament emphasizes social justice. However, an analysis of the Old Testament's concept of social justice shows not only that it is different from what we perceive as social justice but also that it experienced conceptual shifts during the history of ancient Israel. It is well known that the concepts of social justice before, during, and after the monarchy were not the same. Moreover, the Old Testament documents that the social system considered just by one party was considered unjust by another party. This reveals that the fact of a particular form of social organization in a certain historical period does not constitute an uncontested criterion for its validity for that period, let alone for all periods. The Old Testament calls for a comparison of these systems. Such comparison demonstrates that not everything is right in one period and wrong in another.

Special attention must be paid to the fact that Israel was at all times a stratified society in one way or another, and at no time was Israel anything like an international social community. The idea of justice through the establishment of a classless society scarcely finds support in the texts, not even in those about the premonarchic time. Women were never equal. The rights of the poor were always defended, but a demand for the removal of poverty through the equal (re)distribution of wealth, notwithstanding Joshua 13–19, is hard to find. There were always slaves, and foreigners or aliens did not have equal rights in all things. The monarchy is not only considered, intermittently or in principle, as an oppressor (e.g., 1 Samuel 8; 1 Kings 12) but also as the organizer, dispenser, and protector of justice. Furthermore, the hierocratic organization after the monarchy is neither understood as a system of injustice nor evaluated as the better or best implementation of a system of social justice.

The comparison of the varying degrees of justice in the history of ancient Israel's social systems must face the question as to which of the attested systems is better. However, even more it must face the question of how any of its documented social organizations compares with an ideal that can be derived from the potential of Israel's theocratic vision for the shaping of a just society. In view of this, none of the social formations documented in the Old Testament represents a theocratic ideal.

From this deficit, it is normally concluded that such an ideal will only be fulfilled in an eschatological future, and therefore requires the documented expectation of such a future, since it can never be fulfilled in history. But just as in the case of eschatological peace, the relativization of the idea of the eschatological endtime does not mean that the eschatological vision has lost its critical function for social formation in ongoing human history. On the contrary, the theocratic aspect, including its eschatological connotation, represents, especially in the Old Testament, the reminder of the always critical tension between the imperfection of the existing social formations and the theocratic ultimacy. This theocratic aspect reveals both the crisis of any social formation, including those attested in the Old Testament, and the denial of a justification for complacency with any of them. At the same time, it represents both the impetus for the search for better ways, ways always penultimate yet better, and the promise of such ways.

The study of the history of ancient Israel's social formation is important. Yet it is not identical, at least not self-evidently, with the consideration of the function of the Old Testament's explicit theological, theocratic intentionality. This intentionality calls for an Old Testament theology of social justice which in essence must confront the tension between the Old Testament's theocratic claims and — beyond our reconstructions of ancient Israel's social reality — its own social theologies. It calls not only for the comparison of those theologies but for their theological critique in view of the Old Testament's own theocratic claims. This task goes far beyond the often-mentioned prophetic criticism of injustice in the society.

The function of the above statement concerning the deficit of the Old Testament's social theologies has nothing in common with claimed evidence for the Old Testament's theological failure, especially in contrast to the claimed solution of this problem in the New Testament. It is true that a major reason for the Old Testament's theological deficit lies in its understanding of the inseparable connection between Israel the people of God and the historical nation and society of Israel. But quite apart from the fact that the Old Testament is itself aware of the tension present in this connection, the New Testament represents an attempt to take an easy way out by sidestepping, if not eliminating, the question of the social justice of the systems of the ongoing history of nations and societies. From neither its Christology, its eschatology, nor its ecclesiology has it developed a theology of justice for the historical, societal, and international systems. Where Christianity in its own history has attempted it, it has — considering its claims to superiority — fared worse than Israel. Compared with this deficit, the Old Testament confronts the problem, aware of the penultimacy of its answers. Moreover, the fact of this involvement not only outweighs the deficit of its solutions; it accounts for it. Its deficit does not constitute a theological failure, unless one admits the failure of any theology, including the New Testament's, which either inadequately answers the demand for social justice in the systems of human societies or gives no answer at all. This demand is required precisely because of the Old Testament's claim to the reign of God over all at all times.

11. Justice through Corporate or Genealogical Linkage and Justice Based on Individual Responsibility

The Old Testament speaks about the justice of blessing or judgment (or about the degree of the conditions for one or the other) for corporate entities such as Israel and the nations, cities (Gen 18:22-33), and families (Exod 20:5f.), but also about justice based on individual responsibility, in which the individual is either singled out in or separated from the community (as, e.g., in Lev 24:10-23; Deut 24:16; Joshua 6 and 7) or in which the community itself is considered to be based on the separation of righteous individuals from sinful ones (as in Jer 31:27-30; Ezek 3:16-21; 18).

The two, at least different if not basically contrasting, sociological principles pervade the entire Old Testament in a variety of ways. Technically speaking, it would be easy to decide the question of their relationship if one could simply affirm the maxims in Jeremiah 31 and Ezekiel 3 and 18 as the advanced insights which legitimately replace the deficient older principles of corporate justice. But such a method of interpretation is unsustainable. The juxtaposition in the Old Testament of these different principles for the human and divine practice of justice has reserved the right of each, and forces the comparative evaluation of each with the other on substantive grounds. Such comparison will most probably have to confirm the rights, responsibilities, and fortunes of the individual among, or if necessary vis-à-vis, other individuals. It does not seem as if the total evidence allows for a choice in favor of one principle over the other for the perception or actualization of the process of justice.

The difficulty on contextual grounds of a choice between alternatives is reinforced by empirical data reflected in the texts themselves. They make it impossible to ignore the relative correctness as well as the limits of either position. Basic to all texts is the presupposition that there is neither a community without individuals nor an individual without a community. The problem of justice surfaces in the kinds of their relationship.

The corporate entity is, in its rights and responsibilities, in its fortunes and misfortunes, more than the rights, responsibilities, fortunes, and misfortunes of its separate individuals. It is at the same time more than the collective of anonymous numbers in which the individualities of its members would be irrelevant. Conversely, the individuality of one person in distinction to that of other persons is widely regarded in the texts and can be surmised as underlying them. It reflects the understanding of the corporate community as composed of individual members. Yet the split of the community into exclusive parties of righteous and sinful individuals is not only empirically impossible and ethically questionable, it also bears in itself the potential for the destruction of any community, even of the righteous, because the goal of each individual is his own righteousness even as he may serve others.

An Old Testament theology of justice must confront the question of the relationship between the community and its individuals and arrive at justice itself in the interpretation of that relationship. Its basis can be neither collectivistic nor individualistic. It may be called corporate inasmuch as corporateness means the just balance between community and individuality.

12. The Justice of Judgment and the Justice of Pardon

Judgment in the Old Testament is based on the rationality of the just connection of evil acts and their respective consequences. It is an element of justice. This fact need not be specifically documented here. What needs to be pointed out is that events, in which guilty and condemned parties are pardoned, are also considered as acts of justice. They declare an exemption from the punishment stipulated for a crime. Pardon is a particular kind of forgiveness. While not reversing a judgment of guilt and the legality of the sentence for it, it forgives the execution of that sentence. The right to such forgiveness is based on the law's provision for it and normally entrusted to a decision by the highest societal authority. Examples of pardon or aspects of it are found in 1 Sam 11:12f.; 2 Sam 14:1-24; Hos 11:1-9; Job 7:21; and also Gen 50:19f.

Both forms of justice, the justice of punishment and the justice of pardon, are involved in the attempt to overcome or to constrain the consequences of an evil act for the evildoer, one by letting it run its course, the other by turning the evil end for her/him into a good end or by liberating her/him from the evil end. Their tension in the process of justice is generated by the struggle for its true nature. The nature of justice is not equivocal. It is ambivalent. Yet, while its ambivalence forces the — risky — decision in favor of either its one or its other form, it always carries with it the question of the more adequate, the better justice. Justice itself is subject to the criterion for what is good or better. It serves that criterion. The justice of pardon is based on that criterion because it acknowledges that the life of the evildoer is better than his/her death.

13. Justice as Forgiveness of Guilt

Like pardon, human or divine forgiveness of guilt, in contrast to the imposition of it, is an act of better justice. It definitively invalidates the right of the destructive sphere of guilt to run its course, thereby depriving guilt of the basis for its power. Forgiveness is accompanied by psychological effects for the forgiving as well as for the forgiven, but it is not based on emotionality. Nor is it dependent on the insight, repentance, and confession of the sinner, even though it is very often a reaction to such repentance and confession. It results from the decision of the forgiving person or deity, which is itself grounded in the validity of turning evil into goodness. The turning of evil into good is a powerful act of better justice, especially as it rests on a definitive decision.

The just act of forgiveness does not require an institutional judicial setting. It may happen privately between one person and another, or between God and humans, whereby the forgiving party itself carries the burden inflicted on it rather than keeping the burden affixed to the guilty party. Nevertheless, many texts, including those in Leviticus 1–7, point to institutionalized procedures for the actualization of forgiveness. This actualization of forgiveness in set cultic, forensic, or cult-forensic procedures represents a particular aspect of the practice of justice.

14. Justice as World Order, as Ecological Order

By now it is well known that the creation, sustenance, and restoration of world -order, and what we have come to call ecological order, are in the Old Testament considered to be the work of divine justice. This rests especially on the ancient Near Eastern traditions about the establishment of cosmic natural order through the defeat and banishment of chaos. It is fundamental because it represents the just reality without which human history and existence would be impossible. The evaluation of its theological fundamentality is the result of the comparison of the different but related dimensions of reality, and it is based on direct and indirect evidence throughout the Old Testament (cf., among others, Psalms 65; 72:3-7; 85; 89:5-18; Isa 11:1-9; 45:8; 48:18f.; 61:11; Jon 4:9-11).[15]

15. Empirically Verifiable Justice versus Hidden Justice

Throughout the Old Testament, it is assumed that justice must and can be administered in and by Israel's society, and that it is empirically verifiable on the basis of societal ethos and law and through their appropriate procedures. It is also assumed that divine justice is verifiable, either through the divinely ordained institutions in the society or through the divine presence in the cosmos, in history, and in social and individual human existence, foremost by way of the consistent dynamic connection of cause and effect but also by way of interference in that connection for the sake of turning evil into good (e.g., the Joseph novella).

However, the Old Testament also documents, directly and indirectly, that the presence of justice is either hidden in discrepancies between verifiable factors or

15. See H. H. Schmid, *Gerechtigkeit als Weltordnung,* BHT 40 (Tübingen: Mohr, 1968); O. H. Steck, *World and Environment,* Biblical Encounter Series (Nashville: Abingdon, 1980); R. Knierim, "Cosmos and History in Israel's Theology," pages 170-223 in this volume.

hidden altogether. The range, especially of the indirect indicators, is wide and in need of attentive study. The notion that, in the pursuit of its normal societal administration, justice must be sought already indicates that it is hidden within legal cases, not known at the outset, and may still leave a measure of deficit behind even as cases are decided. Or, in societal justice and especially with respect to divine justice, what is verifiable for one party may be inaccessible to the insight of another, be it that the conditions for the verifiability of the same justice are different among different parties or that different parties have different criteria for justice. What may be known as just to one party may appear to be unjust to another, or the justice known by one party may be unknown to another. Furthermore, justice is assumed to be evident to one generation but concealed to another, as is especially evident in the communal complaint psalms. The alternation between evident and hidden justice from one period to another not only shows that a generation's perception of the sudden hiddenness of justice presupposes that its conscious traditional concept of evident justice is currently not applicable; it also implies the question of whether, or to what extent, the traditional concept is (to be) assumed to be merely temporarily suspended — which is often the case — or to be in need of revision. The periodic alternation in the experience of justice evokes either the question of different justices or the question of the relativity of any concept of justice and, thus, of the hiddenness of justice in principle from any form of empirical verification. This question transcends in kind those aspects according to which a fool, e.g., Nabal in 1 Samuel 25, is simply incapable of understanding what is for everyone else self-evidently just.

It is well known that especially the books of Job and Ecclesiastes substantively confront the issue of hidden justice. Their arguments belong to the range under consideration. However, they cannot be the sole basis for the problem of the relationship between empirically verifiable and hidden justice in an Old Testament theology of justice. In such a theology and its sociology, the notion of hidden justice cannot be assumed to have replaced all connotations of the notion of evident or revealed justice. Critical evidence in all Old Testament books points to the validity of both verifiable and hidden justice, yet also to their relativity in relation to and even within each other. By comparing these aspects as comprehensively as possible, an Old Testament theology of justice will itself have to be a search for the Old Testament's own quest for justice, an understanding of which is itself hidden in the Old Testament's statements about it. It must do justice to the Old Testament's own search for justice.

16. Eschatological Justice

Whatever the validity of the future-oriented eschatology of Old Testament texts, especially of their concrete contents, the articulation of this eschatology is for various reasons understandable. The descriptive interpretation of eschatological theology and its various configurations, primarily in the prophetic literature, is done in exegetical work and summarized in monographs. Its evaluation in comparison with the other theologies in the Old Testament belongs to quite a different arena.

The notion of the eschatological revelation of justice is related to the notion of the hiddenness of justice. The counterpart of hidden justice is its revealed state, or revelation. When it comes to the revelation of hidden justice, including momentarily or periodically hidden justice, the Old Testament speaks much more often about such revelations than it speaks about Yahweh's withdrawal into hiddenness. Moreover, it does so without expecting them to happen in an eschatological end-time. The fact that the aspects of the apocalyptic and the eschatological are intertwined, especially in the eschatological texts, does not mean that the two notions are identical and that the two words can be used interchangeably. It only means that what can be revealed at any time will also be revealed in fullness when the new world comes, even as that new event is already now revealed in principle to the apocalypticist. The notion of eschatology, therefore, adds to the notion of apocalyptic the future aspect of a final and definitively new event, and its full revelation with its coming, an event in which, among other things, justice is universally fulfilled and its true nature disclosed.

The question of the viability or necessity of such an eschatological expectation exceeds the range of the discussion concerned with the Old Testament. Within that range, one may have to distinguish between eschatological justice and the justice of the eschaton. The justice of the eschaton may be a justice different from the kinds of justice in the world before the eschaton. Eschatological justice may be understood as (the awareness of) ultimate justice at all times, even as it can only function as the crisis of all justices and as the inevitable necessity for the never ending search for better justice. When one compares the Old Testament's concepts of the justice of the creation and sustenance of the world with its concepts of the justice of and within history, one cannot take for granted that its awareness of the just cosmic order is one of penultimacy, in need of future fulfillment or replacement, rather than one of its ever present ultimacy (cf. Psalm 104 and the priestly Genesis 1) — however hidden or evident (!) that ultimacy may be perceived. Such ultimacy appears in some text traditions to be assumed to exist. Modern natural scientists can say that their task is not to find answers to their questions but to learn how to raise the right questions so that the answers which already exist in the structure of reality may be revealed to them. As far as the issue of justice and eschatology in an Old Testament theology of justice is concerned, it must evaluate in their relatedness the notions of future-eschatology, of ever existing ultimacy, and of the pre-eschatological and penultimate justice, and all this in the context of the epistemological question of their empirical verifiability and/or hiddenness.

Last but not least, the issues of eschatological and ultimate, of pre-eschatological and penultimate justice, together with the issues of revelation and hiddenness, are connected with the issue of God/Yahweh's justice. In the Old Testament, justice is not Yahweh or divine, nor is Yahweh-God dissolved into a specific concept of justice, let alone an abstract principle of justice. But neither is thought of without the other, and neither is considered valid without the other. The question is not only one of theodicy, but also one of *dikaio*-dicy. A theology of justice must address both questions: what does justice contribute to the understanding of, and trust in, God-Yahweh, and what does God-Yahweh contribute to the understanding of justice?

1.-16. The types of justice discussed above and the biblical references given for each type are only selected examples. This list does not claim to be complete. It is important that none of them is exactly identical with the others. Some represent variations of the same or similar conceptual group. Some can be correlated, and some conflict. Most important are both the obvious question of how these types relate to one another and the need to correlate and compare them all so that we may have a basis for their evaluation. There can be little doubt about the complementarity of many of these types. There is also little doubt that the validity of any one of them cannot be taken for granted without regard to the others, and/or without regard to their relationship.

It is not impossible to blend the major contours of these variations into a history of the concept of justice which begins in Egypt and the ancient Near East, extends through the Old Testament (and, e.g., Greece), and enters the New Testament and its time and beyond. Indeed, the reality of such an intellectual history should not be denied.

Nevertheless, our literary-historical data are not definitive enough. Moreover, it cannot be ascertained that a certain variation belonged only to one stage in the development and not also to subsequent stages alongside other variations. With increasing accumulation, the typology becomes synchronically more diversified and complex. The neglect of this fact would lead to a history of an idea which is abstracted from real history, to a construct which exists only in the mind of the interpreter.

Most important is the fact that such a development in the idea of justice involves a critical evaluation of each stage by its succeeding stages, and inevitably either its theoretical subordination or abandonment. The only difference is that such a critical evaluation happens through a historical process rather than through a systematic one. While the former process is not impossible, it has disadvantages. Two have already been mentioned. A third consists in the fact that the Old Testament itself does not cast its statements about justice in the form of the development of an idea. Above all in its canonic level, it contains all the concepts listed above in synchronic juxtaposition and, with few exceptions, presents them to its reader without deciding between differences in validity. Even where in some passages a certain concept is said to have replaced another, as in Jeremiah 31 and Ezekiel 3 and 18, that same concept appears in other passages in full force. The canonic situation calls for the critical correlation and evaluation of all types of concepts of justice. In the following, we shall focus on a few examples.

B. Exemplifications

1. It is not sufficiently acknowledged in biblical theology that the Old Testament clearly distinguishes, terminologically and conceptually, between liberation and justice. The exodus story begins with Israel's oppression and rebellion, and only then narrates (briefly) the exodus itself in Exodus 12–15. Immediately thereafter it continues with the disobedience and sustenance of the liberated, in order to arrive at its most important climax, the covenant and law given at Sinai for the future life of the liberated. The total story is clearly conceptual. In it, the notion of liberation is neither isolated from justice nor identical with it. It is an element of the theology of justice. The theology of justice includes oppression, rebellion, liberation, guidance in the face of distrust, covenant, ethos, law, and more. Inasmuch as liberation is an element in the process of justice, it by no means encompasses all factors that belong to the totality of that process. The process of justice is perceived as a holistic reality of which these factors, including liberation, are parts which dynamically affect each other because it is the need for justice that creates the impetus toward their balanced relationship. Accordingly, liberation is not an end in itself. As the just rescue from, or removal of, injustice, liberation points beyond itself toward the confirmation of justice in its practice by the liberated. Without this continuation and goal, liberation by itself would lose its validity. In this continuation, those involved in the process of justice become grantors of liberation after being recipients of liberation. Liberation is not only to be received, it is also to be granted by the same people. Since it is an element of justice, and since justice is indivisible, liberation cannot divide people into two groups, one that receives it and another that grants it. It unites all in both roles, or it is not just. This aspect is in principle especially emphasized in Deuteronomy. It is also the basis for the prophetic critique of Israel, and occurs throughout the Old Testament's tradition history.

The theological traditions of the Old Testament in which the justice of received liberation points beyond itself to the practice of justice through ethos and law are most noticeable in the theology of Israel's history traditionally called salvation history. But they are also found in the theology of atonement in which the experience of liberation from guilt is followed by the call to holiness, to life in purity, ethos, and law. For example, the twofold structure of the book of Leviticus documents this. Chapters 1–16 call for the establishment of the institution for atonement, and chapters 17–27, through ethical and legal instructions, call for the life of the atoned community in holiness. Perhaps less generally known is another tradition from the time of the first temple in Jerusalem according to which Yahweh, in the celebration of a cultic theophany, endowed Israel with his gift of צדק, of "righteousness," and called upon Israel to live in this gift. This tradition is especially reflected in the psalms (e.g., in Pss 40:10f.; 85; 89; 97; 99; 103:17-20).

In the historical, cult-legal, and cult-theophanic traditions, liberation stands at the beginning of the process of justice as the gift received by Israel, whereas ethos and law follow out of it as a responsibility to be accepted by the liberated themselves because these will not automatically happen.

2. Compared with the concept of justice described above, in which received liberation calls for the subsequent responsible practice of justice by the liberated themselves, a second concept of justice represents a different if not opposite picture. It is predominantly found in texts influenced by the international wisdom tradition. In this concept, the holistic organic process of justice is generated by the responsible just actions of humans. It fulfills itself automatically in their own well-being. Since the process itself is just, well-being is deserved. Well-being is not liberation or salvation granted by someone else, by God for example, either at the beginning or at the end of the process of justice, and without regard to merit or nonmerit. It is the consistent outgrowth of a person's own actions. An individual's personal responsibility is here not her/his responsive action to received liberation or salvation, but the condition for her/his well-being.

Both of the above concepts of justice are found in the Old Testament. Using classical theological terms of the Protestant, especially the Lutheran, tradition, one may label one "soteriological" and the other "legalistic." Their difference cannot be resolved by way of theoretical abstraction, because both exist to this day as types of dynamic reality in human experience. Job's friends are not totally wrong. They represent an internationally prevailing ontology in which reality itself is perceived as a dynamic process through which justice works itself out in the coherent correspondence between the quality of actions and the results of their course. This ontology, which is also the matrix for the conceptualization of laws and legal procedures, is normally called dynamistic. It especially lends itself to the understanding of those biblical traditions in which justice is perceived "legalistically." The question needs to be raised, however, whether the "soteriological" concept of justice reflects only a variation of the same dynamistic ontology, vis-à-vis its "legalistic" variation, or whether it represents a different ontology altogether. This question is not yet resolved and cannot be pursued at this point.

In the meantime, we must account for the fact that the "legalistic" variation of the dynamistic concept of justice is not inherently evil, immoral, unreal, or untrue. Indeed, it is by no means value-neutral, but explicitly rests on the distinctions between good and evil, and on the human responsibility for qualified action and behavior as well. Nevertheless, the two concepts differ or even conflict, not only in theory but also in experience. In view of this difference or conflict, a comparison of the two will have to ask which may include and qualify the other. Once this question is asked, it seems that the "soteriological" concept includes and qualifies an aspect which the "legalistic" does not. It points out that reality, even in human experience, neither begins with nor is based on human actions alone. It always, and not only in terms of human history, begins with and continues to be based on conditions which are *given to* and *for* humans and without which no human activity would be possible. Moreover, it controls or qualifies the "legalistic" concept by saying, on the one hand, that even our most meritorious actions and their beneficial offshoots are nothing but a gift of God, and on the other hand, that even our most sinful actions and their evil consequences will not undo the reality which always remains given to us and for us.

The question may be raised as to what extent the "soteriologically" based ontology of justice collides with the experience of people in the Third World. It can be pointed out that in the present, and perhaps even more in the future, the basic conditions for the mere sustenance of life, let alone for the historical progress of the masses in the Third World, can no longer be presumed as endowed gifts for all which only call for responsible management — if there will be nothing left to manage. Moreover, it can be pointed out that the historical experience of the Third World is, at least thus far, incompatible with the historical experience of ancient Israel in which the process of justice began with their miraculous exodus-liberation by Yahweh, a liberation which was not provided as their active self-liberation and which was granted them before they were called to the practice of justice through ethos and law. The question arises, therefore, whether the situation in the Third World does not call for a reconceptualization of both the "legalistic" and the "soteriological" concepts of justice in the Bible, in the sense that liberation as the beginning of the process of justice becomes an action rather than a gift, but also that doing what is good is the consequence of such liberation rather than the condition for well-being. It seems that what is at stake in a concept of justice is the relationship between doing what is good and liberation. I must confess that I have as yet no answer to these questions, and that I cannot pursue them at this juncture. They seem to be in urgent need of clarification, theoretically and practically.

3. The Old Testament speaks about justice as liberation from social and political oppression, but also as liberation from oppression due to the burden of guilt. Atonement and forgiveness are not sentimental events. They are forensic acts by which, in a cult-judicial procedure, a guilty person is officially declared free of the consequences of her/his guilt. The Old Testament knows of the destructive nature of both guilt and social/political oppression. Its perception of reality is more inclusive than the perception of only one or the other, so frequently found in our history. Indeed, it is guilt — and not just fate — that may generate social and political oppression and the forgiveness of guilt that may lead to liberation from oppression.

4. The theology of the Pentateuch is governed by the covenant theology of Israel's election as Yahweh's exclusive people. The historical perspective of this covenant says that Yahweh, who liberated his people from Egyptian bondage, is going to give them the land of the Canaanites — the same Canaanites who had hosted the patriarchs — as their own possession so that the land of Canaan will become the land of Israel. In its deuteronomic version, and indeed in older traditions, the Canaanites are to be expelled or extinguished, at least subjugated. In this theology, justice means that Yahweh himself, the universal God, both liberates his people and, for their sake, oppresses the Canaanites. He is both liberator and oppressor. His justice consists of his loyalty to his people forever rather than his loyalty to equal justice universally. It is astounding that much of the biblically oriented liberation theology has not taken sufficient notice of this conceptual theological deficiency.

1.-4. The variety of concepts of justice in the Old Testament reflects its awareness of all dimensions of reality: political, social, cultic, psychological, and existential; international, national, group-oriented, and individual; natural and historical; human and Israelite. All are involved in the web of total reality. In this web, no specific dimension is unrelated to all the others. But the nature of these relations is not expressed. Nor is it automatically evident. Indeed, its balance is the problem. The absence of an explicit balance in the relationship of all dimensions of reality to each other is the reason for the rise of the need and concern for justice. That concern is everywhere expressed in the Old Testament. However, its own unbalanced conceptual pluralism reflects unbalanced multidimensional reality itself. The unbalanced situations in both the Old Testament and reality are complementary. Furthermore, we must distinguish between the need and call for justice and the view or experience of fulfilled justice.

C. The Relativity of Justice

Throughout the history of humanity, the struggle for justice arises as the result of complex conditions in which a balanced, sufficient relationship of all vital elements within this complexity is shattered. It arises where שלום, a balanced sufficiency for all things and for all humans, does not exist. It arises where paradise is lost or has never existed and where the eschaton is not at hand. It only arises in an imperfect, broken, and polluted world. It arises in history and because of the imperfect nature of history. Further, it arises out of the complexity of human togetherness and the human inability to establish a balanced sufficiency at the outset. Out of these conditions springs the concern for justice, as criticism, as cry, as exhortation, and as search, with fragile and transitory designs and with merely preliminary actualizations, if any.

Justice is never anything given or known in advance. It is always to be sought, found, and actualized through the balancing of the contentions of many coexisting factors for their rightful place in the whole. This whole may be a family, a town, a nation, humanity, or the world. But its balance is lacking. It may remain traditional and relatively unchanged for some time. But when it is subjected to change, the notion of justice itself and the contents of its truth claims are also subjected to change. This is the deeper reason why neither the Old Testament nor any civilization has the same context or even the same concept of justice for all times, why the contexts and even the concepts of justice themselves are certainly subject to change, and why there is critical confrontation of alternative concepts. It is the reason why, in times of drastic changes that have destroyed the societal equilibrium, the sharp prophetic protest cries out on behalf of the dispossessed and disenfranchised with its warning and even its announcement of collapse. It is also the reason why, e.g., in Job, Ecclesiastes, and apocalypticism, ultimate justice is experienced as hidden. Ultimate justice is the justice of paradise or the eschaton, at best of the cosmos but not of history. The legitimate symbol of ultimate justice is a perfectly balanced and sufficient world. Such a balanced and sufficient world is never realized in this broken, historical world. In history, any justice is only penultimate and relative. It is precisely the ultimacy of the eschatological symbol that reveals the relativity of all our justices and concepts of justice for this world, including those in the Old Testament. Eschatological ultimacy is the crisis of the claim to ultimate truth for our concepts of justice, and the warning for us not to make them into idols for which we might sacrifice everything which and everyone whom justice is to serve.

The relativization by the eschaton of our contexts and concepts of justice means that we never know in advance what justice is in a particular situation. Instead, we must search for it and find it out. Our involvement in the process of justice-finding is indispensable, or else justice does not happen.

To be involved in the process of justice-finding places us in a setting in life similar to the setting that lies behind the Old Testament's case laws. The differentiated forms and contents of these laws, together with those in the ancient Near East, demonstrate that their formulations are the final conclusions, from case to case, of careful analyses of cases, of weighing the evidence, and of comparisons, deliberations, and decisions. The process toward those decisions involves negotiating or contending parties, arbitrations, and — even in criminal judgments — a consensus which satisfies not only as many as possible but especially the critical need that justice be right, "righteous."

It is noteworthy that the Old Testament is keenly aware that the administration of justice and even its very perception are not self-evidently righteous or true. Laws, too, may be wrong (cf. Isa 10:1; Dan 7:25; Zeph 3:4). The judges are, therefore, to judge the people with *righteous* judgment (Deut 16:18). Their judgments are not true by virtue of the authority or power of judges, but by virtue of being righteous. Judges may pervert justice. Even the eyes of the wise are blinded by a bribe, and the cause of the righteous may be subverted. Thus, it is said very emphatically that "righteousness, righteousness you shall pursue" (Deut 16:19f.). (Unfortunately, the *NRSV* translation fails to convey this important distinction by using the words "justice" and "just" in vv. 20 and 18. In v. 18, the Hebrew text uses משפט, "justice," whereas in v. 20 it uses צדק, "righteousness," twice and at the beginning of the sentence for even greater emphasis.) The unit Deuteronomy 18–20 not only teaches about the appointment of judges for the administration of justice. It especially exhorts about the need for "righteous judgment," the pursuit of nothing but righteousness in judgment. This emphatic exhortation or even command reflects the distressing knowledge that in the actual reality of the courts judgments sometimes or often represent the breakdown of righteousness rather than the results of the search for it. Justice can be perverted. It must be right or righteous. In its perception and administration the question of its righteousness is therefore included. Furthermore, righteousness is the criterion for the truth of justice. That criterion is not automatically given. It must be derived from a value system and ever afresh be sought and pursued. In the process toward decisions, priorities emerge which become legal or ethical maxims, principles as encompassing as possible. In this way, justice is found.

The process of justice-finding which the case laws require is essentially a dialogical process based on the communal peace, even as it may involve disputes of contending parties and arguments. It rests on the consensus that not only the better arguments but also the mechanisms by which they are advanced are essential for the practice of justice. However, the question arises, in ancient as in modern times, as to what happens when this normal, peaceful process breaks down because legitimate arguments are ignored, manipulated, excluded, or suppressed by special groups who possess the influence and power to control all others as well as the outcome. This question comes into sharp focus on the issue of violence, its legitimacy or illegitimacy as a reaction against oppression, including the oppressive perversion of the systems of jurisdiction and adjudication. The issue of violence is relevant universally, and is especially pressing for liberation theology and its movement, but also for revolutionary movements in all parts of our globe, and even for counterrevolutionary policies, including policies for concerted violent actions by defenders of conservative values, as in the case of bombings of abortion clinics in the United States.

Along with the discussion in modern ethics, the biblical tradition already reflects the complexity of this problem. Where the Old Testament uses the terminology for violence, it always points to something which is not only destructive but also illegitimate. However, it also is full of texts in which Yahweh's and Israel's violence is considered to be legitimate, and in which under certain conditions so is the violence of foreign nations against Israel. But those texts scarcely ever use the terminology of violence for what is clearly violent. While calling unjust violence by particular names, the Old Testament does not call violence considered to be just by the same names. Its language is not controlled by violence as a phenomenon, be it just or unjust, but by its distinction between the legitimacy or illegitimacy of violence. Its language is, therefore, not constitutive for but relative to the Old Testament's concept of violence. For this reason, the mere quotation of Bible passages in favor of or against violence is useless because any quotation can be offset by a different or opposite one.

The conceptual distinction between just and unjust violence rests on preconceptions which determine what is just and unjust. These preconceptions are, once again, pluralistic and diverse. If one of them rests on the exclusivity of Israel's election or on the absoluteness of the Davidic monarchy, any violence, offensive or defensive, is just, because — and as long as — it serves such exclusivity or absoluteness. If a different preconception rests on the equal rights of all nations and humans, violence that protects these rights against violation is just.

However, all these aspects of "just" violence do not yet address the question of whether violence as such, regardless of any condition, may be considered as a legitimate alternative to the peaceful settlement of conflicts. To this question, the biblical tradition gives no uniform answer. The answer can, however, be approached by the discernment of the better way through the critical comparison of the possibilities. Once this search is pursued, criteria surface. Violence is never as just as the pursuit of the peaceful process and the constant readiness to return to it. The peaceful process for the resolution of conflict represents a basic criterion for the life of the human community and for the righteousness of its justice. Scarcely is there peace without justice, and justice is a condition for peace; but peace is nevertheless the criterion for the righteousness of justice. Violence, any violence, represents or participates in the destruction of peace and peaceful process. This must also be said with regard to the tension in the Bible between the God of war and the God of peace.

Moreover, not only is the justice of violence relative to the justice of peaceful process; its usage and process are also not purposes or ends in themselves. They must point beyond themselves and eventually surrender to inclusive peace. Yet, even this purpose sanctions neither the means of violence indiscriminately nor the same extent of violence at all occasions. In this and other respects, the comparative study of Old Testament texts reveals significant distinctions.

In summary, in the perspective of biblical theology, violence at times appears to be inevitable. It is most probably not coincidental that the Old Testament accepts the phenomenon of violence, both violent action and violent reaction, as a reality in this world. But the justice of violence can be nothing more than a momentary, selective, constrained, and specifically focused reaction, and even then an alien reaction, against a systemic and enduring violation and destruction of peace. It is always accompanied by the question as to the possibility of an alternative peaceful process. It represents a radical emergency measure, a limit situation, in response to an otherwise irreversible emergency condition. It belongs, together with other limit conditions of the human community, to those realities of the world that are not only imperfect but radically broken. Such breakdowns are in no way manifestations of the validity of creation, human life, and the human community. Wherever and whenever possible, they are to be avoided, constrained, and abandoned. With all that has been said we have not yet mentioned those biblical traditions, present in the Old Testament, which are not only about the passive suffering of violence but also about the active endurance of violence without violent reaction, about the submission by the suffering servant to violence, and about God's own patient suffering of violence. These aspects may exceed what humans are willing to bear, but they do not exceed what is possible.

D. The Righteousness of Justice

The Old Testament theology of justice stands at the intersection of contending theologies of justice in the Old Testament. An overarching theology must become involved in the process of comparing, evaluating, and adjudicating of those contending theologies. It must itself become an act of justice. In this process, quantitative and qualitative priorities are found which surpass other priorities, and complementary and conflicting priorities are found as well. It becomes clear that justice is more inclusive than liberation, that justice for the community is the basis of justice for the individual, that a nationalist covenant justice is incompatible with equal justice universally, that without a just balance of the cosmic and global order life on earth, including that of all humans, is lost, and that judgment for the violation of justice is just.

Here in the notion of *just judgment* the quality of justice in its deepest sense appears. I have said above that justice in history is not eschatological. It is part of imperfect reality, involved in polluted and contentious history. This locus is its ontic setting. In this setting, the inevitability of imperfect justice in the polluted world collides with the perfect justice of the pure eschaton. Eschatological justice marks the crisis of and judgment upon the penultimate justices of this world. This judgment is radical, absolute, and uncompromising. In this collision, no imperfection or impurity has the right to continue to exist. The world must be cleansed. Psalm 104, after describing the intact order and wonder of creation, concludes: "Let sinners be consumed from the earth, and let the wicked be no more" (v. 35). True, in this clean order of creation, sinners and the wicked are the unclean spots who ruin the clean reality of the total creation — although they could not have been thought of in the ancient text as destroying the earth's ecosystem itself. The text gives us a glimpse of sin, whatever its actions, as at times measured against the order of creation. Against that yardstick, the radical statement in verse 35 can be understood. Those who ruin the order of creation have no place in it. Perfect, even violent, justice for the sake of a perfect world!

Yet there remains that imperfect justice which in the trial argues on behalf of the opportunity for our world and for us, even as sinners, to continue to exist. Its only argument is that our continued existence in imperfection is better than our nonexistence at all. It does not want this world to be abandoned under the judgment of the eschaton. For this reason, it cannot but plead for patience, constraint, forbearance, compassion, mercy, pardon, and lovingkindness. It is the better justice. In it, God is present in this world because, for the sake of the life of his world, he has, in the collision between the justice of judgment and the justice of pardon, turned from the condemnation of this world to its pardon, and thus remains in and with it.

The justice of pardon and forgiveness is the justice of the God of the Yahwist and the priests, of Hos 11:1-9, of Isaiah 53, and of the book of Jonah. It is the justice of the God who in Israel's liturgy is praised as the one who is "a gracious God and merciful, slow to anger, and abounding in steadfast love, and ready to relent from punishing" (Jon 4:2; cf. Exod 34:6; Num 14:18; Pss 86:5-15; 145:9 [*NRSV* 145:8]; Joel 2:13).

Up to this point, I have scarcely mentioned God. But the God of the Old Testament has been present in everything to which I have referred. When Micah called on humans "to do justice, and to love kindness, and to walk humbly with your God" (6:8b), he must have known that one cannot do justice and love kindness without walking humbly with God. The text certainly presupposes that one cannot walk with God unless one sees God himself walking. The Micah text presupposes the biblical vision of the God who divests himself of his manifest eschatological glory and humbles himself to his polluted and compromised world. In order to keep justice and steadfast love alive, God himself walks by hidden presence in the struggles of this world. This purpose is the reason for God's own ethos of humility. God's own humility entitles us to continue to exist. This gracious justice is the ground without which we would not be, and from which we ourselves are called to walk humbly with God in the pursuit of justice and steadfast love. This vision is not humiliating, but it is humbling because God is always ahead of us. It is the ground by which the Old Testament's search for justice forever lives. It is the only hope for our imperfect world.

FOURTH LECTURE: THE OLD TESTAMENT, THE NEW TESTAMENT, AND JESUS CHRIST

INTRODUCTION

The question may be formulated succinctly: how can we evaluate the individual texts of the Old Testament in the context of the total Christian Bible? Methodologically, this question involves the exegesis of the individual texts and their evaluation within the horizon of Old Testament theology. But it now also involves their evaluation within the horizon of a theology of the entire Bible on the basis of the theologies of the Old and the New Testaments. It involves the task of biblical theology. Furthermore, since the New Testament claims that the revelation of God in Jesus Christ is God's ultimate revelation for all times, all biblical texts, evaluated in the horizon of biblical theology, must also be interpreted in light of the encounter between the Bible and our reality today, which includes the task of biblical hermeneutic.

I. THE RELATIONSHIP OF THE TWO TESTAMENTS, AND JESUS CHRIST

A. From the second century to this day, the Christian church has acknowledged that both testaments together represent the original source and foundation of the Christian truth in the service of Jesus Christ, and that they are mutually open to each other. However, from the very beginning of the Christian church to this day, no consensus has existed as to what each testament means for the other. The basic definitions of the relationship of the two testaments are already contained in the New Testament: the Old Testament either *prophesies* Christ (especially Matthew), or is the *Law* that is surpassed by the *gospel* and the *Spirit* (Paul and Luke) or by the *grace and truth* (John) of Jesus Christ; or it represents the *cloud of believing witnesses* who foreshadow and point beyond themselves to the epiphany of *the community of believers in Jesus Christ* (the letter to the Hebrews). All subsequent definitions are but variations of these basic types.

The ground for these definitions is not so much Jesus Christ as such, but rather the ultimacy of God's revelation in Jesus Christ. This ultimacy is attested in the New Testament, whereas the Old Testament's witness is said to be preparatory or penultimate. The Old Testament anticipates the Messiah. For the New Testament, Christ has come; the eschatological event has happened. These two perspectives are fundamentally different. Accordingly, the Old Testament may be necessary for the understanding of its fulfillment in the New, but the New Testament is certainly necessary for the evaluation of the Old as preliminary, preparatory, penultimate. Even when Christ himself is seen as present in the Old Testament by the New Testament or by Christians, which is not always the case, the Old Testament's witness is still subject to adjudication by the New Testament: its witnesses to events and institutions of salvation are replaced by the witness to the ultimate event of salvation in Jesus Christ. The many laws to which it witnesses, even when based on the old salvific liberation events, are replaced by the one command of love as expressive of the ultimate salvation. Furthermore, the ethnic-national boundary of its believing community is replaced, or at least complemented, by the community of believers drawn from all humanity. In each of these cases, the Old Testament is subordinated to, if not altogether devalued by, the New Testament within a biblical theology and as word of God for us today.

The theological dependence or inferiority of the Old Testament is not overcome when one refers to the traditio-historical continuity of both testaments or to identical or similar motives in them. It is well known that concepts such as liberation-salvation, justice-righteousness, people of God, covenant, and the suffering servant of God pervade the entire Israelite-Judeo-Christian tradition history. Indeed, they represent a continuity of motives in that history. What is less frequently taken into account is that, in the course of their transmission history, these concepts have received quite different places, functions, and meanings within different theological conceptualities. This was already true within ancient Israel, but it was even more true for the transition of such concepts from the Israelite-Jewish community to the Christian community. These changes amount at times to recontextualizations, but at other times to reconceptualizations in contrast to previous or concurrently competing concepts. As long as the significance of such conceptual changes is not interpreted, the reference to the traditio-historical continuity of specific concepts within wider umbrella concepts is relative and insufficient for offsetting the devaluation or subordination of the Old Testament in the New.

The same is true regarding the thesis of the traditio-historical continuity, however perceived, of the two testaments. This very continuity also incorporates the conceptual changes and, hence, the discontinuities of the two testaments. This fact is mitigated even less when one points to the so-called transmission history, the history of the believing communities who transmitted the traditions. All transmitters of the traditions were members of the believing communities and belonged, as we do, to the continuity of the transmission history of the traditions. Each transmitting community believed and believes its own theological concept to be true, regardless of and often in the face of different or opposing concepts. If the transmission-historical continuity were the basis for the equal validity of *what* is transmitted, i.e., the contents of beliefs, the Jewish and Christian communities would not (have to) be separated because all statements in the TaNaK, the Christian Old Testament, and in the New Testament would be recognized as equally valid.

The fact is undeniable that the continuity of the traditio-historical and the transmission-historical development from the Old to the New Testament has, for fundamental substantive reasons, created the split between the Jewish and Christian religions and, therefore, cannot be the conceptual basis for overcoming that split or for overcoming the inferiorization of the Old Testament in a theology of the Christian Bible.

B. In a biblical theology, the factors just mentioned, which set the two testaments over against each other, cannot be ignored. However, at least two major questions remain unanswered which cast additional light on the relationship of the testaments, and possibly even new light. Until these questions are carefully considered, by no means can everything be assumed to have been said.

1. First, do the eschatologically based Christology and the eschatology proper of the New Testament legitimate the abandonment of all attention to the ongoing affairs of this imperfect world? Surely, the ultimacy of the gospel and of love represents the criterion for and crisis of all other salvations and ways of love (let alone any other claim to truth), and reveals the penultimacy of all of them. But does this mean that in the name of the ultimate gospel and the ultimate love, the many realms of this inner-worldly, this-worldly reality are no longer subjects worthy of attention, i.e., the national, international, social, political, and natural realms? With few exceptions, the New Testament pays little if any attention to them. It certainly does not intervene in the structures of the political, social, and international organization of the Roman empire, calling for structural changes or even revolutions as long as the old world lasts and before its end and replacement through the cosmic drama in the second coming of Christ. To a significant extent, it is concerned directly with the coming new world, and where it is concerned with the old world, it focuses on its state under the judgment of the coming new world and on the already eschatological nature of the Christian community and the disciples in it. This focus makes the disqualification and, therefore, neglect of the ongoing affairs of the old world understandable.

a. However, the neglect in the New Testament of the structures of the ongoing old world has become outdated precisely because the old world has continued to exist. This fact is already felt to be a problem in the younger parts of the New Testament. Its permanent existence can no longer be ignored after two millennia have elapsed. The new world has not come as expected, and the old world goes on indefinitely. Whether we like it or not, the fact of the indefinite delay of the parousia reduces the present possibility of appropriating the original Christian expectation of the second coming of Christ to virtual insignificance, as well as its prominent conceptual function in the traditional system of the Christian faith. This fact proves that there can be no valid reason for setting a date for the replacement of the old creation by the new in the second coming of Christ whether by theology or faith, or by the authority of any traditional creed or church or person. Christ may come tomorrow, or in five, ten, a hundred, a thousand, or a million years. The possibility of an *indefinite* delay also means that he may not come at all and that for this reason the affirmation that he will nevertheless come is without ground. Note that I say neither that he will nor that he will not come. I am saying that we no longer have any valid ground for an affirmative position on this question one way or the other.

If it is, therefore, uncertain when or whether the new creation will replace the old in the second coming of Christ, the question of his second coming, and of the breaking-in of the new world connected with it, has become at least relative, if not irrelevant, let alone a ground for Christian certainty. Moreover, the assumption of the second coming, along with the expectation of the end of the old world through the coming of the new, can no longer be considered a legitimate reason for the neglect of the indefinitely continuing old world. Indeed, the condition of this ongoing old world has regained its relevance and theological validity in its own right. It demands our focus and involvement precisely because the assumption of its future replacement by the new world has become relative or irrelevant.

b. What has been said above about the relativity of the concept of the second coming of Christ also applies to the expectation of the impending advent of God's own reign and kingdom in the Synoptic Gospels. It is not absolutely clear which passages in these Gospels, or which elements in them, reflect the position of the historical Jesus and which reflect the position of the early churches behind the New Testament. Most scholars agree that Jesus proclaimed the dawn of the kingdom of God: although it is not yet fully visible, its full arrival has drawn near and is imminent, so imminent that its deadline is close. Its arrival can therefore be announced with certainty. Indeed, the signs of its time, the time of salvation, are already present and visible in Jesus' own activity. One may say more pointedly that the approaching kingdom casts its light toward Jesus just as much as Jesus' activity reflects this light and points toward it. The certainty of its imminent arrival and its already present signs are the basis for the urgent call to accept God's salvation and to live in it now, before the judgment of those who have ignored or rejected it occurs in the actual arrival of God's kingdom.

It is sometimes said that the aspect of the temporal future plays no role or is irrelevant in this expectation. Such an interpretation is scarcely persuasive. It would presuppose that Jesus and the early churches spoke about a kind of nearness of the kingdom that is perpetual, ever the same, and forever invisible, ever near but never here, rather than about the nearness of its already approaching and therefore imminent arrival. The eschatological texts that speak about the nearness of the kingdom do not support such a presupposition. They say that God's reign will break in shortly because it has already drawn near. They speak in terms of temporal future, and their emphasis on its imminence constitutes the urgency of the call. Their reference to this temporal future is not a disposable shell which would have nothing to do with the substance of their message.

But here lies the problem with this temporal concept of the Synoptic Gospels. It is clear, certainly today, that the expectation of the imminence of God's reign was not fulfilled, that the expectation of any temporal future for it is at best relative and is no basis for human or Christian certainty, and that the call to decision has lost its persuasive urgency and force precisely because it can no longer be based on the original certainty of the temporal imminence of the reign of God. An urgent call to decision for the gospel of salvation and for life within it can today only be based upon the certainty that God's reign is always near, although in its totality invisibly, that it is always present and visible in critically discernible qualitative signs, and that it has a future because of its forever nearness and presence rather than its imminent future. This interpretation represents an inevitable reconceptualization of the major tenor in the Synoptic Gospels. But it is not without biblical foundation. The biblical tradition, including the Gospels, knows that God's reign in terms of both his rule and his realm always exists and is always present, whether visible or hidden.

Neither the biblical concept of the parousia nor the equally biblical concept of the ever-presence and ever-nearness of God's reign has anything to do with the idea of an inner-worldly development through the evolutionary progress of world history. The biblical concept of the parousia says that the world and its history will end when God's reign comes, and not that God's reign reaches its culmination in a continuous historical progression. For such an evolutionary ideology, we have at any rate less and less evidence, not only since 1755, 1918, 1945, and the emergence of the current danger of an imminent global ecological catastrophe. Much more important may be the fact that while humanity's existence remains for the most part forever earthbound, for the first time in human history a tension has arisen between the needs of the global population and the globe's finite resources, a tension that from now on will be permanent and will distinguish the nature of future history from all past human history. If anything is predictable, the struggle for nothing more than survival through keeping this tension in balance and preserving humanity from extinction will mark the trajectory of future history, rather than an unending progression in which this permanent limit-condition would be left behind.

The twofold conclusion is inevitable: the idea of the reign of God as an inner-worldly evolutionary progression is just as unbiblical as the biblical concept of its imminent parousia is relative or irrelevant. A traditional theological statement which affirms the end of the world through the coming of the kingdom rather than the coming of the kingdom through the end or culmination of the world is, therefore, insufficient and offers no basis for a biblical theology. By comparison, the affirmation of God's ever-presence and omnipresence depends neither on the idea of evolution nor on the concept of the imminent parousia.

Finally, it must be said that the New Testament is aware not only of the natural structures of this old world but also of its historical and societal structures. As far as nature is concerned, Jesus saw at work in it an ever-present God — a noneschatological view which may be heightened by but does not depend on the expectation of the imminent parousia. The New Testament gives only indirect attention to the structures of human history and of societies and to the powers of this world. It affirms that they are already defeated in Christ's resurrection and elevation to the *Kyrios* of the world and, therefore, are irrelevant for Christians; it focuses on their ultimate demise in Christ's parousia; and while it accounts for them in its explicitly apocalyptic passages such as Mark 13, Matthew 24, Luke 21, and the book of Revelation, it does so because they are pre-stages to the new aeon. In passages such as Rom 13:1-7 and those about the trial of Jesus, it encounters societal structures by advocating loyalty or submission to them. In all these respects, the New Testament does not confront the question of a possible or necessary inner-worldly transformation of these structures through the notion of God's presence in this indefinitely ongoing world.

Jesus' communion with the outcast and destitute is sometimes said to be the significant exception. Indeed, Jesus promises them liberation (cf. Matt 5:3-12; 11:5; Luke 4:16-21, etc.) and practices solidarity with them. In this regard, his activities are an exception and an indirect challenge to the societal systems in which the disenfranchised have neither right nor place. The only problem is that Jesus' promise to them and his personal example are not programs for the social reformation of or revolution against the systems of ongoing human history. They are anticipatory signs for what God will do for them in reality when his reign soon arrives. They are generated exclusively by that expectation and are dependent upon it, because only the coming kingdom will overthrow the insufficient systems of history. Exactly that presupposition, however, has not materialized. The alternative is inevitable that either humanity will have to wait indefinitely for the fulfillment of these promises in the parousia (i.e., against the historical Jesus and at least the Synoptic Gospels), or the promises themselves must be reconceptualized, at least in the meantime, in the sense of the urgent call for the reconstruction of societal structures as the primary mode of God's presence in the indefinitely ongoing human history. Inasmuch as the latter interpretation occurs with reference to Jesus, one ought to admit that it represents a reconceptualization of Jesus' eschatological concept, resulting in something very different from Jesus' concept, and not merely a contextualizing adaptation of it for our own time (unless one dissociates the historical Jesus from the eschatological concept of the Synoptic Gospels and declares him to be a sort of sage who had a social program or a cynic who, while not developing such a program, stood in critical distance from the imperfect conditions of this world). However, whether one opts for the eschatological concept or for its reconceptualization, in either case one envisions the reconstruction of societal and historical structures themselves. Jesus called individuals to decision, but his message of the kingdom envisioned the eschatological transformation of the imperfect or perverted structures of this world. This is more than the ongoing witness concerning these structures by the disciples alone. It is consistent with

Jesus' and the Synoptic Gospels' expectation of the imminent reign of God that Jesus propagated no program for a proper (let alone ideal) political, social, economic, ecological, or international system. Such systems, however, are inevitable not only as long as the parousia is indefinitely delayed but also because of that delay.

a.-b. The relativization or irrelevance of the temporal eschatology found in the concepts of Christ's second coming and of God's reign and kingdom does not invalidate the distinction between the ultimacy and penultimacy of God's reign — as long as the word "ultimacy" presupposes the qualitative distinction between fundamental and relative rather than the chronological distinction between passing time and endtime. The relativization of temporal eschatology only removes the distinction between ultimacy and penultimacy from its conceptual dependence on eschatological futurism. But the distinction regains validity in a reconceptualized sense, which even has biblical antecedents, according to which the "ultimacy" of the "new world" signifies the *claim* to a good and perfect world. This claim functions as a legitimate criterion for revealing the imperfection of our ongoing world, for challenging our assumptions of the ultimacy of its status quo and our excuses with reference to this status, and for devising the vision and the policies for overcoming the status quo in the light of that ever-present criterion, the reality of which is hidden. In light of this, the distinction between ultimate and penultimate is no longer the reason for the neglect of this imperfect world. Rather, it is the reason for critical attention to and involvement in it, an attention that is not confined to the new existence of the Christian community and the disciples, but liberated for the commitment of all individuals to the totality of this ongoing world, including its systemic structures. Moreover, inasmuch as Jesus Christ signifies the ultimacy of God's reign once and for all, the presence of his ultimacy in this ongoing world is constituted by his representation of the ultimacy of God's own reign in it, rather than by the expectation of his second coming once and for all time.

The hermeneutical situation in which we find ourselves today becomes — if not a new then certainly an inevitable — motive for a fresh approach to a biblical theology in which the traditional views of the relationship between the Old and New Testaments appear in a new or more discernible light. Indeed, it is the Old Testament and its theologies in which the ultimacy of God is presented as already constantly involved and present in the affairs of this penultimate world. Does, then, the inclusion of this penultimate world into the ultimacy or totality of God's relationship to the world not have a significance that is at least equal, if not prior, to the notion of the old world and its imperfect concepts of justice and salvation, and therefore, prior to the abandonment of attention to the old world on the basis of the New Testament, and prior to the inferiorization or disqualification of the Old Testament precisely because it is only in the Old Testament that the concepts of justice and salvation are imperfect? Would not such an inclusion call for a new look at the mutual openness of the two testaments in which each needs the other, at times for recontextualization and at times for reconceptualization? What would the ground rules for such an open encounter be? These questions lead to the second major question.

2. What is the relationship between Jesus Christ and God in the New Testament? It is clear that Christology represents the focus of New Testament theology. But it is also clear that Jesus Christ has by no means replaced God in the New Testament. It is correct that the New Testament understands Jesus Christ as the ultimate revelation of the reign of God. But it is also correct that in the New Testament the legitimacy of Christ, let alone the legitimacy of Jesus of Nazareth, depends on the criterion that he fulfills the will of God and in the new world "will also be subjected to the one . . . so that God" — and not Jesus Christ — "may be all in all" (1 Cor 15:28).

The distinction between God and Christ is never dissolved in the New Testament. However their relationship is specifically defined, it is clear that a concept of the nature of the reign of God determines the person and work of Christ at least as much as Christ defines the reign of God. Biblical *theo*logy codetermines New Testament *Christo*logy. In this light, the Old Testament speaks about the reign of God in a way in which the New Testament does not. It speaks about the presence of the ultimate God, even in his hiddenness, in the affairs of this penultimate, imperfect world. It testifies to a God for whom this world and history and everything in it still remain God's one and only world, despite its imperfection and penultimacy.

If a biblical theology means that the two testaments are mutually open, it must account for the Old Testament's witness to the New Testament about God's presence in this penultimate world just as much as it must account for the New Testament's witness to the Old Testament about the ultimacy of Christ's work on behalf of God for this world. It must account for God's reign just as much as for Christ's reign. Or it must account for the full dimension of God's reign through Jesus Christ, in all its aspects, as it is unfolded in the Old Testament and not only in the New. A biblical interpretation of both testaments in light of such substantive theological and methodological considerations would reveal constructive possibilities. In it, a hermeneutic of suspicion would be matched by a hermeneutic of confidence.

II. Exodus 3:7-8 in Light of Biblical Theology

A. This passage is one of the classic texts of liberation theology: "Then the LORD said, 'I have observed the misery of my people who are in Egypt; I have heard their cry on account of their taskmasters. Indeed, I know their sufferings, and I have come down to deliver them from the Egyptians, and to bring them up out of that land to a good and broad land, a land flowing of milk and honey, to the country of the Canaanites, the Hittites, the Amorites, the Perizzites, the Hivites, and the Jebusites.' "

B. These verses contain the first two statements in the Yahweh speech (vv. 7-10) which opens the report about the dialogue between Yahweh and Moses in Exod 3:7–4:17. Yahweh has fully realized the situation of his people ("observed . . . heard . . . know") which was narrated in Exodus 1 and 2, and now announces that he has come down to liberate them out of Egypt and to lead them into the good and wide land of the identified six nations.

The text is concise and clear, despite stylistic variations. Its various aspects are closely connected. Yahweh's intervention is caused by his realization of the oppression of his people. His reaction to their oppression involves the total process of both their liberation out of Egypt and their being led into the rich and wide land of these nations. The text refers to a real impending event. It is a story. The text does not communicate an abstract idea. But without a concept, the story would be without clarity. What is the theological concept in the story?

1. Yahweh's reaction to his people's oppression indicates that without their current oppression there would be no cause for him to lead them out of Egypt. They may have stayed in Egypt forever. Questions arise concerning the relationship in this text between cause and effect on the other hand, and between cause and reason on the other. The answers are obvious on the surface of the text. Yahweh's knowledge of Israel's oppression is the cause for his intervention. His decision to liberate them is the effect. However, in the larger context of the Pentateuch, it is equally obvious that the oppression itself *had* to happen or else Israel's liberation would not have been necessary. Their oppression is the immediate, contingent cause for their liberation. Whether oppression also is the reason or ground for the entire liberation story, as well as its immediate cause, is a different question. It could be that the need for Israel's exodus is in the first place the reason for their oppression, i.e., that Israel, according to the entire Pentateuchal narrative, had to be oppressed in order to be led out of Egypt.

2. Yahweh's reaction to the oppression is to lead Israel *away from* Egypt, and not to create a revolution or a change of conditions *within* Egypt. (For such an alternative possibility, compare the book of Esther in which the endangered Jewish people exiled in Babylonia did not say to the Persians: "Let my people go!") As for Egypt, the death of the current Pharaoh and/or succession by a once again friendly Pharaoh are, for example, not unthinkable possibilities. Not all oppressive conditions are systemic and perpetual. Some, as in this case, are caused by particular individual tyrants who ignore long-established orderly conditions and whose influence disappears when they do. Furthermore, since Yahweh is also in this narrative the universal God of all nations, he could have struck only this particular Pharaoh in order to liberate Israel from him in Egypt rather than strike all Egypt with plagues in order to facilitate Israel's exodus away from Egypt. After all, Israel had been at

home in Egypt for a long period of time extending from the brief period narrated in Genesis 12–50 to the life of Moses in Exodus 1–Deuteronomy 34: 430 years according to Exod 12:40f. (cf. also Exod 1:8, which speaks of the *beginning* of the oppression by "a new king [who] arose over Egypt, who did not know Joseph," whereas Gen 15:13 says that Abraham's descendants "shall be oppressed for four hundred years"). Yahweh's decision to lead Israel away from Egypt is not the only, not even the more obvious, solution to the problem. There are viable alternatives, even in the Old Testament. No such alternative to the exodus is anywhere considered. Again, it seems that the intention to lead Israel away from Egypt is at the outset the conceptual reason for the liberation of Israel for which oppression is the actual cause.

3. When compared with some wilderness traditions, it is striking how directly our text connects Israel's departure from Egypt with the goal of its subsequent migration, the rich and wide land/place of those six nations. No alternatives are considered, not even Sinai. Before the departure begins, the goal is already known and determined. Again, it seems that the entry into Canaan is the reason for the oppression-exodus drama in its entirety. At the outset, the story stands under the concept of Israel's migration to the land promised to the patriarchs! The story of both oppression and liberation serves this specific goal.

4. The promised land is depicted in two ways: it provides a basis for sustenance (a rich land) and for multiplication (a wide land), and it is the land of the six nations. The second depiction points to the tradition of the conquest, while the first points to the tradition of Israel's permanent settlement. To be sure, our text does not speak about the military conquest and the expulsion of those nations — at least not at this juncture. But its own place in the tradition history of the conquest makes it impossible to ignore this implication, and the deuteronomic-deuteronomistic language, especially of verse 8,[16] makes this understanding virtually certain.

5. While the liberation of Israel from oppression is a justifiable element of the concept of Yahweh's justice, the neglect in this and most other texts of the effect of Israel's immigration on the six nations must be noticed. Moreover, the implied presupposition of their subjection and dispossession for the sake of Israel's possession of their land — which reflects the historical situation or claim of the writers! — conflicts with the concept of Yahweh, the God of universal justice. To be sure, in the text Yahweh is the universal God over all nations, but his justice consists of his loyalty to his people. It is not universally equal justice.

1.-5. The concept underlying the text has two roots, both of which are signaled in the text: Yahweh acts on behalf of *"my people,"* not for all people alike; and this action rests upon the theology of Israel's unique election. Further, he intends to lead them to the land of the Canaanites as promised to the patriarchs and to give them that land. More specifically, Yahweh will give Israel this promised land

16. Cf. W. Schmidt, *Exodus,* BKAT II/3 (Neukirchen-Vluyn: Neukirchener, 1983), 140f.

because they are his uniquely elected people. Conceptually, our narrative is determined by and written from the vantage point of the theology of the land of Israel, and the notion of Israel's unique election is the presupposition for this theology. The theology of Exod 3:7-8 is the theology of the land of Israel for Yahweh's own people. All other notions, including the notion of liberation from oppression, stand in the service of this theology.

It should be emphasized that this analysis and its conclusion imply no objection whatsoever to the theology of liberation, let alone a theology of justice. On the contrary, they stand in the service of that theology. They only demonstrate that a *story* of liberation is not self-evidently based on a *concept* or *theology* of liberation. In itself, liberation from oppression is conceptually valid and actually required under any circumstances because it stands for the removal of injustice. However, it is not automatically clear in any given case whether liberation aims at nothing but the removal of injustice, or whether it serves an alien purpose which itself involves oppression of others by the liberated and which discredits the credibility of liberation itself.

Furthermore, it should be emphasized that the criticism of the theological concept just analyzed has nothing to do with anti-Semitism, and must be kept clearly away from possible subsequent anti-Semitic dynamics. However, the renunciation of anti-Semitism cannot mean that for that reason Israel is beyond legitimate criticism. No one, including Israel, is beyond legitimate criticism. The Old Testament knows this very well. For the sake of a balanced perspective, it must also be said that the Christian community is not only unconditionally prohibited from being anti-Semitic but is also prohibited from criticizing Israel *without simultaneously* speaking about its own streak of criminality, which runs throughout its entire history up to the present day. Regardless of whether or not Deschner's view is always correct,[17] the presentation of church history by Christian historians and theologians should not have to wait for the opponents of the church to document that the history of the entire church, especially of the churches calling themselves "orthodox," is also a history of unjustifiable, systemic apostasy and all too often outright criminality — even under the historically prevailing moral and legal criteria, let alone the valid criteria of God's reign — and not only a history of God's revelation and of faith in and obedience to God. By its own very nature, the history of the church in its bare facts involves the struggle for and contention between ultimate values. It is an evaluative history, and for this reason its account must also be evaluative, and not neutrally descriptive. It must include the confessing element. However, confession also includes the full confrontation with and confession of our sins (which the Old Testament demonstrates!) and not only the affirmation of

17. Karlheinz Deschner, *Kriminal-Geschichte des Christentums,* vols. 1 and 2 (Hamburg: Rowohlt, 1986 and 1989). Cf. also F. Battenberg, *Das Europäische Zeitalter der Juden,* 2 vols. (Darmstadt: Wissenschaftliche Buchgesellschaft, 1990).

God's "mighty acts." The worst of all things happens, however, when one party — regardless of which — points at the failures of the other *in order to* conceal its own failures or to divert attention from them.

Last but not least, the critical analysis of this or any other biblical text and the criticism of its theological conceptuality in terms of Old Testament theology, rather than on hermeneutical grounds, are inevitable as long as we, together with the Bible, affirm God as the God of universal justice and salvation. Either we may insist on this affirmation and discern where the Bible confirms or undercuts it, or we may accept the Bible's statements at face value (all is valid because the Bible says it) and forfeit our affirmation of the universality of God's justice and salvation. The choice between these two alternative approaches to biblical-theological interpretation is upon us. Not even the mechanisms of recontextualization or reconceptualization relieve us of this choice. Recontextualization would mean only the application of either one or the other of the two options to narrowly or broadly comparable situations. Reconceptualization would mean the critical and responsible abandonment of one concept for the sake of the other. The alternative remains. But, again, I am only saying explicitly what everyone has always done.

III. The Old Testament, the New Testament, and Jesus Christ

A. The theology of Exod 3:7-8 is not a theology of universal justice and liberation. It is a theology in which the universal God acts against the nations on behalf of his elected people in order to grant them the basis for their livelihood ("a land flowing with milk and honey") and expansion ("a broad land"). This election is exclusive, and inasmuch as the Old Testament elsewhere claims it to be a blessing for the nations, its theology in Exod 3:7-8 conflicts with that claim, because this theology presupposes the impending oppression of those very nations by depriving them of their own good and wide land and free existence.

It is not apparent how the subjection and dispossession of the Canaanites represents a blessing for them. Moreover, this election-land theology also conflicts with the claims in the Old Testament that Yahweh, the God of justice, is a just judge who hears the voices of all involved parties, especially the cries of the oppressed who otherwise may have no access to a fair hearing and judgment, and who "works vindication and justice for all who are oppressed" (Ps 103:6), just as he heard the cries of oppressed Israel. It cannot be assumed that the Canaanites welcomed their subjection and dispossession or accepted it stoically or in humble acquiescence to Israel's divine right, rather than crying out and even going to war against that aggression. Nowhere does the Old Testament take this urgent interest of the other party into consideration in light of its own claim to the universality of

Yahweh's justice. The theology of Exod 3:7-8 stands in the historical trajectory of the ideological paradigm which claims the divine right of nations to the conquest of the land of others for their own life-support and expansion, especially when these needs are caused by the escape of their population from previously oppressive circumstances.

This theology conflicts with, or at least differs from, other theologies in the Old Testament in which Yahweh is indeed acknowledged — by Israel — to be the God of universal justice, e.g., in Psalm 82, the book of Jonah, and the wisdom literature. From the perspective of the New Testament, Israel's possession of the land is at best — implicitly — an issue for the Jewish people. Basically, it is a nonissue because for the New Testament the people of God are not bound by a divinely given land. Inasmuch as Israel's election is recognized and not replaced by the equally problematic Christian community, it is recognized as a servant in God's plan of universal salvation, together with and alongside the Christian community. With regard to the question of the validity of the theology of Exod 3:7-8 and its many identical parallels in the Old Testament, either this theology must be *replaced* by a theology of God's universal justice found elsewhere, partly in the Old Testament and partly in the New Testament, or its own paradigm must be re*conceptual*ized because a re*contextual*ization would only mean the preservation of the same paradigm in historically and societally changing circumstances. A reconceptualization is legitimate precisely because of the claim, found in both the Old and the New Testaments, that all humanity is elected into the blessing of God's universal justice and salvation, ultimately because of the true divinity of God. Inasmuch as Jesus Christ is proclaimed to be the ultimate revelation of the reign of God, he, too, will have to be understood as representing this criterion.

B. The theology of Exod 3:7-8 has its conceptual deficits with regard to the notion of Yahweh's universal justice. However, it has distinctively positive connotations with regard to Yahweh's active presence within human history in the affairs of the nations. To be sure, our text neither says nor implies anything about a transformation of the social and political systems of Egypt and the Canaanite nations. But its focus on Yahweh's presence in inner-historical international processes cannot be overlooked. In this regard, our text points to and stands alongside the many other texts in the Old Testament according to which Yahweh is directly and critically involved within his ongoing creation, within human history, and within Israel's own societal and political system in the struggle for justice as the fulfillment of its election.

Yahweh's struggle for justice in Israel's own historical existence coincides with the purpose of Israel's election and liberation. But the collision of these two factors, so pervasively attested in the Old Testament, demonstrates that the historical and societal actualization of justice by Israel is the standard against which Israel's election is measured and fails (just as much as we Christians fail before the standard of our faith). Israel's election cannot, and did not, distract or exempt it from the critique of its historical and societal system. This critical immanence of Yahweh in Israel's historical system is a decisive theological criterion in its own right which is not controlled by a particularistic concept of election, however much both overlap.

It is one thing to say that Israel's exceptional election demands the exceptional practice of societal justice. It is quite a different matter to ask whether the call for the societal practice of justice is rooted in an exceptional election or in the legitimacy of any society, exceptionally elected or not. The conclusion seems inevitable that the demand for justice and its pursuit and implementation in historical and societal reality are rooted not in Israel's exceptional election but in the legitimacy of any society, including those of the ancient Near East, and that Israel's election represents only the basis for the intensification of that demand. Israel's own admission of its failure to implement justice is, therefore, certainly an admission of the violation of its election and covenant, as the Old Testament texts document; but it is above all the admission of an even greater failure when compared with the demand for the actualization of justice in all societies. This criterion demonstrates that, when it comes to Yahweh's struggle for justice through his presence in this world, his presence in Israel's society is nothing but a paradigm for his presence in humanity. In this sense, Israel's own struggle for justice is a symbol and a paradigm for the same struggle everywhere in humanity, and not a symbol of a claimed justice in the service of Israel's exclusive election. Before the criterion of immanent justice, Israel is just like any other nation. This theological paradigm can be contextualized and universalized, even where it necessitates the reconceptualization of the justice of Israel's election as in Exodus 3. Furthermore, the concept of Yahweh's involvement within historical struggles means that precisely in this domain is his ultimacy revealed, both as the crisis of all historical, societal, and penultimate systems of and claims to justice and as the struggle for better justice as well.

Finally, the combination of the concepts of election and of Yahweh's actual involvement in human history in texts such as Exod 3:7-8 suggests, methodologically, that the critical reconceptualization of its concept of election is preferable to the replacement of the text because of its deficient concept of election. Such abandonment would also mean the unwarranted loss of the other concept, namely, Yahweh's ongoing involvement within the affairs of human history. It might mean God's withdrawal from history.

The understanding of election in Exod 3:7-8 must be reconceptualized. Nevertheless, the legitimate fact remains that in this text the God of the Old Testament remains engaged with the historical forces of this world. It is in this regard that New Testament Christology, eschatology, and ecclesiology have their own important deficiency. They do not say clearly, if at all, whether or not this ongoing imperfect world is still the scene of God's actual engagement with the political and social systems of our history, and not only the scene of crisis and the object of the disciples' witness. Its concept of salvation, for the most part, does not affect this. The New Testament's deficiency is particularly pressing hermeneutically because of the indefinite delay of the parousia after two thousand years of history. This delay throws us back into the systemic nature of this inner-worldly history. At stake is the question of whether this old historical world is still God's world, despite its imperfection, and thus it is once again nothing less than the question of the divinity of God universal. In this regard, the Old Testament makes a contribution to the New Testament in view of the fact that important aspects and texts of the New Testament are in need of reconceptualization.

The interpretation of the crucified Christ is a basic case. It has the potential for understanding God as involved in the systemic social, political, and international nature of our history. But it seems that such an understanding requires not only a recontextualization, but more importantly it requires that its meaning, as expressed in the New Testament, be reconceptualized in light of the reign of God that includes our history.

Conclusion

It seems that the Old and the New Testaments complement each other in that each helps rectify the deficiency of the other and in that each is partly in need of reconceptualization in light of the legitimate emphasis of the other. Both testaments point beyond themselves to the universal, total reign of God in justice, love, and salvation, everywhere and at all times. In a biblical theology and hermeneutic, the inevitable theology of suspicion, which affects each testament, would thus be matched and ultimately surpassed by a theology of confidence.

A discipline of biblical theology, in which the Old Testament is not a priori disenfranchised but in which both testaments are mutually open to each other, continues to be a serious desideratum not only for biblical theology but also for the entire field of theology. Such a theology, and its potential for subsequent hermeneutical and systematic-theological interpretation, even for the disciplines of church history and the history of Christian thought, let alone for the preaching, teaching, and counseling of the church, and for the interreligious encounter, will scarcely succeed as long as biblical interpretation is only based on the paraphrasing exegeses of biblical texts and on their selective hermeneutic. Neither will it succeed as long as it operates only with the method of recontextualization based on the fact that we belong to the totality of the Judeo-Christian tradition.

We must face directly the additional necessity of the reconceptualization of an as yet indefinable number of biblical concepts in both testaments, and this not in light of our own modern ideological preferences but in light of conceptual tensions within the biblical tradition or canon itself. Several movements, which are already highly visible, such as the black, the feminist, and the Third World liberation theologies, express this necessity, with more or less methodological clarity and substantive diversity, and rightly so. But more is at stake with regard to what needs to be done and who must consciously and responsibly do it.

I do not believe that we have seen the full dimension of the problem for biblical studies, a problem for which we scarcely have any precedent. Nevertheless, the task does not at all seem impossible. Whether it is coincidental or not, this task becomes especially pressing at a time in which the entire human race, in all its diverse systems, is for the sake of its survival confronted with the unavoidable necessity of reconceptualizing and reconstructing its traditional value systems rather than only making some recontextualizing adjustments. (Of course, there are people, e.g., certainly in the United States and in Iran, who believe that their nations possess the right value systems and societal structures and that no reconceptualizations are necessary, and who in part hold this belief because they count themselves among the true Christians or Muslims. I will have to leave it to the Jewish people to decide whether or not they have the same problem among themselves.)

Traditional paradigms are at stake not only because of the new world-historical conditions but also because of the many traditional paradigms which have been proven to have been misconceptions at their outset. Moreover, not infrequently, misconceptions, present in the biblical text and urgently in need of reconceptualization, have stood at the cradle of misdirected postbiblical developments, and many continue to this day, because of their "biblical authority," both to block the necessary insight for solving the problems in the Bible and to inhibit the freedom for reconceptualizing interpretation. This fact ought to be clearly seen and admitted.

Ultimately at stake is the question of whether the Bible in the hands of the church, its preachers, laypeople, and theologians, can make a genuine, valid contribution to the global problems facing all humanity rather than only to the Christian community and the life of its individuals. In view of this quest and the fact that responsible people all over the world, without the Bible and the church, are involved in the reconceptualization and reconstruction of the systemic paradigms which guide the life of the human race, one has to wonder how long it will take for the entire community of biblical interpreters to begin to share the burden of others by doing the same kind of work on the Bible itself with at least equal clarity of sight, freedom, and effort. Without such a broadly based breakthrough, there is little hope for the emergence of a viable biblical theology and even less for the Bible's service to humanity. But with it, all the biblical promises, from both testaments, of the God for all humanity in this ongoing world and for its sake will shine with greater clarity, and even the discipline of biblical theology may yet see the light at the end of the tunnel.

Revelation in the Old Testament

Dedicated to Gerhard von Rad[1]

Introduction

An examination of the publications which directly or indirectly discuss the theme "Revelation in the Old Testament" yields the picture of a very nonuniform situation in research, with respect both to how the problems are conceived and to the results of research. Three reasons for this confusion must be mentioned. The first lies in certain preunderstandings (whether theological in nature or belonging to a phenomenology, psychology, or philosophy of religion) under which texts are viewed and evaluated.[2] The second is use of a concern, which is central to and pervades

1. This essay is dedicated to Gerhard von Rad at the completion of his seventieth year of life in heartfelt gratitude and reverence and with the best wishes. It was translated by Dr. Henry T. C. Sun (with the assistance of Dr. Karen Torjesen and under the direction of Rolf P. Knierim).

2. This is, for example, the case with Pannenberg, who says, "For philosophy of religion and systematic theology, the question is that of a self-manifestation of divine reality, one which was not only experienced as such by men of earlier cultures at some time or another, but one which is capable of being convincing for our present-day understanding of existence as the deity's self-confirmation of his reality" (Wolfhart Pannenberg, "Response to the Discussion," in *Theology as History,* trans. W. A. Beardslee, NFT 3, ed. J. M. Robinson and J. B. Cobb, Jr. (New York: Harper and Row, 1967], 231). And although Pannenberg knows of the different forms of the divine self-manifestation, he excludes them because of his criteria: "Other forms of self-manifestation are not able to convince us today of the divinity of what appeared at a time in the past" (232). It is clear that Pannenberg's vantage point from the outset leads to a critical separation between texts which are relevant to this theme and those which are not. A preunderstanding like that of Eliade or Tillich would lead to a different approach to the texts if it were applied to the Old Testament. Eliade: "The manifestation of the sacred ontologically founds the world," and "Revelation of a sacred space makes it possible to obtain a fixed point and hence to acquire orientation in a chaos of homogeneity, to 'found the world' and to live in a real sense" (Mircea Eliade, *The Sacred and the Profane: The Nature of Religion,* trans. W. R. Trask (New York: Harcourt and Brace, 1959], 21, 23). Tillich: "Normative for the appearance of the holy is the relationship of unconditional to conditional meaning" (Paul Tillich, "Reli-

the Old Testament and which is found through exegesis, to interpret the totality of the texts in a uniform way.[3] The third reason ultimately comes from entirely different applications of exegetical methods.[4] It is thereby clear that the theologi-

---

gionsphilosophie," *Urban* 63 [1962]: 70). For the breadth of possibilities, cf. "Offenbarung," RGG[2] 4, 654-72; RGG[3] 4, 1597-1621.

3. This is true, for example, for Moltmann, who says that it is "essential to let the Old Testament itself not only provide the answers, but also pose the problem of revelation, before we draw systematic conclusions" (Jürgen Moltmann, *Theology of Hope: On the Ground and the Implications of a Christian Eschatology,* trans. J. W. Leitch (New York: Harper and Row, 1967], 95). As Moltmann starts with the thesis of the transmigration religion of the patriarchs, he is led exegetically to an understanding of revelation, uniformly prevalent in the Old Testament, which then proves to be fruitful for systematic theology. A comparison of this systematization of the exegetical point of departure with that which is articulated in Lindblom's statements on the subject shows once again how the recourse to exegesis can lead to entirely different systematic points of departure: "So we can determine as a characteristic trait of Old Testament piety that people find themselves, so to say, always and everywhere in a situation in which they have the possibility of coming to know God's will and thoughts and intentions in different occasions," and "[the pious Israelite knew] that God in normal situations would make known to her/him his will and his counsels" (Johannes Lindblom, "Die Vorstellung vom Sprechen Jahwes zu den Menschen im Alten Testament," *ZAW* 75 [1963]: 287). That this historical assertion also has theological significance for an historian of religion, such as Lindblom, is intimated when he says: " 'Theologically,' as it has become fashionable to say today; however, I would prefer to say, from the point of view of the essential uniqueness of ancient Israelite religion . . ." (269). This problem also lies at the heart of the discussion between Rendtorff and Zimmerli concerning the preferential assessment of either history or the Word of Yahweh each relative to the other within the framework of the history of traditions (for this, see below).

4. Thus one has approached the problem from the angle of terminological investigation, e.g., the articles in *TDNT:* δηλόω, 2, 61-62; καλύπτω, 3, 556-92; σημαίνω, 7, 262-65; φαίνω/φανερόω, 9, 1-10; χρηματίζω, 9, 480-82; Friedrich Nötscher, *Das Angesicht Gottes schauen, nach biblischer und babylonischer Auffassung,* 2d ed. (Darmstadt: Wissenschaftliche Buchgesellschaft, 1969); Carl A. Keller, *Das Wort OTH als "Offenbarungszeichen Gottes": Eine philologisch-theologische Begriffsuntersuchung zum Alten Testament* (Basel: E. Hoenen, 1946); Herbert Haag, " 'Offenbaren' in der hebräischen Bibel," *TZ* 16 (1960): 251-58; Lindblom, "Die Vorstellung," 263f.; Frank Schnutenhaus, "Das Kommen und Erscheinen Gottes im Alten Testament," *ZAW* 76 (1964): 1-22. Through the analysis of formulaic expressions and of genres, their settings in life and their transmission history, the attempt has been made form-critically to illuminate the subject matter, either as a whole or one part at a time, with varying results. On the former, cf., above all, Walter Zimmerli, "I Am Yahweh" (1953), "The Knowledge of God according to the Book of Ezekiel" (1954), and "The Word of Divine Self-Manifestation (Proof-Saying): A Prophetic Genre" (1957), collected in *I Am Yahweh,* trans. D. W. Stott (Atlanta: John Knox Press, 1982), 1-28, 29-98, 99-110 (respectively); Rolf Rendtorff, "The Concept of Revelation in Ancient Israel," in *Revelation as History,* trans. David Granskou, ed. Wolfhart Pannenberg (New York: Macmillan, 1968), 23-53; summary of the discussion (and expansion) by James M. Robinson, "Revelation as Word and as History," in *Theology as History,* NFT 3, ed. James M. Robinson and John B. Cobb, Jr. (New York: Harper and Row, 1967), 1-100; cf. also Hans Walter Wolff, " 'Wissen um Gott' bei Hosea als Urform von Theologie" (1952/53), *Gesammelte Studien zum Alten Testament,* ThB 22 (München: Christian Kaiser, 1964), 182-205. On the latter, cf., among others, Artur Weiser, "Zur Frage nach den Beziehungen der Psalmen zum Kult: Die Darstellung der Theophanie in den Psalmen und im Festkult," in *Festschrift*

cal-hermeneutical, systematic-exegetical, and analytical-exegetical ways of developing this subject have not only been handled in a variety of different ways among themselves but also frequently overlap. These general indications of the research situation must suffice here, since a comprehensive and detailed bibliographic and substantive presentation would require a thick monograph. Of course, in addition to what has been said, the question must be raised as to whether the Old Testament's understanding of revelation is at all homogeneous.

For anyone who is concerned with this problem, the research situation outlined above poses the question of how one is to proceed in an appropriate way, because, without a doubt, any one-sided methodological approach will not do justice to this problem. One cannot operate with terms (lexemes) only and leave the form-critical and thematic considerations off to the side, or vice versa. Moreover, it is evident that restricting oneself to certain lexical forms or text groups is a very questionable undertaking. Furthermore, as is well known, one may have to take into consideration the possibility that texts are implicitly concerned with this subject matter even when such a concern cannot at all be registered either terminologically or form-critically. Finally, it cannot be overlooked that the Old Testament's understanding of revelation has to do not only with theology, but also with other conceptual categories, which we designate as ontology, cosmology, psychology, and epistemology. Consequently, the following considerations on the topic must, for the sake of the topic itself, be kept open to the just-mentioned perspectives. The inevitability of the selective use of material should, therefore, remind us to keep our minds open for inquiring further within the total frame of reference of this subject.

Alfred Bertholet zum 80, Geburtstag, ed. Walter Baumgartner, Otto Eissfeldt, Karl Elliger, and Leonhard Rost (Tübingen: J. C. B. Mohr, 1950), 513-31; Claus Westermann, *Praise and Lament in the Psalms,* trans. Keith Crim and R. Soulen (Atlanta: John Knox, 1981), 93-101; Jörg Jeremias, *Theophanie,* WMANT 10 (Neukirchen-Vluyn: Neukirchener, 1965). Finally, the subject has also been handled from a variety of thematic perspectives; cf. Brevard S. Childs, *Myth and Reality in the Old Testament,* SBT 27 (Naperville: A. R. Allenson, 1962), esp. 95f.; John L. McKenzie, *Myths and Realities: Studies in Biblical Theology* (Milwaukee: Bruce Publishing Co., 1963), esp. the chapter "God and Nature in the Old Testament," 85-132; Baruch A. Levine, "On the Presence of God in Biblical Religion," in *Religions in Antiquity: Essays in Memory of Erwin Ramsdell Goodenough,* Studies in the History of Religions 14, ed. Jacob Neusner (Leiden: E. J. Brill, 1968), 71-87; Menahem Haran, "The Divine Presence in the Israelite Cult and the Cultic Institutions," *Bib* 50 (1969): 251-67, a comprehensive critique of the book of Ronald E. Clements, *God and Temple* (Philadelphia: Fortress, 1965), on the same theme.

I. On Language and Worldview

A. On the Significance of Semantics for the Problem

The semantic determination of the fundamental term for "to rev/eal" is by and large clarified. Haag, who may speak for all, says[5] that the root meaning of "to reveal" is preserved most purely in the term גלה in its basic sense of "to disclose," "to unveil" something, hence "to make free and visible something that is covered, veiled, and thereby hidden."[6] Haag then says, "All verbs are taken over from the

5. Haag, " 'Offenbaren'," 251.

6. This understanding is frequently encountered in definitions of biblical and systematic theology and of the philosophy of religion. Cf. Paul Tillich, *Systematic Theology,* vol. 1 (Chicago: University of Chicago, 1951). "Revelation is the manifestation of the depth of reason and the ground of being" (117); H. Richard Niebuhr, *The Meaning of Revelation* (New York: Macmillan, 1941), 101: "When we speak of revelation we mean that something has happened to us in our history which conditions all our thinking and that through this happening we are enabled to apprehend what we are, what we are suffering and doing and what our potentialities are. What is otherwise arbitrary and dumb fact becomes related, intelligible and eloquent fact through the revelatory event" (101); Heinrich Fries, "Die Offenbarung," in *Mysterium Salutis: Grundriss heilsgeschichtlicher Dogmatik,* ed. Johannes Feiner und Magnus Löhrer, vol. 1 (Zürich: Benziger, 1965): "*Revelare* includes a quite distinct perception. It means to remove the velum, the veil, the screen, the cover. It means 'to unveil' what is veiled, to disclose what was hidden, to pronounce it, to make it manifest, so that it is open, opened, so that . . . what was hitherto covered and invisible is carried openly. . . . [It] presupposed that God is a *hidden God,*" if it is said about God ". . . and by this is meant that the hiddenness, the invisibility of God is uncovered and proclaimed, that the hidden God steps forth from his hiddenness, throwing aside, so to say, the veil and manifesting himself. . . . But in the act of revelation something or someone is always made known" (163); "If there is revelation of God to man, then it must be capable of being perceived by the perceiving spirit of men. But then it presupposes perceptibility, intelligibility, truth in the ontological sense" (174). Special reference must be made here to the views of Heinrich Ott regarding the nature and function of theology in connection with the philosophy of the later Heidegger, as Ott understands it. I cite from the lucid depiction by James M. Robinson ("The German Discussion of the Later Heidegger," in *The Later Heidegger and Theology,* NFT 1, ed. James M. Robinson and John B. Cobb, Jr. [New York: Harper and Row, 1963]): "Hence Heidegger speaks of being in terms of *Lichtungsgeschichte,* 'clearing history.' Being, again and again, in different times and ways, clears out the underbrush of thinking so as to make itself clear to thought. If the truth of being is its unveiling of itself to thought, the history of being is the history of these clearings" (26); regarding the binding of ontology and theology: "Only from the truth of being can the essence of the holy be thought. Only from the essence of the holy is the essence of deity to be thought." These sentences could stand also in a book about ancient Near Eastern ontology! "Thus the theological character of ontology . . . is due to the manner in which beings have from the very beginning disconcealed themselves" (35-36); "The being of God signifies . . . an occurrence of unveiling: that God unveils himself to thought as he who he is! that he strikes upon thought as a fate and gives himself to thought as the subject matter to be thought. . . . Thus Ott conceives of God as a being whose being is his revelation of himself, comparable to Heidegger's understanding of being as unveiling" (41-42); "The world that the poet calls up is in fact called up to him by

human sphere and transferred to the God-human sphere. This corresponds to human, and especially to Hebrew, psychology."[7] So he can define the theological meaning (or sense): "Revelation is therefore a participation in or participatory knowledge of God's mysteries."[8] These statements appear to imply that "revelation" is essentially a theological category, and that it is appropriate to speak of revelation only where the word field is applied to the God-human sphere. This becomes even clearer in Rendtorff's statement: "Of the verbal roots relevant here, the LXX regularly renders גלה by ἀποκαλύπτειν, but an examination of the evidence demonstrates at once that the leading understanding of ἀποκαλύπτειν is not theological, but is 'to expose, to unveil' in an everyday sense. This corresponds with the findings of גלה in which the nontheological usage predominates. Where it does appear as a theological term, there is no unified understanding that undergirds it, so that it is unsuitable as a starting point for an investigation."[9] One must ask, however, whether this restriction of the concept of revelation to the theological sector is objectively valid and whether by doing so one might not from the outset obstruct the path to an exegetical comprehension of that which is of primary importance for the Old Testament understanding of revelation, even in a theological sense. Is a theological category (in the restricted sense just referred to) at all at issue in the subject of revelation? Is the view that the terms are transferable from the human to the God-human sphere based in human or Hebrew psychology?[10] Is one not compelled to ask why terms are applicable to both spheres without difficulty? Does not such a question suggest that such a possibility is grounded in a preunderstanding for which "theological" and "profane" are not in principle separate spheres, but are instead parts or modes of a holistic view of reality *(ganzheitliche Wirklichkeit)?* If so, it would hardly be correct to speak of a "transfer"

---

the things themselves in their being. The poet harkens to the silent tolling in things as their being unveils itself. His answer only carries into audible language (so that less perceptive persons may hear) what the things themselves have to say as they speak their world" (50). Cf. the comprehensive discussion of Ott's point of departure in the above-named volume. What is to be said in the current study concerning the Old Testament's understanding of revelation will point out both the common basis with that position and the departure from it.

7. " 'Offenbaren,' " 251.

8. " 'Offenbaren,' " 253.

9. "Concept of Revelation," 27.

10. With this comment Rendtorff's own point of departure in his view of ראה, which indeed is not only a "theological" term for revelation, could also be neutralized above all, if one sees that גלה was also used quite centrally theologically; cf. Haag, " 'Offenbaren,' " 254, according to which 1 Sam 3:7 expresses "the goal of all revelation," i.e., "that people might discern Yahweh." Is it really advisable for the comprehension of the Old Testament's understanding of revelation to exclude one or more lexemes, and thereby to adduce others — or even only one, and that in only one of its confined grammatical forms? Should it not be possible to push this subject into the broader horizon of the Old Testament language, no matter which term one starts from? Which a priori decisions are most appropriate for the issue?

from one sphere to the other and to do so on psychological grounds. This is both because a term would not have belonged originally to *one* sphere over against the other, but rather to a holistically perceived reality *(ganzheitlich gesehenen Wirklichkeit),* and because, in its merely apparent (but not really!) heterogeneous usage, it would not express the difference of spheres, but would express in principle the fact that they belong together in a common fundamental reality *(Grundwirklichkeit).* If the assumption that human speech develops from a preunderstanding and always functions within this preunderstanding is correct, then, with respect to גלה, one must ask from the outset whether this kind of preunderstanding is expressed in גלה, and whether its pervading usage is determined by this preunderstanding or whether its usage in different spheres intends to bring this preunderstanding to bear. Its use in a specific sphere would then mean that what has to be said about that sphere must be expressed in the categories of the term (lexeme) rather than in the specific categories pertaining to that sphere. It would mean that the sphere cannot be understood in and of itself, but only from the presupposition expressing itself in the term. Consequently, one must say that the interest in the use of the term גלה primarily consists in this: to express the becoming visible of something hidden, and that this interest dominates its use with respect to God — as it does in other spheres.[11] The term as such, wherever it is used (including the God-human relationship), would then express an epistemological and ontological intentionality *(Aussageintention).* Its use in this sector would not be determined by the question of whether and how *God* reveals himself, but of whether and how God in the horizon of the human experience of reality is *uncovered, becomes visible.* In other words, the term has its referent in the question concerning revelation, not in the question concerning God. Moreover, generally in the ancient world the question concerning God is not an independent question but part of comprehensive understandings of reality. The reason why neither a transfer of the term to a "theological" realm separate from a profane realm nor a "theological" understanding of revelation is necessary is because the term per se expresses, even in the sector of the God-human relationship, an ontological and epistemological concern, not a theological one. Its theological concern within this sector, then, would be to refer to the God-human relationship as a relevant category in regard to the ontological-epistemological character of that relationship. It must be asked whether this does not already imply a consequence for the totality of the Old Testament's understanding of revelation, which then must be confirmed by the total text corpus, namely, that revelation is not primarily concerned with alternatives such as God or world,

11. On its use with respect to God, cf. Haag, " 'Offenbaren,' " 252f., and, among others, A. Oepke, "καλύπτω," *TDNT* 3, esp. 563f. Oepke seems to me to cut off the problem too quickly when he says, "On the other hand, we cannot take refuge in a purely philological exposition of the relevant passages, e.g., by employing such literal renderings as 'to disclose' or 'to unveil.' For this would imply evasion of the theological issue" (*TDNT* 3, 564).

transcendence or immanence, indirect or direct revelation, history of word or nature, etc., but rather with the result of the becoming visible of the unseen, be it related to the being of the world *(Sein der Welt),* to a hidden truth, or to God. This must in no way be taken to mean that the being of the world *(Sein der Welt)* or the uncovering of truth, e.g., in thinking, is conceptually separate from any relation it might have to God, and that God is reduced to a partial aspect *(Teilaspekt)* of the world. This question seems once again to have more to do with the question concerning God than with the question concerning revelation. Indeed, according to the kinds of understandings of God, revelation is a matter of God's becoming visible in or through all possible modes of the human experience of reality, be it history, language, nature, thought, or whatever else.[12] If the uncovering of the covered, the becoming visible of the unseen, the recognition and understanding of the unrecognized and of that which is not understood constitutes the fundamental concern of the Old Testament's understanding of revelation, then the root concern appears to express itself in what we today call hermeneutic. Last but not least, it becomes clear at this point why the correlate for the revelation of God in the Old Testament is not faith, but sight.

B. On the Significance of Ancient Near Eastern Ontology and Epistemology

Now it is clear that what has been said must be viewed within the broader horizon of ancient Near Eastern ontology and epistemology, to which the Old Testament belonged.[13] Before we turn our attention to the treatment of problems specific to the Old Testament, this state of affairs must be outlined. The historians and phenomenologists of religion describe the fundamental experience of being in antiquity as that of distance. This fundamental experience arises from the confrontation of humans with the powers of the cosmos and the broad expanse of the earth. That ontology and cosmology genuinely belong together is validated by this reality. Jacobsen describes in lively fashion the "feeling of distance" that came about for the Mesopotamians through their experience of the "vast expanse of the heavens."[14] "The religious

12. On the question of the relationships between revelation and "conception of God" in Egypt, cf. Siegfried Morenz, *Egyptian Religion,* trans. Ann Keep (Ithaca: Cornell University Press, 1973), 31-33.

13. Of course, the terms here — "ontology" and "epistemology" — cannot be pressed into the sense of an explicit doctrine of being and recognition, because according to our sense of the word nothing like that can be said to have existed at all in the ancient Near East. Their use in the sense of an implicit understanding of being and knowledge may be justified in view of the absence of a formal doctrine.

14. H. and H. A. Frankfort, J. A. Wilson, and Th. Jacobsen, "Frühlicht des Geistes," *Urban* 9 (1954): 151.

experience of the nonhomogeneity of space is a primordial experience . . . that precedes all reflection of the world."[15] Van der Leeuw says of the sacrament that it plays "in two worlds."[16] The not entirely felicitous expression of "two" worlds is then clarified in that this world is a "sign" of another world. " 'Nature' is a simile *(Gleichnis)*. . . . The simile *(Gleichnis)* is grounded in an original or infinite identity of both worlds."[17] Furthermore, it belongs to the fundamental experience of the ancients that the uniquely Real, the Divine, the gods reveal themselves from within this distance in their appearances — as "sign" or "simile," according to van der Leeuw. According to Eliade, "It is the break effected in space that allows the world to be constituted, because it reveals the fixed point. . . . When the sacred manifests itself in any hierophany, there is not only a break in the homogeneity of space; there is also revelation of an absolute reality. . . . [T]he hierophany revails [*sic*] an absolute, fixed point, a center."[18] "[T]he manifestation of the sacred in space has a cosmological valence; every spatial hierophany or consecration of a space is equivalent to a cosmogony."[19] And Jacobsen says, "Mesopotamians were conscious of both the character and the function of such a power, in so far as they experienced this manifestation in its immediacy, when (or *as*) it was manifested to them from itself and touched them deeply."[20] Jacobsen makes an important distinction, which will concern us presently, when he speaks of the apprehension of the phenomenon in itself *(an sich)* and of its understanding *(Verstehen)* or comprehension *(Begreifen)*.[21]

It is sufficiently known how this preunderstanding expresses itself or works itself out in individual spheres or operations of life. The theocratic city-state, as it appears in the Sumerian temple city (e.g., in Uruk shortly after 3000 BCE), is an epiphany of the universal cosmic-divine reality. For ancient Egypt the same is true. As the deity incorporates himself in the king, so creation is incorporated in the formation of the state. *Maat,* the fundamental principle of world order, discloses itself to the Egyptians first and foremost in cosmological categories.[22] But then, "*Maat* came from heaven in its time and joined itself to those who lived on

15. *Sacred,* 20f.

16. Gerardus van der Leeuw, *Sakramentales Denken* (Hassel: J. Standa, 1959), 113.

17. van der Leeuw, *Sakramentales Denken,* 113.

18. *Sacred,* 21.

19. *Sacred,* 63.

20. "Frühlicht," 151n.11.

21. "To understand nature, the countless and manifold phenomena around men, therefore means to grasp the personalities in these appearances, their characteristic features, their aspirations (what they are striving for), and also the reach of their power. This task does not distinguish itself from the task to understand other humans and to grasp their character, their intentions, the extent of their power" (Jacobsen, "Frühlicht," 146). Of course, this does not always amount to the personalization and identification of the cosmic powers, simply because they are experienced as "powerful creatures of will," though not always so (138, 143).

22. Hans H. Schmid, *Gerechtigkeit als Weltordnung,* BHT 40 (Tübingen: J. C. B. Mohr, 1968), 48.

earth. . . ."[23] It discloses itself in law, in wisdom, in nature, in battle against the enemy, in the cult, and above all in the monarchy and in the act-consequence continuum.[24] Reality, or the Divine, appears in the pyramids, the temple, the emblem, the hypostatized name, the star(s), and/or the numbers. And it may be asked whether in the rite of the sacred marriage it is actually a matter of the deification of humans, and much less the self-realization of God, so as to effect his real presence in the human sphere.

This ancient Near Eastern understanding of the appearance and recognizability of Reality, the Divine, the gods in its broadest extent, rooted in ontology-cosmology-mythology, is the context in which the Old Testament's understanding of revelation finds its home. This general assumption is to be maintained in principle, in spite of the obviously significant deviations in particulars. Since the facts are broadly known, here we can limit ourselves to a few examples. Already Nötscher[25] (following above all a study by Baudissin from the year 1914[26]) has demonstrated that many Old Testament expressions for the seeing of the face of God are rooted primarily in the world of Mesopotamian language and conceptuality. Schnutenhaus has emphasized that the Old Testament's verbs for the coming and appearing of Yahweh (a) are thoroughly dependent on Israel's environment, (b) belong in their diversity to different genres and settings and suggest different spheres (war, nature, Sinai, temple) and aspects (to go out, to come forth, to descend, to march, to raise oneself, to flash, to appear, to shine, etc.) and that (c) the coming of God always has a goal, i.e., it seeks out the one who can see.[27] The common ancient Near Eastern character of the Old Testament's language not only shows that Israel, at least in this respect, had no special concept of revelation, it also necessitates the question whether or not for Israel the experience of "revelation" was viewed essentially in ontological-cosmological and empirical categories. Put theologically, the question is whether or not the revelation of God is more appropriately a matter of the experience of God in the horizon of the human experience of being and knowledge. If so, this would clarify why a special "revelation," such as that of Yahweh, necessitated from the outset a general language for communica-

23. Schmid, *Gerechtigkeit,* 56.

24. Cf. the comprehensive thesis of Schmid, and in view of the act-consequence continuum, the good discussion on pp. 50f. On the problem of the revelation of God in the king in the form of identity, incarnation, or incorporation, cf. Morenz, *Egyptian,* 33-34, 40-41; cf. also Karl-Heinz Bernhardt, *Das Problem der altorientalischen Königsideologie im Alten Testament: unter besonderer Berücksichtigung der Geschichte der Psalmenexegese dargestellt und kritisch gewürdigt,* VTSup 8 (Leiden: E. J. Brill, 1961), esp. 67-90.

25. Nötscher, *Angesicht.*

26. Wolf Wilhelm Graf Baudissin, " 'Gott schauen' in der alttestamentlichen Religion" (1914), now reprinted in Nötscher, *Angesicht,* 193-261.

27. Schnutenhaus, "Kommen." In this one must observe that the verbs for "to come" and "to appear" are forms of expression for the same epiphanic language, the one formulated from the perspective of the act of God, the other from the perspective of the perceiving person.

tion. "Revelation," then, not only would be an expression for the legitimate human experience of God, it also would be the universal evidence for a specific religion. Last but not least, it appears to be inevitable that one must also acknowledge theologically the fact that the Old Testament's language is anchored in the preunderstanding of its environment — and this in its comprehensive breadth. This means above all that every one-sided understanding of the revelation of God is inadequate and that Yahwism is not determined by only *one* kind of experience of revelation, but instead held itself open to the plurality of possible modes of experience. Westermann has already emphasized the affinity of the depictions of Yahweh's epiphany in the Psalter to Babylonian and Egyptian psalms.[28] It is also constitutive for Westermann's distinction between epiphany and theophany that, in spite of all the evident differences, both traditions have to do with the becoming visible of Yahweh (either as he himself or in his works). With respect to the Old Testament's understanding of revelation, the texts do not permit one to ignore one tradition in favor of the other, especially when the definitions of these traditions are as non-uniform as they are in the present situation. In his investigation of a specific genre which he designates as "theophany," Jeremias likewise emphasizes the extra-Israelite origin of the second part of the genre, the tumult of nature, whereas the first part, the coming of Yahweh, could not have originated anywhere else than in the environment of Israel.[29] The work of Jeremias makes one thing absolutely clear (apart from its intention, of course): so long as one restricts oneself to such a partial perspective, one is still far from having gained a perspective of the Old Testament's understanding of revelation in its comprehensiveness.

28. Westermann, *Praise and Lament,* 93-101; for a critique of Weiser, 98-101.

29. Jeremias, *Theophanie,* especially 150f. What is designated by Westermann and Schnutenhaus as "epiphany" Jeremias designates as "theophany." Jeremias's thesis of the genuine Yahwistic origin of the first part of the genre, which contradicts Westermann and Schnutenhaus, is in its proposed form hardly defensible. In addition, his genre definition, strictly speaking, is covered only by the first part of the total structure. But more important is the question how the two parts are related to one another: as occasion (the coming of Yahweh) and consequence (nature's tumult), or as two modes of expression for the same event? In the former, the "coming" would be the appearance — in certain cases not even visible — while the "tumult," a second event, would be the effect on nature. In the second case the "coming" would be visible in the "tumult." This question would require a special investigation.

30. Walther Zimmerli, " 'Offenbarung' im Alten Testament: Ein Gespräch mit R. Rendtorff," *EvT* 22 (1962): 15-31; Rolf Rendtorff, "Geschichte und Wort im Alten Testament," *EvT* 22 (1962): 621-49; also Robinson, "Revelation," 42-62.

II. On the Perception through Word, Event, and History

What now concerns the discussion of our thesis, specifically in regard to the Old Testament, is most directly constituted by the published work of Zimmerli and Rendtorff between 1953 and 1962 and by their common discussion concerning this topic.[30] Under discussion is history and/or word as the kinds of revelation in the Old Testament. While in the final analysis both scholars agree that the two kinds belong together, in the meantime the discussion concerning the clarification of their relationship has reached a deadlock; Zimmerli emphasizes the word of Yahweh which gives rise to and illuminates history (particularly in the self-identification formula I am Yahweh), while for Rendtorff revelation is constituted by history, in which the word is grounded and through which the word is confirmed.[31] Before we return to this problem, we must first concern ourselves with the Old Testament's semantic field *(Begrifflichkeit)* for the understanding of revelation. This is also the point of departure for the works of Rendtorff and Zimmerli, in which the latter begins with a specific use of ידע, the recognition formula *(Erkenntnisaussage)*,[32] while the former begins with a specific use of ראה (נראה Niphal), a term for the appearances of God.[33]

A. Discussion between Zimmerli and Rendtorff

Initially, it must be observed that both scholars, because they have taken their starting point in the empirical-epistemological sphere (i.e., with a conceptuality drawn from human perceiving and human knowing), are in fact moving within the sphere of those same ancient Near Eastern preunderstandings which were outlined above. This state of affairs needs to remain in view, even if it plays only a subordinate role in the work of the two scholars. It points to the religio-historical anchoring of the understandings of revelation. Accordingly, the terms for "to see" and "to know," when set in relation to revelation, must be taken to mean that the concealed element in the event of "disconcealment" is really *seen* and *understood* for what it is. In other words, at issue in revelation is the seeing and knowing by humans of that which reveals itself (or of the one who reveals himself).

1. ראה *and Revelation*

Concerning the term ראה in the context of revelation, the Niphal form נראה, to which Rendtorff limits himself, is a cult-etiological expression for the appearances

31. Cf. Robinson's concluding remark in "Revelation," 62.
32. Zimmerli, "Knowledge of God," 29-98.
33. Rendtorff, "Concept of Revelation," 28-30.

of God in the pre-Yahwistic period. However, it was not adopted as an expression for the theophany of Yahweh. Instead, it appears as the framework for the divine promise speeches. The significance shifts from the manifest appearance of Yahweh to the announcement of his acts. This development is most clearly evident in the form נודעה, according to which one arrives at the recognition of Yahweh in (the experience of) his mighty acts of salvation.[34]

Rendtorff's argument raises a number of questions. First, is the fact that God shows himself, so far as this is expressed through ראה, dependent only on the Niphal form (נראה)? Does not the Old Testament's language also employ the Qal and Hiphil forms for this? Do these forms imply a negation of a theophany event, or do they signify its attestation merely from a different perspective? It appears that the inclusion of the total field of the term is indispensable. Then, however, it is clear that, both for later periods and at central junctures, the Old Testament uses the word ראה quite succinctly for Yahweh's revelation as a humanly knowable appearance.[35]

Second, what does the substantive transition in the narrative from the appearance to the promissory speech about the theophany mean? No doubt at a later time the appearance was pushed into the background by the announcement. But this means that the content of the appearance was no longer the appearance itself, but rather the announcement. God appeared as the speaker,[36] and the revelation was "seen" as a *promise.* (The fact that the promise expresses a content has nothing to do here with the revelation of God in the fulfillment of what is proclaimed as history.) This understanding is confirmed through the preservation of the traditional

34. Rendtorff, "Concept of Revelation," 30-33; cf. Zimmerli's discussion in " 'Offenbarung,' " 17f.

35. Regarding the Niphal imperfect form, Gen 12:7; 17:1; 26:2, 24; 35:9 confirm Rendtorff's claim about the Niphal perfect. Opposed, however, are 1 Kgs 9:2 // 2 Chron 7:12 which are cult-related. Concerning the Qal: (a) perfect, first person sing.: Gen 32:31 (*NRSV* 32:30); 1 Kgs 22:19; Amos 9:1; (b) perfect, first person plur.: Isa 6:5; (c) imperfect, first person sing.: Isa 6:1; Ezek 1:4 (cf. here also the Hiphil participle in Ezek 1:28). Cf. the use of the Hiphil perfect for a thing (Amos 7:1, 4; 8:1) and for Yahweh (Amos 7:7, which is *of course* textually and exegetically problematic) and of the Qal perfect in Amos 9:1. Different forms and perspectives using the same word in the same context! A few attestations for the cultic appearance (Niphal imperfect) of כבוד are found in Lev 9:23; Num 17:7 (*NRSV* 16:42); 20:6; Isa 60:2. Cf. also Exod 24:10f. Cf. the comprehensive discussion concerning the different contexts in which ראה is used, already in Nötscher (*Angesicht,* 22-53); cf. further the ראה tradition in the Old Testament. It appears to be worth mentioning that the report of a first appearance (with נראה) legitimates a late cultic practice, while the prophetic report of a call-vision (ראה in Isa 6:1; 1 Kgs 22:19) legitimates the prophetic message. In no way does the appearance of Yahweh, whether to Micaiah ben Imlah or to Isaiah, function only as the framework for the reception of the revelatory word. It is the necessary, objective evidence expressed in traditional categories for the truth of the (contested) prophetic announcements of judgment.

36. So also Zimmerli, " 'Offenbarung,' " 17.

appearance formula. But this was not always the case in the Old Testament. One might rightly ask why, then, given this shift of significance, the appearance formula continued to be used. Rendtorff says that the formula now qualifies "the *whole* narrative as a manifestation of God."[37] Does this not mean that the *promise* as revealed by Yahweh was indicated by a traditional means and that its *content* should be regarded as revelation? Behind this may stand the question of whether this promise tradition has anything to do with Yahweh. In this case, the fact that the promise is *revealed* would be emphasized, which furthermore means that the revelation happens as a spoken promise.

Naturally, these observations about ראה do not mean that the term can be presupposed to be, throughout the Old Testament, a term for a revelatory event. One must discern whether and where this is the case from the context in which the term refers to the seeing of that which uncovers itself (or something else), of that which — or who — is presupposed to have been hidden.

2. *The Relationship of* ראה *and* ידע

Concerning the relationship of ראה and ידע in the context of revelation, the discussion between Zimmerli and Rendtorff concerning the "how" of revelation, and thereby the knowledge of Yahweh, ignited over the term ידע. Zimmerli had encountered the term through the question concerning the relationship of the self-identification formula *(Selbstvorstellungsformel)* (SF, "I am Yahweh") to the assertion of recognition *(Erkenntnisaussage)* (AK, "They will know"). His result is that the AK which refers to the acts of Yahweh is dependent upon the preceding SF of Yahweh as a person in the cultic proclamation of law or in his proclamation through his witnesses.[38] Rendtorff encountered ידע in Exod 6:3, where the pronounced opposition of ראה and ידע shows that ראה was perceived as inadequate. Accordingly, the speaking about the *appearance* of Yahweh designates a preliminary stage which was separate from the new, Mosaic stage, i.e., from the *knowledge* of the name of Yahweh. Thus, the knowledge of Yahweh has a twofold significance: (1) the knowledge of the name and (2) the self-validation *(Selbsterweis)* of Yahweh in his acts, whereby the knowledge of the name, according to Rendtorff, is essentially already contained in the self-validation through the acts (of Yahweh).[39] The discussion may be reduced to this question: How is Yahweh "seen" or "known"?[40] There are four alternative answers: (a) in his act-promising speeches; (b) in the acts which follow upon the promise; (c) only in acts; or (d) in the traditio-historical unity of both promise and act. Both scholars agree that possibility (c) is to be

37. "Concept of Revelation," 29.
38. "I Am Yahweh," and " 'Offenbarung,' " 24f.
39. "Concept of Revelation," 30f.
40. Zimmerli, " 'Offenbarung,' " 17.

excluded. In the clarification of the relationship of promise and act, Zimmerli inclines to alternative (a), while Rendtorff emphasizes (b) and above all (d).

In view of Rendtorff's exegesis of Exod 6:3, with which Zimmerli agrees, a question arises as to whether in this verse **P** sees the difference between the patriarchal period and the Mosaic period in the difference between the two modes of revelation: appearance (נראה Niphal) and making known (נודע Niphal). Are both modes of revelation valued according to their chronological succession? Or does **P** see the difference between the two periods in the revelation of two different names? Or does he tie the revelation of Yahweh as El Shaddai with נראה (Niphal), while he formulates the revelation of Yahweh as Yahweh with נודע (Niphal)? Rendtorff evidently means the first, although his formulation is not clear: "The appearance of Jahweh [*sic*] is attributed to a preliminary stage, and with Moses something new is inaugurated: [Yahweh] allows himself to be known *as himself*."[41] In view of Rendtorff's emphasis, one must oppose "as himself" to the "preliminary stage," while "the appearance of Jahweh [*sic*]" belongs to "to know." Rendtorff nonetheless seems to place in opposition "appearing" and "as himself," which results in the question posed above. Does וארא . . . באל שדי (Exod 6:3) already say that the name became known through the appearance as such? Rendtorff says that "the verb נראה [I would prefer, here and elsewhere, to speak of the *form* נראה, so as to avoid the danger of suggesting that one is dealing with the total lexeme!] is used in Gen 17:1 and 35:9-11 with the formula אני־אל שדי."[42] This is not entirely correct. In both texts the formula is connected in the first place with the immediately preceding ויאמר. In 17:1 the "saying" can be understood as "appearing," but to accept this in 35:9-12 is more difficult. More likely, for P, it is in both texts, a matter of speech event within an appearance which as such is no longer emphasized, quite apart from the function depicted above. On this account, it is questionable whether, concerning the revelation of the name, the difference for P lies between *appearance* and *making known*. Therefore, it may be asked whether וארא in Exod 6:3 does not refer strictly to the name אל שדי. After all, according to P, God says (v. 2) that he who now introduces himself as Yahweh formerly appeared as אל שדי. Could this mean that for P the traditional formula ראה is used precisely for this concealed revelation of Yahweh under a different name? Then, Exod 6:3 would assert that the difference between the patriarchal and Mosaic periods does not lie in the difference between the revelation of a name as *appearance* and the revelation of a name as *made known,* but in the difference between the revelation of Yahweh (which occurs in both cases) without the proper name *(uneigentliche)* (expressed by נראה Niphal) and with the proper name *(eigentliche)* (expressed by נודע Niphal). The use of ראה and ידע would then express in its own way what the differentiation of the revealed name essentially means: the patriarchs

41. "Concept of Revelation," 30.
42. "Concept of Revelation," 30.

saw Yahweh, but for them he was not identified as Yahweh. This terminological usage implies then — and one must agree in this with Rendtorff and Zimmerli — that for **P** נודע (Niphal) excludes any ambiguity concerning the actual name of God, while this is not the case with ראה. But this still does not mean that in the present text it is primarily an issue of the opposition of the two modes of revelation. The usage of the root ראה throughout the Old Testament underscores this as unlikely. It seems as if P, with this terminological "rule" (Yahweh revealed in the patriarchal period, though under a different name), theologically legitimated the integration of the patriarchal traditions into Israel's history of Yahweh *(Jahwegeschichte Israels)*.

The proposed relationship between ראה and ידע in the sense of both an improper and a proper revelation of the name of Yahweh can also be observed elsewhere. The narrative Judg 13:3-22 is a microcosm for the total problem. The language is precisely chosen throughout: the מלאך־יהוה (vv. 3, 13, 15, 16a+b, 17, 18, 20, 21a+b) is always mentioned from the point of view of the narrator, while the מלאך האלהים is mentioned in verse 9 from the point of view of the narrator and in verse 6 from the point of view of Manoah's wife. The latter is also true for איש האלהים in verses 6, 8, as well as for האיש in verses 10, 11a+b and האלהים in verses 9, 22. The question about the name (vv. 6, 17, 18) is not answered, but indicates that the *identification* of the unknown is a decisive concern. For this, the relationship between ראה and ידע is important. The twofold appearance of the messenger of Yahweh in verses 3-21a is always described with the term ראה (vv. 3, 6, 10, 19, 20, 21a; cf. also vv. 22b, 23). In addition, verse 16b states explicitly that "Manoah did not know that he was the messenger of Yahweh," until he went up in the altar flame. "Then Manoah knew (ידע) that he was the messenger of Yahweh" (v. 21b). For this author ראה and ידע do not represent two subsequent revelatory periods, but two different modes of revelation in the same event. By the end of the story, Manoah, his wife, and the author know that this was a revelation of a messenger of Yahweh. Manoah, the Yahweh-devotee (!, vv. 8, 19), identifies him at the instant of the ascent, that is, in connection with the offering to *Yahweh.* This subsequent identification means, however, for Manoah and for the narrator that the previous unidentified appearance was a revelation of Yahweh as well. In its occurrence, it was a revelation of Yahweh in the form of a visible appearance (which one could name "messenger of God") understood as divine, and seen (ראה) but not identified (ידע). This conception appears to be based, therefore, upon a preunderstanding, according to which Yahweh can reveal himself to the Yahweh-worshipper in different ways. In view of the self-revealing subject, these ways could be spoken of as a unity. In the view of the person who sees the revelation, however, there exists the possibility of a misunderstanding between the seeing of the appearance and the recognition of its identity. It may be asked whether such complementary modes of expression do not attempt to account for two different concerns which surface in the Old Testament's understanding of revelation: the *objective* fact of the revelation of Yahweh, even if a person recognizes it differently, and the *subjective* problem of how a person might recognize the revelation correctly.

The question of the relationship between ראה and ידע in the context of revelation cannot be treated any further here. This would require a separate investigation on a broader basis. What has been said for ראה is also true for ידע. One cannot limit oneself to *one* form of the lexeme, if one wishes to investigate the term in the context of a topic. In view of the relationship to ידע one might merely cite Isa 6:9b: שִׁמְעוּ שָׁמוֹעַ ואל-תבינו וראו ראו ואל־תדעו. Hearing/seeing and understanding/knowing are parallel but not synonymous. Apart from this, the fact that the people are consigned to a misunderstood seeing suggests that the preunderstanding also seems to be that "seeing" means in reality the seeing of the phenomenon of revelation (stronger: the seeing of revelation), but that the seen revelation is not understood and is not identified as the acts of Yahweh. In the context of revelation the term "seeing" is not always used in the way in which the above-cited (and other) texts use it. It can mean "to know" Yahweh as such. In such cases, it is not necessary to speak about "knowing," because the basis for the expected recognition of the identity of Yahweh is already provided by the context. But wherever "knowing" and "seeing" are distinguished, this points either to a problem of identification or to a crisis of revelation altogether. The latter appears to be the case in Hos 5:12-15, where, of course, the term ידע is lacking even though it is precisely the matter of the knowledge of Yahweh which is treated: Ephraim sees (v. 13) its sickness but provides a false diagnosis. The problem of knowledge consists in the misconception of the identity of the one who causes the sickness, which is the reason for the passionate "I . . . I . . . I . . ." (vv. 14f.). Compare the pertinent text by Wolff with regard to the characterization of the knowledge of God in Hosea: "to דעת belongs the embryo of a doctrine of differentiation *(Unterscheidungslehre)* which clarifies who Yahweh is and who Baal is. . . ."[43] It is not always the case that Yahweh is known by his historical acts. That from time to time this itself was ultimately no small problem for Israel will have to be discussed below.

3. *Yahweh and God*

A further reason why one has been unable to move essentially beyond the positions referred to above seems to lie in the fact that in the discussion the difference between אלהים and יהוה has been hinted at here and there but not worked out methodologically. The same is true for the necessary differentiation between the revelation of the name and the revelation of the act. Rendtorff's oft-varying affirmation that "the sight and the experience of the acts of Yahweh brings [*sic*] about knowledge"[44] is characteristic for both. Moreover, the assertion that "the activity itself ought to

43. Wolff, " 'Wissen um Gott,' " 195.
44. "Concept of Revelation," 42.

bring about acknowledgement of God in the one who observes the activity and understands it in its context as an action of Jahweh [*sic*],"[45] fails to clarify how within the connection one arrives at the knowledge of Yahweh, which connection exactly is being spoken of, and why it is precisely Yahweh that should be known. Zimmerli has, of course, already emphasized the emergence of the unknown in the self-identification formula[46] and (in view of many of the texts Rendtorff cites) has correctly asserted that there the knowledge of Yahweh from his deeds is preceded by the making known of his name.[47] But this objection does not prove that it must always be this way, nor is it capable of tracing the relationship between the revelation of the name and the revelation of the deed back to a foundational point of departure; for the self-identification formula must also be investigated to see if it already looks back to an "event-continuum" *(Geschehenszusammenhang)* or presupposes it foundationally, and not only occasionally.

It is well known that the ancient Near Eastern preunderstanding regarding the manifestations of the Divine in all the spheres of human experience is also operative in the Old Testament. The ancient Israelites also see the appearances and acts of God in the appearance of the heavens, in the fullness of nature, in the events of peoples, and specifically in humans. This kind of understanding of revelation is pre- and extra-Yahwistic; but, above all, it has this to do with Yahwism, that even Yahwism could not have existed without it. As an ontological-cosmological pre-understanding to which the knowledge of the Divine belongs, it is the foundation of Yahwism. A נבל who says, "There is no God" (Pss 14:1; 53:2 [*NRSV* 53:1]) denies God in an ontological sense, thereby assailing the common ontology, and deprives himself of the foundation of life. When the Israelites run to Baal in the face of a catastrophe, it certainly demonstrates a confusion with respect to the identity of the acting God, but it also shows that they recognize the act of God in the experience. This requires no further attestations here. According to this preunderstanding, it is perfectly clear that God is manifest and made known in his acts. So long as this preunderstanding is intact, neither a word-announcement (preceding the event) nor an interpretation (following the event) is inevitably necessary, as much as either may be the case. This is also true for the knowledge of the acts of Yahweh, so far as this knowledge refers to divine acts. At this general religio-historical point, Rendtorff's argumentation is fundamentally justified. But how would these divine acts be known as acts of *Yahweh?* Yahweh is not simply God or the Divine. He is — like Jesus Christ in the New Testament — a specific manifestation of God, primarily in a name. How then does one come to the revelation and knowledge of the name? Just as the revelation of *God* in his acts is certainly possible, so the revelation of *Yahweh* in these same acts is certainly

45. "Concept of Revelation," 47.
46. "I Am Yahweh."
47. " 'Offenbarung,' " 24f.

impossible unless the seeing person has known Yahweh's name previously or from somewhere else (such as a narrative context). In this respect the inquiry regarding the name (Genesis 32; Judges 13) is more than an isolated situation. The knowledge of the name implies, therefore, a revelation of a special nature, just as much as it implies a revelation of the name. Now there can be no doubt that the way for a name to become known (whether in self-introduction, through the giving of a name, through proclamation, or through acclamation) is virtually always that of a *word*-event, regardless of whether it is related to a different event (i.e., different from the word-event itself), or whether it announces such an event in advance or interprets it after the event. If the name is not articulated or known as articulated, the identity of the actor remains hidden. At this point, Zimmerli's argumentation for the priority of the *word*-event in the self-disclosure of God as *Yahweh* has its fundamental justification. The recognition of this name is, in principle, prior to the knowledge of the name in his acts — either as its presupposition or as its condition. But this has nothing to do with the explicit proclamation of the name which occasionally precedes an event. The name can be "seen" in the event even without such a preceding proclamation or its subsequent interpretation, if it is known in the horizon of the preunderstanding of the event and defines this horizon. Rather, it has to do with the fact that the knowledge of the name rests on a revelation *sui generis*.

At this point, the inquiry must continue exegetically first in the context of שׁם יהוה. In view of what has been said, Exod 6:3, for example, shows that for the patriarchs appearances were not self-evidently the revelations of *Yahweh.* Only to Moses were these revealed as such in the specific self-introduction of Yahweh (so **P**), i.e., in a word-experience. In Leviticus 18 Yahweh was not manifest as Yahweh in the laws; these have a partially pre- and extra-Israelite origin. Yahweh becomes manifest in the repeatedly spoken self-identification formula. One will have to say the laws do not make Yahweh manifest, but rather the laws receive their revelatory quality in the context of Yahweh's self-revelation. It would also have to be investigated whether the root ידע (or בין in several attestations) refers to the knowledge of the *identity* of God which expresses itself by the name, thereby referring to *this* sort of revelation, and whether terms like ראה and שׁמע are in their respective contexts associated with (the notion of) divine manifestations. That the knowledge of the name is based on a revelation *sui generis* is evident above all in the fact that it quite differently from the unhistorical preunderstanding of divine manifestation is based on historical beginning (so **P**, in another sense also **J**), at least insofar as it became historically significant, specifically in its connection with Israel since the time of Moses. This historical beginning is understood as a word-event. Further, this word-event determines the entire subsequent Old Testament history — not necessarily always as a history of word-announcement but as a *Yahweh*-history, which is based once and for all on the word-event of the revelation of the name. To the extent that the knowledge of the name (a knowledge which is historically determined and which results from the word-event) coincides with the knowledge of God (which is ontologically determined), both together become a presupposition for the Old Testament tradition history, in whatever settings, genres, and relations this presupposition unfolds — be it in the repetitive cult-legal proclamation of the name of Yahweh, in the promise of events in this name, or in the recognition of Yahweh from the events.

Finally, a word concerning the function of the name. Zimmerli has insisted (against Rendtorff) that in אני יהוה or אני הוא "the substantive statements are swallowed up solely by the coming to the front of the 'I', and that as a result in them the 'sovereign freedom' and the 'mystery of the person' are expressed, in which the I discloses itself in its I-character."[48] This is difficult to demonstrate insofar as the I-assertions are usually combined with a statement of an act and thus, so it seems, want to be understood from this point of view. However, in view of the conclusions drawn above, this difficulty solves itself because אני יהוה, notwithstanding its connection with a statement of an act, emphasizes the identity of the one acting in the act as this identity appears in the name. Therefore, one should be more precise: "I-mystery" or "person-mystery" must not, via detour, be understood once more as substantive statements about the nature of Yahweh. It is well known how strongly the Old Testament resisted such inferences about Yahweh's essence on the basis of his name. Nor does Zimmerli think that such inferences are valid. It appears that one must understand the אני יהוה, and thereby the revelation of the name, in the sense of the exclusivity and unmistakability of Yahweh, and, therefore, in the context of the first and second commandments. This concentration on the identity of Yahweh was important not only for periods in which one could recognize Yahweh's acts in history. It was also important for times and situations where this was not possible. In such crises, it was always difficult to recognize Yahweh in his acts. But the knowledge of the name would always remain — often as the sole ground for hope and prayer.

One must also assume that in the revelation of Yahweh as Yahweh two heterogeneous procedures of revelation coincide. The relationship of the general history of religion to the special Yahweh-history as a part of it (yet still unmistakably identified) is mirrored in this unity. The general ontology did not suffice as a foundation for the knowledge of God as Yahweh. This knowledge requires the historical presupposition of the proclaimed name. By contrast, once the name is known, the recognition of Yahweh as God happens in connection with and, by and large, within the categories of the contemporary ontology. Precisely here seems to lie one of the main presuppositions for the capacity of the Yahweh religion to universalization, on the grounds of which Yahweh could absorb such other spheres as creation, nature, law, and wisdom.

First Kings 18:21f. is an example of the interpenetration of God- and Yahweh-

48. " 'Offenbarung,' " 21f.

revelation. First of all, which of the two referred to by name (Yahweh or Baal) is אלהים? It is the proof for *divinity* which is on trial. In both cases, the ordeal by fire serves as the mechanism of proof. This shows that the revelation as *God* for both Baalism and Yahwism can happen in the same way and be recognized under the same presupposition. However, it must also be said that the ordeal by fire as such does not identify God to be either Yahweh or Baal. It proves only what is common to both, and thereby provides no evidence by which to distinguish one from the other regarding his identity. To this extent, it may point *either* to Baal *or* to Yahweh and is thus excluded as a mode of knowing whether the revelation is of Yahweh or of Baal. In other words, knowledge on the basis of the religio-historical ontology, the "seeing" of the phenomenon alone, provides no help at all for the knowledge of the identity of God. This is the reason why there must be two separate fire offerings for אלהים which are distinguished from each other through the identification of each God in the separate invocation of each one's name. God or Yahweh is thus recognized as *Yahweh* from the *context* of the fire-event, the invocation of his name. The interpenetration of the revelation of God and revelation of Yahweh can be determined thusly: Yahweh reveals himself as *God* in the event of the fire, and does so in the context of the prayer to Yahweh insofar as it is Yahweh who reveals himself as God; God reveals himself as *Yahweh* in the invocation of his name, and does so in the context of the fire, insofar as it is God who reveals himself as Yahweh. But this also indicates that only in the combination of both modes of revelation can Yahweh as God and God as Yahweh be revealed. In view of what has been said, it would be necessary to examine throughout the entire Old Testament what the Israelite witnesses wanted to express when, on the one hand, they said אלהים while certainly meaning יהוה, and when, on the other, they said יהוה in the context of speaking about אלהים.

4. History, Word, and Event

That the revelation of Yahweh according to the Old Testament takes place predominantly in historical events, preeminently in the salvific manifestations from the exodus-history on, and also that it takes place as history, needs no further discussion here. This is especially true with regard to Israel's salvific history of Yahweh which stood under the knowledge of the name and with regard to the correlatedness of word and history. If one thereby sees that the revealed nature *(Offenbarsein)* of the name is distinguished from its actual revelation *(Offenbarwerden)* in contingent word- or act-events and that the former precedes the latter, then the question of whether the word precedes the act or vice versa becomes meaningless in the sense of being a basic alternative. If the name is known, an event as well as a word can be recognized as a revelation of Yahweh. Which of these is the case depends on the individual situation, but not on a specific revelatory pattern.

Zimmerli has collected enough material on the word which precedes the event (in different ways). For example, in Josh 21:43-45 and 1 Kgs 2:4, the word is not perceived on the basis of the preceding history but, on the contrary, the history on the basis of the preceding word. On the other hand, Rendtorff has also adduced sufficient examples which illustrate that the word accompanies, or sometimes follows, in an interpretative way the revelation of Yahweh which becomes visible in history. Second Sam 5:1, 12 and 1 Sam 16:18 (!), for example, show that Yahweh was recognizable in events even though there was no preceding word of promise. In Amos 9:7 one could, if one desired, relate the statement concerning Israel to the Yahweh-word which evokes the events. However, the statement about the Philistines and Arameans (*NRSV*) is nothing more than an interpretation of a centuries-long history from the standpoint of Yahweh faith. In Exod 6:3, the relationship of word and history is, strictly speaking, reciprocal. From the perspective of the revelation of *Yahweh* the sequence is: history — interpreting word; whereas from the perspective of the patriarchal religion the sequence is: announcement — history. Rendtorff's argument is especially justified with respect to the manifold ways in which the Old Testament expresses the revelation of Yahweh in the adaptation of non-Yahwistic traditions. In this adaptation, the *demarcation* of Yahweh against the other gods and ultimately the *denial* of their existence can be traced back in principle to the processes of proclamation. The preaching or cultic representation of Yahweh in forms which originally belong to Baalism and the proclamation of the subjection of the other gods through Yahweh are grounded entirely in certain historical processes. In order to see the variability of the relationship of word and event, it is necessary above all to keep in view the Old Testament texts in their full breadth and not to limit its evidence to only *one* category (e.g., historical or prophetic texts).

Now, however, the "revelation as history" thesis in the specific sense of the traditio-historical unity of word and event remains a problem. The thesis was, of course, developed to overcome the choice between revelation as history and revelation as word. Strictly speaking, "as" means that the connection of events or of event and word as such is the mode of revelation, and beyond that, is its *only* mode. This can certainly be established exegetically, particularly where the texts explicitly emphasize such a connection, i.e., where the total history, especially of Israel, is recognized as a manifestation of Yahweh in its totality and unity (cf., e.g., Isa 1:2f.; 5:1-7; 10:23; Amos 4:6-11; 9:7; Psalm 47; etc.). But it may be asked whether or not the mode of revelation (the "how": *as* history) is to be differentiated from its place (the "when, where": *in* history) and from its subject (the "who": God as Yahweh/Yahweh as God); for the revelation/recognition of Yahweh in certain historical events on the basis of the prior knowledge of Yahweh does not yet mean that it is a matter of revelation in event *and* its presupposition and thereby a revelation of *both*. In other words, in revelation *as* history the mode of revelation is history. With revelation *in* history the mode may be something else: an event, a promise, a vision, or a dream in the context of history. With respect to the exegetical factors, it is, however, hardly legitimate either to declare all other modes of revelation irrelevant or to subsume them to the single mode of history. In this way, the essential concern for the modalities of revelation is lost. Furthermore, it appears that by this same process the primary concern in the concept of revelation gets shoved aside as well, namely, the self-revealing subject, more clearly — the identity of the self-revealing God.

Thus, holistic historical connections reveal, among other things, the meaning of history, or even of "God" insofar as "God" has to do with meaning within the framework of a preunderstanding. But with regard to the identity of God (Yahweh), one cannot say that the holistic history reveals Yahweh via that holistic history. Exod 6:3 shows that the holistic historical structure of the patriarchal religion prepared for the continuity with the later Yahweh religion (Maag's God of guidance), but also that this structure still did not lead to the revelation of God as Yahweh to the patriarchs. Furthermore, for **P** the announced history did not reveal the name as such, but Yahweh revealed his name in a mode and process *sui generis,* even in the context of the announced history. The common structure of religion, therefore, reveals the meaning of the total history. This is what made the absorption of the patriarchal history into the Mosaic Yahweh-history possible. But even the unity or connectedness of this holistic history did not yet reveal the name. If, however, the name is known in connection with a *part* of this history, then it is revealed as (the name of) the God of the *whole* on the basis of the structure of experience which all parts have in common.

What has been said shows that the question about the identity of the God who reveals himself, which in the Old Testament is always presupposed, is different from the question about the mode by which he becomes revealed. Now the fact that the God who reveals himself in his identity as Yahweh is always the same does not on that account also mean that the mode by which he becomes revealed is known always and only in one and the same semantic context or in one and the same experience of reality. The context for understanding is flexible and undergoes changes. When, therefore, the Old Testament speaks in an unsystematized manner of modes of the revelation of Yahweh in other than history, of different ways of revelation within history, and of an interpenetration and juxtaposition of different ways (cf. many psalms), this is theologically significant because God's becoming revealed as Yahweh is thereby attested in principle for every possible kind of experience of reality. At this point, the plurality in the word field and in the different genres and settings in life must be seriously considered theologically.

With regard to the *universal* interpretive horizon of revelation, it must be asked, ultimately, whether it is appropriate either to focus on a distinct horizon definitively — be it ontological, historical, cosmological, existential — or to focus on the universalistic perspective of a particular generation from time to time, within the framework of the continuously changing horizon of knowledge.[49] The former leads, as is well known, either to a theological devaluation of the quality of revelation for various Old Testament generations from without, or to a devaluation of many of its stages from a — hypothetical — definitive horizon of reality as seen from within the Old Testament. In contrast, the latter would permit us to accept the Old Testament texts, as well as the Old Testament as such, as universal in their intentional sense, in that a generation or an individual experiences in a specific situation the revelation of God as Yahweh or of Yahweh as God within the horizon of universal reality expected at the time. The significance of that revelation for us today in our horizon of reality could then be explored in dialogue under the label "fusing of horizons" *(Horizontverschmelzung).* A text such as Ps 139:1-16 seems to reflect in principle the diversity of possible horizons, and thereby the flexibility of the certainty of revelation, but nevertheless seems also to reflect the universality of any or all horizons taken together. "God" does not imply here a distinctly fixed universality (not even a history), but each possible kind of universality.

B. The Range of Possibilities

We have already pointed to the word field through which different perspectives of the kinds of Yahweh's revelation were spoken and to the religio-historical categories through which knowledge of Yahweh takes place. At this juncture, it would be necessary at least to point to the full range of possibilities in which Yahweh was revealed to Israel: his saving acts, his covenant, his loyalty, his mercies, his promises, his admonitions, his justice and law *(Recht und Gesetz),* his commandments, his messages, and the manifold worship/cultic institutions. Revelation for humans can happen unexpectedly, or as the answer to the search for and appeal to God. These revelations must be taken seriously in and of themselves, even though they are, of course, all recognizable within the context of the prior knowledge of Yahweh. The oracle of salvation from Eli to Hannah (1 Samuel 1) reveals to her the whole Yahweh in the total horizon of a woman's situation.

A particular question is whether a promise, i.e., a promissory word-event, already reveals Yahweh, even if the fulfillment is still outstanding. In the sense of revelation as promise, this question must be answered in the affirmative. This certainly means that Yahweh is not revealed solely in the unity of promise and fulfillment. Moreover, it does not mean that in the promise alone Yahweh would not reveal himself as yet. The flash of hope, the opening of a people toward an unknown future on the basis of the promise, is no insignificant thing. A great part of Old Testament history was altogether experienced only in this fashion (and one

49. H.-G. Gadamer, *Truth and Method,* trans. J. Weinscheimer and D. G. Marshall, 2d ed. (New York: Crossroad, 1990).

should say that a great part of human history is experienced only in this fashion), i.e., without the knowledge of any fulfillment. It is the distinctive mark of ever-migratory humanity. Inasmuch as hope aims at fulfillment, the question still remains — now for the ancient Israelites — as to whether the promise makes Yahweh so visible that the ancient Israelites know about Yahweh and can rely entirely on Yahweh, and that they, therefore, know about the meaning of life under promise, even if and as long as the fulfillment is not visible (cf. the relationship between promise and faith in Gen 15:1f.).

In light of this example, the *kind* of revelation has a certain contextual value. This means not only that revelation appears in the final unity of all that can be experienced, but also that Yahweh as God appears in contexts where the universal unity as experience of reality is (still) not visible. This contextual value of revelation is also true for the past, for there exists not only the present time of humans cast toward the future, but also the future determined by the past. At issue here is whether the experience with history makes Yahweh so visible that one knows of him as God, even if this history does not stand under a direct promise.

Moltmann touches on decisive points in the Old Testament understanding of revelation, but the subordination of the Old Testament understanding of the world and of itself under the category "history," just as much as Moltmann's subordination of it under the "eschatological outlook in which revelation is seen as promise of the trust,"[50] misses the flexibility of the ontological perspectives within the total arena of the Old Testament. Also, it is not correct, as has been said above, that "the essential difference here is accordingly not between the so-called nature gods and a God of revelation, but between the God of the promise and the gods of the epiphanies," i.e., "in the different ways of conceiving and speaking of the revelation and self-manifestation of the deity."[51] The epiphanic gods were gods of promise, too. Moreover, the ways of speaking about the revealing and self-showing of the deity within the Old Testament are, with respect to Yahweh, not only very different, whereby one can only speak very relatively and incidentally of the devaluation of certain modes to the relative over-valuation of others; taken together, they are also, like the Old Testament, dependent on the environment of Israel. With respect to the relationship between the "coming" of God and his permanent "presence," we are still lacking a fundamental investigation. But in view of the totality of the Old Testament materials (and not only in view of the *hieros logos*-traditions), it is clear that the exclusive dichotomy of "epiphanic piety" and "religion of promise" in Moltmann is untenable.[52] Moltmann's conception, so far as it concerns the Old Testament, can positively and critically be discussed at many points, though it is not possible to pursue it further here.

50. *Theology of Hope,* 44.

51. *Theology of Hope,* 43.

52. *Theology of Hope,* 88f.; cf. the article by Schnutenhaus, "Kommen," on the one hand and the articles by Haran, "Divine Presence," and Levine, "Presence of God," on the other.

Finally, it must be pointed out that for the Old Testament, history as such, in whatever way it is conceptualized, was in no way the only category by which reality was experienced, nor was it the only category of the universal conception of reality.[53] The one-sided emphasis on history can only occur at the expense of a considerable portion of the Old Testament materials.[54] On the contrary, quite apart from other perspectives (e.g., Yahweh's becoming revealed [*Offenbarwerden*] in the act-consequence continuum in the human sphere), one must now point to "nature" as being one of the most important modes of Yahweh's becoming revealed. The manifestation of Yahweh in the control of creation (e.g., according to Gen 8:22f.), in the wisdom of world order (Ps 104:24), in the cycle of birth and death (Ps 104:28-30), in the naming of the stars (Ps 147:4), in the creation of morning and evening (Amos 4:13), in the fullness of the gifts of the earth (Ps 104:10f.), in nature phenomena (Psalm 29; 107:25-29; Deut 7:13), and in the gift of fertility (Genesis 27; 28; 49:24-26; Deut 7:13) — all these and many others make Yahweh known or revealed as the God of the world to the Yahweh worshipper.[55] The Yahweh-faith has laid hold of the revelation of God in nature, not only through its historization but also through the revelation of God as Yahweh in nature as such. Furthermore, one must add that, after all, this horizon of the experience of reality offers itself preeminently to the knowledge of the revelation of Yahweh as a universal horizon.

An examination of the terms אדיר/כבוד and הארץ, in combination with מלא, provides for interesting conclusions. Texts like Deut 33:13-16; Pss 8:2 (*NRSV* 8:1);

53. Here it can only be mentioned that the view that Israel first discovered the category of history in connection with its faith in God proves to be false, as also in other cases, to the extent to which ancient Near Eastern texts are being studied with regard to this question; cf. Bertil Albrektson, *History and the Gods,* Conicctanea Biblica, OT Series 1 (Lund: Gleerup, 1967); cf. also what Westermann has to say about the genealogies, "something of a historical presentation of a form of existence which precedes history" in the sense of the depiction of a "continuous succession of events" (Claus Westermann, *Genesis 1–11: A Commentary,* trans. John J. Scullion (Minneapolis: Augsburg, 1984], 7).

54. It is thereby at least a matter of debate whether one ought to subordinate by design the categories of nature (a problematic term!) or of human existence to a systematically derived concept of history. It is even more unfortunate if one simply overlooks these perspectives because one is fascinated once again by the weightiness of a conception which is also found in the Old Testament. It is unacceptable when Harvey H. Guthrie, Jr., after he has ascertained the faith of the Old Testament as a historical faith, says, "The way in which the J document undertakes to explain the meaning of the Davidic Kingdom in terms of the history that created it makes J the strand of the Old Testament which is not only creative of the faith of Israel but of the idea of history so integral to western civilization" (*God and History in the Old Testament* [Greenwich: Seabury Press, 1960], 143), and when he, after canonizing this point, says, ". . . the wisdom literature . . . could never become a positive servant of that point of view by which the main line of the biblical witness is characterized" (146). Thus, one makes inconvenient witnesses — even Yahweh's — silent!

55. Cf. the broad range of materials in McKenzie, *Myths and Realities,* esp. 85-132.

24:1a+b; 29:5-9; 57:6, 12 (*NRSV* 57:5, 11); 65:10-14 (*NRSV* 65:9-13); 66:2-5 (*NRSV* 66:1-4); 72:19; 85:11-13; 96:3-13; 97:6; 102:16f. (*NRSV* 102:15f.); 104:21, 31; 145; 108:6 (*NRSV* 108:5); Isa 6:3; and others point most clearly to the appearance of the majesty of God, the effect of Yahweh's power in the "fullness" of the earth, i.e., in nature, the history of peoples, and Israel's salvation history. When "nature" and "history" are here juxtaposed, this does not mean that the Old Testament generally subsumes nature under history. If it utilizes a universal expression, then it is "the fullness of the earth."[56]

If one also assumes that Genesis 1 is a(n) (indirect) sort of etiology for the existence of exilic Israel in the form of its seven-day sabbath week, then **P** could thereby select no more universal horizon in which the revelation of Elohim (!), the God of Israel, would be known in the day-to-day reality of Israel. According to **P**, the creation constitutes, of course, the beginning of history which leads to the Israelite cult. But God was not thereby revealed as or through history (what kind of history would this be?), but through the archetype of creation in the context of its likeness to the — ahistorical — week. It is almost an irony: Israel, who through centuries knew the revealed nature of Yahweh in its history, now knew — after the collapse of this mode of revelation — the revealed nature of Yahweh as the creator of the world in each week anew.

C. The Crisis of Revelation

The disclosing of Yahweh always meant that humans were affected as ones who see and know. Therefore, if one wants to speak of revelation appropriately, it is indispensable that we observe as its context the situation of those intermittently affected. For the people so affected, the disclosure of Yahweh is normally knowable and verifiable in its content. This coheres with the fact that seeing and knowing are only possible in the context of a preunderstanding or understanding of reality, however it may be shaped. This verifiability as such is in no way to be judged negatively. In the Old Testament it is not only presupposed to be unproblematic, it also has its substantive justification, if in fact Yahweh has something to do with the reality in which the ancient Israelites found themselves. On this account, revelation always tends toward such verification. Furthermore, it is normal that the horizon for the verification of the situation corresponds to a universal horizon, which hinges on the mutual relationship of Yahweh and God and God and Yahweh. In this way, the universality can be understood cosmologically or historically or apocalyptically (universal-historically), whereby one would have to ask why one is the case and not the others. But just this substantive understanding of revelation is the ground for the fact that again and again in the Old Testament it comes down

56. Cf. also related terms such as פלא, מופת, מעשׂה, etc.

to a crisis of the revealed nature of Yahweh. It generally bursts open at the place where the preunderstanding breaks down or undergoes changes, be it through a different perspective of things or through the radical change of realities. Both signify a breach of continuity. Without the crisis of continuity, there could be, in reality, no crisis of revelation. One of the major problems which the Old Testament presents to us is that for it there is not only continuity but also, and drastically, discontinuity. Accordingly, the place of the crisis of revelation is the place where Yahweh is no longer identifiable in the context of the prior horizons of revelation. Moreover, its essence is that the supports for the preunderstanding — of whichever sort — on the basis of which Yahweh would be knowable have collapsed: no longer does any common denominator (or fusion of horizons) for traditional preunderstandings and present realities exist by which Yahweh would be knowable in the present. Thus, one can say that the crisis of revelation results from the crisis of a common denominator, of a fusion of horizons.

This crisis appears repeatedly in many different ways. It is a constant companion of the history of revelation. A few examples must suffice.

1) The tradition regarding the rebellion in the wilderness — with its central lexeme לון — attests how Israel as a whole viewed Yahweh and Moses as bringers of destruction rather than as bringers of salvation and, therefore, totally misunderstood the history of liberation; cf. Exod 16:3b; 17:3b; Num 14:3f.; 16:11; and so on.

2) The term אות in the Old Testament signifies or indicates that whatever is so designated points not to itself, but always to something other than itself, the properly intended subject of discussion. A "sign," therefore, functions normally as the context of a certain issue. If one compares the function of "sign" with the function of "uncover," i.e., with what is expressed by גלה, ראה, ידע, the following results: "uncovering" makes something visible and knowable, while "sign" confirms what has been uncovered. אות, therefore, has a clarifying, supportive, and confirming function. This shows that a "sign" is necessary in situations wherever something requires confirmation. In its connection with "uncovering," the necessity of a "sign" signifies, therefore, a problem, or even crisis: the non-self-evident nature of that which has been uncovered (cf., among others, Gen 9:12; 17:11; Exod 3:12; 4:8; 10:1; 31:13; Josh 4:6; 2 Kgs 19:29; Isa 8:16-20; 19:19-21).

Here we would have to ask how "faith" is related to revelation. To speak of a faith in revelation in the Old Testament is already linguistically misguided. אמן (Hiphil), in its oldest attestations (Gen 15:6; Exod 4:8; 14:31; Isa 7:9), appears to imply a reliance on a revelation which is known to be dependable and/or on something which, in its revealed nature, is known to be dependable, and which one therefore cannot doubt, ignore, or decline. Even here the modes of revelation are different: in Isa 7:9 it is the David/Zion/Jerusalem tradition; in Gen 15:6 it is the promise which is known to be dependable; in Exod 14:31 it is the "visible" act of Yahweh and Moses.

3) The loss of the ark (1 Samuel 4), i.e., of the manifestation of the presence of Yahweh, resulted in a long-enduring exclusion of the ark from Israel's experience. Although the narrative, written after the (supposed) events, understandably does not say much about it, it could still be asked whether this exclusion had anything to do with a crisis regarding the knowledge of Yahweh's presence during this time. In any case, different elements in the tradition point in this direction. Only after its return to Jerusalem could any defeat of Yahweh (Yahweh in a position of obeisance before Dagan!) be seen as the victory of Yahweh even in his defeat. But that was the revealed nature of Yahweh for later generations, not for the generation concerned with the defeat!

4) What did it mean for the knowledge of Yahweh, as understood by those involved, when Yahweh revealed his guidance of events through perverting strategic, rational arguments (2 Sam 17:14)? Certainly the narrator knew better; he had a transcendent point of view, from which the revelation could easily be known. But does this mean that the question about the knowability of Yahweh is irrelevant for the persons involved in the events themselves? What kind of revelation is this, which only permits the successors to recognize the presence of Yahweh in this process on the basis of knowledge which is obtained and established only after the outcome, without the involved predecessors having the possibility of gaining real knowledge of their situation and how it affected them? For them the revelation would be in crisis in any case.

5) According to 1 Kings 13, Yahweh concealed himself in such a way that he explicitly claims to have repealed his own prohibitive word, spoken to a true prophet, via a second word, given to another Yahweh prophet, and so — only so! — caused the former prophet's failure. Furthermore, in 1 Kings 22 he concealed himself by making the correct knowledge impossible. In these forms of the crisis of revelation, one can clearly see that Israel, when it really had a problem on its hands, had to confront the question of what it meant when it said "Yahweh" who had become its destiny.

6) The bitter conflicts *within* Yahwism over the understanding of the presence and the actions of Yahweh, from Exodus 32 on, speak clearly about the intermittent emergence of the crisis of revelation. We have already mentioned Hos 5:12 (see II.A.2). In the announcements of Hananiah and Jeremiah, Yahweh-word is revealed over against Yahweh-word. The resolution of their contradiction must be suspended. Certainly history will make things clear. Certainly it will be made clear that one of the two Yahweh-words was really revealed from Yahweh and that a person would have been able to act on it. But the answer as to which of these is the correct revelation does not become plain in the prophetic confrontation itself.[57] The sealing and preservation of תורה by Isaiah (8:16) likewise serves, in the arrival of the

57. On the problem as a whole, cf. Gottfried Quell, *Wahre und falsche Propheten,* BFCT 1/146 (Gütersloh: Bertelsmann, 1952).

events, not only to reveal Yahweh as their originator, but also to demonstrate that this arrival was revealed in advance and that, therefore, the prophetic word had really been a revelation of Yahweh. It was on this basis that the tradition accepted the prophets. Most likely, the whole problem of the prophetic confrontation must be seen within a much wider horizon: the rejection of the prophetic message by its hearers and its justification via the call reports of the prophets; the rival Yahweh interpretations by Rechabites, Levites, priests in the Northern and Southern kingdoms, and prophets and prophetic schools; possibly competing theologies such as those of Ezekiel, Deutero-Isaiah, and **P**; and mutually invalidating Yahweh legislations such as Deuteronomy 12 and Leviticus 17. All these (to name only a few aspects) point not only to the tumultuous vitality of the Yahweh-faith but also to the constantly hard-fought question of how the revelation of Yahweh was to be correctly understood. The disagreement between positions which, in these confrontations, often appear to be mutually exclusive cannot be neutralized via the bracket of a total history or a tradition history, however constituted. If, in fact, this were the case, it would also be somewhat easier in our own theological situation to recognize the footsteps of God in our current history. Holistic history as a mode of revelation has only a contextual validity for the respective situations of the subsequent generations (who can only review the whole retrospectively) and for those persons for whom the whole history is actually indispensable for the elucidation of their situation. Yet it is precisely this contextual validity which provokes the question of how revelation can be recognized by those affected *in actu*. In that situation, revelation is very often in crisis.

7) Even in the sphere of wisdom, the recognition of Yahweh, by and large presupposed as unproblematic (as one can observe in the statistics of **אלהים** and **יהוה** in Proverbs, and the Yahwistic bracketing of its individual units), has, on occasion, essentially fallen into crisis, in the context of sapiential preunderstandings, within traditional overestimation of wisdom. "The act of God is not placed in dispute, but rather the human formulation thereof." Qohelet "belongs to those who rebel against an ancient system, who for the sake of truth had the courage to reject old foundations and perceptions, . . . for only where a God who is inaccessible to human comprehension is active does the possibility remain to encounter God himself anew in one of his unforeseen, new acts."[58] For Job, no traditional understanding of God brings revelation into his situation. Only when he can say, "But now my eyes have seen you" — and that is again entirely the old language of theophany! — does he come to his rest.

The crisis of the certainty of revelation shows that the substantive verification of the revelation of Yahweh in the context of human preunderstanding is guaranteed only so long as it, under the specific weight of its contents, neither stifles nor perverts the identity and divinity of Yahweh. Where such a perversion happens,

58. Oswald Loretz, *Qohelet und der alte Orient* (Freiburg: Herder, 1964), 274f.

the contents no longer correspond to "Yahweh." Indeed, there are texts in the Old Testament which assert or imply that "Yahweh" is more and something other than that which converges with human experiences of reality. Job 42:1-6 is one; Ps 73:25f. is another. Above all, one must point to the first and second commandments; for in the claim to exclusivity and unmistakability[59] (cf. the comprehensive "in heaven above, on earth below, and in the water under the earth" Exod 20:4) the identification of Yahweh with anything which may exist in this world is fundamentally rejected. These two commandments already express that Yahweh can be compared only with Yahweh as he reveals himself in his name. Thereby, however, the crisis of any understanding of revelation is already potentially provoked. The real reason why, on the one hand, the Old Testament so strictly distinguishes between the name "Yahweh" and all other reality, and why, on the other hand, it could be so flexible in its horizons of understanding and also overcome the fractures of its traditions seems to lie in the fact that, in the deepest darkness, one thing remains known in Israel: the name which was exclaimed in its midst. Of course, it is also true that the understanding of the name in the context of the first and second commandments in no way permits the independent status of the name over against Yahweh. Certain tendencies in the hypostatizing tradition indicate this danger. In this context, the revealed nature of the name could only point to the *person* (how else should one express it?) known by that name, with whom Israel ultimately is confronted. In other words, the name does not reveal *itself;* it reveals Yahweh. In this, the fact that the people of Yahweh survived even in God's obscurity may be grounded. Therefore, it must be asked whether the revealed nature of the name, in the context of the first two commandments (the demand for exclusivity and noninterchangeability), was not the essential tradition-forming factor for Israel's existence. This has nothing to do with a basic revelation formalism, but very much to do with the fundamental distinction between Yahweh as God in the strict sense of the word and his revealed nature in the horizon of human understanding. This distinction means that God, even in his revealed nature as Yahweh, was understood radically, that he thereby never became a controllable element of our world, but that he encounters humans as God for those humans. Here, ultimately, even a Job would be satisfied.

The possibility of a purely formalistic understanding of revelation does indeed arise here. But already the fact that Yahweh is normally and legitimately experienced in the contexts of the horizons of understanding and of reality negates such a principled formalism. Moreover, the crisis of revelation and the fact of being confronted with Yahweh alone, hence the radicalization of the understanding of revelation, does not mean that from here on no entirely new substantive ascertain-

59. Cf. especially Gerhard von Rad, *Old Testament Theology,* trans. D. M. G. Stalker, vol. 1 (New York: Harper and Row, 1962), 203-19. There is, of course, scarcely a question alluded to in this essay which von Rad has not stimulated in a decisive way through his own work.

ments of God in new horizons of existence would arise. In fact, this is always the case. The conclusion of the book of Job shows this in an almost disappointingly simple way in its statement about Job's return to his original condition.

Of course, the question arises as to wherein lie the ascertainments of such new justification as well as *how* such justification would have to look were it to be legitimate. These questions are so difficult to answer exegetically because the texts do not explicitly address them. But something might be indicated by conjecture. For we may ask whether in the revelation of the name something is not already disclosed for humans which is more than simply the personal over-against-ness of Yahweh in a formal sense. Indeed, the question about the name may imply for the ancient humans more than only their interest in identifying the deity for the purpose of their adoration. The interest in adoration already points to a ground which has something to do with the significance of the God who is to be revealed in his name for humans. One may, therefore, conjecture that the revelation of the name not only affects humans (Schnutenhaus) but also causes the affected humans to recognize that this God is *personally present for them.* The revealed nature of the name means, therefore, the salvific presence of this God in the presence of the affected persons. It would as such already contain what the promise "I am with you" again and again and in all possible situations explicitly asserts. Insofar as the presence of the affected people is always unique from moment to moment, God's presence is inevitably recognized in the horizon of this contingent present, even if the horizon is new. Therein could be grounded not only the justification of ever new substantive ascertainments but also their necessity. Even the question of how God's present may legitimately be substantively ascertained could at least basically be answered in this way: it may be ascertained through the recognition of the present in the context of present salvation. The fact that it thereby often comes down to a continuous tension between the justification of the ascertainment, on the one hand, and the substantive validation of what is ascertained, on the other, points to the nature of the issue under discussion: revelation is not grounded in the certainty of humans, but human certainty is forever grounded in revelation and, therefore, always exposed to the critical control of revelation. In this sense, even the contestation concerning the validity of the knowledge of the revelation of God can reveal God as the one who will never give his honor to another — not even to his best interpreters!

It can hardly be overlooked that the view of things depicted here makes visible, in their relation to one another, an entire spectrum of possible theological assertions which not infrequently seriously contradict each other. The already forgotten debate between Baumgärtel's thesis about the formal promise "I am the Lord your God" (אני יהוה אלהיך) and von Rad's effort to demonstrate the connection between the Old and New Testament in categories of (tradition-) historical realities can no longer be viewed in the sense of the originally opposing positions. Von Rad's own emphasis on the unceasing new interpretations of the acts of Yahweh in the horizon of new experiences proves again to be justified, though not only with respect to Yahweh's historical acts. The interpretive horizon was much more flexible. Ultimately, we have to ask how the reflections in this essay would affect time-honored and contentious problems, such as the relationship between "natural" and "specific" revelation, revelation of the name and of God, knowledge of God historically and ontologically, God in his word and in his acts, and certainty and faith as well. What must be said in this regard certainly far exceeds the scope of this article.

Cosmos and History in Israel's Theology

Dedicated to Claus Westermann

Introduction

It is generally assumed that for the Old Testament a view of reality in which God is closely related to the world and deeply involved in its affairs is fundamental. Indeed, the historical, legal, cultic, prophetic, and wisdom texts of the Old Testament literature amply support this assumption. Our scholarly literature is pervaded by it, and I need not belabor this point. Instead, I want to focus on the more specific questions of what the understanding of the world is in the Old Testament; how God is seen as related to the world; and how Israel experienced reality in this respect. I will confine these questions to two aspects: history and world order.

I. History

A. One aspect that has gained particular prominence in Old Testament interpretation during the last generation is that Israel viewed Yahweh's relationship to the world as uniquely manifested in history. G. von Rad (who for understandable reasons may be quoted on behalf of many) could say that the various theologies of Israel's history "understand the *world* as the sphere of Yahweh's historical action" (emphasis mine).[1] According to this stance, unfolded in von Rad's *Old Testament Theology* as a whole, Israel's own tradition history is the manifestation of Yahweh's salvific presence in the world.

1. G. von Rad, *Old Testament Theology,* 2 vols. (New York: Harper & Row, 1962-65), 2:336-56, especially 341.

This understanding was universalized in the field of systematic theology by W. Pannenberg's concept of revelation as universal history.[2] Most recently, N. Gottwald has reemphasized and reinterpreted this historical aspect in his monumental work, *The Tribes of Yahweh.*[3] For Gottwald, Yahweh was the symbol of the "Israelite Socio-economic Revolution"[4] against the hierarchically stratified ancient Near Eastern societies and toward the establishment of an egalitarian society in which all had equal access to natural resources and to food production. Yahweh functions as the driving force of a socio-historical process toward egalitarianism during the premonarchic time.

B. The assumption that Israel viewed Yahweh's relationship to the world as uniquely manifest in the sphere of history has become, and is, subject to critical objections. First, Israel's historical awareness was not as unique as once believed. Historical awareness also existed among ancient Near Eastern societies.[5] Moreover, we have reason to suspect that, on the one hand, the sources for the emergence of Israel's own historical awareness cannot be found only in its encounter with Yahweh, and that, on the other hand, this encounter with Yahweh contributed to shaping its other perceptions of reality just as much as it contributed to shaping Israel's emerging historical awareness. Second, history itself is not only seen by the Old Testament as the sphere of Yahweh's presence or revelation; it is also, if not above all, seen as the chaos created by humans, including Israel. Finally, the Old Testament, when articulating Yahweh's relationship to the world, knows about realms such as cosmic order, cyclic time, and human existence. By definition, these spheres are not subsumed under Yahweh's relationship to history. Yahweh is related to them in a direct way (or they are related to Yahweh in a direct way), and this is certainly neither necessarily nor exclusively through the medium of history. In other words, history is neither the sole mode of Yahweh's relationship to reality, nor is it the sole mode of Israel's concept of world. The totality of reality was not perceived by Israel under the category of history alone. Moreover, its concept of world or reality was more inclusive than its concept of history.[6]

2. See, among others, the essays by W. Pannenberg, "Redemptive Event and History," "Kerygma and History," and "Hermeneutic and Universal History," in *Basic Questions in Theology,* vol. 1 (Philadelphia: Fortress Press, 1971), 15-136.

3. N. K. Gottwald, *The Tribes of Yahweh* (New York: Orbis, 1979), especially 667-710; cf. also G. E. Mendenhall, *The Tenth Generation* (Baltimore and London: Johns Hopkins University, 1973).

4. *Tribes of Yahweh,* 700.

5. Bertil Albrektson, *History and the Gods* (Berlinkska Boktryckeriet: Lund, 1967); R. C. Dentan, ed., *The Idea of History in the Ancient Near East,* 4th ed. (New Haven: Yale University Press, 1967).

6. Both the fact that the Old Testament, for the most part, is preoccupied with history, especially Israel's history, and the legitimate place of this fact in interpretation remain unaffected

C. Nevertheless, the Old Testament overwhelmingly sees Yahweh as involved with history, both the history of humanity and, especially, Israel's history. The evidence for this fact, especially in the historical and prophetic books and in many psalms, is massive and well known. What does this fact mean? Certainly, it affirms that Yahweh is God of the world of humans. He is not absent from that world, our world. Humans are not alone with their history. Yahweh is on earth, and not only in heaven. Particularly, he is in human history as its salvific force, even through his judgments.

However, what is considered an advantage of the Old Testament, its realistic understanding of God, may be a major deficit. R. Bultmann,[7] F. Baumgärtel,[8] and F. Hesse,[9] among others, have said that Israel's understanding of Yahweh's presence in history is distinctly determined by specific actualizations in its particular history, i.e., Israel's national-political theocracy with its land, temple, and monarchy. This relationship of Yahweh to an elected nationality and its history must be regarded as a witness to a particularistic view of God and of history, which is not commensurate with a universalist view of history, and certainly not with a view of God's presence in history universally.

These theologians would be correct, if what they say were the only thing to be said about Yahweh's relationship to history and about the understanding of

---

by these statements. This fact, however, does not mean that aspects of reality not governed by the aspect of history are absent in the Old Testament; nor can it mean that they are to be ignored or subsumed under the aspect of history because they occur less frequently or belong to the background of the texts rather than to the level of their explicit interests. A reconstruction of the Hebrew understanding of reality cannot be based on the statistical fact that the majority of our texts are concerned with history. Nor can it be confined to the explicit statements of the texts, unless one assumes that the texts intend to speak about reality as such, which is not the case. However, it would be absurd to understand the historical interest of the texts as being identical with their preunderstanding of reality. In fact, one may question whether an appropriate understanding of Israel's concept of history is possible without a sufficient understanding of Israel's concept of reality. That such an understanding must be reconstructed from our texts is obvious, since nowhere has the Old Testament given us a systematic treatise on this subject. Israel's concept of history was believed to have sprung from its experiences with Yahweh, who acts in or as history. The uniqueness of this experience, however, has been undermined. Therefore, the question arises as to what the matrix for the emergence of historical awareness was. In other words, the emergence of historical experience cannot be assumed as an a priori given. It is itself in need of explanation. Precisely at this point, the question arises concerning the relationship of a concept of reality and the emergence of historical consciousness.

7. R. Bultmann, "Prophecy and Fulfillment," in *EOTH,* 50-75; "The Significance of the Old Testament for the Christian Faith," in *The Old Testament and Christian Faith,* ed. B. Anderson (New York: Harper & Row, 1963), 8-35.

8. F. Baumgärtel, *Verheissung* (Gütersloh: Bertelsmann, 1952); "The Hermeneutical Problem of the Old Testament," in *EOTH,* 134-59.

9. F. Hesse, "The Evaluation and the Authority of Old Testament Texts," in *EOTH,* 285-313; *Abschied von der Heilsgeschichte,* ed. M. Geiger, E. Jüngel, and R. Smend, Theologische Studien 108 (Zürich: Theologischer Verlag, 1971).

Yahweh in the Old Testament. However, the Old Testament points to a different understanding. We must ask whether the Old Testament unequivocally depicts Israel's election and its theocratic-political system as the actualization of Yahweh's presence in history in an ultimate sense at all. In light of this question, different aspects come into focus.

1. The Old Testament is itself, in some texts, e.g., Gen 12:1-3; Amos 9:7; Deut 7:6-8; Isa 56:3-5, well aware of the problem of a particularistic understanding of Israel's election. It struggles with this problem. But indeed, one may doubt whether it has succeeded unequivocally in solving it in its concept of election.

2. More importantly, the historical and prophetic literature, inasmuch as it looks at history, looks at the past, the present, and the future. What most of them, particularly the elohistic, deuteronomic-deuteronomistic, and priestly texts, and certainly the pre-exilic prophets, have in common is a keen awareness that Israel's present and future cannot be taken for granted on the basis of its past, in spite of Yahweh's promises and in spite of certain periods, such as the Jerusalemite monarchy, in which one could rely on such inner-historical manifestations. Surely the Old Testament testifies to the theological relevance of the breakdowns of historical eras, the discontinuities in Israel's history, and the abandonment of form after form of its historical existence as the result of Yahweh's judgments, just as much as it testifies to Yahweh's abiding loyalty to his promises. Israel was prevented from looking ultimately at the institutions of its historical existence as the ground of security for its present and future. Yahweh could create these institutions and then take them away, just as he could give Isaac to Abraham and then take him away again. Certainly, Yahweh gave Israel historical existence, but that history could never have any authority in its own right, or be the ground for a predictable future or for the continuity of its historical institutions. None of them, not even Yahweh's own institutions, was sacrosanct. Nor was tradition history sacrosanct, in whatever form one may conceive it. Neither history nor tradition history has divine authority by virtue of being God's creation, or by virtue of its traditionality. The discontinuities in Israel's tradition history are just as telling theologically as the forms of continuity. Israel's knowledge of Yahweh maintains that Yahweh is the criterion of history, both Israel's and humanity's, and not that history is the criterion for and the basis of the presence of God in the world. G. von Rad asserts that "the historical acts by which Yahweh founded the community of Israel were absolute."[10] This statement seems to require reinterpretation, which will be part of the concern of this chapter.

3. Finally, von Rad himself pointed to what he called Yahweh's ever-increasing "hiddenness" and the "history of God's progressing retreat."[11] Here Yahweh is perceived as hiding ever deeper within the historical disasters. Thus, an under-

10. *Old Testament Theology,* vol. 2, 104.
11. *Old Testament Theology,* vol. 2, 374-82.

standing of history as the ultimate manifestation of an inner-historical continuity, especially as salvation history, broke down completely.[12] Israel's history did not simply fail as history, it failed because of Yahweh, so that Israel would look and wait for Yahweh and quit hoping for the future reenactment of its past.

1.-3. To be sure, not all the Old Testament texts reveal this understanding. However, those that do can be taken as the Old Testament's own canon for its understanding of Israel's (tradition) history. They reveal that when looking at its history, or at the history of the nations, Israel encountered Yahweh as the *crisis* of all history. Thus, Israel had to give up mythologizing its own historical institutions and looking at them as the scene of a perfect world. Moreover, Israel had to accept history for what it was, not as the stage of the revelation of God's ultimate glory, but as the realm in which the struggle for the meaning of creation is waged. The vision of the ultimate glory was to be found elsewhere.

II. World Order

The theological interpretation of God's relationship to the world has long been governed, at least in Old Testament studies, by our preoccupation with history. We have believed this preoccupation to be justifiable because of the intensive attention to history in the Old Testament. Under the influence of this preoccupation, however, we have by and large underestimated the role of another aspect in the Old Testament, namely, Yahweh's relationship to and presence in the order of the world. Here I refer to the Old Testament texts regarding the creation and sustenance of the world by God.

To be sure, this aspect does not command as much space in the pages of the Old Testament as does its attention to history. Even so, the texts refer to it much more than is commonly assumed. More importantly, the statistical infrequency says little about the importance of Yahweh's relationships to history and to world order in the total horizon of an Old Testament theology.

A. The Role of Cosmology in Old Testament Studies

Space does not permit us to review thoroughly the literature in which the aspect of cosmology has played a role in Old Testament studies. Serious studies regarding Israel's understanding of the world as space and time, or aspects thereof, are few in number and of a fairly recent date. To be sure, most of our Old Testament

12. See L. Perlitt, "Die Verborgenheit Gottes," in *Probleme Biblischer Theologie, Fest. G. von Rad*, ed. H. W. Wolff (Munich: Kaiser, 1971), 376-82.

theologies deal with the doctrine of the creation and sustenance of the world. Even so, the special aspect of the theological significance of the structure of the world has received little attention. One must go back to the theologies of L. Köhler and W. Eichrodt in order to find explicit paragraphs on this aspect. Many authors ignore it altogether. Three main reasons for this fact can be discerned. None of them can be regarded as acceptable any longer.

One reason is that Old Testament scholarship has understood the cosmologically influenced passages in the Old Testament as reflexes of Israel's encounter with the rest of the ancient Near East. They are not expressions of genuine Yahwism; hence, they are syncretistically compromised and theologically irrelevant. The cyclic worldview, especially, was considered as the paradigmatic expression of the ongoing emanation of the ever-presence of personified divine forces and, therefore, as anti-Yahwistic in principle. The reasons for this view of Israel's uniqueness are well known, as is the theological movement accountable for it. It is certainly true that Israel's understanding of the world as creation was distinctly different from other ancient Near Eastern cosmogonies, especially those of Mesopotamia. Nevertheless, Canaanite perspectives were adopted by Yahwism in central respects, and by no means only in peripheral ones, and not simply rejected. Moreover, the indisputable fact that Yahwism, on the basis of its creation theology, rejected the view of the world as divine drama does not mean that it could not view the cosmic order itself, even the cyclic one, as created by Yahweh.

More than anything else, there is a compelling ground for why Israel had to see cosmic order and Yahweh as related to one another: Israel's agrarian existence in Palestine over centuries from the time of the settlement onward. This fact is fundamental. It alone shows that regardless of where one would draw the lines, e.g., vis-à-vis Baalism, Israel had to accept a worldview that was concerned with cosmic and natural order and with cyclic reality. The adaptation of such a worldview by Israel was as necessary as its agrarian existence was fundamental. It was a necessity resulting from Israel's own existence, and not the more or less unavoidable result of Israel's exposure to its Canaanite neighbors. Moreover, this type of perennial existence had its own structure, which was different from the ups and downs of Israel's history.[13] Yahweh had to be fundamentally associated with this type of existence if he was to be related to Israel's reality in the first place. This type of agrarian existence is the basic reason why we have Canaanite traditions and influences in the Old Testament. Precisely for this reason, such texts need to be reem-

13. When discussing, e.g., the reasons for Israel's complaints and laments, we mention war together with natural catastrophes. This combination suggests that there is no essential difference between the two types of experience. One may ask, however, whether in a natural disaster Israel experienced something that was essentially different from its experience of war. One must also inquire of the reasons for these different types of experience. The same questions can be raised with respect to the hymns in which Israel praises Yahweh's creation on the one hand and his acts in history on the other.

phasized in our interpretation, and not half-heartedly left to the side because they are suspect of fraudulent, syncretistic Yahwism. They must be regarded as expressions of a genuine Yahwism, whether or not this Yahwism directly appropriated them from outside or generated them from within by analogy to generic traditions prevalent in its environment.

A second reason for the neglect of Israel's cosmology in Old Testament theology is the assumption that the notions associated with cosmology, especially as expressed by words such as "cosmos," "land," and "nature," are foreign to Israel's understanding of the world. These notions are either said to belong to the ontological shell which Israel shared with her environment, a shell that contributed nothing to Israel's worldview; or they are said to be dependent on our own textbooks of natural science, the ancestors of which are found in the cosmologies of the Greek philosophers of nature, i.e., the Ionians, Eleades, and Pythagoreans. G. von Rad, speaking for many, could say:

> Discussion of the general concept of the shape of the world and its parts, and of the being of man and his physical and mental characteristics, lies, in our view, outside the province of a theology of the Old Testament, because, like much else, these concepts form a part of the data conditioned of the general culture and mental climate which Israel had in common with the majority of the peoples in the ancient East. But it can never be over-emphasized that our current concept of "world" was foreign to ancient Israel. There are profound reasons for the fact that she did not have at her disposal the equally serviceable concept of the Greek "cosmos." . . . We have to seek the reason for this in the fact that for Israel the "world" was much less Being than Event. . . . Israel did not see the world as an ordered organism in repose. . . .[14]

A critical analysis of this statement would be very interesting. In this writer's opinion, von Rad draws the wrong conclusion from correct observations and legitimate concerns, and ends up designing a theological model in which "the shape of the world" is declared altogether irrelevant for Old Testament theology. As if he wanted to clarify a misunderstanding, von Rad addressed this issue again in a separate essay in 1964.[15] In this essay, he emphasized that we are in danger of insufficiently interpreting Israel's understanding of the world as long as we are merely concerned with its theology of history, and not also with "what we call Nature" (144). "Certainly the faith of Israel did not regard the structure of the universe [*Weltbild*] as a matter of indifference" (146). In fact, Israel's faith in Yahweh the Creator's incomparability generated an understanding according to which the world was seen exclusively as created and, therefore, radically demythologized, and at the same time totally em-

14. *Old Testament Theology,* vol. 1 (New York: Harper & Row, 1962), 152.

15. "Some Aspects of the Old Testament World-view," in *The Problem of the Hexateuch,* trans. E. W. T. Dicken (New York: McGraw-Hill, 1966), 144-65.

braced by Yahweh (150). This worldview can be detected, e.g., in Israel's attitude toward demons, sickness, and death (153). Ultimately, it stood in the service of Israel's own self-identification (155f.). Most importantly, Israel could not exchange it for the view of a "cosmos" that exists in its own right and on the basis of eternal cosmic laws inherent in it (152). It was because of Yahweh that, epistemologically speaking, Israel capitulated in front of the merciless darkness (158f.) which makes a universal understanding of the world impossible.

These reflections are profound and, in many respects, indisputable. However, von Rad closes the door to the theological interpretation of the cosmologically oriented texts at the exact moment he affirms the need for Israel's understanding of "nature." In this regard, he intensifies his position expressed earlier in his *Old Testament Theology.* This position, however, is not convincing. The cosmologically oriented texts deserve a different interpretation, not only because of their statistical visibility but also because they are part of Israel's expression of faith in Yahweh. In this expression of faith, the shell cannot be separated from the core as readily as von Rad proposes. Most importantly, however, why should the "cosmos" and its "laws" have been excluded from Israel's worldview rather than included in its theology of creation, and thereby demythologized just as much as everything else? The question is, then, whether Israel, precisely because of its Yahweh-faith and not in spite of it, had an understanding in which nothing less than the cosmic order itself was seen as created, sustained, and embraced by Yahweh; and if this were the case, why the autonomy of the cosmic order did not result in its elimination. Why should Yahwism have conceded such an autonomy, particularly one concerned with the most universal realm of reality conceivable? The pursuit of this question will open the way to a new and comprehensive interpretation of the theological significance of Israel's cosmology. Such an interpretation should have far-reaching consequences for Old Testament theology and, indeed, for biblical theology.

This conclusion does not affect the legitimate warning that Israel's cosmological erudition was different from ours. This warning is a truism. It pertains to all the aspects of the biblical literature insofar as their interpretation is guided by historical exegesis. Therefore, it is one thing to affirm that Israel's understanding of "nature" and "cosmos" was different from ours, and quite another to deny altogether the existence or relevance of any such understanding on Israel's part. Ultimately, Israel had compelling reasons for such an understanding. The fact that these reasons were profoundly theological in nature should be regarded as the vantage point for the dialogue with modern science.

The third and perhaps most important reason for the neglect of cosmological studies in Old Testament theology has been the subordination of the theology of creation to the theology of history. Especially under the influence of the interpretation of the kerygma of the historical writings, creation was seen as strictly in the service of Israel's history, its land, and its existence. The theology of creation is the etiology of Israel. The virtually unanimous verdict on this issue is overwhelming, and its authority has been virtually canonical. L. Köhler says: "The thought that God created the world is of late date, however. It is not a promise but a deduction from the Old Testament revelation."[16] He also says:

> The creation of the world by God in the Old Testament is no independent fact; creation is intended to be the opening of history. . . . In other words, *the Creation in the Old Testament does not belong to the sphere of natural science but the history of man.* (author's own emphasis)[17]

W. Eichrodt says:

> The creation is thus from the very first integrated into a spiritual process in which each individual event acquires its value from the overall meaning of the whole; that is to say, into history. . . . both the Yahwist and the Priestly writers *make the creation the starting point of a history. . . .* (author's own emphasis)[18]

G. von Rad states: "Creation is regarded as a work of Yahweh in history, a work within time."[19] W. Zimmerli, explaining why in his theology "the section dealing with Yahweh as creator of the world was not placed at the beginning," says:

> It is hardly possible to overlook the fact that in what the Old Testament has to say the "deliverance of Israel from Egypt," an event in the midst of history, furnishes the primary orientation. With this as the starting point, however, Israel comes to speak evermore clearly of the creator, a confession it was called upon to make in its encounter with the fully developed myths of the Canaanite environment. In like manner, the introductory "I believe in God, the Father" in the first article of the Christian creed, which precedes the confession of the "Creator of heaven and earth" cannot be understood without the second article.[20]

B. Anderson summarizes: "In the Bible creation opens to the horizon of the future. Time rather than space, history rather than cosmology is the central concern."[21] One must add that, for all the emphasis on time and history over against space and cosmos, the aspect of *cyclic* time has suffered a fate even worse than that of space in Old Testament interpretation. Its theological significance has been either overlooked or ignored and, for the most part, rejected outright.

16. L. Köhler, *Old Testament Theology,* tr. A. S. Todd (Philadelphia: Westminster, 1957), 85.

17. Köhler, *Theology,* 87.

18. *Theology of the Old Testament,* 5th ed., vol. 2 (Philadelphia: Westminster Press, 1975), 100-101.

19. *Old Testament Theology,* vol. 1, 139.

20. *Old Testament Theology in Outline* (Atlanta: John Knox Press, 1978), 32.

21. *Creation versus Chaos* (New York: Association Press, 1967), 110.

There is no need to affirm the points in these positions that are exegetically well substantiated. Instead, a number of critical observations are in order. First, the proposition that the cosmological statements of the Old Testament are extraneous to its theology is subject to contention on the grounds already discussed. These numerous references are clearly related to Yahweh's relationship to Israel and to the world as well. Of special importance is the aspect of time as it relates to the cosmic space of the ordered world, besides the aspect of time related to history. Second, the thesis that Israel's theology of creation is subordinate to its theology of history, because it emerged after that theology of history and out of it, is fallacious. This thesis equates the systematic relationship of two factors with the chronological sequence of their appearance and, indeed, subjects the determination of the former to that of the latter. This type of argument has no validity. The case seems to be presented better when one points out that, e.g., in the Pentateuch, creation is regarded as the beginning of history, and hence as part of our overall horizon identified as history. In this argument, our sources are said to have a systematic perspective, regardless of the fact that Israel's theology of history is older than its theology of creation. Such a perspective in which creation has its place at the beginning of history implies, on the one hand, that the beginning of history lies in nothing less than the moment of creation and, on the other hand, that creation, inasmuch as it is also a present reality and not merely a past event, is present in the mode of human history. However defensible such an interpretation may be, it is questionable whether it captures all of what needs to be said, let alone what is decisive, about the systematic perspective implied in our sources. The fact that they see creation as the beginning of history does not mean that they also consider actual human history as the ongoing representation of creation. Nor does it mean that creation has no mode of ongoing existence in distinction from or opposite history. Indeed, the priestly account in Genesis 1 not only speaks about creation as the beginning of history. It also speaks about the beginning in the past of a presence which remains an ever-present reality, and does not become a past because it happened in the beginning. This presence has a beginning but is not relegated to the past because of this beginning. Nor is this presence determined by the human history that began with it or grew out of it. Therefore, it must be questioned whether Genesis 1 understands creation only as the beginning of history and exclusively in the service of history. Moreover, it must be asked if Genesis 1 speaks of creation as a reality *sui generis* and vis-à-vis history, a reality that reflects the criterion for the meaning of history just as much as it represents the beginning of history. Our consistent systematic subordination of the Old Testament theology of creation to its theology of history seems to amount, at best, to a truncated view of the Old Testament's theology of creation if not to a reversal of the true relationship of the two theologies altogether.

The defense of the systematic priority of the theology of history is not strengthened when one maintains that in the Pentateuch creation is seen as the etiology of Israel's own history and existence. This may be the case. However, such an interpretation means little as long as it does not address the all-important question implied in it as to whether the purpose of the creation of the world is the history and existence of Israel, or whether the purpose of Israel's history and existence is to point to and actualize the meaning of creation. In the former, creation would have its meaning by standing in the service of Israel. In the latter, the meaning of the history and existence of Israel would be to stand in the service of God's creation of the world. This alternative cannot be dissolved with a "both-and." In fact, many interpreters will readily admit that Israel's election is to serve God's creation. But then one would still have to come to grips with the affirmation that creation is the etiology of Israel (which is not exactly identical with the earlier affirmation), because this affirmation allows for the implication that creation stands in the service of Israel. And as long as this interpretation does not address this alternative, it remains irrelevant for the essential problem. In any case, if the texts themselves should propose or imply that the purpose of creation is Israel, creation itself could at best be understood in a formal function: as the partial realm and the cosmic framework for the self-realization of the people of God. But it would have no substantive value in itself. Therefore, its existence in its own right could be ignored. This is precisely what happened in the field of Old Testament theology and throughout much of our own history. We have lived our own history *in* creation, but without regard *for* creation. Moreover, the question as to what should be the proper foundation of and criterion for such a self-realization of the elect remains unanswered in this interpretation as well. Even if the theological answer given by our texts is not everywhere clear, unified, or even sufficient, even if the question is not fully addressed, and even if our interpretation of the texts must be improved, the interrelationship of the theologies of creation and election in the texts is on the whole beyond dispute. But it seems that any interpretation of this relationship must face up to the Old Testament's theology of creation in its entirety and in its own right, i.e., to its substantive nature which is more than and different from its functional definition alone.

What has just been said is also true for the discussion of the relationship between the theologies of creation and of liberation in the Old Testament. For this discussion, the facts of the *historical* precedence of the latter and of its emergence from the former are again irrelevant. Israel's soteriology undoubtedly preceded and eventually expanded into its protology. But does this fact mean that its protology must stand in the service of its soteriology? Or that ultimately its soteriology came to stand in the service of its protology? The same objections must be raised against the virtually canonical assumption that Israel's experience of liberation was *theologically* fundamental. It is true that in its literature Israel experienced Yahweh as a liberator God and itself as a liberated people, and that this experience became constitutive for the theology of the exclusive covenantal relationship between Yahweh and his people. Does this mean, however, that the theology of liberation had to become the foundation for all of Israel's theology? The composition of the Pentateuch, e.g., does not necessarily support this assumption. In it, the exodus story proper is short and, more importantly, stands in the middle. It presupposes what is said in Genesis, and aims toward Sinai and through the wandering, toward the settlement in Joshua. While it is certainly the presupposition for covenant and settlement, the deliverance was not in itself an end and goal. Even as one recognizes the covenant and the settlement as this end and goal, the question still remains as to what the criterion is by which the meaning of this goal can be determined. Where do we find the theological aspects that illuminate this meaning? Or are we to assume that this meaning is inherent in the fact of Israel's settlement and life in the land as such? On what grounds, then, are we to establish what is theologically fundamental for Israel? On the basis of that which is the presupposition (the exodus) for the following (the covenant and settlement)? On the basis of that which is the goal and fulfillment (the covenant and settlement) of the presupposition (the exodus)? On the basis of that which illuminates and qualifies the meaning of the fulfillment, and with it the meaning of the history and existence of God's people, and if so, what would this be? We must clarify these questions if we want to arrive at a substantial systematic judgment about what is theologically fundamental in the Old Testament. In such a process, the relationship of theological *topoi* such as liberation, covenant, settlement, life in the land, history of the nations, and creation and sustenance of the world must be clarified systematically. This task amounts to nothing less than the discernment of the theological system within the totality of the theological aspects that emerged in Israel's history. Only if we discern such an identifiable systemic coherence in the Old Testament theologies are we entitled to speak of an Old Testament theology in the singular. In such a theological systematization of Israel's historically generated theologies, the Old Testament's theology of history will certainly have its place. Yet, a fresh assessment of the theology of creation in its own right is equally important.

Despite the verdict against the theological relevance of Israel's cosmology in the mainstream of Old Testament studies, aspects of this topic have been addressed during the last two decades with various, and so it seems increasing, degrees of attention to its theological significance. In 1961, S. Herrmann illuminated the pre-stages of Genesis 1.[22] He pointed to the order of cosmic macroforms, to the description of the world in lists, and to heaven as a distinct realm in cosmic space. He also affirmed that Genesis 1 must be considered, along with similar early international endeavors, as a scientific document in its own right, "besides its theological appreciation" (418). In 1962, O. Kaiser showed how the course of the day and the year were understood in Egypt and Ugarit as repetitions of the primordial creation event, and how, out of the experience of the crises of the cosmic and societal order, the idea of a future end of the world that was analogous to its

22. "Die Naturlehre des Schöpfungsberichtes," *TLZ* 86 (1961): 413-24.

beginning emerged.[23] In contrast to the mythological perception of reality which saw the world as a unity, Israel saw the unity in God himself, and the world as creation vis-à-vis God.

In 1964, W. H. Schmidt[24] could, with reference to the interdependence of the order of creation and the cultic order, say that for **P** God is "a god of order" (168). Genesis 1 emphasizes the formation of the creation out of chaos (179). This chapter is deeply reflected theological doctrine (180) in which scientific knowledge and theological affirmation have become a unity (181). However, even though creation and sustenance are distinguished in it, nature and history are not separate realms. Rather, **P** treats "nature like history" (185). To speak of nature means, therefore, to speak of history (187).

In 1965, K. Koch presented a penetrating interpretation of the issue under discussion.[25] He says that in Memphis the creative word secured the presence of the creator in the created, and not only his position vis-à-vis it (264). The divine word and human planning correspond to one another (267). So do the natural and historical realms (268). The unity of the world is grounded in the unity of God (270). The creator God is a *deus revelatus* (260). In the Old Testament, מִשְׁפָּט, צדק and אמת exist before the creation. They are mediated through the heaven, the relay-sphere, from the realm of Yahweh above the heaven to the realm of humans underneath the heaven (275). However, creation is nothing but the preparation for history (278). The self-revelation of God takes place in human history, not through the initial creation (281). Furthermore, although Israel knew of temporary salvific orders, it knew of no fixed cosmos because the chaotically endangered world remains forever dependent on God's sustenance.

In 1968, H. H. Schmid presented the thesis of an all-encompassing world order in the ancient Near East.[26] Its nature is captured by what the Hebrew language calls צדק. Of this world order, the cosmic, political, religious, social, and ethical aspects are parts. For the Old Testament itself, however, "order" is a basically "historical," i.e., an always changeable, reality. C. Westermann repeatedly came close to recognizing the element of cyclic reality in this order. With regard to the genealogies in Genesis 5, he pointed out that the cyclic pattern schematically applied to the description of each generation in the genealogical series. Furthermore, he correctly emphasized both the interdependence of the constant and variable elements in all the phases of the history of humanity and that "there are at work in every event elements of the stable, always and everywhere the same, which

23. *Die Mythische Bedeutung des Meeres in Ägypten, Ugarit und Israel,* BZAW 78 (Berlin: Töpelmann, 1962).

24. *Die Schöpfungsgeschichte der Priesterschrift,* WMANT 17 (Neukirchen-Vluyn: Neukirchener Verlag, 1964).

25. "Wort und Einheit des Schöpfergottes in Memphis und Jerusalem," *ZTK* 62 (1965): 251-93.

26. *Gerechtigkeit als Weltordnung,* BHT 40 (Tübingen: Mohr, 1968).

are common to all humankind at all times and which render questionable a science of history that prescinds from these constants."[27] (See also his books *Beginning and End in the Bible*[28] and *Blessing in the Bible and the Life of the Church,*[29] in which the blessing power of God is described in terms very much reflecting the human life-cycle.) At the same time, Westermann subordinated both the constants and the variables to history: *"Erst beides miteinander wirkt Geschichte."*

This combination of constants and variables has come to play a strong role, *mutatis mutandis,* in two recent publications by O. H. Steck.[30] Steck pays serious attention to the theological significance of the cosmology expressed in Genesis 1. He interprets the intention of the structure of Genesis 1 as guided by the two aspects of cosmic space and cosmic time: the space to which the realms of creation are allocated universally, and the universal time through which the existence of these realms is secured forever. Both together provide the condition for the emergence and continued existence of life (199-223). Steck's interpretation indicates a significant change in orientation, or the possibility for it. Not only are cosmological aspects taken seriously theologically, but the relationship between creation and history in essence appears reversed. In systematic perspective, creation appears as the presupposition for history, even Israel's history (222), irrespective of the fact that the notion of creation grew out of Israel's experience of (liberation-) history.[31]

The argumentation pursued so far raises the suspicion that we may be back in M. Eliade's *Cosmos and History.*[32] Indeed, this topic is exactly what is under discussion. However, "cosmos" can no longer be understood as mythology ("the myth of the eternal return") versus "history" understood as theology. Indeed, it should be understood theologically as cosmic reality, just as historical reality itself is understood theologically. Both cosmos and history are understood nonmythologically under the aspect of Israel's theology of creation.[33] Methodologically, it

27. *Genesis 1–11,* trans. John Scullion (Minneapolis: Augsburg, 1984), 347.

28. Trans. Keith Crim, Facet Books, Biblical Series 31 (Philadelphia: Fortress Press, 1972).

29. Trans. Keith Crim (Philadelphia: Fortress Press, 1978).

30. *Der Schöpfungsbericht der Priesterschrift,* FRLANT 15 (Göttingen: Vandenhoeck und Ruprecht, 1975), esp. pp. 199-223; and *World and Environment,* Biblical Encounter Series (Nashville: Abingdon Press, 1980).

31. Without seeking to be exhaustive, cf. R. J. Clifford, *The Cosmic Mountain in Canaan and the Old Testament* (Cambridge, MA: Harvard University, 1972); R. Luyster, "Wind and Water: Cosmogonic Symbolism in the Old Testament," *ZAW* 93 (1981): 1-10; R. L. Cohn, *The Shape of Sacred Space: Four Biblical Studies* (Chico: Scholars Press, 1981).

32. New York: Harper & Row, 1959.

33. The semantic question of the definition of myth(ology) can be left aside in this context as long as both cosmos and history are seen in juxtaposition and not in opposition, and as long as their common determination as nonmythological is derived from an interpretation of the demythologized nature of Israel's perception of all reality, especially of creation. For the theological understanding of myth, see, e.g., W. Pannenberg, *Christentum und Mythos* (Gütersloh: Gerd Mohn, 1972).

is also no longer appropriate to distinguish between history of religions and theology by assigning one segment of reality to the former, another to the latter. All of reality must be understood theologically as well as religio-historically. Likewise, cosmology in modern natural science cannot remain excluded from theological understanding. In such an understanding, modern cosmology cannot be subordinated to human history on this globe, regardless of how universally this history is conceived. It is a basic fact that our history depends on the existence of this globe in our solar system, while the solar system, let alone what lies beyond it, does not depend on our global history. We could blow up this globe, and the universe around us would scarcely take notice and would go on existing. The fact of our cosmic existence is, therefore, of fundamental theological significance. It cannot be treated as myth, nor can it be relegated to theologically irrelevant natural science, a step parallel to its illicit relegation from theology to the history of religions.

B. The Significance of Cosmic Space and Cyclic Time for the Theology of the Old Testament

In the following, we focus on some aspects of cosmic space and cyclic time that seem to be of particular significance for the theology of the Old and probably the New Testament. A comprehensive treatment is not intended, although it appears to be an urgent desideratum. Nor can the host of passages that would have to play a role in such an endeavor be mentioned. Magnalia must, therefore, suffice for the moment.

While the traditio-historical realities in our texts cannot be ignored, by design they do not constitute the orientation for these reflections. Our descriptions of the traditio-historical processes can illuminate the facts, both the continuities and the discontinuities, and also to some extent where and why certain theologies succeeded while others did not. Tradition history can explain the facticity of the process, even of the theological process. But it seems that it cannot explain as such which of the theologies that emerged in its course becomes the ground and criterion for all the other ones. The Old Testament has not given us an answer to this question. This is the main reason why the Old Testament is not identical with an Old Testament theology. Yet the quest for the theology of the Old Testament is indispensable. This quest must be guided by the search for that theology among the theological traditions of the Old Testament that can be shown to be the foundation and criterion for all the other ones, i.e., of Israel's theological tradition history. In such a pursuit, attention must also be paid to the assumptions presupposed in the texts, and not only to the contingent messages of the texts.

Finally, a theology of Israel's cosmology with all its elements ought to be understood from the outset as predicated upon Israel's theology of creation. Cosmic order is created and sustained by Yahweh. Creation and sustenance do not mean that there is no cosmic order.

1. Creation as Structured by Cosmic Space

The Old Testament traditions do not merely affirm that the world was created by God; they affirm specifically that in its creation the world was ordered as structured space. With regard to Genesis 1, this has always been observed. W. Eichrodt speaks of the "marvellous purposefulness in the structure of the cosmos" and the "architectonic organization of the works of creation."[34] E. Jacob describes the creation in Genesis 1 as "an architect intending to build a house inside which new inhabitants should be entirely at their ease; this house must be substantial, sheltered from dangers, pleasant, with a measure of luxury not forbidden there. . . . The architect is not confused with the creation. . . ."[35] L. Köhler adds: "[Creation] is no enigmatical impenetrable affair; there is no more rational page in the Bible than that which contains the account of creation."[36] This aspect plays an overriding role both in O. H. Steck's *Der Schöpfungsbericht der Priesterschrift,* which carries on the discussion with the works of W. H. Schmidt[37] and of C. Westermann,[38] and in Steck's *World and Environment.* In the latter work, Steck emphasizes this point for the "legion" (141) of examples from the entire ancient Near Eastern and Old Testament literature. He illustrates it once more with Psalm 104 (78-89).

Indeed, the notion of creation as structured space is not only found in the priestly tradition. It is also found in the wisdom literature,[39] the prophetic literature,[40] and especially in the Psalms.[41]

Many of these texts reveal the perception of a structured world in their very

34. *Theology of the Old Testament,* vol. 2, 109.

35. *Theology of the Old Testament* (New York: Harper and Row, 1958), 136-37.

36. *Theology,* 86.

37. *Schöpfungsgeschichte.*

38. *Genesis 1–11.*

39. E.g., Job 38–39; Eccl 1:4-11; and Prov 8:22-31.

40. E.g., Hos 2:23f. (*NRSV* 2:21f.).

41. E.g., Pss 33:4-9; 65:6-14 (*NRSV* 65:5-13); 74:12-17; 89:6-19 (*NRSV* 89:5-18); 104; 136:4-9; and 148:1. The notion is at least recognized, though not unfolded, in L. Sabourin, *The Psalms* (New York: Alba House, 1974), 74, 76, 78. Unfortunately, it plays no role in H.-J. Kraus's *The Theology of the Psalms* (Minneapolis: Augsburg, 1979). Kraus's discussion of the theology of creation in the Psalms is dictated entirely by the correlation of Israel's history with creation, and by the epistemological question concerning the setting from which the knowledge of God, creation, etc., originated: Israel's own history. These observations are certainly legitimate. But they are no substitute for the question as to *what* the Psalms say about creation itself, especially not in a "theology of the Psalms." The indisputable fact that the object of faith is the creator, and neither the act nor the existence of creation (64), does not mean that the substantive understanding of created reality is irrelevant for faith and theology.

own literary structure. They also reveal that the total world is perceived as a structured unity. Just as the texts are holistically conceived as units in which the elements are systematically related to one another, so the world itself is perceived as a universal system, a cosmos, in which every realm has its proper place and function, including humans.

It is well known that this cosmology shows variations in its specifics. But scarcely do such variations relativize Israel's keen interest in perceiving the world as a structured whole. This interest cannot be explained as an aesthetic preoccupation. Nor is the reference to its ancient Near Eastern and Egyptian origins sufficient, true as this may be. The texts before us are deeply embedded in Israel's Yahweh-traditions, and their cosmological interest must have played a profound role in Israel's unceasing effort to understand Yahweh. In these efforts, Israel walked a tightrope. On the one hand, it had to avoid mixing the creator with the created. On the other hand, it had to avoid removing the creator's presence from his creation, or removing creation from the presence of the creator. If, however, that presence understood was above all as creation out of chaos, then it was indispensable that the world was understood first of all as systemically structured space, or else it could not be understood as creation at all. The assumption that Israel saw the unity in Yahweh, and not in the world, is not correct. It confuses unity with uniqueness or incomparability. Against this assumption, we must assert that Israel perceived creation as a structured unity because of Yahweh the creator, and not apart from or in spite of him. It saw Yahweh and the structure of the world as being related in an ultimate way in which the unity of creation was just as important for the creator as the oneness of the creator was for the creation. By his oneness alone, the creator is the ground and guarantor of the unity and wholeness of the world. Without the oneness of the creator, the world would be ultimately chaotic. It would be a "no-world." However, in the unity and wholeness of the structured creation, as opposed to chaos, this creation reflects the presence of the creator in the world. Without this unity, Yahweh would be without a world. There would be no creator. Israel knew about Yahweh's hiddenness, and about anarchy on earth. But never did it say that Yahweh was hiding within the disintegration of his structured creation, or that he was absent from his creation. Israel, therefore, had compelling reasons for adopting a universal cosmology. Ultimately, these reasons were inherent in its own understanding of Yahweh the creator, and not merely the result of its polemical dialogue with Canaan. It is said that Deuteronomy proclaims the oneness of Yahweh, of Israel, and of its land and worship. This is true, but more is at stake. Israel perceived the structure of the world as the ultimate theodicy of Yahweh. If this structure fails, Yahweh fails, and nothing matters any more.[42]

42. On the unity of creation, see W. Eichrodt, *Theology,* vol. 2, 112; L. Sabourin, *Psalms,* 78; and E. K. von Nordheim, "Der grosse Hymnus des Echnaton und Psalm 104. Gott und Mensch im Ägypten der Amarnazeit und in Israel," in *Theologie und Menschenbild, Fest.* Ewald Link (Frankfurt: Peter Lang, 1978), 51-72, esp. 65-66.

In this discussion of the theological significance of Old Testament cosmology, one aspect deserves special attention: the relationship of heaven and earth. It is well known that the Hebrew cosmology distinguished primarily between the macrospheres of "heaven," "earth," and "sea." To these, the sphere of Sheol may be added. It is also well known that this cosmology incorporates subdivisions within these macrospheres and reflects variations and diversity in details.[43] What is of particular interest in this context is the formula "heaven and earth," which occurs about seventy-five times in our texts.[44] This formula was deeply entrenched in the Egyptian, Akkadian, and West-Semitic traditions, and Israel inherited it from them.[45] There is agreement that the formula is cosmological in nature, and that it means the universe in unity, but also that it expresses a bipartite division of the universe, if not a bipolarity or antithesis within it. The problem with these descriptions of the formula is that they explain little.

First of all, there is a tension between two conceptual perceptions of the world. On the one hand, the world is perceived as a structured unity, especially in Israel's theology of creation. On the other hand, the world is perceived as a bipartite structure, as the combination of two separate cosmic realms. The latter perception is expressed by the formula "heaven and earth." In view of these two contending perceptions, the question arises as to why the view of the polarity of the world became and remained prominent, as evident in the expression "heaven and earth," whereas an expression for the perception of the oneness of creation was not similarly developed, let alone given priority over the dual expression for the bipolar view of creation.[46] The prominence of this dual perception of the world is not inevitable. We should, therefore, assume that there was a basic reason for the predominance of the bipolar view of creation which is evidenced linguistically, despite the equally available perception of the unity of creation.[47]

43. For the latest summaries, see H. H. Schmid, "ארץ," *THAT* 1, 228-36; J. A. Soggin, "שׁמים," *THAT* 2, 965-70; Bergmann/Ottosson, "ארץ," *TDOT* 1, 388-405.

44. H. H. Schmid, *THAT* 1, 229.

45. See Bergmann/Ottosson, *TDOT* 1, 388-97.

46. It is obvious that exegetically the affirmations of the polarity and of the unity of creation would have to be grounded on different types of textual evidence, a difficult but intriguing task which cannot be pursued here.

47. This problem was recognized by C. Westermann (*Genesis 1–11,* 101). Westermann's explanation is that languages did not form a word for the larger whole that was meant with the polar expression. Words from later languages, such as the Greek *cosmos,* the Latin *universum,* the German *All,* are *Ersatzworte,* "substitutionary words." Their abstract character demonstrates a limitation of the human *Begriffsvermögen*, "faculty of apprehension." A bipolar expression should reflect a perception of polarity. Such a bipolar perception corresponding to the bipolar expression is not assumed by Westermann. Hence, for Westermann, the tension exists between perception and expression, and not between two competing perceptions. As a result, the problem is merely linguistic in nature. By contrast, I see the problem as substantive in nature, as competition between two perceptions of reality in which one was prevalent over the other. Also, I assume that the Hebrew language was capable of forming one word for the perceived wholeness of the world,

The most obvious reason for the bipolar view seems to be found in the fact that, through its tradition history, our formula was so deeply entrenched universally and so fixed that any further linguistic development toward a uniform expression was either unnecessary or impossible. This argument has considerable weight. One should indeed concede that semantically the formula exerted a force that greatly restricted the possibilities of alternative expressions or of its replacement. Even so, the tension between the two perceptions of the world, i.e., the unity of creation consisting of two realms, remains. Ultimately, the fact of the tradition history of the formula as such does not explain why the totality was seen in two parts.

There is a second reason why the bipolar formula "heaven and earth" is in need of explanation. It is the fact that the structure of the world as depicted in the ancient Near Eastern and Old Testament texts does not necessitate the predominance of a bipolar view and expression. Genesis 1, e.g., could have said in the superscription that God created the realm above the firmament, the realm below it, and the earth. Ps 33:6-8 subdivides between the "heavens," "the waters of the sea," and "the earth."[48] Particularly, the triadic view of heaven-earth-sea or of heaven-earth-netherworld[49] demonstrates that, from a cosmological point of view, the bipolar formula "heaven and earth" was not the only option for expressing the unity of the created world. The bipolar formula represents, therefore, more than a correct systematic formula for the cosmology. We are consequently confronted with a twofold need for explaining the formula. On the one hand, we must explain why the world was seen and expressed in a bipartite division. On the other hand, we must explain why this bipartite division was chosen despite the different cosmological options.

Three things seem clear. First, the formula always presupposes a spatial view of the world. It means above all the bipartite view of universal space. Secondly, this view is systematic in nature. It is more than merely descriptive, and more than the result of an additive enumeration of the sum total of all the realms. Thirdly, the bipartite view of the space of creation is not the only form in which Israel perceived the creation of the world. Therefore, the reason for this view cannot lie in the specific fact that God created the world. It must apparently be sought in concerns and problems with creation itself.

Admittedly, the clarification of this question demands an extensive exegetical treatment which cannot be pursued in this essay. On the basis of what has just been said, however, we should assume that *the formula "heaven and earth" reflects an elementary need for distinguishing between two fundamental realms within cre-*

---

had there been an overriding reason to do so. Furthermore, abstract words (which do not denote nonrealities) are most genuine when they correspond to what is perceived.

48. Cf. Job 38; Exod 20:4, 11; Deut 5:8.

49. Ps 139:7f.; Ezek 26:20; 31:14, 16, 18; 32:18, 20, 24; etc.

ation. This need leads to a systematic understanding of creation as bipartite, or bipolar, universal space. Our formula is the expression of this understanding. Under the influence of this understanding, the expression of the bipartite structure of creation was more important than the expression of its assumed unity, and the other cosmological options were subjected to it at the same time. The paradigmatic text for this phenomenon is undoubtedly Gen 1:1–2:4a (**P**).

What gave impetus to this system? Two aspects seem to be important. The first is cosmological in nature; the second is anthropological and theological. Cosmologically, the formula concentrates on the heaven vis-à-vis the earth at the exclusion of other realms. This concentration indicates the basic distinction of the terrestrial and the extraterrestrial realms, and the importance of the extraterrestrial heaven, specifically for the earth. Both factors amount to fundamental cosmological perceptions. In whatever way the world was perceived as a unity, the extraterrestrial realm "above" the earth had to be considered as separate. This separateness was absolute in the sense that "heaven" was unreachable from the earth. The same was not true for the relationship of the terrestrial realm to the sea or to the nether world. Despite this separateness, however, the extraterrestrial realm of heaven has a direct significance for the earth. In contrast to the sea and the nether world, it is the structured order of the heavenly space that is related to the order of the earth, or to which the order of the earth is related. In this relationship to the heaven as a structured order, the earth itself is ordered and can be perceived as order. This relationship is exclusive, just as the division of the two realms is definite. In their division, each of the two realms is distinct. But in their correlation, "heaven" and "earth" were united in the same order. This view seems to be the cosmological background for the perception of creation and for the formula "heaven and earth."

Related to the cosmological aspect is the anthropological-theological one. It means that, literally, the earth is experienced as the living space for humans, whereas heaven is, in a very specific sense, perceived as the living space of God, especially of the highest god in the ancient Near East, and certainly of Yahweh-God in the Old Testament.

The assumption that God dwells in heaven does not mean that he is identical with heaven, or that heaven is divine. Nor does it mean that Yahweh is not the lord of the earth. Decisive in this aspect is the question of where in the totality of his creation is Yahweh's own living space, and not the question of whether or not he is the creator of heaven and earth. To be sure, the tradition history of the notion of Yahweh's dwelling place shows variations, just as much as the notion of his place in heaven remained prominent throughout that tradition history. In the Old Testament, there is certainly a great difference between the God who "[walks] in the garden" (Gen 3:9 [*NRSV* 3:8]), who "came from Teman" (Hab 3:3) and "from Sinai" (Deut 33:2), "dawned from Seir," and "shone forth from Mt. Paran" (Deut 33:2), who dwells in the temple (1 Kgs 8:12f.) and "roars from Zion" (Amos 1:2), and the God who sits in the heaven and laughs (Ps 2:4), who looks down from heaven (Deut 26:15; Ps 33:13), who "has established his throne in the heavens" (Ps 103:19), who in heaven, his dwelling place, hears prayers (1 Kgs 8:30, 32, 34, 36, 39, 43, 45, 49), whose kingdom comes from heaven (Dan 7:13), who is "the God of heaven" (Ps 136:26; Ezr 1:2; Jon 1:9), whose kingdom is "the kingdom of heaven" (Matt 3:2), and whose will is done in heaven (Matt 6:10). It may be that in some cases, the notion of God's dwelling place on earth excludes the notion of his dwelling place in heaven. In other cases (probably the majority), this is not the case. The Old Testament has not systematized this question. But it is safe to say that, in essence, the Old Testament considers Yahweh's dwelling place to be in heaven, and to be on earth only to the extent to which a holy place on earth, especially a sanctuary, is considered as the extension of the heavenly realm. It is well known that, from the exilic time on, Yahweh's dwelling place was understood ever more exclusively as heaven. But we must realize that its increasingly exclusivistic character is not so much a new development as it is a return to long-held assumptions under specific historical influences. One could say that the postexilic emphasis signifies a return to the basics.

The historical influences that triggered the radicalization of the notion of Yahweh's dwelling place in heaven are well known. They are not only found in Yahweh's withdrawal from his institutions established in Israel. They can also be detected in Israel's ever increasing awareness that, on earth, Yahweh's lordship became contested and polluted, especially through human history, so much so that even the structure of the earth itself became polluted. In light of this awareness, Israel maintained ever more pointedly that there is one realm within creation in which Yahweh's lordship is not polluted, and in essence not even contested, namely, heaven. The theological aspect of Yahweh's dwelling place in heaven is, therefore, a direct correlative to the anthropological aspect of the earth as the realm of humans. On earth, Yahweh and his created order are contested by humans. In this sense, the earthly realm is distinctly different, and separate from the heavenly realm. Moreover, the theological-anthropological aspect of the polarity of heaven and earth corresponds to the cosmological aspect of that polarity. The separation of Yahweh's uncontested space from his contested space rests necessarily on the cosmological polarity of heaven and earth. This cosmological polarity of heaven and earth provides the spatial realms for the tension between Yahweh's universal kingdom and universal human history. The formula "heaven and earth" is based on semantic implications which far transcend its descriptive function for cosmic reality. It expresses in nuclear form the foundational concern of the Old Testament and, we should add, of biblical theology: the concern for the meaning of God's creation as universal cosmic order, especially in view of the acute threat to this order arising from humans on earth.

2. *Creation as Cyclic Cosmic Time*

One basic notion is intrinsic to the understanding of cosmic space in the Old Testament theology of creation: the notion of cyclic time. Cyclic time is that structure of reality in which the same order of the cosmos keeps recurring in a never-ending pattern of successive cycles. Cosmic space not only has a beginning; it also has a time. This time is cyclic. Cosmic space and cyclic time intrinsically belong together. Cyclic time is the permanence of cosmic space, and cosmic space is the order of cyclic time.[50]

Together with the notion of cosmic space the notion of cyclic time has a central place in Israel's Yahweh-theology. The evidence in the Old Testament for this fact is abundant. Israel was aware of the reality of cyclic cosmic time, even as it experienced its ongoing existence as embedded in such cyclic time. Israel related cyclic time to its Yahweh-theology, or Yahweh-theology to cyclic time, and understood cyclic time as one of the major structures in which the world was created and sustained by God-Yahweh. In the context of Israel's creation theology, the focus rested not only on the affirmation that Yahweh was the one who created the world; it rested especially on the question of what kind of world Yahweh had created. The former is presupposed in our discussion; the latter is subject to interpretation.

Cyclic time is different from historical time.[51] It coexists with historical time, but is independent from it. Insofar as cosmic space and cyclic time represent the basic components of creation, creation itself must be understood as coexisting with human history, yet independent from it. Both exist simultaneously. The paradigm for this understanding is again Genesis 1. I take for granted what has often been said, namely, that creation, according to the priestly writer, marks the beginning of human history. However, this interpretation is incomplete as long as it rests its case at this point. Moreover, it leads in a wrong direction altogether when it suggests

50. See Bergmann/Ottosson, *TDOT* 1, 391.

51. The labels "cyclic time," referring to cosmic time, and "historical time," referring to human history, are chosen only for the sake of brevity. We are aware that "historical time" also has a cyclic component, as Westermann has shown. Furthermore, there is reason for ascribing a historical dimension to "cyclic time" as well. To do so would be possible on the ground that cyclic time is understood as the succession of periodic cycles, and not as the permanent repetition of the first and only cycle. This latter conception cannot be documented in the Old Testament. The Old Testament does not speak of an ongoing creation, even though it speaks of Yahweh's ongoing creative acts. But cyclic time itself has a historical dimension insofar as, in the succession of periodic cycles, each cycle is new. The newness, however, lies in the new occurrence of the cycle, or in something new within the cycle, e.g., a drought or an earthquake, and not in the fact of the cycle itself, i.e., in its differentness from other cycles. The cycles repeat one another even as they are successive. We may call this pattern of cyclic time "cosmic cyclic history." But we still must distinguish it fundamentally from the structures of human history, or the divine direction of human history.

that in Genesis 1 creation is related to human history and has no significance of its own apart from, or vis-à-vis, human history. In such an interpretation, the question guiding **P** is said to be history, and creation appears in the service of his understanding of history, especially Israel's history. Against this interpretation, we must assert that **P** does not merely speak of creation as the first in the sequence of historical events, an event that belonged to the past as soon as the next event happened. It is inconceivable that **P** would suggest that the reality he is describing in Genesis 1 no longer exists in his own time. The priestly writer speaks of an event that has remained an ever-present reality throughout all of history, which is an unshakable reality in his own time, and will be an unshakable reality alongside all of human history. This is especially true concerning the cosmology in Genesis 1. Of course, it is also true concerning the capacity of the living creatures to perpetuate themselves, including humans as documented by the genealogies in Genesis 5, 10, and 11. As will be argued later, however, the component of life's self-perpetuating capacity belongs to the theology of creation, and not to the theology of history. It reflects the presence of creation in history, and is not a historically conditioned potential. Therefore, for **P**, creation appears as the unshakable realm of God's presence in the world, in contrast to the course of human history, including his own history. It also appears as the ultimate foundation and criterion from which his conception of Israel's new future will have to be devised.

An appropriate interpretation of the hermeneutic implied in Genesis 1, therefore, must distinguish between two different types of beginning in the act of creation: the beginning of cosmic time on the one hand, and the beginning of human history on the other. The fact that creation marks the beginning of human history does not mean that after that beginning it ceases to exist as a reality of its own. All of creation continues to exist as an ever-present reality alongside and vis-à-vis human history. Thus, creation cannot be understood only as the beginning of human history and as standing in the service of that history. Rather, it must be understood as the place and moment which contains the criterion for the meaningful correlation of cosmic reality and human history, and at the same time for the critical evaluation of human history in light of the ever-present cosmic reality which exists in accordance with its beginning. This cosmic reality is the cosmic order which is constantly present through the cosmic cyclic time. The hermeneutic implied in Genesis 1 presupposes a bipolar reality in which cosmic order and human history confront each other. In this confrontation, history appears to have fallen out of the rhythm of the cosmic order, whereas the cosmic order reflects the ongoing presence of creation. The cosmic order remains loyal to its origin. This ongoing presence of creation is, therefore, an ultimate presence.[52]

52. This statement differs from, e.g., L. Köhler's statement that creation is "an eschatological concept" (*Theology,* 88). For Köhler, *"eschatologisch"* means that the beginning and endtime of human history correspond to one another. See H. Gunkel, *Schöpfung und Chaos in*

Two perspectives in which the presence of creation is expressed are discernible. One says that in creation God-Yahweh through his word established the cosmic order once and for all. This perspective is documented in the priestly theology in Genesis 1 and 9:8-17.[53] But it is also documented in other traditions, such as the Yahwistic version of the Noahitic blessing in Gen 8:21-22, and in passages such as Isa 48:13; Pss 19:1-6; 33:2-7 (*NRSV* 33:4-9); 93:1-2; 95:1-5; 96:10-12; 102:26 (*NRSV* 102:25); 136:4-9; 146:6; Job 38 (esp. 4-11); Prov 3:19-20; 8:22-31; Neh 9:6. The second perspective says God-Yahweh sustains the created cosmic order, especially the boundaries of the sea and the natural order, through his ongoing active interferences. This perspective is documented, among others, in passages such as Psalms 29; 65:6-9 (*NRSV* 65:7-10); 89:6-15 (*NRSV* 89:5-14); 104; 107:33-38; 135:6-7; 148:7-8; Job 9:7; 37:6.[54]

Both perspectives share the focus on the ongoing existence and presence of the cosmic order after its initial creation. In the Old Testament, this ongoing existence and presence is not understood as an autonomous process. It is just as much dependent on Yahweh as the beginning of the world is on God-Yahweh's creative act.[55] Most importantly, this created order continues to exist and to be

---

Urzeit und Endzeit (Göttingen: Vandenhoeck und Ruprecht, 1895), and also W. Eichrodt, *Theology,* vol. 2, 110. According to this interpretation, there is nothing "eschatological" during the time between the beginning and the end. In this sense, the eschatological moments are subordinate to history because they are related to history as moments of history, whereas history itself embraces more than its beginning and end. Furthermore, inasmuch as the "eschatological" only reflects the beginning and end of history, it is subject to the standard of creation because the beginning and end of history themselves are embedded in creation. In this sense, to maintain the ultimacy of the "eschatological" by virtue of the fact that it marks the beginning and the end is once again insufficient. But the eschatological beginning and end are ultimate to the extent to which they represent the ultimacy of creation. The ultimacy of creation, however, exists not only at the beginning and at the end; it is also a present reality. It comprises and pervades past, present, and future. Creation is time, but independent of history. In fact, it is the presupposition for history, and is not only the beginning of history. In view of the perspective of ultimacy, the eschatological perspective is relative.

53. See O. H. Steck, *Der Schöpfungsbericht,* 249.

54. Admittedly, this subject is in need of specific research. It seems that while the heavenly realm is considered established once and for all (Ps 148:1-6), the realm underneath the heavens is in need of continued sustenance (Ps 148:7-12). Also, the separation of these two perspectives of order is not always self-evident. At times, they may converge, such as in Psalms 93; 95; 96. Finally, it is evident that the two perspectives reflect different settings and/or a complex traditio-historical development. In particular, the perspective of the ongoing sustenance of the cosmos reflects the ancient tradition of the persistent periodic defense of creation against the forces of chaos (sea, darkness, death). In their Old Testament form, these forces are still vibrant and in need of constant containment by Yahweh, whereas particularly in the priestly theology, they have lost their force altogether.

55. The tradition speaking of the ongoing sustenance of the cosmos directly documents this perspective. But the tradition speaking of creation established once and for all also documents it insofar as the cosmos exists in constant accordance with and, hence, is constantly determined by Yahweh's initial decrees, and does not exist autonomously.

present in the structure of the cyclic time of the cosmic space.[56] Traditionally, the notion of the ongoing existence of creation has been associated with the notion of the sustenance of the world by God. This notion is derived from the Old Testament itself, and not only from systematic theology. However, the notion of sustenance differs in two respects from the notion of the ongoing existence and presence of creation in the structure of the cosmic cyclic time. On the one hand, it is incapable — strictly speaking — of embracing the perspective of creation as established once and for all without the need for further sustenance. In this respect, the notion is too narrow. On the other hand, the notion of sustenance covers not only those passages that speak of the sustenance of the cosmos; it also covers the passages that speak of the sustenance of human history. In this respect, the notion speaks of more than the presence of cosmic order. Especially, it tends to obscure the fundamental difference between cosmic and historical reality within Yahweh's sustaining activities. In view of this difference, the notion of sustenance cannot be reserved for the cosmic order alone, while in view of the cosmic order itself, it does not embrace all that needs to be said. Consequently, it is advisable that we apply this notion only to the specific biblical traditions covered by it and that we speak of the ongoing or continuous existence and presence of the created cosmic space and cyclic time only to the degree that the focus of the traditions is on the cosmic state subsequent to creation.

The ultimate existence and presence of creation as cosmic order also includes the earth. In fact, this cosmic order exists for the earth, and the earth lives from it, just as the earth is part of it. There are different or separate cosmic realms, but all of them, including the earth, are pervaded by the same order. The structure in which the earth is integrated into the cosmos, and through which its very existence is forever secured, is cyclic. This cyclic structure of the earth's existence represents the permanent presence of the structure of its creation in ever new cycles. In this sense, the earth has a history, just as the cosmos has a history. But the structure of this history of the earth is fundamentally different from the structure of human history on the earth. More specifically, the structure of human existence associated with the cyclic structure of the earth is fundamentally different from the structure of human existence associated with human history.

Indeed, the cosmic cyclic structure of the earth, and of human existence associated with it, existed before the unfolding of human history. Insofar as it coexists with human history, it is the indispensable presupposition and basis for human history. It can continue to exist without human history, but human history cannot exist without it. Moreover, the fact that life, especially human life, is seen as the goal or purpose of creation and of its ongoing existence does not mean that life is the foundation of the cosmic order or that the cosmic order does not exist

56. See O. H. Steck, *Schöpfungsbericht,* 206-13, who speaks of the *"Dauerbestand"* ("perpetual condition") and of *"gegliederte Zeit"* ("time structured according to divisions").

in its own right. On the contrary, life is bound up with that order, or it perishes. We must, therefore, distinguish life and history as the goal and purpose of cosmic creation and its existence from creation and its existence as the presupposition for and foundation of life and history. Both of these aspects only say something about the meaning of the cosmic order, i.e., that it aims at life and represents the support system for life, but they say nothing directly about the meaning of life itself. According to the Old Testament, the meaning of life and history certainly cannot be subservient to the existence of creation. However, neither can the meaning of life and history be separated from or out of tune with that existence, life's very own foundation. To exist in accord with the existence of creation and yet not to be subservient to it is the meaning of life and history which the Old Testament recognizes from its knowledge of Yahweh the creator. The creation hymns precisely reflect this stance (Psalms 8; 19:2-7 [*NRSV* 19:1-6]; 104; 139; 148). In this stance which was derived from the history of its knowledge of Yahweh, Israel expressed the most universal horizon of its Yahweh-theology and, at the same time, the foundational aspect of that history.

The Old Testament amply documents the inclusion of the terrestrial realm into cosmic space and its cyclic order. The various types of seasons are embedded in the cosmic order. They are celebrated in two of Israel's festivals: the feast of harvest or weeks and the feast of ingathering (Exod 23:16-17; 34:22; Deut 16:13). In these festivals, Israel's arrival in this seasonal-cyclic life is celebrated as the fulfillment of Yahweh's salvation history with Israel.[57]

Agrarian existence itself is embedded in the order of cosmic space and cosmic cycle. The number of pertinent Old Testament passages is endless. The Old Testament knows that humans live from the ground while they are alive, just as they come from the ground and return to the ground. The ground is their life space and their permanent home base. Humans themselves belong to the ground because they are of the ground of the earth, and not because they are unavoidably grounded cosmically. Furthermore, human existence is not understood abstractly, as personal existence. It is understood first of all in relation to the ground from which it comes, from which it lives, and to which it returns. Humans do not live from bread alone, but certainly without it they do not live at all. Life from the ground, however,

57. Even the sabbath week is a cyclic system, although it was apparently not derived from the cosmic cycle. See E. Jenni, *Die Theologische Begründung des Sabbatgebotes im Alten Testament,* Theologische Studien 46 (Zollikon-Zürich: Evangelischer, 1956); N. E. Andreasen, *The Old Testament Sabbath,* SBLDS 7 (Missoula: University of Montana, 1972). The hermeneutic in the history of Israel's sabbath tradition, as expressed in the motivations for the sabbath, is telling. On the assumption that Exod 20:11 is an imitation of Deut 5:15 and, hence, represents the final stage in this tradition history, the sabbath week is ultimately authenticated as a cyclic system with reference to creation. See also Gen 2:1-3 and Exod 31:17. In comparison with the earlier authentication of the sabbath week (Exod 23:12; Deut 5:15), this authentication was both more universal and more fundamental. The former could become invalid; the latter cannot.

means life through agrarian existence. Agrarian existence is fundamental, and not tangential, to human existence. It cannot be considered as the residue of a primitive, pretechnological civilization.[58] This factor transcends national and historical boundaries. It is true for all humanity. It is neither confined to Israel's land, nor dependent on Yahweh's history with Israel. On the contrary, it is the presupposition for the fulfillment of the goal of Israel's history in the land. This factor in no way lies outside Israel's Yahweh-theology. Moreover, it is not dependent on human history, but it is dependent on Yahweh's blessing of the ground, i.e., the affirmation of the uninterrupted seasonal cycle (Gen 8:21-22; Hos 2:23-25a [*NRSV* 2:21-23a]; Pss 65:10-14 [*NRSV* 65:9-13]); 104:27-29; 145:15-16; etc.). Agriculture, conceived theologically, is that form of human activity in which humans on earth are integrated into the cosmic life-cycle which owes its creation and ongoing existence to Yahweh. This human integration into the cosmic life-cycle represents a structure of human existence which is different from the structure of human history. In fact, it is the basis for the possibility of human history even as it pervades all of that history. Not infrequently, it provides the conditions for humans to survive historically wrought catastrophes. The structure of this existence is cyclic, and Yahweh's blessing presence in this cyclic structure is more universal and more fundamental than Yahweh's historical acts.[59] The parable of the farmer in Isa 28:23-28 is paradigmatic for the Old Testament's own theological awareness of the fundamentality of the seasonal rhythm in which the farmer's activities of plowing and threshing are meaningful. By looking at what the farmer knows from his God, the parable can conclude that historical catastrophes do not mean the end of history, or of God's presence in history. Is it possible, even for Yahwism proper, that the farmer continues to offer a basis for the understanding of history — if not for its orientation — even as the prophet falls silent?

In an attempt to conceptualize the various Old Testament aspects and traditions pertinent to our subject, we must be aware of several distinctions. First, we must distinguish creation in the beginning from the subsequently ongoing existence of creation. In this distinction, the creation in the beginning must be regarded as the foundational reality in the subsequent existence of the world. Secondly, we must distinguish the cosmic order from human history, even as both began in creation and continue onward. In this distinction, the relationship between cosmic order and history becomes the central issue. It implies the question of whether, in the present existence of the world, the foundational reality of creation is maintained in cosmic order or in history. Thirdly, we must distinguish the relationship of cosmic order and history in the beginning of creation from their relationship subsequent

58. See Gen 3:18-19; Prov 12:11; 28:19; 24:27, 30-34; Isa 5:1; Psalms 65; 104; etc.

59. Certainly, this structure exists within human history. It is even a product of human history. Nevertheless, it is that product in which human history actualizes its own foundation and universal meaning: life on earth for all.

to that beginning. Their relationship in the beginning is seen as integrated, whereas their subsequent relationship is characterized by friction and tension. It should not be difficult to discern what the Old Testament designates to be the point of disintegration: history has removed itself from the rhythm of cosmic order and, thus, has lost contact with the meaning of its own creation. In contrast, the order of cosmic space and cyclic time continues to exist in accord with that meaning. This very order constantly reflects that meaning, knows about it. Humans neither hear the voice nor understand the words, but they know that the voice and words are there. Ps 19:2-7 (*NRSV* 19:1-6) is paradigmatic. Through its cyclic course, the cosmic space, daily and without end, proclaims the glory of God and itself as his handiwork. Yahweh has no difficulties with this realm of his creation. It does his will (Pss 103:19-22; 148:1-6). In this realm, Yahweh is present in a way different from the way he is present in history.

III. World Order, History, and Yahweh

The Old Testament knows about history as well as world order and about Yahweh's relationship to and presence in both. It knows that the structure of world order is different from the structure of human history. It knows that both types of time remain contemporaneous and are experienced as realities each in its own way. Finally, it knows that Yahweh's relationship to and presence in world order is different in kind from his relationship to and presence in history.

A. Yahweh and World Order

The pertinent Old Testament texts show that Yahweh is directly related to and present in the order of his cosmic creation.

This means, first of all, that the distinction between Yahweh and world order is fundamental. For Israel, Yahweh was an identity comparable with nothing else in all reality. Neither was he a mode of world order, nor was world order an emanation or an extension of Yahweh. Yahweh's time is different from the time of the world order. He is God before the creation of the world (Ps 90:2), and he will endure when creation perishes and "wears out like a garment" (Ps 102:27 [*NRSV* 102:26]). Yahweh's place is in the world, yet he is not confined by its order (Deut 4:39; 1 Kgs 8:27; Ps 139:7-12).

In their distinction, however, Yahweh and world order were seen as correlated under clearly distinguishable notions. First, *Yahweh* explicated the meaning of "world order." Under Yahweh, the creator and lord, the world appeared radically deprived of autonomy and of any divine quality. At the same time, the world could be perceived as the cosmic space and cyclic time, the solidly built and furnished universal home, in which life, especially human life, was allowed to exist securely and without fear. Israel's fearless and trustful attitude toward the world was possible only on the basis of its trust in Yahweh. Without this trust, Israel would only have had the deified world as the basis for its encounter with reality; and it would have been forced to feel insecure in it and fear it. It is, therefore, not coincidental that in its hymns Israel praises Yahweh and not the cosmos. Israel trusts in Yahweh, and not in the world order. To the extent to which it is certain of the world order, it is certain because of its trust in Yahweh. This aspect shows that we come to understand the relationship between Yahweh and world order in terms of ultimacy; it is Yahweh and not world order that represents the criterion for the validity of the other. At the same time, Yahweh is perceived not only as an incomparable divine identity but as inseparably related to the universality of any world order however perceived.

Second, *world order* explicated what it meant for Israel to say "Yahweh." The notions of incomparability, identity, or ultimacy by themselves do not explicate the extent and nature of Yahweh's relationship to and presence in reality. They leave room for an understanding of a god without a world, an inconceivable idea for the Old Testament. The notions of world order and history, however, signal both the most universal and the most foundational aspects of reality to which Yahweh is related. They document that Yahweh, the ground of reality, is universally present in reality. He is the God of reality, and not the God of nonreality or an unreal god.

In particular, the created world order has certain qualitative notions which explicate Yahweh's relationship to and presence in it. The fact of creation out of chaos alone represents more than a merely quantitative event. It is a *good* event. The priestly formulation, according to which the whole creation is *very good* in God's judgment is not superficial because the word "good" is a common word. It is a most profound formulation which in essence includes all else that can be said. It cannot be said any better. It is a fundamental theological statement about the world. This goodness is not only true for the order of creation in the beginning. It is also true for the entire time in which this order exists in accordance with its beginning.

The same qualitative notion is implied in the understanding of the fixed, demarcated order as expressed by the word חק, "engravement," "authoritative delimitation." When used in connection with the creation and existence of the world, this word comes close to being *the* Hebrew word for world order. חק, especially when done by God-Yahweh, is always a good action. The reality thus established is also good (Ps 148:6; Prov 8:27-29; Job 26:10; 28:10; 38:10; Jer 5:22). In Prov 3:19; 8:22-31; Ps 104:24; Job 28 and 38, the creation of the world in its order is connected with Yahweh's wisdom (חכמה), or with wisdom as Yahweh's companion. In these and other texts the very perception of the existence of the cosmic order is the perception of an existence in wisdom. This existence represents the presence of Yahweh in his order in כבוד, "glory" (Pss 19:2-7 [*NRSV* 19:1-6]; 29) which may "endure forever" (Ps 104:31) and which only is polluted by one phenomenon: sinners and the wicked (Ps 104:35).

Yahweh's presence in the cosmic order is also perceived in the presence in this order of his righteousness (צדקה/צדק) and related qualities. While many texts implicitly express this aspect (e.g., Ps 65:6-12 [*NRSV* 65:5-11]), some express it directly: "Steadfast love and faithfulness [חסד ואמת] will meet; righteousness and peace [צדק ושלום] will kiss each other. Faithfulness [אמת] will spring up from the ground, and righteousness [צדק] will look down from the sky. The Lord will give what is good [הטוב], and our land will yield its increase. Righteousness [צדק] will go before him, and will make a path for his steps" (Ps 85:11-14 [*NRSV* 85:10-13]). "Righteousness and justice [צדק ומשפט] are the foundation of your throne; steadfast love and faithfulness [חסד ואמת] go before you" (Ps 89:15 [*NRSV* 89:14]). This verse concludes a unit which begins in verse 10 [*NRSV* v. 9]: "You rule [מושל] the raging of the sea; when its waves rise, you still them." In this unit, Yahweh, the conqueror of chaos, is praised as the founder and lord of the world order (v. 11 [*NRSV* v. 10]). Moreover, to the extent that righteousness and justice, the foundation of his throne, also extend to other realms and activities, they must be seen as the criteria for his control of his created cosmic order as well, just as verse 15 (*NRSV* v. 14) cannot be isolated from verses 10-14 (*NRSV* vv. 9-13).

The close connection between the creator and the redeemer in Second Isaiah is well known (Isa 40:12-14, 21-23, 28; 42:5; 44:24; 45:7-13, 18-19; etc.). What matters in this context is that the authenticity of the announcement of the new exodus is substantiated by reference to the creator of the world, and that the event itself, inasmuch as it also is a creation, is characterized by its analogy to the creation of the world. In this event, the existing order of creation is actualized in human history, or human history is reintegrated into the created order of the world: "Shower, O heavens, from above, and let the skies rain down righteousness; let the earth open, that salvation may sprout up, and let it cause righteousness to spring up also; I the Lord have created it" (Isa. 45:8). The same can be said about Hos 2:23-25 (*NRSV* 2:21-23).

We can summarize what has been said so far. Yahweh and the world order are related to one another in their initial distinctiveness. In this relationship, the world order does not appear as good, wise, glorious, and righteous by virtue of its own potential. But it has the qualities and the efficaciousness of the goodness, wisdom, glory, and righteousness of Yahweh, who is present in it as its creator. Because of Yahweh's presence, the world order was considered to be intact; and in this intactness, Yahweh was experienced as cosmically present in everyday reality. The intactness of the world order is not a matter of abstract cosmological theory. It is a fact of experience in exactly those realms of cosmic, natural, and cyclic stability to which all creatures owe their sustained existence. It was intensely perceived, understood, and celebrated. It was the reason for much of Israel's hymnic praise of Yahweh. Inasmuch as the world order revealed goodness, wisdom, glory, and righteousness, it also revealed Yahweh's presence in the world in an ultimate way, and did so more directly than human history ever could.[60] We should not underestimate the high degree of hermeneutical sophistication of texts such as Psalms 104; 148; Genesis 1, and many others. These texts portray the presence of the universal world order in the daily lives of the creatures without any reference to history or interference from it. We would be naive to assume that these people were narcissistic aestheticists who knew nothing about historical catastrophes, social trouble, existential dilemmas, and even the burden of agricultural life as depicted in Gen 3:17-19. They knew about the dark sides of reality. However, in these texts, they fall back on one kind of reality which is also true and present, and which is ultimate and unshakable: the order of creation in which God is present and in which they are at home.

Therefore, it is not coincidental that in many respects, especially in its understanding of the dynamic wholeness of reality in which Yahweh was seen at work and which embraced not only the spheres of individuals, communities, and generations but also the cosmic and historical spheres, Israel relied on the intactness of the process of the world order. Moreover, Israel relied on the intactness of reality because of Yahweh, and not in spite of him. There is ground for suspicion that our scholarly discussion, guided by its insights into the "crisis of wisdom," has tended to regard this view of reality as the primitive and deservedly transitory substratum of a philosophically underdeveloped stage in the history of ontology, a stage destroyed once and for all by Job and Ecclesiastes. This modern trend in interpretation is not without its own problems. It is true that in many crises Israel experienced the breakdown of a holistic process, and along with this experienced either Yahweh's withdrawal from the situation or his presence in hiddenness during these crises. Yet it is not true that these crises cover the totality of all types of reality with their respective experiences, or that the experience of all types of reality reflect such crises. The world of Psalm 104 is not untrue because of Job's situation.

The problem for the book of Job lies in the fact that Job's friends were wrong

60. The notion of the revelation of Yahweh's presence in reality must be distinguished from the notion of the revelation of Yahweh's name. Yahweh's identity in his name is revealed in Israel's history in a particular kind of event: a word-event. And it remains known through the particular tradition history of that word-event. It is revealed neither through world order nor through or as history. However, world order and history reveal, in various ways, the presence in reality of the God known as Yahweh. In the light of these distinctions, G. von Rad's statement is not clear: "the faith of Israel is invariably related to an event, a divine self-declaration in history," "Old Testament World-View," 144. Inasmuch as Israel's faith focused on the self-disclosure of the divine name, it focused on an event and its tradition history within Israel's history. However, inasmuch as Israel focused on the self-disclosure of the known name's divinity, i.e., of Yahweh as God, it focused on the totality of reality, especially on the creation and existence of the world, and not on history alone.

regarding Yahweh's attitude in Job's situation, but were not wrong in everything they said. More importantly, the fact that the wholeness of the world does not exist, or cannot be empirically verified, everywhere and at all times does not mean that it cannot be fundamentally affirmed, in spite of all its chaotic distortions. This affirmation ultimately becomes the basis for the theodicy of Yahweh. In Job 38–39, Job is told that his challenge to Yahweh's justice is evaluated on the basis of the universal order of Yahweh's created and sustained world and not on the basis of his own experience. To the extent that Job saw Yahweh withdrawing from him by withdrawing from the wholeness of his life he was correct. But he was wrong when challenging Yahweh's justice universally. For such a challenge, his experience was not universal enough. His experience cannot be the sum total of wisdom because it does not represent the structure of the whole world, just as he himself is not the creator and sustainer of this structure. Hence, the world order does not depend on his individual experience, but his individual experience may become acceptable if and when the intactness of the world and Yahweh's presence in it is affirmed for him. Yahweh had withdrawn from the wholeness of Job's life. However, he had not withdrawn from the wholeness of his own creation, nor was his creation in chaos because Job's life was in chaos.

One point must be added. The intactness of the world, and Job's presence in it, needed to be affirmed for Job through Yahweh's theophanic speech. From the vantage point of his own experience, Job could no longer experience the intactness of Yahweh's world. This experience had to be revealed to him just as Job himself had demanded this revelation. Nevertheless, the fact that the content of Yahweh's speech to Job contains nothing that empirical wisdom had not said all along is puzzling. Why did what everyone is capable of empirically affirming have to be revealed?

The urgency of the theophany, along with the theophanic mediation of the content of Yahweh's speech, points to the fact that something fundamental was lacking on the level on which the debate between Job and his friends had transpired. On this level, the level of "wisdom" argumentation, empirical data offset and relativize each other. One can say what is correct. Still, one cannot know whether or not what is correct is also true. The friends apparently assumed their correct statements to be inherently true. Understandably, empirical experience for Job could no longer be the basis for its own verifiability. This experience was in need of verification from that which is the critical ground for all empirical experience. Such a basis could not be found in empirical experience itself. It could only be found in Yahweh and in whatever Yahweh would say. Only when Yahweh personally revealed it could that which everyone could empirically know be confirmed as ultimately true. In this revelation, Job does not learn the reason for his personal dilemma. But through it, and only through it, he receives the ultimate confirmation which could not be attained through the empirical experience of reality. His own personal dilemma is not representative of Yahweh's world order, and the world order remains fully intact because of Yahweh's presence in it, despite Job's personal dilemma. This revelatory experience is sufficient for Job. The book of Job provides an answer to the epistemological problem arising from the experiences of chaotic human suffering. It is the problem of how to confirm ultimately what otherwise may or may not be claimed empirically: In the face of the inexplicability of human suffering, God is in this world and the world is in order. Through Yahweh's own theophanic appearance as the creator and sustainer of the world, the order of the world itself theophanically appears in its intactness. This is the book's answer to the crisis of wisdom. This answer reflects a distinctly theological position. With this position, the book of Job appears to be a proto-apocalyptic document.

The distinction between the empirical cognition of the world order and its understanding, explanation, or confirmation is important not only for the book of Job. It is also important for the relationship between the Yahweh traditions and the wisdom traditions in the entire Old Testament. The Old Testament takes it for granted that the world order can be recognized wherever and whenever it exists, not only in heaven but also on earth, not only by Israel but also by all humans.[61] Moreover, it takes for granted that, in the order of the world, the divine presence itself can be recognized by all and not only by Israel, and that the world order points to, and in this case "reveals," the divine creator.[62]

Nevertheless, Israel encountered problems with the assumption of God's revelation or presence in the world order at two points. First, the world order was not everywhere and at all times perceived as intact. Natural catastrophes and the threatening potential of the sea and especially of darkness are cases in point. In these cases, it is not only the world that is perceived as out of order; it is also Yahweh himself who is no longer perceived as present through the order of the world. In passages such as Amos 5:18f.; Zeph 1:15; Joel 2:2-11 (*NRSV* 2:1-10); 3:3-4; Isa 13:10; and Ezek 32:7-8, passages that reflect the tradition of the Day of Yahweh, the structure of the cosmos itself is turned into chaos. Insofar as such darkness reveals Yahweh's glory, it reveals it in Yahweh's hiddenness. The glory itself is indeed recognized only in heaven, not on earth. However, even as the

61. Ps 19:2-7 (*NRSV* 19:1-6) does not contradict this statement. This passage says only that the speech or voice of the heavenly realm is inaudible on earth. At the same time, however, it affirms the existence of that voice. Our text, or author, recognizes the existence of the glory of the cosmic cyclic order with such certainty that he even perceives it as expressing through its very course the meaning of its existence.

62. Paul's statements in Rom 1:18-23 precisely reflect this central stance, and not at all coincidentally. Paul does not say that God's "invisible nature" and "eternal power and deity" are not revealed in the order of creation and, hence, cannot be perceived by humans. He says that humans have perverted the knowledge of God revealed in creation and, hence, it cannot be perceived by humans who, therefore, have made perversion the order of their lives. Paul explains the disorder in their lives by their perverted reading of the presence of God in creation, an avoidable perversion because creation's witness to God is clear. This avoidable perversion is the reason why they are without excuse.

distorted human history is seen as the reason for the cosmic destruction in these traditions, the traditions themselves document that the order of the world is not only the all-embracing framework or horizon but also the substantive issue under concern.

Secondly, Israel encountered a problem at the point where the origin and ground of the world order had to be understood, a problem with God's presence in this order. In this respect, Israel encountered a "merciless darkness"[63] when looking at the world, because its order as such could not reveal the God of the world as Yahweh, perhaps not even as the creator in the strict sense of the word. The darkness alluded to here is different from the darkness of a chaotic world which humans could experientially encounter and describe. It is the darkness encountered by the understanding when it faces the ultimate question of reality. True, the order of the world pointed to a divine origin and to its ever-present ground, and to this extent revealed that origin and ground. But how could order as such, however deeply one penetrated into it cognitively, reveal the identity of that deity? And how could this order reveal by virtue of its existence the identified deity as its creator, distinct from the order itself, rather than as the essence of its own divine nature? When it came to this ultimate question of reality, the world became an ever greater mystery clouded in darkness, despite the glory of its order and the divine presence in it which every eye could see. Ultimately, the world cannot explain itself. This is the last word Israel's epistemology can say, inasmuch as that epistemology is based on empirical understanding.

The reason for the discovery of this dimension of darkness in the world order seems to lie in the tradition history of Israel's own knowledge of Yahweh. From this tradition history, Israel knew that God had an incomparable name and an incomparable identity, both of which distinguished him from everything in the world. From this knowledge, Israel could eventually understand who the God of the world order was. Yahweh was the creator, and the order his creation. Yahweh was the light in the darkness of the ground of the world, and the guarantor of its created order. To know and fear Yahweh was, therefore, wisdom. This wisdom made an enlightened understanding of the wisdom, glory, and justice of the world order possible. This knowledge was certainly no explanation of Yahweh. But it was an explanation of the glory of the created and sustained order of the world.

But once again, even as Israel gained these insights from its own tradition of Yahweh knowledge, the insights themselves did not invalidate what could be perceived empirically. The knowledge of Yahweh's revelation in Israel's tradition did not replace the knowledge of God's presence in the order of the world. Furthermore, wherever Israel perceived Yahweh hiding from the order of the world, it

63. G. von Rad, "Old Testament World-View," 159; and the same author in "Glaube und Welterkenntnis im alten Israel," *Gesammelte Studien zum Alten Testament,* vol. 2 (Munich: Chr. Kaiser, 1973), 255-66.

perceived him hiding from history as well, including its own. In fact, it perceived him hiding from the order of the world because of his hiddenness in or from history. Israel certainly did not perceive him hiding in or from history because of his hiddenness behind the world order.

Ultimately, the emerging origins of this understanding of the meaning of the world in Israel's Yahwism must not be confused with the function this understanding had for Israel. Its function was to let Israel understand both the mystery of the world as creation at home in Yahweh and the meaning of Israel itself as the witness to this fact. Its function was not to show the world order as meant for the exclusive benefit of Israel. The Old Testament traditions that express Yahweh's relationship to the totality of the world ultimately represent those theological concerns of Israel that have to be considered as most fundamental.

B. Yahweh, World Order, and History

The Old Testament says not only that Yahweh acts in history, but above all that Yahweh himself creates and sustains history. More specifically, it sees Yahweh as the Lord of Israel's history and of the history of the nations as well. As is well known, this fact is amply documented, in the sources of the Pentateuch, in the historical and prophetic books, and in the Psalms.

Generally, it is exegetically assumed that Yahweh's intentions for history are salvific, even in those situations in which his judgment is necessary either to prevent history from collapsing or to bring failed history to a collapse in order to enable a new beginning. History was seen as guided by a salvific intentionality despite the frequent hiddenness of this intentionality behind or in the numerous catastrophic historical events. Israel always clung to the conviction that in human actions and decisions there was a meaning and a purpose at work to which those actions and decisions became subservient, even as they determined the course of history. The story of Ahithophel and Hushai (2 Sam 16:15–17:23), Isaiah's view of the Assyrians (Isa 5:26-30; 7:18-20; 10:5-11), Jeremiah's view of the enemy from the north (Jeremiah 4) and of Nebuchadnezzar (Jeremiah 23–28), Deutero-Isaiah's view of Cyrus (Isa 45:1-6; 44:28), and many other examples illustrate this point. Israel was convinced that, ultimately, human actions and decisions were more the result of history than history was the result of human actions and decisions.

At the same time, Israel knew that involvement of humans in history entails being inextricably confronted with a critically discerning factor before which human actions and decisions stand in judgment. Humans may make history, but it is the meaning and purpose of history that judges the historical creations of humans. Thus, human actions and decisions are not deemed good and justified on the ground that they are historical, but human historical involvement is judged in view of how human actions and decisions serve the meaning and purpose of history. History has no ultimate legitimacy or validity by virtue of being history. Its legitimacy and validity are themselves subject to a criterion which is independent of history even as it is at work and can be recognized in history, whether in human history in general or in Israel's history specifically. The criterion for either the truth or the perversion of history, however, is the salvific intentionality to which history is to be subservient, which determines the purpose and meaning of history, and which at the same time is the judge of history.

What has been said amounts to a type of historical consciousness in which Israel distinguished between the historical events and the meaning of those events. Moreover, while it occasionally saw the meaning of history expressed in the events, it frequently protested against, or pointed beyond, the actual course of history precisely because of its perception of true history. The reason for this critical historical consciousness, for this sense of the potential or actual tension between true and perverse history, was undoubtedly the fact that Israel did not perceive the ongoing course of history exclusively as the revelation of Yahweh's great enterprise on earth. Israel also perceived it as the singularly genuine mode for the self-realization of humans on earth. Two questions arise at this point. First, how does the Old Testament understand the relationship between human history and the salvific meaning of history? And secondly, if the meaning and purpose of history is the factor for the critical discernment between true and perverse history, then on what ground does the Old Testament determine what salvation is most universally and most fundamentally?

Generally speaking, the search for the answers to these questions leads us to those texts that reflect the relationship between Yahweh's creation of the world and Yahweh's lordship of history. A few examples may illustrate this point. As far as the history of humanity is concerned, the most obvious case for illustration is the primeval history in the Yahwistic and the priestly versions in Genesis 1–11. The primeval history clearly raises the question of the relationship between creation and human history. The case may not be so clear in the Yahwistic history because this narration emphasizes human history after the fall — paradise on earth lost for humans — while saying nothing about the remainder of paradise itself. Even so, the Yahwist considers human history as fallen out of paradise, the earthly sphere of the order of creation. In this consideration, paradise apparently means more than only the beginning of human history. It is the mirror of true reality, the reality of creation in view of which human history is evaluated. The relationship between creation and history in the Yahwist's view is hardly only chronological in nature. It is systematic in that creation provides the criterion by which the meaning and also the purpose of history, even and especially the purpose of the history of Israel's election, can be determined. Paradise may be lost as history. However, it is not lost as the constant reminder of the true place to which history belongs — creation — nor as the reminder of the fact that history is removed from creation, and not creation from history.

A more specific interpretation of the Yahwistic history would yield further evidence for this systematic understanding of the relationship between creation and history. Suffice it to point out that after the flood Yahweh finds it meaningless to curse the ground again and once more to destroy the living creatures because "the inclination of the human heart is evil from youth" (Gen 8:21). In addition, he guarantees the intactness of the cosmic cycle on earth forever. This guarantee by no means excuses evil human history, nor does it ascribe any legitimacy to its autonomy. On the contrary, by affirming that realm which human history cannot pervert and which, at the same time, is the indispensable basis for the existence of all creatures throughout all history, Yahweh again makes clear that history truly belongs to creation, and not creation to history. Moreover, he makes it clear that, while history cannot destroy creation and creation will not destroy history, history can destroy both life and itself.

The case is even clearer in the priestly version of the primeval history. In addition to what has been said earlier, it is sufficient to mention that the priest knows that the earth is "filled with violence" and that it remains so after the flood (Gen 6:9, 11; 9:1-7). And while he, too, speaks about God's guarantee for the cosmic order (Gen 9:1-7), he adds one more divine decree given for the protection of human life itself (Gen 9:5-6). It is doubtful that the purpose for this protection is to provide the basis for human history. Unavoidably as history springs from life, it is much more probable that the purpose for this protection is to guarantee the continued existence of that realm of the order of creation on earth without which creation itself would be meaningless, i.e., human life. Human life is not a product of human history; it is a product of creation and belongs to the continued existence of the order of creation. In being blessed in creation with the power for its self-perpetuation, human life represents once more the ongoing presence of the order of creation in the sphere of human existence itself.[64] There can be no doubt that the priestly writer sees creation and human history as systematically related, and that, in this relationship, creation appears as the salvific reality to which history genuinely belongs, from which it is actually separated, and in view of which it is evaluated.

64. This understanding is also implied in the Old Testament genealogies, e.g., Genesis 5; 10; 11, in which the constant component reflects the creational aspect, and the variable component the historical aspect, as Westermann has shown (*Genesis 1–11,* 347). Westermann is certainly correct when saying that a science of history which ignores the constant components in the genealogies and, one must add, in the structure of human procreation becomes questionable. One may ask, however, whether this constant component is to be considered an element of human history at all. Instead, it seems to belong to the structure of creation in human existence which is different from and at the same time the presupposition for those components in human existence that belong to its historical structure. Persons are not born and alive because they have individual names; rather, they have names because they are born and alive. Furthermore, humans do not have the right to live because they are historical beings. Rather, they can be historical beings because they have the right to live.

Isaiah, the Psalms, and the wisdom literature speak about the plans and counsels of humans and nations, the political philosophies devised especially by human governments for the purpose of world domination. These policies often conflict with Yahweh's own plan (Psalms 2; 33:10-11; 35; 37; 46; 48; Isa 7:1-9; 8:10; 28:23-29; 29:15; 30:1; 46:11; Job 12:13-25; 38:2; Prov 8:14, et al.). In most of the references, the conflict between the two parties is concerned with their historical plans. One must investigate specifically the presuppositions on which these historical blueprints rest. As for Yahweh's plan, two passages in which this plan appears in the context of creation may be mentioned. One is Job 38:2, where Yahweh's plan refers to his creation and sustenance of the world itself.[65] The other is Ps 33:10-11, where the conflict between Yahweh's counsel and the nations' counsel is mentioned directly after the passage that speaks about the creation of the world: "The LORD brings the counsel of the nations to nothing; he frustrates the plans of the peoples. The counsel of the LORD stands forever, the thoughts of his heart to all generations." Particularly in this psalm, the question arises regarding the relationship between Yahweh's creation and the nations' historical plans which are frustrated by Yahweh. More specifically, what are the objectives of the plans of the two parties, and what are the foundations on which these objectives rest? As for the nations, we may assume what is said elsewhere in the Old Testament, that their objective is to create and control world history, and that the basis for achieving this objective is their reliance on the "great army," the "great strength," and on the "war horse," the "hope for victory" (Ps 33:16-17). By contrast, Yahweh's plan "stands forever, the thoughts of his heart to all generations" (v. 11). What are Yahweh's own thoughts, and what guides them? Verse 5 seems to give the answer, "He loves righteousness and justice; the earth is full of the steadfast love of the LORD." This statement contrasts Yahweh's objectives with the objectives of the nations. Of equal importance is the fact that Yahweh's or his world's[66] love of "righteousness and justice" is mentioned within the passage about Yahweh's creation. It must be understood as the substantive qualification of creation itself. This qualification of creation is apparently the basis that guides Yahweh's thoughts and plans in his conflict with the nations. Psalm 33 as a whole seems concerned with the question of the principles and criteria according to which history on earth is to be governed. In the conflict of governing principles, Yahweh's own criterion is said to be "justice and righteousness." This principle is embedded in and in accordance with his creation of the world. When verse 5b affirms that "the earth is full of the steadfast love [חסד] of the LORD," it most probably refers to the steadfast and loyal presence of justice and righteousness in the stable cosmic condition of the earth itself, and not to the historical plans of the nations. Therefore, our psalm system-

65. See also Prov 8:22-31, where wisdom was established before creation and was at work in it.

66. So K. Koch, "Wort und Einheit," 274-75.

atically relates the theology of creation and the theology of history. In its attempt to validate justice and righteousness as the true guidelines for human history on earth, Psalm 33 must go back to creation and associate "justice and righteousness" (including Yahweh's חסד in the ongoing existence of the cosmic order of the earth) with the creation of the world. Hence, creation theology not only offers the most comprehensive aspect, it also offers the most foundational criterion for the conduct of universal human history and for the critical evaluation of actual human history. History either fails or is justified to the extent that it is in line with the just and righteous order of creation. Yahweh is the God who loves history as justice and righteousness instead of as power and might because he is the creator whose love for justice and righteousness is the basis for the initial and ongoing order of the world. As the creator, "the LORD looks down from heaven; he sees all humankind. From where he sits enthroned he watches all the inhabitants of the earth — he who fashions the hearts of them all, and observes all their deeds" (Ps 33:13-15).

The question of the systematic relationship between the creator of the world and the judge of the nations would also have to be raised with respect to the so-called Yahweh enthronement psalms: 47; 93; 96–99. This question is different from the traditio-historical problem concerning the chronological sequence in which Israel came to know Yahweh as the creator. It arises at the moment in which the notion of the God of history was combined with the notion of the God of creation. From that moment on, the question is unavoidable as to whether Yahweh is understood as the God of creation because he is the God of history, or whether he is the God of history and the judge of the nations because he is the God of creation. At close examination, the answer given or suggested in these psalms should be quite clear. Yahweh is not the God of creation because he is the God of history.

It is true that Yahweh acts in and through history, often in quite mysterious ways. On the whole, however, it seems as if Yahweh's own plan is more effective in bringing the plans of the nations to nought than in implementing the order of his creation in or through human history, or in reintegrating human history into the order of his creation. It seems that the order of creation cannot be restored via human history. It seems that human history cannot bring about or lead to the kingdom of heaven, but on the contrary, human history will come to its end when the kingdom of heaven comes.

C. Israel

However, Israel's experience is exceptional in human history — in psalms, such as 74; 77; 89; 136; 148, and in Deutero-Isaiah (40:27-28; 43:1; 44:24b-28; 45:12-13; 51:9-10; 54:5), creation and Israel's own history are correlated under the aspect of Yahweh's salvific actions. Creation out of chaos is seen as the first in a chain of salvific actions. Here, world order and Israel's history are united under one purpose, liberation from chaos and oppression. Thus, it can be said that Yahweh is the creator of the world because he is its liberator from chaos, just as he is the creator of Israel because he is its liberator from oppression. Therefore, the notion of liberation belongs to both creation and Israel's history. However, this does not yet address the question of the relationship between creation and Israel's history, or specifically, between creation as liberation and Israel's history as liberation. In view of this question, we must again ask whether Yahweh is considered as the liberating creator of the world because he is the liberating creator of Israel, or whether he is considered as the liberator of Israel because he is the liberating creator of the world. Technically speaking, the question concerns the systematic relationship of the passage mentioned above dealing with creation with those dealing with Israel's history.

Once this systematic question is raised, the answer cannot be in doubt. Yahweh is the liberating creator of Israel precisely because he is the liberating creator of the world. It is the creator who is at work in Israel. Deutero-Isaiah refines this by asserting that as he did in the first exodus, so Yahweh will save his people in the second exodus because he is the creator (Isa 51:9-10). His announcement of salvation is trustworthy because the creator is trustworthy (Isa 40:27-28). Strictly speaking, liberation in creation is not only the first in the sequence of Yahweh's historical acts. It is the ever-present foundation and universal horizon for all of Yahweh's subsequent liberating acts in history. Should it not also be the foundation on which and the reality into which history itself is to be finally liberated? If this view of creation is correct, then the liberation and election of Israel cannot be regarded as the purpose of creation. On the contrary, the purpose of Israel's history of liberation was to point to and to witness to the fundamental reality, to God's liberation of the world into the just and righteous order of his creation. Israel was called to actualize this purpose in its own existence.

Above all, two types of existence in which this actualization was supposed to take place in Israel's reality must be listed. The first type into which Israel was called was the מנוחה, the rest in the inherited land, and thus into an agrarian existence that is itself embedded in the cyclic cosmic order of creation. All Old Testament texts that speak about Israel's agricultural existence in the land and Yahweh's blessing presence in it belong to this aspect. The number of references is endless, and the essay interpreting them would be extensive. A text that has been prominent in the discussion of Israel's theological traditions can illustrate this meaning. It is the so-called "Historical Creed" in Deut 26:5-11. This "creed" is actually a תודה, a statement of individual thanksgiving.[67] According to an illustrious tradition of interpretation, this text has been considered as a paradigm for the historicization of myth in Israel, i.e., for the transformation of the ancient Near

67. To my embarrassment, I must admit that I owe the form-critical insight that Deut 26:5-11 is not a "creed" to the systematician W. Pannenberg, communicated in conversation.

Eastern perception of the eternal cycle into a perception of linear salvation history. It is true that, when taken in isolation, the liberation history mentioned in our text reflects an understanding of linear history. But it is definitely wrong to discuss the problem of the relationship between cyclic reality and linear history on the basis of Deut 26:5-11! It is already wrong in view of verses 9-11 of this passage. What is decisive for the passage and its context is the relationship between the past liberation history and the present situation of the worshipper. In this relationship, the past liberation history has led to the situation of living in a land which was given as a gift, a land flowing with milk and honey. And the present situation of the worshipper (Deut 26:1-4) reflects the Yahweh-harvest festival of the firstfruits in which the arrival at this goal was celebrated. It celebrates Israel's arrival in a settled, agrarian existence which is embedded in the structure of cosmic space and its cyclic time. Therefore, the theology of our text reflects, above all and in essence, a cyclization of this history! Salvation history is fulfilled in the blessing of the annual agrarian life cycle which remains forever.

This text also shows that liberation history is not an end in itself, just as it is not the beginning. Israel's history does not begin with its liberation. It begins with its oppression from which it is liberated by Yahweh. Likewise, Yahweh's history with Israel does not end with its liberation from oppression. But its history of liberation ends whenever it arrives at its goal, i.e., the ongoing life in the land in blessing and peace. The theology of historical liberation cannot be considered the fundamental aspect of Old Testament theology. It stands in the service of that aspect which is the goal of historical liberation. In Deut 26:1-11, this goal is life in the land given and blessed by Yahweh. It is life in the actual presence of the order of Yahweh's creation.

The second type of existence into which Israel was called was the implementation of justice and righteousness in its society. In the Old Testament, this implementation is understood both as the actualization of the goal of Israel's liberation history, especially so in the prophets, and as Israel's response to Yahweh's ongoing revelation of justice and righteousness in its cultic traditions, so in the Sinai traditions (Exodus 19–Numbers 10) and in the Jerusalem psalms. The actualization itself ultimately is expected to be in accord with Yahweh's justice and righteousness as the foundations of his world government (Psalms 82; 96:13; 97:2; 98:9; 99:4).

It is well known that, in this aspect, the traditions of Israel's societal laws and the cultic traditions of Yahweh as the judge of the world converge. It is also well known that, traditio-historically speaking, these traditions have heterogeneous origins and have not been correlated systematically throughout the Old Testament. The Sinai traditions, Deuteronomy, and many psalms reflect such systematic efforts. This indicates that the Old Testament tradition history itself does not oppose the need for an all-inclusive systematization of the variety of its societal and legal traditions in the framework of a theology of justice and righteousness. In such a systematization, the traditions expressing Yahweh's universal justice and righteousness as the foundation of his world government apparently represent the most inclusive as well as the most foundational aspects. These aspects occur especially in the psalms from the Jerusalem tradition, but also in the prophetic traditions. In these traditions, however, Yahweh is seen as the Lord/creator of the world, and not only as the Lord/judge of history. More specifically, he is seen as the Lord/judge of history because he is the Lord of the world. Furthermore, the actualization or nonactualization of justice and righteousness by Israel in its own society is subject to the judgment of this judge, on the basis of his worldwide justice, and before a worldwide forum. The critical foundation of the theology of Israel's societal justice is, therefore, Israel's theology of universal justice which is itself anchored in its theology of the just and righteous order of the world. This foundation is not necessarily identical with the historical roots out of which Israel's ethos of justice emerged. But it ultimately becomes the theological foundation for an ethos of universal justice and for an ethos of historical liberation as restoration of justice from perverted justice. In turn, this ethos aims at justice which is in accord with the order of the world. From this perspective, this ethos receives its inescapable force and validity because it is no longer based on particularistic historical movements.

Nevertheless, and precisely because of this criterion, Israel's own history is neither a substitute for the order of God's world to which it points, nor the full actualization of this order on earth. Israel's historical institutions did not replace Yahweh's creation and sustenance of the world. They were supposed to point to that realm of Yahweh's domination. Nor did these institutions ever fully actualize what they were meant to be, i.e., paradigmatic implementations on earth of Yahweh's salvific world order. Throughout the history of its traditions, the Old Testament knows about the tension between Israel's call and Israel's actual existence. Ultimately, Israel's institutions had no mythical qualities even as they were created by Yahweh. They were understood in contrast to mythical legitimations of hierarchical social orders which tend to cement the status quo and to resist the distribution of justice for all. They were meant as instruments for the distribution of Yahweh's own justice, and not as the goal and end of Yahweh's presence in the world. Israel knew that its history and its institutions were to be in the service of Yahweh's work in and for the world, and that Yahweh was not a symbol for the deification of Israel's own history or its institutions.

Nevertheless, it is true that in historical reality Israel's institutions actually tended to act as if they themselves were the goal and purpose of Yahweh's justice. Whenever this was the case, Israel was in crisis — not because of its enemies, but because of Yahweh in its midst. Thus, the salvific historical experiences again and again lost their witnessing clarity and force, and Israel was forced to surrender them. In this ongoing process, Israel experienced the tension between the meaning of its history and its actual history. The theology of the tradition history of Israel is fundamentally characterized by this tension. It presents a people of Yahweh whose history is intended to witness to the presence of the order of Yahweh's creation, but whose history is neither a substitute nor a full testimony for that order. Exactly in this tension between vocation and failure, between the praise of Yahweh's work and the confession of their own sin, emerges the continuity of God's people in history. It is the continuity of those who, through the experience of both their election and their failure, point beyond themselves, as long as the world exists, to the kingdom of God.

D. Old and New Creation

The created world will not exist forever. It is finite. The finiteness of the world comes into sharp focus through the distinction of the creation from its creator. "Before the mountains were brought forth, or ever you had formed the earth and the world, from everlasting to everlasting you are God" (Ps 90:2). "Long ago you laid the foundation of the earth, and the heavens are the work of your hands. They will perish, but you endure; they will all wear out like a garment. You change them like clothing, and they pass away; but you are the same, and your years have no end" (Ps 102:26-28 [*NRSV* 102:25-27]). However, Israel's knowledge of the creator also caused it to speak of a new creation: "For I am about to create new heavens and a new earth; the former things shall not be remembered or come to mind" (Isa 65:17; cf. 66:22).

In a meritorious essay, H.-J. Kraus discusses the subject of creation and new creation and its implications for a biblical theology.[68] Proceeding traditio-historically, Kraus interprets the course of this kerygmatic theme from the early exilic time throughout the postexilic and intertestamental literature to the doorsteps of the New Testament. At the outset, he compares the theologies of the priestly work and Deutero-Isaiah with respect to his topic. The priestly work is said to be guided by a kerygma according to which the initial creation of the world is directly eschatologically present in Israel's cultic realm, especially in the sabbath week (158-59). This "presence of the perfect creation" (*"Präsenz der vollkommenen Schöpfung,"* 159) is also called the "presence of the consummation of the world" (*"Gegenwart der Weltvollendung,"* 159), and even the "presence of the [new creation]" (*"Präsenz der [neuen Schöpfung],"* 175). The priestly writer is said to understand Israel's cultic realm as the quasi-eschatological presence of the perfection of creation, of the new creation (168).

By contrast, Deutero- and Trito-Isaiah, according to Kraus, announce the

68. H.-J. Kraus, "Schöpfung und Weltvollendung," *EvT* 24 (1964): 462-85; reprinted in *Biblisch Theologische Aufsätze* (Neukirchen-Vluyn: Neukirchener Verlag, 1972),151-78, referred to heretofore.

impending consummation of the world as the act of a new creation which is the concomitant symptom of Yahweh's new and final liberation of Israel. This liberation will occur through the universal theophany of Yahweh. It represents the final stage of history into which the nations are also drawn, and along with which the consummation of the world and the new creation will arrive as well (160-68). This prophetic-eschatological view is quite different from the priestly perspective (175-76). Nevertheless, these two aspects, the presence of the beginning and the impending end or the new creation, together represent the background for our understanding of apocalypticism (168-69). The course of the tradition can be discerned especially in the proto-apocalyptic prophetic literature (e.g., Isa 25:8; 26:19; 35:3-7) which represents the bridge from Deutero-Isaiah to Daniel and the intertestamental period (170-71).

Kraus's essay is suggestive. It shows the major traces of the development of the tradition. In addition, it shows how the emerging vision of the future creation appears in this development as a concomitant to Yahweh's consummation of history, which is itself the result of Yahweh's final redemption of Israel. Nevertheless, the essay raises a number of exegetical problems, and ultimately a number of substantive problems concerning the implications of this picture for biblical theology.

A first exegetical remark concerns the theology of the priestly work which reflects the first pole of Kraus's topic *"Schöpfung und Weltvollendung."* Kraus is doubtlessly correct when assuming, along with traditional interpretation, a close correlation between creation and Israel's cultic institutions. He is also correct in pointing out that the initial creation is a present reality and not only a memory of the past. But is he correct when he claims that creation is represented quasi-eschatologically by Israel's cultic institutions, and that these institutions represent the "presence of the perfect creation," the "presence of the consummation of the world," and even the "presence of the [new creation]"? More precisely, are the cultic institutions themselves the presence of creation, or do they simply point to the presence of creation and show Israel to be in accordance with it? In the first case, creation would not be an ongoing reality in its own right because it would have been replaced by Israel's cult. This cult would be the reality of creation, and the cult would not be where creation is, but creation would be where the cult is. In the second case, creation would be recognized as a present reality in its own right, whereas the cult would represent Israel as being in accord with the order of creation. To this extent, one can say that the fullness of creation is present in Israel. But it is the fullness of creation that is present in or mediated through the cult, and not the cult that has replaced creation by being creation itself or even the "new creation." This question may need further research. For the time being, **P** does not seem to say in Genesis 1 that creation exists nowhere except in or through Israel's cult. He seems to know of God's promise of the ongoing existence of the cosmos (Gen 9:1-17), and indeed Israel's sabbath seems to be a sign that points to God's rest from his work (Exod 31:17; Lev 23:3). God does not rest in Israel's sabbath, but Israel's sabbath participates in the rest of God.

The question under discussion has far-reaching consequences. If the cultic institutions themselves are the mode of the presence of creation, then creation would neither exist outside them nor exist as the ground of their existence. This aspect would be the decisive reason for the theological irrelevance of Israel's cosmology in its perception of the world, at least in **P**, if not for the entire Old Testament. It is, however, highly unlikely that **P** represents such a theology. If he did, he would be back in the Canaanite camp where creation takes place, is actualized, and is enacted in the cult.

A second exegetical remark concerns Kraus's discussion of Deutero- and Trito-Isaiah. The problem is both terminological and substantive in nature. Concentrating on the second pole of his topic, creation at the end of history, Kraus uses the terms "consummation of creation" *("Weltvollendung")* and "new creation" *("neue Schöpfung")* interchangeably. These terms, however, do not mean the same thing. "Consummation of creation" means, as Kraus himself describes it in alternating terminology, the perfection of the existing world, i.e., rejuvenation or renewal. This terminology is quite applicable where the texts announce such a consummation via the historical process and as the end or fulfillment of that historical process. The term "new creation," however, does not necessarily carry the same connotation. It can mean an event that happens, instead of history and as the replacement of history rather than via history and as part of history, however final it may be. The differentiation of the two terms is necessary as long as it is not exegetically clarified whether our texts speak of creation as the end of history (in terms of a final stage of history) or in terms of an event that replaces history, or in terms of both. In the first case, the consummation of the world would appear subsumed under universal history. In the second case, history would appear preliminary to the universal aspect of creation, now even more than before, since the newness is not that of a new history but that of a new creation.

As far as Deutero- and Trito-Isaianic eschatology is concerned, the issue is clear even though a development is apparent. Along with Israel's eschatological liberation, the earth is renewed (Isa 40:3-4; 41:18-19; 42:16; 43:19-20; 44:3; 49:11; 51:10). The new event announced by Deutero-Isaiah is the new exodus, not the new creation. As much as creation is concomitantly affected, it is at most the earth which will be turned into paradise again, and not the entire cosmos. Specifically, the earth is renewed or rejuvenated, not created anew or again (cf. also Ps 104:30). This notion is well established in the tradition. In the Canaanite tradition it can be interpreted as a new creation, whereas for Israel it can mean only a renewed or rejuvenated creation. Hence, Deutero-Isaiah announces the renewal of the life-sustaining earth for the purpose of Yahweh's execution of the new exodus. But he does not announce a new creation of the earth, let alone a new cosmic order. It is even doubtful that we should call this announcement the "consummation of the world" because this expression sees something in the future which has not existed before, whereas Deutero-Isaiah, as far as his reference is concerned, seems to see in the future a reactivation of the paradisal origin.

The picture changes in Trito-Isaiah, where Yahweh announces the creation of a "new heavens and a new earth" (Isa 65:17 and 66:22). The object of Yahweh's creation is here no longer the new exodus; it is a new cosmic order which will provide the basis for Israel's life in the land:

> The sun shall no more be your light by day, nor for brightness shall the moon give light to you by night; but the LORD will be your everlasting light, and your God will be your glory. Your sun shall no more go down, or your moon withdraw itself; for the LORD will be your everlasting light, and your days of mourning shall be ended. (Isa 60:19-20)

Indeed, the old cosmic order will not only be replaced by a new one, it will also be replaced by the order of the eternal cosmic theophany. A fundamental change happens in the history of the theophanic tradition: theophany is no longer a recurring historical or cultic event; it is the never-ending presence and revelation of God through cosmic order.

Interestingly, however, Israel's life in the land is described in Isa 65:18-25 entirely in the language of the order of the original creation. It is not the life of the new creation found in later traditions in which death will be no more, or where the dead are resurrected.[69] Even in the new creation, life is perceived as the restitution of the paradisal order of the original creation. Notions of both the new and the original creation converge in this view of the future. Decisive, however, is the fact that this view of the future is entirely guided by the order of creation, and not by the structure of historical existence. Whatever Israel's future history is to be, it will be a history lived in the order of creation. In addition, whatever the future history of the nations is to be, it will appear in the light of the presence of the order of creation in Israel's history.

The question arises as to whether the new creation announced in Trito-Isaiah and from then on must be understood as a concomitant of Israel's emerging history in the land, as the universal extension of it; or whether Israel's future history must be understood as the result of and as based on the coming of the new creation, the coming of Yahweh's kingdom "from above,"[70] i.e., from heaven, just as it exists and is ever present in heaven. This question affects the relationship of eschatology and apocalypticism. Substantively, it affects the problem of whether the new creation appears as the final stage, the completion of the process of universal history, or whether history is ended when its structure is replaced through the integration

69. See Isa 25:8; 26:19; Dan 12:2; Pss. Sol. 3:12; 2 Enoch 65:17. Cf. Kraus, "Schöpfung," 171.

70. Kraus, "Schöpfung," 171. Kraus alludes to this question, but does not discuss its implications.

of the creatures into the order of creation. This question needs further study. For the time being, it seems that, compared with Deutero-Isaiah, Trito-Isaiah represents the beginning of a major shift in which the resolution of historical problems is seen in the new creation instead of in the universalized stage of Israel's new history.

One problem has not yet been addressed. Why is a new creation necessary? This problem will not be pursued here. It is sufficient to point out that the attention ultimately focuses on the newness of creation, and not on the newness of history.

What are the implications of this traditio-historical view of the theme of creation for Old Testament theology, and eventually for biblical theology? Kraus is among those who are certain that "traditio-historical investigation shows the way" for an integrated view of the two testaments.[71] Following von Rad, he proposes as the objective a "history of a thematically oriented kerygma" which is itself based on the ever new "charismatic-eclectic interpretation" of the older traditions.[72] The importance and value of such an endeavor cannot be disputed. It has received its most ingenious execution in von Rad's *Theology of the Old Testament.* However, the question is unavoidable as to whether it alone can provide the basis for an integrated Old Testament theology.

For such a theology, the demonstration of the historical process alone is not sufficient, unless we assume that the process as such is the theological proof of the truth, validity, or legitimacy of the tradition. Moreover, inasmuch as it is a factor of the historical process itself, the reference to the "charismatic-eclectic interpretation" is insufficient, unless we assume that every "charismatic-eclectic interpretation" is true and valid by virtue of being charismatic-eclectic. The biblical tradition in both the Old and the New Testament gives us every reason not to subscribe to this assumption. Moreover, Israel's tradition history has not come to us in the order of successive stages classified historically. It has come to us as a critically accumulated compendium of all the historical stages in which the various and often quite differing kerygmata are juxtaposed. The adaptation and accumulation of these kerygmata, however critically sifted, are themselves supreme results of Israel's tradition history. This tradition history has provided us, therefore, with the variety of charismatic-eclectic interpretations, but it has not endeavored to show us why a particular interpretation is theologically valid — certainly not by the fact that it happened or stands in the tradition! — how its various theological traditions are to be correlated, and what the theological foundation is on which they all belong and which validates them all just as it validates the whole tradition history. In view of these questions, Israel's tradition history has not explained itself. Yet it calls for this explanation and provides the criteria for this explanation out of its own heritage.[73] One may say that these questions themselves belong to the task of

71. "Schöpfung," 177.

72. "Schöpfung," 177.

73. The claim that Jesus Christ is the answer is itself no answer, true as the claim may be

tradition history. But then we must recognize, quite apart from the fact that Old Testament traditio-historical scholarship has not given a prominent visibility to these questions, that Israel's tradition history is subject to a critical criterion inherent in that history, and is not its own validation.

What has been said may finally be illustrated by three questions arising from the discussion of Kraus's essay.

First, what is the validity of the priestly doctrine of creation in view of Deutero-Isaiah's eschatologically oriented prophecy? Does its validity consist only in that it provides, together with Deutero-Isaiah, the historical kerygmatic presupposition for the emergence of apocalypticism? This would mean that the priestly kerygma has no validity in its own right despite the fact that tradition history has ultimately juxtaposed it alongside the other kerygmata. This answer is not good enough. When **P** is juxtaposed with Deutero-Isaiah and the tradition emerging from it, the differences between the two theologies come into sharp focus. These differences weigh even heavier if one assumes that both **P** and Deutero-Isaiah represent approximately simultaneous programs for Israel's return to the land, as well as the renewal and new beginning in it. This problem has many facets which will not be discussed here. Only one point must be mentioned. If we want to correlate the two programs without deciding for one over against the other, then it is necessary to affirm the priestly doctrine in spite of the future-oriented prophecy of Deutero-Isaiah concerning the renewal of creation along with the second exodus. In such an affirmation, however, the priestly message that the order of creation stands as a very present reality despite the historical catastrophes must play a decisive role. In fact, **P** affirms the presence of creation, and of God in creation, and not only its past and future. It is the task of biblical theology to interpret what this affirmation means in its own right, and in relation to Deutero-Isaiah as well.

Secondly, if the Old Testament tradition history developed two kerygmata concerning the future of creation, one about the renewal of the world and the other about the new creation, then the question of their relationship and of the theological function of each in relation to the other must be addressed. A position stating that one was eventually transcended and replaced by the other is certainly insufficient. Nor does a position suffice which relies on nothing more than the fact of the juxtaposition or interwovenness of these kerygmata itself. This position especially may want, in this as well as in other cases, to account for the canonic factor in tradition history. However, as long as it does not explain the kind of relationship between the different kerygmata and the basis for that relationship, it is still caught in a biblicistic approach to biblical theology in which eclectic and charismatic

for the Christian tradition. The fact that Jesus is part of Israel's traditions does not substantiate as such that he is the Christ. Nor does the fact of a new charismatic-eclectic interpretation of the Christ-event substantiate that claim.

interpretation are indistinguishable from arbitrary and chaotic interpretation, i.e., that the Bible justifies every interpretation simply because it is written.

The question in our case certainly involves the relationship of creation and universal history. On the basis of what has been said throughout this essay, this question is not at all new for the exilic/postexilic time. Apparently, it has had a long tradition history. It has been addressed in various settings within Yahwism, and it has not remained without answers. It may be that comprehensive studies can exegetically show that the biblical tradition history finally arrived at an integrated answer. Should it be, however, that the biblical tradition has not given us an answer in unison, nevertheless this tradition history has presented us with its own massive involvement in the question. This fact also belongs to its heritage. In this sense, tradition history calls us to work on the answers to the questions it has raised and left for us. But before we recognize the vast importance of the theology of creation in the Old Testament, we will scarcely be in a position to address this challenge properly.

Thirdly, the Old Testament tradition sharply raises the question of the meaning of Israel in the horizon of creation and history. The fact that Israel's election is seen in this horizon is not a point of debate. It must simply be affirmed. The question is whether the totality of our textual traditions, when seeing Israel in this horizon, describes creation and history as concomitant to and ultimately in the service of Israel's election, or vice versa. Insofar as Israel's particular election represents a meaning for universal human history, the question arises as to what reveals the meaning of universal history in Israel's particular election. Universal history is not meaningful by being universal. But it receives its universality, as well as its qualification, from God's creation of the world which embraces the beginning, the course, and the end of history, and which, at the same time, reveals the meaningfulness or failure of history. The purpose of the elect, however, can only be to point out this meaning of universal history by means of their own historical existence. The problem is that the Old Testament kerygmata themselves do not always unanimously reflect this understanding. Again, tradition history appears as the problem as much as it indicates the directions in which the answers must be found. It does not authenticate itself, but is critically evaluated in light of that which it itself recognizes as the horizon and foundation through which Yahweh determines its meaning: Yahweh's own creation and new creation.

Conclusion

In its most universal and foundational aspects, the history of the Old Testament traditions is profoundly preoccupied with the relationship between cosmic order and human history. Moreover, it is increasingly concerned with the tension between these two realities. This relationship, and especially the tension, between cosmic order and history stands in the center of our own experience at the end of the second Christian millennium. The tension is acute in the threat to human history through the threat to its foundation, the possible destruction of the cosmic order into which the earth is bound. This threat is real, and is generated by human history itself. It is human history that threatens the cosmic order, and not the cosmic order that threatens human history. History certainly has the capacity to destroy itself while the cosmic order may continue to exist. But if it destroys the cosmic order of the earth, history itself ceases to matter and with it everything generated by history, including the existence and concerns of individuals.

The ongoing existence of the cosmic global order must not be taken for granted. The Old Testament already knows that human history can contaminate it, even though this order has no freedom to destroy itself. Furthermore, the ongoing existence of the cosmic global order must not be dismissed in view of the new creation. Whether the new creation is the vision of a future expectation (Isa 65:17; 66:22; 2 Pet 3:13) or of a reality present in the midst of the old creation (2 Cor 5:17; Col 1:15-20), the function of this vision for those who live in the order of the present creation can only be to reveal what creation itself ultimately means. Its function cannot be to reject God's own creation. Therefore, to take the cosmic order for granted or to reject it in view of the new creation is utterly unwarranted and ultimately irresponsible.

By contrast, the ongoing existence of the present order of creation precisely represents the real point of concern. In view of this concern, to be in tune with the order of creation appears as the central task of worldwide human history. This task identifies the criterion from which the meaning or the failure of human history will be determined, i.e., its ultimate fulfillment or its ultimate sin. Scientists increasingly argue that the possibilities for the existence of life elsewhere in the universe are remote. This does not mean that the existence of life somewhere in the universe is impossible or unthinkable. However, it is possible that our globe is the only place in the universe on which life exists, especially human life as we know it. Regardless of whether or not this is the case, the possibility alone is an awesome fact. It means that human history, which itself emerges from and is based on life's existence on this globe, is accountable before the universe for the continuance of the life which inexplicably emerged in this particular spot of the universe. If human history destroys the cosmic order of life on this globe, which is the exceptional place (or at least one of the exceptional places) where this purpose of the universe has become manifest, then it attacks the universe itself, its purpose and the reality of its mystery. For theology and faith, this accountability of history demands a new, fundamental, and large-scale attention to the theology of creation and to the ethos resulting from it.

It is the well-known and ongoing task of biblical theology and hermeneutic to determine the criteria according to which the mutual evaluation of the two testaments can take place. In view of this task, the question arises as to whether there is any correspondence between the theologies of creation in the Old and the New Testament. This question certainly affects the same aspects that are addressed directly or indirectly in both testaments. But it also affects those aspects that are addressed only in one of the two testaments, or at least more directly or extensively in one than in the other. The concerns of the Old Testament wisdom literature are a case in point. The same is true for the extensive preoccupation in the Old Testament with human history as such, and with the history of the people of Israel. On the other hand, the New Testament is extensively preoccupied with God's salvation through Christ for humanity, a preoccupation unmatched in degree by the Old Testament. In addition, it is more preoccupied with the history of the beginning church among the Gentiles, undetermined by Israel's cultic traditions, than with Israel proper. This preoccupation is totally absent in the Old Testament. The New Testament affirms that salvation comes from the Jews. But it does not affirm that it comes through the Jews.

As for the aspect of creation, it is sufficient to repeat what Steck has said:

> The New Testament, unlike the Old, offers no thematically distinct statements about creation, let alone extensive passages on the subject, covering the elemental world of life in its totality.[74]

Nevertheless,

> [The New Testament] does not deny that world, and it by no means overlooks the sphere in which the living have always existed. But it accepts this and includes it, as God's world of creation, in the comprehensive whole of divine activity which reveals its goal in the coming of Christ. . . . Accordingly in the New Testament his coming is not merely perceived by reference to the Old, but also within the framework which the Old Testament itself opens up: the framework of the world's comprehensive dimension of meaning as a whole, both in time and space.[75]

In view of the fact that the New Testament presupposes but does not itself present an explicit and extensive doctrine of creation, the question can be specifically formulated: What is the role and importance of the Old Testament theology of cosmic order, of its ever-presence, and of God's presence in the world through it, for the understanding of Christ? Does Christ represent the presence of the cosmic order of God's creation on which all history rests, including the history of both Jews and Christians, or is he, e.g., only the presence and the future of the new

74. *World and Environment,* 258-59. On the importance of the theology of creation for the total horizon of biblical theology, see H. H. Schmid, *"Schöpfung"* (cf. partial English trans.: "Creation Righteous, and Salvation," *Creation in the Old Testament,* ed. B. Anderson, trans. B. Anderson and Dan Johnson [Philadelphia: Fortress, 1984]).

75. Steck, *World and Environment,* 259.

creation? Even if only the latter aspect were the case, the question would remain regarding the meaning of this new creation in Christ for the ongoing existence of the order of the initial creation, for the relationship between this order and human history, and for the function of Judaism as well as Christianity in this relationship. In any case, the reality of the present order of creation, its relationship to human history, and the function of God's people in this relationship cannot simply be dismissed. The Old Testament does not permit such a dismissal. Nor does the actual historical situation of modern humanity permit it. Such a dismissal would amount to the abdication of any vision of salvation for the current global situation as God's creation in its own right. Moreover, it would mean that Christ himself has nothing to do with the ongoing existence of God's initial creation. He would not be representative of that created order or of its ongoing sustenance. Ultimately, he would be irrelevant for the ongoing history of humanity, i.e., "secular history," and for the dreadful problems confronting humanity's immediate future. In this sense, he would not be the Lord.

In view of these implications, the question is not so much whether or to what extent Christ justifies the Old Testament theology of creation. The question is much more whether or not Christ himself is legitimated by the Old Testament God of creation because it is the God of creation who represents first of all and preeminently nothing less than this reality and its legitimacy. Whether or not the New Testament itself directly and extensively addresses this aspect, the Old Testament's theology of creation would provide the criterion for the most foundational and universal horizon in which Jesus of Nazareth, the risen Christ, appears as the ultimate representative of God's presence in relationship to and concern for his world. The risen Christ of the new creation would appear to be the already existing reconciliation of the tension between creation and human history. This tension cannot be overcome through the order of the initial creation nor through the impetus of human history. But when the tension and friction are already overcome, human history is no longer deterministically condemned to continue in tension with the order of creation. To be witnesses to and for this reconciliation in this world would be the essential reason for the existence of God's people in this world, the foundational reason from which all other reasons derive their meaning. New Testament Christology following the Old Testament doctrine of the messiah, let alone New Testament ecclesiology following the Old Testament doctrine of Israel's election, apparently receives its meaning and legitimacy in light of the Old Testament theology of creation, i.e., of God's world and of God in and for his world.

In light of this, the New Testament ought to be read once again.[76] In such a reading, one will certainly have to be aware of the complexity of the problem

76. For a comprehensive discussion of the New Testament's theological aspects regarding the natural world, see Steck, *World and Environment,* 229-98.

situation. From the methodological point of view, it is apparent that the New Testament must be seen in the context of its own time and of its immediately preceding history. Nevertheless, the fact remains that the context to which the New Testament itself explicitly refers is the Old Testament scriptures, especially the prophets and the psalms. Also, one will have to distinguish between the explicit subjects addressed in the texts and the foundational presuppositions, assumptions, and concerns on which those subjects rest. The interpretation of these presuppositions and assumptions is not only important for the understanding of the texts themselves; it is also important in its own right because it reveals the essential understanding of reality with which the New Testament is concerned. Bultmann may have been wrong in seeing this understanding preoccupied with human existentiality; but he was hardly wrong in attempting to uncover this essential understanding and concern. Finally, the deeply mythological nature of the New Testament texts can only mean that this mythology is interpreted in view of its understanding of reality, but not that it is altogether eliminated from consideration. In this regard, attention to the cosmological statements or assumptions in the New Testament is of special importance. These cosmological perceptions are strongly enmeshed in the mythological concept. This may have been a reason why they have fallen by the wayside in interpretation. However, the mythological and the cosmological perceptions of reality are not the same. The cosmological perception is certainly part of an all-embracing mythical worldview. However, it does not fade away when the essence of the mythical worldview is reinterpreted in nonmythological terms. It will have to remain part of a nonmythological interpretation of the essence of the New Testament's perception of universal reality.

From a substantive point of view, therefore, the cosmological statements or assumptions of the New Testament ought to be interpreted in their own right. Such an interpretation ought to take place because of their theological and christological significance, and not apart from or in spite of it. Numerous questions emerge from such a vantage point. Some of them may be mentioned here. What is the relationship between cosmic space and time and historical time in the New Testament literature? What is the relationship between "heaven" and "earth"? Where is the kingdom already cosmically present, and where is it not, or not fully? According to Matt 6:10, the disciples are to assume that God's will is already being done in heaven, and on this basis they are to pray that it will likewise be done on earth. Does the New Testament assume a cosmic realm in which God's creation has always been intact, over against a realm that is not intact? What does it say or assume about the revealedness or hiddenness of this realm? What is the function of the theology of the cross in view of this horizon?

Moreover, why was it necessary that Jesus be understood as nothing less than the resurrected one? Above all, the resurrection certainly means that the new creation has come into existence cosmically. But what, then, is the relationship between this new creation and that realm of God's initial creation in which God's will has always been done? What is the function of this as yet hidden new creation, the full revelation of which is yet to come, for the evaluation of God's ongoing initial creation into which the order of this earth is bound and from which all creatures continue to live? When waiting for the new heaven and the new earth in which righteousness dwells (2 Pet 3:13), what is the function for those waiting for such an expectation for an ethos of righteousness in this ongoing world?[77]

Finally, the Christian community understands itself as the eschatological human community, the witness to the new creation, as the community who knows that the "perfect world" (1 Cor 13:8-13) is already present but not yet fully revealed. What is the function of this eschatological existence and witness for the understanding of the continued existence of God's initial creation, and for human history? What is the ultimate function and task of Christianity?

It seems that the New Testament has much to say regarding these questions, both in its assertions and in its assumptions. All these questions, and more, are intrinsic to the aspect of God's creation. It seems that this aspect provides the critical basis and horizon for a biblical theology — if there is any basis at all — and at the same time determines both the purpose of the vocation of God's people in this world and the significance of their message to humanity.[78]

77. For an example of the ongoing discussion on this subject, see L. Gaston, "Abraham and the Righteousness of God," *HBT* 2 (1980): 39-68.

78. I am indebted to professor George Coats for his critical discussion of the major part of this paper during the summer of 1981 at Claremont.

Food, Land, and Justice

Introduction

To say that all living beings must regularly eat and drink might be trivial if such a statement were matched by or based on the fact of food being accessible to all. Such a fact does not exist today, nor has it ever existed in the history of life. Hunger always was, and continues to be, a threat to life for many. Further, the regular provision of sufficient food is one of the few elementary concerns of all living beings in their existence.

Thus far in the history of life on this globe, the need for food has not been undercut by its unavailability. The globe's natural resources have always had, and for the time being continue to have, the quantities and qualities in store that are more than sufficient for the needs of all its creatures. On balance, the resources still outnumber the needs. However, this situation is changing. This change of the positive balance between resources and needs represents a new condition in our generation for which there is no precedent in the experience of all previous human history. Its root cause lies in the fact that the geometrical explosion of the global population is rapidly reaching the point from which the globe's resources are being acceleratingly outstripped by mass humanity, outstripped even if the globe's ecosystem — its land, air, and water — could otherwise be kept in balance. It is unlikely that the globe, or any advanced technology for its management, can feed fifty billion people within the next century or two. Compared with millennia of past history, this prospect is fundamentally new, inevitable, and irreversible.

The newness of the growth toward overpopulation means neither that the generations before us should be faulted for not including this aspect in their experience of reality, nor that their own views of the relationship between the earth's resources and the needs of the living are now irrelevant. This means that when confronting the new historical era we must not ignore the views of the ancients, and when considering their views we must not ignore the new historical era. Moreover, since it is obvious that the decisive task for the future consists in managing a balance between the need for food and the provision of food, this intensifies our focus on the question of how the relationship between the need for and the availability of food was considered in the past.

The present chapter is confined to the biblical materials, especially that of the Old Testament. Even so, it can only highlight basic perspectives. The material evidence, especially in the Old Testament, is so abundant that it far exceeds the scope of a single chapter. Indeed, the Ph.D. dissertation by Stephen A. Reed on food in the Old Testament had to be confined to the Psalms,[1] while work on this subject in the other parts of the Old Testament has yet to be done.

The lack of biblical studies on food is strikingly evident in the history of Old and New Testament theologies. Despite the biblical evidence, the issue of food has never received attention worthy of a chapter in a theology, let alone the issue of its function in the whole of biblical theology — as if it were theologically irrelevant! Whatever the effects on the shaping of Western civilization due to the neglect of this concern, especially in the history of the Christian interpretation of the Bible, it is clear that this neglect is the result of the different interests of the interpreters, especially the interpreters of the Old Testament, rather than the result of the Old Testament's own theological perspectives.

Since the need for food is ideally met by the availability of food from the earth's resources, the discussion must focus on the Old Testament's perspective on the importance of food itself, as well as on the importance of land for the provision of food.

I. Food

A. Food in the Lord's Prayer

Before discussing the Old Testament, an observation about the Lord's Prayer is in order. Its Matthean version (Matt 6:9-13; cf. the different version in Luke 11:2b-4), expanded by the later doxological conclusion and used in the Protestant churches, is clearly structured. After the address, it consists of two series of three petitions each. The three petitions of the first series concern God's name, reign, and will. The three petitions of the second series concern those who pray, i.e., the disciples. They are arranged in the following order: first, "give us this day our daily bread"; second, "forgive us our guilt"; third, "lead us not into temptation" (author's translation). We must remember that this prayer is supposed to be the *daily* prayer

1. Stephen A. Reed, "Food in the Psalms" (Ann Arbor, MI: University Microfilms International, 1986), 550.

of the disciples. Now then, from all the concerns that we humans might possibly have, only three are considered paramount to be petitioned for each day: food/bread for today; forgiveness of sins; and protection from temptation. Of these three, the petition for food comes first — before forgiveness of sins, and before protection from temptation. This structure of the prayer calls for a few comments.

1. Whatever the eschatological perspective is in the second part of the prayer, it includes the central concerns of the disciples for their lives on earth — for *this* life.

2. Among these concerns, daily food is not coincidentally considered primary. It appears to be the inevitable presupposition for the rest. If this daily life is lost through the lack of food, the forgiveness of sins and the protection from temptation in this life no longer matter.

3. The recognition that the disciples need daily food does not mean a preferential entitlement for a chosen people in contrast to the rest of humanity that would not be entitled to such food. On the contrary, it means that the disciples are in need of and entitled to daily food, just as all humans are in need of and entitled to it. The disciples are seen together with humanity, and the affirmation of their need for food is grounded in the affirmation of all humanity's need for daily food.

4. Food, "bread," is to be understood literally, as food for the stomach and the sustenance of our physical lives, and not as spiritual food.

5. "Daily bread" means that which we *need* from day to day, and not more, certainly not the surplus destined for the trash can or the garbage disposal.

This understanding of the Lord's Prayer evokes a revealing question concerning the history of Christian theology. Throughout its history, Christian theology has been massively preoccupied with the doctrine of forgiveness, and also — both in doctrine and in moral practice — with the notion of protection from temptation. However, when has Christianity ever developed a doctrine of food supply for all humanity, including the disciples, a doctrine commensurate to the recognition of the place of daily food in the Lord's Prayer and to its fundamentality therein for the doctrines of forgiveness and protection from temptation? The answer is clear. Our tradition has developed no such doctrine. It may be speculative, but one wonders what the impact might have been of such a doctrine on the value systems and the socio-economic structures of the developing Western civilization upon which Christianity has had a formative influence. Indeed, one may also wonder whether under the proper influence of such a doctrine, if only on the basis of the daily (?) practice and sufficient understanding of the Lord's Prayer, we would exist in a world in which forty thousand infants alone die each day of illness and malnutrition.

The important position of the theology of physical food in the Lord's Prayer is significantly offset in the New Testament by the relativization of eating and drinking in favor of Christ — God's spiritual gift of water and bread (John 4:1-15; 6:1-65) — in favor of "every word that comes from the mouth of God" (Matt 4:4), or in favor of the understanding of the Eucharist in which bread and wine point not to the sacramentality of all daily eating and drinking but instead to the sacramentality of Christ's sacrifice for the forgiveness of sins (Matt 26:26-29; Mark 14:22-25; Luke 22:19-23). It seems that, next to the general relativization of the Old Testament, these and similar accentuations or conceptual shifts in the New Testament have prevented, throughout the history of Christianity, the development of a theology of physical food in its own right and also of a biblical theology of food, despite the evidence in the Old Testament and the occasional signals in the New Testament such as Matt 6:25-34; 10:9; 12:1-8; 14:13-21; etc.

In a typical, and not entirely unsubstantiatable, application of this interpretive history, a minister in our time can say in a sermon on John 6:35: "People have at all times wanted bread and games (i.e., the phrase for the Latin *panem et circenses,* which were provided for the masses in the Roman empire). With such eating and entertainment one can attract great masses at any time. Even Jesus stirred attention when feeding the five thousand; but he had to tell the crowd that he had come into the world to offer them eternal food rather than to become their bread king. Whoever eats earthly bread will have to eat again and again, because it suffices only for a moment and one will be hungry again. Whoever eats from the bread offered by Jesus, however, will be satiated in eternity, satiated by God once and for all."

Under discussion here is not God's gift of the bread of eternal life, but with respect to that gift the theological belittling of daily food for the body, and even the contempt for and the mockery of the "masses" and their longing for *panem et circenses.* (As if the feeding of the hungry masses, then and today, even if only on special festive occasions, did not meet an elementary and all too often desperate need which kings and rulers throughout history were responsible to meet!) King Henry IV of France (1533-1610) came to be beloved by his people as a just and fair ruler, and history bestowed upon him the attribute "The Great" because after the ruinous sixteenth-century wars of religion he had the vision, which became a priority for his reign, that every Sunday each family should have a chicken on its table — a luxury at that time, and scarcely a nonluxurious fact even in U.S. society.

But more is at stake. (As if the need of the "masses" for their daily food had nothing to do with the sustenance of all life by God! As if kings or rulers were not required above all else to be bread kings by virtue of their investiture by the deity! As if the human history of migrations, and even wars, was not also a result of the search for food for the masses!) The God of the Old Testament and the God of Jesus Christ, in an expression of daring trust (Matt 6:25-33), is the God who feeds the masses, especially on joyful festivals, in ancient Israel and not only in Rome. If the Christ of the New Testament has little or nothing to do with this God, and only something to do with God's food for eternal life, he would represent less than God's care for his total world at all times. Moreover, when the pastor's sermon concludes by saying, "In order to receive this heavenly food which transcends the earthly self-feeding, one must come to and accept this giver of the heavenly food," one must wonder why anyone who is hungry, let alone the masses, should place in God their hope for being fed. It may be that, for those who have food, the cry "Give me liberty or give me death" represents the highest ideal; but it seems that those who are hungry are prepared to accept any political system that feeds them as long as it does not otherwise murder them. They should not be despised for this "fleshly" attitude, especially by those who are well fed or belong to the minority who have taken upon themselves the way of fasting. Notwithstanding the values of fasting and the merits of monastic life, in the order of creation humanity is not conceived of as a monastic community. The fleshly attitude of the masses reflects the basic truth of their right to life. A religiosity which fails to recognize this truth, or even mocks or belittles it, should take heed. It not only deserves to be ignored by the masses, it also has broken with its own God, the God who sustains all life in this world. The Bible, especially the Old Testament, gives every reason to develop a theology of physical food. The Lord's Prayer and Jesus' references to God's provision of food are imbedded in the traditional God-theology rather than in Christology.

B. Food in the Old Testament

1. Statistics

a. In the Old Testament, the words for the activities of eating and drinking (אכל, שתה) and for becoming satisfied (שׂבע, מלא) number approximately 1,500 references. This count does not include the words for what one eats and drinks, such as bread, meat, water, and wine.

b. In the New Testament, the words for these activities (ἐσθίειν, τρώγειν, φαγεῖν, πίνειν) number about 180 references.

On every three pages of the *NRSV,* the people mentioned in the Old Testament eat or drink four times, whereas those in the New Testament eat or drink twice. The figures are approximate. It must be added that the New Testament passages afford a disproportionate percentage to spiritual (John) or eucharistic (Paul) eating, whereas the Old Testament passages refer with greater regularity to normal human food consumption. The Old Testament evidently pays a great deal of attention to human food consumption, and it does so rather evenly in all its parts. All people ate and drank: rich and poor, young and old, men and women, lords and servants, Israelites and non-Israelites. They all ate and drank daily, and they feasted on many special occasions such as family festivals (Joseph, Gen 43:34), annual and national festivals, and cultic-sacramental occasions for individuals or the community. Their menu was amazingly diverse. During the first third of our century, G. Dalman published seven volumes regarding work and custom in Palestine.[2] Of these, five

2. G. Dalman, *Arbeit und Sitte in Palästina,* 7 vols. (Gütersloh: C. Bertelsmann, 1928-42).

volumes, amounting to two thousand pages, deal with foods and types of food production, most of which are already mentioned in the Old Testament.

More important for us is that they paid attention to the issue of eating and drinking. They spoke and wrote about it in their prose and poetry, their novels and histories, their legislative works, their preaching and illustrations, their prophecies, and their psalms and proverbs. How should we appraise this fact? Were these people overly preoccupied with trivia, with irrelevant things really not worth talking about? Were they too worldly, too bread-and-meat oriented? Were they too fleshly? Or did they consciously realize that eating and drinking must be valued very highly because it represents the foundation for the existence of life and is not at all trivial?

2. Food and Life

a. In the Old Testament, the issue of food and hunger, of eating and drinking, is fundamentally related to humanity as a whole, even to all living beings, and not to Israel alone. It is a human issue which ranks prior to and transcends societal, national, territorial, historical, and individual priorities. Many texts document this fact, especially those related to the creation and sustenance of the world by God. Thus, the Israelites eat and drink, not regardless of whether the rest of humanity eats and drinks but because they belong to humanity. They are entitled to food because they are human, and not because they are Israelites. References to food in these texts point to nondiscrimination from the beginning, not to the elimination of discrimination.

b. Israel had a tradition of sacramental feasting, just like Christianity, which has such a tradition principally in its Eucharist. Of course, from a sacramental meal in Israel one could be fed, whereas one can still starve even when receiving the Christian Eucharist (cf., however, Acts 2:46; 1 Corinthians 8). In Israel, the ritual of a sacrament was associated with or even consisted of a sacramental meal. To be sure, a sacramental ritual meal was a special occasion which had a specific significance. It was distinguished from everyday eating and drinking. From deuteronomic time on, it was, as cultic eating, even separated in kind and place from the kinds and places of profane eating. We can discern the separation of the cult from the processes of daily life, and with it the isolation of sacramental eating in the holy sphere from the original sacramentality of all eating. The potential result was the profanation, and with it the devaluation, of daily eating. The question is whether or not the meal of the sacrament has its ground in, symbolizes, signifies, and points to the sacramentality of every meal, i.e., whether it is holy because all food is sacrosanct, or whether it is holy and separate from regular food by virtue of a special function reserved for the elect. In the former case it reflects the need for and the right of all humans to the food on the creator's table, and in the latter it replaces the importance of daily food and gives cause to neglect the universal need of food. One may question if we have sufficiently understood the relationship between the sacramental food for the few and the daily food for all.

c. What is the basis for Israel's appreciation of food? The Old Testament's appreciation for food is directly related to its understanding of life vis-à-vis death. All living beings are mortal and live under the shadow of death. But instead of focusing on life after death, Israel focused on the conduct and preservation of life itself. The root of this ethos of life under the shadow of death is expressed in Ps 90:12: "So teach us to count our days that we may gain a wise heart."

To be sure, life is experienced as filled with toil and strain (Gen 3:17-19; Ps 90:9f.; Eccl 2:17-23), so much so that the sage in Eccl 2:17 says, "I hated life." Yet in the face of this disillusioned look at the mortality, finitude, and toil of human life, our sage says some amazing words: "There is nothing better for mortals than to eat and drink, and find enjoyment in their toil" (Eccl 2:24); "This is what I have seen to be good: it is fitting to eat and drink and find enjoyment in all the toil with which one toils under the sun the few days of the life God gives us; for this is our lot" (Eccl 5:15 [*NRSV* 5:16]). These passages reveal a legitimization of a realm of life to which every human being is entitled in the face of the shadow of death, despite the toil and vanity of life itself. The foremost entitlement in this realm is the right to eat and drink, and to enjoy them as long as one lives. This right to eating and drinking, and to their enjoyment, is apparently not relative; nor is this statement a cynical one (as in 1 Cor 15:32). On the contrary, the affirmation of eating and drinking is absolute. It reflects the affirmation of the legitimacy of life itself. Life may be mortal and full of vanity, but it is not illegitimate because of its mortality, toil, and vanity. There is, therefore, nothing peripheral, incidental, trivial, or vulgar in eating and drinking. If nothing else, eating and drinking express that life is sacrosanct. They are the sacramental expression of the sacramentality of life in the face of death. This affirmation is not only absolute; it also pertains to all living beings prior to every other affirmation. It is the universal correspondent to the universality of life. All living things must eat or die. Therefore, lack of food denies a person's right to live. It is a fundamental attack against the legitimacy of life itself, against the meaning and goal of the cosmic creation, and ultimately against the existence of God in this world.

This is what our texts dealing with the creation and sustenance of the world through God bear out. Genesis 1 says the universe was built as a cosmic house in which the earth could exist as a greenhouse for one purpose: the provision of vegetation as food for humans and animals. "God said, 'See, I have given you every plant yielding seed that is upon the face of all the earth, and every tree with seed in its fruit; you shall have them for food. And to every beast of the earth, and to every bird of the air, and to everything that creeps on the earth, everything that has the breath of life, I have given every green plant for food'" (Gen 1:29f.). All living creatures are supposed to be vegetarians. This is later updated in Gen 9:3: "Every moving thing that lives shall be food for you; and just as I gave you the green plants, I give you everything."

Accordingly, in various ways, many texts portray the sustenance of life through daily food as the permanent effect of God's blessing the earth in creation. It is because of this meaning and goal of creation that all creatures "look to you to give them their food in due season; when you give to them, they gather it up; when you open your hand, they are filled with good things" (Ps 104:27f.; cf. also Ps 145:15f.).

3. Conclusion

In the Old Testament, regular daily eating and drinking are considered as the actualization, before all else and as the basis of all else, of the sustenance of life vis-à-vis death. As such, they are the most fundamental expression of the legitimacy of life in the order of creation, just as life intrinsically involves the right to eat and to drink. This right to life through food is absolute, or the order of creation is meaningless. Moreover, it belongs to all living creatures universally, especially humans. This universal right has unconditional priority over all particularistic priorities because in it the meaning of the whole world is affected. The right to life through food is derived from the fact of life and the availability of food on earth. We humans have created neither life nor the availability of food. On the contrary, we are the result of life and the availability of food.

The correlated notions of life and food stand in the center of the biblical doctrine of the creation and sustenance of the world through God. They reflect the goal and meaning of the cosmic creation. In light of this notion, the doctrine of creation appears as the criterion of every other Christian or biblical doctrine. The right of all creatures to life through food is not relative or subordinate to Israel's or Christianity's election, to the forgiveness of sins, to the presence of the Holy Spirit, to the significance of Christ, and/or to any of our nationalities or living standards; but any and all of these realities are adjudicated in view of the extent to which they affirm, first of all and most fundamentally, the right of all creatures, especially all humans, to life through food. If they do not do *this,* they attack the goal and meaning of God's creation, and everything else they do becomes irrelevant.

II. Food from the Ground of the Earth

A. The availability of food depends on the availability of actually or potentially fertile land, on agriculture and animal husbandry (save the provision of food by hunting and gathering), and on the production and distribution of food following these activities. Any provision of food requires human, and even animal, activities which involve the organization of increasingly complex systems as populations grow. The emergence of such systems five thousand years ago, along the Tigris and Euphrates in Mesopotamia (the so-called cradle of civilization) and along the Nile in Egypt, was generated by the need to secure food for large populations. The Joseph novella in Genesis 37–50 depicts Joseph as Pharaoh's vizier and organizer of a fourteen-year system for securing Egypt's (!) food supply, a system inspired by God.

Human involvement in the production and organization of food, together with the human need for living space, necessitates their claim to and control of land. It creates a geopolitical factor, and with it not only the question of the distribution of land among different groups but also the question of the relationship of all groups to the land itself. The two questions rest on different presuppositions.

The question of the distribution of land among various persons, groups, and/or nations presupposes that, however land is distributed, it is an object for human claims, control, usage, apportionment. It is the object over which humans meet, more or less peacefully, for its distribution. In such an encounter, however, the land does not contribute its own voice and criteria for the interhuman decisions and settlements. Its fate is decided in the interaction of groups who settle the question of ownership according to their own criteria and interests, which are often alien to the land's own meaning of food for life, especially for all equally. It is decided by modes of interaction of groups, such as acquisition by purchase, by conquest, and by gradual appropriation. These groups, then, speak of property which they dispose of according to their own autonomous counsel. Human history represents an endless chain of types of distribution of and control over land.

By contrast, the question of the relationship between all humans and the land presupposes that the land itself is not an object to be possessed and used according to autonomous human preferences, but a subjective partner that hosts the humans and contributes its own critical standards for human inhabitation and its own distribution, not only in its own interest but also in the interest of humans. In this case, humans would be lessees or stewards of the land, not its owners, and their usage of the land would be governed by what the land contributes to common life rather than by objectives alien to that criterion. At this point, the Old Testament's perspective of the availability of land for food for the living (not of Israel's conquest of the land of Canaan) is of fundamental significance, along with its assertion that "The earth is the LORD's and all that is in it, the world, and those who live in it" (Ps 24:1), and that "the land is mine; with me you are but aliens and tenants" (Lev 25:23).

To be sure, the history of ancient Israel bears out the aspect of Israel's "possession" of (the) land. Israel's patriarch Abraham buys a burial place for his wife Sarah from Ephron the Hittite, "the cave of Mach-pelah, which he owns" (Gen 23:9f.). Israel will and does possess the land of the Canaanites by settlement and conquest, especially so in the deuteronomic theology which is itself based on older traditions. The conquered land is partitioned and allotted to the tribes and their clans in Joshua 13–21. The monarchy developed its own policies of territorial conquest of neighboring nations. Omri "bought the hill of Samaria from Shemer for two talents of silver" (1 Kgs 16:24); Ahab attempts to acquire Naboth's vineyard either by payment or by trading it for a better one (1 Kgs 21:1f.); and so on.

The history of the acquisition of land and property, in unquestionable or questionable legality or morality (cf. Isa 5:8; Mic 2:2), certainly has an important theological dimension. However, when compared with the aspect of the function of the land for the living and with the assertion that "the land is Yahweh's" property (cf. Lev 25:23), it becomes clear that the aspect of human, also Israel's, ownership of the land must be considered subordinate to and dependent on Yahweh's ownership of the land and its function for human life. It is also clear that the support of human life represents a level of significance in Israel's possession of the land which is more fundamental than the theology of the land of Israel.

There is a bumper sticker which reads, "Property is a divine right." Its implicit claim to be derived from the Bible, certainly from the Old Testament, is basically untrue. The opposite is true: Divine property is a human right. Humans are indeed nothing more than stewards of God's earth, not its owners. Whatever the word "God" otherwise means, in this context it means that the earth and its land are subject to criteria and priorities which can be discerned, but not determined, by humans, because these criteria determine humans themselves. What determines all living creatures, i.e., their need for food to live, is fundamental to their right to and stewardship of the earth. This perspective represents the fundamental conceptual level of theological significance already present in the distribution of the land by lot in Joshua 13–21, and also in Naboth's defense of the meaning of his inheritance, a level from which the concept of the possession of land is secondarily derived. Once this conceptual perspective is in focus (which happens by and large through the discernment of conceptualities in interpretation because the Old Testament does not focus on that discernment programmatically), the question is no longer concerned with the modes and legalities of the possession of land as property but with the caretaking and management of the land's own meaning and purpose as the support- and supply system for the sustenance of human life. Thus, the criterion for ethos, law, and justice is no longer rooted in a worldview of irreducible human autonomy but rather in a worldview of irreducible human accountability to the always already given foundation of all life.

Since all life depends on the earth's resources for the provision of food, the caretaking and management of actually or potentially fertile land for the production of food for all equally is conceptually and at least ethically, if not legally, the primary standard for justice in the relationship of humans to the earth. The aspect of justice implies that the correspondence of land and food is fundamental and in opposition to the correspondence of land and hunger, and that all models of ownership of land are relative to the criterion of land for food. As soon as food supply, together with space for habitation, is understood as the just function of the land, the justice or injustice of the relationship of the various historical systems to land can be assessed in view of the extent to which they manage land, above all, for the purpose of food supply and the avoidance or abolishment of hunger. This primary purpose also qualifies the very notion of management or stewardship.

One may differ with N. Gottwald, who sees the ideal system for the just, i.e., equal, distribution of food for all in the premonarchic tribal federation with its God Yahweh, in contrast to centralized empires and monarchies, including Israel's. The question of which system better lends itself for fulfilling this purpose, in antiquity and in the present, may be disputed. But apart from that question, Gottwald is basically correct when pointing to Yahweh's significance regarding food for the living. Indeed, the fundamentality of this conceptuality throughout the Old Testament supports his contention even more extensively than he has accounted for.

In the following, we will focus on the function of the land for the food of all humans in the Old Testament. This focus implies an awareness of the different meanings which the word "land" has, and also of related words such as "earth," "ground," and "soil," not to mention "parcel," "acre/acreage," etc. Similar lexical differentiations can also be found in the biblical languages (γῆ in Greek; ארץ and אדמה in Hebrew). In the following I will discuss that semantic notion in the usage of those words which refer to the ground or soil of the earth. This notion is particularly expressed by the Hebrew word אדמה, "ground, soil, or earth in the sense of ground/soil."

B. Before discussing the relationship of ground/soil to the earth as part of the cosmos on the one hand, and its relationship to growth and food on the other, something must be said about the relationship between ground/soil and humanity. It is not clear whether the Hebrew words for ground, אדמה, and for humanity, אדם, reflect the same etymology.[3] But it is clear that the Old Testament assumes that all humans are made "from the dust of the ground" (Gen 2:7) and that they "return to the ground" (Gen 3:19). Humans are from the ground. This earthly human condition is basic and universal. It precedes all other conditions. Moreover, those who came from the ground and return to the ground live from the ground while they are alive. In life they are related to the ground as their home base. More precisely, humans do not belong to this earth and its ground because they are cosmically restricted to it. Rather, they are cosmically restricted and ground-bound because they are of the ground of this earth. To be an intrinsic component of this earth is the human condition. The earth is not only the *space* for human life; it is the *basis* from which they constantly live. They are, therefore, wholly related to it in their origin, life, and destination.

3. Cf. C. Westermann, "אדם," *THAT* 1, 41-57; Fritz Maass, "אדם," *TWAT* 1, 81-94; *TDOT* 1, 75-87; Hermann Sasse, "γῆ," *TDNT* 1, 677-81; H. H. Schmid, "אדמה," *THAT* 1, 57-60; and J. G. Plöger, "אדמה," *TWAT* 1, 95-105; *TDOT* 1, 88-98.

The awareness in the Old Testament of the relationship to the ground as a basic human condition gives pause once again for the question of whether the modern perception of a subject-object relationship between humans and the earth is not undercut by a view of reality in which human existence and the ground of the earth are interdependent or intersubjective. The question is, of course, raised by scientists of various fields and has also been addressed in a variety of interpretations, especially by phenomenologists of religion such as J. Pedersen,[4] L. Levy-Bruhl,[5] G. van der Leeuw,[6] F. Heiler,[7] S. Mowinckel,[8] and G. Widengren.[9] Our traditional hesitancy to engage in a theology of nature is probably a major reason for failing to recognize a theologically profound ontological and anthropological dimension, either in the Old Testament's texts themselves or in their conceptual presuppositions, according to which the human condition and human existence do not stand vis-à-vis what we call nature, but are an inherent part of it. The replacement of this view by either the subject-object worldview or the view of historical human existence, rather than its correlation with these views, leads not only to the split between human identity and nature with the resulting subjugation of nature by humans but also to human alienation from nature and with it human self-alienation.

The Old Testament's view of reality is different. Its rejection of the deification of nature over and above humans is not based on the concept of a rightful enslavement of nature by humans. It only means that both nature and humans are considered together as created rather than divine, and that they exist together vis-à-vis and dependent on God. Notwithstanding the distinctiveness of each, both belong first of all to each other. In whatever sense humans belong to God, this belonging is not based on their separation from nature or on the opposition of God and humans over against nature. Even if such a conceptuality of opposition may be suggested in Genesis 1 and Psalm 8, it is already effectively undercut in Genesis 2–4. Whatever the creation of humans in "the image of God" means (e.g., their position in the hierarchy of the cosmos and their right to use the plants and to rule over the animals), it means neither that humans are not also created, nor that God and his relationship to nature has been replaced by humans and their reign over nature. The creation of humans in the image of God only refers to human stewardship in accordance with God's own reign over nature for the sake of both nature and

4. J. Pedersen, *Israel: Its Life and Culture,* trans. Aslaug Möller, 2 vols. (London: Oxford University, 1926).

5. L. Levy-Bruhl, *The Soul of the Primitive,* trans. Lilian Clare (London: Allen & Unwin, 1965).

6. G. van der Leeuw, *Phänomenologie der Religion* (Tübingen: J. C. B. Mohr, 1956).

7. Friedrich Heiler, *Erscheinungsformen und Wesen der Religion* (Stuttgart: W. Kohlhammer, 1961).

8. Sigmund Mowinckel, *Religion und Kultus* (Göttingen: Vandenhoeck & Ruprecht, 1953).

9. Geo Widengren, *Religionphänomenologie* (Berlin: de Gruyter, 1969).

humans. This perception of the function of the image of God transcends ancient mythological presuppositions. It points not only to the togetherness of nature and humanity, but also to criteria that determine their relationship in terms of what is common to nature and humanity rather than in terms of what sets them apart from each other. Closer to this view of reality than to a subject-object view of reality is what is expressed by the modern farmer who says that he must live *with* nature rather than *against* it, and also by the modern biologist who says that we humans are, indeed, totally part of nature.

C. The human condition as life from the ground brings the relationship between ground and food into sharp focus. Food is not only the material by which humans live from the ground; it is also a part of the very substance of human life as earthly life. In addition, that which makes the sustenance of human life possible is the life of the ground itself. The ground is blessed. It is empowered to produce life-sustaining food (Gen 1:11f.). It is, therefore, the realm in which and the basis from which humans can live in distinction from the uninhabitable desert (Jer 2:6; Job 38:26). Ground/soil (אדמה) is a terrestrial realm prior to and transcending the boundaries of nations or individual property owners. It is related to the function of food for all life, regardless of the types of human ownership, stewardship, or administration. The totality of the ground is the substance from which humans in their totality live, just as humans in their totality belong to the totality of the ground.

Therefore, all humans depend on the lasting blessing of the ground, the uninterrupted seasonal cycle (Gen 8:21f.). In turn, this seasonal cycle and with it the life of the ground and its production of food are themselves imbedded in and dependent on the cosmic cycle. The fertile land does not belong to us; it belongs to the cosmos and we belong to it. Israel's awareness of the cosmic life-cycle plays a much more fundamental role in Israel's theology than was previously recognized.[10] If it breaks down as in drought (Jer 14:4; Hag 1:11), earthquake (Gen 19:25), war (Deut 28:23; Isa 1:7), famine (Gen 47:13), or locust plague (Deut 28:42; Ps 105:34f.), humans' food supply, and with it the existence of humans as humans, is threatened. The restoration of the seasonal cycle is a cosmic event (Hos 2:10-15, 23-25a [*NRSV* 2:8-13, 21-23a]); Ps 65:10-14 (*NRSV* 65:9-13) gives a vivid example of the effective correspondence between ground and food in the intactness of the seasonal cycle:

10. Cf. R. de Vaux, *Ancient Israel: Its Life and Institutions,* trans. John McHugh (New York: McGraw Hill, 1961); N. Snaith, "Time in the Old Testament," in *Promise and Fulfillment,* ed. F. F. Bruce (Edinburgh: T. & T. Clark, 1963); Eckart Otto and Tim Schramm, *Festival and Joy,* trans. James Blevins (Nashville: Abingdon, 1980); O. H. Steck, *World and Environment* (Nashville: Abingdon, 1980); R. Knierim, "Cosmos and History in Israel's Theology," pages 171-224 in the present volume; C. Westermann, *Elements of Old Testament Theology,* trans. D. W. Stott (Atlanta: John Knox, 1982); B. Lamberty, "Natural Cycles in Ancient Israel's View of Reality" (diss., Claremont Graduate School, 1986).

You visit the earth and water it,
you greatly enrich it;
the river of God is full of water;
you provide the people with grain,
for so you have prepared it.
You water its furrows abundantly,
settling its ridges,
softening it with showers,
and blessing its growth.
You crown the year with your bounty;
your wagon tracks overflow with richness.
The pastures of the wilderness overflow,
the hills gird themselves with joy,
the meadows clothe themselves with flocks,
the valleys deck themselves with grain,
they shout and sing together for joy.

D. As humans are part of the ground and live from it, so they till it. They are farmers. As the ground provides their food, so they work it to provide this food. The Old Testament knows that agriculture is the fundamental economic outgrowth of the earthbound human condition. Agriculture is not an antiquated form of primitive civilization to be replaced by technological civilization. It is the fundamental form of activity by which humans themselves participate in the food-generating power of the living soil.

It is not merely peripheral that the Old Testament presents the man of the first generation as a farmer (Gen 3:17-19, 23), the men of the second generation as a farmer and a shepherd (Gen 4:2), and Noah, the first man after the flood, as "a man of the soil, [who] was the first to plant a vineyard" (Gen 9:20). The proverb says: "Those who till their land will have plenty of food, but those who follow worthless pursuits have no sense" (Prov 12:11; cf. Prov 24:27, 30-34; 28:19; Isa 5:1f.; etc.). With reference to the parable of the farmer in Isa 28:23-28, it may be added that the one who tills the land has a sense of genuine wisdom that may even surpass prophetic wisdom. Jesus Sirach adds, "Do not hate hard labor or farm work, which was created by the MOST HIGH" (Sir 7:15). In Psalm 104, where Yahweh's majesty is described in the framework of the order of his creation, the role of humans (אדם) in this order is pinpointed precisely. They are to cultivate the plants which God causes to grow: "You cause the grass to grow for the cattle, and plants for people to use, to bring forth food from the earth, and wine to gladden the human heart, oil to make the face shine, and bread to strengthen the human heart" (Ps 104:14).[11] No wonder that in Ecclesiastes the

11. Cf. O. H. Steck, *World and Environment,* 78-89, and S. Reed, "Food in the Psalms," 441-49.

one who "hates" life must admit that next to the enjoyment of eating and drinking, one should "find enjoyment in all the toil with which one toils under the sun" (Eccl 2:24; 5:17 [*NRSV* 5:18f.]).

It is amazing how central agriculture was in Israel's Yahweh-theology. In the theology of its seasonal agricultural festivals (Exod 23:14-17, 19; 34:18-26; Lev 23:1-44; Deut 16:1-17; 26:1f.), Israel "cyclisized" history by declaring that its liberation from oppression in Egypt had found its goal and fulfillment in Israel's appropriation of the cyclic-seasonal-agricultural mode of existence in the land.

One more aspect pertinent to agriculture must be mentioned. It is the statement in Gen 1:28: "subdue [the earth]; and have dominion. . . ." This statement has played an unfortunate role in the history of Western Christian civilization, a role that could not have been foreseen by its priestly writer. This statement, which was meant to be an expression of human stewardship over the earth for the purpose of supporting human life, has functioned in our civilization as a legitimation for our exploitation of the earth and for our provocation of the ecological crisis. This is not the only statement that has been misunderstood or adapted for interests alien to its original meaning.

It is evident that the biblical theology of ground/soil and agriculture is intrinsically related to the theology of food, and that, together with the theology of food, it is an elementary part of the theology of the creation and sustenance of the world which focuses above everything else on the basis of life for humanity as a whole. In this theology, the aspect of land as ground/soil is prior to and independent of human history and the historical election of a people. In this order, it has a distinct function — to provide the basis for the food of living creatures. In the biblical view, this function determines the priority of soil for food over all other modes of land use and land possession. In light of this, the relative validity, if not invalidity, of all other claims to land is revealed.

III. Food, Land, and Justice

What do food and the use of soil to provide food have to do with justice? Is there a biblical basis for connecting these notions? The answer is yes, but this is not self-evident.

The problem is that the biblical language for justice is determined by many different contexts. In these contexts, justice is related to different situations, conditions, or kinds of reality which in turn are not systematically coordinated in the Bible. Thus, by reference to justice one can justify virtually everything. One can justify the oppression of the Canaanites by Israel just as much as Israel's liberation from oppression. One can justify individual property just as much as clan, tribal, national, royal, and/or priestly property — even as one says, "The earth is Yahweh's."

It seems to me that we cannot talk about justice reasonably, either in relation to food or to land, unless we adopt a perspective in which only one aspect of justice becomes the criterion for the others, or at least a perspective in which several aspects are related to each other so that priorities can be discerned through their comparison. Such a perspective must be established with reference to two questions. Quantitatively, which are the more, or most, universal or inclusive horizons under which justice is perceived? And qualitatively, which are the more, or most, foundational aspects under which justice is perceived, those aspects which determine others, to which others are relative and on which they depend? Such an approach allows us to coordinate the biblical traditions concerning justice regardless of their statistical frequency and place of occurrence in the Bible.

With this approach in mind, two further questions are pertinent. Is justice related to land and food? And what is the validity of this aspect of justice when compared with other aspects to which justice is related?

A. Is Justice Related to Land and Food?

From the many passages that document such a relationship, three may be mentioned.

1. Ps 85:11-14 (*NRSV* 85:10-13) views the fertility of the land and its yield as a manifestation, an epiphany, of the Creator's justice:

> Steadfast love and faithfulness will meet;
> righteousness and peace will kiss each other.
> Faithfulness will spring up from the ground,
> and righteousness will look down from the sky.
> The LORD will give what is good,
> and our land will yield its increase.
> Righteousness will go before him,
> and will make a path for his steps.

2. Hos 2:16-25 (*NRSV* 2:14-23) expresses the renewal of the covenant between Yahweh and Israel "in righteousness and in justice" (v. 21 [*NRSV* v. 19]) in terms of the restoration of the cosmic ecosystem: "I will answer the heavens and they shall answer the earth; and the earth shall answer the grain, the wine, and the oil" (vv. 23f. [*NRSV* vv. 21f.]).

3. In an instruction concerning the distribution of justice, Yahweh says, "When you reap the harvest of your land, you shall not reap to the very edges of your field, or gather the gleanings of your harvest. You shall not strip your vineyard bare, or gather the fallen grapes of your vineyard; you shall leave them for the poor and the alien: I am the LORD your God" (Lev 19:9-10). This is an expression of justice as related to land and food, and of human stewardship of Yahweh's land,

with specific emphasis on the inclusion of the poor and sojourner in the right to food and with an explicit reference to the fact that nothing less than the identity of the God of Israel is at stake in this inclusion.

B. What Is the Validity of This Aspect of Justice When Compared with Other Aspects to Which Justice Is Related?

1. The order of the world as created and sustained by God vis-à-vis chaos is understood as the presence of God in the world in justice and righteousness. In Job 38–39, God justified himself before Job with reference to the intactness of his creation. This aspect reflects both the most universal horizon of reality and the foundation on which every other reality depends. It is, therefore, the criterion of all other aspects of justice.

2. Land and food intrinsically belong to the creation and sustenance of the world as created order. Above everything else, they pertain to universal humanity and are the basis of and presupposition for everything else in human history. As the fulfillment of the goal and meaning of creation, food and soil succinctly represent the most universal and foundational actualization of justice in this world. Where there is food and soil for all, there is justice. Where there is hunger and lack of soil for food, the justice of creation is compromised, if not indeed replaced, by injustice. The legitimacy or illegitimacy of this world, even the justice of God, if not God's very presence in the world, or indeed God's existence, is at stake with respect to food and the soil which produces that food. In this sense, the theology of food and soil is intrinsic to the theology of justice, just as the theology of justice is elementarily concerned with food and soil for the sustenance of all living beings.

3. This understanding reflects the basis for a concept of a just world. From such a concept, ethical, political, economic, social, and logistical consequences would need to be drawn concerning the production and distribution of food for all and the administration of the land of the earth.

4. The New Testament speaks neither as often nor as directly as the Old Testament about the importance of food in the theology of creation, or about the creation of the world itself for that matter. Quite generally, interpreters explain this restraint by saying that the New Testament does not, and need not, extensively address this aspect because it presupposes and endorses it as self-evident. This explanation is insufficient and lastly incorrect.

It is true that, however infrequently, the New Testament affirms the importance of food in its presupposed theology of creation — with one decisive reconceptualization. In light of the expectation of the new creation in the New Testament, the inherited theology of creation, including its theology of food, is basically relegated to the view of the original and fast-ending old creation, fallen or not. By now, the theology of the new, eschatological creation determines not only the original creation as old and passing; it also relativizes the degree of validity of everything belonging to the structure of the old creation, including food for the living.

As long as this old creation lasts, food for the living is fundamental. Yet since the old creation will soon be ended, and already is ended in the presence of the eschatological signs, daily food has become relative to that different, and decisive, "spiritual" food which nourishes not the mortal but the eschatological or eternal life. Especially, it has for this reason become relative not only for believers, but also for the rest of the creatures if not even a distraction from their urgently expected conversion to the new creation.

The New Testament's and following it Christianity's long history of restraint on the issue of the original creation and the importance in it of food for all living creatures were not caused by the conceptually ongoing predominance of the original theology of creation. Instead, they were caused by a conceptual change in which that original theology became subordinate to the priority of the theology of the new creation. However, the issue of the sustenance of life in the indefinitely ongoing world demands that the fundamentality rather than the relativity of food be again recognized, whether or not the original is replaced by the new creation.

Conclusion

Throughout human history, there have always been hunger and malnutrition. Yet, we seem to live at a juncture in history at which the lack of a global food supply and of an availability of soil for the future food supply of humanity have taken on critical proportions. The mechanisms that are mobilized for coping with this situation depend decisively, in kind and degree, on the clarity with which the problem is recognized and on the priorities that determine our analysis and vision of reality.

The recognition of the problem and priority of food supply is nothing new. In fact, the history of humanity can be interpreted as a history of nations and people in search of food and of soil for food. It is interesting to see how prominently the observation of the fertility of the land ranks in the descriptions of New England by its earliest explorers and settlers.

The world-historical situation catches us in the tension between pessimism and optimism, between dreams of utopia and realistic hope, between self-soothing propaganda and rational prognosis. Tension also exists concerning whether humans possess an inherent inability or ability to manage their present and ongoing life. This tension seems to be genuine, and as long as it exists (and it seems that it will be with humanity from now on) neither an optimistic nor a pessimistic attitude, each repressing the other, is warranted. The neglect of the handwriting on the wall is just as unrealistic as the neglect of the possibilities that still exist. In the current *kairos* the tension itself is our opportunity. But just as the *kairos* will change, so will the opportunity. Whether we can take advantage of the opportunity constructively depends on the present realization of the priorities that constitute the interdependence of the globe and humanity. High and certainly indispensable among them are the provision of food and the preservation of soil for food for the sustenance of the living. Whether or not the Christian and Jewish communities contribute in unison to advancing these priorities among the nations and their peoples will not only determine their relevance for the current state of human history, but also the genuineness of their loyalty to their own claim of their religious truth. The biblical theology of food for all, especially the Old Testament's, is important, not so much because it is biblical or the property of the so-called Judeo-Christian heritage, but because it is the contribution of that heritage to the truth necessary for the life of this ongoing world.

Hope in the Old Testament

Introduction

"Hope," and its terminological equivalent, is one of the great words in our languages. It expresses one of the elementary psychic dynamics in the life of human beings, indeed, of all living beings. The phenomenon of hope pervades the entire human history. In addition, the fact of its existence precedes our reflections, oral or written discourses, and books about it.

Hope is, nonetheless, spoken about throughout history, and certainly throughout ancient Israelite, Jewish, and Christian history. In the history of Christian doctrine it has had, and continues to have, its prominent place, especially in connection with the expectation of the future reign of God in the second coming of Christ, i.e., as eschatological hope. One can scarcely say, however, that the doctrine of eschatological hope and of future eschatology has played an equally vital role for the actual faith of every Christian generation. Moreover, one cannot say that the chapter on eschatology, traditionally the last chapter in Christian doctrines, was always considered the foundational chapter about the Christian faith. Its position at the end of systematic theologies has followed the structures of the classical creeds of the church, which are based on the affirmation of God's reign over the history of the world from its beginning to its axis in Jesus Christ and through the present age of the Holy Spirit to the end of the world in the resurrection and in eternal life. In that structure, hope was associated with the eschatological future of life after death, but for this very reason was dissociated from its relationship to the realities of the current world.

Of course, eschatology or the focus on hope has not always played a lackluster role in Christian theology and faith. In our century, the rediscovery of eschatology — however it is interpreted — has given it a prominent place in theology from the work of A. Schweitzer on. During the past two generations, not coincidentally the generations between the two world wars and after World War II, the subject experienced an explosion of attention. This is documented in the works of theologians such as Barth, Bultmann, Cullmann, de Chardin, Pannenberg, Cox, Braaten, Cobb, and others.

In the horizon of those developments, the issue of hope gained center stage for some time. E. Bloch's *Principle of Hope* drew worldwide attention from 1959 on,[1] and J. Moltmann's *Theology of Hope* introduced the topic into the first rank of the theological debate.[2] But one must not forget that the General Assembly of the Ecumenical Movement had in 1954 already met at Evanston under the topic "Christ — The Hope for the World"; that a 1971 New York conference met under the topic "Hope and the Future of Man" (*sic!,* how our language changes!); and that Pope John XXIII had in the sixties become a living symbol for hope.

To these rather spotty remarks about this development, only one more aspect must be added, namely, the influence of Old Testament traditio-historical studies which found their culmination in G. von Rad's *Old Testament Theology.*[3] Under this influence, Moltmann's systematic *Theology of Hope* became important specifically because it pointed to the roots of the tradition of hope already in the religiosity of the patriarchal history, whose structure is characterized by historical existence as hope and hope as historical existence. In this view, the connection of hope with human historical existence as its decisive notion is of particular importance. While it remains to be seen whether or not, and for what reasons or in what sense, the aspect of history is the sole or dominant aspect to which hope is related, it is clear that under this aspect hope is not only related to an eschaton, let alone an abstract idea, but is elementarily tied to the human experience of all reality. To this relatedness of reality and hope, the Old Testament makes its own contribution, not only in terms of the diverse, exegetically discernible aspects but also in terms of Old Testament theology and its contribution to biblical theology and ultimately to hermeneutic.

At the present time, the focus on the theology of hope seems to have yielded to more pressing concerns. This change in focus cannot mean that the issue has become less relevant theologically and hermeneutically. In fact, when one considers the heightening awareness in our generation of the beginning of the second epoch of human history, which is characterized by the intensifying tension between the globe's resources and the exploding mass of humanity and possibly by the decreasing capacity of the human mind to adjust human behavior to the ever-accelerating expansion of humanity's needs, one may wonder if the retreat from the focus on hope for the future of humanity in this ongoing world is not more an effect of

1. *The Principle of Hope,* trans. N. Plaice, S. Plaice, and P. Knight (Cambridge: MIT, 1986), trans. of *Das Prinzip Hoffnung* (Frankfurt am Main: Suhrkamp, 1959).

2. *Theology of Hope,* trans. J. W. Leitch (New York: Harper & Row, 1967), trans. of *Die Theologie der Hoffnung,* 5th ed. (Munich: Chr. Kaiser, 1965).

3. *Old Testament Theology,* trans. D. M. G. Stalker, 2 vols. (New York: Harper & Row, 1962 and 1965).

resignation, of hopelessness, and of despair of realistic hope, than the result of attention to other issues. It seems that the necessary preoccupation, also in theology, with the ever more pressing affairs of the present and future in and of this world takes place between hope and hopelessness. In their tension, the survival of hope itself is at stake. This alone is reason enough for keeping the subject alive.

In the following discussion of hope in the Old Testament, I will focus on

I. The Phenomenon of Hope and Its Nature, and

II. God, Reality, and Human Hope.

I. The Phenomenon of Hope and Its Nature

A. The Phenomenon of Hope

The subject of hope occurs in the Old Testament both terminologically and substantively.

1. Statistically, the terminology for the word field for what we call "to hope" and "hope" is not overwhelming, especially when one considers that the key term itself occurs in its verbal and nominal forms not more than eighty-four times altogether: forty-seven times for the verb קוה, and thirty-seven times for the two nouns מקוה (five) and תקוה (thirty-two). The root meaning, if not etymologically then at least semantically, seems best expressed with words such as "to be stretched out" or "to be tightened straight."

Semantically associated with the key term is a group of verbs with their nominal derivatives, which is attested in over seven hundred passages. Their variable verbal forms, which are very often in the Piel intensive form just as in the case of the verb קוה, are:

חכה = to wait for (patiently, even hesitantly);
יחל = to wait;
שׂבר = to wait, hope (Piel); to inspect, examine (Qal);
בטח = to feel safe, trust;
דמם = to be, keep, or stand still;
נבט = to look upon, behold (expectantly);
כתר = to have patience with;
צפה = to look at or about, to lie in ambush (attentively);
חסה = to seek refuge;
דרשׁ = to seek, inquire;
דמה = to be still, silent;

שׁאל = to ask for, inquire of;
בקר = to attend to.[4]

None of these semantic cognates is identical with the key term for hope. Each has its own proper notion. But all connote the meaning hope, or hope is one of their connotations. When facing the subject of hope in the Old Testament, it is, as in other cases, important to keep its full range in mind rather than the range as indicated only by the key term for it.

This linguistic phenomenon already suggests an approach to the subject that is circumspective and inclusive from the outset, and not predetermined by specific definitions based only on one aspect, even where one can observe pervading characteristics — which is the case here. One such presupposition must immediately be set aside, namely, the separation of the so-called "theological usage" or the "theological passages" from the "profane usage" or "profane passages" in the biblical texts. However legitimate and necessary those distinctions are linguistically, they may suggest that biblical passages have relevant theological meaning only where they speak about Yahweh or God. In reality, their theological relevance depends on quite different criteria. A passage that expresses nothing at all about God may be profoundly theological in meaning. This entails that phenomenological or anthropological factors are not, in principle or in the order of this chapter, to be considered as devoid of theological meaning. They reflect, on the contrary, the dimension of worldly reality to which theology addresses itself because nothing, certainly in the Old Testament, lies outside the realm of God-Yahweh, whether this is always said or not.

The semantic aspect of the linguistic phenomenon shows us that, first, all words for and in connection with hope are anthropological words. They express a psychic condition which manifests itself as attitude and behavior, and which is, for understandable reasons, observed by humans among humans. Secondly, the word field and its extent throughout the Old Testament, even if concentrated in the prophetic literature, the Psalms, and Job, reveals a picture of a great variety of situations and mind-sets much more than an intention for terminological and conceptual unification or abstraction. It narrates or describes hope in all its complexity, thereby revealing how, in reality, hope appears in the hoping human attitudes. It points out the dynamic of hoping. Thirdly, the words for hope show an attitude in which living beings, foremost humans, are in their respective situations intensely stretching out forward, looking forward, and focusing in anticipation for and in dependence on something or someone to arrive, to happen, or to be achieved. That

4. On the specific meanings of these terms, their occurrences, grammatical variations, and contextual semantics, cf. the respective articles in the lexica and the bibliographical references therein.

attitude presupposes an uncertainty or a tension between the present state and the state hoped for, between the known present and the unknown future, and between the state of desire and the state of satisfaction in its fulfillment. "Hope deferred makes the heart sick, but a desire fulfilled is a tree of life" (Prov 13:12). This attitude is not only an *active* behavior. When hoping, as much as humans are actively involved ("I hope"), they are as much passive. Their activity depends entirely on the open question of whether that which is hoped for will arrive or not.

2. While the usage of words for "hope" is relatively limited, the subject matter of hope can be observed much more fundamentally in the Old Testament writings. The findings can be classified in two categories: a *sociological category* which deals with the goal of humans' hope within the manifold areas of their reality, and a *morphological category* which deals with the forms and concepts in which people have expressed their hope.

a. Hope is almost always *"hope for. . . ." It aims at something.* The textual evidence is endless. The slave longs for the shadow, and the hireling looks for his wages (Job 7:2); the adulterer waits for the twilight, saying, "no eye will see me" (Job 24:15), and a harlot waits for her prey, in the street, the market, and at every corner (Prov 7:12); the wicked "sit in ambush in the villages, . . . their eyes watch for the helpless, they lurk in secret like a lion in its covert, they lurk that they may seize the poor" (Ps 10:8f.); "the wicked watch for the righteous and seek to kill them" (Ps 37:32); society is characterized as "they all lie in wait for blood, and they hunt each other with nets" (Mic 7:2); on the other hand, those in sickness and distress or under accusation wait for recovery (Pss 69:4 [*NRSV* 69:3]; 25:5; et al.), vindication (Pss 37:5f.; 69:7 [*NRSV* 69:6]; et al.), and the possession of the earth (Ps 37:8f.). Humans strive ambitiously for greatness reaching into the heavens (Gen 11:1-9), and haughtily for power and influence (Isa 2:7f.), and their hope is in victory by army, war horse, and chariot (Ps 33:16f.). They hope to be saved by military help (Hos 5:13). They look for justice and salvation (Isa 59:11) and for help (Gen 49:18); they wait anxiously for good (Mic 1:12), for light in darkness (Job 3:9), and for peace and a time of healing (Jer 14:19). The righteous especially expect success (Psalm 1; Prov 11:23), and wait for God's ordinances (Ps 119:43) and words (Ps 119:147). Israel hopes for the day of the Lord (Amos 5:18-20), for the king and the age of peace (Isa 8:23–9:6 [*NRSV* 9:1-7]; 11:1-9), and for the return from exile and reunification in the holy land (Hos 2:17 [*NRSV* 2:15]; Jer 31:17; Amos 9:13-15; Zech 9:12; et al.). Isaiah falls silent and waits for the future revelation of Yahweh (Isa 8:16-18). In a time of upheaval, Baruch cannot seek great things for himself; he can only expect to save his life (Jer 45:5). All creatures have one hope in common: "These all look to you to give them their food in due season" (Ps 104:27). I could go on and on. The passages just referred to were intentionally selected at random. Instead of prematurely elevating one of their various aspects to prominence, or of programmatically grouping the aspects, the random selection shows something about hope that is, in principle, prior to all its diverse manifestations, even as it is operative in all of them. It shows that hope is primarily not an attitude dependent on certain conditions, e.g., ethical or social, but a basic element of the human condition itself. Moreover, it belongs to the condition of all living beings, even of God (Isa 5:7). It exists whether these living beings, including humans, hope as groups or as individuals, and whether they and their hopes are good or evil. But their hopes tend to be realistic, whether their aim is wholesome or destructive. Hope appears as a basic element of the structure of living existence. So Eccl 9:4 says, "But whoever is joined with all the living has hope, for a living dog is better than a dead lion."

This human attitude is always related to reality and reaches out into all of its dimensions, be they the spheres of private life, or of public, political, social, religious life. The objectives hoped for can, thereby, be conceived quite differently. Vis-à-vis the present reality, they can project a new reality, or a modification of the present one, or simply a continuation of the status quo. Hope as a basic human phenomenon is indifferent to such distinctions.

Finally, by its own intention hope is different from illusion and utopia, which are principally unfulfillable. Hope is realistic in that it hopes on the assumption that what is hoped for is possible. If it were not possible, one could not hope for it. Where the possibilities have ended, hope dies. And only death is the end of hope.

b. A word must be said about the forms and concepts in which the ancient Israelites have expressed their hope. It is important to see that, in the Old Testament, hope does not only occur in eschatological texts. As a matter of fact, the language for "hope" does not occur in such texts. Certainly, eschatological texts which prophesy or praise the establishment of the ultimate kingdom of Yahweh in Israel as a new event after the historical catastrophes are still characterized by a tone of triumphant hope. (Cf., among others, Isa 28:16; 8:23–9:6 [*NRSV* 9:1-7]; Hos 2:18-25 [*NRSV* 2:16-23]; Jer 31:31-34; Ezek 17:22-24; 20:32f.; 34; 36:22f.; 37:1f.; 40–48; Isa 40:1-11; 43:1-11; and many others.)

However, other genres of Old Testament literature are strongly governed by such a tone of hope as well. In the historical literature, the history of Solomon's succession to David's throne rests on the hope of the everlasting dynasty (2 Samuel 5–1 Kings 2). The Joseph story (Genesis 37–50) ends by saying that God has turned an evil past into good, and thereby projects a hopeful future for the united tribes in the time of the Davidic-Solomonic dynasty. The Yahwistic work is written from the standpoint of Yahweh's fulfilled promises, and therefore gives cause for hope for Yahweh's future blessings. The priestly document presupposes a theology of hope which aims at preparing Israel for the return to Palestine from exile and for God's dwelling in her midst. Although much more could be said along this line, I will instead point to the Psalms, particularly the Complaint Psalms. These psalms are full of expressions of hope and confidence that God will change the present need of either the individual or the people. Based on hope, they praise God out of the depths. Much of the wisdom literature is based on the optimistic certainty that

"The hope of the righteous ends in gladness, but the expectation of the wicked comes to nothing" (Prov 10:28). The apocalyptic literature, finally, with its beginnings in Ezekiel 38f., Joel, Isaiah 24–27, and Daniel, provides us once more with a different conceptualization of hope. This literature portrays the already dualistic drama of the world in which our old cosmos comes to an end and must make room for the arrival of the new world from heaven.

It is quite clear that the Old Testament does not have only one conceptualization of hope. It has several different ones. They all reach forward into the future, but in different ways and in different types of expectation. *Why is this so?* Probably because the situations of those in hope are different, and hope is always related to their specific reality. It is an answer to it. In the first place a person who is sick and/or accused will not hope for the coming of the new world, but she/he will hope for the restoration of her/his health and/or her/his vindication as long as a chance for them can be seen. This is the hope we often have in the Psalms. Second, a person who has conducted her/his life on the assumption that being righteous is meaningful, in the framework of this assumption, will hope that her/his righteousness will return to her/him in the form of a blessed life. This accounts for the type of hope we have in much of the wisdom literature. Third, the hope of a nation that has attained unity and independence from a long, dark, fragmented past will be concerned with maintaining and improving this result in the future. This is the type of hope we have in the historical writings. It certainly does not disclaim the hope of the sick or the righteous individual, but it responds to a different reality. Fourth, an Israel that has suffered a total political and religious breakdown (722 and 587 BCE) cannot hope for a continuation or simple resumption of its history. It can only hope for a new beginning. This accounts for the prophetic eschatological announcements. Finally, people who realize that the world as a whole is totally and forever evil cannot hope for the rise of a new and perfect historical era in view of this concern. They can only hope, as apocalypticism does, for the coming of a new world. Such hope cannot be oriented individualistically or historically; it can only be radically universalistic and transcendental.

I am trying to say with these examples that the various types of hope in the Old Testament, and for that matter in the New Testament and in the Judeo-Christian tradition, cannot be so easily discounted in favor of one specific type of hope, if hope is to have anything to do with the different types and perspectives of human reality. It may be a significant contribution of the Old Testament to a theology of hope, in that it opens our eyes to the legitimacy of human hope in response to the manifold ranges and areas of human reality and experience, particularly of human suffering. I hasten to add, however, that the acknowledgment of different formations of hope in relation to their respective realities says nothing as yet about the nature or the quality of a hope. As hope takes up, reflects, and responds to reality, in its actual situations and conditions, hope is one thing. It takes living beings seriously where and as they exist. It does not manipulate their existentiality, and it does not speculate. But it is a different question as to what such realistic hope may mean for those in hope and for their relationship to their reality.

B. The Nature of Hope

1. A phenomenological survey shows that the Old Testament does not discuss a theory of hope. It does not have an essay on "hope." However, it continually reports about and describes the living as everywhere hoping, at all times, in all forms, for good hopes and for evil ones, by good people and by bad people, in the depths of the human predicament and in the zenith of their careers. The texts certainly show us hope as a dynamic human event; they also show us the basic structure of the hope-event: With their whole being, people stretch themselves toward the arrival or advent of future possibilities. The future, although it has not yet arrived, is nevertheless possible. Those who reach out for the future cannot force its arrival. Rather, they depend on it. They are active and passive at the same time. Their hope consists in the fact that they take the coming of the possible seriously. They count on it. And with all that, they stand in tension with their present conditions. They walk opposed to these conditions while still living under them. In short, by reaching out for the future possibility, they confront the present reality and challenge the eternal moment.

2. But it would be a mistake to suppose that these general phenomenological and morphological factors already touch upon the real interest of the Old Testament writers, their intentions, their reason for writing about hope, and their own understanding of hope. So far, we have only said that hope is real, that it is related to reality, and that all living beings hope, regardless of whether their hopes and realities are true or perverted, valid or invalid.

We must realize that there are reasons for the Old Testament's attention to the reality of hope and to its connectedness with the diverse realities of those in hope, but we must also realize that it does not indiscriminately equate the reality of hope, the realities of those in hope, or the hoped-for goals and objectives with validity or legitimacy. The words "reality" and "realism" could be — and often are — *e silentio* used as if experienced or hoped-for reality and "realistic" attitudes were codes for truth, as if everything were true that is real. If that were so, the multifaceted nature of reality and realism would mean the equal validity of any reality and hope, and for the same reason their equal invalidity. Both reality and hope would ultimately not only be invalid but also meaningless. It is very clear that the Old Testament not only speaks about the reality of hope in relation to reality, but especially and basically about both of them from the standpoint of validity. We must, therefore, turn to the questions: Which reality and which hope are valid?

With this question in mind, if we turn again to our texts we can make a surprising observation: In many instances in which the texts deal with hope, they explicitly or implicitly raise the question of *whether* human hope is valid or invalid, or *why* hope is valid or invalid. When referring to false human hopes, they only show that they are aware of those hopes as well. They show that for true hope there is no escape from the confrontation with false hope. Both exist side by side. We must assume a difference between realistic hope and valid or legitimate hope. Which hope, then, is valid? Bultmann, in his article on ἐλπίς, correctly says: "Hope is naturally directed to God."[5] This means that hope is legitimate insofar as it is waiting for the arrival of God. "God" as the one expected introduces a distinction from every other object of expectation. This distinction adds a decisive new perspective to our discussion of the structure of the hope-event. Indeed, this perspective is impressively substantiated in the texts. Phrases such as "I wait for you" (Ps 25:21), "wait for the LORD" (Ps 27:14), "we hope in you" (Ps 33:22), "Commit your way to the LORD; trust in him, and he will act" (Ps 37:5) make up about 50 percent of the verbal usage for hope in the Old Testament. One would also have to add innumerable texts that express such hope in God or for God without ever using a word for hope. However, Bultmann's statement is doubly one-sided. First, it suggests that the aspect of future is the only aspect in hope. Second, it does not seriously deal with the question of what it means to say "God." These two issues, however, are of fundamental importance for the understanding of hope in the Old Testament.

a. Regarding the first aspect, the question arises whether it is sufficient to say that the meaning of the present depends on the anticipation of the future, especially the future of God? Wouldn't we have to ask in the first place what makes such anticipation, hope, or expectation possible, especially if hope implies that what we hope for must be possible? It is impossible to expect a certain future possibility to come about as long as there is no possibility for such an expectation. In other words, we are confronted with the question of the cause for or the ground of hope. What makes hope possible? When looking at the confessions of hope in the Bible, especially in the Complaint Psalms, one indeed begins to wonder where these heroes of hope took the strength to say in their often incredible predicament, "I hope *in you,*" thereby assuming that they would not escape into illusions with such an outcry, but would throw themselves into the hands of an almighty possibility! We know that they were not heroes of emotional strength. They all, without exception, fell back on the long history of the mighty acts of Yahweh, on the experience of Yahweh's presence in Israel's midst, and on his words of promise: I am with you! I will bless you! I will give you! I will rescue you! I will lead you! In fact, the Old Testament texts speak just as much, if not more, about those acts and words of Yahweh for the world and for Israel than they speak about Israel's response in praise and hope. They knew that there was a force at work in their midst who was the ground of their existence, without whom they would not have

5. *TDNT* 2, 522.

existed and would not at all have come to where they were. The experience of this force not only allowed for hope, it caused and ignited it. Without this actuality, hope was not possible. Hope for Israel not only means hope *for* God or hope *in* God; it means first of all hope *from* God, in that humans have the fundamental chance, right, and freedom to hope which no power in this world can take away from them.

Hope depends on future fulfillment, but its rationale is grounded in past experience. This experience may be individual or communal, existential, natural, or historical. It is the reason why hope is realistic and not irrational. Moreover, God-Yahweh has a central place in this experience. But even with Yahweh's place in it, the imbeddedness of present hope within the connection of past and future is rooted in the dynamistic worldview which allows for or even generates projection into the future on the basis of past experience.

The highly developed historical consciousness of ancient Israel, the consciousness of a history of Yahweh's acts and words which is the ground for its hope for the future, is a case in point. However distinctively Israelite this consciousness was shaped, one can scarcely overlook the question of its connection with the dynamistic worldview which was not at all unique for Israel. In light of this question, the perception of historical process in which past, present, and future are connected, and in which past experience becomes the present ground for hope in the future, appears to be just one — though a major — offshoot of that dynamistic ontology in which the history of Yahweh's acts and words was perceived as well. One wonders whether the rise of historical consciousness would have been possible without that ontology, or whether it should be understood as a genuinely new and different worldview, which then would have generated the possibility for, and the realism and rationality of, hope.

When, after the catastrophe of 701, the prophet has run out of models from past experience for foretelling the future, he refers to the farmer's activities as a simile for God's historical actions. The farmer, taught by his God, not only demonstrates the connection of his springtime and harvest activities as a basis for hope for a secure future but also demonstrates that his harsh actions connected with both planting and harvesting are themselves based on the same hope, namely, that something good will result from such actions (Isaiah 28). The knowledge of the cyclic natural reality could both offer a rationale for hope and motivate hope, not only for a future but for a good future, whereas the knowledge of history could not. Yahweh was experienced in this natural reality just as much as in Israel's history. Not at all coincidentally, the experience of this reality was institutionalized in ancient Israel's agricultural Yahweh-festivals (cf. Exod 23:10-17; 34:22f.; Lev 23:4-22; Deut 16:9-17; 26:1-11).

What has been said about the ground for hope in the dynamistic worldview, in which the rise of historical consciousness is rooted as well, coincides with many passages about hope, including the hope of animals (cf. Pss 104:27; 136:25;

145:15). This hope in Yahweh has nothing to do with history, notwithstanding the fact that history, both human and Israel's, is in conflict with the ground for that hope.

b. There is yet a second question: What does the Old Testament mean by what we call "God"? For the purpose of this chapter, the question must be reduced to two aspects which control the others. These aspects may be condensed into two words: אלהים, "God," which occurs 2,570 times; and יהוה, "Yahweh," which occurs about 6,830 times.[6]

The word "God" is a generic term for deity. Its background is the polytheistic mythology of the ancient world, which shines through in the grammatical plural form אלהים, in the occasional use of the same word in the Old Testament for the "gods" who *are* or *do* — whereas the one God of monotheism *is* or *does* — and in the fact that it is relatively infrequently accompanied, also in the Old Testament, by a few other words for deity. By contrast, the word "Yahweh" is the personal name of a specific deity who is identified by this name so that this God can be distinguished and ultimately separated from the other gods. Neither word denotes "Lord," which refers to something very different.

Within its monotheistic framework, the Hebrew Bible speaks of the same person, and not of different divine persons, when saying "God" and "Yahweh." Unlike the relationship between God and Jesus Christ in the New Testament which is between two different persons, the relationship between "God" and "Yahweh" in the Hebrew Bible is determined by two different aspects of the same divine person. "God" points to the deity of "Yahweh," while "Yahweh" points to the identity of "God."

While etymologically not ultimately clear, the word for God = Deity stands in the Old Testament for the ultimate personified Highness in reality, immortal, sovereign, and of almighty influence, and especially for God's distinctiveness above and vis-à-vis all humans (cf. Num 23:19; Isa 31:3; Ezek 28:2 + 9; Hos 11:9; et al.). Moreover, the same word for God also stands for the Deity's ethical attitudes of salvation, of justice and righteousness including just judgment, of steadfast love or loyalty, and of mercy and forgiveness in the world. However, the word "Yahweh" stands for the God whom Israel has come to know through its history by name as the true God and as the God of Israel.

The two words complement one another, and are sometimes even juxtaposed (cf. Gen 2:4b–3:23; Exod 9:30; 2 Sam 7:25; Jon 4:6; Pss 72:18; 84:12 [*NRSV* 84:11]; 1 Chron 17:16f.; et al.). While they are certainly also used interchangeably, it is advisable that we be prepared for the fact that their respective usage is often determined by the presence of particular perspectives.

6. W. H. Schmidt, "אלהים Gott," *THAT* 1, 153-67; E. Jenni, "יהוה JHWH," *THAT* 1, 701-7; H. Ringgren, "אלהים," *TWAT* 1, 285-305; *TDOT* 1, 267-84; D. Freedman and P. O'Connor, "יהוה YHWH," *TWAT* 3, 533-54; *TDOT* 5, 500-521.

Hope is hope in the same deity, be it hope in God or hope in Yahweh. But hope in Yahweh as God means the hope in the ultimate reign and influence of God's salvation, justice, loyalty, and mercy, whereas hope in God as Yahweh means hope in this God, known in Israel, who with his personal name vouches for the ultimacy of the divine reign and influence. Thus, the ancient Israelites wait for the loving kindness of God-Yahweh (Ps 33:18-22), for his help (Ps 119:166), for — Yahweh's — light (Isa 59:9; Jer 13:16; Job 3:9), for his peace (Jer 8:15; 14:19), for what is good (Job 30:26), for his justice (Isa 59:11), and ultimately for God-Yahweh himself (Pss 27:14; 40:2 [*NRSV* 40:1]; 130:5; et al.).

1.-2. The nature of hope in the Old Testament comes into focus if one takes into account the presuppositions upon which the ancient Israelites project the goals of legitimate, valid hope. These presuppositions are signaled by the consciousness of the horizon of all reality (and by the possibility of that consciousness), by virtue of which what is ultimately good versus what is evil is discernible. They were shaped in Israel's own history, in all areas of its life, through the focus on salvation and justice, which are the foundation of all good and true life. In hoping for the steadiness or actualization of these goals, they were interested not just in the future for the sake of the future, but in the ongoing actuality into their future, or in their future reactualization, of these values. In this interest, their hope was enforced and legitimized by their knowledge of, and ultimately by their hope itself in, Yahweh-God.

When discussing hope in the Old Testament, the need for the distinction between the phenomenon hope and its nature should by now have become transparent. Phenomenologically, although hope may be true or false, it is still hope. It is, therefore, of programmatic importance that the Old Testament distinguishes between valid and vain hope, and thereby indicates throughout — and not only in Job and Ecclesiastes — that hope is not valid without qualification by virtue of being hope. It is valid by virtue of that which qualifies it, rather than that which disqualifies it. One can say that the legitimacy or validity of endowed hope, endowed in the legitimacy of living creatures, can be either maintained or perverted.

Hope guided by reckless desires and isolated self-orientation, aiming at one's own advantage at the expense of all else, represents the intent to manipulate and to pervert the true meaning of the world, even of God-Yahweh. It may yield success, but it has no legitimacy. The legitimacy or validity of hope is based on the criteria for the true value system discernible in the total horizon of the Old Testament's theologies of creation and also of Yahweh's relationship with Israel. Controlled by these criteria and their own validity, not only are the objectives of hope valid but its attitude as well.

Finally, the valid nature of hope makes it understandable that hope has to do with Yahweh-God, that all hope is theological in nature. It is theological because Yahweh-God symbolizes the ultimate legitimacy on which every legitimate human hope depends without which human hope is relative, regardless of the degree to which that hope is understood to be ultimate. "God-Yahweh" is intrinsic to the nature of hope by indicating that not even legitimate hope is ultimate hope. It is only penultimate hope, always subject to the scrutiny and judgment of the ultimate. Even as humans hope in God, their hope is understood to be generated by God, and not by themselves or their own potential. The dependence of legitimate hope on God's ultimacy emerges especially in texts which indicate that hope in God-Yahweh may differ from hope in presupposed objectives, or which point to a difference between hope and hopes. Hope that would only consist of hopes, hopes for available things as ends in themselves, would be the end of that hope and lead humans to reach beyond the perimeter of known experience. While in many texts the expressed hope in Yahweh coincides with their legitimate objectives, such as recovery from sickness, vindication, restoration of Israel and its land, etc., there are texts in which this coincidence is open. They point to the awareness that hope in God may transcend the horizon of patterned experience, and that God opens up new realities for them.

II. God — Reality — and Human Hope

What is the relationship between hope in or for God on the one hand and hope focusing on reality on the other? I am focusing on four aspects: hope in accord with reality; hope in tension with reality but aiming at its restoration; hope in contrast to reality, aiming at a different reality; and hope in God.

A. Hope in Accord with Reality

Typical for this aspect is Ps 37:1-19, 25, 27-29, 32-40, which can be taken as an example for many other texts of the same nature (I have emphasized those phrases pointing to this aspect):

> 1*Do not fret* because of the wicked;
> do not be envious of wrongdoers,
> 2for they will soon fade like the grass,
> and wither like the green herb.
> 3*Trust* in the LORD, and do good;
> so you will live in the land, and enjoy security.
> 4Take delight in the LORD,
> and he will give you the desires of your heart.
> 5*Commit your way* to the LORD;
> *trust* in him, and he will act.

6He will make your vindication shine like the light,
and the justice of your cause like the noonday.
7Be still before the LORD, and *wait patiently* for him;
do not fret over those who prosper in their way,
over those who carry out evil devices.
8Refrain from anger, and forsake wrath.
Do not fret — it leads only to evil.
9For the wicked shall be cut off,
but those who wait for the LORD shall inherit the land.
10Yet *a little while,* and the wicked will be no more;
though you look diligently for their place, they will not be there.
11But the meek shall inherit the land,
and delight themselves in abundant prosperity.
12The *wicked plot* against the righteous,
and gnash their teeth at them;
13but the LORD laughs at the wicked, . . .
for he sees that their day is coming.
14The wicked draw the sword and bend their bows
to bring down the poor and needy,
to kill those who walk uprightly;
15their sword shall enter their own heart,
and their bows shall be broken.
16Better is a little that the righteous person has
than the abundance of many wicked.
17For the arms of the wicked shall be broken,
but the LORD upholds the righteous.
18The LORD knows the days of the blameless,
and their heritage will abide forever;
19they are not put to shame in evil times,
in the days of famine they have abundance. . . .
25I have been young, and now am old,
yet I have not seen the righteous forsaken
or their children begging bread. . . .
27Depart from evil, and do good;
so you shall abide forever.
28For the LORD loves justice;
he will not forsake his faithful ones.
The righteous shall be kept safe forever,
but the children of the wicked shall be cut off.
29The righteous shall inherit the land,
and live in it forever. . . .
32*The wicked watch* for the righteous,
and seek to kill them.

33The LORD will not abandon them to their power,
or let them be condemned when they are brought to trial.
34*Wait for the LORD*, and keep to his way,
and he will exalt you to inherit the land;
you will look on the destruction of the wicked.
35I have seen the wicked oppressing,
and towering like a cedar of Lebanon.
36Again I passed by, and they were no more;
though I sought them, they could not be found.
37*Mark the blameless,* and *behold the upright,*
for there is posterity for the peaceable.
38But transgressors shall be altogether destroyed;
the posterity of the wicked shall be cut off.
39The salvation of the righteous is from the LORD;
he is their refuge in the time of trouble.
40The LORD helps them and rescues them;
he rescues them from the wicked, and saves them,
because *they take refuge in him.*

The picture is perfectly clear. The life experience of the old man (v. 25) has come down to a very elementary summary. Life is about the difference between the wicked and the righteous. The wicked act falsely, the righteous rightly. Either type reaps with absolute consistency the fruits of its actions, destruction or prosperity. Yahweh fits into the picture without the slightest tension. Moreover, Yahweh takes care that this system remains intact. Occasionally, one may have to wait until a certain fluctuation is stabilized. But this takes place within a relatively short period of time, certainly within a lifetime, and the outcome is predictable. Accordingly, hope in God and hope in the coming reality, expressed both in essence and terminology, are in complete harmony, so much so that hope coincides with certain prognosis and prediction. There are many more texts of this sort, e.g., Psalm 91. Have the composers of these texts ever read the book of Job, or heard anything about the hiddenness of God, or of justification by faith alone?

It would be a mistake to assume with our educated reservations and objections that here speaks a primitive, naive, eudaemonistic works-morale, regrettably all that the wisdom of these people has to offer, a morale that is unaware of all the unsolved problems which are universally expressed. We have learned that such statements are not intended to spread the news of a new discovery by an isolated individual of the best way to a successful life. On the contrary, they intend to affirm — confirmed by the sum total of a lifelong personal experience — a general assumption about the basic order of the world, a basic ontological assumption. The assumption was, and is, that the structure of the world is basically in order. It is not chaotic. Good results from good, and bad from bad. And all that is said about *God* is that he is both creator and guardian of this order. As for humans, their task is to live in accordance with this structure of the world. There is indeed the experience, so our texts indicate, of the integrity of this order in the realms of human life. That is the reason for calling upon humans to be righteous and to have hope. Moreover, hope is possible because the horizon of this intelligible reality allows for the projection of a future that grows logically out of the present. This kind of hope in both God and the prolonged present belongs to the basic structure of humanness. It is based on ontological bedrock, according to which human life is imbedded in the basic order of this world. And "God," as the signal for their ultimate validity, is thus experienced as reaching into the reality of human life. When having such experiences, humans realize that in them the truth of the world is revealed. This reality as experienced appears as salvific foundation of the wholeness of the world and as imbedded in the wholeness of the world. This is the reason for a type of hope that expects, anticipates, and prognosticates the lasting accord of God and reality.

Of course, this understanding presupposes the person's loyalty to the existing order of things, just as Israel's expectations of the same pattern presuppose its loyalty to its covenant with Yahweh. It is very conscious of the criterion that if such loyalty is broken, the continuing existence of the order may not be expected. But it may be expected where loyalty exists.

We have problems with such an understanding, quite apart from the fact that this is by far not everyone's experience. We have learned that, in such an intrinsic connection of God and reality in human hope, God may become a symbol for our material longings. He may become subject to our control and, hence, an idol. This objection is correct. Our own problem, however, is that, while intending to emphasize nothing more than that hope in God must not mean hope in our worldly aspirations and enslavement to the world, we may insufficiently articulate what hope in God has to do with the order of this world and with our reality. If we separate God from reality, we will find it difficult to make explicit which of our material, immanent hopes are theologically legitimate, and under what conditions this is the case, as well as where and why they are not legitimate. The Old Testament points out that, within the framework of a particular perception of reality, hope in God is legitimate and necessary as hope for immanent experiences. It does so by differentiating between legitimate and illegitimate immanent hopes rather than by separating the immanent hopes from hope in God. This kind of discernment is in order where and as long as the world is experienced as intact, and where the horizon of experience is not broken by contrasting experiences.

B. Hope in Tension with Reality

There is a type of hope in which Israel's understanding of God/Yahweh is not covered by its experience, and which aims, therefore, at the reintegration of God and reality. The situations in the Old Testament are numerous and cover a wide variety of experiences. Two types may characterize the pattern.

1. The Hope of Individuals for Restoration

In dozens of Complaint Psalms we have statements such as 38:8-9, 16, 22f. (*NRSV* 38:7-8, 15, 21f.) (emphasis mine):

> 7For my loins are filled with burning,
> and there is no soundness in my flesh.
> 8I am utterly spent and crushed;
> I groan because of the tumult of my heart. . . .
> 15But it is for you, O LORD, that I wait;
> it is you, O LORD my God, who will answer. . . .
> 21Do not forsake me, O LORD;
> O my God, do not be far from me;
> 22make *haste* to *help me,*
> O Lord, my salvation.

What is meant with the situation and with the hope for restoration is expressed in Ps 103:3-5 (emphasis mine):

> 3(the LORD) . . . who forgives all your *iniquity,*
> who heals all your *diseases,*
> 4who redeems your life from the Pit,
> who crowns you with steadfast love and mercy,
> 5who satisfies you with good as long as you live,
> so that your youth is renewed like the eagle's. . . .

People are sick, in deadly danger, and/or persecuted. The order of their life has broken down, but they expect it to be restored soon. The hope is urgent. It is hope both *from* God and *in* God because the word "God" stands for the order of world and life and is, therefore, intensely expected to restore it in the near future.

A considerable portion of the Psalms deals with this situation. It may be that this phenomenon means little to a society that has driven the experience of the old, the sick, the suffering, the hungry, and the dying out of public view. But these texts show a people of God for which the suffering, the outcast, the helpless, the sick, and the dying are at least as much in the center of the community as is the praise of the glory and beauty of divine and human actions. That community knew that the *world* is misshapen and that the body of the community is sick as long as the suffering are not taken care of. Their hope for restoration is not idolatrous. It is a hope that God restores distorted life to its true meaning in this reality.

2. The Hope for Restoration of the Community

Here, too, we have many texts, particularly in the prophetic literature and in the communal Complaint Psalms. Most of them are concerned with the restoration of the exilic Israelite community to the promised land. They expect this restoration from Yahweh. Lamentations 5:8-15, 19-22 is one example:

> 8Slaves rule over us;
> there is no one to deliver us from their hand.
> 9We get our bread at the peril of our lives,
> because of the sword in the wilderness.
> 10Our skin is black as an oven
> from the scorching heat of famine.
> 11Women are raped in Zion,
> virgins in the towns of Judah.
> 12Princes are hung up by their hands;
> no respect is shown to the elders.
> 13Young men are compelled to grind,
> and boys stagger under loads of wood.
> 14The old men have left the city gate,
> the young men their music.
> 15The joy of our hearts has ceased;
> our dancing has been turned to mourning. . . .

(So much for the reference to the situation. Now, in v. 19, follows the reference to the basis for hope.)

> 19But you, O LORD, reign forever;
> your throne endures to all generations.

(Then comes the complaint.)

> 20Why have you forgotten us completely?
> Why have you forsaken us these many days?

(And then the petition for a particular concretization as the expression of hope.)

> 21Restore us to yourself, O LORD,
> that we may be restored;
> renew our days as of old —
> 22unless you have utterly rejected us,
> and are angry with us beyond measure.

Hope in the restoration to God and for the restoration of the days of old go hand in hand. Is this a reactionary mentality which can see in the future nothing but the return to "the good old days"? Scarcely. They do not desire to retreat back into the past for the sake of the past itself. They desire the return to normality as it had been experienced in the past, and they know that normality has not returned despite their confessions of sin. Inasmuch as hope is concerned with the real conditions under which people live, and inasmuch as it is concerned with chaos or normality in these conditions, hope in God as the one who restores normality is legitimate, if God, "the ground of being" (as we so impressively say), is to have anything to do with the real conditions of human life.

In much of our theological tradition, we have grown accustomed to suspect this type of hope of opportunistic and eudaemonistic manipulation of God. However, we may have to reevaluate our stance on this problem. The ancient Israelites themselves felt this same question as well. Again, when expressing hope in material restoration, most of the texts distinguish linguistically between hope for restoration and hope in God. The words for "hope" are overwhelmingly used in expressions for hope in God. "I hope for you" is a standard expression. But the question is also reflected in other ways, e.g., by Hosea. When the people say, "Come, let us return to the LORD; for it is he who has torn, and he will heal us; he has struck down, and he will bind us up. After two days he will revive us; on the third day he will raise us up, that we may live before him" (Hos 6:1f.), Hosea quotes Yahweh as saying, "What shall I do with you, O Ephraim? What shall I do with you, O Judah? Your love is like a morning cloud, like the dew that goes away early. . . . For I desire steadfast love and not sacrifice, the knowledge of God rather than burnt offerings" (6:4, 6). Hosea is saying that hope has no foundation or promise if "God" is nothing but a means for achieving the self-projected, quick material restoration. Hope in God means that humans' material hopes are taken out of their selfish projections and placed into the horizon of that which "God" signifies, namely, the good foundational order of the world: steadfast love, justice, and salvation. This means that the goals, perspectives, values, and attitudes of people who hope in God are scrutinized and changed by the One in whom they are hoping. One can observe not only that hope for material restoration and hope in God are legitimately related to one another, but also that they can prejudice one another. Material hope can use God eudaemonistically, and vice versa: God fulfills the true meaning of material hope, which can mean that he leads it into a fulfillment that was not originally so projected. With all this, Hosea 6 does not reject the hope for immanent restoration. But it differentiates between the ultimate motives and goals. The text leaves no doubt that in this difference not only the validity of their hope but the very identity of God's people is at stake.

C. Hope in Contrast to Reality

Psalm 82 portrays a highly mythical drama. In heaven, the gods of the world have assembled for a divine council, a council concerned with the affairs of world government, as we can safely assume. Suddenly, something astonishing happens. God (*"El,"* understood by the psalmist as Yahweh), the little god of the provincial nation Israel, stands up and accuses the whole pantheon, "How long will you judge unjustly and show partiality to the wicked?" Then he quotes for them from their manual of discipline what their duties would have been, "Give justice to the weak and the orphan; maintain the right of the lowly and the destitute. Rescue the weak and the needy; deliver them from the hand of the wicked." After this evidence of their guilt, he turns, so to speak, to the jury, concluding, "They have neither knowledge nor understanding, they walk around in darkness; all the foundations of the earth are shaken." And finally, he pronounces the sentence: "I say, 'You are gods, children of the Most High, all of you; nevertheless, you shall die like mortals, and fall like any prince.' " Israel says that, on the basis of a trial, its God-Yahweh has deposed the gods of the world, condemned them to death, and assumed sole reign over the whole universe. What was the reason for this revolution? The gods had failed to maintain justice and righteousness on earth. When saying "Yahweh," Israel affirms a concept which governs the universe, the concept of "justice and righteousness," whose criterion of truth is the protection of the disfranchised.

In addition, this God begins to attack the aspirations and policies of the nations, as he had attacked his colleagues in the pantheon. Psalm 33 is a case in point. While praising Yahweh for his creation of the world (vv. 4-9), verse 5 says, "He loves righteousness and justice; the earth is full of the steadfast love of the LORD." The psalm makes a statement about the relationship between the creation of the world and the sustenance of the world, saying that the meaning of creation for the continued existence of the world consists in righteousness, justice, and steadfast love; or that justice, righteousness, and love are the governing principles in which creation is legitimately present in the ongoing world. But then the psalm turns to the realities by which this world is governed, saying, "The LORD brings the counsel of the nations to nothing" (v. 10), and, in verses 16-17, referring to those counsels, "A king is not saved by his great army; a warrior is not delivered by his great strength. The war horse is a vain hope for victory, and by its great might it cannot save." And finally, "Truly the eye of the LORD is on those who fear him, on those who hope in his steadfast love. . . . Our soul waits for the LORD; he is our help and shield." There is a deep conflict going on, the conflict between the aspirations of the nations which aim at running the world with their symbols of power (great armies, great military strength, war horse) and the *assertion* that the world comes to its true meaning only if it is governed by justice, righteousness, and love. Israel disputes the truthfulness of these national ideologies, saying that they destroy the meaning of the world, and Israel affirms that it waits for Yahweh.

Then along come the prophets attacking Israel itself: "For the vineyard of the LORD of hosts is the house of Israel, and the people of Judah are his pleasant planting; he expected [i.e., hoped for, קוה] justice, but saw bloodshed; righteousness, but heard a cry!" (Isa. 5:7). Micah says it very drastically in his word against the landlords and exploiters (3:1-3): "And I said: Listen, you heads of Jacob and rulers of the house of Israel! Should you not know justice? — you who hate the good and love the evil, who tear the skin off my people, and the flesh off their bones; who eat the flesh of my people, flay their skin off them, break their bones in pieces, and chop them up like meat in a kettle, like flesh in a caldron."

To be sure, the Micah passage does not speak about hope. It presupposes that the prophet has lost hope that Israel will ever know justice, just as Yahweh's own hope for justice in Israel has been disappointed (cf. Isa 5:7). These and similar texts reveal the deep contrast between legitimate hope, even Yahweh's, and reality as it is, especially among Yahweh's elect. When Yahweh himself rises against this perverted reality, he does so in the name of the criteria for true reality, the achievement of which was the purpose of Israel's past history. Characteristic of this rebellion of Yahweh against the perverted reality is the fact that the hope for its restoration in the present time has been lost. If there is hope for restoration, this hope must look into the future. At this juncture, at the moment of hopelessness for the present time, it seems that the dimension of the future gains theological relevance in the specific sense of hope in a qualified future — not just hope *as* future, but hope *for* the future of justice and righteousness in Yahweh's new coming.

In its emerging eschatologies, Israel did not expect God because they had hope in the future. They looked to the future because of their hope in God's future coming — unless they had been persuaded on the basis of their past and present experience that God-Yahweh, together with the truth of salvation, justice, and righteousness, had died.

D. Hope in God

The Old Testament testifies not only to the reality of hope. It also testifies to the breakdown of hope. "We look for peace, but find no good; for a time of healing, but there is terror instead" (Jer 14:19). "We wait for light, and lo! there is darkness; and for brightness, but we walk in gloom" (Isa 59:9). "My days are swifter than a weaver's shuttle, and come to their end without hope" (Job 7:6). For Job, the only remaining hope is death: "O that I might have my request, and that God would grant my desire; that it would please God to crush me, that he would let loose his hand and cut me off" (Job 6:8). Moreover, the entire history of Israel pays witness to fading hopes. Even more pressing is the fact that it is not simply hope which breaks down, but God himself finishes it off: "The waters wear away the stones; the torrents wash away the soil of the earth; so you destroy the hope of mortals" (Job 14:19). When God says to Abraham, "Take your son, your only son Isaac, whom you love, and go to the land of Moriah, and offer him there as a burnt offering . . ." (Gen 22:2), he stands against his own promise to give him countless descendants for the fulfillment of which (in Isaac) Abraham had to wait so long.

This example indicates that, as the reason for God's attack on human hope, the reference to human failure alone is insufficient. The problem lies deeper.

But now in contrast to such breakdowns of hope stands the hope in God alone: "Let me have silence, and I will speak, and let come on me what may. I will take my flesh in my teeth, and put my life in my hand. See, he will kill me; I have no hope; yet I will defend my ways to his face" (Job 13:13-15). "Oh that you would hide me in Sheol, that you would conceal me until your wrath is past, that you would appoint me a set time, and remember me! If mortals die, will they live again? All the days of my service I would wait until my release should come" (Job 14:13f.). "For I know that my Redeemer lives, and that at the last he will stand upon the earth; and after my skin has been thus destroyed, then in my flesh I shall see God" (Job 19:25f.). "Whom have I in heaven but you? And there is nothing on earth that I desire other than you. My flesh and my heart may fail, but God is the strength of my heart and my portion forever" (Ps 73:25f.). "So I say, 'Gone is my glory, and all that I had hoped for from the LORD.' . . . But this I call to mind, and therefore I have hope: The steadfast love of the LORD never ceases, his mercies never come to an end; they are new every morning; great is your faithfulness. 'The LORD is my portion,' says my soul, 'therefore I will hope in him' " (Lam 3:18, 21-24).

It is quite clear that in such language "hope in God" is radical (at least on the way to being radical). It does not hold on to set conceptualizations of reality. It reaches even beyond death. It is transconceptual. It focuses strictly on God. It is equally clear that this transconceptuality, this sole focus on God, cannot be explained as a reaction against the breakdown of material, world-immanent hopes. It must rest on an understanding of God inherent in Yahwism from the outset. When Abraham is told, "Go from your country and your kindred and your father's house to the land that I will show you" (Gen 12:1), he must leave behind all the familiar types of experience and go into the unknown, open to any kind of realization/outcome. Then Isaac said to him, "Father!" And he said, "Here am I, my son," and Isaac asked, "The fire and the wood are here, but where is the lamb for a burnt offering?" Abraham said, "God himself will provide the lamb for a burnt offering, my son"; and when "Abraham reached out his hand and took the knife to kill his son" (Gen 22:7f., 10), he must have given up the last bit of any idea as to what he should hope for. But quite apart from those enormously pressing passages, the entire Old Testament recognizes the difference between hope in God and hope in things. As we have seen, this difference could create a division or even a conflict between the two at any moment, and very often did.

What does this radical nature of hope in God mean? It seems that here we touch upon the heart of the concept of hope in the Old Testament. It certainly means that humans have given up using their hopes as crutches by which to support the truth of their lives; that they have given up using their hopes as substitutes which are readily available for competition with the real hope; hence, they have given up living in the twilight between truth and untruth. Their futurologies, their messianisms, their optimisms or pessimisms, and their utopias are demythologized. They do not signify the true meaning of the world by themselves. Bloch's *Deus Spes,* "God Hope," is demythologized also. Hope is no God. Moreover, the God Utopia is ultimately nothing but humans' self-captivity in the projections of their dreams. The hopes must lose their mythic contours and implications under which they hold humans captive within their concepts of the kingdom.

Hope in God alone, however, frees humans from the subduing, determining horizons of their reality; it liberates them from the mythologization of their concepts of reality and unto the ultimately governing validity of the "God" of justice, righteousness, love, and grace. Hope in God alone opens humans for the unseen and unthought, for possibilities beyond patterned experiences, for the rescue and salvation of all who are experiencing danger, terror, suffering, and distress. It means that the horizons and concepts of reality will be created and outlined by that coming justice, righteousness, and love, and not by our fixed experiences of the past. Hope in God experiences new realities.

This hope, though independent of reality, is nevertheless aiming at it. Now, we can look back at what we have said about hope in accord with reality, in tension with reality, and in contrast to reality. Hope in God does not reject the projection of material hopes, anticipations, plans, dreams, expectations, optimisms, and/or futurologies focusing on the realities around us. It does not deny their material focus. On the contrary, it will predominantly call on them inasmuch as we live in a material world, must anticipate a material future, and affect both by our existence. But hope in God sharply differentiates between the legitimacy and illegitimacy of material hopes, between their truth and their untruth, in the light of the ultimate criterion. It is the crisis of hope. It puts before them the entire question of what they truly aim for and how far they reach. Hope in God is not a hope among other hopes, but the truth in them. It judges and transforms them so that they cannot serve themselves (hope for the sake of hope!) but serve only that purpose that is the true meaning of the world. Thus, it reaches into all hopes and realities, everywhere and at all times. It signals the self-realization of God in human experience.

The problem of the Old Testament is that in many texts this differentiation between hope in God and other hopes is not made explicit and that in some it is not present at all. But in a great number of traditions it is referred to often. This ambiguity, and at times even ambivalence, by no means allows us to discard all material hopes. It means only that they must be critically evaluated as to their true or false potential, evaluated in the light of the hope in God to which the Old Testament itself gives witness. The Old Testament has its own hermeneutical problem, which cannot be solved with literalistic, biblicistic, or dogmatic propositions. It can only be approached from the central concern of Israel: its preoccupation with that experience of its reality whom it called "Yahweh." Under this preoccupation, humans exist as creatures who are sustained by hope rather than as those who must sustain their hopes and whose criteria for the validity of their hopes, i.e., justice and mercy and peace, are always on the way to being transcended and reshaped in the encounter with new realities, just as they participate in generating those new realities.

For the Old Testament, hope is a condition common to all living beings, including humans, not merely to Yahweh's own people. And true hope includes the hope in the ultimacy of God-Yahweh.

Since the Old Testament's anthropology is characterized above all else by Israel's reverence for and knowledge of God-Yahweh (which is explicitly documented over nine thousand times, an average of six times per page of the Hebrew Bible), it is necessary to say that Israel's hope in God-Yahweh is an inherent element of this reverence and knowledge, as long as hope in God is considered to be a common condition of the living. In this sense, the Old Testament's reverence for and knowledge of God-Yahweh is at the same time and in its entirety an expression of its hope in God's presence in the ongoing existence and history of the world and of Israel. Inasmuch as the Old Testament speaks about God's acts in the past and the future, one must say that it does so because of their meaning for Yahweh's presence in the ongoing world and human generations, even where he is said to have withdrawn that presence. Hope in God-Yahweh is always hope in his presence, at the very least but not only, in the many passages that document this fact in manifold ways.

This understanding brings into sharp focus the question of the relationship between the Old Testament's hope in Yahweh's abiding presence in creation and history and its hope in his eschatological future. Sole validity can scarcely be granted to eschatological hope with reference to passages such as Jer 31:31-34 and to the ever-expanding hope in the history of the prophetic tradition. However much this aspect with its apocalyptic intensification has its undeniable place in ancient Israel's theological history, and however much its criticism against its contemporary situation is valid, it is not sufficient for discrediting the other aspect about — the knowledge of and hope for — God-Yahweh's ongoing presence in the ongoing world.

This other aspect, which is documented in the Pentateuch, the historical books, the psalms, and the wisdom literature, is also valid. It is valid not only because Israel has retained it in its Bible, rather than eliminate it, with the result that it is finally juxtaposed to its eschatological vision, but also because it massively documents the Old Testament's knowledge of and hope in God's presence in this world — as long as it exists — even if this hope is contextually qualified by the ultimacy of God-Yahweh's presence as portrayed in the eschatological vision.

It is significant, but not coincidental, for the Old Testament's theological self-understanding that the first part of the Hebrew Bible, the Torah, is considered its most important part. However this importance is relativized by the eschatological vision and its arguments such as the human inability to obey the law, the gift of the spirit for enabling such obedience, or the insufficiency of the law itself, the Torah is still the most important part, even under the criterion of that vision for its own significance, because it focuses on God-Yahweh's presence in his world in all its times, on his loyalty to his old and ongoing world. In view of this focus, the hope in the eschatological future, quite apart from the problem of its inner-worldly depictions and of its indefinite postponement, functions as the radicalization of the hope in God-Yahweh's presence in this ongoing world. It does not replace hope. It radicalizes it.

Whatever Luther meant when saying that he would still plant a tree today even if he knew that the LORD were to come tomorrow, his statement means more than that doing today's things remains important before, and probably because of, the eschaton. Does it not also mean, and even more, that the hope in God's eschatological coming serves the hope in God's care for the future of the tree?

The Spirituality of the Old Testament

Introduction

At the beginning, some remarks are necessary about the interdependence of the topic as formulated and the evidence for it in the Old Testament. Everyone involved in scientific research on a subject knows that it makes a great deal of difference whether one approaches the available data under an already defined conceptual framework and a set of questions specifically designed for it, or whether one approaches the data without a clear conception of its nature and contours and of the specific questions that would be evoked by the materials themselves. In the first case, we would ascertain the answers as responses to our own questions, perhaps less but not more; but we would not ascertain those answers that the materials would disclose were we to search for their own questions. We would investigate the materials according to our interest rather than theirs, for our purpose rather than theirs, for the need of our answers rather than theirs. In the second case, we would want to be — sensitively! — in contact with the materials concerned with a certain subject of interest for us, however clearly or generally conceived, but with the intention to find out whether or not our subject is also their subject; and if so, how it is reflected in these materials under their own perspective. We would investigate the materials under the proviso of their interest rather than ours, and in need of their answers to their own questions for our benefit rather than their answers to nothing but our own questions. The differences between the two approaches lie, therefore, in whether the investigation is of our subject or of theirs. Nevertheless, we are inevitably involved in both approaches.

What has just been said in general terms also affects when in the course of an investigation one defines a topic for the object of that investigation. Should the topic be defined at the outset, and thereby predetermine the focus of the investigation as well as its results? Or should its definition reflect the already arrived at conclusions? Or should it reflect the circumference of both the general direction of the approach and the specific shape of the results? The last-named of these possibilities seems to be more adequate, or may even be inevitable. But its greater adequacy does not mean that a thus-formulated topic must be understood as an indication of the complementarity between the findings and our own preconceptions and expectations. It may very well confront us with a different, if not alien, world.

The following chapter is a case in point. It is unnecessary to substantiate the pluralism of approaches to and of conceptual positions on the subject of spirituality, a subject that for good reasons has gained a high visibility in our generation. Nor is it necessary to justify a look at the Old Testament as long as this (part of the) Bible remains an important source for "spiritual" support and renewal for humanity rather than for the Jewish and Christian communities alone. Important, however, is the possibility that from the Old Testament's own perspective on what we call "spirituality," we may gain access to dimensions of that subject which not only expand our knowledge but also contribute distinct, and in part different, aspects to the discovery of the spiritual nature of our existence, even in our knowledge.

Not everything contained in the Old Testament about this subject can be discussed in an essay. Nor is this essay exclusively concerned with the biblical passages that explicitly address the issue of "spirit." The essay is entitled "The Spirituality *of* the Old Testament," not "Spirituality *in* the Old Testament,"[1] whereby the former includes the latter. It is not sufficient to discuss the issue only on the basis of the Old Testament's statements about "spirituality." The Old Testament is in its totality a phenomenon of the "spirit" of which on occasion it speaks. The focus on this phenomenon means that more is at stake than the juxtaposition of various aspects on the subject. Such juxtapositions are easily accessible in biblical lexica which should be consulted in this regard. This essay does not represent another version of that genre, although such work is indeed important.[2] Our reconstruction of the

1. or: "The Old Testament *as* Spirituality."

2. Encyclopedia articles pertaining to spirituality in the Old Testament include: Bertholet and Baed, "Geist: 2. Geist und Geistesgaben im AT und Judentum," *RGG²,* vol. 2 (Tübingen: J. C. B. Mohr, 1928), 940-43; G. Gerleman, "Geist und Geistesgaben im AT," *RGG³,* vol. 2 (Tübingen: J. C. B. Mohr, 1958), 1270-71; R. Jewett, "Spirit," *IDBSup,* 839-41; S. V. McCasland, "Spirit," *IDB* 4, 432-34; N. W. Porteous, "Soul," *IDB* 4, 428-29; L. Rost, "Geist," *Biblisch-Historisches Handwörterbuch,* vol. 1 (Göttingen: Vandenhoeck & Ruprecht, 1962), 534-36; W. H. Schmidt, "Geist/Heiliger Geist/Geistesgaben, I. Altes Testament," *TRE* 12, 170-73. Lexical articles include: regarding רוח: R. Albertz and C. Westermann, *THAT* 2, 726-53; regarding נפש: C. Westermann, *THAT* 2, 71-96; H. Seebass, *TWAT* 5, 531-55; regarding לב: F. Stolz, *THAT* 1, 861-67; H.-J. Fabry, *TWAT* 4, 413-51; regarding קרב: J. Kühlewein, *THAT* 2, 674-81; Rattray and Milgrom, *TWAT* 7, 161-65; regarding חכם: M. Saebö, *THAT* 1, 557-67; Müller and Krause, *TWAT* 2, 920-44 (*TDOT* 4, 365-85).

conceptuality of the Old Testament's spirituality is necessary. This conceptuality can at times be directly observed where the texts address the subject. But it is nowhere discussed *in toto,* neither is it absent where the texts are concerned with other issues. Just as in the case of the Old Testament's anthropology, in which the texts rest on an anthropology without offering us a chapter or biblical book about it, so also its spirituality must be reconstructed in its systemic nature if we want to understand better why the texts say what they say in different contexts throughout the Old Testament.

Finally, the following subdivisions are the result of an attempt to put the evidence into an order that lends itself to reflecting not only the major framework of the conceptuality of the Old Testament's spirituality but also the interdependence of the various aspects within that framework.

I. Spirit and Spirituality, or: Perspectives on Spirituality in the Old Testament and the Old Testament as Spirituality

II. The Nature of the Old Testament Spirituality

   A. Its Focus

   B. Its Expressions and Perspectives

   C. Its Source

I. Spirit and Spirituality

When searching in the Hebrew Bible for an equivalent to our word "spirituality" we are at first disappointed. There seems to be none. However, the reason for this preliminarily negative result is not the unavailability of such a Hebrew equivalent. Rather, it is the direction of investigation suggested by our own preunderstanding of our word "spirituality." For us, especially in a theological and ecclesiastical setting, "spirituality" implies some kind of condition or attitude evolving from "spirit," especially the "Spirit of God." This preunderstanding suggests that we enter the Hebrew Bible through the Hebrew word for spirit, רוח, and expand our inquiry thence to phrases such as רוח יהוה, "the spirit of Yahweh," or רוח אלהים, "the spirit of God," respectively. The result of this etymological approach would stop short of our expectations because it does not carry us to an expression for the subject which we call "spirituality," which would need to be an abstract, conceptual noun such as, e.g., מרוחה. The question becomes unavoidable: does the Old Testament know of "spirituality" as our preunderstanding suggests? Does it speak of it? Or — at least — is it in the Old Testament? If so, how and where do we find it? We are apparently confronted with an inquiry that does not intrinsically hand us the approach to the answer, let alone determine that answer.

On the other hand, it is not clear what is meant when we ourselves speak about spirituality. We have various options in mind, not only from a biblical but also — and probably even more so — from a church-historical, theological, philosophical, or psychological point of view. While using the word as a key signal, we are in danger of not knowing what we are saying and thereby of neutralizing the importance of the subject.[3]

This all means that we are confronted with the comparison of two unknowns. On the one hand, we do not know exactly what we should be looking for in the Old Testament; and on the other hand, we do not know how and where the Old Testament's response to what we are looking for might be found. If anything, this situation signifies the sensitivity of the hermeneutical circle.

This situation suggests an open approach, i.e., an approach in which we try to establish complementarities between our own flexible notions of spirituality and the Old Testament's own course of argumentation. With such an understanding, we can start with the Hebrew word for spirit, "רוח," knowing that this step may only provide a bridge-building entry to the problem, an entry that takes up our preconceived notion or some aspect(s) of it, but which by no means predetermines the full, or final, or even fundamental, answer.

A. Spirituality Corresponding to רוח, "Spirit"

I am seeking to interpret the Hebrew understanding of the word we normally find translated "spirit" in our English translations, and what we should understand when reading the word רוח, or "spirit," in the Old Testament.[4]

1. The Hebrew word for spirit, רוח, belongs to the language of meteorology. It means the moving, agitated air, i.e., the wind. Regarding humans, it is, correspondingly, the human breath in the state of active breathing. This means:

a. רוח, "breath," "spirit," is a physical element. As such, it is part of the human nature and condition.

b. It is that element of the human nature through which the human *physis* becomes vitalized. It is the vitality-giving part of the human *physis,* or if you will, its spiriting element.

3. It cannot be overlooked that the points of view just mentioned essentially reflect the framework of the church-historical traditions and of the modern emergence of psychology within so-called Western civilization. When one looks at different indigenous cultures, especially in Asia, Africa, or Central and South America, one encounters different worldviews and their "spiritualities." By contrast, a reading of the "patients" in "psychiatric" institutions in the former Soviet Union demonstrates that "spirituality," however diversely perceived in other traditions, was a nonissue for them because people were not presumed to have, or to be, a soul.

4. For the following, compare the discussion under the pertinent sections in H. W. Wolff, *Anthropology of the Old Testament,* trans. M. Kohl (Philadelphia: Fortress Press, 1974).

c. Although it is a physical, natural element, and part of human nature, it is distinguished from the human *physis,* or body, which is dust and earth. It is the body's life element. Through the רוח ("spirit as breath"), humans are enlivened, energized, agitated, moved, etc. Without it, they simply die.

a.-c. What has been said so far about the Hebrew word רוח is also reflected in the word נשמה, "breath." Both words complement one another or are interchangeable in this semantic level. Therefore, where advisable, passages using the word נשמה instead of or together with רוח will be drawn into the scope of our discussion.

d. The breath from the air igniting the body to life comes from God and is taken away by God: Yahweh "breathed into his nostrils the breath [נשמה] of life" (Gen 2:7); and, "when you take away their breath [!, רוחם], they die and return to their dust. When you send forth your spirit [!, רוחך], they are created" (Ps 104:29b+30a).

(1) The reason why Ps 104:29b-30a speaks of "their" and "your" spirit lies in the alternating perspectives of the location of the spirit at the moment of its transfer or relocation. At the moment it is taken away from them, it appears as having had its place in them; however, when it is given to them its place appears under the aspect of the one who gives it. But neither formulation implies that the spirit itself is seen as a "human" or "divine" spirit. The two statements provide no ontological discussion of "spirit." Rather, their common denominator is that the spirit essential for human life is given and taken by God, and is not under the control of humans.

(2) Similarly, "breath of life" in Gen 2:7 does not mean a human or divine quality. It certainly has nothing to do with a divine substance in humans. It is the spirit of life but not the spirit of God breathed into humans. It is the spirit coming *from* God, but not the spirit *of* God.

As breath from God, however, the word נשמה is here used in parallel with the word רוח (cf. the parallel *use* of both words in Ps 18:16 [*NRSV* 18:15]; 2 Sam 22:16; Job 34:14; also Gen 7:22; as well as the semantic *congruency* of both in Deut 20:16; Josh 10:40; 11:14; 1 Kgs 15:29; 17:17; Ps 150:6; Isa 2:22, etc.). According to Gen 6:3, the limitation of the endowment with the spirit (רוח) amounts to the limitation of the age of humans. When it is taken away, they die (cf. Gen 3:19) and go back to dust from which they had come (cf. Gen 2:7a; also Pss 49:12, 20 [*NRSV* 49:11, 19]; 90:3).

e. Through the inbreathing of the "breath of life" into the nostrils of humans, these humans, who are otherwise dust from the ground, become "living beings" (Gen 2:7b). The Hebrew word used here for "being" is נפש, which is often translated with the English word "soul." Humans *have* no soul; they *are* living souls or beings because God has breathed the breath of life into אדם, "man" or "human," whom he had formed from the dust of the ground. In other words, the words "man" or "human" (אדם) and "living being" (נפש חיה) have different connotations. אדם is human by virtue of being formed in human *shape*. As such, however, אדם is not yet a "living being." He/she becomes a "living being" only by virtue of the inbreathing of the "breath of life." Without this, he/she may be human by having the human shape, but he/she is not alive.

Apart from the fact that it is God who breathes the breath of life into אדם after he forms him/her, this understanding of the "living being"/"living soul" is important for another reason. It shows that the frequent references in the Old Testament to humans as "living beings" or "souls" rest on the assumption of the absolute dependence of human life on the breath/spirit of life given by God. We may reconstruct this systemic preunderstanding even more precisely. When Yahweh breathes into humans' nostrils the breath of life, and when he takes their breath away (Gen 2:7; Ps 104:29b; and cf. the reversed expression of both aspects in Ps 104:29b and 30a), he appears to function as the initiator, the triggerer, and the terminator of living beings. Not unlike a doctor who has to slap a newborn baby in order to shock it into breathing which continues automatically once started, Yahweh triggers the start of breathing through which the human body becomes, and after which it remains, a living being. At the moment of death, the stoppage of breathing, when someone "breathes her/his last" (cf. Gen 49:33), is seen as breath being "taken away" rather than as "departing on its own."

What is not said is that Yahweh also sustains the breathing of living beings during their lifetime. The absence of such statements scarcely means that Yahweh is merely understood as the triggerer and terminator of life but not also as its sustainer. An analogy would be that God might not be understood as the sustainer of the world because Genesis 1 depicts him only as the creator of its self-perpetuating cosmic order. The God of the Old Testament is not the God of deism. It is much more appropriate to say that, while Yahweh does not sustain the life span of living beings directly through his constant inbreathing (literally from breath to breath), he sustains it indirectly by upholding, rather than terminating, the existence of the cosmic air which living beings organically and naturally breathe once they are connected with it. Their connection with the already and always existing cosmic — no longer chaotic! — air means that each individual's existence as a living being is, before everything else, fundamentally and forever, indissolubly imbedded in and dependent on the order of creation. While this understanding is presupposed, the stated emphasis focuses on the initiation and termination of this connection. Neither humans nor the cosmic air is understood as the creator of living beings. God-Yahweh is. Basically, the texts say neither that humans start breathing nor that the (cosmic) air initiates or forces their breathing. Neither syntactically nor substantively do humans or the air appear as acting subjects by which the living beings come into and remain in existence.

Hence, the understanding presupposed in the central term נפש חיה, "living being," says that humans are, as living beings, spiritual beings. They are spiritual as they live from and are connected with the breath of life that is breathed into and sustains them. They are spiritual as they are alive. Moreover, they are alive as those who depend on the breath of life, and not as those who are independent of that breath and its giver. Their existence as spiritual beings is based on that dependence. This understanding need not be theologized. It is intrinsically theological. It says that the Old Testament's theological conceptuality of spirituality begins with and belongs first of all to its theology of the creation of the world of which humans are a part.

f. In the just-explained sense, all humans, together with all living creatures, live by means of the spirit/breath of life given by God. They are spiritually conditioned in a natural sense, or they are not alive.

This aspect is fundamental in a discussion of the Old Testament's understanding of spirituality. It becomes immediately important as a guard against a quick confinement of "spiritual" existence to a specific and possibly exclusivist "religious" perspective. What it says is that life as such, all life, is spirited, or it does not exist. This aspect points to more than merely one more element of humans' physical ingredients. To be alive is to be inspired, to be energized. Hence, spiritual existence is not only, not even primarily, an internal experience. It is the experience of life as life. The Old Testament concept of the spiritual starts with and is anchored in the concept of life vis-à-vis, or above, death. Life as such, according to the Old Testament, is more than something preliminary or inferior compared with "higher" forms of internalized spirituality, more than something to be taken for granted. It is the basic spiritual reality, a miracle to be marveled at as that which is elevated out of dust and above death.

Ezekiel 37 shows how radically Israel could become aware of this creation of life out of death through the inbreathing of breath. In conspicuous proximity to the conceptualization and language of Gen 2:7, Ezek 37:5f. says, "Thus says the Lord God to these bones: I will cause breath [רוח, not נשמה] to enter you, and you shall live. I will lay sinews on you, and will cause flesh to come upon you, and cover you with skin, and put breath [רוח] in you, and you shall live; and you shall know that I am the Lord." With these words, the passage expresses with these words the physical, inner-historical revival of Israel, and not an internal spiritual one (at least not primarily) or an eschatological resurrection from the dead. How could such a creation of life through the inbreathing of breath be considered spiritually inferior? How could it demonstrate anything but the power and identity of Yahweh? The Old Testament understanding of the breath of life is as theologically relevant as its concept of the spirit of Yahweh or God. This understanding of life is one of the roots of the outbreak of hymnic language and activity, and of the praise of God. In their hymns, which certainly make up a spiritual category, the ancient Israelites act out what they fundamentally are: spirit, i.e., inspired "souls." "In Sheol who can give you praise?" (Ps 6:6 [*NRSV* 6:5]), or "Let everything that breathes praise the Lord" (Ps 150:6). Praising God means that humans recognize that they do not live from themselves, and that they breathe back to God the breath he has previously breathed into them. It is the most fundamental expression of their being alive.

a.-f. With all this, the Old Testament asserts that breath, the spirit of life, is not from humans, although it is in them as part of their natural life. It does not stem from humans and does not depend on them. Rather, their life stems from and depends on it. Their life does not create the spirit, but the spirit creates their life.

2. It is on this basis, and not without or against it, that the Old Testament speaks of the spirit of Yahweh or God falling upon people, especially on the — so-called by us — charismatics. We are aware of the way it depicts Moses, the charismatic leaders during the time of the judges (Deborah, Gideon, Jephthah, Samson, Samuel), Saul and David, the prophets, and repeatedly, charismatic groups (cf. Num 11:25f.; 1 Sam 10:9-13; 1 Kgs 18:4-40; 19:9-14; 20:35-43; 22; 2 Kgs 2; Mic 3:8; Joel 3:1-5 [*NRSV* 2:28-32]; Hag 1:14). That the spirit of Yahweh falls upon or into these charismatics entails, first of all, an intensification of vitality and agitation, an outburst of energy which enables them to rise to or above a particular occasion and to do extraordinary things. They are manifestations of a heightened force of vitality at work in specific circumstances.

This means that the spirit of Yahweh or God is understood on the basis of the same ontological presuppositions as the God-given spirit of life. The common denominator of both is the understanding of the nature of breath or spirit. This shared presupposition cannot be discarded as theologically irrelevant in a specific discussion of the spirit of Yahweh. Consequently, it is wrong to separate the common spirit of life coming from God from the manifestations of Yahweh's spirit, and to emphasize the "charismatic" intensifications as "spiritual" at the expense of the endowment of all humans with the breath of life. The opposite is correct: the God-given, life-igniting, and sustaining spiritual endowment placed in all humans is the provision of the human potential through which and out of which Yahweh enacts his own spirit in specific ways. As far as this ontological perspective is concerned, the spirit *of* God is of the same substance as the spirit of life *from* God. In other words, the worldview behind both expressions is the same. In this respect, the nature of the charismatic experience is not different from that of all humans. Hence, charismatics alone do not represent what the Old Testament has to say about spirit or spirituality and, consequently, cannot be the sole basis on which to discuss the spirituality of the Old Testament.

3. Having said that the Old Testament's expressions of the spirit of life and the spirit of God cannot be separated, we must, nevertheless, recognize the specific notions in the references to God-Yahweh's *own* spirit. Along this line, the intermittent eruptions of the spirit of Yahweh on special occasions in and through the charismatic persons or groups are not only specific intensifications of the common human life-endowment, but also life manifestations of a specific divine identity (cf. Num 11:24f.; Judg 3:10; 6:34; 11:29; 13:25; 14:6, 19; 15:14; 1 Sam 10:6, 10; 19:20, etc.). Complementary to the passages that speak about the momentary

eruptions of Yahweh's spirit are those that speak about the continuous indwelling of his spirit in specific persons, which results in the enlightenment of their mood, mind, and will; in their inspiration to word and/or action; and in their awareness of the presence of Yahweh: "Pharaoh said to his servants, 'Can we find anyone else like this — one in whom is the spirit of God?' So Pharaoh said to Joseph, 'Since God has shown you all this, there is no one so discerning and wise as you' " (Gen 41:38f.); "the spirit of the LORD came mightily upon David from that day forward" (1 Sam 16:13); "The spirit of the LORD shall rest on him, the spirit of wisdom and understanding, the spirit of counsel and might, the spirit of knowledge and the fear of the LORD" (Isa 11:2). "But as for me, I am filled with power, with the spirit of the LORD, and with justice and might, to declare to Jacob his transgression and to Israel his sin" (Mic 3:8). "The spirit of the Lord GOD is upon me . . . to bring good news to the oppressed . . ." (Isa 61:1; cf. Isa 42:1; 44:3; 48:16); the prophet is known as "the man of the spirit" (Hos 9:7); "A new heart I will give you, and a new spirit I will put within you. . . . I will put my spirit within you, and make you follow my statutes" (Ezek 36:26f.). "Then afterward I will pour out my spirit on all flesh; your sons and your daughters shall prophesy, your old men shall dream dreams, and your young men shall see visions. Even on the male and female slaves, in those days, I will pour out my spirit" (Joel 3:1f. [*NRSV* 2:28f.]). Just as it is described as given or announced, so is it most intimately prayed for and expected to be granted, and so it is to reach into the deepest regions of the individual's personal existence. The language of Ps 51:12-14 (*NRSV* 51:10-12) combines a number of aspects involved in the gift of God's spirit: the placing in parallel of heart (see below) and spirit, the "new and right spirit," the "spirit within me"; "your presence" paralleled to the nearness of "your holy spirit"; and "the joy of your salvation" and "a willing spirit": "Create in me a clean heart, O God, and put a new and right spirit within me. Do not cast me away from your presence, and do not take your holy spirit from me. Restore to me the joy of your salvation, and sustain in me a willing spirit."

The range of aspects covered by this selected number of texts — not to mention additional ones — is already extraordinarily broad, and can only be alluded to at this point. In quite general terms, the "spirit of God-Yahweh" is perceived in these texts not only as the vitalizing power as such, but also as that endowment which disposes human(s) toward the fulfillment of God's manifold purposes for the world and for the life of humans, such as wisdom, understanding, counsel, might, salvation, justice and righteousness, help for the afflicted, ability to keep God's statutes, prophetic gifts, restoration from guilt, etc. This general observation means that our own conceptualization of spirituality should be kept adaptable to such a broad variety of salvific aspects, and hence understood as an all-pervading attitude rather than as a limited focus on one specific aspect.

Apart from this attention to the manifold manifestations of the spirit, however, the emphasis on Yahweh's own spirit deserves special attention, because with it the Old Testament focuses pointedly on the divine identity in the phenomenon of the spirit or its manifestations, more so than on the phenomena themselves. This focus is certainly the result of specific reasons which are difficult for us to detect because of the lack of specific Old Testament statements on the problem.

One of these reasons was that the perception of spirit as a mode of Yahweh's own activity and presence increasingly needed to become distinct from perceptions in which the spirit was either an independently influential subject ("spirit of life" as a principal dynamic of the world), only a human potential (Ezek 13:3), or a force used by Yahweh yet not in accordance with his purposes and his identity (cf. Judg 9:23; 1 Sam 16:16 [*NRSV* 16:14], 23; 18:10; 19:9; 1 Kgs 22:21, 23; Hos 4:12; 5:4; Zech 13:2). This range of experiences of "spirit" points to Israel's awareness of critical situations in which the people were either subjected or in danger of being subjected to a spirit of evil or in debate over perceptions of right or perverted spirituality (cf. 1 Kgs 22:19-25; Hos 9:7 versus 4:12; 5:4). "Spirit" and "spirituality" as such were not — and are not — protected, by definition or design, from misperceptions and influences other than those intended.

However, besides this discerning function, the Old Testament's focus on the spirit of Yahweh or God must have had yet another, and probably an even deeper and more genuine, reason. This reason must be sought, as far as I can see, in the ultimate preoccupation of the ancient Israelites with their encounter with Yahweh himself. Under this preoccupation, the perception of the "spirit" as breath had to lose its character definitively as an ontologically genuine subjectivity, however employed by Yahweh, or as a potentially autonomous force altogether. "Spirit" had to become one of the foremost vehicles, which was provided by the common world-understanding, for Yahweh's own presence, especially among his people. To be sure, "spirit/breath" remained essential as a commonly recognized category communicating Yahweh's life-inspiring presence. But apart from the fact that Yahweh had other means of making his presence felt, the emphasis in the expression "the spirit of Yahweh," rather than "Yahweh's spirit," lay in the presence of *Yahweh himself* rather than on the clarification of the mode of his presence.

Isa 31:4 (*NRSV* 31:3) is instructive as a kind of intersection between the two aspects implied in the usage of the word "spirit": (a) the Egyptians are men, and not God; (b) and their horses are flesh, and not spirit. By contrasting the life-creating spirit to the death-ridden flesh, the second line uses the word "spirit" in the sense of a genuine subjectivity, a generic ontic substance of its own. However, by placing the word "spirit" in parallel with the word "God" in the first line, the whole saying binds the understanding of "spirit" to that of "God." And although it does not speak of the "spirit of God," and stops short of saying that the spirit is God, it is on the way to that assertion (cf. Zech 4:6).

The identification of the spirit as the "spirit of Yahweh" or its qualification as the "spirit of God" shows that "God-Yahweh" carried for Israel decisive connotations which were not automatically covered by the perception of "spirit" alone.

These connotations were obviously the result of the accumulated salvific experiences Israel had undergone with Yahweh throughout its history and — to be sure — in many more realms than that of history alone. They were, likewise, the result of Israel's continued orientation on this deity as the life source of its existence, as well as the result of its hope in this deity for its future. At this point, one can understand not only why the "spirit" became a vehicle of Yahweh's own presence but also why the concept of "spirit" was subjected to what it means to encounter and say "Yahweh" or "God." Under this priority, Israel was not so much concentrating on the spirit of life as on the breath of God's own life in Yahweh's revelation. This coming of God-Yahweh through his spirit was far from being understood as making humans divine. Rather, it meant that, for humans, this very God has become a possibility, and even reality, of genuine experience, even a most personal experience, as Psalm 51 and other texts show. It meant that, in such experience, the spirit of life from which humans live appears in its true qualification, identification, orientation, and purpose. The experience of God as God through the spirit meant, at the same time, the experience of the human condition as saved in both its origin and destination. Therefore, the focus on the spirit of God-Yahweh and its gifts portrays for the ancient Israelites the witness to or the hope for the ultimate salvation from the dilemma of failure, lostness, and guilt in the breathing human life, as well as the fulfillment of the destination of their lives. The spirit of God in humans means the salvation of their ultimate meaning as living beings.

1.-3. Our discussion so far of the evidence under the Hebrew word רוח (and partly נשמה) has shown both God's gift of the breath of life and the realization of Yahweh's own life through his spirit in the human condition. This result seems to suggest that in our attempt at conceptualizing spirituality a differentiation exists between what I would like to call a predisposition to spirituality which is the inspired human condition, and spirituality itself, which is the mode of life in which this predisposition specifically unfolds as the presence of God-Yahweh in the attitudes and behavior of humans.

Furthermore, the discussion has indicated that the "inspired" predisposition consists not only of the breathing vitality but also of the endowment with qualitative potentials such as counsel, wisdom, knowledge, fear of God, justice, and good tidings. With this range of perspectives, however, we have already entered the territory of another Hebrew word to which the aspects of such endowment are also closely related and which is equally essential for our understanding of spirituality in the Old Testament, particularly in regard to the side of its human predisposition. This means that from now on we must switch methods. We must depart from our initial etymological method of entry and turn to the semantic method, the study of a word field (or of part of it in our case) by which an issue is variably expressed and in which it is reflected. The word to which we now must turn is לב, "(the) heart."

B. Spirituality Corresponding to לב, "Heart"[5]

It is known that the Old Testament considers — incorrectly! — the heart, the pump in our chest, to be the central psycho-physical human organ — the organ we identify as the brain or central nervous system. However, apart from this anatomical misconception, the Old Testament is supremely aware that there is a center of the human personality in the senses. The word לב, "heart," is the central term in a cluster of related anthropological words covering all the elements by which humans are constituted as persons — the central physical organ as well as the center both of emotional and intellectual ability and of the will.

What is perhaps less known is the fact that our translations often render the Hebrew word לב with English words that are more in accordance with the meaning of this word in its context than with etymological consistency, thereby obscuring that the Hebrew consistently employs the same word לב, "heart." These — basically correct — interpretive translations show that one must consider what a Hebrew writer meant when saying "heart," and not only what he said. With this in mind, we need, first of all, to systematize the connotations implied in the use of the word, and then to draw the conclusions pertinent to our subject.

1. The "heart" is the place, the setting, of the human *mind:* Solomon prays, "Give your servant therefore an understanding mind [לב]" (1 Kgs 3:9; cf. 1 Sam 16:7; Prov 24:12; Ps 45:2 [*NRSV* 45:1]).

2. The heart is the place of *sensitivity* and *emotion:* Yahweh brings forth "wine to gladden the human heart" (Ps 104:15); "Relieve the troubles of my heart" (Ps 25:17; cf. Prov 15:13; 17:22; etc.).

3. The heart is the place of *longing, desire,* and *will:* "You have given him his heart's desire" (Ps 21:3 [*NRSV* 21:2]; cf. 1 Sam 7:3; 1 Kgs 8:17; Isa 10:7; Jer 22:17).

4. It is the place of *intellect* and *rationality:* "The mind [לב] of the wise makes their speech judicious, and adds persuasiveness to their lips" (Prov 16:23; cf. Prov 15:14).

5. It is the place of *conscience:* "Create in me a clean heart [i.e., conscience], O God, and put a new and right spirit [רוח] within me" (Ps 51:12 [*NRSV* 51:10]; cf. Ezek 11:19).

In sum, the heart is the place of mind, sensitivity, emotion, longing, desire, will, intellectual and rational function, and conscience. It is part of the human anatomy. At the same time, as part of the human *physis,* it is the center of the human psyche, just as the brain and central nervous system are for us. One can see here that, for Hebrew anthropology, there is essentially no dichotomy between the physical — literally, the fleshly — and the psychic. Where a discrepancy between the two exists, e.g., where people, "in the stubbornness of their evil will [walk] in their own counsels" (Jer 7:24), it is because the psychic side of the heart is misguided, and not because its fleshly side

5. Compare again Wolff, *Anthropology,* 40f., and F. Stolz, *THAT* 1, 861-67.

is evil while its psychic side is good. Moreover, where the texts contrast "spirit" with "flesh," as in Isa 31:4 (*NRSV* 31:3), they focus on that which perishes versus that which does not perish (living beings die whereas the breath of life does not). For that which perishes the Hebrew text uses the word בשׂר, "flesh," rather than the word לב, "heart." In the heart, the fleshly-physical and the psychic coincide. In other words, the physical heart is the material body in which and through which the psychic heart can unfold itself, and without which it cannot. Thus, the heart is capable of controlling and governing the living human being by plans, projections, dreams, discernment, rationalizations, and judgment, and of responding to its situations in emotions, feelings, longings, and desires. It is the central mechanism for governing existing life. It is the other condition for what I have previously called the predisposition to spirituality, a condition for a spiritual human attitude.

The fact that "heart," the word for the center of human personhood and its functions, is a strictly anthropological term is important. In each case it means the condition for the actualization of persons. This notion is significantly different from the notions of the word רוח, "spirit." This difference leads to questions as to what the relationship is between "spirit" and "heart," and what "heart" has to do with spirituality.

The heart is not only defined by us anthropologically as a central human condition but is described by our texts as existentially actualizing these conditions in human attitudes and behavior. Inasmuch as this is so, we must regard such an actualization as spirituality in its formal sense, i.e., as human spirituality. However, the problem remains as to what this mental or psychic actualization has to do with that spirituality which is an outgrowth either of the spirit of life given by God or of God's own spirit. The activities of the heart as depicted in our texts show quite clearly that spirituality, as the formal phenomenon of psychic-mental activity, by no means automatically implies God-inspiredness. Indeed, it may imply inspiredness by quite different spirits. Thus, "the plans of the mind" (לב) can be futile (Prov 16:1; 19:21); visions can be "of their own minds, not from the mouth of the LORD" (Jer 23:16); the heart is "stubborn" (Exod 8:11, 28 [*NRSV* 8:15, 32]; 9:34; 10:1; Isa 6:9f.; Jer 3:17; 7:24; 9:13 [*NRSV* 9:14]; 11:8; 23:17) or of "stone" rather than of "flesh" (Ezek 36:26f.). Hence, the heart itself needs direction, guidance, and support. This is the function of the parenetic appeal in the deuteronomic time to "search after [Yahweh your God] with all your heart and soul" (Deut 4:29; 6:5; 10:12; 11:13). Furthermore, it is the reason the heart needs to be circumcised (Deut 10:16; 30:6; Jer 4:4; Ezek 44:7, 9) and the reason an altogether new heart needs to be given by God (Ezek 36:26f.; Ps 51:12 [*NRSV* 51:10]; cf. also Jer 31:31f.). In other words, the central human psychic-mental system and its activities may be understood as spiritual. However, this formal spirituality is still prone to all the faults and fallacies of humans. At this point, the concept of spirituality as "heart," as central psychic-mental disposition and activity, points to the need for complementation by that concept which we discussed under the code word "spirit."

We can now compare the notions of "spirit" and "heart." Both are physical realities: the one is a meteorological entity ("wind," and therefore "breath"), and the other is an anatomical one ("heart"). Both become part of the human condition: the one as the source and force of vitality, the other as the center of mind. Furthermore, both are given to humans in the act of creation. However, the "heart," as part of the created human anatomy, is dead along with the body before the breath is given, or as soon as the breath is withdrawn. It has no life of its own, but lives, along with the *physis,* from the spirit of life or of God. By contrast, the spirit is not part of the created human *physis.* It is not even itself created. As a cosmic reality, it exists. As such, it is the gift of life when it inspires the human *physis* to life. Hence, "spirit" signifies the concept of life, God's life, its coming *to* humans and their dependence on it. "Heart," on the other hand, signifies the concept of the central relay-station *in* humans in which the inspired life — or the influences of other "spirits" — can be received, and through which it can be converted into psychic-mental energy and disseminated among the psychophysical channels.

This means that the "heart" is the anthropological complementation to the cosmological or theological "spirit," and as such is structured to be susceptible to the influences of "spirit" and its notions. Human mind and — God's — spirit are structurally compatible. That they are not identical or exchangeable but are clearly distinguished should be evident from what has been said thus far. Hence, while focusing on the central human potential, that of **אדם**, the word "heart" signifies the functioning of this potential under various influences. Just as the heart is always influenced by a "spirit," and is consequently in need of the spirit of life for its own life and of God-Yahweh's spirit for its true guidance and orientation, so the "spirit" is in need of the "heart" to be the relay station for its influences as human attitude. The Old Testament category "heart" is, therefore, an essential element in humans' predisposition for and emergence of spirituality.

A.-B. "Spirit" and "Heart"

With these two words, the Old Testament paradigmatically identifies the human condition as spiritual. They denote the real character of humans as vitalized and "mentalized" living beings, and hence as transcended *physis.* This transcended physis is predisposed to mentally actualizing the influence of God-Yahweh's own life. We realize that the Old Testament concept of human nature is not based on a dichotomy of the spiritual and psychic. On the contrary, the physical is "spiritized" and "mentalized," and as such is alive with reason and perspective. The spirit is the vitality of the physical as it is physically real itself, and as such is present in the physical. And the heart is the human reason governing the *physis,* as it is itself governed by the spirit. In this sense, all humans are beings predisposed to spirituality, or they are neither human nor alive.

This result is supported by another strand of Old Testament statements which call the human condition בשר, "flesh." In view of the interpretation thus far, it is important to note that "flesh" basically means the fleshly and, therefore, mortal substance of a living body (people or animals), the bodily *physis* of a living being. Inasmuch as the word is used in contrast to the dimensions of spiritual life expressed by רוח, לב, and נפש (cf. Gen 6:3; 9:4; Num 16:22; 27:16; Deut 12:23; Isa 31:3; Joel 3:1 [*NRSV* 2:28]; Ezek 44:7, 9; Ps 84:3 [*NRSV* 84:2]; Job 14:22), it distinguishes between the spiritual or inspiring element in the living being and that which is not spiritual as such but is in need of being inspired. On this basis, "flesh" is used as an expression for the qualitative difference between the perishableness of the total human condition (including לב and נפש) and the imperishable nature of God. In addition to the fact that this perishableness is seen as intrinsic to human nature in contradistinction to the nature of God, the natural aspect of this human condition is seen as not unrelated to the aspect of its perversion by humans themselves — in an existential, historical, and ethical sense. Indeed, the aspect of perverse mortality can be observed throughout the Old Testament in the context of its understanding of sin and guilt.

C. Spirituality Corresponding to חכמה, "Wisdom"

Thus far we have outlined the major contours of the presupposition for the Old Testament's concept of spirituality and, ultimately, for discussing the spirituality of the Old Testament itself. For when saying "spirituality," we seem to imply more than a condition of human nature alone. Our usage of the word seems to denote an *attitude* in which humans step forward expressing, applying, actualizing, and implementing their spiritual condition appropriately. Therefore, I would understand spirituality as *the consistent actualization by humans of their spiritual endowment, or their consistent reaction to it in mentality, attitude, and behavior.* Humans' actualization of their spiritual condition by reacting to it or acting it out is nothing foreign to this condition itself. In fact, the spiritual condition intrinsically predisposes humans to such actualization. It is the nature of the spiritual that it mobilizes itself.

With this in mind, I will look again at the Old Testament, asking if, and where, it signals such actualization. In other words, I am again seeking a field of emphasis in which the Old Testament is complementary to our just-updated understanding of spirituality. Indeed, this field of emphasis exists. The Hebrew language has one word above all others which is coextensive with our word "spirituality" as defined above, and that word is חכמה, "wisdom."[6]

6. For the following, compare, among others, G. von Rad, *Wisdom in Israel* (Nashville: Abingdon, 1972); and M. Saebø, *THAT* 1, 557-67.

What is wisdom according to the Old Testament? It is certainly not what some of us might expect: useless, futile, abstract speculation and mere theoretical knowledge. On the contrary, wisdom is practicable and applicable insight, prudence, and knowledge for life. It is the mental activity derived from life and reality and focused on their mastery. Expressed according to strictly Old Testament correlations, wisdom is "spirit" and "heart" put to work. In other words, wisdom is the "heart" put to work by the "spirit" — for the sake of sufficiency or wholeness (שׁלום); for the sake of that which is good (instead of evil); and for the sake of justice, righteousness, love, order, and so on. To these ends, wisdom wisely actualizes the spirit, as it is mobilized by the spirit; it uses the mind discerningly, and the emotions reasonably, in longing and desire, as well as in strategizing, planning, and thinking. Furthermore, wisdom keeps the conscience awake and alert. Hundreds of proverbs in the book of Proverbs and many other passages testify to this understanding.

To be sure, a perverted implementation of the spiritual condition is always possible. It can go so far that even the condition itself is adversely affected. There is a broad word field denoting such perversion. One of these words, the opposite of חכמה, "wisdom," is נבלה, "folly." The fool (נבל) ignores and violates the obvious world order, any normal human behavior, and everything that makes sense. He is wasting his own life as he destroys the life of others. Finally, he destroys — literally — his "heart," and dies (1 Samuel 25). Furthermore, wisdom itself can become perverted if its insights are not in tune with the fundamental laws of reality, especially with the knowledge of Yahweh and his presence in the world. When this happens, the wisdom of the wise perishes (Isa 29:14). This point shows that, for the Old Testament, wisdom is not the activity of the human mind alone. It is as much inspired and guided by Yahweh as it is the result of human insight. But under such guidance, it is the most central and comprehensive form of the human actualization of "spirit" and "heart."

In view of those Old Testament traditions that either separate specific wisdom texts from prophetic, hymnic, legal, and narrative texts, or explicitly point to different types of activities among the different professional groups of the sages, priests, prophets, judges, and so on, it must be admitted that this interpretation of wisdom is not entirely unproblematic. Based on such distinctions, one might be inclined to define חכמה, "wisdom," only in a strictly technical sense and to ascribe to it only the profession of the sages and their respective settings. However, if one considers the total range of inspired and mental activity covered by the word חכמה and the word field related to it, one realizes that the operation of wisdom was understood by the Old Testament neither as restricted to the sages alone nor as taking place in their setting only. After all, the occasional judgments criticizing the wisdom of the sages (Isa 5:21; 29:14; Jer 8:8f.; 18:18, etc.) could not have been but an expression of wisdom, too. More importantly, wisdom is operative in the work of the kings, the lawgivers, and judges, as well as in the insights of the historians, and in the knowledge of the priests and the creators of hymns. Even the prophets themselves represent the operation of wisdom as their messages are combinations of inspirations and their own reflectively formulated contributions. Therefore, in this chapter I am using the word חכמה in the sense of wisdom in operation throughout the Old Testament rather than of wisdom within a professionally identified setting.

We can summarize. The Old Testament word most complementary to our word "spirituality" is "wisdom." Wisdom is the central mental attitude in which humans genuinely go about — or are supposed to go about — their lives within the order of the world.

The consequence of this finding for our reflection on spirituality and the Old Testament is very important. If it is true that the Old Testament understands wisdom/spirituality as the appropriate actualization by humans of their spiritual condition, our question can no longer be "What is the Old Testament *understanding* of spirituality?" or "What does it *say about* spirituality?" This would thereby confine our attention to only those texts which respond to these questions. Rather, we must now recognize that the Old Testament itself, in its entirety, in the totality of its expressions and perspectives as well as in its specific focus, appears as a spiritual phenomenon, a realization of such wisdom/spirituality. Therefore, our inquiry from now on must embrace the entire Old Testament, and hence our topic receives a new and final orientation: we are not only looking for the Old Testament's understanding of spirituality and, hence, for texts speaking about it. More importantly, we also need to assess the nature of this spirituality, the wisdom of the Old Testament texts as they are in accordance with the Old Testament's self-understanding. In other words, we are looking for the Old Testament spirituality itself, about which it explicitly speaks only infrequently. This leads us to part II.

II. The Nature of Old Testament Spirituality

So far I have tried to show that, for the Old Testament, spirituality is first of all a human mental attitude (wisdom) in which the heart, under the influence of the spirit, is put to work for the reasonable mastering of life in the context of reality and under the guidance of Yahweh. With this understanding, the ancient Israelites document that, whatever the specific nature of their wisdom/spirituality is, it is nothing esoteric or separate from that potential which all humans share. Rather, its specificity shares the same ontological and anthropological basis as every other kind of human spirituality. This basis is common and accessible to all. The specific nature of Old Testament spirituality partakes in the common human predisposition. The Old Testament is not spiritual because it is special but because its spirituality is first of all human.

Nevertheless, its human spirituality is of a specific kind which also must be recognized if we want to avoid a one-sided picture. In the following, we will outline the basic traits of the specific nature of Old Testament spirituality. We will do so by concentrating on its focus, its expressions and perspectives, and its source.

A. The Focus of Old Testament Spirituality

The specificity of Old Testament spirituality centers in the One by whom the ancient Israelites were inspired — Yahweh, their God. He is the source and focus of Old Testament spirituality, its life center. This must be said independently of whether or not they explicitly discuss this focus and regardless of how they articulate this preoccupation. Their mind, interest, and intellect, as well as their emotions and concerns — in short, their spirituality — revolves around Yahweh, their God.

The phraseology relevant to this concentration is naturally widespread and diverse. Even so, two phrases in the Hebrew Bible stand out. They are the central paradigms expressing what the rest of the phraseology says under more specific aspects at specific times. The two phrases are: **יראת יהוה/אלהים**, "fear of Yahweh-God," and **דעת אלהים/יהוה**, "knowledge of God-Yahweh." The statistical frequency of these two phrases is great, and we can highlight the evidence with only a few examples of each.

1. Fear of God/Yahweh

a. The deuteronomic-deuteronomistic theology is based on the exhortation to fear Yahweh: "The Lord [Yahweh] your God you shall fear" (Deut 6:13; cf. Deut 4:10; 5:29; 6:2, 24; 8:6; 10:12, 20; 13:5 [*NRSV* 13:4]; 14:23; 17:19; 28:58; 31:12, 13; Josh 4:24; 24:14;[7] Judg 6:10;[8] 1 Sam 12:14, 24; 1 Kgs 8:40, 43; 2 Kgs 17:7, 25, 28, 32-39, 41[9]). Among others, to love Yahweh (Deut 10:12), to serve him and cleave to him (Deut 10:20), to walk in his ways (Deut 8:6), and to follow him (Deut 13:5 [*NRSV* 13:4]) are used as complementary terms. This language shows that, as a human response to the awesome acts of Yahweh in history and nature, the fear of Yahweh is the ethicized attitude of humble reverence and not the shock of terror.

b. In the Psalms, the typical expression "those fearing Yahweh" means either the actual assembly of Yahweh-worshippers (Pss 22:24, 26 [*NRSV* 22:23, 25]; 31:20 [*NRSV* 31:19]; 66:16; etc.), all the people of Yahweh (Pss 60:6 [*NRSV* 60:4]; 61:6 [*NRSV* 61:5]; 85:10 [*NRSV* 85:9]), or those loyal to him (Pss 25:14; 33:18; 34:8, 10 [*NRSV* 34:7, 9]; 103:11, 13, 17; 111:5; 119:74, 79; 147:11).

7. *NRSV* translates as "revere."
8. *NRSV* translates as "pay reverence."
9. *NRSV* translates as "worshipped."

c. The wisdom literature and the texts influenced by the wisdom traditions use characteristic expressions such as "those fearing Yahweh/God" (Isa 50:10; Pss 25:12; 128:1, 4; Prov 14:2; Job 1:8; 2:3; Eccl 7:18), the "fear of Yahweh/God/the Lord/the Almighty" (שדי) (Prov 1:7, 29; 2:5; 8:13; 9:10; 10:27; 14:26, 27; 15:16, 33; 16:6; 19:23; 22:4; 23:17; Isa 11:2, 3; 33:6; Pss 34:12 [*NRSV* 34:11]; 111:10; Job 6:14; 28:28) or just absolute "fear" (Job 4:6;[10] 15:4;[11] 22:4[12]), and "to fear Yahweh/God" (Job 1:9; Eccl 5:6 [*NRSV* 5:7]; 8:12, 13; 12:13; Prov 3:7; 24:21). The importance of the "fear of Yahweh" is demonstrated by nothing less than the fact that the international wisdom, in its Israelite adaptation, was subjected to this fear as its critical focus and foundation. In this sense, the opening of the book of Proverbs states programmatically: "The fear of Yahweh is the foundation [*NRSV:* "the beginning"] of wisdom" (Prov 1:7, author's translation).

d. The previously assumed so-called elohistic narrative strand emphasizes the same aspect in Gen 22:12; 20:11; 42:18; Exod 1:17, 21; 18:21.

e. Furthermore, the laws in the Holiness Code are to be observed in the fear of Yahweh: "You shall fear your God: I am [Yahweh]" (Lev 19:14, 32; cf. 25:17, 36, 43).[13]

2. *Knowledge of God-Yahweh*

Generally, the Hebrew words ידע and דעת mean the discerning human perception arrived at through the activation of the human senses, through investigation and reflection, i.e., the human knowledge gained from perception and experience. As such, knowledge is the result not only of the abstract activity of the mind, but also of the practical experience with its objects. This meaning, broadly attested in the Old Testament literature, shows how closely "knowledge" must be related to our previously developed understanding of spirituality as wisdom.

In a specifically theological sense, the emergence of the knowledge of God-Yahweh seems to have its roots in experiences through which Yahweh made known himself (Exod 6:3; Pss 9:17 [*NRSV* 9:16]; 48:8; 77:15, 20 [*NRSV* 77:14, 19]; 79:10; 88:13 [*NRSV* 88:12]; 98:2; 103:7), his name (Isa 64:1 [*NRSV* 64:2]; Ps 76:2 [*NRSV* 76:1]), or the contents of his manifestations (Exod 25:22; Ezek 20:11; Neh 9:14; 2 Sam 7:21; Gen 41:39; Jer 11:18, etc.). This aspect points to a dialectical structure in the Old Testament's concept of the knowledge of God. While certainly the product of active human imagining about God, it is the active appropriation of

10. *NRSV* supplies "of God."

11. *NRSV* supplies "of God."

12. *NRSV* translates "piety."

13. Compare Joachim Becker, *Gottesfurcht im Alten Testament,* Analecta Biblica 25 (Rome: Pontifical Biblical Institute, 1965); and H. P. Stähli, *THAT* 1, 765-78, with further bibliographical data therein.

God's own self-manifestations rather than a creation of autonomous human imagination.

a. In this sense, the knowledge of Yahweh is, first of all, the prerogative of those who have knowledge of him by virtue of their professional competence: the priests, the rulers, the judges, the wise men, and the prophets (Jer 2:8; 18:18; 28:9; Hos 4:6; Mal 2:7; Isa 11:2; 53:11; Ezek 7:26). They are expected to be capable not only of executing their knowledge of God in their own work but also of teaching the laypeople (Ezek 22:26; 44:23; Mal 2:7), the children (Deut 4:9; Josh 4:22; Ps 78:5f.), and the people (Exod 18:16, 20; Ezek 43:11; Ezra 7:25; Neh 8:12). This understanding of the knowledge of Yahweh is central in the prophetic messages, especially those of Hosea and Jeremiah. They attack the absence of that which is decisive for their religion, among both the professionals who should know better and the people who should have been instructed by those professionals (Hos 4:1, 6; 5:4; 8:2; Jer 2:8; 4:22; 9:2, 5 [*NRSV* 9:3, 6]), and announce a new situation in which such knowledge will prevail (Hos 2:22 [*NRSV* 2:20]; Isa 11:2, 9; 33:6; Jer 31:34; cf. also Hos 6:3, 6; 13:4; Jer 22:16; Mal 2:7, etc.). Hosea 6:6 critically summarizes what Yahweh expects from the Israelites: "For I desire steadfast love and not sacrifice, the knowledge of God rather than burnt offerings."

b. Apart from such mediation, the knowledge of Yahweh is understood as the immediate goal of Yahweh's historical manifestations. The phrases "to know that I am Yahweh" or "Yahweh is God" are formulaic (Exod 6:7; 7:5, 17; 8:6, 18 [*NRSV* 8:10, 22]; 9:14, 29; 10:2; 11:7; 14:4, 18; Lev 23:43; Deut 4:35, 39; 7:9; 11:2; 29:5 [*NRSV* 29:6]; 1 Kgs 8:60; 18:37; 2 Kgs 19:19; Isa 41:20; 45:3, 6; 49:23, 26; Ezek 5:13; 6:7, 10, 13, 14; Pss 20:7 [*NRSV* 20:6]; 41:12 [*NRSV* 41:11]; 56:10 [*NRSV* 56:9], etc.).

c. Knowledge of Yahweh will be gained through the fulfillment of Yahweh's words, especially in the prophetic and prophetically influenced traditions (Deut 18:21f.; Josh 23:14; 2 Kgs 10:10; Jer 28:9; 32:8; 44:28f.; Ezek 6:10; 17:21; 37:14; and many others).

d. The knowledge of Yahweh will at last occur to the nations as well (Deut 4:22f., 29; 1 Sam 17:46f.; 1 Kgs 8:43, 60; 2 Kgs 19:19; Isa 19:21; 43:10; 45:3-6; 49:26; Ezek 21:5; 25:7, 11, 17; Ps 83:19 [*NRSV* 83:18]).

e. Since knowledge is one of the characteristics of wisdom, all the knowledge of the wise and the experienced, together with their wisdom, is rooted, according to the Israelite perspective, in the fear of Yahweh (Prov 1:7, 29; 9:10).[14]

1.-2. The Fear and Knowledge of God-Yahweh

The paradigms of the fear and the knowledge of Yahweh express the central focus of Old Testament spirituality throughout its history and its settings. More precisely,

14. Cf. W. Schottroff, *THAT* 1, 682-701, with more bibliographical data therein, esp. those referring to H. W. Wolff and W. Zimmerli.

just as they express the central self-understanding of Old Testament spirituality, so they point to the entire Old Testament as an outgrowth of this same spirituality.

Furthermore, the fact that the fear and the knowledge of Yahweh appear as the mental appropriations of the "awesome" manifestations in which Yahweh made himself known signals the interrelationship of Yahweh's revelation and the Yahweh-theology or Yahweh-spirituality as it is demonstrated by the Old Testament itself. From this it follows that the theological statement, saying that Yahweh is the central focus of the Old Testament, and the anthropological statement, saying that the Old Testament spirituality gravitates around the fear and the knowledge of God, correspond to one another. Together, they specifically identify the spirituality of the Old Testament.

In this focus, the ancient Israelites, in their own specific way, actualize their insight into the nature of the common human spiritual condition which does not originate from humans (although it is in them) but from God. They do so by mobilizing their vitality and mentality which are provided by God, and by specifically focusing on the vitality of Yahweh's own life (the spirit of Yahweh) coming to them.

Thus, the Old Testament spirituality responds to God-Yahweh in accordance with what he has laid down both in the common human condition and in his specific manifestations to Israel. This is what "fear and knowledge of God-Yahweh" basically means. It is the response of the spiritual human condition to the One who has inspired them, and to the specific modes of inspiration. It is the practice of Israel as humans in their true identity. It is their self-realization in God-Yahweh's work.

B. The Expressions and Perspectives of Old Testament Spirituality

As the foundational orientation for practical spirituality, this fear and knowledge of God seizes upon virtually all the possible aspects of life and reality. It does so both in actions and in available forms of human expression, whereby thinking and language certainly play an important role as manifestations of this kind of spirituality. At this point, our attention to the linguistic types/genres employed in the Old Testament is of great significance. It unfolds before us not only the great variety of linguistic forms but also the preoccupation of the ancient Israelites with a great variety of realms of reality. It is this preoccupation which prompted them to make use of these forms in the first place. Thus, the variety of genres, such as history telling and history writing, novels, legends, chronicles, public and cultic laws, ordinances, commands, prohibitions, declarations, sentences, poetry of all sorts (hymns, complaints, laments, pilgrimage songs, royal and Zion songs, love songs, harvest songs, and others), sayings, prayers, doxologies, confessions, prophecies, reflections, and many others, begins to convey to us a message of its own. This endless variety of expression is in itself a manifestation of the ever-expansive tendency of Old Testament spirituality to penetrate fearlessly all areas of a demythologized reality into which humans are allowed and even called to move. It signifies a universalistic tendency which is prompted in itself by their knowledge of God as the universal Lord.

The intellectual aspect of the Old Testament's spirituality is also of particular importance. This aspect is related to wisdom — particularly as knowledge. The expression "fear and knowledge" is semantically parallel, whereby their denotations synthetically complement each other. The word "fear" or "reverence" denotes the emotional attitude toward God-Yahweh, whereas the word "knowledge" denotes the rational side of the experience of God-Yahweh as well as of his presence in the world. The combination of two distinct aspects in the expression, the emotional and the rational, reflects the assumption of the unity of the human "heart," or psyche, in which neither of these two essential components exists without the other. While the component of knowledge involves more than intellectuality, it does not exclude the human intellect. Intellectuality is an inherent aspect in human knowledge. To be sure, intellectuality is not by definition identical with wisdom. "Better is a poor [and most probably not educated] but wise youth than an old but foolish king, who will no longer take advice" (Eccl 4:13); "Now there was found in it [a besieged city] a poor wise man, and he by his wisdom delivered the city. Yet no one remembered that poor man" (Eccl 9:15). On occasion, especially in Isaiah and Jeremiah, the Old Testament says that for a variety of reasons the (professional) sages and their wisdom, certainly an educated and an intellectual wisdom, fail. Not even wisdom, let alone intellectuality, provides a safeguard against failure. Ecclesiastes and Job know this best.

However, this means that wisdom, even in its intellectual form, needs to be guided by the fear and knowledge of God-Yahweh. It does not mean that the non- or anti-intellectual person self-evidently has the advantage of being wise, or at least of having a predisposition to being wise. When it comes to being wise, the degree of intellectuality, whether low or high, is scarcely a relevant precondition. Nor is it a yardstick for the measure of the practicality of wisdom. Just as for wisdom itself, so the criterion for the validity of intellectuality as wisdom is whether or not it is guided by God-Yahweh. In this relationship, it is basically the fear and knowledge of God-Yahweh that leads to wisdom, rather than wisdom leading to fear and knowledge of God-Yahweh. Wisdom is the result of, not the cause for, fear and knowledge of God-Yahweh. This view of their relationship is especially confirmed by the theological framework in which the references to wisdom (which number more than three hundred in their verbal, adjectival, and nominal forms) are set. These references also show that even where wisdom, whatever its intellectual degree, is relativized, especially due to the absence of fear and/or knowledge of God-Yahweh, it is as such virtually never disqualified. It has its limits, either in human corruption or in the hiddenness of God, but it is not thereby irrelevant or bad. When guided by the reverence for and knowledge of God-Yahweh, wisdom is good and very desirable, indeed extremely so, even in its intellectual version. The picture of the texts is consonant with the inclusion of the intellect in the Old Testament's understanding of לב, "heart," as the result of God's creation of humans rather than as the result of their fall. לב, "heart," by no means refers to the emotions alone!

It is in this horizon that the Old Testament's signals about intellectuality merit attention. On occasion, this aspect is alluded to in passages that narrate or refer to activity in councils which amounts to institutionalized procedures in the search for wise decisions in that questions, controversies, plans, and/or strategies are deliberated in often contentious argumentations. The personnel in these settings represent the experienced and, by and large, professionally educated experts — the intellectual elite of the society.

However, much more is at stake; namely, the intellectuality of the writers of the biblical books, who are for us anonymous. Whoever has attempted even once to analyze the literary composition of an Old Testament text or to reconstruct the conceptuality in such a text (a conceptuality not explicit but operative underneath the text as its coherent design) has not only met difficult challenges but has also encountered the presence of a superior intellectual effort which, so one wonders, has been only infrequently matched by our own interpretive efforts. The intellectuality in the texts is an intrinsic element of the Old Testament's spirituality, of its own expression of the fear and knowledge of God-Yahweh. It belongs to the best of ancient Israel's intellectuality, regardless of whether or not one considers this literature elitist — which I am inclined to assume that it is. In view of the occasional assumption of a populist, prephilosophical standard which shares in the widespread opinion (implicit, if not explicit) that true spirituality has nothing to do with the intellect and that it separates feeling (the seat of truth) from intellect (the seat of falsehood), it cannot be emphasized strongly enough that the entire Old Testament literature, even where it reveals emotion and passion, testifies to the contrary.

In accordance with the plurality of its expressions, the Old Testament spirituality as the fear and knowledge of God-Yahweh is also characterized by a restless and endless interest in subsuming under itself all the issues concerned with life and reality as created and constantly influenced by God. A few examples out of the whole spectrum must suffice:

1. The fear and knowledge of God-Yahweh means the realization of God's mysterious presence in the experiences of either salvific or disastrous historical events or epochs. Ezekiel says time and again that when such events happen "then you shall *know* that I am Yahweh" (Ezek 6:7, 10, 14, etc.).[15] In this sense, from

15. Cf., in addition to the articles of W. Zimmerli referred to above, J. M. Robinson, "Revelation as Word and as History," in *Theology as History,* NFT 3, ed. J. M. Robinson and J. B. Cobb, Jr. (New York: Harper and Row, 1967), 1-100; and R. Knierim, "Revelation in the Old Testament," pages 139-70 in the present volume.

generation to generation Israel was intensively engaged in trying to understand the meaning of its own and of international history for the purpose of gaining orientation for its present and future. This fact is documented by the Israelites' attention to and treatment of the primeval history, the patriarchal-exodus-Sinai-wilderness-settlement-conquest history, the time of the judges, the united and the divided monarchies, their respective falls and exiles, and the postexilic period. In addition to this treatment through history writing by theological historians, the prophets, poets, and lawgivers constantly had their eyes on God's ways in history. They all knew that it would be suicidal not to realize this meaning, as it was suicidal for Pharaoh (Exodus 5f.) and for the international world of neighboring states (Amos 1 and 2).

2. The fear and knowledge of God-Yahweh unfolds in the protective regulations for societal order and solidarity as in the books of Exodus, Leviticus, Numbers, and Deuteronomy. These protective tendencies are one of the matrices and criteria for ethos, especially social ethos. Within this context, to know God meant to realize the difference between good and evil (Gen 2:9, 17; Deut 1:39; 6:18; Isa 1:16f.; Amos 5:14). It meant to know the principles for ethical orientation: "He has told you, O mortal, what is good; and what does the LORD require of you but to do justice, and to love kindness, and to walk humbly with your God?" (Mic 6:8). Jeremiah confronts his king: "Are you a king because you compete in cedar? Did not your father eat and drink and do justice and righteousness? Then it was well with him. He judged the cause of the poor and needy; then it was well. *Is not this to know me?*" (Jer 22:15f., emphasis mine).

3. Fear and knowledge of God-Yahweh unfold in worship and its understanding. From the extensive and diversified tradition, two examples must suffice. In an attempt to draw the line against a false understanding of sacrifices, Ps 50:14 and 23 say: "Offer to God a sacrifice of thanksgiving," and "Those who bring thanksgiving as their sacrifice honor me." Similarly, in an attempt to correct the mechanization of penitence rituals, Joel 2:12f. says: "Return to me with all your heart, with fasting, with weeping, and mourning; rend your hearts and not your clothing." (Cf. also Isa 58:3-5.)

Our understanding of the Old Testament cult is — traditionally — misguided by the assumption that this cult was essentially materialistic in conceptualization and mechanistic as to its performance and intentionality. However, the opposite is true. The essential attitude in which the Israelites were supposed to approach cultic matters and to participate in the cult was spiritual in nature. The repeated criticisms of a materialistic and mechanistic cultic behavior (especially in Deuteronomy, the Psalms, and the prophetic writings) do not indicate an advanced revision of a previously held materialistic and mechanistic understanding of the cult. On the contrary, they criticize and try to correct a materialistic and mechanistic perversion of its always spiritual conceptualization. In other words, while it is true that the Israelite cult could not do without material performances and controlled structures for its ritual procedures — just as no ancient cult could and no modern one can — it is incorrect to regard such performances as ends in themselves, thereby ignoring both their purpose and, on the human side, the spiritual attitude of the participants which was considered indispensable and essential.[16]

Of course, what I have just said in opposition to a materialistic and mechanistic perception of cultic procedures is also especially true for the Old Testament's prescriptions of procedures for the sacrificial cult. The fact that these texts focus on procedures does not permit the conclusion that they do not presuppose spirituality. Whatever the occasional diverse and indeed critical arguments against cultic procedures are — primarily by some prophets, though also in a few psalms and proverbs — they cannot rest on the assumption that those procedures were not themselves also understood to be of an eminently spiritual nature. Any interpretation of those criticisms from within the Old Testament must first of all account for the understanding of the spiritual nature of those procedures.

For example, in the texts regarding sacrificial rituals, such as in the book of Leviticus, it is clear that the objective of their prescriptions is not to describe the human attitude of the laypersons and priests involved. Close attention to their presuppositions, such as a layperson's need for a sacrificial gift and the hoped-for effect of it on Yahweh for the benefit of that person's condition, demonstrates that it is impossible to ignore an encompassing spiritual dimension in which the sacrificial act is meant to be imbedded. Without these presuppositions, a sacrifice would not be undertaken in the first place. They reveal the meaning of the sacrifice and its procedure, which is profoundly spiritual. The sacrifice represents the actualization of this meaning. The awareness of this meaning and the focus on its actualization belong intrinsically together, whereby the latter stands in the foreground and the former in the background of these *texts* — although not necessarily of the performance.

This relationship appears by and large reversed in the book of Psalms. As is well known, many psalms have a cultic setting and especially reflect the patterns of cultic, including sacrificial, procedures. But while these procedures must be exegetically reconstructed (which has been done especially by form criticism) because they stand in the background of the texts, the language of the texts themselves focuses, in expression and mood, on the *meaning* of the cultic events. Thus, neither in the rituals prescribed in Leviticus nor in the Psalms' praises, thanksgivings, complaints, and laments, may the intrinsic coherence of act and meaning, of meaning and act, be severed. Furthermore, the Psalms may not be

16. Recently this has clearly been shown by H. J. Hermisson, in his book *Sprache und Ritus im altisraelitischen Kult,* WMANT 19 (Neukirchen-Vluyn: Neukirchener, 1965). In our context, Hermisson's book is important because its research on "the spiritualization of cultic terms in the Old Testament" (the subtitle of his book) represents a direct exegetical contribution to our present topic.

played over and against Leviticus. Both point not so much to the spiritual side in the relationship of meaning and act, i.e., the side of meaning, as to a spirituality in which act and meaning indissolubly interpenetrate. Moreover, both show, each in its own way, that the fear and knowledge of God-Yahweh lies at the heart of their spirituality.

What has just been said should not entail the neglect of passages such as 1 Sam 15:22; Amos 5:25; Mic 6:6-8; Pss 40:7 (*NRSV* 40:6); 51:18-19 (*NRSV* 51:16-17), in which the heart's spirituality is said to be the true alternative to sacrifices. One should admit that, wherever its roots are and whenever it emerged, there is a strand in the Old Testament that sets the heart's obedience to Yahweh over against sacrifices for Yahweh. One may debate to what extent this strand is on its strongest grounds in its opposition to sacrifices, apart from its certainly true emphasis on the heart's obedience under any circumstances. More important is that just its extreme position indicates what otherwise must be presumed — unless we assume a sacrificial attitude that emphasized performance while dismissing the need for the heart's fear and knowledge of Yahweh — namely, that built into the fabric of Israel's worship was in principle the element of critical discernment between its true and abortive possibilities. This element of contentious discernment is itself an eminently spiritual phenomenon. Its roots should clearly be found in Israel's awareness of its encounter with Yahweh himself, which is the reason for its fear and knowledge of him in the first place. In the awareness of this encounter, it becomes evident that even the best understanding of spirituality may not be taken as a substitute for the encounter with Yahweh himself, or as a shield behind which to hide from that encounter. Yahweh, the ground for fear and knowledge, must not be replaced by fear and knowledge. It is, therefore, inevitable that the Old Testament's concept of spirituality is itself subject to the constantly discriminating question, and the sometimes obviously adversarial debates about its own truth. The Old Testament expresses in these debates that its spirituality as such is no proof of Yahweh's truth but rather is subject to it.[17]

The list of aspects which could be mentioned is endless. Yet I must summarize with the following. Old Testament spirituality, i.e., wisdom as fear and knowledge of God-Yahweh, is always related to reality, and it is constantly moving. It does not consist of one doctrine or doctrinal system, or of one insight only. Rather, it is a process in which many opinions are sometimes, but not always, in dialogue with one another. It is a process in which opinions are constantly in disequilibrium precisely because of their awareness of Yahweh. The fear and knowledge of God-Yahweh drives them to ever new attempts at mastering reality. It is itself the breath

17. On the matter of the conceptual background of the sacrificial laws, cf. R. P. Knierim, *Text and Concept in Lev 1:1-9: A Case in Exegetical Method,* FAT 2 (Tübingen: J. C. B. Mohr, 1992).

of Israel throughout the centuries. Nothing is spared from its touch and interest, from its critical scrutiny of and opposition against chaos, from its purview which is both universal and intimate. The spirituality of the Old Testament as fear and knowledge of God-Yahweh is the phenomenon of an intensely sensitized, heightened mode of human existence.

C. The Source of Old Testament Spirituality

The Old Testament's concentration on what God-Yahweh means to Israel, to humans in their existence, and to the world implies that the Israelites were keenly aware of the difference between the brute facts of life and God's meaning giving presence in them, just as they were aware of the difference between the *physis* as such and its spiritual component in their own anthropology. This awareness provoked the need for the constant distinction between God and the world — not a separation of the two, but a distinction between them. The constant need for distinguishing between God and world had become the situation in which the Israelites found themselves, in which they had to remain, in which they were challenged to the utmost, and in which they had to come forward and respond, trying to discover the truth, to express the truth, to make decisions, and to be obedient. Moreover, it is entirely consistent with this awareness that they were also aware of the difference between what they said about God-Yahweh, on the one hand, and God-Yahweh himself, on the other. The second prohibition of the classical Decalogue stands out as the paradigm for this awareness. This signal for the distinction between their words, assumptions, and writings about God and God himself — of which we have many examples — is another ingredient of the Old Testament spirituality. It indicates that part of their knowledge of God was the awareness of the imperfection of that knowledge, in spite of their constant need and task to articulate it.

At this point, Old Testament spirituality reveals its twofold nature. It is Israel's own knowledge of God-Yahweh, but of such a nature that it is dependent on and controlled by the One who has his own identity and who never becomes an object even for the best of his servants. In this sense, it is correct to say that the Israelites' spirituality is the work of the One whom they know. Just as I said earlier that the Old Testament spirituality is the human self-realization in God's work, so now I must state that it is God-Yahweh's work in their human self-realization. Hence, it is proper to say that the source and force of Israel's spirituality is the presence and work of Yahweh in its life and midst.

The twofold nature of this spirituality, this wisdom as fear and knowledge of God-Yahweh, is paradigmatically expressed in the first twelve verses of Psalm 139. Those who are supposed to know God-Yahweh ultimately must confess that their knowledge of God-Yahweh consists in that the One knows them.

[1]O LORD, you have searched me and known me.
[2]You know when I sit down and when I rise up;
you discern my thoughts from far away.
[3]You search out my path and my lying down,
and are acquainted with all my ways.
[4]Even before a word is on my tongue,
O LORD, you know it completely.
[5]You hem me in, behind and before,
and lay your hand upon me.
[6]Such knowledge is too wonderful for me;
it is so high that I cannot attain it.
[7]Where can I go from your spirit?
Or where can I flee from your presence?
[8]If I ascend to heaven, you are there;
if I make my bed in Sheol, you are there.
[9]If I take the wings of the morning
and settle at the farthest limits of the sea,
[10]even there your hand shall lead me,
and your right hand shall hold me fast.
[11]If I say, "Surely the darkness shall cover me,
and the light around me become night,"
[12]even the darkness is not dark to you;
the night is as bright as the day,
for darkness is as light to you.

CONCLUSION

The spirituality of the Old Testament has a particular function in the intersection of the Old Testament's anthropology and theology. This intersection is characterized by the twofold structure of God-Yahweh's work in or through human lives and human self-realization in God-Yahweh's work, whereby the latter appears to be based in the former. Its particular function consists in its ability for the diacritical identification of true spirituality, of true wisdom, or of the truth of wisdom. The criterion for this discerning ability is the fear and knowledge of God-Yahweh. Since, on the one hand, both wisdom and the fear and knowledge of God-Yahweh are anthropological modes, and since, on the other hand, the nature of true wisdom is qualified by the fear and knowledge of God-Yahweh, the anthropological aspect of the Old Testament's spirituality is theological in nature. It is grounded in the all-pervasive consciousness of God-Yahweh, which is the explicit fundamental presupposition not only for the various theologies *in,* but also for the theology *of,* the Old Testament. This presupposition functions not as a foreword to Old Testament theology, but throughout as the signal for the distinction between God-Yahweh himself and the wisdom of the Old Testament's theologies — themselves expressions of its wisdom spirituality.

However, neither reverence for nor knowledge of Yahweh makes explicit as such the particular contents of that knowledge. The question of content is important for two reasons. First, since wisdom is qualified as true wisdom by the fear and knowledge of God-Yahweh, in order to be able to distinguish between valid and invalid wisdom, one must know not only that God is to be revered and known, but also what the content of the knowledge of God is. In other words, one must not only know *of* the One but also about *what* God-Yahweh is and does. Secondly, since wisdom itself always means wise involvement in the affairs of life and world rather than withdrawal from them, the knowledge of God-Yahweh must state how God is related to and present in his world. When it comes to these necessities, the wisdom spirituality of the Old Testament is pluralistic because it coincides with the pluralism of the theologies in the Old Testament. It belongs, therefore, to the problem of that pluralism, which constitutes the need for the theology of the Old Testament.

Thus, the spirituality of the Old Testament represents a heightened level of the intersection of the theological anthropology and the theology of the Old Testament. By focusing on God-Yahweh as the One, it is the foundational vantage point for everything said in the Old Testament, and the foundational chapter for Old Testament theology in its entirety. By saying that its validity depends on the knowledge of the One God-Yahwch, its own substantive theological pluralism becomes subject to those criteria of Old Testament theology through which the knowledge of God-Yahweh — and hence the true spirituality of the Old Testament — may be discerned. Furthermore, by focusing on both together, i.e., on the One and the knowledge of him, spirituality functions as the catalyst for the permanent need to keep the tension alive between the significance of the knowledge of the One for the critical evaluation of the theologies about God-Yahweh and the significance of the theologies about God-Yahweh for the fear and knowledge of the One. It carries within its own vitality the self-critical, self-controlling, and self-correcting impetus and orientation for human life in the tension between its ultimate and relative experience of God.

The Old Testament — The Letter and the Spirit

Introduction

τὸ γὰρ γράμμα ἀποκτέννει, τὸ δὲ πνεῦμα ζῳοποιεῖ.

"The letter kills, but the spirit makes alive" — so Paul says in 2 Cor 3:6.

In this chapter, he contrasts the existence of Christians with that of the Israelites, the New Covenant with the Old, and the documentation for the New (the human letters written with the spirit of the living God) with the documentation for the Old (the letter written on tablets of stone or with ink).

To be sure, this dualism reflects a contrast already drawn in the Old Testament itself, namely, in Jer 31:31-34. And Paul's statements are in part a christological and ecclesiological midrash on that Old Testament passage. But even as he so splendidly testifies to the splendor of Christ, Paul has left us, nevertheless, with some considerable problems.

First, it seems as though the Christian tradition from Paul's time on has been programmed with the basic assumption that letter and spirit are irreconcilable opposites, so much so that they can be associated with a parallel pair of opposites — death and life.

Second, another consequence of contrasting letter and spirit in Christianity is that the Old Testament has been considered to be the document of a false religion, a religion of laws and the letter, whereas the New Testament represents the true religion — a religion of the gospel and the spirit. More pointedly, under the influence of a Christology which became more and more dogmatized, the Old Testament scriptures were theologically stigmatized as letter under the law, no matter what their letters say and what their spirit is.

I do not want to belittle the importance of this Christology, even as it affects the understanding of the Old Testament. I am aware that the issue is complex, and also that the Old Testament can have different voices in the context of different New Testament Christologies. What worries me is that this specific christological stance has resulted in a captivity of the Old Testament, a bondage imposed on it by an outside conqueror — the church. In this capacity, it can no longer express its own views, including its own way of relating to the Christ of the New Testament, both in letter and spirit. The Old Testament is not liberated from this captivity when it was, or is, gracefully allowed to cast its vote humbly for Christ under the helpful theological control mechanisms of historical Christianity. Under these control mechanisms, it is still far from being entitled to reveal its own self-understanding and to make its own contribution, even to the Christian faith. No totalitarian regime claims to oppress its subjects. It is the nature of totalitarianism that it attempts to liberate its ignorant subjects into the freedom of happily supporting the ideology of the regime, and to teach them that their desire for so-called self-determination is stupid, sinful, criminal, self-destructive, and hence against their own self-interest.

To be sure, much that has happened during the last three centuries, especially in recent decades, was designed to give back to the Old Testament the right of its own voice. But the goal is far from being attained, and the way to the Old Testament's liberation is long and difficult. In this process, we have a decisive responsibility. For we, its oppressors, are the ones who must give it back its freedom.

Within this task, the notions of the letter and the spirit have a central function. For it was under these notions, among others, that the Old Testament was placed in bondage. Hence we must ask what the Old Testament reveals in and of itself when consulted about the letter and the spirit.

I. The Old Testament — The Letter

What does it mean when we say, "the Old Testament — the letter"? It means, first of all, the Old Testament as texts preserved in writing, often derived from oral speeches. In summary, "the Old Testament — the letter" means the Old Testament literature as the sum total of its texts and what these texts say.

This sounds like a simple statement. But here is where we must begin because this is what we have before us; this is where we find ourselves today when studying the Old Testament. This means that no discussion of the Old Testament as letter can ignore the immense results of some three hundred years of Old Testament studies in which the letter of the Old Testament and the Old Testament as letter have been and are being revealed more than ever before. The movement governing these studies has been summarily labeled historical-critical exegesis. This exegesis has not attempted to "criticize" the Old Testament, certainly not more than historical Christianity has done all along. Rather, it has tried to understand it from within, i.e., from its own presuppositions. For all its fallacies, it, more than anything else, has allowed the Old Testament its own voice and is, therefore, irreplaceable. It is, therefore, necessary that we recognize the availability and respective character of the various exegetical methods which constitute historical-critical exegesis and which contribute to the understanding of the Old Testament as letter.

A. The Methods and the Letter

1. The increasing availability of Hebrew, Aramaic, Greek, and Syriac manuscripts, along with those from other languages, which are studied in textual criticism, has opened before us the world of the letter.

2. The discernment of different styles, doublets, repetitions, moods, and messages, which led to the field of literary criticism, has also shown us the world of the Old Testament letter and the Old Testament as letter as consisting of sources, fragments, and independent literary units.

3. The study of the growing compilation of textual traditions up to their final compositions as we basically have them, called redaction criticism, has shown us the growth and history of the letter.

4. The study of forms, structures, or compositions and of genres, advanced in form criticism, has revealed the typical nature of the "letter," and here of not only the written letter, but also the letter of the spoken word behind or before the literature.

5. The study of what is called transmission and tradition history has opened before us the history of the letter throughout centuries. Transmission history focuses on the communities or authors in their settings who were responsible for passing on the contents of the traditions from generation to generation. Ultimately it also accounts for the committing of oral traditions to written texts and the eventual transformation of their respective functions. Tradition history identifies the nature of the particular traditions and describes their continuing identity or their reconceptualization(s) in the process of their transmission.

There can be no doubt what it means when we say today, "the Old Testament — the letter." An enormous panorama of texts, originally from both written and oral backgrounds, opens before our eyes. In this panorama of the letter, we have learned and are learning more, if not better, what the Old Testament says. This must be said in spite of the many things we do not yet know or may never know.

B. The Letter and the Letters

All these methodical studies have shown the historicity of the letter. None of its texts is suprahistorical. Each belongs to and depends on a historical locus.

This historicity accounts for the great variety and diversity of Old Testament voices. Here, therefore, we must speak of the Old Testament as "letters." These voices are discerned diachronically (through time) throughout one thousand years, as well as synchronically (from across all the segments of a single generation). Thus, we have the "letters" for the cult and worship, for the histories, for the prophetic texts, for the proverbs, for the sayings, for the poems, for the novellas, for the laws and instructions, for the hymns and laments and complaints, etc.

We are confronted with a perplexing phenomenon: the letter unveils a pluralism of letters. Even more perplexing is the fact that there is no conceptual unity among them. They do not always merely express the same thing differently. They often say different messages and/or are preoccupied with different topics. Worse, they seldom dialogue, often ignore each other, and even explicitly or implicitly contradict one another — even as they speak about God. As far as their history of tradition is concerned, we should speak of its discontinuity at least as much as we emphasize its continuity. Moreover, as far as the theology of the letter is concerned, we would better speak of their theologies (analogous to what has been said about the New Testament).

C. Summary of "Old Testament — The 'Letter'"

Exegesis has shown us the Old Testament as letter, and as letters. It has taught us to paraphrase what the letters say. The result has been an explosion of knowledge entirely commensurate to the explosion of knowledge in any other field in our time. This result is exciting, stands in its own right, and should not be belittled. Along with it we have learned that the letter, for the most part, does not speak about "law," nor does it understand itself everywhere as "law" or "written code," nor is the gospel/law structure absent, nor is it unaware of the "spirit of the living God." Even more, it certainly does not understand itself as a dead or killing letter vis-à-vis a life-giving spirit.

Nevertheless, the nagging question arises as to what meaning, relevance, and/or validity this explosion of knowledge reveals for us. Is it to justify a self-perpetuation of our ever-expanding scientific bureaucracy? What a symbol for a killing letter that would be! Likewise, I am not concerned about the explosion of knowledge as such, even though I understand its heavy demands on student and scholar. More problematic is the gap between exegesis and theology, the fact that the same exegesis that was supposed to allow the Old Testament theology its own voice has in effect caused the atomization of that theology and, by and large, the loss of a conceptual unity of the Old Testament. Most troublesome, however, is the fact that the discovery of the historicity and pluralism of the letters has led to a relativization, either explicit or implicit, of its revelatory nature and, hence, of its theological validity. Terms such as "inspiration," "spiritual," or "theological" are scarcely considered an integral part of the established exegetical methodology. The texts are considered to be human voices even where they claim to represent revelation. In such cases, we exegete them as claims of revelation, but not necessarily as revelation.

Here we may discover the killing nature of the letter in a new way. Previously, it was a sort of Christian dogmatism that declared the Old Testament to be a letter of death. Is it now our exegetical insight that pronounces the same theological judgment, this time on the basis of the relativistic results from the discovery of the historicity of the Old Testament "letters"? This question leads me to the next section.

II. The Old Testament — The Spirit

In this section, I am not preoccupied with Old Testament texts that speak about the "spirit." Not only are those texts relatively few when compared with the total number of Old Testament texts, but when they speak about the spirit, they voice their own perceptions about it and do not necessarily objectively reflect the spirit's manifestations. Instead, I want to address the spirit of the texts, in the texts themselves, in all the Old Testament texts.

This implies that I am not employing the available exegetical methods in order to interpret a few texts. Rather, I am reconsidering the design of that methodology itself. For it could be that at least part of the reason we perceive the letter as a letter of death lies in our exegetical methods, and not so much, if at all, in the letter itself. Indeed, we may need to speak about a deficiency in the so-called historical-critical exegesis. This method has taught us to interpret texts and what texts say. Its deficiency seems to surface in what I would like to call the insufficiently developed anthropological viewpoint.

To be sure, the task of carefully paraphrasing texts must not be ignored. The important question, however, is what we assume when we say "text," be it oral or written. I hope we are agreed that our texts are not *deus ex machina* products, fallen from the sky, nor have they come from nowhere. In other words, a supernaturalistic or nihilistic understanding of the nature of the texts will not work. Neither will a mechanistic understanding which asserts that they were produced by computers. More important is the observation that the texts were not produced by the events or situations to which they testify. Events do not produce texts. This means that, strictly speaking, a historistic understanding of the nature of the texts is also at fault. We are so preoccupied with the question, "Did what the texts say happened happen?" that we tend to ignore the much more important, and at least the primary, question, "Who spoke or wrote this?"

A. The Human Spirit in the Texts

There can be no doubt that all the texts were spoken or written by humans. This means that the human factor is a constitutive and intrinsic element in each text.

Certainly, our texts reveal very few personal identities and little biographical data of their writers. These people show little self-preoccupation. But our texts do reveal the mental activity of the speakers and writers, and that includes their intellects. To say it pointedly, the activity of their minds and intellects has flowed into their manuscripts, and without that activity, the manuscripts would not have come into existence.

If, however, this activity is behind and in the texts, then the so-called historical-critical exegesis must see to it that the interpretation of such activity is included in the exegesis of a text and not ignored. It must ask what was and is meant, and not only what is said. An exegesis that considers a text only as text, isolated from such human activity, ignores the reality of the text altogether. It might as well be called inhuman.

Therefore, we must become much more aware of a set of methodological/heuristic questions than we have been so far. The major difficulty with these questions is that they seek answers from what is not explicitly stated in the texts, even though such inexplicitness belongs to their essence. At this time, I have not yet systematized the set of questions pertinent to this aspect. For the moment, a few indications must, therefore, suffice:

1. What is the concern behind what is said in a text? For example, what is the concern behind the prohibition: "You shall have no other gods"? The concern is the exclusivity of Yahweh-worship. But what is expressed is the prohibition of other gods. The definition of the concern is not identical with the paraphrase of what is said.

2. What is the problem situation behind the text which prompted both concern and expression? In our example, it is the fact or the danger that other gods are indeed worshipped and Yahweh's exclusivity is lost. Again, the problem situation is not expressed in the text; but it is addressed, which means it is presupposed.

3. What caused a word to be spoken or written? The fact that there is a problem and a concern does not automatically mean that one speaks out on the problem and expresses her/his concern. One can remain silent. Whatever the answer may be in our example, one thing is clear: a prohibition had to be given.

4. What is intended with what is said? Seldom, if ever, do our texts reveal what they want to achieve among those whom they address. Nevertheless, they have such an intention. In our example, the prohibition to worship other gods not only intends to deter the addressees from idolatry. It also, and even more, intends to preserve them in the worship of and loyalty to Yahweh — and that for their own sake.

5. How is what is said supposed to function? This, too, is implied, but scarcely made explicit. The function of a prohibition is quite different from the function of

a parenesis. The latter functions persuasively — it aims at subjective affirmation — whereas the former functions categorically — it aims at obedience.

6. Other possible questions include:

a. What constitutes the composition of a narrative, a legal or prophetic text, a psalm, a sequence of sayings?
b. What are the reasons for unique individualized expressions as analyzed by rhetorical criticism?
c. What are the reasons for patterned expressions?

All these questions — this reading between, behind, in, and under the lines — are important because they help us discover the vitality of the texts far beyond what they literally say. Most important, they allow us to encounter the activity of the human spirit in those texts, and to that extent to encounter our human brothers and sisters. They allow us to participate in their concerns, interests, intentions, methods, problems, and answers to problems and messages. Thus, in discovering the activity of the human spirit in those texts, we discover their meaning. They are not dead, nor killing, unless we declare anything dead and killing simply because it is human. Already in this sense the letter is spiritual, and in the rediscovery of its spirit, the spirit of its human subjects, historical-critical exegesis must be spiritual exegesis. This is part of what I mean by the call to upgrade the anthropological factor in exegesis, an upgrading that will at the same time contribute to its humanization.

I know that the theological sensitivity in many of us smells danger and perceives that this is theologically insufficient. But before we dismiss such a result as theologically irrelevant, I will express a caveat. I believe that a theological anthropology would, indeed, be ill-advised, if it were to dismiss the theological relevance of the phenomenon of the human mind and its activities. To whatever extent our texts reflect God's revelation, this revelation is expressed in the texts only through the participatory or mediating activity of these minds and intellects, as well as hands. To dismiss this fact would not only mean to discount their God-given humanity; it would also mean to deny the experience of God as a human possibility.

B. The Spirit of God and the Human Spirit in the Letter

1. I have already indicated that, in the field of Old Testament theology, it has been virtually impossible to identify any conceptual unity in the Old Testament under which a theology could be conceived. Whether one chooses the concept of "covenant," "gospel-law" (i.e., exodus-commandment), "holiness," "promise-fulfillment," "prophetic religion," "wisdom-religion," "God-human-world," "cult,"

"revelation," "history," "nature," "wisdom," "political and social institutions," "the nature of God and the actions of God," or "creation-sustenance-future hope," all these systems are much more our own than the Old Testament's. Furthermore, categories such as "tradition history" or "canon" are much more formal and functional than conceptual. It seems that, not only for the time being but probably from now on, we must settle for the fact that the Old Testament is not conceptually united. It represents a great variety and diversity, not only of aspects and interests but also of theologies. On the other hand, we must account for the fact that, with the exception of Esther and Song of Songs in their original meaning, the totality of the Old Testament literature is deeply theological. What unites these voices is their encounter of or experience with Yahweh in their experience of diverse realities. This is the preoccupation of the humans of the Old Testament, as well as the distinctive mark of its literature. Because of this mark the Old Testament library was assembled, whereas all the other literature produced by Israel was left aside. Hence the Old Testament reflects the history and sociology of Israel's involvement and fascination with Yahweh. In other words, the letter reveals a spirituality of its voices which had become keenly aware that Yahweh had become their destiny, and not only theirs but that of the entire world. If there is any expression in the Old Testament that comes close to expressing this all-pervading awareness, it is the first and second prohibitions of the classical decalogue, the insistence on the exclusivity and incomparability of Yahweh.

2. This factor is more important than is generally realized, for here the human spirit in the letter testifies to its own inspiredness by Yahweh. This is exactly their self-understanding: paradoxically, where their spirit is at work in their voices, it is captured, ignited, inspired by Yahweh. In this sense, their letter — all of it, and not only those texts that speak about inspiration or quote Yahweh's word — is inspired by their God. This is, I believe, what we should mean when speaking about the inspiration of the Scriptures. There is no reason for us to avoid this assertion, or to be at a loss concerning it. On the contrary, we have every reason to affirm it. And with this affirmation goes the conclusion that, inasmuch as this spirituality is intrinsic to the spirituality of the letter, our exegesis of the letter must take account of it; it must reflect this Yahweh-spirituality. In this sense, it will need to be theological exegesis. Thus, the humanization of our interpretation of this letter will need to show the central theological nature of the letter, just as its theological interpretation will need to show the letter to be an expression of the human spirit.

3. Two important questions arise at this point. First, what is the meaning of the variety and diversity of the voices/letters under their Yahweh-centrality? And second, how do we articulate the difference between Yahweh's spirit and the human spirit in the spirituality of the letter?

a. Let us consider the first question: What is the meaning of the variety and diversity of the voices/letters under their Yahweh-centrality?

It means, first of all, the de-ideologization and relativization of Israel's worldviews. Israel lives and speaks in the worldviews of its time, but ultimately it is not committed to any of them. Israel is in the world but not of the world. The Israelites belong to Yahweh alone. This Yahweh-centrism freed them from ideologies and at the same time liberated them to experience Yahweh in their reality as they experienced it in the plurality, variety, and diversity, which we can observe in the Old Testament. In short, the variety and diversity of the letters must be considered a direct outgrowth of the Yahweh-centrality in their spirituality. In this sense, this variety of letters was inspired by Yahweh.

However, there is another reason for the variety and diversity of the letters; namely, the variety and diversity of Israel's experience. This experience was never the same for all, neither for all those living in a certain generation, nor for all throughout the generations. The history of Israel, and the as yet unwritten sociology of Israel's historical epochs, documents this fact very clearly.

Of particular importance at this point is the fact that the Israelites' articulation of their experience reflects their human vantage point just as much as it reflects their Yahweh-centrism. Although their worldviews were scarcely normative, they were nevertheless *their* worldviews. Moreover, these worldviews, especially in their social-historical context, affected their witness about God and Yahweh. To state it pointedly, the variety and diversity of the letters, including their theology, is not only the result of their inspiration by Yahweh. It is also the result of the inspiration by their own spirit.

Therefore, in the interpretation of the Old Testament letter, one can ignore neither the theological factor, namely, the Yahweh-centric inspiration of the human spirit, nor the anthropological factor, namely, the activity and role of the human spirit in Israel's knowledge of Yahweh. Both are indissolubly related to one another in all the texts.

b. How then do we articulate the difference between Yahweh's spirit and the human spirit in the letter? An answer to this question is obviously imperative. In approaching this question, I will once more look into the Old Testament and ask whether it is itself aware of the question, and if so, what it contributes to answering the question.

At first glance it looks as though the Old Testament is by and large unaware of this problem. The Old Testament seems very self-assured about its possession of the knowledge and spirit of God. But this impression is by and large deceptive.

To be sure, I am not concentrating on those passages in which the Old Testament voices criticize Israel for its sinfulness, especially in the Pentateuch and the prophetic books, although they, too, must be considered. I am more interested, for the time being, in the voices' self-understanding of their own spirituality recorded in the letters.

In its texts about the conflict between true and false prophets, it is clear that Israel's spirituality was confronted with the tenuous understanding of the modes of Yahweh's presence, even as the texts ultimately leave no doubt as to who was right and who was wrong. However, other texts document Israel's awareness that, in many respects, Yahweh's presence was perceived as mysterious, hidden, and beyond being controlled by definitively established societal criteria. This does not mean that this experience of Yahweh's presence was perceived as irrational. On the contrary, it reflected a rationality which accounted for the knowledge that saying "God/Yahweh" meant including a type of experience which cannot be measured exclusively by the patterns of reality generated by the human mind alone.

A few texts which signal this type of awareness may be briefly introduced. The prophets themselves, especially Isaiah and Jeremiah, testify to the hiddenness of Yahweh and his plans and wait for the Lord, sometimes in agony. The Old Testament history writers portray the most venerable of their saints as quite unsaintly (Abraham, Jacob, Moses, Saul, and David). Solomon prayed for a heart of wisdom; that is why he became wise. The sages who in Proverbs so emphasize "the fear of Yahweh" are greatly puzzled by the mysteries of God's ways. One of them says, "The human mind plans the way, but the LORD directs the steps" (Prov 16:9). The psalmist says, "O send out your light and your truth; let them lead me" (43:3), or "Teach me your way, O LORD, that I may walk in your truth . . ." (86:11). (Much more should be said. This chapter of our Old Testament anthropology has scarcely been studied at all.)

I do not mean to imply that the Old Testament voices do not speak with great self-assertion about God and about knowledge of God. However, when they speak to our problem, they articulate a distinct awareness of the difference between Yahweh's spirit and their own spirit, in and because of their knowledge of God/Yahweh and not apart from it. Moreover, one must add that the variety and diversity of their witnesses implicitly testifies to this same fact.

In this kind of self-awareness, these voices begin to confess their sin and to pray for guidance, for a clean heart and mind, for wisdom, for revelation, and for God's own spirit. They extend themselves in waiting and hoping for God. They know that their knowledge of God is above all else an awareness that Yahweh "proves," "tests," "searches," and "knows" them, i.e., their hearts and minds (Pss 26:2; 139:23). They are aware of the difference between Yahweh's spirit and their own spirit in their self-experience, and they articulate this difference. These people knew that their religious self-consciousness alone did not yet demonstrate at all the presence of Yahweh's spirit.

This awareness of the difference between Yahweh's spirit and the human spirit ultimately reveals the nature of this human spirit in our letters. These letters say their witness to God is only a witness, and no substitute for God himself. As a witness it is dependent on being justified through the One to whom they witness. Thus, they demythologize their own human spirit, even as it testifies to God, and admit, to the glory of God and certainly to no one else's glory, that the articulations of their witnesses are preliminary because the wholeness cannot yet be said or seen.

Thus, by pointing beyond themselves, they document that the spirit of Yahweh is at work in their human spirit.

Thus, these letters call us, their readers, to join along on the way. They invite us to probe them in light of what they say and in light of the One to whom they point, just as they probe us regarding whom we point to in what we say. I believe that, as we discover the nature of Old Testament spirituality, we will discover new avenues for relating it to the nature and structure of New Testament spirituality. Out of such relating, a dialogue could emerge in which the Old Testament contributes as much to the understanding of the New as the New Testament contributes to the understanding of the Old. To the extent to which we facilitate that dialogue, we will learn how much they all are our brothers and sisters who teach us the steps of faith.

Israel and the Nations in the Land of Palestine in the Old Testament[1]

Introduction

Let me tell you, first of all, what I do not intend, and what my real objective is.

I am lobbying neither for the Palestine Liberation Organization nor for the United States Nazi Party, nor for the Jewish Defense, or Anti-Defamation, League. I am not lobbying for any branch of the United States government, nor for the government of the state of Israel, nor for any of the Arab governments, and certainly not for our oil companies. I am not on any of their payrolls. I am not analyzing Mr. Sadat's or Mr. Begin's positions; and I do not want to give an account of the history of the problem because that history is the very reason for the problem.

I do want to inquire whether the biblical tradition can offer us insights that may help us shape a theologically grounded position in the current chaos. Such an inquiry I take to be a task intrinsic to our Christian ministry, at least as much as our involvement in other public and worldwide affairs. Such a task cannot be left to political or economic interest groups. It calls for the Christian voice.

I intend to consult the Old Testament primarily, if not solely. The Old Testament is important for such an endeavor for two reasons. First, it is the Old Testament and not the New Testament that speaks directly to our problem. To the extent to which the biblical tradition plays any role at all in the current ideologies, it is the Old Testament. Because the Old Testament is part of our canon, one way or another we must come to grips with it.

1. Lecture given at the Lutheran Theological Seminary, Gettysburg, Pennsylvania, on May 18, 1978, during the critical months of negotiations between the governments of Egypt and Israel for peace in the Middle East. With minor adjustments, this chapter represents the content and style of the oral presentation.

I am aware that I am running the risk of missing what has been called the christocentric criterion in all Christian and biblical theologizing. But I prefer to give the Old Testament its own say in the hope that it may tell something which is in the spirit of Christ. I prefer this route to the other in which the New Testament speaks for the Old Testament, thereby depriving it of its own voice and authenticity, which is exegetically and theologically no longer acceptable.

The decisive reason, however, for inquiring into the Old Testament about our subject is the second. It is only through the Old Testament that we can affirm today that the God of Jesus Christ, or Jesus Christ himself, has anything directly to do with the present situation.

Do you remember the day of President Sadat's visit to Jerusalem in November of last year (1977)? His visit coincided with the Islamic holy day on which Muslims celebrate the event narrated in Genesis 22, i.e., the Old Testament story about the substitution of animals for human sacrifices. And with respect to that story, Sadat pleaded: Let us stop sacrificing human lives and make peace!

What a constellation! A Muslim celebrating and proclaiming to Jews an Old Testament message — and that in a move of utmost importance on the global political scene. Where in these events is Jesus Christ whom we confess to be Lord? If Jesus Christ has anything to do with these events today, either he is present through Yahweh, the God of the Old Testament, or he stands inactively in the corner of present world history, as a provincial particularist, while Yahweh works for peace in the world.

Finally, I propose that we focus on the topic in a new way. Throughout two thousand years of Christian history, from at least 70 CE on, Christians have had no reason at all to pay attention to the encounter between Israel and the nations of Palestine. It was simply not their problem. To be sure, they have always had an interest in the Holy Land for their own sake, inasmuch as it was the land of their Lord. This interest was part of the motivation for the Crusades. The problem became acute for Christianity only in our century, with the rise of Zionism, as a Jewish problem. As for the Jewish people, it arose in a specific way, namely, as the call for the return of the diaspora to their land. What was important for the Jews was their return to their land after more than twenty-five hundred years of exile, and their claim of independence in that land after twenty-five hundred years of dependence on foreign empires. Even for them, their relationship to the other inhabitants in the land was at best a secondary concern. To the extent to which Christians addressed themselves to the Jewish return to and claim on the land, they reflected on the theological, political, or historical legitimacy of that claim, and on its relevance or irrelevance for Christians.[2]

2. This is basically the point where we are today (1978), and what our publications reflect with very few exceptions: the theology of the *land.* See, among others, W. Eckert, N. P. Levinson, and M. Stöhr, eds., *Jüdisches Volk-gelobtes Land,* Abhandlungen zum christlich-jüdischen Dialog

W. Brueggemann, in the "hermeneutical reflections" concluding his book, reflects precisely the status quo of our present theological or hermeneutical position when he says, "It is clear that, since the recent wars of the state of Israel, Christians cannot speak seriously to Jews unless we acknowledge (the) land to be the central agenda. While the Arabs surely have rights and legitimate grievances, the Jewish people are peculiarly the pained voice of the land in the history of humanity, grieved Rachel weeping (Jer 31:15)."[3]

I would like to submit to you that this definition of the "central agenda" is no longer sufficient. We not only have to speak to the Jews (if at all), we also have to speak to the Arabs and to the world! Moreover, we must, finally, address ourselves to a strand in the Old Testament tradition and to a new problem we have never really faced before, namely, the relationship of Israel and her neighbors *in* the land. In view of this problem, the question of Israel's claim on the land is only an overture.

To be sure, it is an overture in its own right! I must reaffirm what others have said. Israel's right to exist in Palestine in freedom and independence, as a political entity, is a settled issue and no longer subject to discussion. I mean this not in the sense of acquiescence to established facts but out of the convictions of a Christian theologian. The reasons are twofold. The first is the history of more than three thousand years of Israelite presence in Palestine and the fundamental religious conviction that Israelite identity is tightly bound to that land. This conviction was never given up, and the many forced exiles never invalidated it. The second is the Holocaust! Hitler's — final — attempt to extinguish the homeless Jews epitomized their fundamental peril as long as they are not the sole masters of their own destiny.

Of Israel's right to exist as a state, there can be no doubt. And if, because of this position, I come into conflict with representatives of Arab nations or of the Palestine Liberation Organization, I shall continue to resist and to contradict them, just as we — members of the theological faculty at Heidelberg — did in 1965, when West Germany assumed diplomatic relations with Israel (in 1964!) and the Arabs studying there confronted us, saying, "You are either their enemies or ours," and broke off all relations with us for years when we did not give in to their pressure.

In this sense, Israel's claim to the land is a "central agenda." Nevertheless, why is it only an overture to the other issue, Israel and the nations in the land? The answer is that Israel's claim on the land does not yet address that other question. That question, however, reflects the heart of the problem, for other nations have also lived in that land and had a claim on it. Furthermore, the Old Testament itself has an explicit theology on that question. Let me, then, proceed to that theology.

---

3 (München: Chr. Kaiser, 1970); from twenty-two articles, not one deals with "Israel and the Nations in the Land." The same is true for W. D. Davies, *The Gospel and the Land* (Berkeley: University of California, 1974); P. Diepold, *Israels Land,* BWANT 95 (Stuttgart: Kohlhammer, 1972); and W. Brueggemann, *The Land,* OBT 1 (Philadelphia: Fortress, 1977).

3. W. Brueggemann, *The Land,* 190.

I. A Survey of the Old Testament Picture

First of all, I want to define the subject more precisely. We are not dealing with Israel's relationship to the foreign nations outside Palestine, of which the Old Testament speaks very often. Nor are we dealing primarily with the social and legal status of foreigners, strangers, or sojourners, who happened to migrate through or to live in the land already occupied and governed by Israel.[4] Instead, we want to concentrate on those Old Testament traditions that document Israel's relationship to other people *in* the land with regard to her own claim on the land.

This focus immediately brings to our attention that strand in the Old Testament tradition which says not only that Yahweh has promised and given the land to Israel but also, quite distinctly, that Yahweh has given the inhabitants of the land into the hand of Israel, and that Israel was supposed to dispossess, expel, and/or extinguish them, and did so wherever and whenever it could.

As for this promise and command of Yahweh, we must recall, among others, Gen 15:18f.: "On that day, the LORD made a covenant with Abram saying, 'To your descendants I give this land, from the river of Egypt to the great river, the river Euphrates, the land of the Kenites, the Kenizzites, the Kadmonites, the Hittites, the Perizzites, the Rephaim, the Amorites, the Canaanites, the Girgashites, and the Jebusites.' " A list of ten nations! "I will give you not a *tabula rasa,* a white spot on the map. No, I will give you *their* land." A similar list of nations occurs in Deut 7:1-2: "When the LORD your God brings you into the land that you are about to enter and occupy, and he clears away many nations before you — the Hittites, the Girgashites, the Amorites, the Canaanites, the Perizzites, the Hivites, and the Jebusites, seven nations mightier and more numerous than you — and when the LORD your God gives them over to you, and you defeat them, then you must utterly destroy them. Make no covenant with them and show to them no mercy" (cf., moreover, Deut 20:16f.). These two passages are not exceptions. Similar passages pervade the entire body of pertinent Old Testament literature and represent the central factor accompanying Israel's claim on the land.[5]

Accordingly, Joshua 1–11 portrays Israel's conquest of Canaan not as a settlement in the land but as a conquest which led to the expulsion and extinction of its population. See Josh 6:21; 8; 11:14f.; and 10:40-42, which states: "So Joshua defeated the whole land, the hill country and the Negeb and the lowland and the slopes, and all their kings; he left no one remaining, but utterly destroyed all that breathed, as the LORD God of Israel commanded. And Joshua defeated them from Kadesh-barnea to Gaza, and all the country of Goshen, as far as Gibeon. Joshua

4. For this, cf. A. Bertholet, *Die Stellung der Israeliten und der Juden zu den Fremden* (Freiburg: J. C. B. Mohr, 1896); and the articles on גר, נכרי, תושב, and זר in *THAT, TWAT,* and *TDOT*.

5. For more references, cf. A. R. Hulst, *THAT* 2, 321.

took all these kings and their land at one time, because the LORD God of Israel fought for Israel."

It is interesting to note the verbs that are used in describing Israel's treatment of the other nations:[6]

a. to blot out, annihilate (כחד, Hiphil), Exod 23:23
b. to ban = to utterly destroy (חרם, Hiphil), Deut 7:2; 20:17 (cf. Joshua 6–12)
c. to strike, beat, defeat (נכה, Hiphil), Deut 7:2
d. to break down (נתץ), Deut 7:5
e. to dash in pieces (שׁבר), Deut 7:5
f. to hew down (גדע), Deut 7:5
g. to burn (שׂרף), Deut 7:5
h. to tear down (הרס), Judg 6:25
i. to cut off (כרת, Hiphil), Deut 12:29; 19; Josh 11:21; 23:4
j. to destroy (שׁמד, Hiphil), Deut 7:23f.; 9:3; 12:30; 31:3f.
k. to finish off (כלה, Piel), Deut 7:22
l. to destroy (אבד, Qal, Hiphil), Deut 7:20; 8:20; 9:3
m. to clear away, drive out (נשל), Deut 7:1, 22
n. to clear away, drive out (ירשׁ, Hiphil), Josh 3:10; 13:6, 12, etc.
o. to clear away, drive out (גרשׁ, Piel), Exod 23:28-31
p. to throw into confusion (המם), Exod 23:27

I have referred to only sixteen different Hebrew verbs. There are more.

The Old Testament tradition is overwhelmingly explicit in stating that before Israel there was a multitude of nations in Canaan, and that, coming into the land, Israel attacked, expelled, and extinguished these nations, i.e., "cleared them out" — and did so under the promise and command of Yahweh. Of course, historical research, supported by the Old Testament itself, has shown that the historical course of the events is not entirely consonant with the events in, e.g., the book of Joshua as that book portrays it (e.g., Josh 12:7-24 and Judges 1 for a comparison). Hence we must now proceed to what we can reconstruct from history.

II. The Historical Picture

The traces of human presence in Palestine reach back 200,000 years. Human skeletons have been found in Galilee and Carmel between 100,000 and 9,000 years old. Between 9000 and 6000 BCE, humans lived there in caves; from 8000 BCE on,

6. Cf. Götz Schmitt, *Du sollst keinen Frieden schliessen mit den Bewohnern des Landes,* BWANT 91 (Stuttgart: Kohlhammer, 1970), 13f.

they began to live in villages, and at least Jericho was a fortified city by 7000 BCE. Later, for a period of 1,800 years, namely, from 3000 to 1200 BCE (the Bronze Age), Palestine experienced a tremendous cultural explosion which culminated in the creation of hundreds of cities, and initiated what is called the Canaanite Age. This is also what our biblical records reflect when they speak of the land of Canaan (Gen 11:31; 12:5; 13:12; 16:3; 17:8; 23:2, 19; 31:18; 35:6; 36:5f.; 37:1; 42:5; etc.). "The Land of Canaan" is the technical term which summarily expressed the fact that, in a development of nearly 2,000 years, populations had settled in the whole land, cultivated it, and created a flourishing civilization — the bronze culture — so much so that, in spite of all its ethnic diversities and the absence of a central government, the culture was one. All this was the work of the Canaanites who had cultivated the land and made it their own. Canaan and the Canaanites, the land and its people, were inseparable. The Old Testament tradition is distinctly cognizant of this.

Late in that period, sometime during its last third, the patriarchs appeared in the land of Canaan. They were few, migratory, and never became fully sedentary. When they sojourned for a while, they stayed on vacant soil, apart from or at best in peaceful coexistence with the inhabitants — except for occasional quarrels about wells for their flocks. They were foreigners, sojourners in a land that firmly belonged to others. Abraham bought a field near Hebron including a cave which was basically to be used as a burial place for his wife and himself.

But then, from Joshua on — Moses never entered the land — Israel appeared on the scene, and within 300 years the land that had been "the Land of Canaan" for almost 2,000 years became "the Land of Israel." By the time of David and Solomon, the land was governed by Israelites as totally as it had been previously governed by Canaanites. Even more was this so because the land was now united, at least initially, under the central government in Jerusalem.

To be sure, Israel's unity broke apart after Solomon's death, but not Israelite control of the land. But in 722 BCE and in 586 BCE, respectively, that control was lost; it remained so until 1948 and 1967. For some 2,500 years, the land was a province under foreign powers (the Babylonians, the Persians, the Greeks, the Romans, Constantinople, the Arabs, the Turks, and the British Mandate). During this time, Israel possessed the land no more and no less than other people living there. However, Israel has always maintained a claim on the land, a claim to its sole possession! And that claim rests on the time when Israel indeed had possession of the land. More precisely, Israel's claim to the sole possession and control of the land rests on the time — and theology — in which it took the land over from its former inhabitants and possessors, the Canaanites. That was the time from 1200 to 900 BCE, the Early Iron Age, the time from Joshua through David and Solomon. It was the time of conquest, settlement, and integration of the land. During these three centuries, in the process of conquest, settlement, and consolidation in the land, Israel's relationship to the inhabitants of the land was shaped once and for all. This factor is fundamental, and all the subsequent articulations of that relationship are only variations of the same stance.

We must, therefore, take a closer look at historical and theological developments during that time. A summary of studies on the subject shows the following reconstruction. During the generation of Joshua, the Hebrew tribes appeared in the land of Canaan in diverse movements. Some, especially Benjamin and Ephraim-Manasseh, came across the Jordan, perhaps conquered some cities (Joshua 6–12), and settled essentially peacefully in the southern and middle Palestinian mountains (cf. Josh 17:14f.). Others, like Judah, came from the south and settled — also peacefully — in the southland. There is some reason to think that some northern tribes in Galilee arose from within and overthrew part of the Canaanites there (this would be a correct point in Mendenhall's thesis — *The Tenth Generation*).[7] Initially, these movements were not coordinated. The tribes were basically acting on their own initiative; they were autonomous and largely separated from one another.

After some time, however (fifty years), they formed what has been called the Israelite tribal confederacy. Our understanding of the nature of this confederacy and of the cause of its creation has been controversial. But gradually we are getting a clearer picture, a picture that is somewhat different from previous assumptions.

It now seems that the main reason for the confederation of the tribes was nothing less than the plan for a united takeover of the land from the Canaanites. These tribes had lived in the land for some time without gaining significant ground. Among themselves they had one thing in common, namely, that they were Yahweh worshippers. This Yahweh-worship brought them together at intertribal sanctuaries, especially that at Gilgal (others were at Tabor, Shechem, and later Shiloh). It was probably at Gilgal that the religious interdependence of the tribes prompted a religio-political confederacy with a strategy of a comprehensive attack on the whole land and its inhabitants.

Two sets of texts belong to this setting. The first is the report of the programmatic distribution of the land to the tribes by the lot-oracle in Joshua 13–19.[8] It reflects the divinely proclaimed right to a share of the total land for each of the tribes. The second can be found in Exod 23:23-33 and 34:11f. These two texts rest on a common tradition of a conquest-covenant ceremony, also from Gilgal, in which Yahweh said to the assembled, "I will hand over to you the inhabitants of the land, and you shall drive them out before you. You shall make no covenant [peace] with them and their gods" (Exod 23:31b+32).[9] Here we have the origin of the confed-

7. G. E. Mendenhall, *The Tenth Generation* (Baltimore: Johns Hopkins University Press, 1976), esp. 19f. On the whole, cf. now R. DeVaux, *The Early History of Israel* (Philadelphia: Westminster, 1978), esp. 153-290 and 488-682.

8. Cf. Götz Schmitt, *Frieden,* esp. 81f., and the work by Sh. Yeivin, *The Israelite Conquest of Canaan* (Istanbül: Nederlands Historisch-Archaeologisch Instituut, 1971).

9. Cf. E. Otto, *Das Mazzotfest in Gilgal,* BWANT 107 (Stuttgart: Kohlhammer, 1975), 298.

eration and, more importantly, the origin of the claims on the land and especially of Israel's relationship to its inhabitants: "You shall make no peace or covenant with the inhabitants of the land." The question that cannot be clearly answered is which of the two traditions in our texts reflects the original meaning of this prohibition:[10] the one which says, "Destroy them or drive them out!" or the one which says, "Subject them"? In either case, Israel was prepared to take control — either by the subjection or by the annihilation of the inhabitants (Deut 20:10-20). Moreover, Israel was forbidden to grant the Canaanites any arrangement which would guarantee their security and settled existence in their homeland.

The rest is history! In the plains of Jezreel, the Canaanites were attacked. In the country, many cities were conquered (part of the list of Joshua 12). Gibeon escaped the catastrophe. It became subservient through deception. However, even then many cities remained free and were subjugated only in David's time, which finally saw the fulfillment of the program. Judg 1:27f. reports their inability to drive out the Canaanites and, thus, indirectly confirms the existence of their claim to the land. Yahweh explains this inability: "I will not drive them out before you because you have not obeyed my command not to make any covenant with them" (cf. Judg 2:1-3). Their continued existence in the land is the result of Israel's disobedience of Yahweh's command to drive them out, and not of their own inability to do so!

Thus, the land of Canaan became the land of Israel. Those who had formerly lived in it in freedom now became extinct or — at best — "aliens," "sojourners," "foreigners" in their own land. Under the *pax Israel,* the self-determination of the survivors of those who had lived there came to an end once and for all.[11]

III. The Hermeneutical Problem

It should be clear by now that this fundamental strand in the Old Testament tradition raises a severe theological problem for us, a problem that far transcends the question

10. Cf. G. Schmitt, *Frieden,* 41-45.

11. This assessment is not invalidated by the fact that Palestine or parts of it were time and again under the dominion of the various foreign powers before and during Israel's time. To be sure, no one in Palestine was granted "freedom" and "self-determination" whenever such circumstances were prevalent. However, the foreign dominions, even when they included Israel, affected neither Israel's claim to be domestically in sole control of the land nor Israel's execution of that claim whenever possible. As far as the conquest itself is concerned, Israel did not intend to conquer Canaan in order to liberate the Canaanites from foreign powers. We are, therefore, concerned with the relationship of the nations existing side by side within the land, especially with Israel's own view of that relationship, regardless of the dependence/independence of the land on/from foreign powers.

of Israel's exclusive right to the land. Can we ignore the fact that the land was no vacant countryside, but that it was densely settled, populated, and cultivated? Is it enough to say that these documents must be understood in the context of their time, where the search for land by migrating nations implied the right to destroy other nations, by divine manifest destiny? Is it theologically sufficient for us that the texts repeatedly motivate the program of "no peace with the inhabitants of the land" and of their expulsion and annihilation, by polemicizing against the cultic abominations of the Canaanites (who at the time of the conquest did not even know Yahweh) or by warning about the acute danger of the Israelites being enticed to apostasy? Once again, is it an inescapable theological conclusion for us that the Canaanites had to be annihilated because they happened to have had a different religion and were not part of the chosen covenant people? This question is raised with respect to a theological strand of the Old Testament itself, and not only with respect to our theology today in contradistinction to an Old Testament notion that is supposedly justifiable within the historical context of its own time. But just when we concede that the texts must be accepted in the light of their own time and culture, what about the witness of the same Old Testament that the same God who destroyed the nations for Israel's sake is a blessing to the nations through Israel?

What about the one-sided perspective from which the case is presented to us from Israel's vantage point, exclusive of and against the life of those nations? Their voice is not heard while their very existence is at stake! Is it sentimental to ask what those Canaanites, who are said to have been dispossessed, expelled, annihilated, and/or subjected, would have said about their fate? We don't hear those voices anymore! Were they not there — the desperate cries of women and children being slaughtered, of men whose property was taken away and whose cities were burned to the ground? Do we not have to recognize two claims on the land, even as they may conflict — and this *because of* the God of Israel and of Jesus Christ, and not *in spite of* him?

This matter about the conflict of two claims on the land cannot be taken lightly, not even from the perspective of Old Testament theology. Technically speaking, in terms of Old Testament genres, this conflict between two claims reflects the legal genre of litigation or trial in which two opposing parties meet in court before a judge. The Old Testament is very aware of this setting, which was an essential part of Israel's own legal institutions. More importantly, the Old Testament — especially the prophetic tradition — knows of Yahweh as the judge who justly distributes justice. In the context both of Israel's legal institutions and of the understanding of Yahweh's just judgment, it would be inconceivable that someone who is attacked and deprived of freedom and life would not have the right to plead his or her case in court, and would not be heard and eventually rehabilitated and restored. Judges who listen to one side only are said to be corrupt! Even though they may be corrupt, and especially where they are in fact corrupt, Yahweh himself will see to it that equal justice, justice for all, is upheld. He hears the cries of the oppressed. Therefore, an interpretation of the conquest that ignores the cry of the Canaanites for help, a cry not represented by the Old Testament because it pleads only Israel's case, is in fundamental conflict with the Old Testament understanding of God as the just and merciful judge.

What about the sidestepping of this issue in our exegetical and hermeneutical literature, as it theologizes about "the holy war in ancient Israel," "the Yahweh wars of Israel," or the "divine warrior" tradition? G. von Rad said Israel's holy wars were basically defensive wars. I submit to you that the overwhelming evidence testifies to the contrary, at least as far as the conquest tradition is concerned.[12] G. E. Wright attempted to justify the tradition of "God the Warrior" by interpreting it as a metaphor, an image for God's mighty interference on behalf of his people — a spiritualized understanding, as it were.[13] However, our texts do not talk in images. They are not metaphors or allegories for spiritual realities. They refer precisely to what they described: historical events and people! It may be a bitter pill for us to swallow, but it is time that we face the facts!

Another point must be recognized. The Old Testament tradition sees the conquest of Canaan as intrinsically linked to the preceding exodus from Egypt and the wandering in the desert. The conquest cannot be seen in isolation. It is the final step in Israel's liberation from oppression and slavery in Egypt into the freedom of its own existence and history. With this, Israel proclaims a God who is involved in historical processes, liberating people from oppression by others. This proclamation is a fundamental theological insight — and a legitimate one at that — if God has anything to do with the real history of this world. In light of this insight Israel's claim to its own land in freedom from oppression and self-determination is legitimate.

The only problem is that exactly at the moment in which the Old Testament says that Yahweh liberated Israel from homelessness and oppression, it also says that, precisely for that purpose, Yahweh commanded Israel to annihilate, dispossess, and oppress others. Yahweh, by liberating Israel, destroyed others! The programmatic justification for Israel's liberation from oppression is turned into a programmatic justification for the oppression of free people by Israel, a fate that was explicitly much worse than anything Israel had suffered in Egypt.

This is a major problem in the Old Testament which affects our reading of the biblical understanding of the nature of God — and our understanding of God's presence in our history as well. For if we should assume that God justifies our oppression of others for the sake of our liberation from oppression by others, we have, at best, a particularistic and nationalistic God who is not the Savior of all;

12. Cf. F. Stoltz, *Jahwes und Israels Kriege,* ATANT 60 (Zürich: Theologischer Verlag Zürich, 1972).

13. G. E. Wright, *The Old Testament and Theology* (New York: Harper and Row, 1969), 121-50.

or, at most, we worship a God of oppression, a demon, which is the exact contrary of what the biblical tradition intends to say about God — even in the Old Testament.

It is at this point, the understanding of Yahweh-God, that the decision must be made concerning the Old Testament statements about Israel's relationship to her neighbors. We must ask whether the understanding of the "God of the conquest" and the "God of Israel" is the only understanding of God in the Old Testament. The answer is obviously no.

To be sure, in a statistical sense, the far larger portion of the Old Testament deals with Yahweh's relationship with Israel and Israelites — just as we spend most of our time preaching about the relationship of Jesus Christ with ourselves, our church, and our country. Just as we are, so these people were concerned with their own affairs.

However, the Old Testament without a doubt contains a significant variety of voices in which Yahweh-God is understood as the God of universal justice, righteousness, peace, and salvation. This picture is not systematized in the Old Testament. It reflects Israel's faith on the move throughout the centuries. Its diversity reflects the plurality of settings in which and of perspectives from which it was presented. This fact should be taken seriously as an expression of living theology and faith. A book along these lines is not yet written, and I will be rather sketchy with limited examples.

It is normally assumed that the prophets were the first to pronounce Yahweh's salvation for the world, and not only for Israel. Read Isa 2:1-4. The nations of the world shall come to Zion, and there they shall no longer learn war! "Salvation aims at the peace of the world, and not at an Israelite empire."[14] In Isa 49:6b Yahweh says, "I will give you [Israel] as a light to the nations, that my salvation may reach to the end of the earth" (cf. Isa 60:1-3; 66:23).

The prophets are not the only voices. There are the Psalms. Psalm 96 praises Yahweh, the creator of all the earth, for his salvation to the nations "from day to day," who rules and sustains the world with righteousness and truth (v. 13) and equity (v. 10). According to Psalm 82, Yahweh has become the sole God of the universe because he is the defender of the weak and afflicted — universally! Psalm 33 says "[Yahweh] loves righteousness and justice; the earth is full of the steadfast love of the LORD" (v. 5) and "A king is not saved by his great army; a warrior is not delivered by his great strength. The war horse is a vain hope for victory, and by its great might it cannot save" (vv. 16-17).

The study of words such as "justice," "righteousness," "fidelity," "truth," "peace," and "salvation" reveals time and again that Yahweh is not a destroyer of anyone outside or inside the land. He is the source and protector of life for all.

14. Author's translation from Th. C. Vriezen, *Theologie des Alten Testaments in Grundzügen* (Wageningen, Holland: H. Veeman and Zonen, 1956), 311f. (Eng. trans. = *An Outline of Old Testament Theology* [Oxford: Basil Blackwell, 1960], 360f.).

Furthermore, the novella about the prophet Jonah teaches that Yahweh is a universally merciful God, not only for Israel but also for Nineveh!

Finally, we must consider the Yahwistic history and theology. The Yahwist is especially important because his witness is preprophetic and reflects the time after the completion of the conquest. In this time, the Yahwist testifies to a God who is concerned with the blessing of all the nations (Gen 12:1-3). For him, "Yahweh" means blessing for humankind. Within this purpose, Israel has a role — not to rule, oppress, drive out, and/or annihilate but to represent that blessing for the nations. Thus, when writing his patriarchal story, he writes a sort of anti-story to the story of the conquest: peaceful coexistence with the inhabitants of the land as sojourners in Yahweh's land (Lev 25:23). Moreover, the people with whom the patriarchs come into contact are blessed: Abraham intercedes for Sodom(!) (Genesis 18) and for the ancestors of the Moabites and Ammonites (Gen 19:37f.); Lot (Edom!) is offered the choice of land by Abraham (Genesis 13); Abimelech the "Philistine" and Isaac make a "covenant" and coexist in "peace" (Gen 26:28-31); the Aramean/Syrian Laban says to Jacob, ". . . I have learned by divination that the LORD has blessed me because of you" (Gen 30:27); Jacob and Esau are reconciled (Gen 33:1f.); and Egypt is blessed for Joseph's sake (Gen 41:49, 57). The patriarchs in the land, and all with and around them, are blessed: Moab, Ammon, Edom, Aram, Philistia, Egypt, and the Hittites in Hebron (Genesis 23).[15]

CONCLUSION

Imagine a symposium of all the theological voices in the Old Testament on the question of Israel's relationship to its neighbors in the land, especially the original inhabitants and owners! It would take some time until they all would concentrate on this subject from their respective agendas and perspectives. But I am sure that a considerable number of those theologians would raise their eyebrows and tell the "holy war and get tough with the inhabitants of the land" party that this position is simply out of tune with what it means to say "Yahweh" — and ultimately "Israel." This position may have had a past, but it has no present and no future. If they could not persuade the war party, they would rather risk a schism than yield to this theology and ethos! Indeed, they would want to give "the Canaanites" their right to exist, their self-determination, and their dignity, because of Yahweh the God of all and because of Israel's identity as Yahweh's people.

What I mean with the simulation of such a symposium is that the Old Testament, with the plurality of its voices, is on its way, a restless way, to a better

15. Cf. H. W. Wolff, "Das Kerygma des Jahwisten," *EvT* 24 (1964): 73-98; reprinted in *Gesammelte Studien zum Alten Testament,* ThB 22 (München: Chr. Kaiser Verlag, 1964), 345-73.

understanding of God and his people in the world. Precisely because its voices are diverse, they call upon us to read them with discernment. The result cannot be in doubt, especially if we allow for the voice in the New Testament as well.

In this chapter I have been concerned with the preparation of a Christian witness to the presence of God today in the Arab-Jewish conflict. Such a preparation must come to grips with the Old Testament position on Israel's relationship to the original inhabitants of the land. The result is that the theology of annihilation and subjugation cannot be justified. It ignores the rights of the other nations, and ultimately God's truth itself.

With regard to the present situation, this means two things. First, just as the Old Testament is struggling for its theological identity among various options, so Israel today is confronted with the quest of its identity. And this is important for us because an Israel that would side with the call to be a light to the nations would be of utmost theological significance for Christianity. Second, as Christians we should have a witness! Its essence should be the refusal to be partisan. Positively speaking, it should support and affirm the rights of both parties, their dignity, their existence, and their self-determination, however difficult that road may be in *"Realpolitik."* In such a witness, we will learn how important for us the Old Testament is in its testimony about the presence of God in the real affairs of our world. Moreover, by affirming justice and peace equally for all, we will also encounter in those affairs of the world the footsteps of Jesus Christ, the Lord.

On the Theology of Psalm 19

*Dedicated to Klaus Koch**

I. Exegesis of Psalm 19[1]

In order to establish the basis for the interpretation of the psalm's theology, a closer look at its pertinent exegetical aspects is in order, especially in part A. I will begin with a translation which attempts to render the text as closely as possible.

A. Translation[2]

v. 1 To the choirmaster. A melody of David.
v. 2 The heaven[3] is reporting the glory of El,
and the work of his hands the firmament is announcing.
v. 3 Day to day outpours speech,
and night to night discloses knowledge.
v. 4 There is no speech, and there are no words.
Not being heard is their voice.

*Dedicated to Klaus Koch, who in 1952-53 introduced me to Old Testament exegesis and who has become a wonderful personal friend, on the occasion of his sixty-fifth birthday, in gratitude and with best wishes for his years to come.

1. It is unnecessary to recount in detail why the extant text of Psalm 19 is considered to consist of two parts — subsequently referred to as A and B. But their juxtaposition in one text unit continues to be in need of interpretation. It affects the theology of the psalm itself, and also its place in Old Testament theology. The following study will focus on the aspects primarily connected with these problems.

2. In this chapter the versification of Psalm 19 refers to the Masoretic text (MT). MT verses 2-15 correspond to *NRSV* 1-14.

3. For השמים, I am using the collective singular meaning.

v. 5a To all the earth goes forth their sound,
and to the end of the world their words.
v. 5b For the sun he set a tent in them,
v. 6 and it, like a bridegroom exiting his chamber,
it rejoices, like a warrior, to run a course.
v. 7 From the end of the heaven is its exit,
and its turn above their ends,
and nothing is hid from its heat.
v. 8 The law of Yahweh is complete, restoring vitality.
The testimony of Yahweh is reliable, making wise the simple.
v. 9 The precepts of Yahweh are right, gladdening the heart.
The order of Yahweh is pure, causing light for the eyes.
v. 10a The saying[4] of Yahweh is clean, standing forever.
v. 10b The judgments of Yahweh are truth, they are righteous altogether —
v. 11 the ones desirable more than gold and fine gold,
and sweeter than honey and overflowing honeycomb.
v. 12 Also your servant is warned by them.
In observing them is plenty of reward.
v. 13 Errors — who detects them?
From hidden ones acquit me.
v. 14 Also from insolent ones spare your servant:
they may not rule me.
Then I shall be complete and innocent of great crime.
v. 15 To favor be the sayings of my mouth,
and the whispering of my heart before you —
Yahweh, my rock and my redeemer.

B. Exegetical Observations

1. On Psalm 19, Part A (vv. 2-7)

a. Verse 2 opens with a basic statement about an ongoing activity of the heaven and the firmament. This activity is vocal and linguistic. It consists of actual speech and takes place simultaneously with the text's statement about it, i.e., at the present time of the text. The heaven's reporting connotes, in addition to the connotation of speech, the aspect of a past fact which happened before the current reporting about it. This connotation calls for attention because, if we were to translate מספרים as "describing," we might expect their report's object, the glory of El, to be the focus of a description of his present activity rather than of a report about his past activity. But

4. Reading אמרת for יראת, cf. v. 15aα + β.

while referring to a past activity, verse 2a at the same time presupposes the attribute of El's present glory. It praises El's present glory by reporting his past act.

The twofold temporal aspect expressed and presupposed in verse 2a is reinforced by verse 2b, the announcing by the firmament. Again, the announcing happens through speaking which is, just as the heaven's reporting, public, indeed, speaking in the cosmic public. In announcing "the work of his hands," the firmament refers to creation not as a presently ongoing work but as the original act by El, once and for all time. It announces the origin of the presently existing creation, and with it its own origin as well as that of the heaven's. Gunkel correctly spoke of the praise of "jener uranfänglichen Gottestat."[5] The distinction drawn by Westermann between reporting and describing praise is directly relevant for verse 2.[6]

The parallelism of verse 2a and 2b is obvious, as is its chiastic structure,[7] which is perhaps prompted by the emphasis on the object of the announcement, "the work of his hands." This work constitutes El's glory reported by the heaven. Although the text refers to his glory as reported by the heaven first (v. 2a), it presupposes that in the chronology of the events the recognition of El's work (v. 2b) precedes and prompts the recognition of his glory. However, the text's reference first to the glory points to the conceptual priority of the qualitative result for El's own attribute before and over the quantitative cause in El's work. It indicates that even in the praise of the work (v. 2b) it is El who is praised and not the work for its own sake, let alone for the sake of those praising. The hymn of heaven and firmament is *Gotteslob* in the praise of God's action, the praise of the work of "his hands," not action-praise regardless of whose action it is, and not at all *Naturbeschreibung*. In it, those praising divest themselves of the claim to glory just as they speak about themselves as El's work.

The nouns "heaven" and "firmament" are closely related cosmologically. "Firmament" is clearly specific, whereas "heaven" is more than strictly synonymous to "firmament." It is important that both speak neither about El's person nor to him. They speak about his glory and work. The text presupposes their knowledge of both El and his work. One may ask whether they have come to know El only through his work, or whether they can identify him as the God of this work because they have already known him. This question has logical, ontological, religio-historical, and speculative implications, and any answer may be inconclusive. However, the distinction between the two kinds of knowledge — see in verse 3b! — and the alternative possibilities for the origin of the knowledge of El-God suggest that the assumption of something like a primal form of natural revelation

5. H. Gunkel and J. Begrich, *Einleitung in die Psalmen,* 4th ed. (1933; reprint, Göttingen: Vandenhoeck & Ruprecht, 1984).

6. C. Westermann, *Praise and Lament in the Psalms,* trans. Keith Crim and Richard Soulen (Atlanta: John Knox Press, 1981).

7. Cf. Dahood, *Psalms I, 1–50,* AB (Garden City, NY: Doubleday, 1966), 121.

in the cosmos (God revealed to the cosmos through his work in the cosmos's self-reflection) cannot be unambiguously derived from this text. Nor is the subject of revelation at issue for this verse of the psalm, or its author or reader. Whatever the source of the psalm's knowledge of the cosmos's praise of God is, the text focuses on the fact of that praise, and not on the source of its own knowledge of El.

Together with the already-mentioned aspect of cosmic time, the references to "the heaven" and especially to "the firmament" point to the text's understanding of their particular position in the spatial order of creation. In addition to what is generally known, it presupposes that El is above the firmament,[8] that the sun, moon, and stars — not mentioned, but see verses 5b-7! — are underneath the firmament while belonging to its realm, and especially that the space of heaven and firmament is above and independent of the earth, which is mentioned in verse 5a. This location is the presupposition for the distinction in the text between the effect of their hymn extending to the earth below (vv. 4-5) and its function for the ears of El above. While the text does not speak of an immediate access of heaven and firmament to El, their presupposed spatial proximity to him is certainly operative in the text's statement of their praise. It is closer to him than the distance to him of the earth and its humans.

b. The statement in verse 2 is specifically unfolded in verse 3 whereby the grammatical elements in both verses correspond to each other. "Day" and "night" interpret "heaven" and "firmament"; "outpouring" and "disclosing" interpret "reporting" and "announcing"; and "speech" and "knowledge" interpret "the glory of El" and "the work of his hands." Whatever the switches in perspective are, the contextuality of both verses is beyond doubt.

The continuous (participle) reporting and announcing is said to happen through an ever new (iterative imperfect) outpouring (of speech) and disclosing (of knowledge), whereby the statement of each vocal-verbal activity in verse 3 apparently refers to both statements of the praise in verse 2. In the same way, the (outpouring of) speech and the (disclosing of) knowledge in verse 3 each refer to both the glory of God and the work of his hands in verse 2. The praising of verse 2 is in verse 3 said to happen through the instrument of speech which verbalizes the content of its knowledge. However, except for the formal expressions in verse 2, the specifics of that known content are not substantively explicated, at least not in verses 2-5a. This silence already points to verse 4.

The relationship of "day" and "night" to "the heaven" and "the firmament" is more complicated. While the praising by heaven and firmament is obviously *meant* to happen through the elements of day and night, day and night are not cosmologically identical with the heaven and the firmament. In effect, the text switches from a

8. Cf. Kraus: ". . . to God, who is enthroned above the heavens (cf. Ps. 29:9, 10)," *Psalms 1–59,* trans. H. C. Oswald (Minneapolis: Augsburg, 1988), 270; von Rad, *TDNT* 5, 502-9.

statement of praise by heaven and firmament to a statement of praise by day and night. In this regard, the meaning of the relationship of verses 2 and 3 is ambivalent. One may resort to the argument of artistic poetic freedom. But poetry need not create such tensions, neither generally nor in this case. The text could have continued after verse 2 with a reference to praise by the sun, the moon, and the stars, as in Job 38:7 and Ps 148:2-4. Instead of speculating about alternative explanations for the ambivalent relationship between verses 2 and 3 (such as both realms praising together or one realm delegating the praise to the other), we may ask why the text switches from one praising subject to the other. The answer is found in the switch from the spatial aspect of heaven and firmament to the temporal aspect of day and night. This switch is necessitated by the participially expressed praise in verse 2, and by the praise occurring between the temporal poles of original creation and of the present time of the text. The spatial aspect of heaven and firmament does not lend itself to expressing the temporal continuum of the continuous reporting and announcing of God's glory and work. This continuum, connoted in the verbal forms of verse 2, must be and is unfolded in the statement about the activities of day and night in verse 3. Compared with this need, the switch in perspective from one praising subject to a different one is relative, especially since day and night are also perceived as elements of creation. Basic for the relationship of verses 2 and 3, therefore, is the temporal aspect in the cosmic praise of El, compared to which the switch in the spatial aspects is not at issue. This temporal aspect is decisive precisely because the praise of El is perceived as the present and unending continuation of the cosmos's original reaction to its creation (cf. Job 38:7).

Why does the text refer to day and night rather than to month and year, or to the (sabbath) week? The reason for this choice probably lies not so much in the sense that they are the shortest units of cosmic time without which months and years could not exist, as in the traditional perception that day and night represent the original establishment of the division of darkness and light out of the darkness of chaos into their temporally ongoing spatial rotation — if it is thought of as rotation, a cosmic order that precedes the division into months and years, but can be seen as the basis of the sabbath week. They are the fundamental divisions of cosmic time (see vv. 6-7; also Genesis 1, where they precede even the creation of the firmament).

Finally, verse 3 also explicates something already implied in verse 2, namely, the addressee of the cosmic praise of El. Day and night address neither El, nor the earth, nor humans. Each addresses the successor of its own kind: Day to day and night to night.[9] These formulations refer to what is traditionally called the chain of transmission, an interpretation that must be qualified. One should expect the formulation "day to night and night to day," which would not change the poetic rhythm. If poetry has anything to do with the production of meaning, true or untrue meaning,

9. Kraus, *Psalms,* 270f.

which today is frequently emphasized in a hermeneutic which neo-romantically highlights the importance of poetry (over against prose), the formulation of verse 3 should be expected to be subject to the meaning of what it says, rather than to a poetic freedom that may say what it does not mean. The appreciable fact of poetic freedom again does not explain why the poetry expresses two separate chains of transmission — probably perceived to be simultaneously going on in parallel, instead of one chain in which day and night alternate — perhaps in rotation — as one would expect. This is to be compared with the visualization in verse 7. The extant visualization is certainly linear, not cyclic. But to assume an anti-cyclic tendency behind it seems to be beside the point. The Old Testament tradition knows about cyclic reality, and its often claimed denial of that reality should especially not be assumed for this text, particularly in the direct context of verses 5b-7. Also under such a tendency, our text would have sacrificed the empirically and inevitably realistic description of one rotating continuum combining both day and night to an ideologically based *status confessionis* against any heresy of cyclic motion. The grammatical objects in the text point to a different answer: Day belongs to day because each day outpours speech, whereas the disclosure of knowledge belongs to the night. The background of this idea would require a separate study. Suffice it to say that the Old Testament, especially in the wisdom tradition, is clearly aware of the correlation of knowledge and speech in the sense that knowledge precedes speech and, especially, that it is hidden whereas speech is in the open (cf., among others, Job 10:7; 34:35; 35:16; 38:2; 43:2; Ps 139:1-18; Prov 3:20; 8:8-9, 12; 10:14; 11:9; 12:23; 13:26; 14:7; 15:2, 7, 14; 17:27; 21:11; 26:10). Ps 19:3 seems to be a variation of this concept in the sense that the night discloses the knowledge in hiddenness whereas the day pours it out in speech. The reason for the day being mentioned first in verse 3 should be sought not only in the priority of the day over the night, but especially in the context's emphasis on the speaking of heaven and firmament in the cosmic public. The separate events of speech and knowledge account for the dominant criterion in the poetic formation of the text. Strictly speaking, the text refers to two separate chains of transmission: one of speech from day to day, and one of knowledge from night to night. Yet it presupposes that both chains are conceptually related in the correspondence of day and night and of the speech of knowledge and the knowledge of speech.

c. Verse 4a, taken literally, contradicts verses 2 and 3. That verse 4a is meant epistemologically rather than ontologically is stated in verse 4b, which interprets verse 4a. Although they happen, speech and words do not exist in the sense that their voice is not heard.

For Weiser, verse 4a refers to every *human* speech, whereas verse 4b refers to the voice of the cosmos which can be heard in every human speech:[10] "There is no language nor are there words in which their voice is not heard." Weiser's interpretation would amount to an understanding of verse 4b as a relative clause

10. *The Psalms,* trans. H. Hartwell, OTL (Philadelphia: Westminster, 1962), 198-99.

to 4a. However, בלי is in itself nothing more than a particle of negation, in our case negating נשׁמע. Its additional understanding as a relative clause particle, or the implication of a missing but assumable additional relative particle, is highly problematic. Yet the text is syntactically straightforward. Verses 4a and b represent two asyndetically juxtaposed (by contrast, cf. the conjunctions in vv. 2b, 3b, 5a) independent negated sentences, one nominal and the other verbal, in which the אין in the two nominal clauses corresponds to בלי נשמע, while the nouns אמר and דברים correspond to קולם. The "speech" and "words" are the language of "their" voice in verse 4b. Hence, just as verse 4b is expressed by the suffix on קולם, so verse 4a also refers to the vocal and linguistic activity of the heaven and not to "any language" of humans.

The problem of the relationship of verse 4a and 4b consists, then, in the *inexplicit* relationship between the seemingly contradictory statements of the pair, rather than in the assumption of a missing relative particle between them. Since one should assume that the (writer of the) text is aware of its self-contradiction, one must conclude that its form is intended, and interpret this intention. It is apparently prompted by the poetic deficit arising from the objectifying ontological statements in verses 2 and 3. It confirms this deficit by saying that such speech does not exist epistemologically, while precisely with the same argument defending the validity of the earlier statements against the objection that the cosmic praise cannot exist if it is not heard. The intellectual awareness operative in the text, the ability to analyze and synthesize arguments, to bring them into dialogue, and to express the results in condensed poetic form, is enviable.

The context, which speaks of the linguistic activity of the cosmos alone, supports our agreement with the traditional translation of verse 4. Last but not least, the hearing of their "voices" (v. 4b) would require human ears, not human speech and words. The Hebrew psychology was sophisticated enough to require the correct expression of the same mode of perception, and its articulations in poetry should not a priori be expected to be free of such requirements. As for poetry itself, verse 4 documents once again the control by the intellect over what is said, also in psychological matters, over and above the freedom of expression in the name of poetry.

The conclusion that the cosmic voice is *not* heard by humans points to another important consequence for the interpretation of verse 4. This lies in the fact that the text neither addresses nor presupposes the issue of revelation, which is greatly strained in this regard. If anything, verse 4 indeed stands in the way of such an assumption. Whatever enables humans to make objectifying statements such as in verses 2 and 3, verse 4 makes it clear that this human knowledge — the text's knowledge! — is not the result of revelation, in this case through audition, just as verses 2 and 3 say nothing about the cosmic praise being for human ears. The significance of this understanding will be discussed below.

d. Verse 5a returns to the statements of objective fact in verses 2 and 3. The plural suffixes in קום and מליהם as well as the nouns which they modify resume the introductory statement about the reporting praise of the heaven, the nouns themselves being synonyms, one for "voice" (v. 4b) and the other for "words" (v. 4a). Regardless of whether one sees in verses 2-5a an ad hoc literary creation or the result of successive accretions, this entire subunit is governed and tightly held together by the terminology for vocal/linguistic expression. In this terminology, a threefold conceptual preunderstanding is operative in which "voice" or "sound" (קול, v. 4b, or קו, v. 5a) is the acoustical carrier of the act of "speech" (אמר, vv. 3a, 4a) and its concomitant activity of "speaking" (expressed in variable aspects by the verbs: ספר piel, v. 2a; נגד hiph., v. 2b; נבע hiph., v. 3a; and חוה pa. Aram., v. 3b), which in turn consist of "words" (דברים, v. 4aβ, מלין Aram., v. 5aβ). This systemic usage of speech terminology shows once again how uniformly the text is focused on the fact of cosmic praise, not only in its surface but also conceptually.

The predicate in verse 5a introduces another specific aspect of this praise, this time not about its modalities but about its extent — yet not about its effect! (Cf. the difference in the statement in v. 7b.) Their sound goes forth to all the earth, and their words to the world's end. Instead of saying that both reach El above, the text says they reach down to make contact with the earth. This is scarcely because El is here perceived as dwelling on earth, e.g., in Jerusalem, and scarcely because the heaven intends for it to reach the earth. The text speaks about the sound (sing.), not about the heavens (plur.). *It* goes forth. Read together with verse 4, the meaning can only be: the sound and its words go forth to the whole earth despite the fact that they are not heard on earth. What, then, does verse 5a say? Scarcely that it is an "unintelligible," "strange sound" which, however, the singer hears, while it is "inaudible" for the rest of "the entire creation."[11] Why should the psalmist hear the sound and understand its words which go out to the entire earth and to its end? Does this text presuppose a special revelation for the psalmist which is inaccessible to everyone else? A simpler answer is preferable. The text, still focusing on the cosmic praise also, says nothing more than that this daily and nightly sound and its words are not confined to the space above the earth but also extend to the total space of the earth — even as it cannot be heard by anyone. It pervades heaven and earth, the universe. The question of whence the psalm, or the psalmist, has this knowledge is not at issue, neither in the text nor in its presuppositions.

e. Verses 5b-7 contain a reporting praise of God in verse 5b and a basically descriptive praise of the sun itself in verses 6-7.

Verse 5b refers, as does verse 2b, to an act of God at the moment of creation — however, this time to a specific act. The text distinguishes, as with שמים and רקיע in verse 2, between the tent and — presumably (בהם) — the heaven. Not reported is the creation of the sun. But the tent was created for the sun, not like the firmament of Genesis 1 which was created for the separation of the waters. The

11. Kraus, *Psalms 1–59,* 271f.

creation of the sun may or may not have been presupposed in an originally independent hymn about the sun, but it is not at issue in the extant text (vv. 5b-7). The extant text presupposes the existence of the sun, and reports the creation of the tent in preparation for what it has to say about the course of the sun itself.

The tent is "the night quarters,"[12] the resting place, of the sun. The imagery suggests that it is staked out at the ends of the heaven as they reach the ends of the earth (verse 7), and that it spans underneath the earth. It is clear that this imagery is meant to be metaphoric. The text cannot be unaware that the sun is too hot for a tent (v. 7b). The metaphoric usage of the tent corresponds to the similes in verse 6 in which the sun itself is compared to a bridegroom and to a warrior, a bridegroom leaving his chamber, חפה, a parallel but not a synonym for tent, and a warrior running a course. Indeed, the interpenetration of metaphor, simile, and substantive terminology and concepts shows poetic freedom at work in this part of the poem.

Why does the text only speak about God's creation of the tent? This creation is not an end in itself. The text says emphatically that it is "for the sun." The statement about its creation has no substantive significance beyond that purpose. The text's report about the setup of the sun's nightly resting place reflects the answer to questions such as: Where is the sun during the nighttime? Whence does its bridegroomlike appearance freshly emerge every morning and where does it go after its daylong, hot, warriorlike run? What is the nature and function of its nightly subterranean location? And especially, does that place still belong to a realm of chaos remaining after creation? Does the sun itself belong to creation during the day and to chaos during the night? In answer to this question, the sun in its daily run exits from and returns to its tent, not chaos. Its tent is itself "set up," created. This tent was only and specifically set up for the nightly rest of the sun. It is not chaotic but set up once and for all time as the permanent home in which the sun can rejuvenate itself for its ever new daily course. Just as its original setup is the chronological presupposition for its permanence, and just as its creation is the logical presupposition for its existence, so is it in both respects the presupposition for the sun's daily course from the creation of the world onward. Likewise verse 5b is the textual presupposition for what is said about the sun's own course in verses 6-7 (emphatic והוא in v. 6a). This course is not said to be the object of God's creation. It happens at the sun's own initiative. But it is possible only because it daily depends on what was and remains set up for it. The text's concept of original creation is the basis for the permanent subjective life and activity of the sun. At the same time the tent itself has no such subjective life.

The statement about the setup of the tent in its subservient function is apparently prompted by the conceptual presupposition behind the statement about the sun's course during the daytime in verses 6-7. Presupposed is that the sun moves in a daily circle in which it spatially and temporally passes through the two spheres

12. Kraus, *Psalms 1–59,* 272.

of day and night. Verses 6-7 speak only about the sun's course during the daytime. What they don't say but presuppose is that even its stay during the nighttime is part of the created order of the total daily movement of the sun. Specifically, even during the night it is not absorbed by the night nor is the night its home. Verse 5b makes explicit the presupposition that is operative in verses 6-7. While it could say, "he set up a tent in the night," it says, as if to shy away from such a statement, "he set up a tent in the heaven" — if that is what בהם means.

f. H. Schmidt[13] interprets the relationship between verses 2-5a and 5b-7 in the sense that the latter part represents the quoted content of the heaven's praise referred to formally in the former part. Verses 5b-7 are spoken by the stars, the "Gestirne." This assumption is the rationale for Schmidt's reference to the poet. The content is reported by the poet, and the poet has heard it, "vernommen." Of course, "blocked ears cannot understand them [the stars]; the poet's ears, however, can understand them very well."[14] Poetry as revelation to the poet! Schmidt's interpretation is intriguing but scarcely defensible. Apart from the fact that there is no explicit evidence for it, he must exempt the poet's ears from verse 4b's "it is not heard," and interpret this word to mean understanding, "verstehen," rather than hearing. However, that verse says שׁמע and not ידע or בין, which is correctly interpreted by Kraus in the sense that the speech and words of the heavenly powers are "inaudible."[15] The text gives no indication that the poet can understand what others can only hear. It does not speak about the reception of an understandable text. It emphasizes that nothing at all can be heard, let alone understood. We must conclude that verses 5b-7 represent the poet's own text, not his quotation of the cosmic praise.

There is reason for suspicion that verses 5b-7 might originally have been an independent hymn about the sun, or a fragment of such a hymn. They praise the sun itself rather than recount the praise of El by it as in verses 2-5a. Also, apart from the fact that nothing is said about the creation of the sun, verses 2-5a do not cosmologically describe the functions of heaven and firmament as do verses 6-7. Even if מעשׂה ידיו (sing.) in verse 2b includes the creation of the sun, this aspect is precisely what is not expressed in verses 5b-7. While an analogy can be seen between the extension of the cosmic sound and words to the earth in verse 5a and the extension of the sun's heat also — presumably — to the earth, this analogy is offset by the fact that the former cannot be heard while the latter is certainly seen and felt. Also, the reference to the creation of the tent is too exceptional to belong to the elements traditionally mentioned in the statements about creation. It is in this sense unique in the Old Testament. It is not reasonable exegetically to say that the tent belongs to the works implied in verse 2 which praise God for their creation.

13. H. Schmidt, *Die Psalmen,* HAT 15 (Tübingen: J. C. B. Mohr, 1934), 31.
14. H. Schmidt, *Psalmen,* 31.
15. *Psalms 1–59,* 272.

Nevertheless, the connections between verses 2-5a and 5b-7 in the extant text outweigh the differences. Terminologically, the lexemes יצא in verses 5aα and 6a and קצה in 5aβ and 7aα and b link the hymn about the sun proper directly with the end of the preceding hymn, particularly on the basis of the aspect of the "ends" of the earth. In addition, the sun as well as the sound and the words "go[es] forth." בהם in verse 5b refers to the heaven of the preceding text, which is also mentioned in verse 7a.

Conceptually, verses 2-5a and 5b-7 are united in both their spatial and temporal aspects and within the latter by distinguishing between the original beginning and its subsequent permanent daily order. They are also united concerning what happens in the cosmic realm outside and independently of the earth and concerning the reach of the respective activities down to the earth. Last but not least, they may be conceptually united in the sense that the sun's creation is not mentioned in verses 5b-7 because it is presumed to be implied in 2-5a, especially in 2a — even though this interpretation admittedly stretches the evidence to its limits if not beyond. Finally, the two parts of verses 2-7 are united in the theological concept of God's original creation of the cosmic realm and its own subsequent permanent reaction to that creation as an expression and manifestation of their complete conformity with it.

Without reading more into the extant text (vv. 2-7) than the evidence allows, one can conclude that in it, whether its composition is original or the result of the combination of two separate poems, the hymn about the sun represents an additional aspect to the report and description of the praise by heaven and firmament. This aspect was added under the common conceptual denominator of the psalm's — and psalmist's — own praise of God for the order of the cosmic realm which presently exists as a daily reality and which is based on the permanence of its original creation. And in praising God, the psalm — and psalmist — focuses on the cosmos's own reaction to its creation.

2. On Psalm 19, Part B (vv. 8-15)

a. Verses 8-15 contain the psalmist's offering of praise for Yahweh's Torah. Its structure consists of generic elements, each in specific form. Verses 8-11 contain a descriptive praise of Yahweh's Torah itself, and verses 12-15a, a personal prayer to Yahweh. The prayer includes a personal affirmation of the Torah's function, for the psalmist (v. 12), i.e., the function of Yahweh's judgments in it, a petition for forgiveness of "errors" (v. 13), and a petition for being spared from the influence of insolent ones (v. 14a).[16] The latter is concluded by a predictive self-affirmation of a positive verdict (v. 14b). And the whole prayer is concluded by another petition for Yahweh's pleased or favorable acceptance of the psalmist's words and whispered

16. *Atnach,* to be transposed to בי; Kraus, *Psalms 1–59,* 268.

thoughts (v. 15a), which is supported by an expression of personal confidence (v. 15b).[17]

This generic structure, however, is generated in its sequential order by a chain of conceptually related typical motifs which shift from aspect to aspect as the text progresses. The shifts in complementary aspects are possible on the basis of the text's conceptual unity in the psalmist's focus on his relationship to Yahweh.

b. The descriptive praise of the Torah (vv. 8-11) is clearly structured. According to Weiser, its sentences "exhibit the same structure. In each [of vv. 8-9] . . . first a characteristic peculiarity of the law is described and then a specific effect produced by the law. . . ."[18] The accumulation of attributes for the Torah itself, for its qualities and beneficial effects on the life and mind of the individual, leads to an expression of abundant comprehensiveness in complementary aspects. Verse 10 is different. While still speaking about Yahweh's Torah, it speaks about the Torah's own intrinsic qualities rather than about its effect. Nevertheless, verse 11, as it unfolds the reference to Yahweh's judgments in the Torah (v. 10b), still speaks about their effect, if only in terms of their subjective desirability rather than of their objective outcome. Verses 10-11 focus distributively on the plurality of aspects of Yahweh's judgments in the Torah, all of which are desirable. Moreover, it is their desirability which in verse 11 (an apposition to v. 10, which at the same time concludes vv. 8-11) is extolled twice (v. 11a and b), each according to degrees of comparison in which the compared inferior object (gold and honey), already most valuable by itself, is referred to a second time under the specific aspect of its superlative quality.

c. The implicit subjective aspect of the desirability of Yahweh's judgments provides the motif for the transition from the descriptive praise of the objective effect of the Torah to the psalmist's personal prayer in verse 12, in which he himself is the subject and the judgments of the Torah are the object. Indirectly, the personal aspect was already prepared in the statements about the Torah's effect on the life and mind of the individual. In his personal prayer, the psalmist, who devoutly calls himself "your servant," first of all explicitly applies himself (by גם with following *makkeph*) to what had been said before, and then turns the focus of the Torah's effect on him toward its warning function as an additional reason for the desirability of Yahweh's true and righteous judgments (v. 11). It is further enhanced by the outlook at the reward for their observation (v. 12b).

d. The direction introduced by the aspect of "warning" — against dangers — in verse 12a is developed in verses 13-14 under the aspect of increasingly severe kinds of dangers. To begin with, there is the problem of (conscious) acts that turn out to be "errors" committed unwittingly, שגיאות (v. 13a). They are "hidden." Not taken into account is the fact that the Torah may help to reveal an "error"

17. Cf. E. S. Gerstenberger, *Psalms, Part I with an Introduction to Cultic Poetry,* FOTL 14 (Grand Rapids: Eerdmans, 1988), 100, with some modifications.

18. *Psalms,* 201.

after it happened. The focus is on errors that are and remain hidden, which for this reason constitute an uncontrollable adverse influence on a person's life and must therefore be removed. Against such "errors," the Torah can warn, but it cannot prevent, let alone forgive, them. In light of such situations, the perspective continues to switch, now from the Torah to Yahweh himself, who alone can forgive the errors, if not prevent them. Yahweh declares the person free from them. The frequent English translation of נקה (piel) as "to acquit" is easy to misunderstand. It suggests that an accused is declared to be innocent. But the inadvertence of a committed error does not constitute a state of objective innocence which would be confirmed by Yahweh's acquittal. It constitutes a state of objective guilt concerning which Yahweh declares the guilty person free from its destructive consequences. Just as the erring person is not innocent, so is his/her liberation from the guilt of his/her error not an automatic event or process. It can only happen through a declaratory act of God through which the bond between the fact of guilt and its automatic destructive consequences is severed, so that the guilt loses its power to initiate those consequences because it has lost the right to do so. Moreover, because this severance can only happen through the interference of Yahweh, and because Yahweh is not understood as another automatically functioning mechanism for it, Yahweh's interference must be especially appealed to, i.e., petitioned. As traditional as the petition in verse 13b is, it is expressed because it is substantively necessary, not because it is traditional.

e. There is another, even greater danger about which the Torah can inform Yahweh's servant but from which only Yahweh himself is capable of sparing him (v. 14a): the influence of insolent ones, זדים, people consciously and grossly irreverent, as the לצים of Ps 1:1b. Again, being "spared" — now not from the consequences of errors but from a conscious attitude under the influence of insolent ones — requires more than the servant's own observance of the Torah. One might expect the Torah to be capable of protecting the servant from this obvious danger merely by instructing him to stay away from it. Indeed, instruct him it does. But our petition apparently presupposes a problem which the Torah, for all its consciousness-raising function, cannot solve; namely, to protect him from himself, from his own inability to be "spared" from the influence of insolent ones. This kind of protection requires Yahweh's personal companionship. It requires Yahweh's own ruling over him so that "they may not rule me" (v. 14b).

After verse 13, verse 14 reveals another astute awareness: the dynamics of the potential and actual influence of groups on individuals in the community's social psychology. This psychological influence is so strong that it affects the servant's psyche in a way that is beyond the Torah's instructing abilities. At the same time, verse 14 also reveals the strong dogma of the separation of the individual servant from the insolent ones. This separative "sparing," חשך, is considered so important that no one less than Yahweh himself must function as a societal force protecting each of his servants from, in this case, the luring attraction of the insolent ones. Again, the servant's petition for Yahweh to spare him is more than perfunctory. It is grounded in the servant's own interest, and in Yahweh's own interest as well. "Then," and only then, "I shall be" both "complete and innocent of great crime" (v. 14b).

The word פשׁע connotes the consciousness of one's act or behavior, just as the servant is conscious of the nature of the insolent ones. This connotation is the opposite of the unwitting errors of verse 13a. It is a heavier "sin" and, therefore — expressed pleonastically — a "great crime." One may say that insolence is the crime, while its conscious nature in this text qualifies it as a great crime. The text distinguishes between different kinds of sin which have different degrees of severity, and its movement from the less to the more severe sins reflects its hamartiological system.

f. The transition in the text from the objective description of the qualities of Yahweh's Torah to the personal prayer needs attention. It is not self-explanatory, even though the combination of the two elements is traditional. It seems that the text turns to personal prayer and the devout expression "your servant" at the moment in which the enjoyable function of the Torah no longer enhances the normal preconditions of a person. Rather, the judgments of the Torah and ultimately Yahweh's own immediate coming forth are necessary to save the servant from life's dark sides and dangers. A psychology may account for the turn to personal prayer in which the human condition is seen not only in its teachability but also in depths beyond the reach of beneficial instruction. When it comes to these spheres, Yahweh's personal help beyond its mediation through instruction is necessary. One of the important problems in Old Testament studies not sufficiently pursued consists in the theological reason for many expressions of so-called personal piety as personal encounter with God.

The words "complete" and "innocent" in verse 14b are synthetically juxtaposed. They are not synonymous. איתם means "I am complete" or "perfect," not "blameless" as, e.g., in the *NRSV,* which expresses the negation of something negative, as with the word "innocent." The text, by combining the affirmation of the positive notion "perfect" with the negation of the negative notion of guilt in "innocent," takes care that each aspect protects the other from a potential deficit.

The particle אז, "then," placed emphatically, not only refers to the consequence of the servant being spared. It also reveals his presupposed aspiration that stands behind his petition to be spared and ultimately behind his total praise of Yahweh in verses 8-14; namely, to be complete and innocent. Just as "plenty of reward" in verse 12b reveals the aspiration of a positive end for his life due to his observance of the warning function of the Torah's judgments, so, in petitioning to be free from the consequences of errors and to be spared from being ruled by insolent ones, he aspires to become ultimately and personally complete and innocent. One cannot avoid saying that the decisive motive in both the praise of Yahweh's Torah and the prayer for Yahweh's help is Yahweh's servant's interest in reward, completeness, and innocence.

To this extent, the servant petitions that the expressions of his mouth and heart may be favorable before Yahweh on whom he relies as his rock and redeemer (v. 15). The word רצון denotes "favor," "delight," and/or "pleasing," whereas the *NRSV*'s translation as "acceptance" is a connotation of only the first meaning. The petition asks that Yahweh be favorably disposed to the prayer, and therefore accept it, and not that he accept it whether he is pleased or not. But it also presupposes the awareness that the pleased acceptance of these "sayings" cannot be expected to be automatic, on the basis of the magic of its presentation or content. The preceding prayer, indeed the entire psalm, depends on whether or not Yahweh will receive it with favor. Verse 15 is a prayerful petition about the psalm. The psalm lives from the awareness that the judgment on its validity does not rest on the psalmist's own judgment of its content, composition, and/or poetry, not even on the depth of his self-examination. That judgment must be left open and surrendered to the sole prerogative of Yahweh's own opinion and decision. Thus, more than the petition for Yahweh's personal help in the dangerous spheres of his life, the servant's total prayer is ultimately in need of Yahweh's personal saving decision. In the end, he can present his petition with confidence in the hope of its favorable reception because of one thing of which his tradition has assured him: Yahweh is his rock and redeemer. This he can affirm, but nothing more.

II. Theology of Psalm 19

A. Problem of the Theology

The problem of the theology of the psalm as a whole lies in the combination of its two parts, A and B. This combination is particularly difficult to interpret because the reasons for it are infratextual, not explicit, and because any intratextual signals of the correspondence between the two parts are outweighed by signals of their mutual distance. The exegetical tradition in which verses (1)2-7 and 8-15 are presented as two separate psalms[19] accounts for their essentially different nature. But it does so at the expense of their combination in the extant text, which is a hermeneutical fact in its own right. The reasons for this combination cannot be considered accidental.[20] This interpretation is also valuable for an additional reason. Even if we had to interpret two separate psalms, however closely juxtaposed or distantly placed in the Psalter or in the Old Testament, the problem of their relationship would still exist, certainly in light of their significance within Old

19. E.g., Kraus, *Psalms 1–59,* 268f.; H. Schmidt, *Psalmen,* 30-31, 32-33; Weiser, *Psalms,* 197-200, 200-204.

20. So, e.g., Kraus, *Psalms 1–59,* 269; Sabourin, *The Psalms: Their Origin and Meaning,* vol. 1 (New York: Alba House, 1969), 179; Gerstenberger, *Psalms,* 101-3.

Testament theology. In that light, the difference between their direct combination and their separateness is relative. Moreover, the fact of their direct combination in Psalm 19 only highlights the need for the interpretation of their relationship.

B. Significance of Psalm 19B

It is generally recognized that the psalm as a whole cannot be older than the concept of the Torah in 19B. Torah is "the exclusive, written revelation of the will of God that is read publicly (Deut 31:9-11) and privately (Josh 1:7; Ps 1:2)."[21] It is most probably the Pentateuch available and read after the time of Ezra. Of particular importance is the form-critical aspect of the psalm's genre and setting. Gerstenberger has defined it as a personal prayer which "was used . . . in a liturgical framework of community worship," and which combines "two different strands of theological tradition. As a pattern of ritual prayer, such combination of hymn and petition is widespread and very old."[22]

C. Reason(s) for the Combination of 19A and 19B

Gerstenberger's interpretation points out that the combination of 19A and B is not the result of an isolated decision by an individual poet. Rather, its literary combination is the result of the influence of a tradition of a pattern of communal ritual prayer, also of the individual, from a traditional setting in which stands the congregation of the Second Temple. The fact that this tradition is already found in the ancient Near East is particularly important. It shows that the combination of cosmic aspect with personal prayer is not unique to ancient Israel. In this light, the combination of 19A and B cannot be said to have been forged ad hoc by an individual poet's uniquely new theological perspective, because its theological perspective was already presupposed in the transmission and adaptation of the traditional combination. Of course, unless we assume that, as long as theological perspectives and their conceptualities, changing in the process of transmissions, are automatically authorized by the tradition and by the transmitting religious communities, they are not worth discussing, the explanation of the reasons for their combination is just as necessary for any stage in the tradition and transmission history of this combination as the explanation of their specific perspectives.

The conclusion that the reasons for the combination of 19A and B are already found in its antecedent tradition history shows that the substantive aspects from that tradition cannot be ignored, and that the psalm's interpretation on the sole

21. Kraus, *Psalms 1–59,* 273.
22. *Psalms,* 102.

ground of the extant psalm's setting and the identifiable concerns in that setting is too restrictive. We also must interpret the hermeneutic of the extant text in light of the contribution which its traditional pattern makes to it.

D. Psalm 19B — A Yahweh Psalm

It is clear that 19B is a Yahweh Psalm. Self-evidently it could have functioned in the Second Temple congregation but scarcely outside Israel. It is also clear that 19A, through its combination with B, also functions as a Yahweh hymn.[23] It is not at all self-evident that the text of 19A can, taken separately, be considered a Yahweh Psalm. Its content is unique in the Old Testament, and where it has analogies, such as in the phenomenology of Psalm 29, it points together with them more to an extra-Israelite origin than to a genuinely Israelite origin, conceptually and textually. Sabourin's assumption that "it is quite possible . . . that Psalm 19 was composed as one poem by the same author,"[24] and his argument in support of it, stands on weak ground. Particularly foreign is the usage of the word "El" in verse 2a. Psalm 19A is an El hymn. Given the facts that "El" in an independent psalm about the cosmos and its creation could scarcely be presumed self-evidently to refer to Yahweh, and that traditionally "El" was at least as much the personal name of a deity as it was a generic title for deity, one must ask why a late Israelite poet, in order to avoid ambiguity if not outright syncretistic implications, would not have preferred to use in his own setting the word יהוה as in Psalms 8 and 29, or at least אלהים for יהוה as in Ps 82:1 or Genesis 1 (Torah!), especially in the context of 19B.

Despite its traditionally patterned function, the text of 19A in its postexilic setting must have required an *e silentio* preunderstanding shared by the individual and the congregation that the *spoken* word "El" must be *understood* with discernment, not as referring to the foreign deity but to Israel's God whose name is Yahweh. To be sure, this hermeneutical discernment was necessary at any rate since the extant text uses "El" regardless of whether the word was adopted from an older text or chosen ad hoc, of which the former is easier to assume.

E. Interpreting the Meaning of the Combination of 19A and B

The combination of 19A and B is substantively interpreted in different ways. Sabourin, referring to Tourney, mentions the Israelite sage's easy transition from

23. See Gerstenberger, *Psalms,* 101: "only through the accretion of vv. 8-15 did the psalm [i.e., vv. 2-7] become a Yahweh hymn."

24. *Psalms,* 179.

the aspect of the physical world to that of the moral world.[25] Quoting Ringgren, he refers to "actually two manifestations of one and the same divine will" in God's handiwork and God's law.[26] Yet, either motif is too remote and especially too general for explaining the specific connection of the cosmos' praise of God with the psalmist's particular praise of God. The conceptual presuppositions which are exegetically discernible do not support these assumptions.

While separating 19A and B on the ground of the presumed irreconcilable difference between visualization ("Anschauung") and mere thought ("nur Gedanke"), H. Schmidt saw in the connection of 19A and B an essential stage in the history of Israel's religion in which the aspects of nature and the law ("Gesetz") were juxtaposed on the basis of the common denominator of the mysteriously lively ("das geheimnisvoll Legendige")[27] which reveals the glory of God in both. But as much as this common denominator may appear to be the motif in Psalm 19 for combining A and B, it was not — so one must understand Schmidt — sufficient to prevent the tension between these two vehicles of revelation or ways to experience God. Hence, the intellectual history of Israel is determined by the alternation between their amalgamation and their being set in contrast and — so one must add — not only by that alternation but also by the tension between *Anschauung* and *Gedanke*. However the relationship between nature and law is interpreted, Schmidt's assumption of the mysteriously lively as the common denominator is, once again, too general a background for the explanation of the combination of 19A and B. As much as it is a mystery, the text speaks about the clarity of the cosmos's praise of God and the clarity of the Torah. Moreover, unlike Psalm 8, it gives no indication that the psalmist's subjective experience of the revelatory mystery plays a role in what is said.

For Weiser, the two parts were linked together by "the idea of the divine order constituting the[ir] spiritual bond."[28] This divine order is an "idea," and the "spiritual bond" linking the two parts (for Weiser, not of the order, but of the text) together is apparently the qualified mode of the idea. The compositional idea of the text is a human idea which is, however, spiritual. It is the spiritual perception of the poet. The spiritual quality of the poet's idea lies in the fact that "the grandeur of Nature reveals to him . . . the majesty of its Creator."[29] Furthermore, "our poet holds a view on these matters which is entirely his own."[30] It lies likewise in the fact that "for the poet the law is the point at which an encounter takes place with the living God who reveals himself in the law. . . ."[31] It is this revelatory inspiration

25. *Psalms,* 179.
26. *Psalms,* 179.
27. *Psalmen,* 33.
28. *Psalms,* 201.
29. *Psalms,* 198.
30. *Psalms,* 198.
31. *Psalms,* 202.

that prompts this poet to discern the common denominator, the same divine order in both nature and law, "this harmonious, uniform vision, achieved by a comprehension of Nature based on faith"[32] as well as in "the characteristic peculiarities attributed to the law."[33] It prompts him to link the two parts together.

Weiser's references to revelation, inspiration, and the poet's role in them are scarcely at issue in the text. At any rate, they do not explain the peculiarity of this composition because they are true for all psalms. Furthermore, even if the aspect of divine order plays a role in the linkage of the two parts, we would still have to explain their relationship, because the "order" of the "law" is not the "order" of the "cosmos." H. Schmidt's understanding of their tension is very different from Weiser's understanding of their harmony in the poet's vision. Weiser would have had to explain the function of each part in relation to the other. For this explanation, even of the text's traditional pattern, the reference to a common denominator such as a divine world order is important. But at best it points to the formal aspect of the ancient worldview, which is by no means the poet's unique property. Yet it does not explain why and how cosmos and law are related in that worldview.

The aspect of the presupposition for the substantive relationship of 19A and B is directly addressed by Kraus. After criticizing the frequent exegetical interpretation of God's revelations through both nature and law (interpretations that resonate Kant's "star-studded sky above me" and "the moral law within me"), Kraus says part B emphasizes that which part A cannot achieve: ". . . we do not recognize God from the works of creation. Indeed, a powerful message comes our way, but we do not understand it. The glossolalian ciphers of transmission in the heart of nature, which praise and teach the Creator, no one can perceive. The cosmos celebrates God's כבוד, but it does not teach his will. . . . In the תורה — there God is perceivable, that is where we recognize who God is. That is where the manifestation of God's will readies us. It effects what nature is not able to effect: it leads us as the עבד־יהוה. . . ."[34]

According to Kraus, Psalm 19A stands in its own right as a testimony to the cosmos's own praise of God. But since humans cannot hear and understand that hymn, it cannot teach them the will of God. In view of this deficit, 19B was added. Psalm 19B supplements the decisive aspect missing in 19A. The psalmist considers 19A not with regard to what it says — at least not in verses 2-3 and 5-7, but once again with regard to whether or not humans can learn and recognize from the cosmos the will of Yahweh. With respect to this decisive question put before 19A — whether it addresses this question itself or not — the answer must be no. Only the Torah teaches, reveals, and makes known that will to humans. The psalm is, therefore, composed with reference to the question of which of the two creations

32. *Psalms,* 200.
33. *Psalms,* 202.
34. Kraus, *Psalms 1–59,* 275f.

reveals the will of Yahweh to humans. It is the language of the law, not the language of nature, which reveals that will. Specifically, Psalm 19 is composed from a perspective antithetical to the assumption present in the tradition behind 19A that the cosmos, the work of creation, can and does teach humans the will of God. According to this interpretation, Psalm 19 should be understood as a late Israelite critical distantiation from a concept in the history of religion according to which the deity reveals itself through nature, a distantiation prompted by the finalized concept of Yahweh's revelation exclusively through his law. We need not emphasize that this view of the religio-historical development is the direct opposite of the one expressed by Schmidt.

Kraus's interpretation is scarcely sustainable. While speaking of the transmission, immanent in nature, of the knowledge of the Creator and his work, it does not explain why 19A focuses on the cosmos rather than on any other part of nature, especially on earth. Furthermore, Israel's environment, and the Old Testament as well, knows that "God's language is read in nature,"[35] even in the cosmos (see Psalms 8; 29; etc.). Kraus's interpretation of the relationship of 19A and B would at least have to document that the psalm represents a critical rejection of a widespread basic notion within Israel's own theological tradition history according to which Yahweh is well recognized in his works of nature as well as in his works of history. Last but not least, we must again ask: Is 19A concerned with the issue of human understanding at all? Moreover, from the perspective of 19B, is 19A handled with reference to that issue? Or is it, while *e silentio* presuming such understanding as a matter of fact, concerned with something different, which is also the reason for its combination with 19B? Gerstenberger's interpretation shows nothing of an adversative function for 19B over against 19A and comes closer to the point: the outlook of 19A is "very objective, distant, and meditative. The only visible *interest* [my emphasis] is to describe the marvellous skies and celestial bodies, to let them sing — in a mysterious, superhuman way — the glories of El and witness to the all-penetrating power of the sun."[36]

F. The Relationship of 19A and B

How then are we to interpret the relationship of 19A and B? Since the text does not address this question, we certainly must reconstruct its presuppositions. Quite generally, such reconstructions, while always practiced, are often insufficiently controlled methodologically. Whatever they end up being, these reconstructions are sometimes even justified by the maxim of the so-called multivalency or polysemic nature of texts — a modern but by no means new trend. Under this disguise,

35. Sabourin, *Psalms,* referring to Jirku, 179.
36. Gerstenberger, *Psalms,* 101.

a text can be said to say or to presuppose or to mean whatever the exegete's eye beholds in it, and more. Yet, distantiation and discernment are possible. In our case, some interpretations, such as the ideas of revelation, the mysteriously lively, the divine will, the complementarity of the physical and the moral, the epistemological complementarity or contrariness of nature and law, or the poet's spirituality, infer presuppositions which may or may not be in the background this text shares with all or many texts, but which are not operative in it in the sense that they do not directly constitute those aspects that generate the concept of this individual text. Or these interpretations rest on observations of elements in the text, such as morphological data or a particular verse like verse 4, which are taken for the text in its entirety. It seems necessary to protect the conceptual reconstruction from over-interpretation by restricting it to, and having it controlled by, what the text expresses as a unit — in our case, by what appears to be the focus of what is said in each of the two parts of Psalm 19.

G. The Conceptual Basis of 19A and B

Psalm 19A speaks about the daily and nightly praise of the glory and work of El by the heaven and the firmament and about the daily run of the sun out of and back into its tent, which El has set up for it in the heaven. All these subjects are united under the presupposed conceptuality of the cosmic realm. This part focuses on God's daily praise specifically by the cosmic realm above and outside the earth. Specific aspects, such as the relationships of heaven, firmament, and sun; of the original moment of creation and its permanent time; of day and night; of sun and tent; of the modes of expression and their continuous happening, etc., are clearly subordinate to the main focus. Also subordinate to it are the statements that although their hymn reaches the earth, it is not heard there. These statements show especially that the text is interested in stating the objective fact of the cosmic praise of the creator-God, despite the human inability to hear it which makes it seem as if this praise does not exist. In other words, the text is interested in stating this praise as an objective fact, and not that it is known, or understood, or revealed! The text emphasizes the praise of God itself, not the revealed knowledge of it. Such an emphasis on revealed knowledge would then either be complemented or contradicted by the statement about the knowledge of the revealed Torah! Psalm 19A reveals a distinct emphasis on the independence of the cosmos from the earth, and of its own praise from that of humans. It speaks about the cosmos's own relationship to God in its daily response of praise for its creation; and while this relationship is not immediate, i.e., there is no direct address, it is separate from that of humans. It has its own living existence.

Psalm 19B presents the praise of Yahweh's Torah and its effect on human life, as well as an individual's prayer to Yahweh affirming the Torah's warning function and petitioning for Yahweh's own help in dangers from which not even the Torah can shield Yahweh's servant. Verse 15 concludes 19B, and in the context the whole psalm, with a petition that Yahweh be favorable to the servant's sayings and with an affirmation of personal confidence in Yahweh. The conceptuality of 19B, to which various aspects are complementarily subordinate, focuses on the completeness and innocence of the life of Yahweh's servant (v. 14b), not coincidentally stated at the end, for which Yahweh's Torah is generally completely sufficient while Yahweh's personal protection of the servant is specifically petitioned. Yahweh's Torah is presumed to be existing. The event of its gift, or creation, or revelation is neither reported nor at issue. At issue is the completeness of Yahweh's guidance and protection for the completeness of human life, especially the life of the individual servants of Yahweh. Yahweh's guidance through both his Torah and his personal intervention is the condition for the completeness of human life, and for that reason is praised.

If there is a common conceptual denominator for the combination of 19A and B, it is, besides the fact of praise, the aspect of completeness. Just as the life of the cosmos is complete before God its creator in both its order and its response to that order, so the life of humans on earth, especially of Yahweh's servants, is expected to be complete through the ongoing influence of the Torah and of Yahweh's own protective interference. The praise of the cosmos is already complete because it represents the permanent state of its undisturbed creation. By contrast, life on earth is incomplete, endangered, and in need of complete instruction, attention, and support to effect its completion. This incompleteness is constant. Its support must, therefore, be a constantly present companion rather than, as in the case of the cosmos's original creation, a perfect fact in no need of further instruction and support.

It is probably not coincidental that the aspect of completeness appears as the common denominator for 19A and B. The deeper reason for it may be seen in the concept of creation itself referred to in A, which mirrors the glory of El. This concept signifies the complete order out of chaos, which also includes the earth and human life. It may well be that the ultimate interest behind 19B, including the function of Yahweh's Torah, lies in the criteria for providing the conformity of human life to the order of creation.

All other aspects in 19A and B are more disparate than complementary. Their disparity reveals something about the nature of their relationship. It is attributable to the separate realms of the cosmos and of human life on earth, and to the different conditions under which the cosmos and humans exist in relation to God-Yahweh. Hence, rather than looking for signs of complementarity, we should perceive the disparity of 19A and B as conceptually genuine. Each party, the cosmos and humans, has its own relationship to God-Yahweh, which is predicated by its own distinct conditions, and each party praises God for its own different reasons. This becomes evident above all else in the case of Yahweh's Torah: Humans need it, the cosmos does not. The cosmos's praise of God for its existence is based on its creation, not on the gift of the Torah. Humans praise Yahweh for their guidance by means of the Torah and by Yahweh himself, apart from the question of whether or not the cosmos teaches them something as well.

This finding indicates that Psalm 19 does not intend to teach two foundations of morality for humans as expressed by Kant. It expresses the human knowledge about the cosmos's own ethos, but says neither that the cosmic order is the prototype of human life nor that it actually teaches humans. In this sense, Kraus's criticism is justified.[37] He is also correct in seeing the importance of the Torah's function for the servant's life. However, he misses the point when saying that the Torah supplants the cosmos because it is *intelligible* whereas the cosmos is not, and when deducing from this exegesis the general idea that the Torah achieves what nature cannot.[38] In fact, part A's statements about the cosmic praise of the work of El's hands and his setting up of the tent show that the knowledge of this praise teaches the psalmist at least that the cosmos was created by God. In this sense, one could say that even according to this text, its language is understandable although its words cannot be heard. However that may be, Psalm 19, rather than being combined under the question of what the vehicle is of revelation for human lives — namely, the Torah only or both cosmos and the Torah — seems to be conceptualized in the sense that its two parts are juxtaposed under the aspects of genuinely distinct existential conditions in which the cosmos and God on the one hand and Yahweh and his servants on the other hand are related — regardless of what one reveals for the other.

The separate foci, which account for the juxtaposition of the two distinct aspects, have a deficit. They have prevented an expression, or at least a transparency, of what each aspect means for the other. This deficit should be admitted, and the interpretation from this point on should not attempt to extrapolate harmonizing consequences from the psalm. Instead, it should place the psalm into the context of the entire Old Testament and attempt to evaluate what its two foci and their juxtaposition mean in that context.

H. General Aspects

Under this objective, the following general aspects, if only preliminary, seem to be pertinent.

1. In referring to God's original creation and to the creation's, including the cosmos's, response, our text is not alone in the Old Testament. It is profoundly imbedded in the tradition and theology of the available, written Torah, and also in the cultic traditions of the prayers, especially the petitions of the individual.

37. Kraus, *Psalms 1–59,* 275f.

38. Kraus, *Psalms 1–59,* 275.

2. Many Old Testament texts make it clear that Israel, together with its environment, knows about the cosmos and its life, not only from the Torah but also from the observation of the natural which has even flowed into the Torah. In this respect, Israel shares with its environment the common knowledge of God's creation of the world, and of the knowledge and the praise of God.

3. The Old Testament does not confirm the exegetical assumption that Yahweh-worshippers understand the relationship of God and world only via their instruction through the Torah, especially if "Torah" means the Pentateuch. They are instructed not only about nature but also about their lives, by history and by nature and/or creation as well, although their knowledge of God's name, Yahweh, is predicated on the linguistic tradition of the disclosure of that name to Israel. An extrapolation from Psalm 19A saying that nature would not reveal the work of God would encounter significant objections from much of the Old Testament and its worldview. It would also mean that, in 19A itself, the cosmic nature is said by the psalm to know about its creation and its order, whereas the very text that makes this statement would deny the same knowledge, or participation in the cosmos's own knowledge, by humans.

4. In light of the entire Old Testament, the separateness of each party's praise for its own reasons, in 19A and B, cannot be taken as programmatic. While important in its own right, it is contingent upon — so to say — the existential focus of each party. This separateness is transcended in the Old Testament, even in the Torah, by the testimony that Israel joins the cosmos in its praise of God's creation just as our psalm joins the cosmos's praise. It is also transcended by the testimony that the cosmos or nature in various ways witnesses to and is in support of the Torah — at least in its wider sense (see, e.g., Deut 4:32; 28:23-24; Job 20:27; Pss 50:6; 89:6 [*NRSV* 89:5]; 109:89; Jer 2:12). The latter aspect would have to be more extensively considered in light of the relationship between creation and Torah in Israel's theological tradition history.

5. The Torah is perfect, except for its limitations appearing in 19B. It is the salvific, life-giving gift of Yahweh enlightening the mind, enjoyable, and desirable. It is not a burden. What is not addressed in these formal qualifications is the great variety of its contents and concepts. The goodness of all these contents and concepts is presupposed. Yet, if one compares some of those substantive aspects, e.g., the particular relationship between Israel and the nations, on the basis of Israel's election as a manifestation of the justice and righteousness of the universal God-Yahweh, one will find in the Old Testament itself voices which advocate justice and righteousness equally for all as the criterion for the truth of the universality of Yahweh, rather than the relationship of Yahweh and his people Israel as the criterion for Yahweh's justice and righteousness. Such a problem is not recognized in Psalm 19B, but it exists. Its existence constitutes a tension between the formal claims to the perfection of the Torah and the substantive notion that the universal deity of Yahweh is based on his universally equal justice, rather than on the truth of his justice being based on his relationship to his people.

6. Finally, it is interesting that, in the tradition of the exegetical discussion, verses 12b and 15b have scarcely received any penetrating interpretation. One must wonder why this is the case. Weiser acknowledges these passages,[39] but then one page later he circumscribes reservations from prophetic and New Testament perspectives against "the limits which are set to this type of godliness" and the "uncertainties of the law."[40] Kraus, whose descriptions of the self-understanding of the Torah are paradigmatic, refers to verse 12b with the short remark that "such a life, led by the direction of God, knows that it is richly rewarded," and is altogether silent about verse 14b.[41] Such an interpretation appears both as if the understanding of the servant's completeness and innocence were in no need of exegesis, and further as if in the horizon of the Old Testament — totally apart from considerations influenced by the New Testament — the problem would not exist of whether this consequence of completeness and innocence ("then"), resulting from being spared by God and observing the law, is based on and guaranteed by these conditions or whether it, while also being a legitimate outgrowth from such conditions, cannot be and is not regarded as the only way of Yahweh even with the best of his servants. What, in terms of Old Testament theology, would it mean if the expressed consequence, the "then," also brings to light the servant's ultimate intention — to be complete and innocent? Would or could it mean that the psalmist's servanthood for Yahweh is to be in the service of his own perfection rather than, however perfect, in the service of Yahweh? Both the intentionality of the aspired consequence and its exclusivistic possibility if not actually doctrinal nature are not made irrelevant. Rather they are relativized and even contradicted by alternative voices from various parts of the Old Testament.

Postscript

In his "Überlegungen zur Theologie des 19 Psalms,"[42] A. Meinhold considers what he takes to be the four parts of the psalm (verses 2-5a, 5b-7, 8-11, 12-15) as conceptually united by the aspect of the happening of the word of God or the happening of God as word ("Das Wortgeschehen Gottes," 119, 134). This happening is said to take place as speech about God ("Rede von Gott"), as God's own speech ("Rede Gottes"), and as speech to God ("Rede zu Gott"). And it has in Psalm 19 received its two dimensions, the cosmic and the personal, through the combination of the psalm's two parts by the redactors.[43]

39. *Psalms,* 203.
40. *Psalms,* 204.
41. Kraus, *Psalms 1–59,* 275.
42. A. Meinhold, "Überlegungen zur Theologie des 19. Psalms," *ZTK* 80 (1983): 119-36.
43. "Überlegungen," 130.

Meinhold's essay is significant because it represents a case study that suggests programmatic viewpoints for the interpretation of the theology of the Bible. Rather than listing many details on which our exegeses agree, and some on which they differ or conflict, I am focusing on his thesis that the psalm's composition and theology are constituted by the concept of the happening of God's word or of God's happening as word. Several aspects need to be discussed.

First, Meinhold's argument raises the suspicion that his thesis rests more on a concept adopted from systematic theology than on exegetical observations. His opening reference to G. Ebeling's definition of theology — namely, the scientific explanation of the word of God — which Meinhold also applies to the task of Old Testament theology, causes the suspicion at the outset. Throughout his essay, it does not become sufficiently clear that in the dialogue between exegesis and systematic theology, his conclusions are controlled by the former rather than the latter.

Secondly, the suspicion is reinforced by Meinhold's focus on *three* modes of the word of God happening: the speech ("Rede") about, of, and to God. At the same time, Meinhold speaks about the *two* dimensions of the cosmic and the personal — which happen to coincide with the traditional exegetical subdivision of Psalms 19A and B. Yet, in turn, he speaks about the *four* parts of the psalm.

It is clear that the first and the last two parts address, respectively, the two dimensions of the cosmic and the personal. This means, however, that the focus on these two dimensions unites and controls the two aspects addressed in either dimension. Hence, the two-partite dominates the four-partite composition of the psalm. But Meinhold needs more than two parts or else he cannot accommodate his three modes of God's word so central to his interpretation. If the psalm is governed by the aspect of two dimensions, this aspect controls the other aspect of the three modes of God's word regardless of the extent to which they play a role in the text. The dominance of the threefold mode of God's word can only be upheld if the psalm's two-partite dimensionality is relativized and the psalm is considered to rest on more than two parts.

Thus, and now for form-critical reasons, not on three but on four parts. However, also the four-partite consideration of the psalm conflicts with the aspect of the three modes of God's word. The second of these four parts, about the tent for the sun and the run of the sun in verses 5b-7, fits into none of Meinhold's three modes of speech about, of, or to God. It refers at best in verse 5b to the psalmist's, not the heaven's, speech about God, but then in verses 6-7 to the sun's re-*action* rather than praising speech about the work of God. Not coincidentally, this part plays no explicit role in Meinhold's substantiation for his thesis. But it exists!

Thirdly, Meinhold's thesis can, of course, point to some evidence in verses 2-5a, 8-11, 12-15. But this substantiation is gained at the cost of other distinctions also evident in the text. For example, the psalmist's praise of Yahweh's Torah, of God's own word, certainly refers to a linguistic phenomenon. But this gift is not of the same kind as the "happenings" of the word in the rest of the psalm. It is an already existing written text, as opposed to the oral speeches of the heaven and the psalmist. Meinhold uses the nouns "word" ("Wort") and "speech" ("Rede"), whereby all three modes of God's word are characterized as speech. But he clarifies neither the relationship between word and speech nor the different kinds within his speech modes of the word — with confusing questions remaining: only the word of God's creatures is speech, whereas God's own word is text. Within the umbrella concept of God's word are the heaven and humans united through their speech *about* as well as *to* God, in contradistinction to the text of God's own word, so that one could not simply juxtapose speech about *and* speech of *and* speech to God? Or are the heaven and the sun, on the one hand, and the psalmist, on the other hand, united in their re-*action,* including speech and action, to both the work and Torah of God? Or is the distinction relevant between the psalmist's quoted speech on the one hand, and his reference only to both the speech of the heaven and the word of God on the other hand? Or is it relevant that the reference to God's own "speech," the Torah, is first of all the psalm's own speech about God's own word? Which of these distinctions in the text controls the others? And do Meinhold's distinctions unquestionably reflect the distinctions dominant in the text and decisive for its theology, or are they imposed upon the text from systematic theology?

As far as the Torah itself is concerned, it represents not just God's word about his acts as well as his words but first of all the witness *about* those words and acts. It is, speaking in Meinhold's terms, the happening of God's word about God's speech(es) and work, just as the heaven's speaking about God's work is this happening. To reserve, under the blanket of the happening of God's word, the Torah as the sole mode of God's own word in contradistinction to any word about or to God, is fraught with ambiguity despite the fact that it is Yahweh's Torah. Deuteronomy is Yahweh's Torah, but as the speech-instruction of Moses about Yahweh rather than Yahweh's own speech. Are verses 8-11 unaware of this fact?

Fourthly, what has been said thus far brings into sharper focus the problematic imposition upon a text of a systematically conceived word of God theology, whereby the modes of God's word are, on some textual indicators, compartmentalized in such a way that each mode is not only distinct but also exclusive rather than inclusive of the others. Yet a systematic-theological understanding of the Bible as the happening of the divine word, or as the happening of God as word, will have to assume that each mode is present in the others, be it in the form of speech about, of, or to God, and that all are equally explicated as word of God. In this case, the distinction of the three modes, and even the recognition of their importance, becomes subservient to the claimed conceptual unity of a text, regardless of whether or not, or to what extent, the system of the text itself is based on that unifying conceptuality. The claimed unity theologizes the text without necessarily interpreting its theology; and the modes of God's word in their distinction serve in this claim as systematic-theological presuppositions. But it does not demonstrate that these modes are the systemic aspects by which the text is generated.

Fifthly, the subjection of the psalm to the commanding aspect of the three modes of word about, of, and to God suggests that the composition of the psalm and its theology rest in principle on *formal* criteria. It suggests that substantive indicators such as who speaks — or acts — and how, and what is spoken about, and their relationship, while worth mentioning, play a subordinate role but are not constitutive for the structure of the psalm's theology — as if speakers, tone (praise!), and contents were relative as long as there are word and speech. It may be that the formal factors, especially on the surface, govern the structure of a text. This can only be found out through comparison with the other indicators, of which many are also discernible in Psalm 19 and which Meinhold mentions. One may well expect the substantive rather than the formal indicators of the psalm to be of importance, especially in the interpretation of its theology. After all, when coming to the New Testament church, Meinhold cannot avoid saying that the witness of Psalm 19 is neither identical with nor analogous to the New Testament witness.[44] Nevertheless, it represents a continuity and a likeness in function because the speaking God is the same in both.[45] This argument shows directly that the formal aspect of function, as continuity and likeness, appears to Meinhold to be dominant despite the acknowledgment that the contents within this continuity are neither identical nor analogous and may even be contradictory. What is the validity of continuity if God's word is not the same?

What Meinhold indicates concerning the psalm's relationship to the New Testament also applies to the relationship between the formal and the substantive aspects in Psalm 19. For this discussion, the formal aspect of the three modes of God's word is not sufficient.

Finally, one must question whether the search for a principle unifying all aspects is at all on the right track. This question is especially pertinent for the interpretation of the two parts, A and B, of the psalm. The peculiarity of the psalm seems to lie in its attention to two different realms, i.e., the cosmic and the human. Whether or not, and in what sense, these two foci are formally and substantively complementary or rest on a common denominator seems to be beyond the psalm's present concern. The most persuasive answer as to what constitutes the combination of its two parts is provided by the traditio-historical explanation: The older tradition(s) in verses 2-7 which spoke only about God's praise and reaction to God's work by the cosmos were complemented by the human, the servant's own praise for God's gift of the Torah already at hand and of God's personal guidance. The servant joins the cosmos in the ongoing daily praise of God, and each party praises God for its own reasons. The servant has inherited a text about the cosmos's praise.

44. "Überlegungen," 134-35.
45. "Überlegungen," 135.

Missing in that text is his own praise. It is the recognition of the absence of his own praise in that text which accounts for his addition of his praise of God's already existing gift to him to the inherited text. This transmission-historical factor generated, traditio-historically, the combination of two theologically relevant foci: the praise of God by the cosmos and by the psalmist. The psalm's theology consists of these two legitimate foci, but their not more than parallel juxtaposition also accounts for the questions not addressed in this theology, and in this regard for the psalm's own theological deficit.

The Composition of the Pentateuch

Introduction

Ever since Wellhausen's *Die Composition des Hexateuchs,*[1] the study of the composition of larger blocks of Old Testament materials has been a legitimate scholarly endeavor, and it has played an increasing role during the last two generations. The latest publication to date concerned with composition is E. Blum's monumental dissertation, *Die Komposition der Vätergeschichte.*[2]

It is immediately clear that methodologically quite different things are done under the term "composition." The term is used in literary-critical, form-critical, redaction-critical, rhetorical, stylistic, and other types of interpretation. The same is true for the term "structure," which, in addition to its use in the fields just mentioned, has become the main label for entire fields such as structuralism and structural linguistics.

The following discussion is not concerned with the appropriateness of these words for certain fields of study.[3] Nor is it concerned with distinctions between the words "structure" and "composition." Rather, it focuses on the proper determination of the parts within a literary unit and on their relationship — in our case the super- or macrostructure of the Pentateuch.

Whether or not, and by what criteria, the Pentateuch must be considered as a literary unit may remain an open question even though the traditional source-critical and traditio-historical arguments in favor of a Hexateuch have decisively

1. J. Wellhausen, *Die Composition des Hexateuchs und der historischen Bücher des Alten Testaments,* 4th ed. (Berlin: Walter de Gruyter and Co., 1963).

2. E. Blum, *Die Komposition der Vätergeschichte,* WMANT 57 (Neukirchen-Vluyn: Neukirchener, 1984).

3. On this point, see my comments in "Criticism of Literary Features, Form, Tradition, and Redaction," *The Hebrew Bible and Its Modern Interpreters,* ed. D. Knight and G. Tucker (Philadelphia: Fortress; Decatur: Scholars Press, 1985), 123-65.

lost ground since M. Noth. The Pentateuch certainly points beyond itself. Nevertheless, there is sufficient ground for the study of its composition even if this literary unit should be part of a larger historical work in which the priestly and deuteronomistic works were combined.

It is known that the Pentateuch in its basically extant form is the result of a long and complex growth process of oral and written traditions which extended throughout centuries. It is also known that this process essentially did not come to its end before the fifth century BCE. What is presumed, but not sufficiently studied, is the final result of this process at that later period in Israel, this "baroque" phenomenon as G. von Rad called it. For good reasons traditional historical exegesis has been preoccupied with the layers and developments predating the latest composition. At the same time, it has behaved as if the final composition was not worth discussing. The reason for this neglect is probably because this layer is presumed to be self-explanatory, a matter for laypeople. Another reason might be that its complexity betrays the disintegration or convolution of originally "pure" generic traditions and literary authors, or even that its late date associates it with the "ritualistic" and "legalistic" interests of Jewish religiosity which is considered "inferior" to early Israel's great traditions and thereby irrelevant for the knowledge of the Old Testament's religion or theology.

It is worthwhile to point out these influences on scholarship. But neither their ideological prejudices nor their historical assumptions provide a valid basis for true and ongoing scholarly work. Indeed, the interpretation of the extant Pentateuch is an urgent necessity, not only because its final composition represents another important historical datum in the Pentateuch's and the Old Testament's tradition history but also because attention to this stratum provides an important starting point and control mechanism for studying the Pentateuch's tradition history itself.

It is not the intention of this paper to engage in critical discussion with publications that focus on the same subject. In any case, these publications are few in number. The absence of critical discussion results from the basically different method in this chapter and the results derived from this method, and not from intentional neglect of the valid scholarship of others. The results may differ from or concur with those of others. In either case, they rest on the approach to the material and not, at least not primarily, on the history of research thus far. The test for the method and its results has to be the literary phenomenon of the Pentateuch itself.

This essay can only address the major questions. Much detail must remain unsaid for the time being; and some aspects that should be mentioned may be missed. It is, hopefully, a beginning.

I. The Main Parts of the Pentateuch

A. Pentateuch?

The canonical shape of the Pentateuch, i.e., its division into five books, is just as much an obstacle to the recognition of its literary structure and genre as the shape of its literary sources has always been. Whatever the reasons for this fivefold division, and its canonic-theological implications, this shape cannot claim to reflect the formation of the Pentateuch that is intrinsic to its literary nature. Indeed, at important points the canonical shape has destroyed the literary structure of the whole. Inasmuch as this intrinsic literary nature is theologically relevant, its own theological relevance is more important than the theological relevance of its canonical shape.

The division between Genesis and Exodus is for obvious reasons a primary division. The division between Numbers and Deuteronomy is also justifiable. But it cannot be considered on the same level as the division between Genesis and Exodus. For a variety of reasons to be discussed below, Numbers and Deuteronomy belong decisively closer together than Genesis and Exodus. The case is even clearer regarding the divisions between Exodus and Leviticus and between Leviticus and Numbers. Both divisions cut to pieces the literary unit of the Sinai pericope by associating one part of this pericope with the narrative leading to Sinai (so in Exodus) and another part with the narrative following the time at Sinai (so in Numbers).

The fivefold division of the work suggests, structurally speaking, that its five parts belong together on the same, and highest, macrostructural level. If it were to suggest a different interpretation, such an interpretation is not self-evident, and it still conflicts with the self-evidence of the equal level of each part suggested by the fivefold division. Most importantly, however, the fivefold subdivision, should it structurally mean anything at all, conflicts with the different structural levels to which certain blocks belong in the literary unity of the work. Indeed, it stands in the way of a proper understanding of the hierarchical nature of the work's composition. This composition consists of a variety of different levels in which the parts of the work are related to one another. Moreover, no interpretation of the composition of the "Pentateuch" is appropriate which ignores the fundamental importance of these different structural levels to which the parts of the work belong and which constitute the relationship of these parts. In view of this methodological maxim, a fresh look at the problem is in order.

B. The Bipartite "Pentateuch"

We begin with the observation that the books of Exodus through Deuteronomy are held together by the narrative about Moses from his birth until his death. This observation is important for our understanding of the composition of the "Pentateuch." This work consists of two parts: the time before Moses (Genesis) and the time of Moses (Exodus-Deuteronomy). A number of additional observations support and specify this conclusion.

1. The book of Genesis covers the time span from the creation of the world until the death of Joseph, an exceedingly long time (more than 2,000 years) narrated in roughly 25 percent of the total text of the Pentateuch. In 75 percent of the total text of the Pentateuch, the books of Exodus-Deuteronomy cover the time span of Moses' life, 120 years. The extent of material allotted to each of the two time spans is extremely disproportionate, a factor that must be considered programmatic and not merely the result of the relative availability of information for the two parts of the work.

2. The work regards each of the two time periods as coherent in its respective part, in Genesis on the basis of genealogy, and in Exodus-Deuteronomy on the basis of Moses' life, an aspect not unrelated to genealogy. By contrast, the work sees a hiatus between the two time periods which is unparalleled within each of the two parts. Exod 1:6-8 makes the hiatus explicit by referring, on the one hand, to the death of Joseph and his generation and, on the other, to a new king who did not know Joseph and to the increase of Israel's descendants between the two eras. This passage establishes the link between the generation of Joseph and the generation of the Israelites under the new Pharaoh, but it says nothing about the duration which elapsed between them, but which it quite obviously assumes. Exod 12:40 knows it precisely: 430 years.

3. The scenarios of the two blocks must also be considered as separate. The story of the Israelites in Egypt and in the desert is clearly distinct from the story of the patriarchs and their ancestors in Mesopotamia, Syria, and Palestine. Whatever the divisions are in each of the two stories, they are less significant than the divisions between the two of them. The division between Genesis and Exodus-Deuteronomy is therefore fundamental, while all other divisions within the "Pentateuch" are subservient to it.

4. What, then, is the relationship of these two parts? It should be evident that the Pentateuch focuses heavily on the time of Moses, and compared with this focus only preliminarily on the time before Moses. Further, since in its historical perspective both times are connected, the conclusion is inevitable that the Pentateuch as a whole is a work concerning the time of Moses in which Genesis, the time before Moses, is the introduction, the prelude, the preparation, or the prehistory. The book of Genesis is not the center of this work, nor is it equal in perspective to Exodus-Deuteronomy, in spite of the extent to which it is read and discussed. Nor is it meant to be understood apart from the following main work. It is the introduction to the time of Moses and receives its meaning from Exodus-Deuteronomy.

Nevertheless, this prehistory is not unimportant. It shows that the time of

Moses must not be understood in isolation. On the contrary, the time of Moses must be understood in world-historical perspective as the culmination of the long process of world history in one short period. The Pentateuch is the story, or history, of the time of Moses in the light of universal creation and history, or the history of universal creation and history culminating in the time of Moses.

5. In the following, we will bypass discussing the composition of the book of Genesis[4] and focus on the composition of the main body.

II. The Composition of the Moses Story

A. The Macrostructure of Exodus-Deuteronomy

What is the super- or macrostructure of Exodus-Deuteronomy? In order to answer this question, we proceed as before by first defining the dominant blocks of the material to which all the other blocks are subordinate. Methodologically, the guiding question is: What are the criteria according to which this work is organized? Under this question it is immediately clear that our traditional exegetical methods do not provide the primary tools for determining the structure of this work. For the macrostructural level, something like concept criticism seems to be of primary importance since the work on this level appears to be organized conceptually.

1. Two blocks stand out as primary units: Deuteronomy and the Sinai pericope from Exodus 19–Num 10:10. This leaves us with two other primary units: Exodus 1–18, and Num 10:11–36:13. Thus, the Moses story consists of four primary parts. Before discussing the nature of these parts we will ask how they are related to each other.

2. Statistical data are relative. Yet what they indicate should not be ignored. The Sinai pericope alone represents some 42 percent, almost half, of the total text. It is by far the largest of the four units. When combined with Deuteronomy, which amounts to more than 26 percent, both units make up 68.5 percent of the text. By comparison, Num 10:11–36:13 covers about 19 percent, and Exodus 1–18, the smallest of the four blocks, about 11.5 percent of the text. At first impression, the Sinai pericope seems to be the most important of the four blocks, followed by Deuteronomy, whereas Exodus 1–18 and Num 10:11–36:13 appear to be in some sense subordinate.

3. This first impression is reinforced by additional observations. One is geographical and topographical in nature and the other chronological.

a. The entire Moses story is based on the migration of the Israelites from

4. For this composition, see now G. W. Coats, *Genesis: With an Introduction to Narrative Literature,* FOTL 1 (Grand Rapids: William B. Eerdmans, 1983).

Egypt to the land of Moab, "beyond the Jordan" (Deut 1:1-3; Num 33:49, 50-56). The itinerary tradition is the well-known backbone of this story. Indeed, it is the primary device for the organization of the fourfold macrostructure of the story. In light of the itinerary, the Moses story focuses on the primary importance of two locations above all others during the migration: Sinai and the plains of Moab. The migration story is governed by the arrival and events at these two locations. Consequently, the two other parts of the Moses story (Exodus 1–18; Num 10:11–36:13) must be considered as pre-stages or presuppositions to their respective goals, and as leading up to and being subservient to these goals. This picture reveals, as in other places where itineraries are used, much more than an interest in the mere listing of the itinerary stations. It reveals a systematized understanding of the migratory process which is heavily controlled by theological priorities. Lastly, it shows that the Moses story is conceptualized as a migration story under two foci to which the other parts represent the prelude and transition, respectively. On this basis, the macrostructure of the Moses story looks as follows:

I. From Egypt to Sinai	Exodus 1–Num 10:10
A. Migration to Sinai	Exodus 1–18
B. Events at Sinai (note the programmatic statement in Exod 19:3)	Exodus 19–Num 10:10
II. From Sinai to Moab	Num 10:11–Deuteronomy 34
A. Migration to Moab	Num 10:11–36:13
B. Moses' Testament	Deuteronomy 1–34

It may be mentioned at the outset that this structure, clearly the end result of a long traditio-historical process, is quite unlike any structure that can be found in the tradition history of the same core material in the Old Testament.

Before this view of the macrostructure can be further discussed, it must be recognized that already the jahwistic-priestly narrative of Numbers 22–36 also speaks about the events in the plains of Moab. It is possible to consider a structural subdivision of II. as consisting of: A. Migration of Moab, Num 10:11–21:35, and of B. Events in the plains of Moab, Num 22:1–Deuteronomy 34. In this case, II.B. would consist of: 1. Preliminary events in Numbers 22–36, and 2. Moses' Testament in Deuteronomy 1–34.

For the time being, however, it seems to me that the combination of the deuteronomistic with the jahwistic-priestly narrative about the stay in Moab has mounted to a structure according to which Numbers 22–36 has been relegated to being the concluding part of the forty years' migration (cf. Deut 1:3; 2:7; 8:2, 4; 29:5; Josh 5:6, 10-12). On the other hand, Deuteronomy 1–34 not only represents the analogy to Sinai (I.B.) but focuses on the decisive condition for the impending conquest of and settlement in the promised land proper after Moses. The retrospection in the introductory units Deut 1:1-5 and 1:6–3:29 — especially from the perspective of the date of Moses' final speech — seems much more to include the text of Numbers 22–36 than to exclude it by looking only at Num 10:11–21:35.

On the surface, the structure appears symmetrical, but there are important semantic differences. In both I. and II., the migration (A.) leads to the main destination (B.); but what happens at each destination also looks back at, reflects, and integrates the meaning of the migration. However, the situations presupposed in I. and II. are not the same. In I., the liberation story aims at the Sinai story and the Sinai story actualizes the liberation story. The role of the liberation story (I.A.) is thereby different from the role of the second journey story (II.A.). Even though this story (I.A.) — more specifically the story of the oppression, the exodus, and the beginning of the migration — is not an end in itself but points to its first and most important fulfillment in the Sinai narrative, it is certainly also perceived as constitutive. This is not the case for the second migration (II.A.).

Interestingly, the Sinai pericope does not reflect on the already narrated murmurings of the Israelites. The situation is very different in II. While II.A., the forty-year migration in the wilderness (Num 14:33-34; 32:13; Deut 2:7; 8:2, 4; 29:4 [*NRSV* 29:5]; cf. also Exod 16:35; Josh 5:6), arrives at the concluding events in Moab in Numbers 22–36, II.B., Moses' last will or testament, is above all necessitated by the crisis that had erupted during the migration (II.A.) after Sinai (I.B.) — namely, Israel's repeated failure to react appropriately to its liberation/covenant experience. It is this kind of failure which Deuteronomy confronts through its exhorting and admonishing parenesis. With qualifications, one could say that the first part of the Moses story (I.) focuses on Yahweh's acts, whereas the second part (II.) shifts in focus to the problem of the human response to these acts.

This understanding of II.A. is programmatically expressed in the deuteronomistic introduction to Deuteronomy (Deut 1:6–3:29), which reviews the migration from Horeb to Hermon under the aspect of four crises: at Horeb (1:6-18), at Kadesh (1:19-46), *en route* from Kadesh to Zered (2:1-15), and from Zered to Hermon (2:16–3:29). It is another, and quite unique, theologically systematized understanding of that period.

What has been said also helps to bring into sharper focus the relationship between the whole of I., the exodus and Sinai story, and II.B., Moses' testament. While both the Sinai story (I.B.) and Deuteronomy (II.B.) refer to the oppression/exodus event (I.A.), Deuteronomy specifically represents an updated, additional interpretation of the Sinai event (I.B.) without reinterpreting the exodus event itself. Deuteronomy has no problem with the exodus event. But from that time on it must confront the problems that arose with the Sinai event. This function of Moses' testament shows that Deuteronomy is no replacement for the Sinai-pericope. On the contrary, it reaffirms the Sinai pericope as its own foundation. Deuteronomy submits to the preeminence of the Sinai pericope, and by doing so points to that pericope as the central piece and most important part of the macrostructure of Exodus-Deuteronomy.

A final observation concerns the relationship between the periods of encampment in I.B. and II.B. on the one hand, and the periods of migratory movement in I.A. and II.A. on the other. If our observations so far are correct, we should conclude that the periods of local encampment are considered more important than the periods of movement. This conclusion far exceeds a passing significance. It is in tune with the fundamental assumption of the entire Old Testament tradition according to which the basic structure of Israel's existence is sedentary, and not migratory. This sedentary existence is not transitional. It is final. The migratory existence, even the one of the patriarchs, is not final. It is transitional, preliminary.

b. Chronological observations reinforce what has been said thus far. In this context, we cannot discuss all the extant chronological data and the literary-historical and traditio-critical problems associated with them. We will confine the discussion to the data relevant for the macrostructure of the Moses story. The data concerning Moses' life will be discussed later.

The chronological data are interspersed in the material. They complement the macrostructure observed in the itinerary system. Exod 12:1f. mentions the first date. Passover is to be held in the night before the fifteenth day of the first month, the night of the exodus. This instruction establishes the cultic calendar, grounds it in the presupposed Babylonian lunar cycle, and represents the basis for the numbering of years in this stratum of the Israelite tradition. This tradition is priestly. On this basis, Israel arrives in the wilderness of Sin "on the fifteenth day of the second month" (Exod 16:1), i.e., one month after the day of exodus. On the day of "the third new moon" (Exod 19:1), i.e., after a month and a half, or forty-two days, of migration, Israel arrives at Sinai; and on the twentieth day of the second month of the second year (Num 10:11), i.e., after almost a full year of encampment, Israel departs from Sinai.

In part II.A., the migration to Moab, we find only the reference to the forty-year period of wandering, but no longer a date that would specify any event during this period within the cultic calendric system. The shift for this period from the cultic calendar to the forty-year period is more than coincidental. It reflects the negative value already asserted for that period in the narrative II.A., and not only in Deuteronomy 1:6–3:29. In addition, this shift neglects the positive value asserted for the periods I.A. and I.B. — in I.A. specifically from the day of the exodus on.

Into this positive calendric schedule, the document of Moses' last will and testament (II.B.) is finally also bound: "In the fortieth year, on the first day of the eleventh month, Moses spoke . . ." (Deut 1:3). By this statement, the forty-year period from the passover-exodus date in I.A. until the end of II.A. in Numbers 36 is connected with the new event II.B. On this day, the positive conclusions are drawn from the negative results of the previous period from "Horeb" on.

It is generally assumed that Deut 1:3 comes from the hands of the priestly redaction. It is also generally assumed that in the deuteronomistic tradition of the book of Deuteronomy, Moses is giving his farewell speech and that in this edition the references to "today" reflect the day of his farewell speech. For the priestly redactor in Deut 1:3, however, "today," namely, day one of month eleven of year forty, is the day of Moses' death. With this statement, the priestly redactor reinterprets all other references to the day of Moses' farewell speech so as to mean Moses' last will and testament on the day of his death. This testament includes not only his farewell speech but also the other testamentary activities such as, among others, the installation of his successor Joshua and the Song and the Blessing of Moses.[5] Thus, the redactor changes the genre of the deuteronomistic farewell speech to the genre of the last will and testament of a dying person. Thus, the book of Deuteronomy becomes based on the structure of the genre "testament," and no longer on the generic structure of a farewell speech. Last but not least, this final event in Moses' life becomes an integral part of Israel's cultic history.

In summary, the absence of specific dates in II.A. confirms what has been said about this part in the topographical discussion. In addition, the specific datings present in I.A., I.B., and II.B. confirm what has been said in the topographical discussion about these parts. The datings specifically point to the importance of these parts of the Moses story, just as the negative forty-year period reflects the negative side, even of Moses' own life, which was not the case in I.A. (Exodus 1–18). It is clear, however, that neither the datings nor the periods dated determine by themselves the importance of the dated events. The arrival in the wilderness of Sin (Exod 16:1) is not as important as either Israel's encampment at Sinai or Moses' testament. Moreover, the fact that Moses' testament happened on one day while Israel's encampment at Sinai lasted almost a year is most probably based on the idea of the duration required for each event. However, this difference does not by itself indicate a priority of one over the other. The importance of the parts of the total story lies in their conceptual relationships, which emerge from their topographical and chronological orders.

B. The Individual Parts

1. Introduction

The next step in the discussion would be to interpret the composition of each of the four parts of the Moses story on a further level of subdivision. In this chapter, this task cannot be addressed for each part. For obvious reasons, the two parts that deserve preferred attention are I.B., the events at Sinai, and II.B., the testament of Moses. What is most important concerning the latter has already been indicated.

5. Cf. Deut 26:17, 18; 27:1, 4, 9, 10, 11; 28:1, 13, 14, 15; 29:9, 11, 14; 30:2, 8, 15, 16; 31:2; 32:46, 48. The priestly hand in Deut 1:3 is now contested especially by L. Perlitt, for whom the verse is deuteronomistic, in *Deuteronomium,* BKAT 5 (Neukirchen-Vluyn: Neukirchener, 1990), 15-17.

What needs to be addressed is the problem of the composition of the Sinai pericope, which is the longest and most central part of the Moses story. To this task we now turn.

2. The Sinai Pericope

a. By combining a calendric and a topographical statement, Exod 19:1-2 reports that Israel arrived in the wilderness of Sinai and "camped there in front of the mountain." This statement sets the stage for the basic structural organization of the entire Sinai pericope in the final form of our text. This organization develops out of the distance between the two mentioned localities: the camp and the mountain.

Clearly enough, Exod 19:3 begins by saying: "Then Moses went up [עלה] to God." According to verse 7 he came down into the camp: "So Moses came [ויבא] [and] summoned the elders. . . ." Verse 8b resumes: "Moses reported [lit., returned] [וישב] the words of the people . . . ," and according to verse 14 he "went down" (וירד). Again, Moses went up (ויעל), verse 20bβ, and "down" (וירד), verse 25, and up (נגש), 20:21b, and down (ויבא), 24:3, and up (ויעל), 24:9, and down (וירד), 32:15, and up (ויעל), 34:4, and down for the final time (ויהי ברדת), 34:29.

The regularity of this ascent-descent pattern is blurred within the block Exod 32:15–34:4. After coming "down from the mountain" (32:15), Moses says to the people, "I will *go up* to [Yahweh]" (אעלה, 32:30b). Exod 32:31 continues, "So Moses *returned* to [Yahweh]" (וישב). According to 33:4, the people "heard these harsh words." This leaves it unclear whether they heard Yahweh's words spoken on the mountain to Moses (which is an improbable assumption to make of the text), or whether they heard Moses after his return from the mountain (which may be presupposed, but is not said), or whether 33:4 assumes a Moses-speech conveying the Yahweh-speech (33:1-3) that was spoken at a different place, namely, in the tent outside the camp.

Exod 33:7-11 speaks about the ongoing encounter between Yahweh and Moses whereby Yahweh speaks to Moses "face to face, as one speaks to a friend." This encounter takes place in the tent outside the camp. Exod 33:12-23 contains a dialogue between the two of them, according to the context (vv. 7-11), in the tent. The dialogue is continued in 34:1-3, and in 34:4 Moses "went up on Mount Sinai" again.

Thus, Moses is said to have gone up but not to have come down. At the same time, he is presupposed to be in the camp (33:4), but it is not said from where he came. The interruption of the clearly expressed ascent-descent pattern certainly results from the combination of different literary strata or of text accretions in which different signals come to work together. Exod 32:15 and 34:4 belong together because of the tablets Moses brings down and the new tablets he takes back. Both passages mention the mountain. By contrast, 32:30-31 has Moses going up —

returning to Yahweh for intercession and without the new tablets — and 33:4 fails to mention that Moses came down again. Finally, 33:4–34:3 is the only block in Exodus 19–39 where Yahweh speaks to Moses from within the tent.

These factors suggest that, in the final redaction, the literarily heterogeneous block 32:30–34:3 was not successfully integrated into the ascent-descent pattern, despite a signal indicating such an integration in the statement "I will go up" in 32:30b. The final redaction has combined conflicting signals. Based on 32:30b, one might account for an additional ascent-descent cycle. However, based on the unsuccessful integration of the block 32:30–34:3, one may prefer to consider 32:30-35 as an accretion to the older ascent-descent tradition which, in the process toward finalization of the text, was not fully upheld and became, along with other texts, a subordinate element in the block 32:15–34:4. With this *caveat* in mind, we can now summarize.

b. Six times Moses goes up to the mountain, and six times he comes down into the camp. Whenever he is on the mountain he receives an instruction from Yahweh, and whenever he is in the camp he conveys it to the people. While the response of the people to Moses is mentioned repeatedly, it is returned by Moses to Yahweh only once, in 19:8b. The ascent-descent pattern must be considered as the basic structural signal for the organization of Exodus 19–39. According to this structure, the text consists of six major cycles, each of which has two subdivisions: the first, the instruction report, narrating the event on the mountain; and the second, the compliance report, narrating the subsequent event in the camp. While the ascent-descent statements introduce the two parts of each cycle, the contents of the cycles are governed by six distinctly different concerns. These concerns distinguish the cycles from one another and reflect the progress of the events. The structure may, then, be presented as follows:

I. The initiation of the covenant	19:3-8a
A. Ascent for instruction	19:3-6
B. Descent for compliance	19:7-8a
II. The theophany	19:8b-19
A. Ascent for instruction	19:8b-13
B. Descent for compliance	19:14-19
III. The confirmation of the mediator	19:20–20:20
A. Ascent for instruction	19:20-24
B. Descent for compliance	19:25–20:20
IV. The document and ratification of the covenant	20:21–24:8
A. Ascent for instruction: the document	20:21–24:2
B. Descent for compliance: ratification	24:3-8
V. The instruction for the tabernacle	24:9–34:3
A. Ascent for instruction	24:9–32:14

	B. Descent for *interference*	32:15–34:3
VI.	The second tablets and the compliance	34:4–39:43
	A. Ascent for instruction: second tablets	34:4-28
	B. Descent with tablets for construction compliance	34:29–39:43

As is well known, this structure unites — sometimes violently — a variety of different literary strata and aspects of which only the most striking may be noted. The classical Decalogue (Exod 20:1-17), introduced as a speech of God, interrupts the narrative flow about the descent situation in the camp from 19:25 to 20:18. Resulting from its position in the narrative in Deuteronomy 5, the positioning of the Decalogue in Exodus was a logical choice. Nevertheless, it conflicts with the functions of all the compliance elements in the Exodus narrative, except for Exod 40:1-15. In none of these elements does God speak to Moses or the people while they are in the camp in order to give substantive instructions, except in the case of the Decalogue. Exod 40:1-15 and Leviticus are exempt from this rule for good reasons, which we will discuss below. Also, the position of the Decalogue in III., the confirmation of the mediator, has little, if anything, to do with that confirmation. While the deuteronomic notion of God's speaking the Decalogue to the people caused the positioning of the Decalogue in III.B., it severely conflicts with the meaning of the compliance reports and of part III. in the structure of the narrative in Exodus.

c. The literary-critical and traditio-historical problems of the so-called Covenant Book are well known. It should be noted, however, and precisely for contextual reasons, that this block of material belongs to IV.A., to Yahweh's instruction given to Moses on the mountain, and not to a compliance report or any other context apart from this instruction. The reasons for the position of the Covenant Book in IV.A. are certainly in need of interpretation.

It should also be noted that in one part of V.A., namely, in Exod 24:9-18, the ascent pattern starting in verse 9 is extended. After ascending together with Aaron, Nadab, Abihu, and seventy of Israel's elders (vv. 9-11), Moses is called to ascend (further!) to God on the mountain. He goes with Joshua while leaving the elders behind to wait with Aaron and Hur (vv. 12-14). Finally, Moses goes up (even further! and without Joshua!) for six days, to be called by Yahweh from out of the cloud on the seventh day and to go into the cloud and up onto the mountain for forty days (vv. 15-18). That is where and how he received the instruction for the sanctuary!

It is clear that the passage 24:9-18 is meant to extend the regular ascent pattern, and not to interrupt or replace it. In its present composition this passage portrays a sort of hierarchical reality of localities — and times, i.e., seven days and forty days — in five stages: (1) the camp, (2) a higher level with Aaron, Nadab, Abihu, and seventy elders; with Aaron and Hur, (3) a further higher level with

Joshua, (4) another higher level with Moses alone (?) outside the cloud, and (5) the highest level with Moses, certainly alone with God, in the cloud.

It is unnecessary to list the heterogeneity of many elements in Exod 24:9-18, but it is amazing how successfully these disparate materials were combined under the guidance of a configuration of the hierarchical order of Israel's representatives between Yahweh and Israel, an order that literally places them at different levels on the mountain. Moreover, while Moses belongs to all levels of this hierarchy, nevertheless he stands above all of them, and he alone stands with God on the very top of the mountain. Does this configuration reflect a reality in Israel's cultic history or a program for Israel's cult? And if so, what reality or program is it, and from what time and place did this picture originate?

d. However, more important than what has been said so far is the fact that, in parts V. and VI., the ascent-descent pattern has combined elements of quite different nature and origin. In V.A., the just-discussed conceptual unit Exod 24:9-18 is, in its entirety, nothing but an expanded ascent statement analogous to all the other ascent statements. This statement functions as the introduction to the Yahweh instruction for Moses in Exodus 25–31. The traditionally so-called jehovistic block, Exod 24:9-18, has been combined with the priestly text Exodus 25–31 to form a united structural entity.

But that is not all. This entire ascent narrative does not end in Exod 31:18, as is universally assumed under the magical influence of literary-critical criteria. It ends in Exod 32:14. Not until Exod 32:15 does Moses descend from the mountain. Certainly, the perspective in Exod 32:1-6 switches down to the camp. But 32:7-14 switches right back to the situation on the mountain, to Yahweh's speech to Moses about the situation in the camp (vv. 7-10) and to Moses' successful intercession (vv. 11-14). The passage 32:7-14 shows that the momentary switch in perspective in verses 1-6 is a necessary literary device used to demonstrate to the reader that Yahweh had become aware on the mountain of what was going on in the camp. This device is, nevertheless, subordinate to Moses' place on the mountain. Literary-critically speaking, the deuteronomic-jehovistic narrative unit, Exodus 32–34, has been split into four parts with new functions. Its first part, 32:1-14, was combined with the previous combination of 24:9-18 and chapters 25–31 to form a unit about the events on the mountain (V.A.). Its second part, Exod 32:15–34:3, narrates Moses' interference in the camp (V.B.). Its third part, Exod 34:4-28, has Moses back on the mountain again for the Yahweh instruction of the commandments and for the gift of the second set of tablets (VI.A.). Its concluding part in Exod 34:29-35 functions as the expanded introduction to the compliance report according to which the elements of the sanctuary are manufactured and the sanctuary is set up (VI.B.).

The combination of different literary strata under the dominant ascent-descent pattern has led in parts V. and VI. not only to the disruption of the originally coherent priestly narrative tradition in Exodus 25–31 and 35–40 but also to a substantively modified flow of the narrative from V. to VI. The priestly portions in parts V.A. and VI.B. belong together as ascent and descent for the narrative about the sanctuary. This narrative did not require a twofold ascent-descent. In fact, the ascent-descent pattern did not belong at all to the original priestly narrative. Rather, the priestly sanctuary narrative was inserted into the narrative governed by the ascent-descent pattern.

One result of this insertion was that both the jehovistic-deuteronomic and the priestly narrative units were split, and the respective parts of one narrative were combined with the respective parts of the other under the influence of the jehovistic-deuteronomic ascent-descent pattern to which the priestly narrative had to yield and for good reasons. The other result was a bifurcation in which its two foci nevertheless complement one another. This bifurcation consists of the focus on the sanctuary on the one hand (V.A. and VI.B.) and of the focus on Israel's anti-sanctuary and the resulting crisis of the tablets on the other (V.B. and V.I.A.). In this bifurcation within the combined text, however, the crisis of the tablets is combined with the story of the sanctuary in V.A. and VI.B., as well as the story of the anti-sanctuary in V.B. If this observation is correct, one may conclude that the creation of the anti-sanctuary narrated in Exod 32:1-14, while representing within V.A. the counter-story to the simultaneous instruction for the sanctuary, created the crisis, namely, the destruction of the tablets which in the combined story were related to the sanctuary as Yahweh's very own contribution. The *real* crisis, for which the story of the golden calf is only the cause, consists of the destruction of the tablets that were given by Yahweh in conjunction with his instruction for the sanctuary. This crisis explodes in V.B., the narrative about the destruction of both the anti-sanctuary and the tablets. After that is done, the story can continue in VI.A. with the new ascent for the instruction and the writing of the second set of tablets, and in VI.B. with the descent in which, as in V.A., the tablets are combined with the sanctuary.

In summary, the aspects of the sanctuary and the tablets complement one another as the two central components of the sanctuary despite their bifurcation caused by the combination of different literary strata. This complementation, which excludes and destroys the anti-sanctuary, represents a major conceptual integration of traditio-historically quite different cultic traditions contained in the jehovistic-deuteronomic and the priestly texts, respectively. Historically, it seems to be a late phenomenon which must have been generated by the priestly tradents.

e. What is the intention of the sixfold ascent-descent narrative? It shows Moses as the decisive mediator, literally, the "go-between" between Yahweh and the people. Specifically, Moses is the mediator of the total process and not only of the covenant. What is the nature of this process? How are the six ascent-descent cycles related?

The first four cycles are connected by the covenant motif. They reflect the process of making the covenant in which Moses is the mediator between Yahweh on the mountain and Israel in the camp. In each step of the process, Yahweh takes the initiative, and Moses and/or Israel follow suit. Cycles five and six are connected under the sanctuary motif. They reflect the process of making the sanctuary, again initiated by Yahweh on the mountain and mediated through Moses to Israel in the camp. How, then, are cycles I.-IV. and V.-VI. related? The covenant narrative I.-IV. has lost its independence and has become subservient to the sanctuary narrative. It is now the introduction to the narrative about the sanctuary in the center of Israel's camp (Exod 25:8; Numbers 1–2), as opposed to the older tradition which had the tent of meeting set up outside the camp (Exod 33:7; Num 12:1-15). The covenant is the condition and preparation for the establishment of the sanctuary in Israel's midst.

Connected with Sinai, the original priestly narrative had only the story of the tabernacle; it had no Sinai covenant story. The priestly tradents included the jehovistic-deuteronomic covenant story with their priestly narrative of the sanctuary story. The combination of these two traditions reveals the following theological program. The ultimate goal of Israel's encampment at Sinai during its migration from Egypt to the promised land is not the covenant — as important as it was as a precondition — but the permanent sanctuary as the place of Yahweh's presence or appearance in Israel's midst, along with the organization of Israel as a strictly theocratic community around this sanctuary. At the same time, this goal provides the prototype for the ultimate meaning of Israel's existence as a settled community in the promised land.

In the sixfold ascent-descent cycle, the emphasis lies clearly on the sanctuary narrative. It is not surprising that the older covenant narrative is much shorter than the sanctuary narrative; indeed, it remained shorter and perhaps became more truncated in the transmission process than it may have been before. It is equally unsurprising that, under the influence of the priestly redactors who controlled the combination of both narratives, it was the priestly portion of the total narrative that continued to receive accretions, apparently over several generations, and not the jehovistic-deuteronomic portion.

Lastly, the monstrous structure of the tabernacle itself can only be understood in light of Israel's permanent settlement in the promised land. As important as its origin at Sinai is as a fundamental legitimation, it cannot be understood as the sanctuary of an essentially migratory community. True, it had to be carried, and a large organization had to be set up for this service (Numbers 4). Further, it is true that after being initially erected (Exod 40:1-17) and taken down (Num 10:17), the tabernacle-sanctuary apparently was meant to be erected repeatedly whenever Israel encamped for any length of time, "whether it was two days, or a month, or a longer time, that the cloud continued over the tabernacle" (Num 9:22; cf. also Num 9:15-23). Nevertheless, besides Exod 40:1-17 and Num 10:17, which refer to its initial erection and taking down at Sinai, there is no further statement which explicitly says that the sanctuary was ever again erected and taken down. It is always the "cloud" that settles down, rests, or is taken up. The text emphasizes that the sanctuary had to be carried, and de-emphasizes that it was erected and taken down — with the single exception in Exodus 40. One wonders why. At any rate, even the implied repeated setting up of the tabernacle cannot mean more than the scenario of a transitional situation in which the tabernacle was understood to be on the way to its final destination, to be erected there permanently, and not to be carried again once Israel, organized around it, had arrived at this destination and settled down permanently. Seen from the vantage point of Israel's anticipated permanent settlement, the message is that the legitimate sanctuary had to be the Mosaic tabernacle from Sinai and no other!

f. A word must be said about the position of Exodus 40 in the Sinai narrative. The unit consists of three parts: a new Yahweh instruction to Moses to erect the tabernacle "on the first day of the first month" — New Year's Day of the second year! (vv. 1-15) — Moses' compliance (vv. 16-33), and the occupation of the sanctuary ("tent of meeting" as well as "tabernacle") by Yahweh (vv. 34-38).

Since this unit refers only to the sanctuary, it belongs at most to cycles V. and VI. of the ascent-descent pattern. However, the question arises whether it belongs to this pattern at all. On the one hand, Moses is in the camp and no longer on the mountain for the Yahweh instructions. On the other hand, the unit is clearly set apart from the preceding compliance report (Exodus 35–39) by a summary of that report in 39:32-43 and by a new Yahweh instruction concerning the erection of the manufactured sanctuary at a specific date. Finally, if one recognizes the parallelism between the instruction and compliance concerning the construction (Exod 24:9–39:43), on the one hand, and the instruction and compliance concerning the erection (Exodus 40), on the other hand, the sum of all indicators suggests that the total narrative of Exod 24:9–40:38 is governed by two conceptual aspects: the manufacture and the erection of the sanctuary. In view of this conceptualization, the ascent-descent pattern is relegated to a secondary structural level. It is confined to the manufacture narrative, whereas the narrative about the erection of the sanctuary, together with its occupation by Yahweh on New Year's Day — a conclusion that has its counterpart in the conclusion 39:32-34 — is a separate and highly special event, even for that day itself.

g. We are now in a position to ask the final question concerning the macrostructure of the Sinai pericope. What is the relationship of the text discussed thus far, Exodus 19–40, to the rest of the Sinai pericope from Leviticus 1 on? It seems that the decisive signal for this question is given in Lev 1:1: "And the LORD summoned [ויקרא, in addition to the usual וידבר] Moses and spoke to him *from the tent of meeting*" (my emphasis). This statement is programmatic. Up to this time Moses had to go up to the mountain to receive the instruction and to bring the instruction back to the camp. The distance between Yahweh's and Israel's location had to be bridged. This was inevitable as long as there was no sanctuary in Israel's midst.

We have already mentioned that the idea of the sanctuary in the midst of the camp conflicts with the older tradition of Yahweh's coming down and encountering

Moses and the Israelites "at the entrance of the tent" outside the camp (Num 12:5). The conflict is apparently also programmatic. It reflects the difference between opposing claims concerning the legitimacy of the location of the true, the only true, Yahweh sanctuary. This difference cannot be decided on the basis of Moses' authority, which belongs to both traditions. Moreover, Num 12:4-5 shows that the final text has not totally resolved the conflict.

Lev 1:1 contends that the legitimate sanctuary is the one which had its pattern (תבנית, Exod 25:9, 40; 26:30; 27:8) genuinely revealed *on* the mountain, and which represents the place to which Yahweh's revelation moved *from* the mountain. This sanctuary represents the continuity of the localities of revelation: from the mountain to the tabernacle. The older tradition of the tent of meeting outside the camp could not compete with this massive claim. This claim confirms what we said earlier about the importance of Sinai when compared with the exodus. It was only at Sinai that the liberated community was organized around the sanctuary as a cultic-theocratic community and prepared for its final settlement. While the exodus community was on a migration led by the pillars of cloud and fire (Exod 13:21-22; 14:19, 24; 16:10), the Sinai community of the priestly tradition was on a pilgrimage organized around the sanctuary, the place of the revelation of the glory of the God from Sinai, the place to which the cloud had become related (Lev 16:2, 13; Num 9:15-21; 10:11-12; 12:10; 14:14; 16:12).

Lev 1:1 signals the highest level in the macrostructure of the Sinai pericope. According to this structure, the total narrative consists of two parts: the revelation from the mountain (Exod 19:3–40:38) and the revelation from the "tent of meeting" (Lev 1:1–Num 10:10). This structure reveals a fundamental theological program. It speaks of two stages of revelation in which the first was preparatory and preliminary and provided the condition for the second stage, the ultimate goal of Yahweh's revelation. As long as Yahweh could not speak to Moses from the sanctuary in Israel's midst, he had to speak from the mountain in order to provide the condition of his move from the mountain to the sanctuary in the camp. Once that condition was accomplished Yahweh moved down, and the period of the revelation from the mountain was replaced by the new period of revelation in which Moses still remained the exclusive mediator.

From this point on, Yahweh would call on and speak to Moses from the sanctuary in Israel's midst, and no longer on Sinai. The mountain belonged to the past. The presence belonged to the sanctuary. Its legitimacy and identity were secured by the continuity of the revelation of the God from the mountain. And now Yahweh could give the ultimately decisive instructions concerning the ongoing life of Israel. These instructions have two foci: the provision of the atonement institution for the continuous liberation from the destructive burden of guilt and pollution (Leviticus 1–16), and the regulations for Israel's societal life as a "holy" community (Leviticus 17–27). The Sinai pericope aims at the book of Leviticus. This book is the center of the Pentateuch.

In conclusion, we can present the structure of the Sinai pericope:

I. The Revelation from the mountain	Exod 19:3–40:38
A. Preparation: the covenant (four ascent-descent cycles)	Exod 19:3–24:8
1. First	Exod 19:3-8a
2. Second	Exod 19:8b-19
3. Third	Exod 19:20–20:20
4. Fourth	Exod 20:21–24:8
B. The goal: the sanctuary	Exod 24:9–40:38
1. The construction of the sanctuary	Exod 24:9–39:43
a. Instruction	Exod 24:9–34:28
1) Fifth ascent	Exod 24:9–32:14
2) Descent: the crisis	Exod 32:15–34:3
3) Sixth ascent	Exod 34:4-28
b. Compliance-execution	Exod 34:29–39:43
2. The erection of the sanctuary and the appearance of the glory	Exod 40:1-38
II. The Revelation from the tent	Lev 1:1–Num 10:10
A. Instruction of communal life	Lev 1:1–27:34
1. Concerning atonement	Lev 1:1–16:34
2. Concerning societal life	Lev 17:1–27:34
B. Preparation for the pilgrimage	Num 1:1–10:10

This structure must be understood as part of the larger structure of Exodus-Deuteronomy, and ultimately of the twofold "Pentateuch." It is hoped that this discussion justifies the conclusion that the Sinai pericope, the end result of a long traditio-historical process, is in its final form the expression of a profoundly systematized theological understanding which shaped the historical narrative. This achievement reflects a distinct setting, i.e., priestly, and the concerns of a specific historical period, i.e., exilic — postexilic. It belongs to, and in part is similar to and yet distinctly different from, the theological blueprints that can be discerned in Ezekiel, Haggai, Zechariah, Deutero- and Trito-Isaiah, the deuteronomists, and Ezra-Nehemiah. We know little if anything about these priestly authors and their specific time and location, but without careful attention to their final Pentateuchal work we will know even less. It is just this attention to their ongoing work which took place within their own circle over several generations that may give us a few more clues about its authors, as well as a heightened appreciation for the potency of their thoughts. That their work was an ongoing process can also be seen, among many other instances, in the fact that at various places in Leviticus, including Lev 27:34, Yahweh still, or once again, speaks to Moses from the mountain, in clear conflict with Lev 1:1. Finally, a better understanding of the end result of the traditio-historical process may provide some safeguards against insufficiently substantiated assumptions regarding earlier stages of that process and, ultimately, a new basis for the study of the tradition history of the Pentateuch itself.

III. The Genre of the Pentateuch

A. Possible Genres of the Pentateuch

With few exceptions the question of the genre of the Pentateuch has not played a significant role in critical Old Testament scholarship.

1. The oldest tradition in which these books have been understood as a unit defined them as Torah.[6] This definition reflects the nature of the five books as the earliest and most authoritative unit of the tripartite canon in the Jewish tradition. But it is scarcely sufficient for determining the generic nature of the work. Ultimately, all parts of the Old Testament are Torah. Although it includes different generic forms, the term "torah" in its broad and functional sense says nothing about the specific generic form of the Pentateuch. With respect to genre, the term "torah" conceals more than it reveals.

The question of genre involves more than only technical curiosity. It may well be that the genre of the Pentateuch constitutes the decisive basis for the authority of the Pentateuch-Torah over the other parts of the Old Testament. The assumption that the Pentateuch-Torah is most authoritative does not mean that it is authoritative because it is torah. It means that there is something else that makes this Torah especially authoritative. The Torah is the result of its authoritative basis, but it is not the ground of its own authority. What is the authoritative ground of the Pentateuch-Torah?

The picture changes when the Pentateuch is called the torah of *Moses*.[7] This definition still does not indicate a genre. However, it qualifies this torah as the most authoritative because it represents the legacy of Moses. The Pentateuch is not distinct because it is torah but because the personal authority of Moses, and ultimately the claimed authorship of Moses, constitutes the Pentateuch as a unit and its torah as distinctly authoritative regardless of its generic form. This distinc-

6. Cf. J. Sanders, *Torah and Canon* (Philadelphia: Fortress, 1972); B. Childs, *Introduction to the Old Testament as Scripture* (Philadelphia: Fortress, 1979), 128-35; R. Rendtorff, *The Old Testament: An Introduction*, trans. John Bowden (Philadelphia: Fortress, 1986), 131f.

7. The phraseology referring to Moses as the decisive person for the authority of the law(s), their communication and writing, and the book of Torah is diverse. From the numerous references, a random sample may be given: Exod 24:4; Lev 26:46; 27:34; Num 15:22-23; 17:5 (*NRSV* 16:40); 30:17 (*NRSV* 30:16); Deut 4:44; 31:9, 24; 33:4; Josh 8:32; 22:5; Judg 3:4; 1 Kgs 2:3; 2 Kgs 14:6; 18:12; 21:8; 23:25; 1 Chron 22:13; 2 Chron 23:18; 25:4; 30:16; 33:8; Ezra 3:2; Neh 1:7; 8:1; 10:29 (*NRSV* 10:30); Sir 24:23; Matt 8:4; Mark 1:44; 12:26; Luke 2:22; 24:44; John 1:17; etc.

tiveness of the Pentateuch-Torah due to the person of Moses increasingly became all-important, not only for everything already contained in the tradition (which for much of the material was originally not the case) but also for everything new that was in need of supreme authorization.

The constitutiveness of Moses for the Pentateuch-Torah is directly relevant for the question of the literary genre of the Pentateuch. If the generic forms of torah and the Torah itself were relative to the authority given them by Moses, one must ask if the constitutive importance of Moses himself did not have to be expressed in the Pentateuch in a literarily typical and ultimately generic way. We must ask what constitutes the importance of Moses rather than what constitutes the importance of the Torah. Furthermore, we may assume that this question was not alien to the final authors of the Pentateuch and that we can find the answer in their work. We will return to this question later.

2. Of the few theories concerning the genre of the Pentateuch or Hexateuch that have been proposed, none has survived, at least not intact.

a. G. von Rad explained it as the baroque kerygmatic narrative — unfolding the ancient cultic creed in Deut 26:5-11. A. Weiser explained it as the outgrowth of the ancient covenant-cult festival. However, one cannot say that a serious attempt has been made to explain the whole of the Pentateuch or Hexateuch as the narrative form of the covenant formulary.

b. B. Childs following J. Sanders[8] emphasizes the reality of Torah while saying, "Clearly Genesis was conceived of by the final redactor as the introduction to the story of Israel which begins in Exodus."[9] He says the first five books "provided a critical norm of how the Mosaic tradition was to be understood by the covenant people."[10] At the same time he says, "The claim of Mosaic authorship functioned as a norm by which to test the tradition's authority."[11] In the first of these two statements, the norm for the Mosaic tradition is the Pentateuch. In the second statement, the norm for the tradition's (the Pentateuch's?!) authority is the Mosaic authorship. Which is the norm for which? If Moses is the norm for the Pentateuch, how is this reflected in the work as a whole? It is doubtful that Childs has answered this question, despite his justifiable attention to the canonic level and to the final redactor. Moreover, if the Pentateuch is the norm for the Mosaic tradition, in what sense is it the norm for the covenant people? Is it the norm in the sense that it is "the story of Israel which begins in Exodus," and to which Genesis is the introduction? Is this the explanation of the sense of its normativity? Nevertheless, this formulation comes relatively close to a generic definition. It is intriguing that Genesis is considered the introduction to the whole which follows.

8. Sanders, *Torah*.
9. Childs, *Introduction,* 130.
10. Childs, *Introduction,* 131-32.
11. Childs, *Introduction,* 134.

But the "story of Israel" goes beyond the Pentateuch. In this "story," Exodus-Deuteronomy would be the *beginnings* of the *history* of Israel. If we ask, however, what constitutes these beginnings of Israel's history, we are back at the question of whether the history of these beginnings constitutes the Mosaic authority, or whether the Mosaic authority constitutes these beginnings. In short, what is constitutive. The beginnings? Israel, with Moses? Moses for Israel? Or something else? For the beginnings, for Israel, and/or for Moses?

c. It is commonplace in interpretation to define Exodus-Deuteronomy as being concerned with Israel. This *opinio communis* is subject to critical scrutiny. Indeed, it seems to be much more the result of the critical-historical reconstruction of the historical origins of Israel than the result of the interpretation of the literary nature of the Pentateuch. In this critical reconstruction of Israel's historical beginnings, Moses has played an ever-decreasing role which is the exact opposite of the ever-increasing role asserted for Moses in the traditio-historical process resulting in the Pentateuch. From the time of the deuteronomists on, the Pentateuch was referred to with regard to Moses, and not with regard to Israel or Israel's history. This role of Moses which finally increased to monumental proportions could be neglected in critical scholarship because the final literary picture reflects neither the reality of Israel's historical beginnings nor the portrait of the historical Moses. The history of research about Moses presented by R. Smend[12] and E. Osswald[13] and the analysis of the Moses traditions in the Pentateuch by many others, most recently in a brilliant way by H. Cazelles,[14] are exceedingly revealing. This history and analysis has been governed virtually exclusively by the historical question regarding what we can know concerning the historical Moses and the portrait of Moses *before* its final shape in the extant Pentateuch. Only a single publication discusses that picture throughout the entire biblical tradition and beyond.[15]

Due to the prevalent historical interest, the importance of Moses in the late form of Exodus-Deuteronomy has played no role in modern scholarship, including Cazelles' article, and the late form of the Pentateuch itself has not been worth studying, neither literarily nor historically. It is, then, quite typical when O. Kaiser can have a beginning student, speaking for many, exclaim: "The Pentateuch is not Mosaic, but a mosaic!"[16] One wonders how such a beginner can arrive at such a sophisticated judgment. Also, K. Baltzer, who in my opinion is basically on the

12. R. Smend, *Das Mosebild von Heinrich Ewald bis Martin Noth,* BGBE 3 (Tübingen: J. C. B. Mohr, 1959).

13. E. Osswald, *Das Bild des Mose in der kritischen alttestamentlichen Wissenschaft seit Julius Wellhausen,* Theologische Arbeiten 18 (Berlin: Evangelische Verlagsanstalt, 1962).

14. H. Cazelles, "מֹשֶׁה," *TWAT* 5, 28-46.

15. H. Cazelles, *Moïse, l'homme de l'alliance* (Paris: Desclée & Cie, 1955); German edition: *Moses in Schrift und Überlieferung,* trans. F. Stier and E. Beck (Düsseldorf: Patmos, 1963).

16. O. Kaiser, *Introduction to the Old Testament,* trans. John Sturdy (Minneapolis: Augsburg, 1975), 44.

right track, can say that the Pentateuch contains essential elements of the genre "biography" but that "die geschlossene Form einer Biographie [ist] hier weitgehend aufgelost."[17]

d. Against all these assumptions, it should be asserted that the serious study of the literary form and genre of the extant Pentateuch, and with it the study of the portrait of Moses, is just as necessary as the study of the historical Moses or of the Moses in the pre-Pentateuchal traditions. In such a study it may just happen, for beginning students and scholars alike, that the Pentateuch appears to be much more Mosaic and much less a — chaotic — mosaic than O. Kaiser's beginner assumes.

Recognizing that statistics are relative, Moses is mentioned more often than Israel in Exodus-Deuteronomy — some 510 against 460 times (according to a rough count based on Mandelkern). But one needs to read the entire narration from Exodus through the end of Deuteronomy with attention to the question of how the relationship between Israel and Moses is depicted, i.e., who is in the foreground and who is in the background; who is important for whom; who is decisive and who is, if not negligible, then at least relative; who depends on whom; whose story is it and whose is it not, or whose is it only secondarily. The evidence for the answers to these questions is so overwhelming that one need not even bother quoting references which number in the hundreds. It is perplexing how the scholarly tradition could say that Exodus-Deuteronomy narrates the story of Israel, contrary to what these books demonstrate and contrary to the self-understanding of these books in the subsequent tradition history. We must be prepared for the thesis that *the Pentateuch is not the story or history of Israel's beginnings but the story of the life of Moses which is fundamental for the beginnings of Israel's history; that it is the vita, or the biography, of Moses.* It is not coincidental that the older traditions mean the torah of Moses, and not simply torah, when referring to the Pentateuch.

B. The Pentateuch as Biography

1. With the possibility that the Pentateuch is the biography of Moses we introduce an interpretation that demands, if only briefly in this chapter, a few methodological clarifications.

a. The genre "biography" has recently been introduced into the discussion by K. Baltzer.[18] Following upon some forerunners who pointed out the biographical nature of some Old Testament materials, Baltzer has defined the genre specifically and associates a broad spectrum of the Old Testament literature with it, or with elements of it. Baltzer's work is of fundamental importance for one reason above all others. Old Testament research, particularly in form criticism, has focused on

17. K. Baltzer, *Die Biographie der Propheten* (Neukirchen-Vluyn: Neukirchener, 1975).
18. Baltzer, *Die Biographie*.

the corporate reality of Israel to such an extent that its attention to individuals and their relationship to and role in their communities has not been only neglected but sometimes outright disclaimed. This one-sided sociological model can no longer be defended, not only because of the great individuals in Israel's history but also because of the place of each individual in Israel's community. Israel was not an amorphous mass of anonymous numbers. Attention to individuality has nothing to do with an individualistic concept of society. Whatever the sociological and theological importance of Jeremiah and Ezekiel 3 and 18 may be for the view of the relationship between the individual and the community, these books do not mark the beginning of Israel's attention to individuals. Indeed, we will not properly understand Israel's concept of community as long as we do not understand the place and role of individuals in the community.

The roots for Israel's awareness of individuality should be much more carefully studied. Israel recognized that individuals were born, lived, and died, and that each had a name, a life story, and above all else a pedigree. One of the inevitable roots for all life stories, narrated or not, was the genealogy, a richly documented genre in the Old Testament. Against this common background, the life stories of individuals which we possess must be understood. They are quite numerous. They are the biographies of individuals who had become important for their communities, for their traditions, and ultimately for Israel and its history. There are a variety of aspects which are important for such life stories, including clan, hero, royal office, types of nonroyal office, messiah, prophet, and perhaps others. The telling or writing of a life story is an easily identifiable tradition throughout the entire Old Testament tradition history which had — for understandable reasons — different forms and different settings. Baltzer's work raises some problems, but it addresses a gap for which research has been long overdue.

b. Based on the pattern of the Egyptian tomb inscriptions, Baltzer presupposes for the genre a strict or closed set of patterned elements according to which a biography, i.e., the biography of a public servant, had to be constructed. This methodological assumption not only evokes the question of the historical relationship between the Egyptian tomb inscriptions and the Old Testament biographies. It also raises the broader question of the possible variety of forms or structures and of matrices or settings in which and out of which biographies could emerge, a question that cannot be pursued at this time. Another question has to do with the apparent interdependence of different genres such as tomb inscriptions, biographies, royal inscriptions, chronicles, annals, historical novels, and histories.[19] Last but not least, the question is of utmost importance whether we must understand every genre as the programmatic application of a consciously preconceived pattern, or whether we may at least also understand genre as the result of processes in which typical

19. On this aspect, cf. the lucid discussion by John Van Seters, *In Search of History* (New Haven/London: Yale University Press, 1983).

forms or structures of oral or written narrations emerge. The question is whether a *defined* genre stands at the beginning of a narration or literary work, or whether the generic definition of some such works may also be an a posteriori abstraction. What is the relationship between Baltzer's "Ideal-biography" and a "Real-biography"?

c. Autobiographical and biographical literature is found, with qualifications, in ancient Egypt and among the Hittites,[20] and in the Mediterranean world in a long development from pre-stages in Homer on down to Roman times.[21] Characteristic for this literature is the correlation between personal life *(bios)* and work, the importance of the spirit guiding the personal life for the work, and the public relevance of the work. The development also shows that autobiography and biography as genres were possible only under societal conditions, especially in monarchies, in which the society's fate was decisively influenced by the character, the accomplishments, and the fate of an individual.

The fact that the full-fledged genre appears late in the Mediterranean world, from the Hellenistic period into the Rome period, does not prove that this development is irrelevant for the Israelite literature because the former is later than the latter. The question is whether an analogous generic development can also be observed in the history of the older Israelite literature, and especially in the development of the Pentateuchal traditions themselves in which Moses had become ever more important until he finally became the solely decisive individual for the entire history and community of Israel.[22] Such an analogous generic development toward the biography of the all-important Moses is particularly relevant with regard to the historical circumstances under which Moses could become more important for

20. Cf. Van Seters, *History,* 118f., 128-30, 145, 165, 181-87, 192, 219, 221.

21. Cf. V. Pöschl, "Autobiographie," *Lexikon der Alten Welt* (Zurich/Stuttgart: Artemis, 1965), 414-17; C. Andresen, "Biographie," *Lexikon der Alten Welt* (Zurich/Stuttgart: Artemis, 1965), 469-73; G. Misch, *A History of Autobiography in Antiquity,* trans. E. W. Dickes (Cambridge: Harvard University, 1951); and A. Momigliano, *The Development of Greek Biography* (Cambridge: Harvard University, 1971).

22. For the development of the form of the Egyptian biographies, cf. Van Seters, *History,* 181-85. Most important is what Van Seters says about their complex structure: "And what is most important for form-critical considerations, both private biographies and royal inscriptions often have the same complex structure with a variety of genre elements included within the same work, each appropriate to the general *Sitz im Leben* in which it is used. Prose narration may be combined with poetic forms, especially hymns and prayers. Both genres may contain lists or legal enactments, and even elements of wisdom" (185). Van Seters's description demonstrates very clearly what is *not* constitutive for the genre: the "complex structure" — in terms of style and genre elements — is a mosaic, to use Kaiser's term. But the mosaic says nothing about whether it is chaotic or generic. This fact is especially important where the mosaic, as in the case of the Pentateuch, is the result of a complex traditio-historical process. The complexity of this process does not mean that in the final stratum, or in any of its earlier literary strata, a generic identity and homogeneity are impossible because the complexity of the tradition history would only allow for generic disintegration into chaos.

Israel than any other individual in its history, i.e., after the end of the monarchy. After the monarchy and because it had been vanquished and the biographies of the kings had come to an end, de facto and with regard to the fundamental validity of those available, Moses could rise above them all. Moreover, his biography could once and for all replace theirs as the life story of the person whose importance for Israel was more fundamental than theirs and who preceded them.

d. In order to provide a clearer access to the question of the biographical nature of the Pentateuch we must raise two questions. What is constitutive for the genre? And how are the person and his/her work related in the genre?

Regarding the first question, Baltzer and Van Seters, with some variations, have presented the arguments on the basis of the Egyptian biographies. According to their description, the biographies present persons as figures of a public function or office and their work as an accountability report (to the gods or to posterity) for their conduct in this office. Constitutive for the biographies are the installation report (so Baltzer; not mentioned by Van Seters); the reference to the installing authority, the king, and to their good relationship with that authority; and the description of their assignment and its execution.

Variables in the genre include (and here we already include aspects from the Old Testament biographies): (1) the narrations or statements about birth and death. Not all biographies contain birth narrations or birth statements, although reference to the genealogical relationship is virtually universal. For obvious reasons, the autobiographical farewell speeches in which persons leaving public office account for their conduct in office contain no death report. Probably for other reasons as well, we have to distinguish between *ante mortem* and *post mortem* biographies; (2) the variable arrangement of the material in chronological, topographical, or some other systematic order; (3) the aspects of different offices, or various aspects of the same public function or office; predominant among the aspects of office are the person's conduct of foreign and domestic affairs, and the relationship of the office to the cult; (4) the degree to which a biography appears in the context of a wider history; (5) the length of the narration; (6) the length of the life narrated; and (7) the styles in generic elements used in the narration.

e. The second question of how person and work are related in the genre is important above all because the ancient biography is constituted by the correlation of these two factors. The ancient biography is no *Entwicklungsroman*.[23] In this relationship between person and work, one can see not only that the individual person does not disappear behind the work but also that the work would not exist

23. The modern understanding of biography as an often highly individualistic and psychological development is perhaps another reason, besides the focus on corporateness, why Old Testament scholarship has hesitated to speak about biography. A further reason for this hesitancy seems to have been the theological interest in the kerygmatic nature of the texts in which the focus is on Yahweh and not on persons. But the focus on Yahweh means neither that there are no human life stories nor that Yahweh is absent from such human life stories.

without the individual person. At the same time one can see that the subjective traits of the person's individuality, insofar as they play a role at all, stand in the service of the objective conditions of the person's task as a public servant. One can detect, and should expect, a correlation between the references to an individual's life and the conceptualized presentation of work, function, or office. How this correlation looks can only be discovered from case to case. We can now return to the Pentateuch.

2. Of all the criteria just listed for the ancient genre of biography, not one is absent in Exodus-Deuteronomy. All the elements of biography, including the variables, are contained in that narration without exception. These elements need not be recounted here. Nor is it necessary to list the statements of the authors, such as, e.g., Deut 34:7-12, which explicitly state the importance of Moses the person, or the references to his various functions or offices, or even those references which note his subjective traits. Exodus-Deuteronomy without the person of Moses would not exist. In fact, this work is not only framed by the narrations of Moses' birth and death; throughout it is pervaded by and based upon the central importance of Moses.

a. What is more important than the biographical elements is the conceptual coherence in Exodus-Deuteronomy constituted by those biographical elements. In its twofold structure, with two subdivisions in each of the two parts, this narration represents in a systematized order the work of Moses, Yahweh's servant for Israel, utilizing the framework of his life from his birth until the day of his death. This systematized structure is cast into the topographical and chronological order of the sequence of the events. In each of the four major parts, Moses has a specifically different function as the narration progresses. Deuteronomy alone, the testament of Moses, is a distinctly biographical element of the whole Moses story. Here, for the last time, he functions, as in the older parts, as the executor and interpreter of Yahweh's instructions and as the dispenser of his public responsibility. In the narration concerning the journey from Egypt to Sinai he is both the receiver and executor of Yahweh's instructions, the Mediator. Nowhere does Moses disappear behind his work because he is Yahweh's servant, or behind Israel because Yahweh's and Moses' work take place on behalf of Israel. On the contrary, Moses' work and Yahweh's work, indeed Israel itself, would not exist without the person of Moses. Israel's existence was bound to Moses, and the proposal that Yahweh could have chosen someone else is speculative in view of the literary narration, apart from the fact that it would only affirm the importance of a person anyway. Moses' work is intrinsically related to Moses as a person, and the person of Moses stands in the service of the conditions of his work. The biographical data and the conceptual organization are interwoven. They are indissolubly intertwined.

b. Moreover, the work of Moses is not narrated by means of the juxtaposition of two or four stages on the same level of importance. It climaxes in the Sinai pericope in which Moses is literally the go-between, first between Israel in the camp and Yahweh on the mountain — ultimately alone with Yahweh! (About whom in the Old Testament was Israel capable of saying such a thing?) — and then between Israel around and Yahweh over the sanctuary within the camp. He is much more than the leader of a migratory group. He is the Mediator κατ' ἐξοχήν — prophetically and priestly — for all time. Beyond the second most important event, i.e., Moses' testament, the Sinai pericope pinpoints the culminating event in Moses' "life": his "work" in less than a one-year period. The narration of Moses' life is not an anthology of unrelated stories or periods. It may be a mosaic, but this mosaic is eminently structured topographically and chronologically, and, most important of all, is conceptually prioritized. The picture presented here conflicts with Baltzer's statement that the closed or fixed form of biography is by and large dissolved in the Pentateuch. That statement reflects the tradition of tradition-critical scholarship on the Pentateuch in which one ultimately could no longer see the forest for the trees, as the saying goes. It seems much more certain that the biographical genre is clearly evident precisely in its final and very much expanded form.[24]

c. Moses died 120 years old. According to Exod 7:7 he was 80 years old when he spoke to Pharaoh. This statement must be understood biographically. It refers to Moses' public appearance and not to his vocation-installation. It focuses the reader's attention on the understanding that the Moses biography proper, encompassing the last third of his life, begins with his public appearance. This distinction within the total biography rests, perhaps, on the older well-known distinction between the secret vocation or anointment of Yahweh's servants and their public appearance. One can see here a shift in the tradition history of the Moses biography from one biographical element to another: from the installation to the public appearance; or again, from the commission to the compliance-execution. Likewise, it ought to be noted that Moses' public appearance before Pharaoh subdivides the section "From Egypt to Sinai" (Exodus 1–18) into two parts: the time before his appearance and the time from that appearance on. This subdivision is not necessarily required by the older structure of the narration.

Finally, Exod 7:7 does not dislodge the twofold/fourfold macrostructure of

24. Baltzer, *Biographie,* 38. Baltzer is probably correct when assuming that there were several Moses biographies in earlier stages of the tradition. However, this assumption proves nothing regarding the absence or presence of the same genre in the final Pentateuch. But when Baltzer separates the salvation-historical and the biographical traditions in Exodus-Deuteronomy and says that the decision as to which elements belong to which tradition cannot always be made with certainty (39), he has a good argument as far as the analysis of the traditions behind the final Pentateuch is concerned. For the final Pentateuch, however, it is quite clear that this alternative does not exist because all those originally non-Mosaic salvation-historical traditions have been — redaction-historically speaking — framed by, and thereby placed under, the authority of Moses. This massive Mosaization is especially clear in the priestly parts of the Sinai pericope and in Deuteronomy.

Exodus-Deuteronomy. One might suspect that the statement is a signal by which the public life of Moses from Exod 7:7–Deuteronomy 34 is bound together in contradistinction to the preparation for that period in Exod 1:1–7:6. This understanding would be an overinterpretation of the function of Exod 7:7 which confines Moses' (and Aaron's) appearance to their speaking to Pharaoh. Thus, it marks the beginnings of the 40 decisive years of public life, while it relates this beginning to Moses' and Aaron's encounter with Pharaoh, together with the statement that Aaron was 83 years old at that moment. Exod 7:7 is confined to the story of the rebellion against the oppression which precedes the exodus story proper.

d. What has Genesis to do with the biography of Moses in Exodus-Deuteronomy? If Genesis is not a part of that biography, the "Pentateuch" as a whole cannot be the biography of Moses. Can or must Genesis be understood as part of this biography?

We have discussed the major arguments for the twofold macrostructure of the Pentateuch. Basic to that discussion is the argument that the two blocks are related and not juxtaposed as unrelated narrations. Genesis is the introduction to the *Vita Mosis*. Hence, the two parts interpret one another. Their relationship means, basically, that the life and time of Moses, the period of one person's generation, cannot be properly understood in isolation from all of human history, indeed from the creation of the world. It can only be understood in this horizon. Conversely, creation, human history, and the patriarchal period cannot be properly understood if not seen in the light of the life and work of Moses.

Specifically, the relationship between Genesis and Exodus-Deuteronomy means that in the work of Moses for Israel, especially in Moses' mediation of the revelation at Sinai as well as in his testament, the program is laid down by which Israel is called to be the paradigm for humanity in God's/Yahweh's creation. The decisive person for mediating this revelatory paradigm is Moses. Thus, just as Moses is seen as the single most decisive person for Israel's history and existence, so is he the decisive person for all of humanity's history and existence.

This person appeared in the course of, and at a distinct point in, Israel's history and human history, i.e., during Israel's oppression in a foreign land, and before its entry into the promised land. That point in history is obviously viewed as more than a passing historical moment. It is perceived as the axis of Israel's and human history before and after it, as the watershed mark and forever the fundamental point of orientation for Israel's and human history, even as it is itself a moment in history.

This interpretation is substantiated when one realizes that the exilic-postexilic writers of the Pentateuch, even those who proceeded to write the subsequent history of Israel — i.e., the deuteronomists — did not regard history as progressing to ever higher culminations after the life of Moses, up to their own time and beyond. On the contrary, they saw history culminating, once and for all, centuries earlier in the life of Moses, and themselves constituted, called, and evaluated from that vantage point.[25] When talking about Moses they did not talk about themselves, but when talking about themselves they talked about Moses. To be the Israel of *Moses* was the criterion for their identification. This criterion was at the same time the basis for their claims to universal validity.

Genesis is an intrinsic part of the biography of Moses, of the biographical genre that came to be structurally developed in the context of a universal-historical perspective, and even a creation-historical perspective. This stage in the development of the genre is obviously late in Israel's history. One would have to ask, however, where the roots of this structure are found within Israel's history, as well as in the history of the ancient Near East. This question cannot be pursued at this time. Here it must suffice to point to the subsequent development of the biographical genre which is visible, e.g., in the Chronistic work where, as in the Pentateuch, the movement begins with Adam but, unlike the Pentateuch, culminates in the time of David and Solomon, who built the temple. One is reminded of the gospels of Matthew, Luke, and John in which, with variations, the life and especially the public ministry of Jesus are set up in a more (so Luke and John) or less (so Matthew) universal perspective. One would have to look at other biographies or histories (e.g., Eusebius's *Vita Constantini* and his *Ecclesiastical History*) and perhaps at the correlation of both. The patterned, generic composition of the *Vita Mosis* in the Pentateuch may not have been the first of its kind. It certainly was not the last.[26]

25. The observation is inevitable that, for the Christian perspective, its *Mitte der Zeit* (Conzelmann, *Die Mitte der Zeit,* BHT 17 [Tübingen: J. C. B. Mohr, 1960]), or its axis of history in history (different from K. Jasper's eighth-century BCE prophetic axis time of world history), is the time of the life of Jesus or the event of resurrection (Pannenberg) which is in antithesis to the Pentateuch. This Christian thesis comes into sharp focus only when one understands it as the direct antithesis to the Pentateuch's thesis: Jesus versus Moses.

26. Since the first appearance of this essay in 1985, two extensive publications about the composition or formation of the Pentateuch have gained center stage: Erhard Blum, *Studien zur Komposition des Pentateuch,* BZAW 189 (Berlin: Walter de Gruyter, 1990); and Suzanne Boorer, *The Promise of the Land as Oath,* BZAW 205 (Berlin: Walter de Gruyter, 1992).

More than my own essay, both — with different results — specifically focus on the problem of the concept govenring the Pentateuch's composition. Decisive for its concept is the presupposition that it aims at the possession of and life in the promised land by Yahweh's exclusively elected people. On this presupposition, the Pentateuch provides both the history of Yahweh's elect, particularly led by Moses, to the border of the promised land, and the foundational condition for the life in the land laid down before its conquest.

The Book of Numbers

Introduction

In his recent book *The Old Testament: An Introduction,* Rolf Rendtorff states, "Of all the books in the Pentateuch, the Book of Numbers is the hardest to survey. . . . It is even difficult to decide how to divide it."[1] Rendtorff is only the most recent in a long line of interpreters who have said essentially the same: Gray, Snaith, Noth, de Vaux, Levine, Childs, Budd, et al.

Nevertheless, all interpreters inevitably divide it anyway. Everyone acknowledges the need to discern its structure or composition from its super- or macro-structure — the highest level — throughout the various levels of its infrastructure. Since we do not even have a clear idea of the superstructure of the book of Numbers, I shall focus in this discussion on that question only.

Most commentators divide Numbers into three parts, but their divisions vary. Most posit the conclusion of the first section to be 10:10, but some see it at 10:36 (Noth, Coats), while others at 9:14 (Budd). The conclusion of the second section is usually assumed to be at 20:13; 21:9; 22:1; or 25:18. Commentators cannot even agree that the third section ends at 36:13, the final verse of the book. Budd, e.g., views chapter 36 as an appendix.

The structure of Numbers is obviously anything but self-evident, and much more effort and methodological awareness must be invested in this task. We may have divided the book of Numbers, but we have not necessarily discovered its divisions.

Brevard Childs may be correct in saying, "The biblical editors seem less concerned with this literary problem than are modern commentators."[2] Whether

1. R. Rendtorff, *The Old Testament: An Introduction,* trans. John Bowden (Philadelphia: Fortress, 1986), 147.

2. B. Childs, *Introduction to the Old Testament as Scripture* (Philadelphia: Fortress, 1979), 195.

or not this is the case, and where, is subject to serious study and not to conjecture. Indeed, the only serious study published thus far which focuses on our problem — and which promptly contradicts Childs by claiming that Numbers does have a "convincing and meaningful structure" — is the Ph.D. dissertation by Dennis T. Olson written at Yale under the supervision of Childs himself![3] (What a testimony to the integrity of this doctoral supervisor, who approves the thesis of his student who contradicts him — especially if he might not be completely persuaded!)

Olson's thesis differs sharply from all others, proposing that Numbers has two parts: chapters 1–25 and chapters 26–36. His theory is based on the shift of focus from the old generation who experienced the exodus and Sinai to the new generation who replaced the old in the desert forty years later. Consequently, it is based on the theological distinction between the disobedience of the old generation and the obedience of the new. The texts that signal the beginning of each section are the two census reports in chapters 1 and 26.

This is not the place for a critical review of Olson's thesis. His work contains many astute observations, and deserves credit for being the first to address its subject squarely rather than casually. These observations will force future interpreters to be more critically conscious when addressing this subject than has been characteristic of past attempts. Further, I agree with Olson that Numbers indeed contains only two main parts, not three. However, his thesis neglects a number of alternative structural signals, and, most importantly, is in conflict with additional signals directly pertinent to his very premise. Let me, then, address the issue of structure.

I. The Superstructure of the Book of Numbers

A. Its Place as a Subdivision of the Pentateuch

One might ask whether Numbers is not simply the result of a more or less pragmatic subdivision of the Pentateuch into five convenient parts, a subdivision that could not avoid severing 1:1–10:10 from its organic connectedness with the preceding Sinai pericope. It is certainly true that Numbers is no independent literary entity. If the structure of Numbers is relevant in its own right, then it is so only in distinction from and in tension with the superstructure of the Pentateuch, especially of the Moses biography which comprises Exodus through Deuteronomy.

Such distinctions and tensions of overlapping structures are possible and can be observed especially in composite literary works in which different literary strata

3. Dennis Olson, *The Death of the Old and the Birth of the New: The Framework of the Book of Numbers and the Pentateuch,* Brown Judaic Studies 71 (Chico, CA: Scholars Press, 1985), 1.

have been amalgamated. Each literary stratum imported its original structural system into the new composition. The editors or authors of such compositions were evidently much more concerned with this literary problem than Childs may want to concede. But he is correct in the sense that these editors/redactors/authors, when synthesizing different strata, including their own, often did not erase the original structures of adopted traditions. Apparently, they were not always concerned with the effects of the resultant overlapping and conflicting structures on modern commentators. Therefore, whether or not the book of Numbers reflects a structure in its own right, different from its position in the Pentateuch and subordinate to it, must be discerned from the evidence in the book itself.

B. Structural Integrity of Numbers

Numbers has subdivisions. The discernment of the levels to which they belong is complicated by many obviously conflicting signals in the surface of the extant text. As yet no one has proposed that because Numbers has thirty-six chapters, it therefore has thirty-six major parts. Nor has anyone proposed fifty-five major parts on the evidence of fifty-five distinguishable literary units (perhaps no one has even bothered to make such a count). It is clear that these fifty-five literary units are cast in larger multiunit blocks, themselves distinguishable as higher structural levels.

It is equally clear that Numbers was not organized on the basis of the juxtaposition of different literary strata (**J** and **P**) or of traditions, however defined. The extant text of Numbers owes its basic structure to the priestly writers who, beginning in chapter 11 and continuing throughout the narrative, interwove their own respective contributions with the Yahwistic traditions. In this, however, all literary strata are knit together through the coordination of units, and even interwoven within the units themselves. The final tapestry reflecting the various strata testifies that considerations other than literary-historical were responsible for the formation of Numbers. The authors apparently did not set out to write a "History of the Pentateuchal Literature"!

Neither can it be posited that the references to Moses in fifty-one of the fifty-five units are clues to the structure of Numbers. The same is true for the sixty-six Yahweh speeches reported throughout the text. In twenty-six instances, a Yahweh speech opens the unit, but in forty cases it occurs within a unit. The four chronological indicators in 1:1; 7:1; 10:11; and 33:38 are equally unlikely bases for determining the structure of Numbers.

More significant are the topographical and geographical indicators which pervade the book and punctuate the ongoing movement of the Israelites. They are based on the genre of itinerary. This genre consists of lists of *local* names oriented topographically and of lists of names of *territories* oriented geographically (e.g., the desert of Sinai and the plains of Moab). The lists of such names follow the sequence of stations and territories in a march, journey, pilgrimage, or campaign.

Such lists represent one of the two elementary components of narratives about such marches in accordance with an itinerary. The other component is defined by the terminology for decampment and encampment, especially by the verbs **נסע** ("to decamp") and **חנה** ("to encamp") — e.g., they decamped at this place and encamped at that place. The entire book of Numbers is a narrative which rests on the basic elements for a long movement of what is called a "camp" (**מחנה**) along many locations and through larger territories, thereby focusing specifically on the longer or shorter intervals between encampment and march.

Despite its importance, however, the itinerary-movement narrative does not reflect the agenda under which the book of Numbers is composed at its highest level. A comparison of the entire book with the itinerary narrative in chapter 33 renders the structural differences strikingly clear. Numbers 33 is a concise report of Israel's total pilgrimage along forty-one locations, from its initiation at Rameses to its arrival "in the plains of Moab" (N.B.: the context indicates forty arrivals/encampments in forty years!). Of the forty-one place names, thirty-eight are topographical, while only three refer to territories (the wildernesses of Sin and Sinai and the plains of Moab). But even the three territories appear in this text to be nothing more than further local stations, like all others in the sequential order of encampments and decampments.

Structurally, the narrative of Numbers 33 consists at its highest level of forty parts. By no means can the same be concluded about the function of the geographical and topographical signals for the entire book. In Numbers, the topographical indicators are first of all subordinate to its geographical indicators, especially the desert of Sinai for 1:1–10:10, the plains of Moab for chapters 22–36, and the territories in between: the wilderness of Paran (10:12; 12:16), the land of Edom (20:23; 21:4), the Negeb (21:1), the lands of Moab (21:11, 13, 20; 22:1), and the lands of the Amorites (21:13, 21, 31). The dominant geographical indicator would suggest a narrative structure of seven parts based on the march through seven territories. However, many who subdivide on the basis of geography note only three parts: Sinai, Moab, and the combined regions in between. This discrepancy between exegetical claims and textual evidence demonstrates that considerations other than territorial ones account for the threefold subdivision of Numbers by those commentators, despite their claims for the geographical criteria. They assume a system of composition in which each of the two decisive encampments — at Sinai at the beginning and in Moab at the conclusion — is equally structurally significant to the march through the five other regions in between. In other words, Sinai and Moab are more important than each of the other five regions taken individually, and consequently for other than geographical reasons.

The tripartite subdivision by commentators is on the right track. But it does not go far enough. It fails to account for structural factors that supersede the aspect of geography and even the aspect of the unquestionable preeminence of the two encampments at Sinai and in Moab. The preeminence of these two over the other encampments in the territories between Sinai and Moab already indicates that the aspect of those combined territories does not rank on the same structural level as the aspects referential to Sinai and Moab. The aspect of the combined territories must be connected below the surface of the extant text to either Sinai or Moab according to a perspective which unites it with one of these two alternatives. What is this perspective? This question implies the possibility that Numbers has a bipartite — and not a tripartite — structure. But it can be answered clearly only when an explanation can be found for the preference for a bipartite structure. Apparently, the constitutive conceptual factors for the structure of Numbers must be identified through the clarification of the relationship of its three major components. This clarification indeed provides clear conceptual criteria which reveal that Numbers rests on a bipartite structure. The criteria surface when those factors that to date have not received the attention due their importance are taken into account. They reveal two fundamentally different functions within the three major components, and thus the highest possible level of structural distinction; and they enable us to discover the relationship between the two major parts and the relationship of the transitional part either to what precedes it — Sinai — or to what follows it — Moab.

Associated with the encampment at Sinai is the aspect of the organization of the camp. This organization is cultic-military in nature. The nature of this encampment for the purpose of organization differs from the nature of every other encampment in Numbers. This aspect is, in the extant text, presupposed for the entire movement after the departure from Sinai. In relation to this subsequent movement, it functions as the preparation for that movement. Conversely, the movement itself is evidently associated with the aspect of a military campaign and no longer with the aspect of organization; and it functions in relation to the preceding organization as the execution of the prepared campaign. From 10:11 on — the departure from Sinai — the entire sequence of events, including the events originating from the camp in the plains of Moab, is understood to be the execution of the campaign prepared at Sinai. Together with the part about Moab, the other major component about the transitional phase and territories belongs, therefore, in the narrative of the execution and not the organization of the campaign. As was suspected earlier, the distinction between the transitional phase and Moab, however important, does not belong to the highest structural level in Numbers.

The book of Numbers indeed has two parts: the conceptual aspects of the preparatory organization and the execution of the campaign. These two aspects complement each other as the two basic elements of a report or narrative about a campaign. Numbers is a conceptual unity in its own right — it is the saga of a campaign. Moreover, since this campaign belongs to the type of migration from one territory to another rather than to the type of campaign which returns to its point of departure after completion, it should specifically be characterized as the saga of a migratory campaign.

II. Genre, Setting, and Intention

Does this twofold structure — campaign preparation and campaign execution — belong to a narrative genre?

For the sake of brevity, I will set aside the question of whether the narrative belongs to the types epic, saga, or legend. More important is the question about the type of movement portrayed in Numbers. It is certainly a migration — the movement of a nation from one land, in Numbers from Sinai, to another, the promised land. But what kind of migration is it? Types of movements characterized as (business) trip,. (private/tourist) journey, travel, wandering, hike, or march are insufficient or beside the point.

The second section — from 10:11 through chapter 33 — is clearly governed by the agenda of a military campaign. The same is also true, however, for the first section, especially when one considers that the first four chapters outweigh the remainder of the first section in structural significance. Of these four, chapters 1 and 2 programmatically narrate the story of the exclusively military organization of the draftable males of the twelve tribes (excluding Levi), which consists of their conscription and mobilization into the outer camp arrayed around the already existing and erected sanctuary. The organization of the outer camp is described in chapters 3 and 4, followed by a description of the mobilization of the Aaronides and the Levites (the sanctuary personnel) into the inner camp for the service of the sanctuary. The organization in all four chapters is defined as the preparation — according to the plan and instruction of Yahweh and under the supervision of Moses — for the impending campaign. Moreover, explicit attention is paid to the alternating camp formation: quadrangular for the encampment, linear for the march. Not coincidentally, Num 10:11-28 reports that the tribes naturally assumed that linear formation when they decamped from Sinai and began the campaign.

It is astounding that the latest, otherwise valuable, publication on the theology of warfare in ancient Israel by Millard C. Lind,[4] like virtually all others on the subject before it, completely ignores at least Numbers 1–2. By contrast, it must be said that Numbers 1–4 occupies an eminent place in the theology of warfare in ancient Israel. Even more specifically, these chapters speak not so much about the campaign of the tribes with the sanctuary in attendance as about the campaign of the sanctuary with the tribes in attendance. They address the organization of the sanctuary camp under the leadership of Yahweh the Campaigner in the sanctuary,

4. Millard Lind, *Yahweh Is a Warrior* (Scottdale, PA: Herald Press, 1980).

accompanied by his host, the militia of Israel. They certainly do not address themselves to tribal warfare.

It has been said (Kuschke, et al.) that Numbers 1–2 reflects an artificial agglutination of two genuinely separate traditions — a pilgrimage camp on the one hand and a military camp on the other, an agglutination that has no ground either in reality or in traditional ideology — and that the text is a kind of narrative of a pilgrimage with military protection. Evidence for such an assumption is scanty, and the context reveals a different understanding. The matrix for the concept of a sanctuary camp campaign — to which both the cultic and military aspects are intrinsic — can be discovered immediately adjacent, in the older Yahwistic portions of the second section of Numbers. The motif is crystallized at the beginning, in 10:33-35:

So they set out from the mountain of Yahweh —
three days' way.
And the ark of the covenant of Yahweh went before them —
three days' way,
to seek out a resting place.
And the cloud of Yahweh was over them by day,
and whenever they set out from the camp.
And whenever the ark set out, Moses said,
"Arise, Yahweh!
Let your enemies be scattered
and let those that hate you flee before you!"
And when it rested he said,
"Return, Yahweh, to the ten thousand thousands of Israel."
(author's translation)

This passage reflects the situation of a cultic campaign in which the ark — the ancient symbol of the presence of Yahweh — leads the host of Israel. This vision has nothing to do with an artificial emulsion of pilgrimage and warfare, and is the opposite of a pilgrimage protected by a military contingent. The priestly writers of Numbers 1–4 had only to adopt the older Yahwistic tradition of the cultic campaign — the ark campaign — to expand upon their own tradition, while sculpting the expansion in their own way. In doing so, they certainly did not introduce a societal concept of separation between clergy and military under conditions of warfare. On the contrary, they considered Israel's militia to be in the service of cultic warfare.

The Yahwistic tradition in the second portion of Numbers speaks only about the campaign itself. Nowhere does it describe the preparatory organization of the camp for that campaign, let alone by Yahweh himself! This is exactly what the priestly writers did in the first portion of Numbers. They expanded the available Yahwistic narrative about the campaign with their own narrative about its preparation, implemented by Moses in accordance with Yahweh's own plan and instruction. In the course of this expansion, the tabernacle replaces the ark, literally by "intaking" it. The twofold narrative pattern of preparation and execution, instruction and implementation, which thus emerged can also be found in the priestly narrative about the instructions for and the construction of the tabernacle in Exodus 25–40. It reveals an intention by the priestly writers to emphasize both essential elements of these operations: not only the execution but also its preparation — especially as designed by Yahweh; not only the preparation but also its execution — as supervised by Moses.

The narrative genre of cultic campaigns is not unique to the priestly writers. It belongs to a tradition history of such narratives in which sometimes one, sometimes the other, and sometimes both, of its two components is/are used. Nor is the campaign report genre unique to Israel. The Mesopotamian campaign reports speak — as far as I have observed — only about the campaigns themselves. Egyptian sources report about both the planning stage in Pharaoh's court and the execution of the plan. Not emphasized in most of these reports is the cultic nature of the campaigns in which cultic symbols play a role. However, the presence of such symbols in campaigns and the religious perception of such campaigns are documented throughout history up to our own century.

Whatever the case, the priestly vision of the sanctuary campaign from Sinai to Moab and beyond is based not only on this broad tradition history of campaigns and their cultic-religious undergirding but on the tradition history of Israel's own narratives about the Yahweh wars.

It is self-evident that the twofold pattern of the narrative genre emphasized by the priestly writers conforms to the twofold pattern of preparation and execution of campaigns in the historical reality of warfare. But it is also clear that, if the setting of the narrators or reporters were at any time identical with the setting of those who were involved in the actual preparation and execution of campaigns, it could only have been so at the origin of this narrative genre. At best, the narrators were originally companions of the campaigners (the *Kriegsberichterstatter,* "the war correspondents"). From that point on, the group of people or the institution which employs this narrative genre becomes a setting in its own right, with its own tradition history. Such a setting and such a tradition history can be observed for Israel's history of literature, and possibly for the history of its oral traditions. In this history, the priestly writers have their own relatively late place. From it, they inherited the generic narrative pattern. In addition, as can be seen in the book of Numbers, they reshaped the older tradition of Israel's campaign from Sinai to the plains of Moab under the influence of their own theological program, and thus narrated the story of Israel's first movement toward the land as the prototypical event.

Their addition to the Yahwistic narrative, chronicling the preparation, reveals at least something of their theological program. If the campaign itself from Sinai forward was — according to the Yahwistic narrative — fraught with delays and conflict, one factor was not responsible for these delays and conflicts: its preparation by Moses according to Yahweh's own plan and instruction. Moreover, in the light of this preparation, the fact that Israel's disobedience and lack of trust led to delays and conflicts becomes all the more understandable.

We may assume that, with their emphasis on the preparation phase, the priestly writers had a message in mind for their own time: if the conquest, or reconquest, of the land is to have any promise of success, it must avoid the failures recorded in the Yahwistic saga. An epiphanic campaign must instead be prepared for, with the host of Yahweh, the militia of Israel, mobilized around the sanctuary, ready to follow Yahweh's lead in Yahweh's own reconquest of the land.

We still do not know for certain the historical date for at least the beginning of this concept of the — presumably — Aaronide writers, and I do not want to commit myself to my own speculations. However, one thing is clear: The assumption that the ideas of these chroniclers of Israel's repossession of the land — after 701, 640, 586, 539, or 515 BCE — had nothing to do with Yahweh the Warrior or the theology of warfare is subject to serious revision.

Conceptual Aspects in Exodus 25:1-9

*Dedicated to Jacob Milgrom**

Introduction

As with any text, the meaning of biblical texts consists not only in what they say on the surface but also in the unexpressed thought underneath the texts, yet generative for and operative in them. Unless texts are meaningless, they are semantically conceptualized linguistic structures in which expression and thought converge.

In exegetical work, the difference between a text's explicit statements and the inexplicit thought presupposed in and for it has always been felt. Such an awareness exists even if it is more often the result of common sense than of an approach directly suggested and consciously applied through exegetical method. In more recent developments, the study of the "composition" of small as well as large texts has become virtually commonplace. Yet it is not clear to what extent "composition" analysis is preoccupied essentially with the surface of texts rather than with both their surface and the conceptualities beneath their surface. One may say that the structure of a text is more than its surface composition. If exegetical work wants to explain a text, it must explain its structure. It must, therefore, not only discern its surface composition, but it must also consciously reconstruct the conceptuality beneath its surface. That the latter task is more difficult and hypothetical cannot be used as an excuse for evading it. Its execution must be controlled by signals in the text itself. Of course, this sort of reconstruction of the conceptualities of texts has everything to do with the explanation of the texts themselves and nothing to do with a reconstruction in which texts serve only as irrelevant,

*The following attempt at understanding the *Geistesbeschäftigung* in one of our biblical texts rather than merely describing what it says is dedicated to Professor Jacob Milgrom, an admirable scholar and a gracious person, with my best wishes for a good life in the years to come.

dispensable shells through which to traverse to the real thing, the vision of meaning in the abstract idea.

In order to exemplify this task, in the following I will discuss some conceptual aspects in Exod 25:1-9. Some of them focus on the place of verses 1-9 in their larger context, and some on verses 3b-7 specifically.

Initially it must be said that verses 1-9 of Exodus 25 are selected exclusively for demonstrating the objective of this essay. Their selection does not depend on well-known literary-critical assumptions and even less on a claim that these verses represent a self-contained literary unit in the extant, or so-called canonical, text. Nor has it anything at all to do with the practicality of delimiting a passage for the sake of convenience, a choice — however practical — that does not belong to exegetical work.

I. The Structure of Exodus 25:1-9

Contrary to the virtually universal renderings in the commentaries, verses 1-9 are not a unit structurally. One may surmise that, as soon as this is stated, everyone knows it to be true, and also that by and large the influence either of source-critical positions or of practical convenience prevents a correct representation of the text's structure. Failure to take this structure seriously is particularly astonishing where attention to the extant text is emphasized.

However the larger context is discerned, it is clear that a distinct literary unit begins Exod 25:1 with the narrative formula, וידבר יהוה אל משה לאמר ("The Lord said to Moses"). This unit ends in Exod 30:10 and not in Exod 25:9; 31:17; or 31:18. The unit Exod 25:1–30:10 is a narrative about a speech of the deity to Moses (during Moses' forty-day encounter alone with the deity near or at the top of the mountain). Structurally, this unit consists of two parts: the narrative introduction in 25:1 and the narrated speech in 25:2–30:10. The narrated speech happened in the narrator's past. The quoted speech, described generally, is an instruction which also consists of two parts: the command to Moses to speak to the Israelites in 25:2aα and the content of this commanded speech in 25:2aβ–30:10 (which Moses is to transmit to them after his descent from the mountain). Furthermore, the content consists of two parts: the call on the Israelites for a gift of materials (תרומה) together with the prescription to make a sanctuary in 25:2aβ-9, and the detailed prescriptions for the manufacturing of the parts of the sanctuary as well as the priestly, Aaronide, vestments in 25:10–30:10.

Thus, the structural diagram of Exodus 25:1–30:10 is as follows:

A Narrative about a YHWH Speech to Moses	25:1–30:10

I. Formulaic narrative introduction	25:1
II. The speech — an instruction	25:2–30:10
A. The commission to Moses (to transmit the received speech)	25:2aα
B. The content of the speech	25:2aβ–30:10
1. The call for an offering and — by interpretation — its purpose	25:2aβ-9
2. The instruction for manufacturing	25:10–30:10

This structure is anything but a simple, ultimately simplistic, "outline" or "table of contents." It demonstrates an order of different conceptual levels stratified semantically in the fashion of an inverted pyramid, in which each level is related to all others even as all levels are collapsed in the same literary level of the extant macrounit. The fact that all the identified structural parts are juxtaposed in the extant literary level, or the so-called composition, does not mean that they are, therefore, conceptually coordinated on the same level. Their relationship is one of superordination and, correspondingly, subordination. This structure demands much more than our usual recognition of the redactional or compositional technique of the writers. It especially prevents us from quickly setting aside the "redactional framework" as a mere shell for the important essence of the text — as if we possessed any essence without this framework!

II. Critique of Utzschneider's Treatment of Exodus 25:1-9

Before discussing some of the conceptual aspects in this structure, a comparison with a similar attempt may be helpful. In his important work, *Das Heiligtum und das Gesetz,* H. Utzschneider,[1] who distinguishes between the cohesion *("Kohäsion")* of the text surface and the infratextual coherence *("Kohärenz"),* recognizes distinct elements, such as those in Exod 25:1, 2aα, 2aβ-8; 39:43, as signals typical of the cohesion of the Sinaitic texts. Moreover, he states that the "Handlungsrolle des Mose erweist sich damit als das bestimmende Movens im *thematischen* Aufriss der sinaitischen Heiligtumstexte" (emphasis mine).[2]

However, his apparent conclusion that the text's infratextual, its "thematic," coherence, i.e., its concept, appears in the identified surface signals is problematic. Verse 1 is not an address *("Anrede").* An address, such as "Moses, Moses," would be part of a narrated speech. Such an address may be presupposed for the beginning of 25:2aα, after verse 1. If this were the case, it would represent a specific structural

1. *Das Heiligtum und das Gesetz* (Göttingen: Vandenhoeck & Ruprecht, 1988).
2. *Heiligtum,* 145.

element of the deity's quoted speech. The failure to define verse 1 correctly leads at the outset to a false reconstruction of the *Schema,* the infraconceptuality of the entire narrative, namely, as a fourfold thematic pattern in which address, commission, content, and effect belong to the same conceptual level. This interpretation misreads not only the pyramidic nature of the infraconceptuality but also the signals in the surface text itself.

Furthermore, Utzschneider's inclusion of Exod 39:43, which expresses the "Darstellung und Reflexion des Effektes," certainly belongs to the typical bipartite priestly narrative pattern of commission and execution. However, this fourth element, i.e., the effect, belongs to the execution report and stands vis-à-vis the first three elements, all of which belong to the commission report. It is not a fourth element in the same report. In terms of both cohesion and coherence, Exod 39:43 belongs to Exodus 35–39, not to Exodus 25–31.

Finally, Utzschneider says that Exod 25:1-10 and 28:1-5 "zentrale Überschrift- und Gliederungsfunktionen wahrnehmen. Sie sind gewissermassen 'Kopfstücke' für die dann folgenden Textkomplexe."[3] Apart from his association of verse 10 with 25:1-9, Utzschneider's equating of the function of 28:1-5 with that of 25:1-9 is, at best, defensible only if one ignores the functions of 25:1, 25:2aα, and especially 25:3-7 (the call for a gift) for the entire following text until 30:10 (and beyond). Ignoring 25:3-7, one would have to take 25:8-9 as covering no more than Exod 25:10–27:21. But 25:3-7 may not be ignored, not only because verses 8-9 function as the explanation for the call but also because that call itself includes the materials needed for the manufacturing of priestly vestments prescribed from Exod 28:1 on. Hence, Exod 28:1-5 represents only the second part of the instructions for all manufacturing in 25:10–30:10, at best from 25:8 on. It is not the conceptual opposite to Exod 25:1-10, or verses 1-9, or especially 2aβ-7. Exod 25:1-10 cannot uniformly be called a *"Bauanweisung,"* not even one directly *"an 'die Israeliten.' "*[4]

III. Hermeneutical Conceptuality of Exodus 25:1-9

The structure shown above reveals a highly developed hermeneutical conceptuality on the part of the narrator. Two aspects will be highlighted in the following.

A. The Unit as Narrative

First, the entirety of 25:1–30:10 must be identified as a narrative about a (divine) commission or command to transmit a call for a gift, a directive to make a sanctuary

3. *Heiligtum,* 190.
4. *Heiligtum,* 41.

from that gift, and an instruction for the manufacturing of its parts and of the priestly vestments. It is a narrative, not just instruction — let alone law. Its narrative character determines the entire text, not only Exod 25:1. It presupposes the anonymous narrator-writer for all its subsections. The scene of the narrated speech includes the actants; namely, the commissioning and instructing deity, the recipient of the commission, and, *in absentia,* the intended Israelite addressees. At issue are the gift of the materials, the making of a sanctuary, and the manufacturing in detail — a one-time event!

Unless "law" is understood in its broadest sense, the differing generic characteristics of this narrative and the deity's speech must be accounted for. Furthermore, both of them fundamentally differ from those laws that are concerned with Israel's permanent existence, regardless of their apodictic or casuistic forms. The focus on a one-time event might best be understood as a precedent-setting prescription to be followed verbatim in similar cases of one-time sanctuary constructions. However, in my opinion it should not. At any rate, this focus in principle sets apart the instructions about the sanctuary from the instructions about the sacrificial procedures in Leviticus 1–7, despite the well-known stylistic similarities in the two cases.

Decisive, however, is the fact that the whole is *narrated* instruction. Why is this so? Specifically, why is the instruction narrated as given by the deity to Moses rather than by Moses to Israel? This question is not answered by reference to Exod 35:4-19. It becomes particularly relevant when one considers the literary-historical possibility that the instruction existed in an earlier, original layer without the extant narrative framework. The emphasis on the narrative framework and the conceptual implications in it are scarcely peripheral. They point to the hermeneutical situation of the redactors, obviously from the Aaronide denomination, in which the authority of their own claims to the legitimate priesthood at the one and only sanctuary was not secure. Their claims were in competition with the claims of others and had to be established by reference to the irreplaceable original revelation *to Moses* of the plan for both the sanctuary and Aaron's priesthood. For the authentication of this claim, neither an earlier form of instruction without the extant narrative framework, the reference to the tradition of the eponymous Aaron, nor the reference to Moses himself was sufficient.

Whether actually presumed or theoretically presumable, an original form of the sanctuary instruction alone, even if it had its origin among the Aaronides, could not have been beyond the contestability of claims by other priestly parties, regardless of whether those claims belonged to the pre-exilic or exilic time. Even if it had been considered "law," or revealed law, that sort of authority and its tradition would not have authenticated the claims of the Aaronides in their own time vis-à-vis the claims of competing groups.

Nor could their recourse to their ancestor Aaron substantiate such a claim. In the tradition, Aaron's own relationship to the legitimate sanctuary was compromised, as the Pentateuch very clearly shows (Exodus 32–34). Aaron had to be relegitimated. This had to happen (and indeed happened) either through a reconceptualization of the tradition in which he had been compromised, or at least through a conceptualization juxtaposed to the compromised tradition. Such an attempt intended to erase the shadow on Aaron and to restore, or even to establish, his unblemished credibility.

Even so, Aaron's authenticity could never have existed without Moses. For Aaron's relegitimation, his reinstatement into an unblemished relationship with Moses was certainly indispensable. This recourse to the Moses-Aaron chain of authenticity is traditio-historically significant. It implies that the authentications of all sanctuary traditions and their priesthoods from the time of Israel's settlement on (not only those in the north) had become relativized, if not compromised. No priesthood during the centuries after the settlement was beyond controversy. Only one person in Israel's tradition emerged as being beyond contestation: the person of Moses. In the traditio-historical process, he alone turned out to be above all Israel and not merely at Israel's beginning. Still, for the authentication of a priesthood through its indispensable connection with the establishment of a sanctuary, not even Moses could have been perceived as having the authority to commission such an establishment.

In modern times, the decision to build a sanctuary is made by a religious community for the sake of its gathering for worship. However, religio-historically, a sanctuary was in principle the dwelling place of the deity on earth, and only for this reason the place for humans to gather. In order to be authentic, such a sanctuary, a מקדשׁ and its מִשְׁכן, had to be initiated by the deity. The decision to build it, as well as its design, belonged to the deity, not to humans on behalf of the deity. Programmatically, even the biblical tradition speaks about the establishment of Israel's sanctuaries in terms of revelation narratives, at least in terms of reactions to revelation. The narrative introduction in Exod 25:1, heavily prepared by 24:15-18, belongs to this conceptual tradition. The aspect expressed in it reflects at the outset the decisive rationale on which the Aaronides' exclusive claims to Israel's sanctuary tradition could be authenticated. Without this introduction to Exod 25:2–30:10, as in similar introductions in the Sinai pericope, the rationale would not exist. The content alone, by virtue of being only an instruction without identifying its instructor, would be insufficient.

The traditional concept of the hierarchically stratified chain of authority, from Yahweh via Moses to Israel, is especially important for the beginning of the narrative about the Sinaitic sanctuary, Israel's first. This is directly expressed in the text. In it, not only the initial but the basic actant is the deity.[5] Another aspect implicitly presupposed in Exod 25:1 and throughout the narrative is the hermeneutical position of the narrators. With the explicit reference to the priests in Exod 27:21 and Exod 28:1f. only after the instructions for the sanctuary itself, the identity

5. Against Utzschneider who says, "Mose erweist sich damit als das *bestimmende Movens . . .*" (emphasis mine). *Heiligtum,* 145. In fact, in Exodus 25–31 Moses is no "Movens" at all.

of the narrators becomes — not coincidentally — evident. The sequence in the text from sanctuary to priesthood is, once again, conceptual. It is unlikely that this reflects merely the temporal sequence of the two major stages of the total operation. An assumption of such a temporal sequence would mean that all objects to be manufactured, at least those for the priests, can only be made in successive order rather than simultaneously by different people or groups. On the contrary, the sequence of the text means that while no sanctuary is without its priesthood, the priesthood is the consequence of the sanctuary rather than the condition for it. Yet one would overlook the self-interest of the narrators, their own vantage point, if one were to assume that this interest only begins where they begin to speak about "Aaron and his sons." In fact, quite logically, it begins with their narrative about the instructions for the sanctuary (from Exod 25:1 on). Without first focusing on the sanctuary, their own authenticity would be without ground. Therefore, when reading the text's composition conceptually, one has to read it from the subjective perspective of the narrators, even as one must understand their objectifying perspective. This means that Exodus 28–30, as well as other texts about the origin of the narrators' own tradition, must be read as underlying Exod 25–27. It is this origin of the narrators' tradition that is authenticated in Exod 25:1–27:19.[6]

Of course, rather than implying an ad hoc affirmation of his importance by the priestly writers, we should assume that the narrators' recourse to Moses' singular position in Israel as the mediator without equal of the deity's revelation presupposes a traditio-historical development in which Moses' fundamental importance had already emerged. This development is already complete in Exodus 19–24, which I maintain to be older than what follows and on the basis of which I take the priestly text to have been expanded such that the entire Sinai pericope peaks in the instruction for the construction of the sanctuary and ultimately its erection in Exodus 40. Through this expansion, Moses became the mediator of the sanctuary tradition, for which his role as the mediator of the covenant turned out to be the pre-stage. The question of the development of the Moses tradition in its entirety seems to be in urgent need of a fresh focus and approach.

Finally, the traditio-historical question of the medium by which the revelation is received is also significant. It is one thing to paraphrase a sentence such as "Yahweh spoke to Moses," but quite a different thing to explain it. On this question, Utzschneider has recently pointed to the combination of the conceptions of oracle and law in the tradition.[7] Yet, when comparing the Moses tradition and the oracular

6. It should be obvious that this reading of the text concerned with the hermeneutic of the Aaronides differs from a reading in which the texts are examined for their contribution to our historical reconstruction of the Aaronides, as is essentially the case in M. Haran, *Temples and Temple-Services in Ancient Israel* (Oxford: Clarendon Press, 1978), 84-111, especially 84-92. The two approaches are complementary, although each must rest on its own kind of evidence.

7. *Heiligtum,* 145-51.

tradition in their interpenetration, one will probably have to assume that the oracular tradition became absolutized in conjunction with the absolutization of the role of Moses, rather than that Moses grew in importance as the oracular element grew, if at all, in its own tradition history.

B. Place and Significance of Exod 25:2aβ-7

The second conceptual aspect in the structure concerns the particular place of the call for a gift in Exod 25:2aβ-7 and its purpose as expressed in verses 8-9 in the form of the instruction to make a sanctuary. I here refer to Exod 25:2aβ-9, II.B.1. in the structure given above.

The justification for placing verses 3-7, the call for the gift, before the instructions for manufacturing (25:10f.), and even before the basic directive to make a sanctuary in 25:8-9, seems self-evident. Perhaps this is the reason no one has bothered to explain it. It is not unthinkable, however, that the narrative could have been organized such that the architectural prescriptions, from Exod 25:10 or even from verse 8 on, preceded the call for the materials. After all, it should be expected for a planned building project, that a list of materials as in 25:3-7 is not established and an order for their procurement as in 25:2aβ+b issued (however voluntary the necessary תרומה is), unless the purpose for which the materials are to be used is known and has already been specified. In addition to the types of materials, under normal circumstances the quantity of the various required materials also plays a role, for economic reasons. This aspect does not appear in verses 3-7. This shows that the catalogue of only the types of materials[8] presupposes the

8. John Durham speaks of a "catalogue of opulence" (*Exodus,* WBC 3 [Waco, TX: Word Books, 1987], 354). "Opulence" in Durham's statement refers to the quality of all the materials in the "catalogue" (a defensible interpretation), not to their quantity; their quantity is infratextually presupposed but not referred to or indicated as are the qualifying connotations of the materials listed.

The genre term "catalogue" is correct inasmuch as it refers to a systematized written list. However, the sort of catalogue given in Exod 25:3-7 is not an inventory of the materials themselves. It is, rather, an order of types of materials by which the materials themselves are to be separately grouped or assembled when given. Institutionally, in terms of setting, this typologizing catalogue points — as in our context — to a stage in the process of giving. After the gifts are received, they are identified, separated, and placed, each according to its respective type. After this stage is completed, the counting of each type of material can begin, which will show whether the received quantities are sufficient. Only after the materials are typologically organized can the manufacturers begin their work.

We have every reason for saying that historically the text about the Sinai event is fictitious. But in form-critical perspective, in terms of genre and setting, the text is anything but fictitious. On the contrary, it reflects the institutionalized reality of such collections, indeed a specific stage in their procedure, and it is the generic expression of that reality.

The question of the order itself, the composition of this typologizing catalogue (which

assumption that they will be given in sufficient quantity. This assumption, implicitly operative in verses 3-7, is confirmed both indirectly by the text's statement about the voluntary nature of giving in verse 2b and directly by the narrative about the overabundance of the given materials in Exod 35:20-29 and 36:2-7.

Since the acquisition of materials for a building project presupposes the knowledge of their required types and even quantities, under normal circumstances, one can call for the acquisition of such materials only after the design of the building is complete. Therefore, the justification for placing the call for (an offering of) materials before the publication of the design is by no means self-evident. It must be explained.

This opens the possibility of explaining alternative conceptualities in the structures of texts. A structure in which the design *precedes* the call for the procurement of the materials would point to the *planning* stage in the procedural sequence of a project. By contrast, a structure in which the design *follows* the call for the procurement would point to that state in the total procedure in which the already completed plan is promulgated for the implementation or execution. Exod 25:1–30:10 exemplifies the latter structure. The difference between the two structures is not coincidental. It rests on the distinction between the procedure involved in a planning stage and the procedure as it is reversed from the moment the plan begins to be implemented.

Applied to our text, this distinction means that the call for the gift of materials could not be reported unless the design of the project were reported first. However, this does not correspond to our text's structure. If the design is presupposed to be complete and ready for implementation, it is now announced in such a way that the call for the materials precedes the instruction about the design, just as the procurement of the materials must precede their usage in manufacturing the objects for which the design must be at hand. This is the sequence the structure of our text reflects. Therefore, this structure is derived from and aims at the procedural sequence for the beginning of the implementation of the design presumed to be previously completed. It does not reflect the sequence of steps during the planning stage (so to say, in the administrative or architectural bureau), nor does it reflect the procedure of the actual manufacturing. It belongs to the stage *between* the planning and the actual manufacturing, i.e., to the start of the implementation of the plan through its logistically ordered pronouncement.

We have good reason for assuming that these distinctions in the text's structure reflect distinct institutionalized steps in the reality of construction projects, both in ancient Israel and in the ancient Near East, and indeed throughout history.

---

must be institutionally prepared before it can be applied to the arriving materials, and the preparation of which requires administrative theoreticians) is not further discussed here. Although there is some truth to the usual interpretation of the order of its "descending sequence of value" (Durham, *Exodus,* 354), a closer analysis reveals a more complicated picture.

They reflect typical societal settings, particularly of society-wide enterprises, and are generic expressions of those settings. They belong to the basic genre of reports or narratives about construction projects. The basic distinction in such reports, namely, between the prescription for the work and the description of the work, is generally recognized or supposed to be known. Thus far, however, the specific distinction between the planning process and the order in which the completed plan is announced for the sake of the public start of a project has played no role in the structural interpretation of such texts.[9] The two distinguishable types of composition point to two distinguishable typical subsettings preceding the manufacturing process in a total project: the planning stage (in architectural bureaus) and (the commission of) the publication of the plan (by a commissioning authority).

One may even venture to explain why our text's composition is based on the commission to publicize the project rather than on the structure of the planning stage. When considering the nature of Exod 25:1–30:10, namely, the revelation to Moses by the deity about what Israel must do, one must realize that this communication is governed by the procedure of the implementation of the deity's plan, not by the procedure of the deity's own planning. This text does not speculate about the process in the deity's mind or council! It narrates the revelation, the pronouncement of the result of that process for the sake of its implementation. Whether this focus was consciously intended by the writer or resulted from his patterned preunderstanding is beyond our capabilities to discern. Relevant, however, is the role of Moses as the commissioned communicator. It corresponds to the role of grand viziers in royal offices who must be assumed to have had administrative responsibility over a project from the point at which they publicly announced it. Our highly mythological text corresponds primarily to the earthly setting of a royal palace in which a vizier was commissioned by the king to begin the implementation of a plan, by communicating to the public the sequence of the necessary steps as a precondition for the actual work.

Furthermore, the communicative function in the sequence of the two major types of the content of the commission points to the focus on the implementation of the plan. Thus, one should assume that the call for the gift from all Israelites must be made before the instructions for the designs of the objects are handed to the workers, especially to the supervisors of the work. Last but not least, the communicative function of this stage of the process is discernible in the diction of the total text. Not only does the text constantly say, "you shall make," thereby expressing that what is indicated shall be made, for the most part it prescribes the details of the objects. The diction or style and the specifications are directed to the workers. It belongs to the generic style of instructions for workers which — along with the tradition of models or diagrams, analogous to our "blueprints" — spell

9. Cf. also Utzschneider: "Vergleiche mit der reichen ao. [*sic,* ancient oriental] Bauinschriften-Literatur fehlen bisher weitgehend"[21] (the footnote refers to B. Levine).

out verbatim how the work is to be done at the construction site. Exod 25:10–30:10 speaks only about the deity's communication of the design to Moses. Yet one has to infer that it presupposes the understanding of a process in which the commissioned vizier gives the prescription for the design to the working people before their own work starts (reflected in Exod 36:8f.). Even so, our text belongs to the instructional setting. It is not, like Exod 36:8–39:34, a building report *("Baubericht")* proper. Strictly speaking, it is a narrative about the instruction for a building project that is commissioned by the highest authority. Whatever the setting and time of the priestly narrators was, their narrative reflects, in its highly mythologized form, the tradition of this narrative genre and its setting.

Science in the Bible

I. Introductory Remarks

This chapter focuses on science *in,* not science *and,* the Bible, on the presence and role of science in the Bible itself rather than on the relationship of modern science and the Bible. This focus is important because the scientific aspect is just as much a part of the religious nature of the Bible as the religious aspect is inevitable in modern science. Science as well as faith, faith as well as science, belongs to both the Bible and our own time. As we need clarity about the relationship of faith and science in our own time, we need clarity not about faith in the Bible as opposed to science today but about the relationship of faith and science in the Bible itself. And since we normally speak about the Bible as a book of faith, we especially need greater clarity about the role of science in the faith of the biblical generations.

The arrangement of the biblical books in the Christian canon, their contents, concepts, and intentions, demonstrate beyond doubt that neither the Bible as a whole nor any of its books was designed as a dictionary, or as dictionaries, of science, even where parts of them are scientific in character or reflective of the state of science at the time. They were not meant that way for their time, and are not meant that way for our time. The biblical books and the Bible as a whole are theologically oriented literature which focuses on the relationship between God and the world and the world and God. The Bible speaks neither about God in isolation from the world nor about the world in isolation from God. It speaks about God's relationship to the world and the world's relationship to God. It presupposes that there is neither a God without the world nor the world without God. By speaking about God's existence for and presence in the world, it focuses on the question of the meaning of the world and gives its witness to the presence of truth in it. In this sense, the Bible presents its view, and views, of reality, its worldview(s).

There is massive evidence that the biblical writers were not only concerned with the knowledge of God but also with the knowledge of the world. Their knowledge of God's presence in the world became transparent through their knowledge of the world. That is the point where "science" became inevitable, especially for the generations of the Old Testament.

To whatever extent we speak about science in the Bible, the evidence is irrefutable that the scientific knowledge of the biblical writers reflects the state of knowledge at their own time, more than two millennia ago, and even the development of that knowledge during several hundred years. It reflects, so to say, the ancient editions of real and imaginable scientific dictionaries, but certainly not the editions of such dictionaries for our time. The difference should come as no surprise. Also important is the other recognition that the biblical writings may not indiscriminately be dismissed as nonscientific because they represent outdated stages of knowledge. Scientific knowledge and practice are constantly changing, and their character is not determined by the difference between what is outdated and what is up-to-date.

The knowledge of the ancients has been called prescientific because of, e.g., their mythological worldview. Such a judgment is relative, if not inaccurate, because it ignores factors in that knowledge, even of their myths, which very much belong to the criteria for any, even a modern, definition of science. Rather than presuming one of the specifically modern definitions, it is advisable that we focus on those characteristics in the biblical literature which are symptomatic of any scientific thinking, knowledge, and practice, such as:

(i) *Rationality* in argumentation, e.g., about the relationship or interdependence of things in space and time within a system of thought, as in the argument about the dynamic process from cause toward effect. Job's friends were not only wrong, nor was Job only right;

(ii) *consistency* in the relationship of conceptual thought and its expressions in language;

(iii) *verifiability* of thought by observation of external factors, e.g., confirmation by external evidence, especially by mathematics, the exacting disciplines of geometry, cosmology, biology, geography, etc.;

(iv) the *predictability* of recurring conditions, e.g., days, months, years, annual seasons, on the basis of cosmological knowledge rather than on the basis of the regularity of past experience alone; the predictability of everything based on mathematics, including the predictability of the successful completion of projects, e.g., large buildings, water-supply projects, particular production processes requiring mathematical formulas, and so on. One has to distinguish between predictability, prognosis, and prophecy in the biblical literature;

(v) the *implementability* of theory in and its confirmation or nonconfirmation by practice.

More could be said, e.g., about evidence for analytical and synthetic thinking and the relationship of both to the visionary, mythopoeic, or poetic perception of reality.

It must be said, however, that the biblical writers' understanding of the presence of God in reality, of the truth of the world and of the totality of reality, was neither confined to the scientificness of their thought nor everywhere based on this criterion. For that sort of understanding, more was at stake than only what numbers could add up to, reason objectify, language express, or practice implement, especially where the articulation of the distinctiveness of GOD within everything that was perceived as and called "heaven and earth" was involved. Lastly, the scientificness of their understanding was necessary for reaching out as far as and wherever possible toward a nonchaotic understanding of, and life in, the nonchaotic order of God's world. Yet it was at the same time and for that very reason not more than an important instrument for helping to discern the truth of God and truth in the world, without being the criterion for either that truth itself or its own truth.

The subject would require a comprehensive treatment suited to fill a tome. Such a treatment does not exist. In an essay, we can only begin to face the breadth of what ought to be considered, and even that in magnalia only. In the following, we shall select a number of aspects that may be indicative of what, and what more, is involved.

II. Aspects

A. When speaking about science and, or in, the Bible, many think about creation science. The confinement of the subject to this aspect is totally unjustifiable. So much may be said at once, however, that after 360 years of condemnation for defending Copernicus's discovery of the heliocentric system Galileo Galilei (1564-1642) was in the fall of 1992 rehabilitated by Pope John Paul II: The sun does after all not revolve about the earth as the Bible assumes, but the earth revolves about the sun.

Galileo did not become right when the pope acknowledged his theory but he, together with Copernicus and Kepler, has been right all along whereas the church had all along been wrong. It may sometimes take generations, but an appeal to data from science in the Bible, where one wants to insist on their timeless validity at all, has eventually to yield to the scientific evidence of newer data. Such yielding has nothing to do with the loss of faith or truth in the Bible. It only brings faith or truth up to date. Also, in its geocentric cosmology the Bible did not become incorrect when this incorrectness was discovered. What was discovered was that it had been incorrect in its own time. The assumption that statements of the Bible which no longer reflect our time were nevertheless correct in their own time, because they were made for that time and in its context, is indefensible. The geocentric cosmology was developed in and for its time but was wrong even during that time. Not everything in history, or in the history of science, was correct or true because it was said in the context of and for the needs of its time! Finally, the Bible's geocentric view was not unscientific because it was wrong, but its scientific theory was wrong because it rested on the insufficient state of cosmological knowledge at its time.

In the late summer of 1955, I offhandedly remarked, as young pastors do, to the men's class of my congregation that I find it entirely conceivable that we will someday be flying to the moon; to which one of my two senior presbyters replied that this will never happen because the Lord will not permit it. My presbyter was correct in assuming that the Bible would consider such a human hybris impossible and impermissible. He was not correct in assuming that the Bible's state of scientific knowledge could not become outdated or that the state of faith based on the Bible could not be on the side of modern science rather than in contradiction to it because of biblical science. At least, I did not have to suffer Galileo's fate.

B. Before any other aspect, we need to pay attention to the biblical languages and written texts without which the Bible would not even exist. These languages are clearly, logically structured, and the texts based on them are for the most part the result of intensive intellectual activity: of conceptualized thought, disciplined composition, and rational argumentation as in *the ancient science of rhetoric.* They are everything but impressionistic, in their poetry as well as in their prose. Languages are the products of structured thought, and as media of communication require disciplined learning. Already in Old Testament times, a public person did not just speak, he/she had to be "knowledgeable in speech" (1 Sam 16:18).

What is true for the art of oral speech is even more true for the art of copying and especially of creative writing. In antiquity certainly, and up to and into modern times, the masses could not write let alone compose literary works. Those who could belonged to the cultural elite. The writers of the biblical books belonged to the class of the educated; they were the academicians of their time.

There is evidence that certain parts of the biblical books represent scientific work directly, while other parts reflect scientifically controlled operations in society indirectly. This distinction is analogous to the difference between scientific, i.e., scholarly, publications and practical operations of a scientific nature in our time. Most important, however, is the fact that in ancient as in modern times, science consisted of the sciences of many fields. Only if we realize that the sciences are not confined to natural sciences and that even the natural sciences consist of many fields can we begin to encounter and appreciate the breadth of science in the Bible.

C. The clearest case of scientific literature in the Old Testament exists in those lists in which individual subjects or objects belonging to the same group are collected and identified. This type of list belongs to a very widespread practice in the entire ancient Near East and has been called *the ancient science of lists.* Their basic form, nothing more than the listing of names or items, is simple, but they are everything but simplistic. They are the products of organized efforts to comprehend individually distinguishable identities as belonging together in conceptualized group entities, to order their listing according to certain systematized principles — analogous to the catalogue systems in our modern libraries based on *library science* — and to consider them classified in distinction from other, different types of groupings. These lists represent the intentional effort to collect all available data, and to order or recognize the order of the manifoldness in which reality is encountered.

Standing out among the lists existing in the Old Testament are those about: the nations as in Genesis 10; Israel's tribes, referred to very often, especially in the form of the sons of Jacob as in Gen 35:23-26; the clans of the tribes as in Numbers 26 and 1 Chronicles 1–9, all mostly in genealogical form; royal heroes and officials as in 2 Sam 8:16-18 and 20:23-26; territories and the towns and fortresses of their borders as in Joshua 15–19 or Num 34:1-15; itineraries of local names in territories as in Numbers 33; and material objects such as offerings in Exod 35:21-29 or of booty from military campaigns as in Num 31:42-47.

These types of lists, or their usage in narratives, represent systematized, controlled, basically verified or verifiable condensations of knowledge, very often institutionalized and functioning for the sake of theory and practice. They represent the nuclear forms of the *sciences of ethnography* both national and international, *administration, geography and topography, economy* and *warfare,* the *logistics* for various types of operations and, so we have reason for assuming, of the *biological sciences.*

D. Another clear case of scientificness in the Old Testament exists in the literary compositions of its *legal,* including *cult-legal, corpora.* The most prominent examples are Exod 21:1–23:19; Deuteronomy 5–11 and 12–26; and Leviticus 1–7. These compositions, which have their antecedents in some ancient Near Eastern law codes such as Hammurabi's or the Hittite law code, represent legal systems organized for administration. They presuppose not lawyers or judges but systematizing legal theoreticians who did not just issue individual laws from case to case or adjudicate cases or, as in the sacrificial cult, priests who performed sacrifices. The composers of these corpora had their specific setting and function. They wrote in their chambers, not where judgment was held or animals were sacrificed! And they wrote in light of the demands of the time and for the purpose of societal unity by establishing legal uniformity. Their works represented in their own time the *field of law as a science.*

E. What is true for the law codes is also true for the history works in both Testaments. Concerning the Old Testament, we can only refer to the most evident ones. The five books of Moses (the Pentateuch) present the history which begins in creation and aims at and culminates in the public life, work, and function of Moses, the most important person since creation, for Israel and the world. On the basis of Moses' Law in Deuteronomy, the books of Joshua through 2 Kings (the so-called deuteronomistic history) present the history of Israel from Moses' successor Joshua on until a generation after the fall of Jerusalem in 587 BCE. The books of Chronicles and Ezra-Nehemiah are similar works. In the New Testament, especially Luke's Gospel and the Book of Acts present the history of Jesus, including his pedigree (Luke 3:23-38), and focus particularly on his public life and death and the history of the movement of the early Christian mission until Paul's arrival in Rome.

These and other works belong to the *ancient science of historiography.* They focus on sometimes huge and sometimes shorter periods of the past, and virtually always lead up to their authors' own time. They are coherently structured literary compositions designed to reflect the many and diverse actual events as coherent developments. They were conceptualized from certain vantage points and, therefore, with plots and for a purpose, so that the authors' own interpretations of the meaning of their history pervades their narrative of what happened. They represent everything but storytelling, or only collections of stories. The materials for these histories had to be collected by the authors, but the authors themselves were historians.

The sources on which the authors had to rely were diverse. Many, such as lists, annals, or earlier works, were written; others were oral sources. To be sure, not all their sources meet the criteria for historiography in the modern scientific sense of the word, criteria that were already established by the Greek historian Thucydides in the later fifth century BCE. Yet although these criteria for the use of sources and for saying what happened have legitimately been delimited, the nature of the works of our biblical authors belongs to the erudite study of historical epochs by those authors and to the ancient science of historiography.

F. Although they are not scientific in nature themselves, many Old Testament texts presuppose or draw on science existing in society. In this respect, our sources offer only indirect but nonetheless enough evidence not only for our reconstruction of fields of science in society behind the texts but also for the fact that they informed the texts themselves.

There is the *science of biology* which was at its time clearly distinguishing between the subdisciplines of *anatomy, botany,* and *zoology.* There also is evidence for differentiated *psychological* knowledge, but the extent to which it was organized as a system of knowledge remains an open question. However, the *anatomical* knowledge of humans and animals was certainly systemic, as the language shows and as the texts about the dissection of animals for sacrifices presupposes. Of course, it was less perfected than ours. They were, e.g., unaware that the heart is only a pump and not the seat of thinking and emotion. Systemic also was their *botanical* knowledge, as not only the remarkable terminology but also evidence for their clear distinction between classes of plants show. In *zoology* they had classified the diverse animals of the air, the sea, and the land, subclassified diverse kinds of wild and domestic animals, and still further classified at least the latter ones according to types, sex, age, function, and so on and, of course, according to clean and unclean. The terminology is again remarkably wide.

What reveals the scientific background of the biological data in the texts is the fact that these data must be understood as being used in the texts on the basis of a clear, differentiating, analytically and synthetically classifying knowledge of the biological world. Indeed, one may with good reason postulate the existence of *catalogues* of biological science in ancient Israel on which references such as in Genesis 7; Psalms 104; 148; Job 38–39, and others rest.

G. We know that there were medical doctors in ancient Israel, among whom priests were included. Of course, the one healer above all — and, so we have to understand, in the work of all — was God (Exod 15:26). Diagnostically, the Old Testament knows about a significant breadth of specifically identified physical illnesses, beginning but not ending with blindness, lameness, diverse skin and sexual diseases, diseases of physical organs, strokes, wounds, and more, and also of psychopathological conditions.

Therapeutically, medicine answered with an array of treatments by oils, balsams, bandages, specific waters, and other natural-based medications. It knows about mouth-to-mouth resuscitation, whereas surgical practice does not seem to have been basically established. Important, however, were preventive practices, quite obviously officially established and enforced policies, such as "temporary isolation, quarantine, burning or scalding of infected garments and utensils, thorough scrubbing and smoking out of houses suspected of infection, and scrupulous inspection and purification of the diseased person after recovery (Leviticus 13–14)" (quoted from the valuable article on "Medicine" in *Encyclopedia Judaica,* vol. 2 [Jerusalem: Macmillan, 1971], especially 1179-80).

One will have to allow that the state of medical knowledge discernible in the Old Testament was not always the same during more than eight hundred years in ancient Israel's history. But when we come to science in the extant Bible, it is clear that already in pre-Christian times a host of medical knowledge for prevention, diagnosis, and therapy of illnesses had been developed and accumulated which by far exceeded the abilities of the average person. In both detail and comprehensiveness, and in terms of erudition, this body of knowledge and practice required the profession of the trained physician and amounts to the state of *medical science* at the time.

H. In Exod 25:3-7, the Israelites are to be asked by Moses to offer the types of materials for the construction of the sanctuary and its furnishings, and according to Exodus 35 they bring these materials. A detailed interpretation of the scientific knowledge behind this text, a knowledge presupposed to be operative in the text and known by its readers, would by far exceed the limits of this essay. Only a few aspects may be highlighted.

The text itself is a systematized, comprehensive list of the types of materials needed for the operation. How does such a list come into existence, where, at what stage of the operation, and by whom? It reflects the reality in the planning stage of such operations in the rooms of the planners, normally after the specific blueprint is ready and the question arises about what materials are needed and to be procured. It belongs to the *science of management and logistics* which has not at all received its deserving attention in biblical interpretation, especially on the subject of science in the Bible. Yet it is this field which is most discernible in the institutionalized operations, especially from Israel's statehood on, which stand as settings behind many Old Testament texts.

1. For the monarchy, already the organization for the administration or management of the state required a conceptualized system which in one sense replaced the way the premonarchic tribal confederacy functioned and in another sense was superimposed over the older one. This organization was a matter of both theory and practice. It involved the specialization of departments and their coordination, such as — foremost: the religion and its cult (the first temple in Jerusalem and the sanctuaries in Dan and Bethel were royal sanctuaries), law and justice, the royal administration of the tribes, treasury, economy, international relations = foreign policy, state-owned holdings in the land, industry (especially for state projects) and the military for warfare and its maintenance in peacetime. All these institutions can be observed behind a host of Old Testament texts.

The Israelite monarchy was without doubt rationally and systematically organized, in analogy to the other ancient Near Eastern states, and was, as the Jerusalem traditions show, especially in the Psalms, thought of as being the implementation of divine order on earth. Its only difference from the surrounding nations was its monotheistic theology, which served an even stronger tendency toward the organization of an integrated and united society. Not coincidentally, the book of Deuteronomy is understood as the program for Israel under the concept: one God — one people — one land. This kind of theoretical conceptualization amounts to a particular form of the ancient religio-political systems. It represents the ideological basis for *political science,* especially for the *science of government.* And the sciences of management and logistics serve, among others, the implementation of political and governmental sciences.

Two areas for management and logistics will be mentioned. One involves the operation of state buildings, the other the operation of warfare.

2. The biblical references to the temples in Jerusalem are known. Of particular importance for our topic are the narratives, either about the plans for construction or for both plan and construction, which we have in 1 Kings 5–8; 2 Chronicles

2–5; and Ezekiel 40–43. We will, however, focus on the other narrative about the Sinai-desert sanctuary in Exodus 25–27 (28–31:11) and 35–40. This narrative might be taken less seriously than the others because its existence is highly unlikely for that time and place. Under discussion, however, is the scientificness of its conceptualization, which reflects the reality of such operations, not the historicity of its existence and the question of the meaning of this "historicizing" narrative. Even in its highly mythological form, this narrative reflects the structure of the total management — and logistics — process of such operations in reality, from its very beginning stages until the moment of the deity's occupation of the sanctuary.

The report — so to be called because it intends to reflect reality accurately — focuses on the two major stages of planning and execution. In the planning stage, the deity commissions Moses to summon the Israelites for the offering of materials. The deity's decision to have its sanctuary built is presupposed. A call has to reach all Israelites for this offering. It includes the information about the types of materials needed. Then, so in this case, the deity reveals to Moses — to the king in the ancient Near Eastern tradition and in Israel — the verbatim description for the blueprint of the sanctuary. Before construction, there has to be a detailed, exact blueprint, which in historical reality is drafted in the offices of architects.

The drafting requires the comprehensive knowledge of the required types of materials, of the mathematics for the design of each structural component and the composition of all components, i.e., technological knowledge for the layout of the entire premise. It involves scientific knowledge for the theory, production, and functionality of the works of art. Furthermore, it involves managerial and logistical planning, such as selecting and recruiting the experts who function as foremen of the construction crews, as in Exod 31:1-11. Of course, the text presupposes that those foremen and artists will receive the blueprint for construction after their appointment and before they go to work.

The execution implements the planned project. Its place is the site for the construction, no longer the sides of decision and commission and — in reality — of the architectural offices. Now the society is asked to provide the supplies. The supplies have to be collected, in one way or another, at their own respective locations, transported and deposited at the building site in the order of their types — an eminent logistic task of its own. Then the experts are actually called to set up their particular sort of work. Then the people bring the materials, and the construction, with the plan on hand, takes place, and is completed, and the building is ready for occupation.

It is very clear that the narrative reflects in its entirety the concepts for the management and logistics of the total operation, just as in modern times. The rationality and sophistication of this conceptualization are obvious. If analogous conceptualizations of theory and practice of such sorts in our time have anything to do with science, our biblical texts reflect *the science of architecture and construction, and their management and logistics*.

3. In Numbers 1–2 we have the clearest of all references in the Bible to the organization of an army in preparation for a military campaign. The surface of the text reflects the background of such events. It reflects *the management and logistics of military science.* The operation is conceptualized in two stages: the registration or conscription of the draftable men and the mobilization or induction of the draftees into the camp.

The registration involves a monumental process. Since it presupposes the tribal system for basic divisions — envisioned in the militia, not a professional army — the registration had to be organized and supervised by a representative officer of each tribe. It involves the subdivisions of each tribe. Within this system, each qualifying person must individually register — apparently being entered by name in a registration list — which requires writing registrars. The lists then serve as the basis for adding up the numbers of the personal names stage by stage: from the family (or clan) to the tribal numbers and finally to the total number of all tribes. This process had to be organized, supervised, and executed by many persons with different functions and at different places. We do not know whether such a process ever took place in ancient Israel or in an ancient nation for military purposes. That census for taxation took place must be assumed. Nevertheless, the imagined structure of the process reflects the scientific theory for it. It certainly indicates the purpose for which actually existing genealogical lists could also be used.

After the registration, which does not happen in the camp, the draftees are called up into the military camp. They are inducted or mobilized. The camp is laid out according to plan, either in a quadrangular or a rectangular pattern, which is the layout for the encamped and defensive order. When on the march, the tribes are in linear formation. Three tribes are encamped on each side, all around the sanctuary. The location of the sanctuary, in the center of the camp, is not determined by the location of the tribes, but rather it determines the location of the tribes. Their function is to protect the sanctuary. The real campaigner is the deity, accompanied by its host. This religio-centered imagery should come as no surprise, and the organization of the camp should for that reason not be called unscientific unless we want to declare any organization for military warfare up to our very present time unscientific because it claims to act on behalf of God.

I. We return to Exod 25:3-7. This passage reveals, as do many others, more evidence for science in the Bible.

Its reference to the availability of metals for the production of metal objects presupposes not only the expert knowledge of the management of the total metallurgical process, a science by itself, but also the differentiated knowledge of metals themselves, including their different values and usages. The use of words for pure metals such as gold, silver, copper, tin, iron, and lead, and for alloys such as bronze (copper mixed with either tin or lead or antimony), signals a knowledgeable distinction of each metal, and when used in cluster for a series of metals such as gold-silver-bronze, a knowledge of their relationship systematized in a value system within which each metal has not only its commercial but also its functional value. In the transition from the Bronze to the Iron Age, about 1200 BCE, gold held the highest value commercially and for the production of art works, whereas iron became most valuable for the production of arms and — where affordable — plows. Such systemic knowledge and its application are indicative of the *science of metallurgy.* See "Metals and Mining," in *Encyclopedia Judaica,* vol. 2 (1971), 1428-34, and similar biblical dictionaries.

When Exod 25:4 refers to "blue and purple and scarlet stuff," one has to ask what kind of expertise was necessary to gain the original materials for it and to process them through differentiated stages to the final product in order to realize the extent and level of expert knowledge in both theory and practice, for the total process which stands behind such a biblical reference. The same must be said for the background for the many sorts of jewelry listed in a passage such as Isa 3:18-23, for the *science of jewelry.*

Exod 25:7 refers to precious stones such as onyx, bdellium, amethyst, jasper, beryl, smaragd, rubin, lapis lazuli, chrysolid, diamond, sapphire, amber, coral, pearl, etc., as do other passages, also in the New Testament. Their physico-chemical formula was not known, but that they belonged to a special category expressed by the formula "precious stone" (2 Sam 12:30; 1 Kgs 10:2, 10; and more often) points to the state of the *science of mineralogy* at the time.

J. Because of limitations of space, we can only allude to *philosophical science* in the Bible. The extent to which philosophy in modern times is acknowledged as scientific, not speculative but based on empirical disciplines and logic, is mirrored in the philosophical nature of many biblical texts, also insofar as it includes God in the rationality of thought. What is philosophical depends thereby much more on the kind of thinking, the *Geistesbeschäftigung,* than on the format, especially when compared with the format of treatises from Greek philosophy on. Even there, however, the Socratic dialogue was an appropriate philosophical form.

The books of Job and Ecclesiastes represent philosophy. Their discussion focuses on the issue of a conceptualized worldview and its problems, a worldview that stands behind virtually the entire Old Testament and many texts in the New Testament. It is the so-called dynamistic ontology which says that reality is a dynamic process from beginning causes to their corresponding ends. The fact that this ontology had in the Old Testament already become subject to contestation, modifications, and complementation means neither that it has been abandoned in the wake of the historical development of philosophical discourse nor that it is not also, alongside complementary or alternative propositions, empirically verifiable, then and today.

K. What, then, about creation in the Bible? After what has been said thus far, which is only part of what ought to be considered, it should be evident that the scientific aspect in the Bible's references to creation must not be considered in isolation from the totality of the state and function of science in it. It is part of the total state of the development of science in the times to which the biblical literature belongs. It presupposes the total context of those times; and without it the claims to the understandability and validity of the biblical messages could not have been made transparent.

Also, while significant, the references to the creation of the world are actually very few when compared with the overwhelming attention of the Bible to the other concerns which are preoccupied with the affairs in and of this ongoing world as in the Old Testament, and specifically with things of the Christian existence as in the New Testament. Besides Genesis 1–2, they are essentially found in Isaiah 40–66, in Job, in a few psalms, and some other passages, and in the context of particular arguments in not more than twenty passages in the New Testament. Information is available in every biblical concordance and dictionary.

One must distinguish between the place and function of the creation and the massive preponderance of the Bible's attention to the presence of God in the ongoing existence of the created world. It is significant that the great breadth of the state of scientific knowledge in the biblical texts and their background reflects the Bible's constant and unlimited attention to the presently ongoing reality, at least to the totality of reality *after* creation, in terms of past, present, and future, rather than to the beginnings of this reality.

When the question arises about the scientificness of the Bible's knowledge of creation, it is clear that its statements are not scientific simply because they are made by the Bible. Quite apart from the fact that variations exist that cannot be harmonized, it must be said that, except in part for Genesis 1, scarcely any of the biblical statements about the creation event fulfill the criteria for being derived from, based on, and reflective of what can be said in light of the mathematically certifiable data available at the time. Besides saying that it was the one God who created the world as order out of chaos — the notion of order being derived from verifiable observation of the structure of the cosmos — their imageries of the mode and process of creation are genuinely mythopoeic and influenced by ancient Near Eastern traditions. Their mythopoeic nature does not mean that there is therefore no truth in it; it only means that the roots for its knowledge lie in what *imagination produces,* in prose as well as in poetry, rather than in knowledge based on scientifically obtainable data.

The preponderance of mythopoeic imagery is perfectly understandable in light of one of the basic human questions concerning the *whence* of the amazing existence of the cosmic order in the midst of and despite the also existing reality and possibility of universal chaos. It arises at a time when verifiable access to those primordial beginnings was not at all available and when even what could scientifically be said about them could not be said on the ground of what one knew about those beginnings but only on the ground of inferences or conclusions for them from what one knew about the present order, including the presence of God in this present order. Nevertheless the mythopoeic imagery, and the need for it, of the mode and process of the creation event also means that it cannot avoid being compared with the stages of accurate knowledge, being controlled by and, where necessary, being replaced by that constantly developing knowledge.

Genesis 1 was not written for a scientific dictionary — neither for an edition of its own nor an edition of our time. It represents the start of the work of the Pentateuch, the conceptually unified work that was subdivided into the five books of Moses (Genesis to Deuteronomy). Genesis 1 cannot legitimately be read in isolation from that total work. Rather, it aims above all at the establishment of Israel's sabbath week culminating in the sabbath day itself, just as creation in six days culminates in God's sabbath day. It aims at anchoring one of the two distinctive marks — next to circumcision — by which especially the postexilic community of Israel is above all else identified, in the event of the creation of the world. See Exod 20:8-11; 31:12-17. Clearly, the seven-day pattern dominates the structure of Gen 1:1–2:4a, so much so that eight distinct works of God had to be accommodated within six rather than eight days. The historical origin of the seven-day week lies, as far as can be said, in Israel's own history, somewhere in the ninth or eighth century BCE, but not in the scientific state of cosmological knowledge of that or any other time as in the case of the annual, monthly, and daily cycles. This pattern, unique among all other creation traditions, wants to say that, unlike the other cycles for the permanence of which the "greater" and "lesser" light are universal signs, the sabbath is not constituted by a cosmically verifiable order and permanently indicated by the regularity of its signs of sun, moon, and stars; rather, it is constituted by a unique, noncosmic order of creation and indicated by Israel's own sabbath week. The roots for the complementarity of the creation week and Israel's week lie in Israel's concept of its own election.

Nevertheless, Genesis 1 reflects in other respects that level of scientific knowledge which is derived from the knowledge at the time of the presently existing structure of the cosmos: each part is in its proper place within the whole and in relation to all other parts. It is the result of an intensely reflected effort to present the origin of this structure as a clear, conceptualized system, as the implementation of a design for a cosmic architecture in which God is as much presupposed to have been the architect as God is said to be the sole executor of the design through nothing other than execution by God's word. In order to focus on the origin, however, it had to narrate the event as a sequence of successive stages rather than to describe the permanently existing order. In transposing the description of the existing order into the narrative about its origin, it had to narrate this origin as a sequence of events that was itself clearly structured. As in actual constructions of buildings, what is to be done must be done in proper sequence because each phase is at the same time presupposed by its preceding phase and the condition for its following phase. The sequential order in the structure of the narrative reflects the *scientificness of the management* in actual construction processes. The details are, or should be, explained in the commentaries and lexica.

The creation of the cosmos aims at the creation of the earth as its center, especially its land, and ultimately of humans as the purpose of all creation. Of great importance is the fact that the creation is seen in the basic, also scientifically established aspects of *space and time.* Any discussion that considers Genesis 1 only under the aspect of time and not also under the aspect of space misreads this chapter at the outset.

Also important is that creation is seen as the beginning of both the permanently ongoing stable cycles of the cosmic order on which the ancient Near East's and Israel's calendric system is based (which — in turn — is the basis for Israel's permanent agricultural existence in the land) and the development of the forward-moving but unstable and always-changing human history. In creation lies the beginning of the cyclic as well as the linear structure of time within the structure of cosmic space. And the existence of humanity is imbedded in and structured by both the ongoing cosmic order which we call the order of nature (not "natural order"!) and the march of human history. One can see that human imbeddedness in the cosmic order is not only the basis for the possibility of any human history but also the yardstick for its truth and survivability.

The cosmology of Genesis 1 — seeing the earth as the center of the universe, raised out of the chaotic waters still underneath and around it and protected from the same kind of waters above it by a solid bowl with solid windows, a bowl underneath which sun, moon, and stars were placed — represents just as much the scientific, essentially astronomical information of its writers as it has been outdated for centuries by now. That astronomy is operative in the text of Genesis 1 means only that this text, too, presupposes astronomical knowledge in terms of both space and time, not that this knowledge stands only behind Genesis 1. Indeed, quite a number of Old Testament texts rest on the ancient *science of astronomy.* We must only notice that the use of astronomical knowledge in Genesis 1 and the entire Old Testament excludes its astrological application, which was widespread in the ancient world but banned in Israel. Heaven and the stars were not divine. They were indeed demythologized, seen as serving humans rather than as governing them and being worshipped by them.

In contrast to the outdated elements in the cosmology of Genesis 1, the narrative's concept of the *sequential* creation, from the cosmos to the earth, on earth from water to especially fertile land, of life from the sea — to the air — to the land animals to humans, including its knowledge of the variety within and the distinctiveness of each type, is essentially as we see it today, even with the help of Darwin. Had their state of information given them the evidence we possess that these types evolved one out of the other, there is no reason for disputing that they would have said that God created it this way.

Genesis 1 says that the world was created in six days — of twenty-four hours each — and that God rested on the seventh day. It says nothing about how long ago that happened, nor does the Bible say anything of that sort anywhere. That it happened 5,755 years before 1994, according to the Jewish calendar, is the result of later interpreters in the Jewish tradition adding up chronological data from diverse contexts filtered out of the Hebrew Bible. We know that the universe is much, much older, its origin going back to sometime between ten and eighteen billion years ago, that a mathematical game such as with Ps 90:4 is beside the point. Any insistence on the necessity of adhering to the biblical state of cosmological knowledge stands only in the way of our own awe, reverence, and love of God and what it means for us to speak about the truth of God and in light of our constantly increasing knowledge of the awesome vastness of the universe and the secret of its origin, of the wondrous precariousness of this little planet in our solar system at the outermost fringes of one of millions of galaxies, a planet that is our only home. The universe, and this earth entrusted to us — and their God — are immensely greater than the writer of Psalm 8 could ever have imagined.

Conclusion

It cannot escape attention that the discussed aspects of science in the Bible are almost exclusively found in the Old Testament with scarcely any background in the New Testament. This difference is not coincidental, and the reason for it would not change if one were to discuss a few instances, e.g., the phenomenon of rhetoric, which demonstrate scientificness also behind the New Testament writings. Its basic reason lies in the fact that the books of the New Testament in their extant form, except the Gospel of John, focus on the eschatological condition of the world, humanity, and Christian community in view of the impending end of this world in the second coming of Christ and of its replacement by the new creation. In light of this expectation, especially the Christian community was called to consider its existence and to prepare for the second coming and the appearance of the new creation, already a reality in a certain kind of its existence.

This temporal eschatology has not been fulfilled, just as none of the temporal eschatologies in the prophetic writings of the Old Testament was fulfilled as stated and conceived. Its hope for the ultimate consummation of the world was just as much scientifically unverifiable as the biblical texts about the origin of the world as such were always unverifiable but could only be inferred from the experience of the existing order of the world. If, by analogy, our current knowledge of this existing order is a basis for inferring the hope for the future of this world, this cosmic future appears to be open for a very long time — save a cataclysmic event of a natural sort or the destruction of the globe by ourselves. At any rate, the history of the past two millennia and the current state of our scientific knowledge conflict with the expectation of the second coming of Christ and with the replacement of this world by a new world in a temporally conceived eschatology.

In the meantime, the created world has been and is going on. And it seems to be better, if not decisive, that we focus on God's presence and the ultimate meaning of it in the affairs of this ongoing world. After all, the Bible teaches us that God was at the beginning and will be at the end because God is always and everywhere present, rather than that God is present because God was at the beginning and will be at the end. When it comes to this awareness, the Old Testament's attention to the affairs of this ongoing world, to the question of the truth in it, the truth in and for it, including its attention to scientific knowledge for the better understanding of that truth, serves a decisive function for the human race, certainly for the Christian community. Appreciation of the Old Testament in the Christian canon amounts to its fundamental rather than only peripheral importance, an importance unlike any it has had in the history of the interpretation of the Christian Bible.

There is only one basic difference, a fact that neither the biblical faith nor the scientificness in or behind it ever imagined. For the biblical generations it was inconceivable that the existence of this earth in the structure of the cosmos, at least of life on this planet, could ever end by human hand itself rather than by the hand of God alone when it "wears out like a garment" and God "changes it like raiment, and it passes away" (Ps 102:27). Up to our very own generation, even the progress of science throughout the history of humanity could be understood as the implementation of the God-given human facilities within the never-touchable solid foundation of the cosmic order of this earth and all life on it. With our generation, and from now on, this history has come to its end. From now on, the question will not only be science *in* or science *and* the Bible but the role of God in view of the human ability to destroy God's earth and to commit the suicide of the human race, whereas previously the existence of this earth was reserved and forever guaranteed. As far as the Bible is concerned, the question of science *in* or *and* the Bible is by now surpassed by and depends on the question of the task and ability of us humans to uphold the creation of this earth for us in the face of our own ability to bring an end to it before any other kind of end. What this means for our reading of the Bible and, still, its potential for us, is an entirely new and as yet scarcely even recognized problem.

On the Contours of Old Testament and Biblical Hamartiology

I. Hermeneutical Considerations

A. On the Contemporary Situation

1. Reality and Intelligibility

It may be characteristic of our time that the subject of sin and guilt has come to elude intelligibility while the reality of evil pervades this planet at least as intensively as ever before. Everyone stares into the face of evil daily. Evil affects every human being in one way or another. This reality may defy rational explanation, but it can certainly be recognized. One need not be a pessimist to say that the idea of the perfectly good human being, or of progress toward that end, is unrealistically utopian.

The initial impression may be that sin and guilt are a forgotten or repressed subject. Alternatively, they may reflect an antiquated understanding of the human condition, which has been replaced by modern models which more accurately explain the frailties of human nature. Both of these impressions are deceiving because they negate the dark side of the human condition. Yet these reactions do not simply represent immoral attitudes. They reflect a mechanism by which human nature attempts to shield itself from self-destruction. Yet this very mechanism has its limits. Whereas it denies one's, one's group's, or a society's own dark sides, it is propelled toward the constant awareness and unveiling of the dark sides of others. The need to justify oneself goes hand in hand with the need to point out the sins and guilt of others. Admission of one's own sin and guilt, without at least the certainty that it is not self-destructive, conflicts with the necessity for one's self-protection and survival. In our human relationships, other people's sins are everywhere known and expressed: unforgotten, unrepressed, unsilenced, unaltered, and even unforgiven. When it comes to ourselves, to me, the issue of recognition, admission, and intelligibility is a very different matter.

2. Secular and Theological Language

The impression that the recognition of sin appears antiquated rests, of course, on the fact that the word "sin" belongs to the traditional religious and theological vocabulary of the wider Christian and Jewish communities. Essentially, the word is no longer part of the languages of our secularized societies. Its removal from secular discourse points on the one hand to the fact that the religious and theological dimension in secular reality has been forgotten and on the other hand to the actual presence of this dimension in secular reality in the guise of a secular word field. This word field seems to be, but is not, unrelated to the religious and theological dimension. The secular word field and our perception of it do not prove the absence of the religious dimension of the subject matter of sin and guilt.

3. The Nature of the Secular Word Field

The subject matter of sin and guilt is included in our linguisticality. It may be *infra*textual or *infra*terminological, but one cannot say that this dimension plays no role in our modern word fields. These broad word fields for negative facts range from words such as "error," "mistake," "oversight," and "deceit," across the total spectrum to words for different kinds of nonviolent crimes such as "fraud," "bribery," "theft," etc., to words for violent crimes such as "assault," "rape," "homicide," "murder," "genocide," and so on. The terminological catalogue which reflects a systematized understanding of these negative facts is endless.

Each of these word fields includes a scale for the evaluation of severity of action. They distinguish between acts of persons with and without negative impacts on others, between the limited and wider range of those impacts, between kinds of unintended and willful "sins," and between conscious and inadvertent acts that subsequently turn out to be "sinful," with more or less severe consequences. And depending on each particular societal system, they reflect in different ways the distinctions between and interpenetrations of private and public accountability for deficient actions, be they immoral, unethical, or illegal. They reflect distinctions between acts and attitudes as well as between institutionalized prosecution as opposed to adverse personal or social consequences outside the reach of judicial institutions, and much more.

These word fields, which include the grammatical typology of the words, their verbal and nominal forms, point to the following:

a. Each word field primarily consists of qualifying terminology. These words express the negative quality of actions, behaviors, and attitudes rather than describe the actions specifically. While presupposing what happens and connoting the concreteness of the kind of happening, they disqualify the happening in kind. They reflect the perception of the intrinsic connection between typical acts and their invalidity. They disqualify these facts typologically rather than as isolated cases. The description of acts and their consequences must be distinguished from the typologized expressions by which these acts and their consequences are disqualified.

b. On occasion, the qualifying notions include or are complemented by quantifying references as, e.g., genocide or mass murder.

c. Strictly speaking, the typologized disqualifying terminology does not amount to abstraction or generalization. As long as the word "crime" refers to a real act, it is not abstracted from that reality. The disqualification of that act has nothing to do with abstraction from it. Nor does typologizing an act as a crime mean generalization in the sense that the act is deprived of its specificity. In fact, the specificity of a criminal act is the presupposition for labeling it as a crime in the first place. The disqualifying and typologizing nature of the terminology is rooted in the differentiating perception of the specifics of real experience and the arrangement of these specifics in value systems.

d. No single word has its meaning in isolation from its word field. The meaning of each word functions in its relationship to all others in a semantic web that amounts to a system, or to competing systems, of stratified disqualifications which reflect the negative side of a society's, or societies', positive value system(s).

e. For the most part, these systems and their linguistic expressions appear to be understood in our modern societies as secular, i.e., nonreligious and especially nontheological. As if the religious dimension and its theological shapes are clearly separated from anything secular because things happen in secular fashion. As if sin does not happen in secular reality; conversely, as if secular disqualifications do not point to sinfulness in the religious and theological senses. As if words have a theological meaning only when used with the word "God," in contrast to their nontheological meaning when referring to secular facts for which the word "God" is not used. Unfortunately, this implication is even suggested by the composition of articles in dictionaries of the biblical languages in which the theological and nontheological usages of words are nicely compartmentalized. As if a theft is not also sin and more than merely a crime or simply a theft, and as if sin is not an act secularly committed as a theft.

f. Especially, as if the (dis)qualification of any act, behavior, attitude, or condition of the mind has nothing to do with the question of truth or untruth. I say this despite the impossibility of knowing ultimate truth; ultimate truth endures as a questioning signal, always casting us beyond our qualifications by reminding us of our limitedness, relativity, and imperfection.

The notion of truth must be distinguished from the notion of meaning. In given contexts, things are meaningful or meaningless, or more or less so. Murder is meaningful. What is the truth of such meaning?

The notion of ultimate truth is not irrelevant because ultimate truth is unknown. It signals that the truth claims in our qualifications and disqualifications stand in principle under question and reservation. They are relative, and the books on any of them are never finally closed. Nor does the relativity of our (dis)qualifications mean that they are for this reason irrelevant or untrue. Although their truth can only be relative and imperfect, imperfect truth is still better than the abrogation of the claim to truth altogether and the replacement of this claim simply by what appears meaningful in a certain context.

If the knowledge of the reality of God has anything to do with the knowledge of truth absolutely or relatively, and if the question of truth is intrinsic to all value judgments, then there is no secular value system without a religious as well as a theological dimension. Wherever, whenever, or however secular facts are disqualified, the religious and theological dimensions of sin and guilt are at issue.

B. Biblical and Contemporary Hamartiology

An analysis of the place of sin in the diverse value systems of the current secular world — where it is secularized! — does not assume that any current system holds the criteria for the approach to biblical hamartiology. Nor does such an analysis assume that a properly conceived biblical hamartiology provides the sole criterion for current conceptions of sin and guilt. The relationship between biblical and current hamartiologies belongs to the discipline of biblical hermeneutic.

1. The Encounter

The hermeneutic of biblical hamartiology is part of the mutually open encounter between the value systems of the biblical literature and of our own time. In this encounter, neither system is a priori normative for the other. Rather, they inform each other, and that which is normative can only emerge from the encounter itself. Thus, whether the dialogue in the hermeneutical circle begins from the current or from the biblical standpoint is relative. The issue of the dialogue's beginning must be distinguished from the principal issue, namely, that which is substantively under discussion in the encounter itself.

2. Biblical Hamartiology

The hermeneutic of biblical hamartiology requires the representation of biblical hamartiology in its own right. This hamartiology is an essential part of biblical theology. It is indispensable because it represents the decisive contrast to biblical soteriology. Also, hamartiology and soteriology together represent the bipolar span intrinsic to the biblical theology of justice and righteousness. Without hamartiology, the biblical soteriology and theology of justice and righteousness cannot be properly understood. Hamartiology and soteriology may be interpreted individually. Still, their separate interpretation does not mean that they are not mutually reflective of each other.

3. The Biblical Literature

As it should be, biblical hamartiology is interpreted on the basis of the biblical literature alone. Of course the interpreter consciously attempts to distantiate her/his inevitable subjectivity in the process of her/his interpretation.

Nevertheless, the awareness of the hermeneutical task alongside the biblical task remains significant. As long as the Bible is involved, no minister preaches or teaches theology or religion without hermeneutical interpretation. Just like the practitioners, the theoreticians cannot exempt themselves from constant attention to the hermeneutical practice of biblical interpretation. This is so not only because the theoreticians provide support for the practitioners in the hermeneutical task. The real reason is that theoretical biblical work is never separated from the hermeneutical circle in the first place.

4. Interdisciplinary Aspects

In the interdisciplinary theological discourse itself, the widespread *incommunicado* between biblical and especially systematic theologians is not primarily the result of the experience of the distance between the biblical and modern worldviews. It is the result of biblical scholars' insufficient presentation of a coherent conceptualization of the total biblical literature, or at least a framework for such a system. Because of this deficiency, biblical and systematic theology have not been able to meet at the crossroads of a systematized biblical theology.

5. Biblical Pluralism

Finally, attention to the hermeneutical consequences of biblical theology will confirm what any credible concept of biblical theology itself will have to involve. Any conceptualization of biblical theology must allow for the interpretation of the pluralism of theological aspects in the biblical literature. Specifically, it must allow for the interpretation of the relationship of these aspects, so that this theology may legitimately be called *biblical* in the sense that it does not rest on some selected aspects or elements, such as words, texts, books, concepts, or traditions, at the expense or neglect of all others. In such a design, biblical theology or any subject within it, including biblical hamartiology, will be a critically constructed biblical-theological value system which, of course, has nothing to do with unification, let alone harmonization. Finally, any such theology as a whole can then truly encounter the critical construct of a modern value system.

II. On the Method for a Biblical Hamartiology

What has just been said sheds light on the question of method for a biblical hamartiology. It is clear at the outset that neither the Old nor the New Testament, let alone both together, represents an explicit systematization of their hamartiological terminologies, statements, and concepts. It is equally clear that the compartmentalized and juxtaposed interpretations of their diverse hamartiologies, e.g., the words for sin in dictionaries and monographs, or the texts about and concepts of sin in **J**, **D**, **DtrH**, **P**, Amos, Hosea, Isaiah, the Psalms, Proverbs, etc., as well as in the Synoptics, John, Paul, etc., do not amount to a biblical hamartiology. This is true regardless whether or not one considers such a hamartiology in the singular desirable or necessary.

In order to determine the focus for this subject, distinctions must be made about what is constitutive for the biblical hamartiological question and what is, while not irrelevant, subsidiary.

A. Socio-historical Aspects and the Substantive Aspect

As in any aspect of biblical theology, biblical hamartiology above all else comprises *what* the biblical texts say about sin and guilt together with these texts' operative conceptual presuppositions. Such a hamartiology also recognizes the diversity of the biblical books in the one Bible, in the Christian tradition especially the fact of the two Testaments plus or minus the intertestamental books.

This focus on the substantive aspect of the Bible is specific. It cannot be replaced by other subsidiary concerns, despite their own legitimacy.

1. Genres

Clearly, the biblical texts speak about sin within genres such as accusation, indictment, judgment, confession, and so on. However, while every genre points to a typical context in which sin plays a concrete role, no genre reveals as such what sin is or how it is understood.

2. Settings

Similarly, the texts point to settings in which sin is addressed and disqualified as sin. These settings must be distinguished from the situations in which sin is assumed to have happened. The setting for the adjudication of a crime is separate from the situation of the committed crime. Still, no typical setting reveals the specific content of an act or condition whereby it is formally disqualified by an implied or stated evaluation as sin.

Sin happens and is confronted in a variety of social settings. It is realistically experienced in those settings; by no means is it experienced in cult or worship alone. It appears in the contexts of public ethos and law, political systems, international relations, personal and family life, etc. Nevertheless, neither the specific nature of sin nor the reason for its disqualification is revealed by any of these settings. Whether defined by a certain setting or society at large, what the content and nature of sin are is a question distinct from where and how it happens and is adjudicated.

3. History

The fact of the history of diverse statements and perceptions about sin is also subsidiary to the question of what sin is said and perceived to be. Just as in the case of the history of the biblical religion, or the history of the theologies in the Bible, the history of the Bible's hamartiology must be distinguished from a biblical hamartiology. While each aspect is legitimate, the description of the historical development of the biblical notion of sin does not reach the heart of the biblical hamartiological problem.

We may be able to give a roughly adequate rendition of the history of ancient Israel's society, as well as a history of the early Christian communities. We may even be able to portray the historical development of the biblical literature as part of those societal histories, even as they were influenced by the various ancient cultures before and throughout biblical times. Even so, these questions remain: On what basis can any of the Bible's diverse hamartiological positions be considered true? Should all of them be considered equally true? What are the implications for a biblical hamartiology? No hamartiological phenomenology, including its historical perspective, is sufficient for confronting these questions.

B. Substance Criticism

The biblical texts not only narrate, describe, and prescribe. They also qualify. In doing so, they claim to be true. This claim is the fundamental element of their *raison d'être*. The undeniable evidence for this element is derived from an inner-biblical hermeneutic in which value judgments are not only made but assumed to be true.

1. Genre, Setting, and Tradition

When this aspect is accounted for, it becomes clear that sin is not defined by the specific genres and settings in which it is confronted. Neither is sin disqualified with reference to tradition or reversal of tradition. For example, in Deut 24:16 a new legal maxim is decreed:

> Parents shall not be put to death for their children, nor shall children be put to death for their parents; only for their own crimes may persons be put to death. (Cf. Jer 31:29-30; Ezekiel 18.)[1]

The validity of this new maxim does not rest in its newness or in its reversal of the traditional maxim, or on the ground that changing times call for changing principles. At stake is whether the abandoned maxim is in effect understood to have been imperfect, even wrong, in its own time; also at issue is whether the new maxim is in effect understood to be perfect and right in its own time. Lastly, it needs to be clarified whether either maxim was held valid universally and exclusively in its own time. Evidently, neither maxim was restricted to its own time. This means that both were conflicting throughout Israel's history; neither was considered valid exclusively. Last but not least, their authoritative juxtaposition in the canon has intensified the conflict because both maxims, reflected in passages from the complete span of Israel's history, have been handed down to posterity without any arbitration of their contradicting distinctness. Canonically, they relativize each other, which is known from the critical study of their tradition history anyway.

2. Tradition Criticism

The legacy of the biblical tradition — and transmission — history provides no answer to the question whether all hamartiological disqualifications are equally relevant, valid, or true. In fact, it generates this question. It is also the reason for the necessary substance-critical evaluation of these disqualifications. The history of the Bible's hamartiology is no substitute for a biblical hamartiology. It only demonstrates the history of and, to a certain extent, the reasons for hamartiological continuity and change. But this history does not show why any continuity or change should be considered valid with regard to any current condition.

One can safely assume that in an imagined symposium of the representatives behind the hamartiological positions in the Bible, the existing agreements and differences would very soon break out. No position would remain unquestioned or uncontested by others, be it older or newer, valuing tradition or advocating new ideas, secular or theologizing — with increasing conflict as the arguments are more specifically exegeted. No harmony or uniformity would emerge. What would emerge is the question of which arguments are more and which are less fundamental, and a heuristic process in which all positions could be compared and interrelated. This process would inevitably lead to the substance criticism *(Sachkritik)* of each position, and to the recognition of the relative validity — not irrelevance! — of each position, and even to the indefensibility of certain positions.

1. Biblical quotations are from the *New Revised Standard Version,* except where noted.

Just as in the extant canon, the hamartiological diversity of the biblical tradition history provides another reason for this substance-critical demand and hence for substance criticism of the traditions themselves. An adequately conceptualized biblical hamartiology falls short unless it is based on the interpreters' assessment of the Bible's hamartiological positions through their substance-critical comparison. Unless this assessment is done by the interpreters themselves, there are only diverse hamartiologies in the Bible. No biblical hamartiology will exist, and the Bible itself, including its hamartiological unintelligibility, will do nothing more than provide the reason for its ever-increasing irrelevance. Its relevance with regard to sin, or any other issue, will no longer be discovered anew.

3. The New Testament Tradition

The substance-critical comparison of the Bible's hamartiologies comes into sharpest focus when those of the Old Testament are compared with those of the New Testament. In comparison with the Old Testament, the New Testament's position is fundamentally different. And in virtually all Christian interpretations, the subject of sin is but part of the total theological evaluation of the Old Testament from the perspective of the New Testament's Christology, soteriology, eschatology, and ecclesiology. Whether considered in terms of prophecy and fulfillment, law and gospel, the law of the letter and the law of the Spirit, or prototype and antitype, the history of the believing community in the historically earlier paradigm is not only old in light of the new revelation; it is basically subordinate if not inferior *in toto.* In light of the end stage, it is never more than a pre-stage, despite its individual significance.

This a priori substance-critical judgment programmatically vetoes any implication that the practically universal scholarly assertion of the Old Testament's right to its own terms may mean that it is in certain respects equally as valid as the New Testament, let alone more valid. One may, therefore, speak about an Old Testament and a New Testament hamartiology. But a biblical hamartiology of both testaments inevitably depends on the question of whether the Old Testament's hamartiology is to be substance-critically prejudiced by the one in the New Testament, or whether this prejudice is itself subject to substance-critical assessment. Such an assessment can only be made through the evaluation of how the two testaments mutually critique and complement each other.

III. On Old Testament Hamartiology

The problem of an Old Testament hamartiology is structural and systemic in nature. If it is to be a hamartiology in the singular, it must confront the question of how the Old Testament's various hamartiologies, along with their infratextual concepts, are to be related by the interpreter. The task is complicated. It begins by presupposing the known results of exegetical work on the total Old Testament, not only with regard to sin. In the following, a number of the major systemic aspects necessary for the development of an Old Testament hamartiology will be discussed.

A. The Word Field

It is well known that the Old Testament does not have a singular word for sin like *hamartia* in the New Testament. Neither did such a word ever exist in the Old Testament's tradition history. Terminologically, sin in the Old Testament is encountered in a very broad word field. Any interpretation must account for the meaning of this field.

1. Terminology

The interpretation of the word field must be distinguished from interpretations of individual words. Word studies remain an indispensable prerequisite. The results of such studies are found in monographs, articles, and theological word dictionaries. They give statistical and etymological information, the semantic range, synonyms and antonyms, combinations in word clusters or text compositions, the meaning of verbal and nominal forms, their usage in text genres and their various societal settings, and so on. This sin vocabulary of more than forty words, and quite apart from the broader range of disqualifying language, points to an enormously differentiated spectrum of disqualified or disqualifiable actions, conditions, or situations. It reaches into every sphere of human life.

As disqualifiers, the individual terms are formal terms. Clearly, they presuppose and refer to actions, behaviors, attitudes, processes, or results. Yet what they express is the invalidity of such events or conditions rather than specific description. They specifically disqualify individual situations according to the type of event or condition. Hence, they disqualify typologically. Among the various typological aspects we find the following:[2]

a. חָטָא ("to miss") denotes the negative result, or failure, of an action or behavior.

b. עָוָה ("to become/be guilty") points to the course of negative conditions from the beginning of an action to its final result.

c. פָּשַׁע ("to commit a breach") points to the nature of an act itself within social and international relations (as in Amos 1–2). It is, therefore, also a legal word for crime.

2. For the sake of brevity, only a portion of the word field is presented here.

d. חָמַס ("to act violently") points to the violent nature of an act.

e. אָשַׁם ("to become subject to [the obligation of] guilt") points to the consequences of a state of guilt.

f. נָבַל ("to be foolish" or "to act foolishly") refers to an act or behavior with deadly consequences because it rips the fabric of communal relations to pieces, particularly in the realm of sexual mores (e.g., Genesis 34; Judges 19–20; 2 Samuel 13), but also in other respects where foolishness is the opposite of wisdom (Proverbs). The meaning of this word reaches much deeper than the modern meaning of the same word. Its depth reflects taboo-based values. The same can be said for words such as תּוֹעֵבָה ("abomination") or זִמָּה ("shame"). The Old Testament, and not only Far Eastern cultures, speaks of shame! Guilt and shame are not mutually exclusive aspects in the Old Testament. Nor is shame only a psychological condition in the Old Testament ("to be ashamed"). It is also an objective ("shameful") condition. These words point especially to the violated taboos of the cultic realm. טָמֵא ("to be/become unclean") has a similar function.

g. רַע ("bad," "evil") is the opposite of טוֹב ("good"). רַע points to the most encompassing meaning of sin. Again, the weight of what is considered bad or evil corresponds to the English word "evil" much more than the English word "bad."

These disqualifiers are formal and typological. This does not mean that they are therefore abstract. Already the relationship of their verbal and nominal aspects points to the correspondence between personal involvement and the nature of that involvement. Despite their individual emphases, each form of expression signals the experience of negative events, conditions, and forces rather than a world of ideas abstracted from events and their characteristics. The Old Testament's hamartiological terminology is intrinsically connected to the concreteness of sinful reality. Decisive in this terminology is, therefore, not the difference between concrete and abstract, but the inherent relationship between facts and their evaluation. This terminology is essentially empirical in nature.

2. The Word Field

In the Old Testament, this varied terminology is never conceptualized as a comprehensive doctrine of sin. Still, no Old Testament hamartiology can bypass the question of the meaning of the Old Testament's word field. When this question is raised, the articulation of the meaning of each word in the word field does not suffice as an answer. What is necessary is the correlation of the individual words' meanings, so that the meaning of the web of the total word field may be reconstructed. At this point, we can only hope for the completion of this task in someone's future work.

Clearly, the assumption is untenable that the meaning of any word has nothing to do with the meaning of any other, e.g., that an act of violence is not a crime, or that a crime does not imply both guilt and consequences, or that guilt has nothing to do with a shameful activity as well as the sense of shame, etc. Also, the assumption that such words do not have legal as well as ethical, social/communal as well as individual, cultic as well as civil, religious/theological as well as secular implications is unwarranted. The word field itself raises the question of whether it reflects one coherent or many conflicting views of reality.

This question remains necessary even though the texts offer no systematic treatise on this topic. The Old Testament, unlike the New Testament, does not offer a holistic hamartiology because of its lack of explicit conceptual systematizations in general, despite clearly recognizable systematizing tendencies. This absence does not mean, however, that the Old Testament's view of reality is nothing but fragmentary or chaotic. Until the view of reality underneath the complex word field is interpreted, any judgment about the nature of the Old Testament's hamartiology is premature.

B. The Texts

In order to understand the aspects of sin signaled by the vocabulary, the text units and larger text corpora are more important than the individual sentences which in arrangement, content, and substance serve those units. The text units demonstrate the difference between the verbal and nominal forms in the terminology. They offer both narratives of sinful events and formally disqualifying definitions of sin. The latter are found most prominently in declaratory statements. Such statements focus either on the nature of an act as in Lev 11:42, "they are detestable," or on the nature of the consequences as in Jer 26:11, "This man deserves the sentence of death." In the latter example, the specific action is mentioned, "because he has prophesied against this city." In this example, one must ultimately ask: Who actually is sinning, Jeremiah or his accusers?

Three observations are of general significance:

1. Words and Texts

Words for sin in the texts are just as important for understanding the texts as the texts are for understanding the individual words. Where used, the words express the conceptual foci which control what is said about them in the texts. For example, one cannot narrate a story about a criminal action and call the action "good." The texts express the concrete circumstances to which the formally and typologically disqualifying words are tied.

2. Conceptual Common Denominators

The indissoluble correlation between words and texts reveals the common conceptual framework in which both facts and their qualities are perceived as the two essential aspects of the same reality. Each fact has a quality, and each quality exists in a concrete fact. Hence, each quality is factually concrete.

3. Texts with and without Words for Sin

Many texts use words for sin. Other texts report aspects of sin without using the terminology (e.g., Gen 4:23-24; 11:1-9). These texts are governed by identifiable infratextual hamartiological concepts. Indeed, there is no nonconceptual text, whether in terms of concepts that control individual texts or in terms of text groups. And inasmuch as text and context complement rather than exclude each other, the issue of Old Testament hamartiology, too, must lastly focus on the hamartiological concepts in the texts if it is to address the central issue.

C. Conceptual Aspects

Conceptually, the Old Testament speaks about different kinds and degrees of sin and guilt. The mere juxtaposition of their individual interpretations in a sort of anthology amounts more to a hamartiological anatomy than a hamartiology. At issue is the extent to which the individual understandings of sin are already related in the Old Testament itself. Equally at issue is whether the process of relating can be completed through interpretation. In the following, the focus will be on the major conceptual aspects. It is inevitable, for the time being, that these aspects be discussed vis-à-vis the major sections of the Old Testament.

1. The Primeval History

The Pentateuch is a history work which extends from creation to the death of Moses. In it, the primeval history composed of **J** and **P** (Genesis 3–11) contains a basic orientation for the Pentateuch and beyond. G. von Rad has said that it narrates God's reaction to "the increasingly grave violation" of God's order.[3] W. Zimmerli has said that "it illustrates uncannily the rapid growth of evil."[4] In these formulations, the words "violation" or "evil" and "increasing" or "growth" deserve special attention.

The narrative speaks directly about a variety of violations and evils. It does not say that the violations and evils are increasing or growing — except in the introduction to the flood story. Nevertheless, we correctly interpret the concept of growth in this reported variety. We interpret more than what the narrative says, and our interpretation amounts to more than the sum of the narrative's aspects. It amounts to a hamartiology.

3. G. von Rad, *Old Testament Theology,* 2 vols. (New York: Harper & Row, 1962), 1:155.
4. W. Zimmerli, *Old Testament Theology in Outline* (Atlanta: John Knox Press, 1978), 169.

Clearly, the movement of the narrative does not imply that one kind of violation belongs to the past when a new kind of violation appears. Rather, the kinds of violation progressively accumulate. All are present by the end of the primeval history, and remain an ever-present reality not only throughout the following history narrated in the Pentateuch and during Israel's history, but also throughout the totality of human history. From the text's perspective, the hamartiology of the primeval history is the paradigm for the growth and function of evil in human history.

What, then, is the nature of humanity's sin? Every new kind of violation, evil, or sin is the actualization of the possibility of self-destruction intrinsic to the human condition. This self-destruction is effected by continually breaking away from what is known to be the goodness of the order which is provided for and sustains human life. This order is not derived from humanity itself, but from the deity vis-à-vis humanity. The self-destructive actualization is self-inflicted. For its sinfulness, nothing and nobody but humanity itself is responsible, because it alone has actualized the possibility; it is not subject to an inevitable fate. And since this sinfulness pervades all humanity, no individual — except Enoch and Noah (Gen 5:24; 6:8-9) — or group is judged righteous. All partake in humanity's self-destructive existence and would not continue to live except for the reality of patience toward humanity's existence.

Even so, there is no guarantee that humanity will continue to exist. Despite the deity's hope-giving promise in Gen 9:8-17, the possibility remains that at some point in human history, humanity itself may rush into the abyss rather than hover indefinitely along its brink. The continuation of sinful human existence, after the insufficient remedies attempted in the flood and the Noahitic covenant, belies any confidence in the perpetuity of this precarious balance.

Within this basic conceptuality, two major types of sin and their consequences are primarily discerned.

a. Limit-Condition Disobedience

One type of sin consists of the humans' disobedience to their creaturely limit conditions. These limit conditions have been established for them by the deity. When humanity challenges these limits, adverse consequences result for human existence. Women have enmity for the cursed serpent, experience pain in childbearing, and are emotionally and socially dependent on their husbands (a fact which is only now gradually and limitedly changing in the global perspective). Men face lifelong arduous toil for food gained from among the thorns and thistles of the ground, which is cursed because of them. Such a break with the proper human place in "the garden of Eden" (Gen 3:23), or with the good order of creation (Genesis 1), affects existential human conditions which exist prior to and regardless of all historical changes.

b. History

The other type of self-destructiveness consists of those sins which occur within the realm of humanity's historical development. This type of self-destructiveness is based on, but not identical with, the succession of generations and the increase in population resulting from this succession.

As humanity increases — this increase is considered a blessing — more people are involved in sinful actions and more are affected by their consequences. Before the flood, the sins include: murder in the family (Gen 4:1-16), the legitimation of blood talion to the extent of programmatic revenge among groups (4:23-24), procreation of children through the union of divine (!) and human partners (6:1-4), and the ruination of the earth through the violent way of "all flesh" (6:11-13). After the flood, sin continues in the violation of the taboo of parental nakedness (9:20-25; cf. 19:30-38), and in the total human involvement in the decision for and execution of the construction of a "heaven-scraper" with the resulting dispersion of humanity through the deity's dissolution of the common language (11:1-9).

Although the narrative projects a historical development, its sociology presupposes that every mentioned type of sin remains pertinent throughout this development. It amounts to a phenomenology of the progressive accumulation of the realms of sin. All societal entities are involved: individuals, families, groups, and all humanity.

a. + b. Kinds of Sin

Like the terminology, the kinds of sin vary greatly. All appear to be similarly grave. Yet, because murder is the criterion under which someone in the Old Testament is declared guilty of death, it must be considered the gravest of all sins. Murder is also that violence which ruins the earth and signals the ultimate contrast to the goodness of its creation; it represents the implosion of the social fabric of humanity and its explosive destructive effects on the earth.

Murder is not the only time the death sentence is applied legally. The deity's sentence of death by flood for humanity's social and ecological violence is also a legal decision. It is based on the illegality of violence. Yet violence (חָמָס) is not condemned because of its social and ecological effects but because this sort of destruction represents the severest sort of crime. Other aspects regarding the degrees of severity of sin will be pursued later.

2. *Act and Condition*

The hamartiology of the primeval history shows what can also be observed in other texts such as Isaiah, Hosea, Jeremiah, the Psalms, and Proverbs: the interdependence of acts and condition, or sins and sin. Sins are not only perceived as momentary, isolated acts or occasional aberrations from presumed human goodness. They are also perceived to be manifestations of a condition in humanity which lends itself to sinful as well as good behavior. In effect the human condition is understood to be less than capable of resisting evil influences and upholding what is good. The experience of sins calls attention to sinfulness, and the perception of sinfulness is confirmed by the experience of sins.

In the Old Testament, the distinction between sinfulness as a human possibility and as a basic, ontic human condition is fluid. The reason for this fluidity seems to lie in the fact that the texts focus on empirical observation rather than on ontological theory. This remains so even where the texts border on an ontologically based understanding, such as in the dynamistic ontology *(Tatsphäredenken)* in the Old Testament emphasized in K. Koch's work. As reflected in its attention to the endless chain of sins, the Old Testament understanding of human nature as basically sinful is not rooted in the awareness of sin as an a priori ontic condition. Rather, it is rooted in the accumulating and intensifying amalgamation of all sinful acts into an indissoluble web in which humans, individually and corporately, become inextricably ensnared. It becomes their nature and destiny to the extent that they can only sin and sin again. As they sin, they become addicted to sinning.

For example, Hosea's language rests on the experience of this dynamistic reality: "Their deeds surround them" (Hos 7:2); ". . . they sow the wind, and they shall reap the whirlwind" (8:7a); "Their deeds do not permit them to return to their God. For the spirit of whoredom is within them" (5:4); "Ephraim stumbles in his guilt" (5:5), and so on. Similarly, the community's curse against the man who sets up a graven or molten image "in secret" (Deut 27:15) is not only a substitute for its inability to punish the person for his sin; it commits that person to a destiny of concrete sinful acts, attitudes, and behavior which keep the crime hidden. The person's secret act creates a concrete sphere of inescapable sinfulness which in turn forces upon that person sinful act after sinful act. The fact that "there is no one who does not sin" (1 Kgs 8:46) — "no one" referring to each individual human — does not mean that each person is not sin*ful* as well. It means that both act and condition mutually affect each other. Together they belong to the reality of human existence. This reality is destructive, and the fact that it holds every individual equally in its grip does not excuse any person from her/his responsibility in this reality.

3. Act and Mind

In the Old Testament's understanding of the interdependence of sinful acts and sinfulness, the distinction between mind and act, the psychic and physical, the attitudinal and behavioral, or the internal and external, holds a central place. This is observed especially in the attention to the human psyche as the sphere in which the human condition is most closely experienced. This attention is most clearly reflected in texts that speak about the human heart, its desires and plans, and so on. Again, the primeval history offers such observations.

The general correlation between mind and act is portrayed in a variety of ways. For example, they "saw" — a psychic factor — "and took" (Gen 3:1-14; 4:1-8; 6:1-2). Ham "saw . . . and told" (9:22); here "telling" is an act. These texts portray the continually sinful activity of the mind which prompts the subsequent act either in action or word. The same dynamic occurs in individually different cases. It can also be derived from Gen 6:5 (**J**) and 6:11-13 (**P**). Here humanity is irredeemably wicked, and "every inclination of the thoughts of their hearts was only evil continually" — note the accumulation of psychological terms! Then humanity is evaluated as hopelessly corrupt and violent. In this instance, the process from mind to act no longer refers to individual acts but to a characteristic human pattern.

Gen 4:23-24 and 11:1-9 refer only to acts. In our interpretations, we often focus on the state of mind behind what the texts say. The texts may each imply a state of hubris, but they do not narrate it. The first passage focuses on what Lamech is said to have done, and the second passage focuses on what the monolingual humans said (and by inference, did [11:5]). The focus on acts alone in these two texts is noteworthy, because the converse is not narrated. There is no text in the primeval history that refers to the state of mind alone without also stating its external behavioral actualization.

This anthropological hamartiology is entirely empirical, nonspeculative, and nonideological. Even where it speaks about every continually evil "inclination of the thoughts of their hearts" (Gen 6:5), it refers to an attitude observable in humanity and not to an ontic precondition — such as paradise lost. This condition is not inevitable. It is a fact for which humanity remains liable despite divine forbearance. Not coincidentally, Cain is called and expected to be able to "master" the anger which is "lurking at the door" (4:7).

4. Greater and Lesser Sins

One of the most important chapters in an Old Testament hamartiology is the analysis of the Old Testament's recognition of the differing levels of severity of sin and sinfulness. Every sin and sinfulness is not equal in weight. This recognition comes to light in various ways, especially in the legal text corpora which focus on typical individual cases. The differentiating perspective and the focus on cases have nothing to do with what we negatively label as casuistry and legalism. With regard to sin and sinful acts, just as in the total arena of ancient Israel's social formation, the ethical and legal sides are intertwined. The root cause for the stratifying perspective lies in the experience that not every sin is equally destructive, especially socially. The fact that everyone sins does not mean that every sin is deadly. A thief is a sinner but is not a murderer. The differentiation between kinds and degrees of sin and the focus on the specific cases resulting from this variety show that this hamartiology is based empirically on the realities of human life rather than in ideological abstraction from those realities.

In the evaluation of sin and guilt by the society, the differentiation between kinds and degrees of sin serves to provide limits on punishment. The criteria for any punishment are commensurate with the assessment of the destructive effects of the sin it seeks to curb. However, despite the differing assessments, no degree of sin and guilt is without real consequences. This is true even where sin is said to be forgiven. No freedom from sin through forgiveness, especially through the comprehensive forgiveness in Christian theology, means that anyone or any community, including any elected community, is therefore free from both sins and their consequences during life on earth. Whatever the merit of forgiveness may be, it becomes a docetic claim unless it is correlated to the fact that all humans must face the consequences of their sins in one way or another in this life.

a. Relationship of Act and Mind

One kind of differentiation of severity can be observed with regard to relationship between act and mind. For example, in the primeval history, the sinful acts carry more weight than the states of mind in which they originate. Although the human mind is evil from youth (Gen 8:21), its destructiveness becomes particularly effective when it is released into concrete action. Lamech's boasting about his already committed barbarism and humanity's decision to make bricks and build a city and tower (4:23-24; 11:3-4) are both speech acts. Still, the emphasis is on the acts, not the states of mind. Likewise, Cain is cursed for his act, not for his state of mind (4:10-12).

The texts about unwittingly committed sins (e.g., Lev 4:2, et al.) speak of conscious acts which even with the best of intentions turn out to be wrong. Here the sin is understood to exist in the (result of the) executed act and not in the mind. Thus, compared to the act or its result, the state of mind in which the act is committed can represent either an aggravating or a mitigating factor. But it is never as decisive as the act itself, especially its result. The relationship in the Old Testament between sinful act and state of mind deserves careful study. Nevertheless, an Old Testament hamartiology based on state of mind, or an ethos of attitude *(Gesinnung, Gesinnungsethik),* without accounting for acts, is scarcely defensible.

Of course, the connection of mind and act is also evidenced in the wisdom tradition. As elsewhere, this tradition sees this connection as a fact of human existence. Although it distinguishes between mind and act, it considers both as functioning interdependently in the person who is a living "soul" (נֶפֶשׁ). A sentence such as "the soul of the wicked [רָשָׁע] desires evil" (author's translation of Prov 21:10a) presupposes that the desire — a psychological notion — of the wicked is caused by what he/she is, meaning his/her identity, or his/her soul. He/she desires evil because he/she is evil. A person may become evil by acting in evil ways or may act in such ways because he/she is evil. Neither case is a reason for exculpation.

b. Relationships between Acts

The acts themselves, too, are considered to be of graded severity. Cain's murdering and Lamech's limitless revenge rank among the most severe criminal acts of violence. In Israel's legislation, they belong to those deserving the death penalty (cf. Exod 21:12-17). A scale of severity is the basis for the composition of the pertinent parts of the Covenant Book in Exod 21:12–22:17.

On the scale of sins, the most grave of all is pervasive violence, the apex of which is certainly murder. It is the reason for the flood, a fundamental judgment the deity promises not to repeat. The extreme gravity of murder is pointed out in the barbaric crimes of the neighboring nations in Amos 1–2, regardless whether one interprets these actions as breaches of international treaties or only as excessive warfare. Breach of treaty does not necessarily happen barbarically. It is the barbarism that is the reason for the announced harsh punishment of the nations, both in international warfare and in Israel's social injustice.

Both Amos 1–2 and Isa 10:5-19 seem to presuppose a distinction between what we call acts of war and war crimes, or between the inevitability of war and the norms for its controlled practice. In the Old as well as in the New Testament, whether or not war should or may be considered sin depends on criteria independent of its general acceptance or its divine ordination. Whether accepted or rejected, warfare represents mass killing and mass destruction, and belongs to the phenomenon of all-pervasive violence. It is the most radical type by which humanity takes itself, qualitatively and quantitatively, to the brink of extinction. Thereby, the excesses of war in Amos 1–2 are sins which are distinctly foremost in their severity.

c. Sin beyond Societal Reach

Not every sin is criminal and subject to punishment or remedial action. The number of situations is endless where sinful behavior in words or acts lies outside the reach of institutionalized societal mechanisms.

The wisdom tradition is especially pertinent in this respect. It is not so much concerned with the institutionalized containment and curbing of sin and guilt as with the avoidance of sin by the individual "child" him/herself, before and regardless of the society's reaction to it. Next to its positive value system, the wisdom tradition is concerned with the art of staying and turning away from evil. The book of Proverbs is the primary case in point. The scoffers are ensnared by their own behavior (Prov 1:22-33). The sluggard ends in poverty, the wicked in calamity, and the adulterer in destruction and disgrace (6:6-11, 12-15, 20-35; cf. 16:25-33; 17:1-12, 14, 15, 19, 20, et al.).

Whereas some of the avoidance instructions ("do not . . .") imply or refer to legal prosecution (e.g., 22:28; 23:10), most of them refer to sinful thoughts, words, and actions outside the court jurisdiction (3:27-31; 4:4-17; 5:1-14; 9:8; 20:13, 22; 22:22, 24, 26; 23:3, 4, 6, 9, 17, 20; 24:1, 15, 17, 19, et al.). These instructions delve into the endlessly varied scope of the daily life of the individual. Here evil is always a possibility waiting to spread like a cancer; even stupid thoughtlessness is no negligible matter but one with evil effects. Despite this type of independence from legal consequences, evil still has very damaging influences on social and personal life. Thus, the avoidance instructions are not a code of rules. Rather, they are collections of examples which attempt to inculcate in the individual a mind-set of prudence which is always cognizant of evil's effects and intent on keeping those effects at bay.

Also, these instructions are not only concerned with words and acts. Their concern is foolishness as it decays the mind itself. These concise proverbial forms are the expressions of the intellectual concentration on the difference between the constructive and the destructive dynamics in life, namely, the difference between wisdom and foolishness. The fact that they often focus on negative realities has nothing to do with a pessimistic outlook. Clearly, they are balanced by a consistent focus on the positive. The overarching intent is the protection of the positive through the prevention of the negative. In this way, destructive dynamics are to be kept from ruling life.

The wisdom instructions do more than merely describe facts. They qualify and disqualify those facts. Their preoccupation with good and bad quality reveals the basic experience that the process of valuation is intrinsic to reality and life; life is not value-neutral. Therefore, the instructions are not moralistic, nor are they derived from abstract moral codes. They are neither pessimistic nor optimistic in outlook. Their ethos is realistic, generated and shaped by the experience — everyone's, not just a particular community's — that the dimensions of life themselves are always evaluated as better or worse, or good or evil. In this ethical realism, evil is consciously confronted. Its neglect or indifferent treatment would amount to conspiracy with it.

The opposite terms "good" and "evil" are used most generally. They do not signal the highest kinds of values. Nor do they replace all other differentiations within the value system by seeing reality simplistically as either right or wrong. Rather, they function comprehensively for the basic and decisive distinction between all different kinds and degrees of goodness and badness. Passages having to do with the knowledge of good and evil and the search for that which is good (e.g., Gen 3:5, 22; Deut 1:39; Isa 1:16-17; 5:20; Amos 5:14-15; Mic 3:2; Heb 5:14) reflect no momentary rhetorical intuitions. They stand on the solidly established tradition in which the distinction between good and evil belongs to the most important, fundamental, and at the same time most challenging task of the human mind on behalf of human existence.

The form of parallelism in Hebrew poetry lends itself to comparing and differentiating among different perspectives. These parallelisms are in no way whimsical. They are the result of intense reflection, and each condenses in strikingly appropriate short form the substance of a complex and complicated process which otherwise would have to be narrated in a story.

aa. Antithetically Parallel Statements For example, in Prov 10:12 ("Hatred stirs up strife, but love covers all offenses"), the effects of hatred and love are juxtaposed antithetically. Their juxtaposition amounts to a systematized comparison of opposing values. It begins with the observation of each behavior and its effects, and arrives at the recognition of their distinct values through mutual comparison. The two types of events happen separately. The proverb compares their opposite natures and brings the difference between destructive and constructive attitudes and behaviors into sharp focus. It thus provides the basis for the correct choice between the two (cf. 10:13, 14, 25-28; 14:1-19, et al.).

bb. Synthetically Parallel Statements A person may return "evil for good." But that person will find that "evil will not depart" from his/her house (Prov 17:13). Here and in similar cases, the synthetically formed proverb reflects the conceptualized understanding of the direct correlation between the nature of an act and its consequences. In this case, the evil consequence is irreversibly intensified by means of the unusually evil act. This person has not simply done something evil; the person has violently broken the correspondence between a good action and its good effect by answering good with evil. Thus he/she has turned a good process into an evil one, not only for the affected victim but especially for the perpetrator.

cc. The "Better" Sayings The so-called better sayings are especially important. These proverbs rest on an intellectual process in which the values of experiences are distinguished through their comparison in terms of their relative relationship. Prov 16:8 ("Better is a little with righteousness than large income with injustice") does not say that righteousness is better than injustice. Nor does it say that little is better than large income. It focuses on the difference between little and large income with respect to the different conditions for the acquisition of each. It only calls the little "better" under these conditions; and the large income is not called evil outright. Such observations reflect the virtually resigned realism which abstains from moralization in the face of the facts of human existence (cf. 15:17; 16:19; 19:1, 22; 28:6; Eccl 9:7).

While the situations called "better" normally belong to what is good, not all less than good situations are therefore assumed to be evil. They may simply be less good, as in Prov 22:1, "A good name is to be chosen rather than great riches, and favor is better than silver or gold." (Cf. 1 Cor 12:31; 13:13.)

The mechanism for comparing and discerning differing values in the "better" sayings addresses the dimensions of experience which are so impenetrable that they defy clear-cut evaluation as wrong and right, or evil and good. They can only be evaluated in terms of compared and related values. These are the dimensions situated between the clearly recognizable opposites of good and evil. They represent a range of experience which is susceptible to the influence of either good or evil but also depends on additional factors. Amid these expressed nuances, these comparisons direct attention to what is better and away from what is worse.

This sort of evaluation through comparison is fundamentally different from abstract, timeless moral principles. It provides a distinctly empirical basis for value judgments regarding sin and guilt. In addition to other types of comparison, the "better" sayings relativize values and place realistic restraints on the individual judgments which arise from specific moral stances.

5. The Relativizing of Ontology

The ontological concept of the coherence of evil acts, attitudes, and behaviors, along with their evil effects and guilt-determined destinies, pervades the entire literature of the Old Testament throughout its history. In the course of that history, however, other typical kinds of experiences accompanied this view of reality. Although they did not replace the coherence ontology, they did succeed in providing competing views. Thus, the coherence ontology could no longer function as the sole criterion for discerning truth and falsehood. In the wake of these experiences, Israel's ontology became conceptually pluralistic. For this reason alone, the Old Testament theology, including its hamartiology, does not depend on any particular ontology.

As new insights emerged, they on occasion even claimed primacy over the traditional concept. Yet the coherence concept continued to be considered valid, so that old and new coexisted, opposing, complementing, and ultimately mutually relativizing each other. While one concept is considered true with respect to certain types of experience, other concepts are considered equally true for other types of experience. No single concept is verified as true for all types of experience. The issue left unresolved by this pluralistic phenomenon of concepts is whether or not a value system relating these competing concepts may be discerned by substance-critical comparison. Such comparison would demonstrate their stratification in a system of greater and lesser validities, or in a system of hamartiological "better" sayings.

Two major exceptions to the concept of strict coherence and proportionality of evil act and effect have already been mentioned: the replacement — or claims to it — of the principle of corporate responsibility by individual responsibility in Deuteronomy, Jeremiah, and Ezekiel, and the primeval history's theology of the never-ending continuation of life on earth — expressed in the deity's promise — in spite of the perpetual evil in humanity. In these cases, the concept of effects proportionate to sin is superseded by the focus on reducing either the quantitative extent or the qualitative dominance of destructive forces. Alongside these two perspectives, other exceptions to the coherence concept are apparent.

a. Abraham

In the narrative of Abraham's intercession for Sodom (Gen 18:22-33), the problem put before the deity is not only whether the righteous will be destroyed with the wicked (v. 23). Primarily, the deity must consider the possibility of the corporate salvation of the sinful city on account of a few righteous citizens. With respect to the innocent, the principle of corporate punishment is considered contestable at the outset. In the broader Old Testament perspective, this initial contestation certainly led to the principle of the separation of the righteous and sinners, most notably in legal and judicial administration. Yet the story itself considers no such separation. Indeed, it suggests that the principle of corporate punishment be replaced by the principle of corporate pardon on account of the righteous minority. The only debate is how far that minority may be downsized. Abraham's deity is forced to acknowledge a real and inevitable problem of communal existence. The deity must de-ideologize the deity's abstract principle of justice in view of this problem. Ultimately the deity must admit that the principle of corporate sparing is "better" for "the judge of all the earth" than the principle of corporate punishment. The resulting concept is that, in communal existence, the justice of pardon outweighs in value the justice of punishment of the community's sin.

b. Hosea 11:1-9

In Hosea 11:1-9, Yahweh judges elected Israel; no distinction between righteous and sinners is expressed. In this passage, the replacement of the justice of judgment by the justice of pardon represents the radicalization of the concept just analyzed in the Abraham narrative. This concept affects the very identity of the judge as deity, as it reflects the conflict between these two kinds of justice in the ongoing reality of the community. Who but the one who says, "I am God and no human" (author's translation of v. 9), can replace punishment with pardon without controlling or removing the ongoing destructiveness of evil? Just as in the primeval history, the passage wonders at the ongoing existence of the community despite its ongoing sinfulness. This wonder is intensified by the assumption that the elect ought to be "better" than humanity in general.

c. The Joseph Novella

The gravest of sinful events in the familial realm is depicted in the Joseph novella (Genesis 37–50): Joseph is sold into slavery by his brothers. Legally, this is considered a capital crime (cf. Exod 21:16).[5] Once committed, lied about, and hidden, the crime seems to have become nonexistent within the family. Yet its dynamic course continues through the decades in another country. Finally, it is revealed that in this course the dynamic of evil has been overtaken by the dynamic of good; Joseph yields his right and power to punish his brothers to the "better" right and power already established through the complete reversal of the course of evil. When Joseph says, "As for you, you meant evil against me; but God meant it for good" (Gen 50:20),[6] he acknowledges the dynamic presence in a process which breaks the autonomous coherence of evil act and evil consequence by turning it into a process of goodness and which, therefore, represents the better justice. Joseph accepts this better justice as the ethical basis for his own judgment of forgiveness.

d. The Jonah Novella

As is generally known, the consistency of evil processes can also be broken by repentance. Such repentance is variously expressed as a change of mind, attitude, and behavior, and by institutionalized modes of confession of sin, sacrificial acts for atonement, and remedial and, where necessary, punitive acts as well. The number of cases is large. This possibility exists not only for Israel. For example, it is also realized by Nineveh, when the Ninevites obey their king's command that "all shall turn from their evil ways and from the violence that is in their hands" (Jon 3:8-10). No faith in Yahweh is required, nor is the positive activity of doing good. The rituals of penitence suffice. The Ninevites have to cry to God and, more importantly, turn away from evil, especially violence. And God repents.

e. Exodus 34:6-7

Exod 34:6-7 reflects the precarious attempt at striking a balance in the deity's relation to the succeeding generations, especially within a family:

5. This text describes the brothers' mentality (Gen 37:4) as well as their word-act (vv. 18-20). Nevertheless, the act of selling Joseph into slavery is decisive and thereby disqualified as the most grave sin.

6. Here I use the *Revised Standard Version.* I think it more accurately translates the Hebrew רָעָה and טוֹבָה as the opposites "evil" and "good."

> Merciful and gracious, slow to anger, and abounding in steadfast love and faithfulness, keeping steadfast love for thousands, forgiving guilt and crime and sin, but who will by no means clear the guilty, visiting the guilt of the parents upon the children and the children's children, to the third and fourth generation. (author's translation; cf. Exod 20:5-6; Num 14:18; Neh 9:17; Ps 86:15; Jon 4:2)

What is clear in this passage is that the influence of the positive factors outweighs the influence of the destructive factors, both in degree and duration. Still, neither entirely eliminates the other. What is not clear is how the complexity of real experience can be aligned according to these specific differentiations. Here doctrine is on the way to projecting a reality which does not suffice for the complex struggle in lived experience of conceptualizing the relationship between righteousness and sin.

f. The Separation of the Righteous and Sinners

The same tension with experienced reality also exists in the concept of the separation of a holy, or sinless, community from the human community, and in the concept of separation of righteous individuals from sinners. Attempting to implement the opposites of good and evil in the structures of societal life runs into insurmountable obstacles. Israel's election is valid. But the entire Old Testament overwhelmingly testifies to the fact that the elect community was at no time in its history without sin and guilt. It never was what it was called to be. Nor has Christianity ever been what *it* was called to be. In light of the central claim of Christianity, this is an even more serious deficiency.

As soon as any such elect community is established, sin and guilt will soon reappear. Even the attempt at separating the righteous from sinners within the same community, be it the human or the elect community (as hailed by Psalms 1; 119; etc., and advocated by Ezekiel, Habakkuk, Trito-Isaiah, Malachi, et al.), does not succeed in extricating the so-called righteous from their own communal and personal sin. Ps 19:11-13 knows this well. Not even when "I perceived their end" (Ps 73:17) proves definitively the experience of the separation of the righteous and sinners. "Their end" is not always one of evil, different from the end of the righteous. Empirical skepticism waits in the wings.

g. Empirical Skepticism

> The same fate comes to all, to the righteous and the wicked, to the good and the evil, to the clean and the unclean, to those who sacrifice and those who do not sacrifice. (Eccl 9:2)

> All go to one place; all are from the dust, and all turn to dust again. (3:20)

These passages begin with the definitiveness of human mortality. Neither birth nor death separates the righteous from sinners. Within the given life span,

> There is a vanity which takes place on earth, that there are righteous people who are treated according to the conduct of the wicked, and there are wicked people who are treated according to the conduct of the righteous. (8:14)

Job says, "I . . . a just and blameless man, I am a laughing stock," whereas "the tents of robbers are at peace, and those who provoke God are secure" (Job 12:4, 6). This breakdown of the coherence between act and consequence, not even prevented by God, is very different from God's replacement of evil with good in the Joseph story. Any statement such as "I have been young, and now am old; yet I have not seen the righteous forsaken or their children begging bread" (Ps 37:25) is relativized by the fact that the wicked can have this same experience (Job 21:7-26). Another relativizing fact is that righteous individuals, too, suffer periods of affliction even as Yahweh "rescues them from them all" (Ps 34:19).

What, then, is the difference between the lives of the righteous and those of the wicked? And, "what is the Almighty, that we should serve him? And what profit do we get if we pray to him?" (Job 21:15). Is the difference between the righteous and the wicked negligible in this mortal life? Does the only valid answer lie in the hope of a future people with a new heart (Hos 2:14-23; Jer 31:31-34; Ezekiel 37), who will live in the prophesied eschatological history? Ultimately, do we have to look to a new creation which is nonetheless conceived in this-worldly terms? In this new creation, "Your people shall all be righteous; they shall possess the land forever" (Isa 60:21; cf. 60; 65:17-25; 66:22-23). Here the sinners shall finally be destroyed. Or does the answer lie in a total replacement of this old world by the cataclysmic apocalypse of the heavenly world as expected in the book of Daniel?

Whatever the validity is of eschatology and apocalypticism in the Old Testament, and whatever the function of those hopes is for present comfort, they cannot function as alternatives to and escapism from humanity's and the elect's deep and inescapable entanglement in the destructive, all-pervasive power of sin and guilt in this ongoing world. This ongoing world has thus far outlasted all eschatological and apocalyptic visions. After all, any theological history constructed from the Old Testament in which the eschatological and apocalyptic worldview is assumed to have replaced worldviews based on the ongoing world is an illusion. Very clearly, the Old Testament's noneschatological worldview runs historically alongside the rise of eschatology and apocalypticism down to the latest sources and beyond them to this day. The noneschatological always remains in competition with the eschatological-apocalyptic worldview. It is in this competition that the struggle to cope with the continual fact of evil in this indefinitely ongoing world becomes most apparent. What, then, is the validity of empirically based skepticism?

It cannot be denied that the empirical observations raised especially in Job and Ecclesiastes are true. They show the reductionism in any formula which attempts to define and manage the modes of the reality of evil in a set ontological system. Evil cannot be conceived as an ideology, an abstract homogeneous system. Evil is chaotic in nature, and for this reason defies a homogeneously defined or systematized ontology. Such homogeneity falls apart in light of experience. Nevertheless, empirical skepticism has its limits, too. First, the experience that the destinies of sinners and the righteous are indistinguishable does not mean that the other experience is not also true: that sinners reap evil whereas righteous persons live in well-being. Actually, both Job and his friends were right. Second, empirical skepticism's correct observations especially about the profitable life of evildoers are quite superficial. They account for what is on the surface and before the eyes but not for the guilt-based effects, which remain hidden. They do not address the inner life of the sinner, who at best must repress the sinful nature of his/her acts and live a hidden life which determines all else that he/she does, says, and appears to be. Such a person might, at worst, become neurotic or paranoid.

Third and most important, however, is the experience-based fact that nowhere in the Old Testament, including its skepticism, are sinners no longer identified as sinners. Nowhere has the difference between them and the innocent become irrelevant. Neither is the lifestyle of sinners ever endorsed. It is always rejected, regardless of its good or evil outcome. This rejection is based on their acts, behavior, and attitude, and never on the consequences or the coherence of act and consequences. It, therefore, amounts to the primacy of one's acts over their results. Hence, good is done and evil is avoided for their own sake rather than as means to ends. This fundamental viewpoint of doing good and turning from evil for their own sake prevents the experience of the coherence of act and consequence from becoming an instrument of self-interest. In no way can self-interest determine what is good; rather, what is good is maintained as the criterion for what one does and who one is. Good and evil are not determined by any relativized version of the dynamistic ontology. Sinners do not identify what is evil, but evil identifies sinners. And the course of evil is not identified by the fact of the course but by its evil quality. This *lack* of good quality in any form and at any state of the course's development is determined by those realities that are experienced as destructive rather than constructive.

D. The Prophets

Much more may be said about the prophets' confrontations with sin and guilt than can be mentioned here. What is most important at the outset is that the prophets' appearance not be seen in isolation from the other parts of the Old Testament. Israel's encounter with sin and guilt existed before, during, and after the prophets.

Even during their own time, they were not the only ones confronting this reality. In their respective historical contexts, they either announced the end of Israel's history in the land — sometimes with last-hour warnings to fulfill the conditions for survival — or announced and projected Israel's new beginning. In the early postexilic period, they were involved in both salvation prophecy and judgment of their communities and the world. Throughout their appearances, their messages addressed the meaning of history, especially the meaning of Israel's election. For the prophets, history is the unfolding of the tension and ultimately the conflict between the bestowed history of salvation, and Israel's and the nations' violation of that gift. It is this critical sin- and guilt-laden failure to adhere to the meaning of history in goodness, and the vision of a radical new beginning of a good history, culminating in the vision of a new creation, which sharply characterizes the prophetic foci. Above all, the prophets force uncompromising attention to the critical difference between good history and destructive, evil history in this ongoing world. They appear — often alone, lonely, and at grave risk — at those critical moments of transition from one epoch to the next, in which good and evil historical courses collided.

The place of prophetic appearance marks the difference between the prophets and the historians of the historical works. Both groups focus on history. Both are concerned about humanity's sinful distortion of the God-given conditions for a wholesome course of history. However, whereas the historians, not to mention the sages, communicate their evaluations indirectly, in distantiation from the actual scenes, the prophets interfere with the events directly, provocatively, and confrontationally.

The results are on record. The nature of history has not changed since then, neither through the works of historians nor through prophetic interdictions and announcements. Yet their joint realization that human history hangs precariously in the balance precisely because of the threat posed by the powerful influence of human sin and guilt has always been and continues to be true. This analysis is the abiding legacy of historians and prophets, even as they attended to ongoing history despite its endangerment.

The pre-exilic prophets announced the downfall of the nation of Israel and the demise of international powers. The reasons for these announcements, especially against their own nation, are given in their indictments. Their real message, the announcement of judgment, must not be overlooked. Also, it must be clear that these prophets were not teachers and preachers of ethics. Nevertheless, their indictments are the decisive factor, because they contain the rationale for these devastating announcements.

There is no need to recount these indictments in detail. For the most part, they elucidate Israel's own manifold rending of the fabric of social and legal justice. This rending was manifested in social, legal, and ethical corruption and in Israel's perversion of the integrity of its Yahweh-religion and its institutions, through all kinds of sinful acts, falsehoods, haughtiness, and the deeply corrupted corporate mind.

The prophets' critiques began with their intense clashes at the highest national levels of the Israelite monarchy — Nathan, Gad, Elijah, Amos, Isaiah, and Jeremiah — with the upper echelons of the society's institutions: the kings themselves, the princes, priests, other prophets, legislators and judges, and sages. These clashes continued down to all the people corporately and individually. Virtually no individual, group, or institution in the organized state was found blameless (e.g., Jer 5:1-5).

In their indictments, the prophets do not establish new norms. They presuppose and refer to the basic norms of the society's tradition, which represent the heart of the Old Testament's legal, cultic, and wisdom traditions. God Yahweh "has showed you, O human, what is good; and what Yahweh requires of you: To do justice, to love kindness, and to walk humbly with your God." (Author's translation of Mic 6:8; cf. Amos 5:24; Isa 1:16-17; Jer 5:1, et al.)

Already, the indictments distinguish between prophets, teachers of wisdom, priests, legislators, and historians. They do not speak in the forms of description, report, or doctrine about these distinct groups and their actions. In their sharpest form, they speak *ad personam.* They accuse directly. In these accusations, two factors are especially important. First, they focus on the sins that are actually committed or on the norms that ought to be, but are not, actualized. The prophets do not define justice. They say that it must be done. The verbs in the texts highlight this aspect: "*To do* justice, *to love* kindness, and *to walk* humbly with your God" (Mic 6:8); "*let* justice *roll down* like waters . . ." (Amos 5:24); "*seek* good, and *not* evil . . . *hate* evil, and *love* good" (5:14-15); "*wash* yourselves; *make* yourselves clean; *remove* the evil of your doings from before my eyes; *cease to do* evil, *learn to do* good; *seek* justice, *rescue* the oppressed, *defend* the orphan, *plead* for the widow" (Isa 1:16-17); ". . . find one person who *acts* justly and *seeks* truth" (Jer 5:1). Of course, this emphasis on acts or practices was not new! Just as the prophets do not define justice, they do not explain specifically how it should be done. Instead, they focus on actual situations and say that justice is not being done. This focus represents the most direct confrontation with the reality of sin and, inevitably, with sinners. Herein lies the reason why those prophets were so intensely rejected by the people.

This rejection is in no way the last word on the issue. The fact remains that the *practice* of the known doctrine is emphasized by the prophets as the decisive criterion for that doctrine's realistic nature. Doctrine that demands the enactment of an objective becomes an abstract ideology if its adherents fail to enact that objective. At worst, doctrine then becomes a shield of professed orthodoxy behind which one can hide the quite opposite nature of one's own actions. The behavior is thus hidden from the objective of the doctrine itself and from the deity. By criticizing the separation within doctrine of its objective from the demand for the practice of this objective, the prophets insist that both object and verb, content and practice, are the constitutive parts of doctrine itself. Hence, doctrine as such loses its integrity if its ethical thrust is neglected (cf. Jer 7:1-15).

Second, the prophets focus on the victims of injustice, namely, the oppressed, exploited, and disfranchised: the poor and needy (Amos 5:10-12), and orphans and widows (Isa 1:17). Socially, economically, and legally, they represent the endangered species within the society. Attention to them was not new in Israel's tradition history, nor were they the only reason behind the prophetic indictments. Still, in these indictments, this attention carries a particular weight. More than any other group, they had become especially victimized by the historical development of the state system. Their disfranchisement represented the disintegration of justice and social solidarity. Thus, the plight of the poor and oppressed symbolized the crisis of Israel's election more than any other societal aspect.

Next to Israel, the prophets and their schools also criticize the nations. In this critique, the nations are denounced as enemies of Yahweh's universal reign, and particularly for brutal acts and autonomous human behavior; see the books of Amos, Isaiah, Nahum, Habakkuk, Zephaniah, Obadiah, Ezekiel, Deutero- and Trito-Isaiah, Joel, Trito-Zechariah (12–14), and Malachi.

E. God Yahweh

1. Theological Hamartiology

There is no kind of sin mentioned anywhere in the Old Testament that would not be considered sin against God, especially against Israel's God Yahweh. The fact that this has not been explicitly discussed thus far is intentional. More is at stake than the necessary avoidance of a monotonous repetitiveness in referring to God Yahweh, which would devalue the significance of these references for the understanding of the presence of God Yahweh in Israel's experience of sin. It is clear, however, that the anthropological side of the Old Testament's hamartiology is fundamentally theological in nature.

2. The Deity

As with other Old Testament subjects, the knowledge of Yahweh adds something to the experience of sin and guilt which is not yet evident in that experience as such. One does not need a deity in order to realize that an evil act has consequences and a crime deserves punishment. Much of what is said in the Old Testament about human sin could be said without referring to the deity. Human sin is a matter of empirical verifiability. Yet, neither should we assume that discussion of the divine aspect has become irrelevant because it is perceived mythologically. We should not assume that the deity is perceived as a *deus ex machina* who supernaturally and mechanically interferes in the affairs of this world, or an abstract idea by which sin and guilt can be recognized for what they are. Also, we would do well not to say that sin and guilt are truly recognized only when we theologize the notion. Apart from the fact that theologization is itself not, and has not been, above the danger of sinfulness, sin and guilt are themselves perceived to be inherently religious and theological. Where they are encountered, they are always encountered before the deity. This does not mean they are encountered before the mythological visualization of the deity, but that they are engaged before the *divine presence* within the myth.

The awareness of sin and guilt as sin and guilt against God can only be circumscribed. It means that their destructive nature is inexcusable, regardless how specific sins are rationalized. It means that the coherence of act and consequences is not just a matter of the widespread experience of an autonomous process. It is equally a matter of the presence of inescapable justice in, and the just quality of, that process. This just quality is widely evident in the texts. And although many sinners may live and die in comfort, the fact that they are called sinners means that this judgment represents the inescapable identity of their existence, indeed of everyone's existence. It reflects the assumption that ultimately justice is legitimate even when it is only a claim and not always empirically recognized. Wherever and whenever it is experienced in the course of events the legitimacy of the claim is demonstrated; but this legitimacy does not always depend on empirical verification. It is true whether or not it is verified in experience. In the irreducible ultimacy of this claim, the judgment against sin is present in the sinner's life in this world. It is the presence of God which cannot be obscured by any course of events or manipulated by any human challenge to this claim.

This presence signals the impossibility of human autonomy, including the subjectivistic control over what sin and guilt are and are not. And it is the rational ground for human faith and hope in God and for the fear of God as well, as in Psalms 73; 139, et al., even when the way of the wicked does not perish (cf. Ps 1:6b).

Last but not least, the Old Testament's awareness of sin as sin against God means that sinners are personally confronted by God in their sinfulness. This is most intensely expressed in passages such as Psalms 6, 32, 38, 51, 102, 130, 143, and 139:1-18. As in the prophetic indictments, this personal encounter allows for no escape into self-distantiated theorizing about sin. The many texts in which the individual and the community confess their sin are ample testimony that the subject of sin and guilt is anything but an abstract idea.

The awareness of sin as sin against God comes into sharp focus where its destructive influence is miraculously — yes, miraculously though not supernaturally — experienced as contained, reduced, and even turned into goodness apart from any human action or intention. The whole primeval history, Abraham's pleading with Yahweh, the Joseph novella, and the portrayal throughout the Old Testament of Israel's experience with Yahweh highlight this awareness. It is also highlighted by the aspect of historical periodization, in which at one point humanity and at many points Israel, both individually and corporately, are caught by the effects of their sins. Yet at the same time they are enabled to start anew without the burden of past guilt. Even in today's reality, who is ever really allowed to be free of the past once he, she, or they have lived through it? Save the prophesied period of the sinless people of God — a historical period which has not arrived to this day — this kind of periodization attends to the presence of God in the framework of human history as long as it lasts. It represents another mode of the justice of the claim that the effects of guilt do not last forever but are confined to certain periods (Judges; Isa 40:1-2, et al.) or to certain generations (Num 14:20-35; 26:63-65; 32:6-15; Deut 1:34-36).

Though there is forgiveness of sin, this does not mean that sin is ever forgotten, said not to have happened, or understood not to continue to be a destructive possibility. The one who forgives bears and suffers the burden of suffered violation her/himself, thereby relieving the sinner at least forensically by declaring that the sin has lost its right to oppress or destroy the sinner's life and future. Who, having suffered violation, can also suffer its effects so that the guilty are free to live, even in death, except God? If there is liberation from a guilt-determined fate, it is through the suffering of God, who "is bearing [נוֹשֵׂא] guilt and crime and sin" (author's translation of Exod 34:7). The suffering servant of Isa 52:13–53:12 is the human image of God because of whom Israel is forgiven, just as the presence of the suffering God in human history is the reason why this history continues to exist despite the burden of its guilt. The reality of the forgiveness of guilt has to be a fundamental part of any theology of liberation.

F. The Hamartiological System

1. Comparison

It has already been pointed out in II.B.2. that the representatives of the Old Testament's hamartiological aspects never compared the wide range of their differences as well as their similarities. Had they ever done such comparison, would their acknowledgment of both difference and similarity, along with their unanimous profession of Yahweh, the one God of Israel and the world, be their last word? There is no reason for such an assumption. In fact, they would probably have been left with the necessity of comparing their notes if for no other reason than their awareness that they were handing their experiences down to future generations. In such a process, criteria would, and do, emerge which represent the basis for the major contours of an Old Testament hamartiology. These criteria concerning sin and guilt are both quantitative and qualitative.

2. *Quantifiers*

Quantitatively, the Old Testament speaks about the sins of individuals, families, clans (Korah, Dathan, Abiram in Numbers 16), tribes (Benjamin in Judges 19–20), Israel both north and south, and the nations and humanity as a whole. Some of the sinful acts happen at different places and times, but none can be said to happen apart from all others.

3. *Qualifiers*

Qualitatively, not all sinful conditions are equally severe. The evidence has already been discussed, and the significance of levels of severity must not be sidestepped or declared theologically irrelevant. It mirrors worldly reality. There are differences between a son who fails to honor father and mother (Exod 20:12), a stubborn and rebellious son (Deut 21:18-21), and one who strikes or curses his father and mother (Exod 21:15, 17), even though the death penalty is to be applied in each of the three latter cases.

In the classic Decalogue (Deut 5:6-21; Exod 20:2-17), the degree of severity in each prohibited offense is quite apparent. Some are subject to the death penalty; others have less severe consequences. And the prohibition against coveting may not be prosecutable at all.

4. *Quantifiers and Qualifiers*

When quantitative and qualitative aspects are correlated, it becomes clear that even the most severe case of individual guilt affects the community, Israel, or humanity less than the barbaric violence occurring among the nations. Its effect is also less than humanity's murderous violence, which affects all people as well as the individual (cf. Amos 5:13; Mic 2:3).

Similarly, the corporate evil imagination of humanity's mind (Gen 8:21) appears to be a greater threat to humanity's self-destruction than an individual's isolated murderous act. While such isolated acts are severe in the extreme, they do not directly lead toward destruction of humanity's existence. Their consequences fall basically back on the individual sinner, as the wisdom literature, with its attention to the individual, shows, as does the tradition history of Israel's judiciary. At any rate, the Old Testament knows very well that it is relatively easy to single these individuals out, while it is practically impossible to weed out systemic corruption in entire groups, societies, or humanity.

The destructive weight of sin and guilt appears to be heavier the more sin and guilt affect all equally. This is the reason for the heightened responsibility of leaders, lawgivers, judges, priests, sages, counselors, administrators, prophets, princes, and kings. If any of these is corrupt, the rest of society suffers. This weight is heaviest when sin and guilt are seen as inherent in the condition and history of humanity, particularly in the form of continual violence. More than anyone else's, humanity's sin affects not only humanity's own existence; it affects the earth, save — in past times! — the earth's cosmic security, and hence the order of creation created for humanity as its only home. When compared to the severity of the destruction of the order of creation, all other kinds of sin and guilt are relative (e.g., Job 38–41). If that order is destroyed, all other destructions, whatever their own varying degrees of severity may be, become altogether irrelevant. In light of this evaluation, it is quite logical when the Old Testament ultimately speaks of a new heaven and earth (e.g., Isa 60:10-22; 65:17-25; 66:22-23).

Destruction — of what is good, just, wholesome, blessed, and salvific — is the common denominator for all kinds of sin and guilt. It is the qualitative criterion for recognizing and naming sin as sin. The experience of such destruction is the basis for human sin language. The Old Testament's sin language reflects the ethical or moral code embodied in its laws; but neither the laws, be they commands, prohibitions, or case laws, nor the ethos or morality is the basis for their own existence. The roots of their existence lie in the experience of the difference between destructive evil and constructive goodness. These roots are ontological, historical, sociological, and existential in nature. Customs, laws, morals, and ethos evolve from these roots. For this reason, they have nothing to do with moralizing.

As the expression of the all-pervasive and ineradicable presence of evil, the primordial chaos sweeps into the creation through human existence and history. After making its way back into the creation, it continually threatens this good order. As long as human existence and history last, the constant containment of and resistance to chaotic influences are, therefore, a basic and inevitable necessity. More is impossible, less unallowable. Containment and resistance are defense mechanisms; they are not ideals. Still, they are realistic mechanisms and cannot be neglected in favor of positive thinking alone, despite the fact that overcoming evil with good is a better way than solely fighting evil. Human initiatives and institutions of all sorts and on all levels are intended to and do serve the purpose of advancing what is good and preventing what is evil.

Nevertheless, the Old Testament knows how fragile the promise of these initiatives and institutions is. And when it constantly speaks about the presence of God *in* all these efforts, i.e., about God's constant, burdensome, tiring, suffering labor at all places and times for the sake of the good order, it points to the fact that the continuing existence of humanity and its earthly basis are more than the result of human creativity and effort. They are the wondrous presence of an undeserved gift. The God of the Old Testament is wrestling with the imperfect human existence and history, under imperfect conditions, and is hidden in this imperfection.

5. Israel and Humanity in the Old Testament

Israel is elected to be the answer to humanity's sinful, destructive course. The story is known and need not be recounted in detail: from the election out of the nations with the promise of the land and multiplication, via the exile in Egypt and the liberation from it, to Israel's organization at Sinai as a holy nation, and on via the preparation for and the campaign itself toward the promised land until the conquest and the gift of the good life in it. On the basis of all these gifts, Israel is to be Yahweh's "treasured possession out of all the peoples . . . a priestly kingdom and a holy nation" (Exod 19:5-6).

Among the Old Testament texts, the prophetic texts contain the record of Israel's failure to live up to and maintain the conditions of its election history. Israel failed specifically with regard to internal societal justice and exclusive loyalty to its savior God, Yahweh, and the purity of Yahweh's cult. The history of Israel's election is accompanied by the history of Israel's sinful failure throughout all its periods down to the latest period covered by the Old Testament literature.

The extent to which Israel's rise in the midst of humanity functions as the tentative realization of the formation of a new humanity extricated from sin and guilt is seriously questioned in view of the tension between Israel's election and failure. At best, this tension functions as a basic signal that the tension itself rather than its resolution must be permanently confronted and sustained as a paradigm for humanity, as long as humanity exists. This does not mean that such a role is unimportant. Quite the opposite is true. Israel would thus be the symbol not for a new but for the old, imperfect humanity through the toleration of the tension at the crossroads of election and failure, rather than escape from this tension. It would be a symbol for humanity's own possibility of enduring this same tension between its own election and failure as its basic mode of existence. In and through the actualization of this possibility the onslaught of chaotic destructiveness is contained and the victory of evil prevented.

However, apart from the fact that this paradigmatic model has not belonged to Israel alone, it is not supported by many aspects of the Old Testament's concept of the relationship between Israel and humanity. Essentially, in the Old Testament, Israel is not understood as the symbol for the self-realization of humanity's own potential. Israel is understood as the new humanity, as God-Yahweh's own people. The destiny of the rest of humanity depends on the nations' acknowledgment of this understanding.

When one asks whether and where in the Old Testament Israel is considered to be elected for the sake of humanity or humanity for the sake of Israel, the answer is divided at best. One can say that the wisdom of Proverbs, Job, and Ecclesiastes, including wisdom's Yahwehization, is true for Israel because it is true internationally. Also, the ability of the king of Nineveh and his nation to repent and remove evil is recognized by the novelist of the book of Jonah without the requirement that this king become a devotee of Yahweh and a follower of Israel. The king recognizes the truth in Jonah's (i.e., in Israel's) message. Still, the truth of the need to remove evil is not Israel's truth alone.

The Pentateuch, at least some of the prophetic books (meaning the canonic, not the false prophets), many psalms (e.g., Psalms 2, 110, 132), and many other examples show the opposite picture. In the Pentateuch and the subsequent deuteronomistic history, Israel's election is both the purpose and aim of creation and the condition wherein the nations can be blessed or cursed. The status of the nations depends on whether they bless or curse Israel. The programmatic introduction to the patriarchal history, which points far beyond that segment of Israel's history, consists of Gen 12:1-3 and not only of Gen 12:1-2.

Similarly, the story of Israel's liberation from Egypt is not based on the concept of a God who liberates all oppressed equally because oppression is universally unjust. It is seen as the actualization by Yahweh of Israel's exclusive election. Yahweh liberates Israel because they are Yahweh's people. It is not an example of Yahweh's liberation of all oppressed people everywhere. Nothing about Yahweh's universal liberation is spoken of or presupposed. According to the story's concept, particular election does not serve universal liberation. Rather, liberation serves particularistic election particularly.

It is not surprising, then, that this particularistic liberation theology has not led to a conceptualization of humanity's societal formation in which all people who are subject to constricting social stratifications, such as women, slaves, aliens, sojourners, and the masses in every nation, would gain the status of equal freedom.

Moreover, Israel is not liberated from Egypt in order to be liberated from slavery. Israel does not leave Egypt in order to attain freedom in any other land. The departure serves the purpose of the march toward the promised land. The liberation from Egypt, as well as the Sinai experience and the following campaigns, stands in the service of the march toward and conquest of the promised land. The Pentateuch could not be what it is without this concept.

Most importantly, the divinely ordained conquest of the divinely promised land of "Canaan," so the expression in Genesis, and the dispossession of the Canaanites can by no means be understood as a demonstration of Israel's election for the beneficial blessing of the Canaanites, for which they should have blessed Israel and become worshippers of Yahweh. Conversely, it is nowhere said, except for the attempt in Numbers 22–24, that the Canaanites cursed Israel. Hence, in light of their experience vis-à-vis the conquest, why are they cursed when they do no more than fail to bless Israel and become Yahweh worshippers?

As long as one reads the texts exegetically, i.e., for what they say and conceptually are, rather than reading into them counter-conceptualizations regardless of their own claims, the conclusion is inevitable that the exclusionary election theology represents an insurmountable crisis for the Old Testament's claim to Yahweh's universal justice. It equally represents a crisis for the integrity, conceptual coherence, and credibility of the Old Testament's hamartiology in all its correlated and compared aspects. The exclusionary election theology contradicts the Old Testament concept of God's universal, indivisible justice, and that the violation of universally equal justice, especially by violence, is sinful. It destroys the affirmation that Israel's God, Yahweh, does not violate justice. Also, by subjecting the theology of creation to the theology of exclusionary election, it discredits the claim that Yahweh is truly and justifiably the universal deity. Lastly, it represents the most serious theological perversion of the notion of God and, thus, the most serious among all possible and actual similarly sinful theologized ideologies. In the Old Testament's hamartiology, we have to account substance-critically for the fact not only that its hamartiological aspects are subject to a differentiating value system but also that some aspects considered just and good are unjust and evil. For decisive reasons, the theology of creation is not only the widest framework of the Old Testament theology; it is the basis of and criterion for the validity of Israel's or any election. It is also the criterion by which sin can be diagnosed in the deepest sense of the word; it is the violation of the totality of creation and the presence of God in this totality.

It must be very clear that this criticism has nothing to do with the traditional evaluation of the total Old Testament as inferior from a New Testament, or Christian, vantage point. Nor does it have anything to do with anti-Semitism. It in no way protects the New Testament and the history of Christianity from the same kind of criticism. This criticism aims to prevent the theological or any other kind of ideologization of GOD for the sake of any group's self-interest, be its formation national or religious. The Christianization of GOD, which already begins in the New Testament and is known from two millennia of Christian history, is just as subject to this criticism as the Israelitization of GOD observed in the Old Testament.

Finally, although Old Testament hamartiology is methodologically systematic, it must not aim at any sort of codified system, once and for all times set in stone. In the first place, the amount of aspects is unmanageable for such a system. In the second and more important place is the fact that a system would stand in the way of what is decisive: the evidence that sin and guilt are constantly encountered in reality and must constantly be confronted, evaluated, adjudged, contained, and avoided as much as possible by what can be learned from the tradition of the "better" sayings. Old Testament hamartiology functions heuristically.

IV. Old Testament Hamartiology in Biblical Perspective

At first glance, it looks as though the hamartiology of the New Testament is in many respects little more than a continuation of the hamartiological concept of the Old Testament. The New Testament sin vocabulary exceeds well over a dozen

Greek words. These verbal and nominal forms are rendered in English by the words "sin," "trespass," "transgression," "ignorance," "lawlessness," "wickedness," "disobedience," "ungodliness," "impiety," "badness," "injustice," "misdeed," "wrong," "guilt," and "debt." All are disqualifying terms, and the word field demonstrates the awareness of a wide range of acts, behaviors, and attitudes. Phenomenologically, the occurrence of sin in the New Testament is similar to that in the Old Testament.

The same can be said about the kinds of sin mentioned throughout the New Testament, and its ethical instructions against sin, be they apodictic or parenetic. Nevertheless, the conceptual presupposition for the evaluation of sin and sinful existence in the New Testament is fundamentally different from that of the Old Testament. Sin in the Old Testament is understood to be a constantly ongoing encounter with its many forms in an indefinitely ongoing world. In contrast, in the New Testament sin is understood from the perspective of the new world which has once and for all arrived in Jesus Christ in this old world. Through Jesus Christ, the old world appears fundamentally judged as the world of sin and at the same time reconciled to God and forgiven once and for all.

The New Testament's concept of sin presupposes its eschatologically based Christology which says that the eschaton has arrived and will therefore soon fully appear in the second coming of Christ. Except probably for the Gospel of John — but not the first letter of John (cf. 1 John 1:17, 18, 28; 4:3) — the temporal notion of the eschatological second coming of Christ is intrinsic to the New Testament's worldview. It cannot be regarded as a discardable shell. Most of what is said in the New Testament about the urgency and radicality of human existence, especially about the lifestyle of Christian believers, is said because of and not apart from this temporal eschatology. This worldview says: The eschaton, already present in this old world, has not yet fully replaced the old world but will soon replace it, because the evil old world contradicts the total presence and reign of God in the world. The New Testament says, as the late Professor Schlink correctly rendered to the chagrin of many at Evanston in 1954, that this old world ends when the Lord comes. The new world does not come when the old world ends.

During the time between the first and second coming of Christ, the ἐκκλησία of Jesus Christ is already the eschatological community in the midst of the old world. It no longer exists in the tension between good and evil in the old world. It exists in the tension between the new and the old world. Since its existence is determined by the new world, however, it no longer exists in sin but in the state of forgiveness. It is, therefore, called and empowered to sin no more and to live in accordance with the characteristics of the new creation of which ἀγάπη is primary.

While the ἐκκλησία and its members still commit sins, they will be forgiven because all sin has already been forgiven once and for all through the death of Christ. Actually, they are not *simul iustus et peccator* but *iustus quamque peccator;* each is righteous though a sinner. Their one-time baptism realizes this state (Rom

6:1-4; 1 Cor 12:12-13; Gal 3:26-29; Col 2:9-13), as does the Lord's Supper (Matt 26:28; Luke 22:19-20; 1 Cor 11:24-26). Their eschatological existence means that sin can no longer destroy them and restrict their freedom in the newness of life. Sin and guilt, whatever their kinds are as indicated by the word field, have forever lost the right of their claim. Their power can, therefore, also be overcome: "Do not be overcome by evil, but overcome evil with good" (Rom 12:21).

The New Testament view that sin and guilt are no longer factors that determine the structure of believers' existence is radical and has extensive implications. While these factors still exist and must be confronted, human life is in principle not captive to the conditions caused by sin and guilt. Therefore, humanity is always free to break away from them, not so much toward what is good as back to the newness of the eschatological condition. And while it is inevitable that the experience of this reality be personally accepted "by faith," it is clear that the freedom from sin is not constituted by this acceptance. Rather, the possibility for this acceptance is constituted by the reality of forgiven sin.

The Old Testament's hamartiology does not match this radical understanding because it does not rest on the New Testament's eschatological Christology and ecclesiology. As has been stated, the Old Testament is at odds with itself especially with regard to the texts in which the sins of the nations or of humanity are evaluated in light of humanity's relationship to the exclusionary election of Israel. Yet the New Testament's hamartiology has its shortfalls, too. Two major ones must be mentioned.

First, despite the fact that the Christian believer is forever forgiven and free from this world, he/she is still inescapably subject to its concrete structures. This is true apart from the fact that Paul has said so in Rom 13:1-7. When committing any sort of sin, the believer must concretely bear its consequences, notwithstanding eschatological forgiveness. He/she is free to confess specifically, whether before others or privately. This type of confession is distinct from any abstract general confession, as in the formulaic rhetoric of the churches' liturgies. The believer is also free to suffer the consequences in one way or another, regardless whether this freedom is ever enacted or not. In any case, the consequences must be concretely borne.

Thus, the believer is not only fully back in the structures of existence of this old world or of the reality portrayed by the Old Testament's hamartiology; he/she has never left these structures. The New Testament is aware of this reality; this awareness runs alongside its emphasis on the new life. Yet it is scarcely sufficiently portrayed or clarified in the New Testament, especially with respect to the tension between the new life and the concrete experiences of the structures of the old world. This kind of neglect has dangerous potential. It may mean — has meant and still does mean — that good Christians shun, or assume exemption from, the consequences of their sins precisely because they may think they have this right since they are forgiven. It is no triviality if one points out that the mentality created by the comfort of forgiveness is often one of the root causes for playing it loose with the public law of our secular societies.

Many examples could be given from the New Testament. As a case in point, the righteousness of the disciples must exceed that of the scribes and Pharisees or they will not enter the kingdom of heaven (Matt 5:20). This means either that this standard of righteousness is no longer relevant for those justified by faith, whether they fulfill it or not, or that nobody enters the kingdom of heaven. Another case arises when the Christ of the Sermon on the Mount says,

> . . . do not worry, saying, "What will we eat?" or "What will we drink?" or "What will we wear?" For it is the Gentiles who strive for all these things; and indeed your heavenly Father knows that you need all these things. But strive first for the kingdom of God and his righteousness, and all these things will be given to you as well. So do not worry about tomorrow, for tomorrow will bring worries of its own. Today's trouble is enough for today. (6:31-34)

When this statement is read in the context of Matthew, tensions arise. For whoever today as well as two thousand years ago is not anxious for food, drink, and clothing for tomorrow not only neglects the reality, e.g., of the workers described in the parable of the vineyard but is even so focused this-worldly and will therefore not enter the reign of heaven, eschatologically justified by faith or not.

Second, along with the concept of complete forgiveness, the New Testament's temporal eschatology causes insufficient attention to the importance of the concrete consequences of sin. The early Christians originally expected the second coming of Christ during their lifetime. After experienced delays, they still expected it soon. Since they already belonged to Christ's eschatological presence, they were called upon to live in accordance with this presence, all the while expecting the final parousia of God's reign. With this decisively forward-looking orientation, exemplified in the urgent call in the Synoptics for timely repentance, it was inevitable that the affairs of the rapidly ending old world had to be bypassed because the disciples already no longer belonged to it. It is, therefore, programmatic rather than parenthetic that the affairs of this world, the political, social, economic, military, and international affairs of the Roman empire and the troubled experiences of the non-Christian human masses in these affairs, play no role in the New Testament.

After all, the Lord's Supper is not understood as a worldwide food program, a program however cynically pursued by the emperors' *panem et circenses,* but the celebration of Christ's death especially for the forgiveness of sins. And the opening sermon of Jesus in the synagogue of Nazareth in Luke 4:16-21 is understood, together with the other words and miracles of Jesus in Luke, as the signification of the exceptionality of his appearance, but not as a program for the social liberation of all poor in the world, the release of all prisoners, the medical healing of all blind, and the revolutionary overthrow of the structures of human societies. Moreover, the New Testament, when compared to the Old Testament, is virtually devoid of any relationship with science or culture in the ancient world.

After two millennia, it has become clear that Christ has not come again and that, therefore, one cannot say that he will come sooner the longer his return is delayed. More importantly, it has also become clear that the entire temporal eschatology was, to say the least, a relative, indeed irrelevant, concept from the outset in its own time. It is not a constitutive factor of Christian existence. The Gospel of John draws the consequences, not without, however, considering the whole of the old world undividedly as one of darkness.

Whatever the contribution is of nontemporal eschatological existence to the conditions of humans, the fact is irreducible that the disciples, like all humans, were ensnared in the concrete conditions of this ultimately imperfect world and its sinfulness, just as most of the Old Testament's hamartiology portrays it. This entanglement includes the deity's remedial presence in all affairs of human history, not only in the existence of the disciples or the churches. To downplay the theological significance of this fact amounts to an unrealistic utopia, a utopia whose hope of fulfillment lacks a sufficiently realistic basis. It also amounts to — at least the danger of — a theology in which Jesus Christ has replaced God, and in which the theology of the universally present reign of God is reduced to a Christology of Jesus Christ's presence in the church. By comparison, the Old Testament's hamartiology, focusing on the deity's presence in and involvement with the totality of the structures of this ongoing world, re-enters the discussion with full legitimacy and force.

Excursus: On Q

The debate about the Jesus community of **Q** is in full swing among New Testament scholars. I am not a participant in the discussion of the reconstruction of **Q**, neither in the agreements nor in the differences of opinion. On the basis of one reconstruction,[7] I wish to focus on some substance-critical observations regarding the picture of Jesus in that community itself, especially concerning the aspect of evil.

According to **Q**, the lifestyle of Jesus realized the ideal of God's rule as the basic reality in which there was no "force of evil" (2). Accordingly, Jesus was constantly on the go, implementing the ideal from case to case (note the attention to each case!); he practiced what he preached (4). Hence, he "earned no money," "had no change of clothes or provision of food" but "counted on life's necessities

7. James M. Robinson, "The Jesus of the Sayings Gospel **Q**," Occasional Papers of the Institute for Antiquity and Christianity, no. 28 (Claremont, CA: The Institute for Antiquity and Christianity, 1993), 1-18. In this essay, Robinson mainly discusses the trajectory from the **Q** community to early Christianity.

being provided without his working . . ." (3), "leaving it to God to care for the practical side of things" (4). He went "from house to house, from hamlet to hamlet, knocking on doors" (5). When someone opened and he, after saying "Shalom," was "received hospitably" (5), he, in addition to curing sick people, "laid out his thoughts, and motivated a few to abandon their customary lifestyle and join up with him" (4). He advocated an alternative lifestyle which, though utopian, realized the reign of God. The systemic nature of this realization of the kingdom of God means that "the activation of the good exposes the basic impotence of evil. The apparent prevalence of evil thus is unmasked as an unreal sham" (6, n. 48), and the temple cult and the state religion are "by implication defrocked" (7).

This lifestyle of the Jesus of **Q**, claiming to stand for the practice of the realization of the reign of God, does not withstand scrutiny. To be sure, a utopia or ideal can, at least approximately, be realized in a radical lifestyle. It is not unrealistic by definition. Also, doing good does unmask evil, including evil in the state religion and in the temple cult. Whether or not, or to what extent, evil is therefore also unmasked as an "unreal sham" and its "impotence exposed" may be left an open question.

Left aside may also be the fact that this lifestyle, just as that of the later "Christian" disciples, has nothing to do with direct participation and involvement in the affairs of human history such as those of the Roman empire. The problem appears in the lifestyle itself as a symbol for the reign of God, including its implications for the exposure and overcoming of evil.

The exposure of evil through this lifestyle does not mean that every other lifestyle is therefore nothing but evil. Nonutopian lifestyles may be less good than the perfect ideal. Nevertheless, they may still be genuinely good. If the radical utopian lifestyle represents the criterion for the distinction between goodness and evil, everything else is evil because the radical, utopian goodness of the reign of God is the criterion by which this world is radically adjudged as evil in its totality. Whether this worldview is rooted in temporal eschatology, apocalypticism, or a philosophical idea of ultimacy, it is clear that this view is at least analogous to or a variation of the worldview on which the New Testament rests: In contrast to the reign of God and/or the reign of Christ, this old creation is evil in its totality. The lifestyle of the Jesus of **Q** has nothing to do with the regular conditions of human life in the indefinitely ongoing world. In contrast to this Jesus lifestyle, everyone's settled existence — inevitably hard daily work for one's own and one's family's material sustenance and a roof over the head, raising children and taking sustained care of one's old parents, maintaining the social and legal relationships in Shalom with the local neighbors in the towns and hamlets and so on — is not only set aside but appears as inauthentic forms of God's reign on earth. Indeed, this lifestyle calls people out and away from all these conditions in the name of the reign of God. This radical lifestyle maintains its validity only if in view of it all other lifestyles are considered nothing but sinful. And should this call be evaluated critically, the question is not only in what regard all other lifestyles are evil and in what regard they are not, but especially whether or not this ideal itself is justifiable.

This sort of utopian lifestyle, with its implication that all other lifestyles are evil, amounts to a concept of the reign of God which not only totally fails to lend itself to universal human application and to revealing everything else as evil; its own authenticity is compromised by a type of practice — on earth and in this life! — which, while insisting on the personal practice of the ideal of God's reign, turns the care for one's own practical needs over to the responsibility of God and other people.

Any ideal of the reign of God practiced in separation from the commonly acknowledged involvement of God in all practical concerns is an indefensible understanding of that reign. By definition, an ideal understanding of God's reign accounts for the fact that God works in and through humanity's practical concerns. God's care for worldly matters is therefore not considered evil. On the contrary, God's concern for this world is just as good as the practice of any ideal, if not better. Therefore, the practice of the reign of God by humans must involve them in good worldly matters just as much as in ideal ones. Human withdrawal to nothing but the ideal amounts to the separation of a nonworldly from a worldly reign of God on earth, and the self-authorized abandonment of God's hard work in this world. This may lead to the possibility of self-righteous sectarianism in the name of the ideal within and at the expense of the human race. Dualism and docetism loom ahead, if they have not already arrived.

Indeed, this idealized lifestyle may be considered the height of cynical contempt for fellow humans and God's own work through their practical work. The disciples' lifestyle included knocking at people's doors, expecting the hosts to do God's practical work of providing food and housing in exchange for instruction and invitation to the disciples' ideal lifestyle. Yet, if this invitation were heeded by all, there would be no hosts with food and shelter. Everyone would be constantly on the road and asking one another for sustenance. Yet, no one would have anything to give.

This concept and practice of the reign of God is not only unrealistically utopian; it amounts to a program for the destruction of any valuable basis for the social formation of the human race as well as any material and practical support for the indispensable livelihood of the human community. It represents the denial of the universal human need to possess the basic requirements of livelihood as the precondition for giving to others. It is a program for human existence in heaven — and what kind of heaven would that be — but not for God's reign on earth. It neglects the basis implied in the theology of creation. Its radicalism stands against the concept of God's constant care for all humans in this world, through the daily labor of all, including God's own elect, whoever they may be. It misrepresents the true, at least decisively better, understanding of God's reign to which it claims to be totally committed, and its real possibilities for human discipleship.

Aside from some positive potential, the worldview of **Q** exemplified in the lifestyle of Jesus in principle amounts to world estrangement *(Weltenfremdung).* It may also function as the basis for hostility toward this ongoing world *(Weltfeindlichkeit).* It certainly has very little to do with the worldview of the Old Testament, and its Jesus is much more removed from his — only Hebrew — Bible than he appears to be in the Christologized Synoptic Gospels.

By contrast, one may adduce the parables about the farmers, the laborers in the vineyard, and business people. One may also bring forth Paul's statements in 1 Thess 2:9; 4:11-12, and especially in 2 Thess 3:6-12. These are the two oldest letters of Paul, written at about the same time as **Q** (C.E. 50-51). Paul, speaking not in the name of Jesus but in the name of Christ, commands the Gentile Thessalonian Christians to "keep away from believers who are living in idleness" (2 Thess 3:6). They are called to imitate Paul, who was "not idle" when he was with them (v. 7). Indeed, Paul, Silvanus, and Timothy "did not eat anyone's bread without paying for it, but with toil and labor we worked night and day, so that we might not burden any of you" (v. 8).

What is decisive is that Paul considers this work ethos as *imitatio Christi* (v. 12)! The remaining issue is whether this work ethos imitates God's own practice of God's reign on earth. There is no question that it is quite different from the practice of the ideal of **Q**'s Jesus and the **Q** disciples. When compared, it becomes apparent that the work ethos represents God's reign and practice more authentically. It is inevitable that **Q**'s discipleship lifestyle, with its withdrawal from worldly matters to the practice of an unrealistic utopian ideal, be considered less authentic than personal individual involvement in the totality of God's involvement in this world. The latter is the better criterion for authenticity and the better basis for the discernment of the difference between good and evil.

Excursus: On Economic Justice in the New Testament

What has been said about the lack of attention in the New Testament to the systemic affairs of this world and the reasons for that absence seems to be undercut by many references to economic realities in the New Testament. Very often, these references are taken by Christian interpreters as the foundation for an economic ethos for humanity. The claim of the validity of this ethos is based on the fact that the ethos is derived from the New Testament; it is, therefore, Christian. We Christians are incorrigible. Unless something is said in, confirmed by, or extrapolated from the New Testament, it is either less valid theologically or not valid at all. The classic example is that the Old Testament must be approved by the New Testament, whether explicitly affirmed or with some qualification. Of course, it could never be independently as good, let alone better, than the New Testament.

In a recent essay, the latest among many on these issues, Jörg Baumgarten writes about the topic "On the Way toward Greater Economic Justice — The Contribution of the New Testament to the Current Discussion about Economic Ethics."[8] This essay is relevant for biblical hamartiology because it deals with an aspect of affairs in this world, namely, how the emphasis on greater economic justice mirrors the need for the reduction of economic injustice.

Baumgarten's succinct article correctly notes that the early Christian statements about work and economy no longer reflect our conditions today. In light of their basically eschatological orientation, neither literal nor partial adaptation of these statements is a viable option for today (473). He then describes the New Testament's own insights.

These insights focus on the economy of the circle of (Jesus') disciples, which confined itself to *satisfying the basic material and immaterial needs,* which Baumgarten documents with many references (473-74). Luke expanded this orientation to the ideal of the needs of the early Christian community for goods necessary for daily life. The ideal focuses on the tension between private and communal property rather than on a concept of communal economy (474).

Thus, poverty is not idealized; it is taken seriously. The care of the poor is important (474). The marginalized in society are God's special concern (477). Private property is accepted but dishonest competition criticized. This is exemplified by the cleansing of the monetary and mercantile perversion of the temple (475). Wealth by itself is not rejected. Rather, it is subjected to ethical responsibility. Trust in wealth is rejected as antithetical to trust in God (475-76). The positive criterion is responsible stewardship (476).

The model character of the early Christian community is particularly evident in its communal lifestyle, exemplified in the appointment of seven deacons to care for the poor (474), and in the collection for Jerusalem (476). The practice of regular tithing is not important (474).

Although I appreciate and support Baumgarten's focus on the New Testament's own view of things, the New Testament viewpoint itself calls for further discussion. Most of the aspects of economic justice called for in the New Testament are not uniquely Christian. Whether they are derived from their contemporary Jewish or Gentile societal ethos, the emphasis on the care of the poor, rejection of dishonest competition, support for the marginalized, rejection of mercenariness in the temple, the acceptance of private property and wealth, and even the call to decide between trust in God and trust in mammon were adopted and not invented by the early Christians. These principles were obviously sharpened by the shape of the Christian conscience. However, they were not adopted because they were Christian but because they belonged to the better common human ethos, which was

8. Jörg Baumgarten, "Auf dem Weg zu grösserer wirtschaftlicher Gerechtigkeit. Der Beitrag des Neuen Testaments zur gegenwärtigen wirtschaftsethischen Diskussion," *EvT* 53 (1993): 470-79.

true for the Christians, too. For advocating their validity, one did not need the New Testament or its Christology and eschatology. One would go to the original sources of this ethos. One important source is the Old Testament, especially its international wisdom ethos as found, e.g., in the prophets, the Psalms, and the laws, where the worldview framework is evidently based on a much broader scale.

Especially problematic is the fact that the New Testament evidence shows that the responsibility for the application of principles of economic justice in society at large is left to the discretion of individual Christians. The churches themselves are basically concerned with the task of inner- or intercongregational economic justice. The collection for Jerusalem was meant for the church, not for the city of Jerusalem. A strategy for economic justice beyond the churches in the cities, the Roman empire, or internationally is never articulated or implied. The assumption that the New Testament's picture of economic justice within the church represents the basis for an economic strategy in the larger society is exegetically undocumented and subject to critical scrutiny. Almsgiving by individual Christians in the wider community does not amount to a strategy for societal economic justice. And the absence of the law of tithing, a society-wide tax, already signals the churches' withdrawal from societal economic involvement.

Why did the churches withdraw from the wider economic framework rather than remain within the traditional societal economic ethos? Why did they adopt the concept of economic justice for themselves without continuing to participate and even lead toward greater economic justice in society at large? Did they not hedge themselves in over against society with regard to economic concerns in the areas of politics, social stratification, warfare, international affairs, etc., as well? Was it not their eschatological worldview which caused them on the one hand to adopt the public ethos, shape it to serve that worldview, and use it as far as it lent itself to the organization of the church as the eschatological community as long as its existence in this world was inevitable, and on the other hand caused them at the same time and for the same reason to be separate from involvement in the systemic affairs of this old, passing world? If so, are we correct in assuming that the New Testament's ethos for the economy of the church can be directly extended into the secular realm, as if the basis for the two economic strategies were the same? Is it not true that the strategy for economic justice in an ongoing world is different from, indeed in opposition to, the economic strategy of an eschatologically oriented community? An economic strategy conceived in light of the impending parousia is very different from a strategy for humanity and its open future. It seems that the New Testament's confinement of economic concerns to the church and lack of attention to economic justice in the secular realm are programmatic rather than incidental results of its understandable preoccupation with its own affairs. Hence, the New Testament's portrayal of economic justice is no basis for a concept of secular economic justice. The assessment of this portrayal involves more than the facts that ancient economic conditions are unlike ours and a literal adaptation of the New Testament's statements is not viable for us. And more is necessary than a paradigm shift via biblical hermeneutic from the New Testament's economic concept to ours. The eschatological foundation for the New Testament's economic paradigm itself is under question. Unless the Christian church sets aside the presupposed eschatological exclusivism and rejoins the human community and its economic ethos — by making its Christian contribution to that ethos — the understanding of the reign of God in the economic arena of humanity remains compromised if not self-contradictory.

This analysis of the New Testament's economic ethos affects Baumgarten's other statements about the function of eschatology specifically, the aspect of humanity universally, and the relationship of the two testaments. Of course, the eschatological perspective forbids the possibility of the organization of paradise on earth (478). But this is not enough. This eschatological perspective itself stands in the way of economic justice on earth. Furthermore, it makes the need for economic justice in the ongoing history of the planet irrelevant. For this need, the Old Testament's widespread assumption of the ongoing world — until it wears out like a garment (Isa 24:4; 51:6) or is destroyed by ourselves — and God's laboring presence in it for the sake of justice is a clear theological basis. Taken by itself, in distinction from some later prophetic texts such as in Trito-Isaiah, Daniel, et al., this worldview contains no hope for the restoration of paradise, nor is it restricted by an eschatology of a new creation. For this Old Testament view, paradise is lost, and this world goes on whether a new creation will happen or not.

Baumgarten nevertheless surprises when he speaks about the restoration *(Wiederherstellung)* of the integrity of creation as the task of the global economy. Perhaps this challenge amounts to a realistic utopia. Still, it comes suspiciously close to a notion of a historical evolution back toward an original inner-worldly order of creation.

There can be no doubt that a better way toward economic justice for all humanity is an essential tenet of any theology of creation. However, this tenet is rooted in the biblical theology of the creation and sustenance of the world regardless of its eschatology. It can be rooted in the New Testament's Christology only to the extent to which Jesus Christ can be understood as the incarnation of God's presence in the ongoing world, rather than as the one who announces the world's end and thereby the irrelevance of its historical structures. At the very least, one cannot say that, in this respect, the New Testament's Christology is sufficiently developed.

Finally, when Baumgarten speaks of humanity (477-79), he begins to use the term "biblical" *(biblisch)* to refer to both testaments. It is possible that although he focuses on the New Testament specifically, he implies that much of what is under discussion is also attested in the Old Testament. This issue is not clearly addressed. More important is the fact that — save its exclusionary election theology — the Old Testament represents the theology of the creation and sustenance of the earth and humanity much more directly than the New Testament, without and before the existence of the New Testament. The Old Testament's creation and sustenance theology remains the basis for whatever is said about creation and sustenance in the New Testament. In this regard, the Old Testament can rest its own case, without needing to be legitimized by anything in the New Testament. We have good reason for saying that the first article in the Christian Trinitarian creed not only points, religio-historically, to the chronological sequence of essential aspects of the Christian faith. It is more than the first article, which one quickly recites in order to pass on to the important affirmations. It represents, theologically, the foundation and the basic criterion for the validity of everything that follows.

The aspect of economic injustice is an essential part of biblical hamartiology. In biblical theology, the reality of economic injustice is confronted by the ethos of justice and the call for justice in the economic realm. Even if there is no ideal, the call for steps toward modes of greater economic justice everywhere for all survives. This ethos and the call for this practice belong to the legacy of the Bible's confrontation with sin in human history. For the confrontation with the reality of economic sin in the total arena of humanity, the New Testament's model of economic justice for the eschatologically oriented church provides no basis. The basis for at least containing, if not reducing, economic sin within the sinful structures of all humanity exists in the Old Testament.

V. Open-ended Conclusion

A. Specific Aspects

Little has been said thus far about the many specific aspects considered sinful by the Bible. A list of these aspects would be long. In the New Testament, there are cases which are considered anathema, such as sin against the Holy Spirit (Matt 12:32; Mark 3:29; Luke 12:10; Acts 5:3), not loving the Lord (1 Cor 16:22), or preaching a gospel other than Paul's (Gal 3:8-10). They will not be forgiven.

In the Old Testament, every violation by Israel of Yahweh's exclusive rights such as exclusive worship of Yahweh, Yahweh's imagelessness, Yahweh's name, the sabbath, and so on, would have to be mentioned. These aspects belong to the theology of Israel's election as Yahweh's holy people. The extent to which and the reasons why all or some of them are, are not, or should not be considered valid for all humanity are already a problem within the various positions of the Old Testament. They are even more of a problem when considered within the horizon of biblical theology in which some, e.g., monotheism, and the name and imagelessness of God, appear as valid, while others such as the sabbath law and the laws of purity do not, particularly for Gentile Christians.

Similarly, in both Testaments there are codes of virtues and vices which can neither be ignored nor said to mean something which they neither say nor mean. It would be difficult, e.g., to find a biblical position advocating the liberal sexual mores of our own time with regard to male and female homosexuality, the function of intercourse, divorce, any form of population control, or even abortion. All these mores are considered sinful in the Bible. The fact that these biblical judgments reflect the influence of certain traditions in the cultural environment of their times means little. All it means is that these widespread cultural mores have been adopted into theological biblical concepts. They became Yahwehized and Christologized.

However, their theological adoption under the names of Yahweh and Christ does not show that their validity self-evidently lies in the fact that they have been substantiated theologically. Many things have been theologically substantiated invalidly. Their validity, relativity, or irrelevance depends, therefore, on the validity of the theological concepts in which they are imbedded. Just as our mores are not valid by virtue of the fact that we determine them, neither are the biblical moral injunctions validated by virtue of being in the Bible. Only when the biblical theological concepts themselves are critically compared and evaluated will we gain a clearer picture of their proper place in the total value system of biblical theology and its hamartiology.

B. Toward a Biblical Value System

The synthesis of a biblical value system involves attention to specific kinds of problems which deserve further extensive and detailed study. Only three of these problems may be mentioned at this point.

1. There is the question of the relationship between the system of positive values and the hamartiological system of anti-values. In the Bible's own theological positions, neither system is unrelated to the other. One must even say that the recognition of the anti-values within the Bible's own theological positions depends on the Bible's own sense of the positive values. Nevertheless, modern experience demonstrates that behavioral patterns considered wrong by one party are considered right by another. What functions as a positive value system for one party functions as an anti-value system for the other party. The societal result is no longer the conflict between an agreed-upon value system and its opposite, but the conflict between opposite claims of positive values.

When heuristically applied to the Bible, this modern experience confirms what is already known exegetically: The Bible's position from which sin is determined as sin does not yet confront the reason why such sinful positions are considered by their own advocates good, just, and even theologically true. King Ahaz is threatened by Isaiah (Isa 7:1-9). Ahaz's strategy is evaluated as sinful by nothing more than Isaiah's opposing strategy. The fact that Ahaz's strategy is in no way also considered a legitimate stance of faith is not explained simply by our a priori agreement with Isaiah. Many of the so-called false prophets were Yahweh prophets, too. In our texts, they represent an anti-value system. They themselves claimed to be believers, not sinners, and to represent a positive value system, especially theologically. There are plenty of similar examples.

The evidence shows that the biblical hamartiology cannot be confined to acknowledging a system of anti-values derived from not more than the canonically stated positions. This hamartiology must confront the fact of the adversarial nature in much of the Bible's theological pluralism. Hence, it must do more than merely describe what is said or presumed to be invalid or sinful. It must explain why in any conflict of claimed positive value systems one or the other is good or evil, better or worse.

2. The biblical texts operate on the distinction of the categories of sinfulness and righteousness, or sinners and righteous people. One should assume that these distinct categories reflect the common social consciousness. A question by far not fully explored is whether or not and to what extent persons who commit an act or behavior which is commonly presumed wrong are just as clearly conscious of their wrongdoing as everybody else.

This question has nothing to do with the case of inadvertent sins, acts committed in good faith which afterward are recognized to have been wrong. The distinction between sinfulness and righteousness focuses on the self-contradiction in persons', or a society's, consciousness who act or behave wrongly in full knowledge of their wrongdoing. They know both what they do and that it is wrong. The following questions point to a perspective which thus far has not been sufficiently clarified: Is Cain presumed to have known that his envy was evil? Does the fool (נָבָל) act foolishly in clear consciousness of his foolishness? Is Lamech aware in both his act and boast that he does the wrong thing?

Exegetically, one has to infer that in many instances (e.g., in David's original involvement with Bathsheba and his betrayal and murder of Uriah) the acting person had to know that the action was under no circumstance justifiable. Such a person could not refer to any value system, or to a conflict of value systems. When David is condemned for his sin, what role is played by the fact that he not only committed the acts but did so consciously — the adultery unintentionally and the murder intentionally? There is enough evidence that the aspect of consciously committed sin, sin committed despite the clear knowledge of its nature, plays a significant role in the texts, and that this aspect cannot be disregarded because the texts may not address it directly. This aspect is at any rate very often indicated contextually and presupposed to be directly operative in what is said.

When the crucified asks God to "forgive them; for they do not know what they are doing" (Luke 23:34), would he have asked for the same if he had to say: "even though they know what they are doing"? In the biblical hamartiology, the role of consciousness in either committing or avoiding sin cannot be ignored. And in the interpretation of this hamartiology, it is, after all, significant that we, collectively and individually, perpetuate lifestyles fully conscious of their ruinous nature.

3. Also important is the difference between a common denominator for characterizing all kinds of sin and the Bible's attention to specific norms in light of which sins are recognized. To interpret all sins as basically destructive or as manifestations of the lost world is one thing. True as this interpretation is, it cannot replace the Bible's attention to the fact that in real experience not all destructive events are equally destructive. The endless number of narrated cases, of specific norms, maxims, laws, prohibitions, and commands, and of parenetic admonitions and exhortations rests on a variety of specific norms.

When saying that Cain killed Abel, the story does not say what we interpret, that he committed a destructive act. It says that "your brother's blood is crying to me from the ground!" and that the ground "has opened its mouth to receive your brother's blood from your hand" (Gen 4:10-11). To reduce this murder to nothing but the common denominator of a destructive act would amount to not more than a truism. It would deprive this kind of act of its particular nature and its norm.

The range of observable norms is wide, and their reasons differ, especially when one considers their various settings in Israel's society and history. It should be evident, however, that attention to norms and to what is normative has nothing to do with moralizing, unless everything considered to be moral is labeled as moralizing. The necessary recognition of norms behind the references to sinful violations demonstrates that sins are rejected for deeper reasons than the fact that they are committed. And the variety of norms points again to the need not only for their identification but for their synthesis in a normative value system through which their particular kind of validity may be discerned. With such a goal in mind, we may be able to see more clearly whether all norms have their place in a coherent system, or whether we will also have to speak of incompatible normative systems.

The place of all ethical instructions and hamartiological judgments in biblical theology must be distinguished from the hermeneutic of biblical theology for our own time. This inevitability is the result of changes due to the historical process. It is true neither that everything remains valid despite the changing times nor that everything is only valid within its specific contexts. Validity depends on why something is true, or more true, for all and in all reality, not on changing or unchanging times. Neither traditionalism, modernism, nor post-modernism is sufficient ground for validity.

The hermeneutical problem already begins in the first chapter of the Bible with the blessing of multiplication and human rule over the earth. This chapter assumes the beginning of humanity, literally of a few people or only a couple, not an overpopulated earth on which the masses ravage the earth's resources like armies of locusts the cornfields. Had the Creator God of Genesis 1 been confronted with such overpopulation, it is virtually certain that this God, in order to implement the word of blessing as a blessing effect, might have said, "be fruitful," but scarcely, at least not without any qualification, "and multiply, and fill the earth." Without qualification, this blessing may turn into a destructive disaster. The same is true for "subdue" the earth. Whatever this word does and does not mean, it must be considered in view of today's use of the earth by humans, but no longer in view of its use more than two millennia ago. The change in how the earth is used is certainly caused by the necessarily different formula due to the changed quantitative relationship between the human masses and the earth's resources. But the reason for this change lies in the qualitative difference between the blessedness or nonblessedness of human life on earth. This difference is always the same, and for its sake the change in the use of the earth by humans is necessary or the blessing is lost.

C. Summary

Whatever the positive contributions are of the aspects of eschatological and apocalyptic ultimacy and of a realistic utopian hope for the realization of human existence, the evidence is undeniable that for as long as this world exists, elect of all traditions are together with all humans irretrievably interwoven in the concrete conditions of this imperfect world and its human sinfulness. To neglect this fundamental fact amounts to an unrealistic utopia, a utopia whose hope for liberation from this entanglement is a hope without a sufficient basis. In any case, the Old Testament's hamartiology, focusing on the deity's critical involvement in culture, history, and existence in the structures of this ongoing world, for the sake of what is good or better and against what is evil or worse than good, re-enters into our perception of reality in full validity and force.

The nature and legitimate substance of the Old Testament's hamartiology contribute a basic aspect to the conditions of human existence, an aspect essentially lacking in the New Testament even when one acknowledges that the New Testament, too, especially in the Synoptics, is mindful of creation. But it cannot be overlooked that in the New Testament the notion of creation has become subordinate to the concept of the new creation. It no longer has the same function that it has in most of the Old Testament.

The Old Testament's hamartiology complements the hamartiology of the New Testament just as critically as the New Testament's hamartiology complements the Old Testament's hamartiology. Both Testaments agree that no human is free from the destructive influences of sin and guilt. Also, and more importantly, sin and guilt are neither the ultimate reality of creation and history nor the ultimate fate of humans. The experience of God in both Testaments means that the right to be liberated from sin and guilt not only ultimately replaces the justice of subjection to their consequences. It also outweighs and overcomes the rightful consequences of experienced judgment within the course of mortal human life. The total range of this agreement as well as the mutually critical hamartiological complementarity and correction of the two Testaments has not been addressed by the Testaments themselves. This project, in principle and in detail, represents the task of a fully developed biblical hamartiology, but it is beyond its contours.

A Posteriori Explorations

One may debate whether or not, or to what extent, something like a comprehensive Old Testament theology is possible or even advisable, especially in view of the manifold directions currently under way in Old Testament studies. Such a debate would have to revolve around the issues of the theological nature proper of the task, a coherently conceptualized system based on an understanding of that task, and the practicability or possibility of its comprehensive execution.

I. On Possibility and Practicability

A. Problematic Preconceptions

Aiming at a comprehensive execution represents a formidable problem. Not only would one have to account for all Old Testament texts; one would also have to consider all exegetical data in each text. The quantity of such an endeavor exceeds the lifetime of any scholar. Even Karl Barth could not complete his work. It is not coincidental that no Old Testament scholar has presented a comprehensive Old Testament theology in the strict sense of the word, not even Walther Eichrodt.

Despair at the magnitude of a comprehensive execution is, however, an insufficient argument for retreating to a principle of more or less extensive magnalia on the Old Testament. Whatever the merits of magnalia may be, they do not guarantee that all voices of the Old Testament are taken into account, that none falls by the wayside. When we talk about the Old Testament, or the TaNaK, we talk about all its voices, not just about a few major ones — quite apart from the question of what we define as major. The claim to all-inclusive comprehensiveness is not invalidated by our difficulties in executing it.

An Old Testament theology, even if it were comprehensively executed, may for this very reason be impractical for its readers. Who reads, or has the time to read, all of a voluminous tome, let alone the total work of many tomes? Laypeople? Pastors? Seminary students? Old Testament Ph.D. students? Old Testament professors? Professors from other theological let alone nontheological fields?

What may be impracticable is still not impossible, neither for authors nor their readers. Readers depend on the availability of the authors' work to begin with. For scholarly authors to acknowledge the need for a comprehensive Old Testament theology may amount to the admission of a utopian hope. We know, however, that there are possible as well as impossible utopias, possible as well as impossible dreams. It is not inconceivable that someday, if not an individual, a team of like-minded Old Testament scholars will organize a comprehensive Old Testament theology using methods similar to those by which research projects in the modern sciences are organized. Such a project is, to my knowledge, currently not on the horizon. And I am not preparing its execution.

B. The Alternative

1. I am essentially concerned with something different, compared to which a comprehensive execution is relative. I am concerned with our competence for theologically interpreting each Old Testament text or subject within a comprehensive, all-inclusive Old Testament horizon. To call for an all-inclusive execution of Old Testament theology is one thing; to require the inclusion of the total horizon of the Old Testament in the theological interpretation of each of its texts or subjects is quite a different task. The former call may or may not materialize, whereas the latter requirement is inevitable as long as any of the Old Testament texts or subjects is assumed to be representative of the entire Old Testament rather than isolated from this entirety. We can, even with the highest degree of probability, interpret the message and theology of a specific text or subject and still fail to understand its meaning, let alone its truth, as long as we do not consider it in the horizon of the entire Old Testament.

It must immediately be said that the requirement just stated is based on the inevitable fact that each interpretation of a specific text or subject happens in some sort of wider context systemically perceived. This is not invalidated by the other fact that nobody is at every moment, if at all, conscious of all factors pertaining to this wider context. In this respect, knowledge at least of the system of the magnalia is important. Still, the inevitable imperfection in actual interpretation may neither undercut the requirement nor discourage us from pursuing it. It only signals the always preliminary nature of our knowledge of the truth of God also found in the Old Testament — and in both testaments for that matter. Settling for this preliminary nature is better than not dare say anything at all.

2. The often-heard methodological program "From Exegesis to the Sermon"

is a case in point. This program, and its didactic implementation, may be a formulaic shortcut for something meaning more than what it says. Nevertheless, there is reason at least for suspecting that the direct, straightforward application of an exegeted text to an analogous contemporary situation is considered to be the proper method for biblical preaching. If only a text's exegesis is reasonably well done, it is ready for application today, or the better it is exegeted, the clearer its truth for today. Such a methodological proposition, or its unreflected application, is indefensible.

To be sure, we know, for example, from prisoners, prisoners of war, some of the recent hostages in Lebanon, and from many types of personal experiences that the reading or just the recitation of memorized Bible passages — should someone be fortunate enough to have been exposed to an educational system of compulsory, of course mindless, memorization! — has an immediate, often literally life-sustaining impact on a person's dreadful condition, or directly provides the decisive comfort in the final days and hours of a dying person, and not only for that person alone. And who, when asked by a dying person to read to her/him Psalm 23, would not do so — without any exegesis and any further interpretation? Exactly this was requested of me by Mrs. Muilenberg on her deathbed, and done without any interpretative baggage. By contrast, when I asked young people if they knew a Bible passage and a teenager answered "yes, Psalm 23," I responded by venturing into the whole gamut of interpretative problems, of if's and but's — and lost the teenager! Whoever has seen the abysmal conditions of the masses in the slums of São Paulo and heard how sociologist Barbara Hüfner-Kemper reads Psalm 23 with women groups there will certainly from such a moment on refrain from dismissing such direct, literal reading outright and from claiming that it is invalid unless it is accompanied by a theoretical discussion of the criteria for the "correct" reading of a text. The list of cases for this sort of reading is endless.

Clearly, any appropriation of a biblical text or idea rests on its adaptability to a person's, or a generation's, own situation. The fact that it is done directly does not mean it is therefore invalid or untrue. Indeed, its unmediated appropriation may in an existential situation reflect the universal biblical truth, or a level of it, so precisely that any subsequent analysis can only confirm its understanding. Nevertheless, adaptations of texts also rest on the adaptors' selfish motives, which are not commensurate with the texts' own hermeneutic. Who would not want to justify her/his selfish motives with the Holy Scriptures?

Decisive is not the difference between one mode in which texts are adapted directly, and another mode in which they are only appropriated after being processed through the full range of a methodologized interpretation; decisive in both modes is the difference between the truth or its perversion as they emerge from the encounter of the text and its adaptor. And because neither of these modes guarantees a valid result in principle, the truth or validity of a direct adaptation cannot be presumed at face value, by virtue of the fact that such adaptations are possible and happen, not even in view of the always existential conditions — which is a truism at any rate. Direct adaptations, too, are therefore in need of accountability, whether such accountability precedes or follows the adaptation of a text or idea. For this accountability, however reliably executed, the methodological reflections provide the instrument.

By far not all biblical texts are directly adaptable in the sense just discussed. Any experienced pastor, priest, or rabbi knows that in the care of people the number of texts that lend themselves to specific situations is limited, and that even within that limited range he/she must still search for the "right" text. When we come to the ongoing practice of biblical interpretation for today and to the availability of *all* biblical texts and subjects for today, including all Old Testament, the Jewish TaNaK's, texts, most of them are not applicable directly. The practitioner who on a weekly basis is confronted with a text, often from a lectionary, knows not only that the text does not always express what ought to be preached; he/she also knows that the better a text is exegeted, the less its direct adaptation is possible.

In principle, there is no two-step path from the exegesis of a text to not more than its direct appropriation in a sermon. Even where it seems that such appropriation is or can be done, it is done through an interpretative filter which controls both the exegesis and the sermon. The only question is whether or not a preacher is aware of employing this filter and accounts for its employment, not whether or not he/she uses it.

No preacher can speak of the wrath or anger of God in the Old Testament without an interpretative filter. He/she speaks either about the Old Testament's god of wrath — as compared with the New Testament's god of love — or about the wrath of God in the New as well as in the Old Testament and in the context of God's love, mercy, and justice in both, and about this wrath even as a mode of God's justice if not even God's love. The first example represents a virtually ineradicable and irresponsible distortion of the image of God, especially in the Old but also in the New Testament, whereas the second example represents an appropriate understanding. In neither case does the understanding of God's wrath rest on the exegesis of a specific text or on this specific notion in isolation from the other aspects.

3. Our interest must be in our accountability for what we do, not in interpretation without accountability. I am referring to pastors, priests, and rabbis for more than practical reasons. Regardless of the extent of their scholarly expertise when compared with that of specialists, they are de facto involved in the problem of the same nature. Indeed, they represent the testing ground for the clarity or unclarity of the specialists' teachings. In the face of the same kind of problem, the difference between specialists and practitioners disappears.

A practitioner may want to employ the blueprint for a direct process from the exegesis of a text to its application in a sermon. Yet if he/she accounts for what is actually happening during her/his movement from exegesis to writing — not yet delivering — the sermon, he/she will have to acknowledge that this blueprint is an illusion. He/she realizes that the more carefully the text is exegeted "on its own terms," as we say, the less it can be applied without being filtered through and balanced by not only *con*textual but also *inter*textual and *infra*textual conceptual and ultimately panbiblical qualifications. Or: he/she realizes that the more he/she needs to say what he/she wants to say, the less a text may accommodate her/him; the less it does so, the better it is exegeted.

I never cease to wonder why, after the reading of a text for a sermon, the preacher's sermon has little if anything to do with the theology and message of this text. There are all sorts of reasons for this widespread split between a text for a sermon and the sermon about it. I do not believe, however, that the decisive reason lies in the lack of sufficient exegetical schooling (much as that may also be the case) or in the lack of time for careful exegetical preparation (much as that is certainly the case), and that the split could be healed if only exegetical training would be intensified and more time set aside for actual preparation — both of which would certainly help. The decisive reason for the split seems to be quite rational, although often only subconsciously felt or repressed; namely, that the clearer a text is understood exegetically, the less it is directly applicable unless it is filtered through panbiblical qualifications. Should this suspicion be true, the practitioner finds her/himself in the same situation as the biblical interpreter who is at the same time exegete and panbiblical theologian. And we have not even mentioned the hermeneutical task.

That both are confronted with the same kind of problem means that the difference between specialist and practitioner is relative, not a matter of principle. The difference lies in their respective functions and settings, not in a dichotomy of scholarship and practice. With their respective expertise, they complement and check rather than oppose each other. The practitioner does not, and cannot, evade filtering an exegeted text or a biblical subject through its panbiblical qualifications — however perceived and quite apart from whatever other filters he/she uses. A biblical exegete may say that a panbiblical interpretation of a text or idea is beyond her/his task. In such a case, he/she not only is of less than sufficient assistance to the practitioner but also is nothing more than an exegete of smaller or larger texts. He/she is not a biblical interpreter in the full sense of the word, let alone a biblical theologian who tries to interpret the texts and subjects in their panbiblical theological horizon.

4. Nothing is being said here against the necessity of the best possible kind of exegetical work, also by the practitioner. On the contrary! Any neglect of competent exegesis increases the risk of superficial generalizations, outright subjectivism, the subjection of the biblical legacy to our autonomous ideologies, and ultimately the irrelevance of the Bible for our time and the future. With regard to the function of exegesis in Old Testament theology and for hermeneutic and preaching, what *is* being said is that the focus of our common attention will have to shift

from an emphasis on exegesis alone to *the relationship between a text or subject and its qualifications to be gained from within the panbiblical horizon.* Under discussion for both the practitioner and the biblical specialist is *the relationship between the fields of biblical exegesis and biblical theology, specifically the interpretation of the theological qualifications of texts to be gained from within their panbiblical perspectives.*

For this task it is helpful but not indispensable that we produce or have at hand a comprehensive Old Testament or New Testament or biblical theology. In the practice of biblical interpretation, neither the scholar nor the preacher says everything at the same time. Instead, what is necessary is both the accountability and competence for the need of interpreting a biblical text or concept or sentence or word in the horizon of its panbiblical qualifications. Compared with this constantly ongoing task and practice, the hope of eventually producing a comprehensive Old Testament or New Testament or biblical theology is relative. It is relative not only because the ongoing interpretation does not stop, waiting until all problems are solved and published, but especially because the true setting of biblical interpretation is its ongoing actual practice rather than books about this practice.

Not coincidentally, biblical interpretation from the times of the Bible onward has always happened from case to case, from situation to situation. None of the biblical writers themselves is assumed to have had a comprehensive tome at hand, let alone a biblical theology, which would have provided the basis for the advocacy of her/his case. However much these writers depended on traditions, their works were ad hoc theologically oriented case productions. They are analogous to our case studies and to the work of the preacher in her/his even oral settings — certainly not to the work of the biblical theologian, not even to that of the biblical exegete as long as he/she does not preach. The exegete, however, *re*-presents the cases of the biblical writers. This *re*-presentation of the cases is important theologically, not only because the cases are applied theology but also because they reveal the distinctiveness of each case among the various theologies.

5. Notwithstanding anything said, the interpretation of individual texts and subjects still requires the inclusion and application of all aspects of the panbiblical horizon. It requires the development of a network in which all theologies, of the Old Testament, of the New Testament, and of the total Bible, become constructively related, compared, and evaluated. This requirement goes beyond the work of the exegete, beyond the kind of exegetical work in which one detects a network indicated by signals in which texts are connected contextually within the same text corpus, or in which different text corpora are connected intertextually as, e.g., by the deuteronomistic hands in the Pentateuch, in the deuteronomistic history, in the prophetic books, in the Psalms, and in some of the wisdom literature. Rather, this requirement rests on the fact that even where a literary network exists pointing to more than the mere juxtaposition of works, the con-

ceptual pluralism of the combined theologies still exists, too, within such a literary network.

The deuteronomists added their own theological concept, or put it over, the concepts of the works they had at hand, but they did not eliminate the differences between those concepts. In the extant text, their own concept turned out to be just one among several different concepts. These differences must be accounted for. The deuteronomistic theology can by no means be considered normative for all others simply because it exists or because its voice is present everywhere or because it represents the predominant force in the societal formation of its time or one of the final stages in the development of the TaNaK. The deuteronomistic theology is only one among the others, and just as much subject to theological qualification as any other theology in the TaNaK, including any blanketed by it.

Unless we, the heirs of this legacy of theological pluralism, can justifiably say that this pluralism is all we need for a sufficient understanding of each of our respective Bibles, we need more than what the biblical writers did and what exegetes do. This work is always done in the practice of biblical theology; *therefore, the primary task of the biblical theologian is to provide the instrument for this work.*

The task of developing and operating with an all-inclusive network of the biblical theologies is markedly different from the past search for a unifying principle, a center, or a harmony. It focuses on the relationship of these theologies, whether or not, or in what respects, a conceptual unity or center is identifiable. Moreover, it focuses on the systemically stratifiable order of their relationship, which can be established by qualifications or evaluation discernible through their comparison. The task especially presupposes that unifying signals such as God, Yahweh, canon, tradition history, word of God, inspiration, spirituality, revelation, and others — all truisms as much as they have their own significance — neither address nor solve the problem of biblical diversity and sometimes divisiveness. Pluralism anywhere and at any time can amount as much to anarchy as to symbiosis.

Nor has this task anything to do with the creation of a theological system abstracted or removed or separated from the reality of the biblical messages and their theologies. Not only is it controlled by that reality; it particularly focuses on the reality of *Geistesbeschäftigung* of these messages and their theologies, and on their own thoughts operative in their words. Ideas, thoughts, and concepts can reflect an abstract worldview. As long as they are operative in human existence and history, they are not abstract. And as long as we need to understand words or texts or actions, we need to understand their guiding ideas, thoughts, concepts, and motives and even to reconstruct them for our understanding as long as they are not made explicit.

6. The focus on the relationship between texts and concepts and their qualifications from within the panbiblical horizon means that for discerning the kinds of this relationship, the other kind of relationship must be developed, i.e., the relationship of the biblical theologies themselves. This development constitutes the

task proper of Old Testament, New Testament, and ultimately biblical theology, and its specific contribution to the total process of biblical interpretation.

The task just discussed is not invalidated by someone's insufficient familiarity with all aspects of the biblical horizon. For practitioners in ministry, this deficit could be alleviated at the outset in the crucial setting of their theological education in which a curriculum would have to provide a reasonable basis at least for the awareness of the contours of all major theological concepts but also for the mechanics in the subsequent process of their comparison and evaluation. For such a basis, a basis for professional competence in ministry, some rudimentary knowledge of exegetical tools, combined with an exegetical course in either Genesis, or some psalms, or some passages of Amos or Jeremiah let alone Isaiah, does not go far enough. The task of practicing Old Testament theology is not invalidated by our educational systems. Our educational systems are called into question and challenged by the task.

II. On Systematizing and the Systematic

How should a coherently conceptualized system for implementing the task look?

A. Delimitations

It should be clear that, as far as the theology of the Old Testament is concerned, its material basis is the Old Testament alone — regardless of its extent in the Jewish, Roman Catholic, Orthodox, or Protestant editions. The criteria for its conceptualization must be gained from within it, not from the New Testament or a dogmatic or a philosophical system. The Old Testament's theological validity does not depend on any outside criterion, not even for Christians. On the contrary, the validity of the biblical theology of Christians depends on the Old Testament's own validity.

It should also be clear that the conceptualization of Old Testament theology is not based on a confessional stance, and that it presupposes, but is more than and different from, the description of the Old Testament's data.

It should, finally, be clear that Old Testament theology must be distinguished — not separated — from Old Testament hermeneutic. Everyone must be aware of the hermeneutical circle in the totality of interpretation, of its intersubjective nature. Yet within that circle, the distinction between "it" and "us" must not be blurred or collapsed or dissolved. Old Testament theology conceptualizes the Old Testament's own reality, whereas Old Testament hermeneutic conceptualizes — for Christians together with New Testament theology — our encounter of that reality with our reality.

B. The Criteria

1. The description of the Old Testament's data is the indispensable presupposition for the conceptualization of Old Testament theology. Included in it is the description of the theologies of the texts. Customarily, the task of such description is identified, among others, with the task of exegesis. For this reason, I have in the preceding chapter specifically focused on the issue of Old Testament theology vis-à-vis the issue of exegesis.

2. However, in order to provide a sufficient foundation for the practice of Old Testament theology, we need to free its conceptualization from the maxim that this practice may only be pursued from the exegesis of text units and from what they explicitly state. Two aspects are involved:

a. One of them lies in the fact that text units are not the only outlet through which theologically relevant aspects or concepts appear and can be perceived. Notwithstanding our knowledge of the semantic order of words in sentences, and of sentences in small and macrounits, it must be said that sentences and words are not altogether meaningless unless they occur in specific contexts. The meaning of sentences and words is also already predetermined by significations that are inherent in their traditional usage. Specific words are not used coincidentally in their contexts or at random. They are often deliberately chosen not only because they fit their context but also because they contribute something to it which otherwise would not come into clear focus. Often they determine that focus in the sense that their context must be formulated in their light. They represent conceptual signals. It is difficult to deny this contribution to texts especially of key terms such as "peace," "justice," "righteousness," "knowledge of God," "wisdom," "rest," "the day of Yahweh," and "sin."

It is neither impossible nor illegitimate to discuss a theological notion or any notion or concept in its pan-Old Testament horizon on the basis of a word or phrase or sentence. Whether or not such discussion is coherently conceptualized depends on our attention to the choice of the same signal word across the body of the Old Testament's language, in and despite this word's varying connotations or even notions, and not on our registration of only those variations. The choice of such signal words is not accidental. It rests in the fact that they themselves have had their history. Semantically, the fact of their availability and choice adds something to their variable meanings in different contexts that is not yet signaled by those variations alone. While it does not point to a unity or originality of meaning in the variety of a word's meaning, as may falsely be assumed to be found in its etymology, it does point to something like the meaning of a united focus on a subject.

Indeed, the choice of the same word throughout the variety of its meanings points to the focus on the same subject despite that variety, to the constant in the variety. This focus on the constant is not self-explanatory. It constitutes a problem which must be addressed.

What is said about words must especially be said about word fields. In their word field verbs, nouns, and adjectives function in a system of relationships of notions and connotations. This system is not abstract. It reflects the actual linguisticality in which the usage of terminology — *language* — operates out of its conceptual basis — *langue.* The word fields point directly to those conceptual systems which themselves function even more clearly when juxtaposed to word fields whose conceptual systems stand in opposition to them.

The individual words of a word field occur separately across the Old Testament, intertextually, but also intratextually, in various forms of word clusters of two, three, or more words in the same text. The occurrence of such clusters reveals conceptual systems within which each word has its meaning directly. They represent the conceptual backbone of texts, and they must be interpreted in their own right just as much as the place and function of sentences in a text.

The problem of Kittel's New Testament dictionary or of the Old Testament dictionaries by Jenni/Westermann and Botterweck/Ringgren is not that they represent word studies — as if word studies were wrong. Quite apart from the question of whether these dictionaries are to provide not more than a historiological and sociological phenomenology of words, their intrinsic deficit may be that they describe the semantic changes of a term in its various contexts but do not explain the usage of the same word — despite those different contexts. Moreover, in these dictionaries, the plurality of a word's meanings does not itself become an issue for further semantic reflection. Such reflection would have to be beyond the relativity of the many meanings of a word. It would have to explain the significance of the plurality of meanings of the same words, especially when such plurality exists in the same society at the same time. It has become quite customary for religious people to greet one another by saying "peace," or even "shalom" — although one does not say "eirene." In using the same word, there certainly is a united focus on the same subject of peace. However, is it beyond doubt that everyone means the same when using this word, even in a wish for someone else? And we have not even touched the problem of the usage of this word in other areas, such as, e.g., domestic and international politics. In their respective languages, both testaments of the Bible use the same word. What does it mean that this word has so many different, and in some respect opposite, meanings?

Not coincidentally, and quite legitimately, a sermon may be preached about a sentence or a topic signaled by a key word just as well as it may use a text. Its conceptual coherency and theological validity depend on none of these approaches. If exegesis is strictly defined as the critical paraphrase only of text units, it is too restrictive a basis for the practice of Old Testament theology.

b. Access to the practice of Old Testament theology must also be freed from an exegetical practice or maxim which is governed by nothing more than attention to what the texts say, to the texts' explicit statements. Nothing is said against the speaking texts, or against the messages of the texts. Yet the assumption that texts only speak but do not also think represents a fundamental misjudgment of the nature of any text. Where the distinction between the stories of the Bible and its ideas plays the role of an either-or, of an alternative between two mutually exclusive modes of reading, one operates on an indefensible theory of the nature of language, a theory that cannot be upheld — neither in the exegesis of texts nor in any sort of discourse.

At issue is the relationship between a text's explicit statement and its, though very often inexplicit, conceptual presupposition which is nevertheless operative in it, accounts for its coherence, and without which a text may be read, recited, re-narrated but cannot be understood and explained. The relationship between a text and its concept rests in principle on the correspondence of both and on the transformability of a concept into an expressed exemplification or vice versa. Where the Old Testament speaks conceptually, such as in the expression "Yahweh is merciful," it is not difficult to find a story about such mercy, and vice versa.

Of particular importance is the fact that in many texts about narratives of events or speeches, about poems, proverbs, laws, etc., the conceptual presuppositions are at best only signaled by words, phrases, and the composition, but they remain unaddressed. Every exegete knows that the infratextual conceptuality must in such cases be reconstructed. Such reconstruction results always in more than what the surface text says or suggests, and often in something quite different.

The story of Moses' vocation in Exod 3:1–4:17, e.g., is frequently understood as the paradigm story for God's universal liberation of oppressed people, the people referred to in the expression "Let my people go!" When the question is raised of who "my" people are, one is led to the analytical question of whether the God of this story liberates the Israelites because he liberates all oppressed everywhere and at all times, or whether he liberates them because they are his people whereas he does not likewise liberate all oppressed. It quickly becomes clear that the latter is meant in the text and the former not. As much as this story is a liberation story which reflects the concept of liberation, too, it basically rests on and is qualified by the concept of Israel's election and would not exist without this concept.

The cases for the need to reconstruct the infratextual concepts are legion. This consciously methodologized endeavor is actually an inherent part of the exegetical task. It directly serves the understanding of texts and has nothing to do with an interpreter's launch into the world of abstract ideas beyond and apart from texts. To be sure, we will have to distinguish between conceptual presuppositions directly operative in texts and those indirectly operative in them, such as from the worldview common to all texts. In either case, the concept must be identified and its function in the text explained.

The identification of concepts and the reconstruction of their infratextual existence are of paramount importance for the practice of Old Testament theology. If texts are to be related, compared, and evaluated, it must essentially happen on the basis of their conceptual relationship and comparison. All texts are subject to societal and historical conditions. Whether or not their conceptuality remains the same or changes with changing conditions is an open question. Also open is the question of why, and how, a traditional concept is legitimately upheld in a new context, or why, and how, it is legitimately abandoned and replaced by a different one in a new situation or a different setting. To whatever extent the role of the story is defined in Old Testament theology, the basis for its understanding and for the understanding of the relationship of the stories lie in the concepts of the stories. Unless one wants to advocate the relevance of only the endless number of individual stories and messages, one has to face the importance of conceptualities. Without this focus, the interpretation of the theology of any text would be a mute issue, and even more so the practice of Old Testament theology. If there is a legitimate quest for Old Testament theology, it must be based on the explanation of its theologies, on their comparison, i.e., the interpretation of their relationship, and on their evaluation resulting from such comparison.

3. Little needs to be said about how one compares. Comparison starts by raising comparative questions. The questions arise from the subjects to be compared and are controlled by those subjects. Once raised, the questions generate the search for answers which must be worked out because in the Old Testament they are not readily, if at all, available since the questions themselves are not raised. Comparison may either involve or be followed by the evaluation or qualification of the compared issues. If it only describes differences and commonalities without also evaluating them, it does not go far enough. In this event, evaluation or qualification would be an additional step following comparison. Regardless of how comparison is defined, the evaluation of what can be comparatively described is, for theological reasons, indispensable. Evaluation is through the comparison of the quantifiers and qualifiers found in the compared issues. In this work, the interpreter is on her/his way to becoming a biblical theologian in her/his own right.

Comparative work is in effect already practiced in the working processes of many Old Testament publications, but rarely ever in explicitly methodologized ways, and often not at all. Seldom does any type of Old Testament scholarly publication emphasize the programmatic importance of comparison and evaluation as a specific element of the method of interpretation, whether they are about exegetical methods, commentaries, introductions, or Old Testament theologies. The lack of an explicit focus on the comparative method amounts to a remarkable deficit in biblical studies at a time when comparative studies in virtually every field are receiving center stage.

Certainly, the comparative study of religion is not new. In the history of this discipline, not only the description but also the evaluation or qualification of the compared differences has played a decisive role. The conceptualization of the future development of this discipline involves many questions, including: Will the element of evaluation or qualification continue to be a part of the work of this discipline? If not, why should its work be confined to descriptive comparisons alone? And what is the higher validity of such self-confinement? As for the Bible, everyone recognizes its theological pluralism. Yet it is doubtful whether we have thus far realized the full methodological consequences involved in the recognition of this fact. Perhaps unwittingly we are still too much influenced by assumptions from past theological eras which say that biblical theology is meaningless since its truth cannot be discerned unless we can in the Bible's pluralism define a unifying center or concept or principle. The comparative method, however, when applied to the Bible's theological pluralism, points to a different direction, and to the discernment of the biblical truth.

Last but not least, the comparative method is not a modern one at all. It has been an instrument in thought and language, often quite intentionally employed, in all human cultures throughout known history, also in the Old and New Testaments.

4. Once set in motion, the comparative method inevitably leads to the understanding of a network in which the various theologies are no longer considered in isolation but interrelated, and in which their place, significance, and degree of validity can be distinguished in view of their relativity — not their irrelevance! — to each other. In this process, any notion of their univalency becomes a mute issue, and not every valency in multivalency appears as *equi*valency.

I realize that the image of a network is ambiguous. Rather than suggesting a unilevel arrangement of the coordinates, it is meant to point to their connectedness in terms of higher and lower as well as the same levels. Working out these kinds of connectedness enables us to recognize or determine priorities and subordinations in addition to coordinations. What emerges is the systematization of otherwise not more than juxtaposed, and frequently not even coordinated, theologies and theological notions.

Also ambiguous are the images implied in words such as "hierarchy" or "stratification" of meaning. They could, but are not meant to, suggest an order of authority which is statically fixed and even institutionally reinforced, and which, once established, would turn the heuristic nature of the working process into its opposite by functioning as a pre-established process, i.e., one which would not only have to be confirmed by the findings but would also control the direction of the questions for those presupposed findings. By contrast, hierarchy or stratification is only understood to refer to the relationship between strata of meaning and validity as discerned through the heuristic nature of the comparative process. This nature, for more reasons than the individual interpreter's imperfection, is scarcely ever final. It is always open to new and better insights.

Nevertheless, the preliminary nature of the discernment of a hierarchy of meanings and validity renders its construction neither impossible nor illegitimate. The comparative method and its discernment of priorities are not discredited by the preliminary nature of their results. One may say that precisely because the method is set, it facilitates the ongoing improvement of the results.

I have called this task systematic theology (so also in B. Ollenburger's choice of a title for his introduction to my proposal in *The Flowering of Old Testament Theology,* ed. Ben C. Ollenburger, Elmer A. Martens, and Gerhard F. Hasel [Winona Lake, IN: Eisenbrauns, 1992], 465). I see no need for abandoning this label. I know of no book on Old Testament theology that is not explicitly or implicitly systematic. This kind of work does not and must not presuppose a system which is or would be preconceived. It is, on the contrary, an inevitably heuristic device, not for answering existing questions but for developing the questions themselves; namely, those questions that arise from but are not — at least not in principle — answered by the Old Testament or New Testament or the Bible. By applying this device a system comes into being. The modifier "systematic" must therefore be taken to include the systematizing process leading to the system or systemic conceptualization. In contrast to a pre-established system, the conceptualization discussed here is in principle open to improvement since it depends on the ongoing heuristic process. The fact that this system depends on that process does not make it therefore unsystematic.

This kind of work can be done by everybody and can be improved with increased attention and experience. When it is taken up by many interpreters, the discipline of Old Testament theology in the scholarly and practical fields will take on a very different shape than the one we have seen thus far.

For the time being, systematizing studies in this direction are more important than the complete execution of a system, which at any rate would have to evolve from many paradigmatic studies. On many issues, not only those of the Old Testament but also those which are urgent for our time, Old Testament and eventually all biblical studies await treatment. Such issues include the relationship of war and peace; of the complementarity or divisiveness in pluralism; of traditionalism and change; of the cosmic, global, and historical; of space and time; of humanity and societies and Israel and individuals; of the protection and killing of life; of liberation, justice, and judgment; of wealth and poverty; of power and powerlessness; etc.

Such studies may be generated by our own concerns as well as by those of the Old Testament. We do not exclusively have to focus on the Bible's questions and concerns. We may also bring our own concerns to the Bible, including those not directly addressed by it. The legitimacy of practicing biblical theology depends on its potential to cast light on any serious question raised by itself or by us, not on our focus on the Bible's questions alone, regardless of our own questions. Ultimately, biblical theology should provide the matrix for constructive biblical thinking on all matters of reality, be they approached from the Bible's or our own concerns.

5. Two qualifications are necessary for the requirement just stated.

a. First, this requirement still belongs to the task of Old Testament or New Testament, or biblical, theology proper. It does not yet belong to the task of biblical hermeneutic simply because we bring questions to the Old Testament that it does not address. As long as we study the Old Testament's own answers to our questions instead of confronting its answers with our own answers to those questions, the distinction between Old Testament theology and Old Testament hermeneutic is not blurred.

b. The second qualification must deal with the impression that this requirement, by involving more than the Old Testament says or thinks, may lead *eis allo genos,* to a kind of transbiblical theology which would be removed from the biblical agenda and perhaps even be speculative. The verdict against compromising or abandoning the Bible's agenda and against a sort of speculative, biblically launched transbiblical theology is certainly legitimate. However, this verdict does not apply as long as our questions do not replace the biblical agenda but are raised in light of and together with it; and as long as the answers, hypothetical as they very often have to be, are accounted for rationally, based on evidence, rather than being the product of subjective speculation dissociated from such evidence.

Legitimate as the verdict is for its own reasons, it is not a response to the possibility that, on the basis of and within an Old Testament network or system, issues may be raised and answers found which are neither explicitly addressed nor thought of by the Old Testament. We should realize that within its own world experience, certainly as it developed historically, more issues could have been addressed than were, notwithstanding the enormous breadth of those addressed. Had more been addressed — and the post-TaNaK development in the Jewish interpretation of the TaNaK testifies to this — they would not only belong to the totality of the Old Testament's concerns but would also have to become part of a systematizing Old Testament theology. These considerations mean that the nature of the Old Testament's, or the canon's, agenda, its foci, is contingent rather than fundamental, and that the fundamental potential even of its own agenda is wider than what is actually addressed. They also mean that our inclusion of additional issues into an Old Testament theological system is not discredited because they are ours and represent nothing more than possibilities.

c. Consider the following example. The modern advocacy of intentional population control and abortion is a case in point. The Old Testament does not address these issues, presumably because it considers them at the outset unworthy of attention. There is more than peripheral evidence that, had it had to confront the advocacy of planned population control and especially of intentional abortion, it would clearly have rejected both their advocacy and practice.

The reason for this assumable rejection must be carefully located. It lies in the Old Testament's own basic perspective, supported by additional factors in its theological anthropology, which, simply speaking, says that the fullness of the earth is forever sufficient for sustaining the growth of humanity even to its own fullness. From this vantage point the growth of humanity is experienced as and said to be a basic blessing. And while the actualization of this blessing through humans need not be reinforced by legal or ethical commands to *multiply* — which is different from the question of the need for procreation of heirs in family law — it is self-evident that it must not be undercut by attempts to restrict or even reverse the blessed growth of humanity.

However, had the Old Testament been confronted with the experience of a mass of humanity that has outgrown, or is about to outgrow, the earth's potential for sustaining this mass, the question is perfectly open as to whether it would have called, or continued to call, such a state of affairs a blessing; indeed, whether it would not have advocated an ethos in favor of restricting population growth precisely because of the development of humanity as a blessing rather than a life-destroying curse. Even the issue of intentional abortion — what of contraception which was not available — appears — *horribile dictu* — in a different light from this vantage point, especially when considered with respect to that same sacrosanctness and need for the protection not only of unborn but also of all born human life throughout the total life span of humans.

The vantage point of a humanity outgrowing the fullness of the earth is nowhere in sight in the Old Testament. It only belongs to our most recent common consciousness. The absence of this aspect does not mean, however, that nothing can be said on the questions of population control and abortion in the parameter of Old Testament theology. Of course, a bit more is necessary for such work than a few biblical quotations.

Necessary is the insight that the Old Testament's assumable rejection of population control and intentional abortion is not based on an indiscriminate blanket application of its principles of the sacrosanctness and blessing of human life, regardless of the actual conditions of this life. Indeed, the sacrosanctness and blessing of human life are caused and predicated precisely by the Old Testament's vantage point of the existing conditions in the growth of humanity in relation to the earth's potential for sustenance. When blessing by saying "be fruitful and multiply," the God of Genesis 1 focuses on the first few humans in creation, not on an overpopulated earth. This contextually presupposed focus is based on solid exegetical grounds, taking the text literally, i.e., on its own terms. It must not be ignored as if it were nonexistent or irrelevant. It exists, and is the decisive precondition for what is said. No one who ignores this precondition has the right to claim loyalty to the biblical text and its concept. The Old Testament's rejection represents the negative consequence from its positive application of these principles in light of the actual conditions.

The Old Testament's negative position is prejudicated by those conditions. Should those conditions turn upside down, the Old Testament's position would have to be expected to become reversed, too, precisely because and in defense of the same principles rather than apart from or despite them. In the Old Testament, the principles of sacrosanctness and blessing of human life are not put forward *in abstracto,* as abstract ideas, separate from and regardless of the presupposed and often stated real conditions. On the contrary, the application of these principles is predetermined by the conditions as considered by the text for the time under discussion. Its unidirectionality is relative, not absolute. Unless we see evidence in the Old Testament that this contingent unidirectional position would have replaced its basic principles of sacrosanctness and blessing and become instead the principle itself regardless of the conditions under which sacrosanctness and blessing may be upheld and regardless of its self-contradiction on the matter of principles, we will have to conclude within the framework of Old Testament theology and in defense of the Old Testament that under reversed conditions it would have reversed its position stipulating significant differentiations or qualifications from then on.

The entire picture would have to be worked out in detail, which would have to be done by Old Testament theologians. It seems, however, that the basic contours of its network can be recognized from within the Old Testament where the relationship of the various notions can be systematized. Expressed theoretically, the formula for this network may be stated as follows: The two principles of the sancrosanctness and blessing of human life — the question of their own relationship being left aside for the moment — are the criteria for the direction of their ethical (and probably legal) application under essentially different, especially opposite, conditions; whereas the different conditions are the criteria for modifying the application of the basic principles so that these principles can be upheld.

The case just discussed exemplifies — in part — the fact that interpretation in terms of Old Testament theology must do more than exegesis does and that such interpretation is based on the Old Testament alone. It does not depend on the New Testament's vantage point. It is not prejudiced one way or another by our own preferences or positions, although it is clearly caused by our problems and concerns. It is neither descriptive nor confessional, and the basis for the evaluative discernment in it is its rational mode of argumentation.

6. What has been said is especially relevant for the relationship between biblical theology and the other theological disciplines, particularly but by no means only systematic theology. The trench, if not rift, between biblical theology and fields such as systematic theology, ethics, homiletics, religious education, let alone church history, pastoral care, and counseling, et al., is wide. Indeed, each of these fields coexists beside the others in a sort of pluralism that reflects more its autonomous separateness than the interpenetration of all. The problem is aggravated in the Christian tradition by the separate worlds of Old and New Testament interpretation, and by the virtually ineradicable neglect of the Old Testament in any Christian discourse. As if the world and theological truth began with Jesus or Jesus Christ and early Christianity! And as if the Old Testament, or TaNaK, would not contribute to the New Testament and its theology of the reign of God and to the legitimacy of Jesus Christ just as much as the New Testament contributes its aspects about that reign and that legitimacy to the Old Testament!

D. Consider this example. The formal and confessional affirmation of the centrality of Jesus or Jesus Christ contributes nothing to the clarification of why this is or should be so, and how this affirmation can be substantiated. Indeed, functioning as an a priori confessional statement, it stands in the way of any clarification by allowing only the repetition of those answers that support what is already presupposed. Yet it does not at all replace the need for its theological clarification, which provides for its foundation and leads to conclusions that are at essential points different from those normally heard.

The question of the meaning and truth of Jesus Christ, when considered in the horizon of a panbiblical theology, is far from sufficiently answered, at least by biblical theologians. It concerns everyone who reads the two testaments together. In the horizon of a theology of both Testaments, the question of the meaning and truth of Jesus and especially of the New Testament's theologies of Jesus Christ for the Old Testament cannot be bypassed. It is doubtful, however, whether the known traditional answers beginning from early Christianity on rest on sufficient questions. They all rest in one way or another on the assumption of the principal difference between God's revelation in Jesus Christ and all other revelation, or on the principal difference between the meaning of Jesus Christ for all reality and all other meaning of reality. Of course, the meaning of Jesus Christ is considered to be revealed in the New Testament, which means that any contribution to that meaning by the Old Testament — which does not speak of the Jesus Christ of the New Testament — is always, in principle, inevitably, and at the outset for one reason or another not more than preparatory, preliminary, antithetical, at most unequally relevant if not irrelevant altogether. The Old Testament appears, in theory and practice, as inferior.

This state of affairs is not only very unsatisfactory. It is unjustifiable and stands decisively in the way of the conceptualization of a panbiblical theology comprising both testaments.

In order to lay the ground for such a conceptualization, it ought to be postulated at the outset that for the interpretation of the meaning and truth of Jesus Christ, the Old Testament represents not an unequal context but an equal one that is just as vital as the New Testament. Of course, this postulate must and can be substantiated. It is based on the fundamental notion that in the New Testament Jesus Christ is considered not to have replaced God and God's total reign but to represent God and God's reign. Only in view of this basic criterion can the meaning and truth of Jesus Christ be accounted for.

Therefore, if we want to substantiate — in terms of biblical theology — how Jesus Christ represents God and God's reign, the New Testament alone is an insufficient basis. We must have the best possible idea about this notion, an idea that must be derived from both Testaments. This requirement means neither that the Old Testament would have to be assumed to speak about Jesus Christ, explicitly or implicitly; nor that there are no differences and even opposites between the two Testaments' concepts of the reign of God; nor that the New Testament's interpretations of the modes of fulfillment of the Old Testament in Jesus Christ are sufficient;

nor that the recognition of any kind of traditio-historical movement from the Old to the New Testament, or from its own to the New Testament's kerygma, is sufficient, though it is a religio-historical fact, half true as it is. What the requirement does mean is that the Old Testament is a priori equal to the New Testament as part of the same basis for the documentation and study of God and God's reign, and that the two Testaments are in principle open toward each other for our comparison of their concepts of that reign, which results in mutual agreement, in complementarity, and in mutual criticism. In this process, both the significance of the New Testament's Christology for the Old Testament and of the Old Testament's theology for the New Testament's Christology can be discerned. Such work may well generate a new dawn for a serious collaboration of Old and New Testament scholars and for a new rise and shape of biblical theology.

For a promising contribution by the interpreter of the Old Testament to the interdisciplinary theological discourse, it is insufficient that he/she says that her/his only task is to exegete the texts whereas the representatives of the other fields must make sense of the exegetical results. Such a demand on the other fields is not only impractical but insufficient. One cannot expect experts in other fields to be equally expert in the full range of Old Testament studies; and one should not expect them to systematize Old Testament studies while experts in Old Testament studies claim to have nothing to do with systematization, i.e., with constructive thinking beyond thinking about their exegetical task. Unless Old Testament scholars offer the other fields systematized conceptual studies as a basis for their own systematizing tasks, the hope for a constructive interdisciplinary discourse remains elusive for this reason alone, quite apart from the question of whether or not, and how, the representatives of other disciplines react.

III. The Theological Nature Proper of the Task

A. Its Distinctiveness

1. The theological nature proper of the task of Old Testament theology is constituted by the fact that the Old Testament is theological literature and, hence, by the need to interpret this characteristic. This characteristic distinguishes the discipline from the other disciplines of Old Testament studies. It involves a set of questions which are distinctly different from and go beyond the questions raised by those disciplines, although they emerge from their work and include the results of that work. These questions are crystallized in the following questions: What is meant in the Old Testament's language and perception of God-Yahweh? And in what sense, or why, may this language and perception with respect to the Old Testament's own criteria be discerned as true or valid?

2. The theological questions of the task involve above all else the substantive aspects of the discussion. They represent the primary aspects for the conceptualization of the proposed method of comparison and its practicability, and are the criterion for the appropriate application of the method itself. They are the what and why questions: what is said, thought, presupposed, and why; what does comparison show, and why; and what constitutes the truth or validity in any of these whats, and why? With the focus on the Old Testament's substantive subject matters, Old Testament theology is a discipline in its own right, not usurped by other disciplines of Old Testament study.

3. Consider the following examples. The fact of the traditions in any tradio-historical process can as far as possible be described and explained, but what constitutes the truth or validity of this fact, and why are questions not answered by the description and explanation of this fact? Not even the Old Testament's tradition history, considered as a whole, demonstrates as such the reason for its validity; it still belongs to the field of religious history.

We describe and explain the processes in ancient Israel's societal formation, which has been one of the tasks of form criticism. But is, or was, any societal formation in human history, however consistent or inconsistent in its historical development, true simply because it happens? Or is it true because a certain generation had in its own time a certain perception of its formation, or because of the way it was perceived in retrospect by later generations? Is human history true as it exists, or as it is perceived, or to the extent only to which there is truth in history? What would that truth be, and why? And how could it be discerned?

Why should anything any believing community says be true? Because it is said by a believing rather than an unbelieving community? Or because such a community only speaks to and for itself, and not to and for anyone else? Does not any truth claim of the believing community have to rest on the truth for the total human race in the first place? What sense does it make when one speaks of the Bible not only as the Book of, but also for, the believing community? Since when is the fact of faith or believing a valid argument for the truth of what is believed? Do believers not advocate different, often opposite, beliefs, precisely as, rather than apart from being, believers, and precisely because of their belief in one and the same God? Does the credibility of believers not depend on the truth of their beliefs to begin with? What may that truth be?

In the second place, is any belief itself true because it is a belief, regardless of what this belief is, of what else is, has been, or may be said? Or is it true because it responds to believers' peculiar historical, societal, or personal conditions — a mode of explanation that often seems to answer all questions? Does each of these conditions not offer the alternative between different beliefs? And does it not necessitate the elucidation by the comparison of the more or less defensible beliefs, especially as the believed answers are very often preshaped by ill- as well as well-founded subjective interests?

Since faith is for each individual certainly a very personal matter, is therefore my claim to the validity of my faith based on my subjective judgment? What sense does it make for me to claim that what I personally believe is subject to *my own* judgment regardless of whether or not my *judgment* is true for more than myself? Do I believe in the truth of God regardless of that truth for all or because I, too, may believe what is true for all? Do I believe in the truth of God because I believe or because I believe in its truth? Again: what may that truth be?

Ultimately, why should the symbiotic, umbilical connectedness of belief and believing of community or an individual self-evidently be true? Are not the societal dynamics of the believing community just as much the matrix for the ideas of its beliefs as its existing or generated beliefs become the matrix for its societal dynamics? Does this circular movement from believing to belief and from belief to believing prove anything more than the fact — a truism — of this dynamic of social formation? Have those social formations not also been captives of blindness and have they not led into disaster precisely because their circular self-incurvation kept them isolated and solidly captive on the wrong path?

Are not all, belief, the believing or any other community, and both together, imbedded in the relativity of history? Are they not all too often radiating more than critically confronting the modes of *Zeitgeist?* Are they self-evidently the salt of their time, or is the time their salt? Do they signal only the true and not also the untrue path? What are the criteria for their truth, the truth of their societal dynamics or their ideas, or of both united in a circle, at any of their moments or in the total process of all moments? Etc., etc., etc. The theological question proper is not answered by any of these factualities. Are these questions not true for the Old Testament as well as the entire Bible?

B. Major Aspects

1. In the Old Testament, the aspects of what we call facts, meaning, and truth are interwoven. It narrates or describes events or conditions in the forms of factuality. It is aware of and refers to its often controversial discussion about their meanings, and is with regard to both the facts and their meaning concerned about truth.

Despite their constant interwovenness, these three factors appear in the Old Testament as distinctly different. The Old Testament knows that all facts have meanings which, in their respective contexts, can be recognized as meaningful. But it also knows that their meaningfulness may be understood differently by different parties. The book of Job may be mentioned as but one of many examples. Meaning, even meaningfulness, is itself pluralistic. Because of its pluralism, not everything that is meaningful is therefore also self-evidently true. The concern for truth is distinct and inevitable. It evolves from and happens within the Old Testament's consciousness of the pluralism of the meanings of the facts. It is an indispensable element of the Old Testament's epistemology which is decisively sharpened by the function of its knowledge of God, itself crystallized in the intersection of the Old Testament's debate about monotheism versus polytheism. The question of truth is not solved by the fact that this debate exists, or by the fact of the Old Testament's position. But it is signaled in this debate as the distinct and decisive question.

The distinction between facts, meaning, and truth is not new in Old Testament interpretation. It has in various modifications, more or less explicitly, always played a role. Our conscious attention to it, however, is particularly called for because it affects our own state of discussion, especially with respect to the understanding of meaning. Our focus on the discovery or production of meaning, as discussed in fields such as, e.g., semantics, structural linguistics, hermeneutic, or semiotics, is certainly meaningful. When we come to the interpretation of the Bible, however, this sole focus provides an insufficient framework for facing the Old Testament's concerns which culminate in its concern for truth. Unless the question of truth or validity is confronted, the decisive concern of both Testaments is missed in interpretation.

The question of truth must above all else be methodologized in Old Testament theology. It amounts to the task of discerning the criteria for sifting out the truth in the facts and their meanings, and also in the theologies within the Old Testament itself. In pursuit of this task, the observation cannot be avoided that the Old Testament has in its own beliefs, often about the same facts, arrived not only at the same or complementary concepts but also at different and even opposite ones.

This observation is especially aggravated by the fact that the different belief-concepts are no longer presented to us in their original — meaningful — contexts but in their so-called canonical context in juxtaposition, by which their original context and its meaning are relativized if not abandoned and replaced by a new and different canonical context and its pluralistic meaning. Whatever canonic criticism means, if it wants to be relevant theologically, it must deal with the issues involved in the task of Old Testament theology. The conceptualization of this task is the presupposition for the theological relevance of canonic criticism, quite apart from its potential in other respects.

That the knowledge of truth, also the biblical knowledge, is not absolute but relative, does not have to be learned from philosophy or skepticism alone. We know it from the Bible, the better the more seriously we read it. "Our knowledge" — even our religious knowledge at its best — "is imperfect." . . . "but when the perfect comes, the imperfect will pass away. . . ." "Now I know in part; then I shall understand fully, even as I have been fully understood. So," under the irreducible premise of this imperfect knowledge, only the second-best of all the best things can be said, namely, that "faith, hope, love abide, these three; but the greatest of these is love" (1 Cor 13:9-13). The study in the Old Testament of the subject of revelation confirms, among other things, that the knowledge of God is revealed imperfectly, too. It is relative.

2. It is quite clear that the Old Testament's language of God and Yahweh

points to more than its production of meaning. It signals the basic awareness of the presence in all reality of what we call truth, the affirmation of identifiable truth that qualifies any meaning, and the autonomy of the presence of truth vis-à-vis any human appropriation of it, including Israel's own affirmations. The Old Testament knows — somewhere — that even its most sacrosanct confessions and theological affirmations are subject to the judgment of God, and are not themselves divine.

The truth of God, or God as truth, is in the Old Testament discerned through the awareness of the relationship between God and world and world and God, but neither through the awareness of God alone or world alone. The Old Testament speaks neither about God nor about the world. It speaks about the relationship of the two.

The interpretation of this relationship is, of course, one of the foremost subjects in Old Testament theology. There seems to be an imbalance, however, in our attention to what was *meant* when the Old Testament said "God" or "Yahweh" as compared with our ability to interpret its understanding of the world. Interpretations of the former aspect are also available. Yet, one has the impression that the importance of this aspect is generally insufficiently recognized. When it comes to the explanation of the *meaning* of the Old Testament's God language, all seems *e silentio* presumed to be clear; nothing has to be explained because everyone knows now what it meant then to say "God" or "Yahweh." Of course, one enlightenedly affirms that God was perceived mythologically, as a person who dwells in his penthouse on top of the universe, and that this ancient perception can be assumed by us to be outdated, especially since it represents no more than a disposable shell which has nothing to do with the substance inside it, a substance which has not changed and is known, as it was known, by everyone.

Is that sort of affirmation true? Had, and has, the "shell" really nothing to do with the "substance"? Was it not an indispensable substantive component in the Old Testament's — or for that matter in the ancient Near East's — understanding of the relationship between the deity and the world, i.e., a part of the substance itself which at its time could not, and as "shell" of whatever concept today cannot, be disposed of? Are we to assume that, after discarding the ancient "shell" of God language, we now have a God language without a "shell"? If not, without the ancient one, what would that "shell" be? Is it the locale of God behind and after the black holes in the centers of the galaxies signaled by the pulsars? so the admirable British theoretical physicist Hawking. Or in the process of evolution? If behind the black holes, where is God here and now? If in the process of evolution, is God the evolution itself — why then use two different words for the same subject? — or *in* the evolution — how is "God" to be distinguished from evolution?

If "God" is to be understood without any "shell," then and today, what was, and is, meant? According to the Old Testament, in what sense may God and Yahweh be discerned as truth, as the truth in reality in whatever changing ways reality is understood? What do God-Yahweh and Yahweh-God contribute to the Old Testament's understanding of reality? What did it mean for the Old Testament to say "God"?

We use the word "God" because we have inherited it from a linguistic tradition thousands of years old. It was not coined by the early Christians, nor by the ancient Israelites before the Christians. It belonged to the common linguistic repertoire for deities by which the ancient Near Eastern cultures expressed their worldview. The ancient Israelites adopted it. Without it they would not have known the word "God." But while they must have had an idea what it meant to say "God," we ourselves continue to use the word without knowing what their idea was. While their usage of the word was a linguistic expression generated by and imbedded in their understanding of its meaning, our usage of it rests on the tradition of the word alone, transmitted to and adopted by us, regardless of and even apart from an understanding of its meaning. One of the most self-evident yet startling questions that we may be or are asked is: What does the Bible mean, or what do you mean when saying "God"?

The word — the most important word in our religious language? — has become an autonomous rhetorical mechanism uprooted from meaning, which is a prime example for the autonomy of a kind of rhetoric that does not reflect reality. Instead of pointing to its meaning, the meaning of the word has become an empty shell. Had we not inherited the word "God" from the past, would we invent it? And if so, as an expression for the meaning of — "what"? And should our meaning of "what" be expected to correspond to the *meaning* rather than only the *usage* of the word "God" in the Old Testament? Should we not be compelled to ask what this word meant in the Old Testament rather than repeat it as a given in the text without understanding its conceptuality? Can we expect anyone today to take our insistence on the importance or even the authority of the Bible seriously as long as we do not make transparent the meaning of the most important word in the Bible, the word "God"? Whatever the relevance is of the Bible as the word of God, we cannot clarify that relevance unless we clarify what the Bible means by the word "God" itself.

What has been said affects our understanding of the Old Testament's monotheism. Our merely formal recitation and affirmation of this word as the antithesis to the word "polytheism" is insignificant. The Old Testament uses neither word, but it has their concepts. For the explanation of these concepts, it is not enough to reference the fact of its rejection of the Canaanite syncretism with its especially sexual connotations. Nor is the meaning of these concepts explained with reference to the fact that monotheism means the existence of one God whereas polytheism means the existence of many gods.

How should any reference to the difference between the two concepts suffice as long as the meaning of the word "God" is not explained in the first place? "Poly" — what? "Mono" — what? What is the concept of "theism"? If "theism" has anything to do with the meaning of and the truth of reality in which God and world are thought of existing together — God is perceived as reality, too — what is the contribution of "theism" to the understanding of reality in the Old Testament? What is the Old Testament's understanding of the truth of God "him" — (so the Old Testament's language) — self, or of God as truth? In what sense is God true and valid?

Since reality is pluralistic, is it therefore not also *poly*theistic? Why, then, should *poly*theism be wrong and *mono*theism right? Does *mono*theism represent a conceptual antithesis to an understanding of reality as pluralistic? If so, in what sense would reality have to be understood as one, or as one reality among the plurality of realities? If not, what is the decisive difference between *mono-* and *poly*theism as the reality of deity in the totality of reality? Is it — not the world order itself, but — the truth of the world order (perceived to be for the benefit of humans) in the midst of the potential or actual chaos of the pluralistic reality, i.e., the truth for which *poly*theism can lastly not account because the gods throw the truth of that one world order back into chaotic divisiveness instead of maintaining the diversity of this order in its oneness, or the diversity as one order? As long as we do not *explain why* God "him"-self is true, and *why mono*theism is a true concept, we neither explain the Old Testament's foremost theological assumptions nor do we make these assumptions transparent for modern understanding. These questions are not yet explained with reference to the religio-historical development from polytheism toward monotheism. That development is a fact. Why it was, and should be, considered true is a different matter. Within the theological task proper of Old Testament theology, much more intensive attention to these questions than is normally realized remains a serious desideratum.

Someone may ask whether the reach into this dimension of the questions does not amount to a biblical philosophy, or a philosophy of the biblical truth. Indeed! And what would be wrong with that? Would it not, while focusing on the Bible, be in contact with philosophy of religion and with philosophy in principle, as biblical philosophy's contribution to those fields? Would it not, together with these fields, be concerned with the questions of reality, world, facts, meanings, language, and truth, including the Bible's own foci and positions on these matters in each of its testaments?

3. Last but not least, the Old Testament speaks just as essentially about humans' direct personal encounter with God as it speaks about their indirect knowledge of God through their experience of the relationship between God and world. One experience is personalistic or existential (I/we-thou), the other is context-oriented. One focuses on us or me, the other on the world that is of concern for us or me. Both aspects coexist, and in interpretation neither may be left aside in favor of the other. What is to be explained is their relationship. In what sense is the objective knowledge of God affected by the subjective encounter with God? And in what sense does it affect this personal encounter? Which of the two kinds of

experience is the basis for the truth of the other? Does their truth consist in their mutual reinforcement? Or are they to be considered as mutually isolated, as separate experiences of the truth of God, whether or not they reveal separate truths? Is there a personal encounter with God regardless of an encounter with the world? Or is there an encounter with God through the encounter with the world regardless of a personal encounter with God? Why must each complement the other? Whoever is familiar with the total breadth of the Old Testament literature will realize that these questions are inevitable, precisely in light of that breadth.

For the Old Testament, the direct encounter with God is not confined to humans alone. But humans have an exceptional position in it. This position depends neither on the fact that the Old Testament is human literature written from human perspective, nor on the statistical fact that it speaks about the encounter by humans more often than the one by other creations (and about the encounter by the Israelites more often than the one by other humans). Rather, it depends on humans', including the Israelites', assumption not only that humans stand at the top of the pyramid of creation but especially that the rest of creation was created and is sustained for the benefit of humans, a benefit culminated in and defined by Israel's election as revealed in the Torah. Humans are seen as the purpose of the creation of the universe. However the specific significance is perceived of the direct encounter of God with humans and humans with God, in the Old Testament it is clear that it is not perceived without the knowledge of the human position in God's world.

As humans and certainly also the Israelites know God from God's work of and presence in the world — a knowledge revealed to Israel either through the "Torah of Moses" or through the Torah if the entire TaNaK is perceived as Torah — they know themselves as the ones who, in and as part of this world, are encountered by and encounter God personally. The modes, forms, settings, and contents of these encounters are well documented. In none of them is God encountered without the awareness of God's world. But the personal encounter amounts to the human accountability to God in the context of God's world and not in separation from this context.

Conversely, as humans encounter God personally, they cannot encounter a god without a world. They encounter God in their awareness of the world as the indispensable context for their knowledge of God. Moreover, as humans encounter God, they are caused to encounter and to know God's world, and the question of the truth of God's world.

Therefore, the categories of personal encounter and human knowledge represent two different types of human experience. These two types are intrinsically related in the sense that each involves the other in its totality. In this relationship, the criterion for distinguishing is not based on the difference between encounter and knowledge — be it encounter with God versus knowledge of the world or encounter of the world versus knowledge of God. Rather, the criterion for distinguishing is based on the difference between the role of God both known and encountered through both the knowledge of and encounter with the world, and the role of the world both known and encountered through both the knowledge of and encounter with God.

To this basic distinction, the distinctions between knowledge and encounter as such are relative — again: not irrelevant. Those relative differences represent complementary modes within the totality of the human experience of reality. In this totality itself, the difference between God, the truth in the world, and the world, the place and time of God's truth, is fundamental. Neither of these modes of experience can exist without the other. The experience of God involves the experience of the world as the place and time of God's truth just as the experience of the world involves the experience of God, the truth in the world. And while the sequential order of the two fundamental types of experience, of God and world, appears to be just as relative as the sequential order of their modes of encounter and knowledge, i.e., mutually reversible, the principal, and decisive, order of their relationship seems to be their mutual interpenetration and substantive correspondence. This relationship represents one of the essential characteristics of the aspect of spirituality in the Old Testament, and of the Old Testament's own spirituality. It is, therefore, an essential issue in Old Testament theology, especially its theological anthropology.

On Gabler

Introduction

It is self-evident that a program for Old Testament theology presupposes an awareness of the history of this discipline. However, the history of the discipline and the program for it belong to different genres. The program requires that the Old Testament subjects themselves be discussed. In this discussion, elements from the history of the discipline may be left behind, as well as entire systems of interpretation, or even the systems of the past altogether.

What has just been said is also true for the difference between the Old Testament's history of theology or religion and the theology of the Old Testament itself. While each of these two approaches is legitimate, they are not identical because each is subject to a distinct agenda. The history of ancient Israel's theology, including the history of the transmission of its theological traditions, belongs to the genre of history writing. In this genre, the question of the validity of each stage or voice or of the total history may or may not be raised and answered. As soon as the question of validity is raised, both a comparative method and substantive criteria for comparison have to be developed by which not only the various theological concepts and messages of each setting but also the total history itself may be evaluated, including the extant "canonic" level(s) of the Old Testament. In view of this question, an approach via the history of the Old Testament's theologies is relative because every historical observation remains subject to the questions why and how it is theologically valid. The task of Old Testament theology, as of any theology, is constituted by the substance-critical approach.[1]

1. Standardized expressions for the German *Sachkritik* and *sachkritisch* do not — yet — exist in English. What is meant by these German terms is the substance of the problem at issue *in* a text, idea, concept, etc. Therefore, I am using the expressions "substance criticism" and "substance-critical" in the just-mentioned sense. After all, the root meaning of the word "*sub*-stance" is: a stance *under* something. *Sachkritik* aims at discussing that "stance."

In the discussion about method in Old Testament, New Testament, or biblical theology, the alternative between the historical and the topical approach has been prominent and controversial. The alternative is not new, and the discussion about it has recently converged with the question of its beginning more than two hundred years ago; namely, when Johann Philipp Gabler separated biblical theology as a discipline independent from dogmatics. Of all biblical theologians of past centuries, Gabler's name is the one still mentioned today. Indeed, it cannot be accidental that the editors of the 1992 volume *The Flowering of Old Testament Theology,* an anthology of approaches from 1930 to 1990, added a reprint of Gabler's seminal address at the University of Altdorf as an appendix.[2]

In this his 1787 inaugural lecture as a professor of theology before the constituents of the University of Altdorf, a Protestant (Lutheran) establishment from the late sixteenth century a few kilometers southeast of Nuremberg in Bavaria, Gabler presented his program for the separation of biblical and dogmatic theology on the ground that each has a distinct agenda. Compared with our time in which these disciplines — as well as Old Testament, New Testament, church history, and practical theology — are completely separate, with professors normally holding chairs for one field only, Gabler's program was remarkable. In its own time, and at the occasion of an inauguration (!), it was proposed within a tradition in which the fields in theological faculties were not separate. Every professor had to lecture in each field.

Gabler, too, was inaugurated as a professor of theology, especially of dogmatics. Given the variety of fields in his professorship, he could have chosen any subject from one of those fields or any combination of those fields. His choice of the relation between the Bible and dogmatics demonstrates not only the critical importance of this subject, especially in his Lutheran setting, and the state of affairs on the subject at the time, but also his own genius in proposing a new or at least advanced approach to this long-standing problem and its central importance for all theological disciplines.

I. Recent Interpretations of Gabler's Lecture: A Review

In the history of its interpretation, it has for a long time been said that Gabler's lecture defines biblical theology as a historical discipline in the sense of the history

2. John Sandys-Wunsch and Laurence Eldredge, "J. P. Gabler and the Distinction between Biblical and Dogmatic Theology: Translation, Commentary, and Discussion of His Originality," *SJT* 33 (1980): 133-44. Excerpted in *The Flowering of Old Testament Theology,* ed. Ben C. Ollenburger, Elmer A. Martens, and Gerhard F. Hasel, Sources for Biblical and Theological Study, no. 1 (Winona Lake, IN: Eisenbrauns, 1992), 493-502.

of ancient Israel's theologies. But recently it has also been emphasized that Gabler, when defining biblical theology as a historical discipline, speaks about more than the study of the Bible under the perspective of history; he also aims at a historically based method through which the truth of the Bible must be filtered out, especially that truth which is valid for all times. Thus, in whatever sense Gabler understood the historical genre of biblical theology and however indispensable he considered it to be, it was for him not an end in itself.

A. W. G. Kümmel says:

> With these programmatic declarations Gabler not only clearly emphasized the *historical* [Kümmel's emphasis] character of "biblical theology," but also recognized the need [more: "the necessity" for the German *Notwendigkeit,* a must for Gabler, also according to Kümmel] of distinguishing [more: "separating" for Kümmel's *Scheidung*] the several modes of teaching [better: "the individual forms of doctrine" for Kümmel's *der einzelnen Lehrformen*] in accordance with their historical sequence, and saw that the normative character of the biblical writings only becomes evident when this historical approach to them [correct to: "*this* historical reality of them" for ***dieser*** *geschichtlichen Wirklichkeit* (Kümmel's emphasis)] is taken seriously.[3]

Kümmel emphasizes the historical sequence of the individual forms of doctrine as the basis for the emergence of the normative character of the biblical books in Gabler's program. What the nature of that normative character is, Kümmel does not say.

B. R. Smend[4] summarizes Gabler as saying that biblical theology "has to trace the statements of the biblical writers back to their universal ideas *(notiones universae,* also *notiones purae).*" The collection of these ideas produces something which Gabler calls " 'biblical theology in the narrower sense of the word,' an intermediate thing between biblical doctrine and dogmatics." Quoting Gabler, Smend says that this "pure biblical theology separates through *philosophical critique the true basic ideas* from their modifications by the[ir] era[s] and produces through this *philosophical* operation a *foundation for the pure Christian doctrine of religion*" (Smend's emphasis).[5]

3. Werner Georg Kümmel, *The New Testament: The History of the Investigation of Its Problems,* trans. S. McLean Gilmer and Howard C. Kee (Nashville/New York: Abingdon, 1972), 100-101. Translated from *Das Neue Testament — Geschichte der Erforschung seiner Probleme,* 2d ed. (Freiburg/München: Karl Alber, 1970), 118-19.

4. Rudolf Smend, "Johan Philipp Gablers Begründung der biblischen Theologie," *EvT* 22 (July 1962): 345-57.

5. Biblical theology "hat, die . . . Äusserungen der biblischen Schriftsteller auf allgemeine

In a prior article of the same year,[6] Smend says that the developments at Gabler's time had threatened a "theological axiom" (169) which at that time was basically not contested: the normative character of the Bible for dogmatics. Because of these developments biblical theology, as a discipline between exegesis and dogmatics, was moved into a predicament from which it has not escaped until today. Thus, Gabler requires two biblical theologies,

> . . . one on the other and one on this side of the gap, one that describes the theology of the biblical writers historically accurately [*historisch getreu*] and another that represents what is still valid and normative in it and can be adopted by dogmatics. (170)

Gabler calls the first one the "true" biblical theology (i.e., historically true); he calls the second one, which stands more on the side of dogmatics, "pure" biblical theology. What is, therefore, normative, or the canon within the canon, in the theology of the biblical writers? According to Smend, Gabler's answer is: "Those certain and indubitable universal notions which uniquely have usage in dogmatic theology," not, however, what only "belongs to a certain time, place, and kind of people" (170).

In Smend's view, Gabler calls for two different theologies on the two sides of the gap between the Bible and dogmatics, one being historically descriptive and the other doctrinal. Doctrinal biblical theology, representing the pure doctrine of the Christian religion which still functions as the normative basis for dogmatics, is achieved by the separation of the universal ideas from their era-, place-, and people-restricted, and therefore contingent, modifications.

Smend does not discuss whether the two different biblical theologies are also separated because of this gap, or are somehow related. He does not elucidate Gabler's view on the relationship between historical and doctrinal biblical theology. Also, one may assume that for Smend, Gabler's doctrinal biblical theology is to be structured as a system of doctrines applicable to the dogmatic system, and at least as such not in the form of a history of doctrine. Whether in historical biblical theology the requirement for "historically accurate" description refers to the critical reconstruction of the placement of the biblical ideas in historical sequence or to the description of their "historically" contingent distinctiveness, Smend does not

---

Vorstellungen (notiones universae, auch notiones purae) zurückzuführen." This collection of these ideas produces something which Gabler calls "**die Biblische Theologie im engeren Sinne des Wortes,** . . . ein Mittelding zwischen Bibellehre und der Dogmatik." And quoting Gabler, he says that this "reine biblische Theologie hingegen sondert durch *philosophische Kritik die wahren Grundideen* von den Modifikationen des Zeitalters ab und liefert durch diese *philosophische* Operation eine *Grundlage zur reinen christlichen Religionslehre*" (347-48).

6. Rudolf Smend, "Universalismus und Partikularismus in der Alttestamentlichen Theologie des 19. Jahrhunderts," *EvT* 22 (April 1962): 169-79.

say, and the question is open. Furthermore, Smend refers to Gabler's focus on the Christian religion, instead of religion in general. Yet he does not discuss whether or not Gabler defines the nature of the Christian religion specifically. Finally, for Smend, the difference between Gabler's historical and doctrinal biblical theology rests on the distinction between contingent and universal ideas. Are, therefore, all universal ideas by definition for all times and as such indicative of the Christian religion of all times? Or is there in Gabler's theology a difference between universal ideas of one sort and of another sort?

C. H.-J. Kraus,[7] after discussing Gabler's statements about the historical character of the discipline, including its historical periodization, i.e., the "periodization of the biblical history" (*Periodisierung der biblischen Geschichte,* 53), says that dogmatics can only begin after biblical theology worked out by historical-critical exegesis is completed. To this Kraus himself adds that one has to ask how its "fitting order" may look. In this respect, Gabler has given no answer. In the end, it looks as if Gabler is aiming at a procedure for collecting the opinions of the divine persons which already is directed toward the order of the Lutheran *loci* (53-55).

For Kraus, the aspect of historical periodization is taken for granted. The idea of evolution has entered biblical science from Herder and Eichhorn. He therefore recognizes Gabler's distinction between the Old Testament's and the Christian form of doctrine. He especially raises the question not only of the appropriate order of the universal ideas — which Gabler does not explain — but also of the relationship between the historical (as understood by Kraus) and the substance-critical. And since he suspects that Gabler aims at the order of the *loci,* he surmises that Gabler's definition of the "historical character" *(genus historicum)* refers only to the method for the differentiation of the stages in the historical periodization, but not to his total concept.

D. O. Merk[8] explains that the historical character of biblical theology represents Gabler's decisive methodological statement (34), and that this historical discipline must be executed both analytically and synthetically (36). Only on this basis — including the universal notions — can those opinions be identified "which . . . refer to the staying form of the Christian doctrine, . . . to the religion of all times . . . the *dicta classica.* . . . From them alone can those 'universal ideas' . . . be sifted out" which alone are useful in dogmatic theology (37).[9] Based on historical analysis

7. Hans Joachim Kraus, *Die Biblische Theologie — Ihre Geschichte und Problematik* (Neukirchen-Vluyn: Neukirchener Verlag, 1970), 52-59.

8. Otto Merk, *Biblische Theologie des Neuen Testaments in ihrer Anfangszeit,* Marburger Theologische Studien, no. 9 (Marburg: N. G. Elwert, 1972), 31-45.

9. German: Those opinions "welche . . . sich auf die bleibende Form der christlichen Lehre

and synthesis, those universal or pure notions, or *dicta classica,* must be singled out which represent the New Testament's unchanging doctrine of salvation, *the* religion for all times, the divine form of faith (40). Still, biblical theology in its stricter sense can only be established when from the *dicta classica* those universal notions are singled out which alone are useful as the foundation for dogmatics. Dogmatics accommodates them in accordance with the changing requirements of the times, but their content remains the same "because it is gained by the principles of historical criticism" (37).

Merk, too, says that Gabler considers biblical theology as imbedded in the history from the Old to the New Testament, including the Apocrypha. Hence, the canon's boundaries dissolve. Nevertheless, biblical theology focuses on what the writers thought about divine things. This task, executed with the help of secular *(profan)* historical criticism, becomes especially calibrated through the position of biblical theology opposite dogmatics.

Thus, according to Merk, Gabler seems to speak of three biblical theologies: one of historical nature, one consisting of the *dicta classica,* and one of those universal notions in the *dicta classica* that are useful as the foundation for dogmatics. As these three theologies successively emerge, distinct kinds of universal notions also emerge. Are these kinds discerned on the basis of their historical development, or on the basis of their conceptual, substantive differences and of their usefulness for dogmatics?

E. H. Boers[10] attributes the critical function of Gabler's program for the developments in the field since then to its "clarity" (25). Gabler wants to reestablish the Bible as the foundation of all, including dogmatic, theology (27), rather than to create a separate discipline as an end in itself (24-26). For this purpose, he identifies biblical theology as *historical* in the sense that the Bible's subject matter exists as "a fixed body of material from the past" (33), and as *systematic* in the sense that it has to work out "the stable, unchanging ideas" from within this body (24, 27, 32, 33). For discerning those ideas, the distinction between religion and theology is most basic (30), because biblical religion represents "the unchanging, divine revelation," whereas theology represents different and changing theologies (25, 30, 31, 32).

Through his method, Gabler arrives at two theologies, a "true" one in the broader sense which is to provide "a fully comprehensive system of biblical theology, a true picture of the biblical religion" (34), and a "pure" one in the narrower sense which will present "the unchanging biblical teaching which was

---

beziehen" (37), "auf die Religion aller Zeiten . . . die *dicta classica.* . . . Aus ihnen allein können die **allgemeinen Vorstellungen** (notiones universae) eruiert werden" (37).

10. Hendrikus Boers, *What Is New Testament Theology?* Guides to Biblical Scholarship: New Testament Series (Philadelphia: Fortress, 1979), 23-38.

valid for all times, purified of those concepts that were limited to particular circumstances" (34). The total discipline could then mediate "between the biblical religion and dogmatic theology" (31); it is "something in between, participating in both" (33), or "an intermediate discipline with the task of transforming the biblical religious thinking into the form of a theological system" (37). It has to "philosophize about all matters concerning the divine on the basis of the Bible" (37).

The main points in Boers's argument are his understanding of the historical discipline in the sense of dealing with a "fixed body of material from the past" rather than with the history of that body, and the central importance of the category of "religion" in all, including biblical, theology. The universal notions represent the "religious" dimension. Are they all of the same kind?

F. In Sandys-Wunsch's interpretation,[11] too, "the task of biblical theology is to work out what the truth contained in Scripture is" (147). For this task, religion and theology must be distinguished. Unlike theology, religion contains "timeless truths," and those truths are found in Scripture alone (146). Indeed,

> Only ideas which are common throughout the Bible are the true doctrines of religion. . . . Such a biblical theology then is religion. (148)

Essential for the execution of this task is Gabler's idea of history which is "concerned with the whole outlook of an age, its ways of perceiving and expressing truth" (146). Gabler assumes "that every age including his own has its particular and limited ways of expressing the truth it has discovered" (146). Hence, "what is historical is secondary to what is true"; the Bible is a "revealed source of truth," parts of which are by Providence "trans-historical" (147).

> When he says that biblical theology is of historical origin, then, what he means is that it should by proper investigation of the documents in the Bible aim at isolating their purely historical characteristics in order to eliminate them and leave the truth exposed. History on its own has no significance for biblical theology. (147)

For Sandys-Wunsch, the historical "origin" of biblical theology lies not in the genre of a fixed body of literature from the past, as in Boers's interpretation, but in Gabler's idea of history. This idea focuses on the "whole outlook of an age" rather than on the periodization of the successive ages. But since "only ideas which are common throughout the Bible are true doctrines of the Bible" (148), history, in the sense of the specific character of distinct ages as well as that of their historical

11. Sandys-Wunsch and Eldredge, 144-58. This commentary and interpretation is by Sandys-Wunsch.

development, is irrelevant for the aspect of religion in biblical theology. Sandys-Wunsch's interpretation means, as does Boers's, that Gabler's concept, including its attention to the historical dimension, focuses on the systematization of substantive doctrines rather than on the systematization of history. Still, these questions remain: Are *all* universal ideas common throughout the ages? What is the nature of "the Christian" in Gabler's concept of religion? And what is "Christian" specifically?

G. According to J. Hayes and F. Prussner,[12] Gabler distinguishes between true, pure, and dogmatic theology. The first has to contain "the comprehensive presentation of the total religion of the Bible" based on exegesis and "done in a historical perspective" (63). Its task is "purely descriptive" (63). The second, in its narrower, or pure, sense, has to be "a systematic presentation of God's eternal truths or unchanging ideas found in the Bible which [are] valid for all times" (63). It moves from the descriptive to the "normative task" (63).

For isolating the timeless ideas, Gabler offers four criteria: Not all biblical writers stand on the same level; many things in the biblical materials were intended by God for only a limited historical time; much in the Bible must be seen as the authors' attempts to be understood rather than the expression of timeless truths; and universal notions are more reflective of pure doctrine than particular ideas (63-64). On the basis of pure biblical theology, dogmatic systems can then be produced.

Hayes and Prussner say that Gabler clarifies neither how to move from true to pure biblical theology, nor how to distinguish the particular from the universal (64). But he does postulate, *inter alia,* "an intermediate stage or stages between exegesis and dogmatic thought" (65). And Hayes and Prussner assume that "Gabler's own thinking was moving in the direction of a 'history of religion'" and "find him . . . not only laying the foundations for Old Testament theology as a distinct science, but also anticipating, as it were, the 'history of religion' approach" (66), although he does not specifically endorse a separate study of Old Testament theology (65).

Hayes's and Prussner's brief discussion highlights important distinctions in and for Gabler's method. But they do not explain how the two different biblical theologies are related. By saying that the second one aims at systematically presenting "God's eternal truths" and that Gabler is moving toward a " 'history of religion,'" they either overlook the question of how the systematization of doctrines and the systematization of their history are related in Gabler's concept, or mean to say that Gabler's program is deficient by not addressing this problem. And again these questions remain unanswered: Are all universal notions equally for all times? What is "Christian" in religion? And what in the Christian religion is specifically Christian?

12. John Hayes and Frederick Prussner, *Old Testament Theology — Its History and Development* (Atlanta: John Knox, 1985), 62-66.

H. B. C. Ollenburger[13] takes aim at the history of interpretation from Wrede on, in which Gabler's legacy has been

> seen as having given biblical theology a purely historical character, so that it enjoys a "complete separation" from dogmatics. (38)

Ollenburger situates Gabler in the context of his time, and argues that "biblical theology generally has moved in a direction quite contrary to Gabler, and that Gabler's proposed method has no counterpart in the present" (42). He "has no methodological disciples in the discipline of biblical theology" (46).

Pointing to Gabler's distinction between exegesis and — philosophical — explanation, and the universal and temporal, Ollenburger says that Gabler ultimately aims at a "Christian theology that (a) is suitable for its own time, and (b) rests upon an unchanging foundation of biblical truth." Biblical theology addresses the second aspect of Christian theology: "theology . . . must rest upon the abiding truths of revelation which it is biblical theology's task to articulate" (39).

According to Ollenburger, Gabler's program has been for too long misunderstood. Yet, understood correctly, his program nevertheless is obsolete in the current discussion because of his insufficient distinctions between the historical-temporal and the timeless, and between the purely descriptive and the philosophically grounded criticism (47).

In his analysis of Gabler's program, it is clear that Ollenburger does not view Gabler as inaugurating a biblical history of religion approach. Also, Ollenburger emphasizes more than other interpreters Gabler's aim at a *Christian* biblical theology. However, Ollenburger does not explain how that which is specifically Christian is brought to bear in Gabler's concept of biblical theology. When referring to this theology as the "unchanging" foundation of biblical truth he, too, does not address whether it is only Christian truth which is unchanging in the Scriptures or all biblical truth, including that ascertained in Gabler's first theology. Should the latter be the case, what is the difference between unchanging *Christian* truth and those unchanging truths that are also ascertained exegetically, but are *not* Christian in origin?

I. M. Saebø[14] points out the large gap between religion and dogmatic theology at the time of Gabler's address. The Bible, as the collection of the *dicta probantia,* had become an auxiliary science to dogmatics; this was the wound resulting from the theological crisis of the church. Gabler responds by placing theology in the

13. Ben C. Ollenburger, "Biblical Theology: Situating the Discipline," in *Understanding the Word,* JSOTSup. no. 37 (Sheffield: JSOT Press, 1985), 37-62.

14. Magne Saebø, "Johann Philipp Gablers Bedeutung für die Biblische Theologie," *ZAW* 99 (1987): 1-16.

arena of religion *(den Bereich der Religion)* through the establishment of biblical theology as a historical science (7). Also new is Gabler's distinction between historical *(überlieferungsmässig)* and didactic *(philosophisch)* (7).

Historical biblical theology argues historically. It is, considered by itself, always in accord with itself (8). In this respect, Gabler is concerned with the correct separation of the contingent and variable from the universal ideas which by divine Providence were meant for all times. His reference to the universal notions presumably corresponds to his formerly stated "always in accord with itself" (9).

The transition from Gabler's first to his second theology is characterized by the focus on substance-critical *(sachkritische)* considerations in the second theology. Something *(einiges)* will have to fall by the wayside because it was only meant for people of a particular era *(Zeitalter)* but not for the constant form of the Christian doctrine and, hence, for us (10). Gabler's aim is, therefore, to establish the *dicta classica* as the theologically secured minimum of biblical theology in its narrower sense. This minimum represents the bridge between the total area of the historical biblical theology and the total area of dogmatic theology.

Saebø's interpretation, augmented by passages on Gabler's biography and on the further development of his work, contains many insightful observations. Especially important is his attempt to show Gabler's interest throughout his lecture not only in necessary distinctions but also in the coherence and unity of his concept of Christian theology. Nevertheless, Saebø's interpretation cannot escape the questions which already have implicitly or explicitly surfaced in this review.

What precisely is meant by "historical" *(überlieferungsmässig)?* Does it mean the conveyance of the unchanging, historically given texts, or the interpretation of the transmission itself in these texts? Does it mean that historical work has to identify (and eliminate) the contingent in the texts, whereas the universal ideas must be identified — in the second theology — by substance criticism, rather than historical criticism? Or does it mean that what is always the same is the *separation* of the contingent opinions from the universal ideas in Gabler's second biblical theology? Does substance criticism occur only from his second theology on? Are all universal ideas for all times, and for this reason Christian? If so, is there a specific norm for the Christian character of the *dicta classica?* Are those ideas that belong to a particular era *(Zeitalter)* individual opinions of biblical authors or are they indicative of "era-restricted" universals? Does Gabler distinguish between a theology of Christian biblical *dicta classica* and a selection from those *dicta* which should be the basis for dogmatics? One thing seems clear: Saebø does not say that Gabler's concept aims at a history of the biblical theologies or of biblical religion. Saebø's attention to the coherence of the lecture through its two major biblical theologies leads him to say that the lecture aims at establishing a theology of the substantive doctrinal system of the biblical religion.

Another remark on Saebø's contribution is necessary. All interpreters, including Saebø himself (3), state in unison — sometimes with a somewhat deploring undertone — that Gabler never presented the execution of his program. But Saebø adds to this statement that Gabler's strength was his many occasional papers — as well as his always well prepared lectures for his students. These papers were his virtually exclusive form of doing theology, namely, on concrete issues. Whatever the disadvantage may be of the absence of a *magnum opus* on biblical theology, it may well be outweighed by the application of its program to concrete issues. Compared with such concretizations, which reflect the concreteness of the biblical books themselves, an executed biblical theology may itself appear as a rather distantiated abstraction. Gabler is remembered for his program, without its execution. Whether or not his legacy would be equally intensively remembered had he executed his biblical theology is an open question.

A.-I. Conclusion

If a symposium were to take place of the just-reviewed authors about Gabler's lecture, based on the *genus historicum* as the rule for its interpretation, and if these and other authors unfortunately not included in this review were placed around the conference table either in the chronological order of their publications or in any other order, all would first legitimately point out that they had said more about the "universal ideas" than has been discussed in the just-given review. If proceeding in order, they would collect and classify their interpretations, with due recognition of their essential points, and compare them.

One result of such a symposium can be predicted with certainty. It would be the same as the supposed result of conferences of the Old Testament's authors, the New Testament's authors, and all authors of both Testaments. Gabler has said it well: ". . . it is clearly revealed wherein the separate authors agree in a friendly fashion, or differ among themselves" (Sandys-Wunsch and Eldredge, 142). The last word before adjournment would be: To whatever extent Gabler, just as the issue of biblical theology, merits attention, the sum of the discussion requires more work.

II. Discussion of the Major Issues

Understanding Gabler's lecture depends as much, if not more, on the question of its total conceptuality as on the clearly visible forward-moving composition of its parts and the higher or lower degree of clarity, or the explicitness or implicitness, of some of his statements. Next to specific clarifications, it centers around the following set of questions: What are the basic focus and the purpose of the total lecture? What is meant by "historical" and "history" in the lecture? What is the meaning of the "universal notions" for Gabler? How are Gabler's — at least — two biblical theologies related? What is the function of dogmatics in Gabler's concept of biblical theology? The discussion of these questions will have to keep the whole lecture in mind lest it disintegrate into disparate entities.

A. What Are the Basic Focus and the Purpose of the Lecture?

This question arises with reference to both the introduction and the main body of the lecture when it discusses biblical theology specifically. This covers some 60 percent of the lecture, including its short conclusion.[15]

1. In the *introduction,* the immediately arising question is how its long opening sentence is related to the title of the lecture and to the rest of the introduction.

a. The focus of the *opening sentence* is different from that of the title. The title focuses "On the proper distinction between biblical and dogmatic theology and the specific objectives of each" (134). The opening sentence focuses on something else. It refers to the unanimously affirmed consensus by all "pledged to the sacred Christian [things]" (134) (*Christianis sacris addicti,* 180). This pledge specifically affirms that "the sacred books, especially of the New Testament," represent two things: They are "that one, most clear source from which all true and certain recognition of the Christian religion may be derived" (134) (*unus ille et limpidissimus fons, ex quo vera omnis et certa religionis Christianae cognitio haurienda sit,* 179-80), and "that sacred sanctuary to which we uniquely take refuge in so great the ambiguity and vicissitude of human knowledge" (134) (*sacrum illud Palladium, ad quod in tante humanae scientiae et ambiguitate et vicissitudine unice confugiendum nobis sit,* 180) — "if we aspire to a solid understanding of the divine matters and want to grasp a certain and firm hope of salvation" (134) (*si ad solidam rerum divinarum intelligentiam adspiremus, velimusque certam firmamque salutis spem concipere,* 180).

Gabler speaks about — and to — Christians. He says "we" — the Christians who have become dedicated to what is specifically Christian. They all profess

15. Throughout the rest of this chapter, I will be quoting Gabler's lecture in English; often this will be followed by the original Latin. If the paginated English quotation is *not* followed by the Latin, *or* if it is followed by the *un*paginated Latin, then the quotation is adopted verbatim from the translation by Sandys-Wunsch and Eldredge (134-44). If the paginated English quotation is followed by the *paginated* Latin, then the English quotation will be different from Sandys-Wunsch's and Eldredge's; it will reflect my own variation from Sandys-Wunsch and Eldredge. For the Latin original I will be quoting from: Johann Philipp Gabler, "De justo discrimine theologiae biblicae et dogmaticae regundisque recte utriusque finibus," *Kleinere theologische Schriften* (Ulm: 1831), 179-93. This is the same Latin text that Sandys-Wunsch and Eldredge use.

without dissent — who are those who would take no exception whatsoever to what he defines? — that their true and certain recognition *(cognitio)* of the Christian religion may be derived from the biblical books, its clearest source — interestingly, he does not say "sole" *(solus)* source — for the purpose of gaining a solid understanding *(intelligentia)* of the divine matters, and a certain and firm hope of salvation. At the same time, these books offer protection from the vicissitudes of human knowledge *(scientia)*.

Not theology but religion. Not just religion but the Christian religion. And the true and certain recognition of it. And that in the sense of the intelligibility of its divine matters with particular regard to "our certain and firm hope of salvation." And all that in the face of the dangers by rational human knowledge. All of it "true," "certain," "solid," "certain," and "firm." At issue are the certainty of the Christians' *understanding* of divine matters and their hope of salvation through their clear *recognition* of this kind of Christian religion. For this understanding through this recognition the biblical books, especially of the New Testament, are the one most clear source and at the same time the sanctuary offering protection from the vicissitude and ambiguity of only — human — knowledge.

For this recognition, the sacred books are indispensable. However, they are only the *source* for the understanding of divine matters and this hope of salvation. They are not the *ground* of such understanding and hope. Indeed, Gabler does not explain what the *ground* of these is in his lecture. And they are the *source* only insofar as they provide *this* understanding, and not because they provide all other sorts of knowledge.

Unless we assume that this statement is nothing more than an advanced rhetorical reassurance for his audience of his loyalty to the Christian cause expressed in orthodox terms, which stands despite whatever else he is going to say — an unfounded assumption at best — we should expect that this statement gives at the outset the basic concern, focus, and purpose of his lecture.

How, then, is this focus related to the different focus of the lecture's title on the distinction between biblical and dogmatic theology? The answer can only be that the title represents that point of clarification which is particularly necessary to confirm the affirmation in the opening statement. The title serves this purpose, notwithstanding whatever Gabler subsequently says about biblical theology and its distinction from and relation to dogmatic theology. It aims at establishing the specific nature of the doctrine of the Christian religion in the Bible. It aims at the recognition and understanding of the substantive biblical doctrine of the Christian religion.

b. The opening statement also foreshadows *the rest of the introduction.* Its references to both the doctrinal consensus and the vicissitude of human knowledge trigger questions about the reasons for contention, fatal discord, and dissension. Of Gabler's four reasons for this discordant situation, three have explicitly to do with the Scriptures: their own obscurity in terms of both words and concepts, incorrect or even arbitrary exegesis, and — in the fourth place as the transition to the lecture's main body — the bad mixture between "the simplicity and ease of biblical theology with the subtlety and difficulty of dogmatic theology" (135).[16] The third reason, inattention to the distinction between religion and theology, does not refer to the Scriptures. It refers to the basic importance of the aspect of religion in the Scriptures expressed in the opening sentence. When this distinction is neglected, the aspect of religion as *the* genuine category of decisive biblical substance is lost. Therefore, all four reasons cause the breakdown of the consensus about the Bible as the source for this substance.

The first three reasons affect the recognition of the biblical substance directly; the fourth, while also affecting this recognition, rests on the additional aspect of the different characters of dogmatic and biblical theology. The neglect of this difference between these two disciplines adversely affects all other reasons for the confusion within biblical theology itself. The "bad mixture" of biblical and dogmatic theology prevents the Bible and biblical theology from being the "source" and *refugium* in its own right, regardless of whether biblical interpretation is in itself confused or not. Therefore, when Gabler, in his title and the main body of his lecture, focuses on the distinction between biblical and dogmatic theology, it means more than the mere discussion of the relation of two disciplines in a theological faculty. It is an attempt to restore the Bible as the legitimate source for the recognition of the Christian religion's understanding of the divine, and its hope of salvation. It is an attempt to rescue the Bible not only from the dangers of human knowledge but also from its subservience to dogmatics. Strange as it may be, of all threats to the Bible as the source and *refugium,* for Gabler dogmatic theology is the greatest. Its separation from biblical theology through the separation of the latter from the former is, therefore, the most urgent task.

After being concisely defined, the four reasons for the discord are subsequently more specifically explicated. The first two explications (about obscurity in and arbitrary exegesis of the Bible) are conventional, and the fourth is formal, preparing the main part. The third explication, about the difference between religion and theology, is important. "Religion is namely the divine doctrine conveyed in

16. Gabler's expression *male mixta* (180), or "badly mixed," in this context amounts to a pleonasm, since any mixture of the two theologies is for him bad. Sandys-Wunsch and Eldredge translate — meaningfully — "inappropriate combination" (135). Gabler also speaks of the "readiness to mix completely diverse things" (137) *(studium miscendi res plane diversas).*

The other issue in this statement requires interpretation. When speaking of "the simplicity and ease of biblical theology," he cannot possibly mean that his method for this theology and its execution are "simple and easy." In fact, they require competent scholarly work which is complex and difficult, as Gabler's description of the method shows and as he himself says. "Simplicity" is used as the opposite of "subtlety." It means that biblical theology is simple and easy in the sense that it descriptively states the biblical facts, whereas dogmatic theology explains them in the ongoing dialogue with its contemporary intellectual environment.

the Scriptures; teaching . . ." (182) (*Est enim . . . religio doctrina divina in scripturis tradita; docens* . . . , 182).[17] It teaches "what each Christian ought to know and believe and do in order to secure happiness in this life and the life to come. Religion, then, is every-day, transparently clear knowledge. . . ." It is "for the common man" (136).

Since "religion" is what every *Christian* must know ". . . for possessing the happiness of this and the future life" (135) (*ad tenendam huius et futurae vitae felicitatem,* 182) — this "happiness" being the earlier mentioned kind of "hope of salvation" experienced in life — "religion" is again understood by Gabler in the qualified sense of the word. It is the *Christian* religion. This religion is "conveyed" (135) *(tradita),* i.e., in the Scriptures "unalterably passed on" as divine doctrine for its readers. Hence, it teaches them as *divine doctrine*.

Yet Gabler speaks about the Christian religion *in,* not of, the Scriptures. This religion is the Scriptures' own divine doctrine. That doctrine teaches. What does it teach? Later he says it teaches the doctrine of salvation. This divine doctrine is the clear, transparent, everyday knowledge "for the common man." It is clear, or simple, not because it is unscientific in contrast to scientific theology, and only for simple-minded rather than for all people, but because its substance is unadulterated by any other influence, including dogmatics. For Gabler, dogmatics does often have an adulterating influence on this divine doctrine as the two are inappropriately combined.

Gabler distinguishes religion and theology in terms of their different functions. He means neither that religion plays no role in theology, nor that everyone's knowledge of religion exists apart from the Scriptures. On the contrary, he means that religion represents the essence of the theological enterprise, and that this enterprise is based on the theology of the Scriptures. In the theology of the Scriptures, the essence of the Christian religion within the Scriptures is worked out. He does not speak about a nonbiblical nature of religion as opposed to the biblical nature of biblical theology. Inasmuch as he speaks later in his lecture about the different "forms" of religion in the Scriptures themselves, he does so in order to

17. This translation differs from Sandys-Wunsch's and Eldredge's: "Religion is passed on by the doctrine in the Scriptures, teaching. . . ." Their translation misses the important adjective *divina* ("divine") after *doctrina* or — respectively — before "doctrine." Also, Gabler, in discussing the difference between religion and theology, clearly defines each. First, he defines them in terms of what their individual *natures* are. Second, he defines them in terms of what they *do.* Thus, the definitions for religion are: it *is* the divine doctrine, and as such it *teaches.* After this sentence, Gabler again — by the connecting adverb "consequently" *(igitur)* — defines religion in terms of what it *is:* "every-day, transparently clear knowledge" (136). This knowledge is the result of religion's teaching the divine doctrine conveyed in the Scriptures, which every Christian "ought to know and believe and do . . ." (136). By contrast, Sandys-Wunsch's and Eldredge's translation means that Gabler only says what religion does, without saying in their basic sentence what it is. In Gabler's text, the definition of what each discipline does is subsidiary to the definition of its nature.

distinguish the unique nature of the Christian religion from those forms in the Scriptures that are not uniquely Christian. However, although the "common man" is expected to know the unique nature of the Christian religion, he or she cannot be equally expected to possess the much more complex knowledge of fundamental religious differences, even and especially in the Scriptures. This sort of knowledge requires the scholarly discipline of theology.

Hence, in contradistinction to the function of religion as the knowledge expected of the "common man," the function of theology, be it biblical or dogmatic, is characterized by the complex demands for scientific discourse among scholars. This discourse also pertains to the discernment of religious differences or different religions. The discipline of theology, therefore, requires academic expertise that not everybody can afford. Gabler's statement does not imply that scientific theology has nothing to do with working out in both biblical and dogmatic theology the unalterable, clear, simple, everyday knowledge of the divine doctrine of the Christian religion of salvation. In fact, exactly that task may in both disciplines be the supreme test for their intellectual integrity or deficiency.

Together with his three other explications, Gabler's explication of the difference between religion and theology is directly connected to his opening affirmation. It becomes clear that the progress of his discussion remains controlled by his focus on that affirmation, and that the purpose of his lecture is to clarify the way toward restoring the Bible as the source for the knowledge of the Christian religion as the divine doctrine of salvation by developing the appropriate biblical theology for that clarification.

Should this interpretation be correct, the question already arises at this point as to whether his discussion of the first stage of biblical theology can at all sufficiently be understood without his discussion of the second stage of "stricter," also "biblical" theology. It appears that the first stage is a mere stepping-stone — inevitable and distinct, yes, but nothing more than that — toward the goal of his "true" theology, in which the concern of his introduction comes to its conclusion. If indeed it is a stepping-stone, the first stage only offers the necessary distinctions and synthetic requirements for providing the plateau from which to ascend to the top or proceed to the heart of the answer to the basic problem. Unless Gabler's focus in the first stage of his biblical theology departs from the focus of his introduction, it seems that his discussion of this stage is controlled by the focus expressed in the introduction and in the stricter theology as well. At any rate, an interpretation suggesting that: (1) the first stage of his biblical theology is his ultimate objective, compared to which the second stage is only indirectly or relatively important, and (2) that the first stage alone represents his program, in which his goal is a historical biblical theology — because the stricter theology is substantive and not also historical in nature, and only functions as a mediating bridge between the real biblical and dogmatic theology — is very questionable.

2. The body of Gabler's lecture, together with its conclusion, consists of

another introduction and a bipartite presentation of his program for biblical theology.

a. The *introduction* to the body begins with the definition and discussion of the difference between the scientific disciplines of biblical and dogmatic theology. It continues with a call for attention to "those things that have been said up to now" (138):

> that we distinguish carefully the divine from the human, . . . that we establish some distinction between biblical and dogmatic theology, [and then] . . . after we have separated those things which in the sacred books refer most immediately to their own times and to the men of those times from those only [*modo*] pure notions which divine providence wished to be characteristic of all times and places, let us . . . construct the foundation of our philosophy upon religion and designate, . . . the objectives of divine and human wisdom. (138)

This introduction ends with the announcement of the procedure in two stages. We must "on the one hand correctly maintain the just mode of the cautiously to be portrayed notions of the sacred authors" (138) (*partim iustum modum notionum auctorum sacrorum caute informandarum recte teneamus,* 185). We must also "on the other hand legitimately establish their dogmatic use and its own objectives" (138) (*partim earum usum dogmaticum, huiusque fines rite constituamus,* 185).

The middle section of this introduction shows, through both its explicit connection with his previously discussed focus and its reformulation here, that Gabler's design for biblical theology is — next to its relationship to dogmatics — guided by one decisive objective: the careful distinction of "the divine from the human [things]" (138) *(divina ab humanis dilegenter dignoscamus).* Why is this objective decisive? Because the fundamental issue for the correct understanding of all the "sacred books" is the accurate distinction between what is divine in them and what is merely human. God's word versus human word. This question lies at the heart of the consensus of Christians, and also their discord, precisely because the sacred books themselves do not clearly reveal what is divine and what is human within them.

What is the guideline for the answer? It is separating "from the temporal things [*secretis iis, quae . . . tempora*] . . . these strictly pure notions" (136) (*eas modo notiones puras,* 185) which are "characteristic of all times and places" (136). In order to discern the difference between the divine and the human, first one must look at what is eternal and what is temporal. The discernment of the difference between eternity and temporality is the epistemological road toward the theological knowledge of the difference between the divine and the human. This means that the difference between eternity and temporality can be found out from the sacred books. But the difference between the divine and the human can only be logically concluded *for* the sacred books after the difference between eternity and temporality *in* the sacred books has been determined.

Yet, by what criteria can the eternal and the temporal themselves be distinguished? Does Gabler mean to distinguish the temporal and the eternal notions within the individual texts and their respective marks by observing the history of their ideas? Does he stand in a trajectory of, e.g., Herder shortly before and Hegel shortly after him? If so, what kind of design would be necessary for his biblical theology? A design for a history of ideas demands more than the recognition of the chronological sequence of individual ideas and the distinction between the temporal and eternal notions within each. Following if not preceding this kind of distinction, it would have to develop those steps by which the relationship between the temporal and eternal can be shown as a forward-moving process of the transition from one stage to another, a process from its beginning to its end, in which the changing relationship of the two notions becomes evident, and which itself is characterized by this changing relationship. Does Gabler want to distinguish, and lastly, to separate the temporal from the eternal notions within each individual text? Or does he want to describe their changing relationship in a historical process? Clearly one understanding of Gabler's design must be set aside: that he hypothesizes a contrast between the temporal biblical ideas at the very beginning of the total historical process and the eternal ideas at its very end. And of course, this kind of hypothesis would have nothing to do with Gunkel's *Schöpfung und Chaos in Urzeit und Endzeit,* even if Gabler intends this. The contrast between a temporal, contingent, and primeval time and an eternal endtime has nothing to do with the conceptual analogy of the two times. Also, the hypothesis of this kind of contrast would not accommodate the main concerns in Gabler's program. It would allow neither for the distinction between the temporal and eternal ideas in each stage of the biblical texts nor for the determination of their relationship throughout the development of all stages. Finally, the hypothesis of this kind of contrast is absent from Gabler's concept because he assumes the coexistence of the temporal and eternal ideas in all texts and their stages, even in the New Testament, rather than the existence of the temporal only at the beginning and the eternal only at the end, and rather than an evolution from only a temporally characterized beginning toward only an eternally characterized end. If he thinks about a history of the biblical ideas, he can only have meant a history of the ongoing relationship of the temporal and eternal ideas, and the transformation of their relationship in the historical process.

As will be discussed below, for Gabler the universal notions are the decisive instrument for distinguishing and separating those biblical ideas that are above the temporal and contingent ones. This being the case, one will have to ask whether or not his lecture demonstrates a design not only for distinguishing the universal from the temporal notions but also for describing and explaining a history of the universal notions. Lastly, his biblical theology culminates in the focus on the importance of these notions. He certainly needs the contingent ideas for distinguishing the two kinds. But it does not seem that a history of the contingent or temporal ideas would have been as important for his system of biblical theology as a history of the universal ideas — if he had a history of the biblical ideas in mind. A critical question is, then, whether Gabler demonstrates the necessary method for a history of the universal notions, a history that describes their ongoing process from stage to stage, from notion to notion, which at least lastly ascends to the emergence of those notions that represent the Christian religion of salvation for all places and times.

Or, does he, before studying the Scriptures, already know that he must look in his study for their own doctrine of such a history in order to be able to conclude from his results what is distinctly temporal and what is distinctly eternal in that history — and in order to have a biblical theology? Would he in this case not have to propose, as the basic objective of his theology, a history of the biblical ideas based on the history of the biblical books rather than or regardless of his declared goal of separating the temporal from the eternal ideas in each book? Is he after a history of ideas or after a typology of substantively classified doctrines?

But more is at stake: Why does he focus at all on the categories of — temporal and eternal — time and place? Why does he not focus, e.g., on the person of Jesus the Christ as the ultimate fulfillment of a history of ascending divine revelation, based on the category of the incarnation? Does he, a Lutheran professor of theology, not know that Christology and soteriology are the ground and reason for knowing what is divine in the Scriptures and therefore also eternal, and not the result of the distinction between the temporal and eternal?

Whence is his choice of the category of time derived? Does it not come from what he already firmly knows, presupposes, and affirms with all Christians; namely, that the Christian doctrine of salvation in the sacred books is purely divine and therefore also for all times and places? Gabler wants to *discover* what in the Scriptures is human and what is divine. He claims to arrive at this *discovery* by *discovering* what is temporal and what is eternal. In fact, he already knows the result of what he wants to discover. He will discover the eternal because he knows what is divine, the temporal because he knows what is eternal, and the human because he knows what is temporal.

Therefore, does his method for the process of discovery not depend on his already firmly held doctrinal presupposition? Is not the logic of this process in effect designed to lead, step by step, to the proof of the result expressed at the end of his lecture? Does not the proof of this result actually control the method for the procedure toward this result from the very outset — despite his claim to arrive at the result *through* the procedure? Is his method genuinely heuristic or actually nothing more than a method of — not dogmatic but inner-biblical — proof-texting? Is not the structure of his total lecture conceptualized from the perspective of his conclusion at the end of the lecture; namely, the arrival at a system for the doctrinal classification of the biblical books? In the discussion of his lecture, Gabler has received much credit for the integrity of his strictly objective, historical-critical method in the first stage of his theology, which is said to be uninfluenced by substance-critical criteria, whereas the substance-critical nature of its second stage has been generally recognized, but with little consideration of the question of whether or not that stage is seen by Gabler also to be exegetically based. Is an interpretation of Gabler's method on target which says, suggests, or implies that its first stage is free from substance criticism and its second stage is beyond historical-critical exegesis? Has his lecture at times not received on the one hand more, and on the other hand less, credit than it deserves?[18]

For implementing the distinction between temporal and eternal ideas, Gabler, concluding his second, specific, introduction proposes "that on the one hand [*partim*] we hold firmly to a just method [*iustum modum*]" for "our interpretations of the sacred authors; and on the other [*partim*] that we rightly establish the use in dogmatics of these interpretations and dogmatics' own objectives" (Sandys-Wunsch and Eldredge, 138). His proposal of this bipartite procedure, probably better called these two complementary procedures, might look as if he means that what needs to be done "on the one hand," the interpretation of the sacred authors, is exclusively confined to the first stage of his theology, whereas the use of these interpretations is "on the other hand" equally exclusively, without any further biblical interpretation, confined to its second stage.

Clearly, from his discussion of the second stage on, Gabler speaks of the "dogmatic use" of the opinions of the "holy men," and of the different "goals of biblical and dogmatic theology" (142). However, it is also clear that in the second stage of his program, he still calls for the investigation and organization of nothing but biblical arguments in its first and even in the beginning of its second, final part. The second stage is not meant to be exclusively confined to the discussion of the use in dogmatics of the biblical interpretations established in only the first stage. It represents to a large extent the completion of his program for biblical theology. Therefore, the two stages of Gabler's program do not reflect the progression from biblical to dogmatic theology, but the concern for the difference between the two types of theology basically pervades both stages, in accordance with his earlier statements about their "bad mixture" and although this concern is for understandable reasons not everywhere equally explicit.

b. The first stage of the bipartite biblical theology

This stage (138-42) focuses on the careful "gathering" of "the sacred ideas," including, where necessary, "fashioning" them if "they are not expressed in the

18. The latest opinion on this question says that, according to Gabler, "Biblical Theology should rediscover the 'historical meaning of the Bible.' He and other scholars of similar orientation (e.g., Georg L. Bauer) were convinced that God revealed himself in nature and in history as a cosmic soul, which eventually concentrated in Jesus Christ, so that in their view Biblical Theology was almost identical with a philosophy of history." Petr Pokorny, "The Problem of Biblical Theology," *HBT* 15 (June 1993): 83-94, especially 83.

sacred Scriptures" (138-39). This "gathering" must itself happen in two "parts" *(partes):* (1) "the legitimate interpretation of passages pertinent to this procedure," and (2) "the careful comparison of the ideas of all the sacred authors among themselves [*inter se*]" (140).

However, before Gabler starts unfolding these two parts (140ff.), he once again prefaces their discussion by two main qualifications. One of these qualifications is important for his biblical theology.

First, the qualification with regard to inspiration is peripheral. He essentially says that all the sacred writers have to be equally revered "because of the divine authority that has been imprinted on their writings." Second, and more importantly, he says, "it is of no consequence under what authority these men wrote, but *what* they perceived this occasion of divine inspiration clearly transmitted and *what* they perceived it finally meant" (139, emphases mine). He makes this statement in the context of the question regarding the use of the category of inspiration for dogmatics. It is obvious, however, that this statement is relevant for his biblical theology. The uncontested fact of the inspiration of the authors of the sacred books, and of the books themselves, including the authority of that inspiration, contributes nothing to the clarification of their differences. Indeed, seen in light of the opening part of his lecture, the facts of inspiration and authority reinforce or even generate discord among Christians with regard to the sacred books. This is precisely because all are inspired equally and have authority equally. Hence, the validity of the substance of *what* they say does not depend on their inspiration and divine authority — in which case each of their different or opposite ideas would be equally authoritative and no doctrinal distinctions would be useful — but the degrees of inspiration and divine authority depend on the different degrees of validity of their ideas. It is, therefore, out of this understanding that Gabler directs his focus instead to the other qualification which is important for the biblical theology: the "form of religion" (139) *(religionis forma).*[19]

With respect to the "form of religion," he distinguishes between the two main parts of the Bible that do "not . . . attest to the same form of religion" (139): (1) those of the "old, itself elementary, formula" and (2) "others . . . of the newer and better Christian formula" (139) (*antiqua, eiusdemque elementaris, formula . . . recentioris et melioris formula Christiana,* 186). Note his choice of words when comparing: As opposites he uses "old" and "elementary" — Christian expressions for the characterization of the Old Testament as part of the Christian Bible — versus the "newer and better" and the "Christian," rather than the "New Testament" formula. When he speaks of "the newer and better Christian formula,"[20] one is

19. Here as elsewhere, I am using the basic rather than the syntactically required form of the Latin text.

20. The usage of the term "formula" refers to more than the formal side in the word "Testament." In accord with the "form of religion" and in the context of what Gabler says, it

directly reminded of his expression "especially of the New Testament" *(nova praesertim formula)* in the opening sentence of his lecture.

From this main distinction, Gabler draws a principal consequence for the organization of his biblical theology: It "is necessary . . . that we separate the individual periods of the Old and the New religion" (139) (*seiungamus necesse est . . . singulas religionis antiquae et novae periodos,* 186). This means that on the basis of the separate treatment of the two forms of religion, the old and the new, equated with the Old and the New Testament, Gabler then requires the separate interpretation of "each of the authors" (139) within each Testament.

This preface to the material discussion of the two "parts" in the first stage of his biblical theology reveals two important aspects. The first aspect is his focus on the authors of the biblical books, to the extent to which they are important for the gathering and individual identification of their ideas, as well as for the identification of the two basic forms of religion, even if their ideas at times have to be "fashioned" because they are not expressed. It is clear that work serving this focus demands much more than describing and re-narrating the biblical stories; it requires something quite different from talking about the biblical heroes of faith. It demands the clear recognition or, if necessary, the reconstruction of the concepts in the texts. Gabler's biblical theology aims at a system of concepts of the biblical texts.

The second aspect is that he separates the treatment of the two Testaments on the ground of the presupposed substance-critical distinction that the Christian formula of the New Testament is "better" than the "elementary" formula of the Old Testament. Gabler knows, as everyone does, that the Old Testament precedes the New Testament historically. But his judgment that the New Testament is "better" is not derived from his knowledge that it is "newer." It is derived from his Christian stance based on the New Testament, including its statements about the Old Testament. He accepts this basis at face value. On this ground, he knows in advance where that which is eternal, and therefore purely or truly divine, and that which is merely temporal, and therefore human, will be discovered — at least decisively if not exclusively. His presupposed and explicit substance-critical position, which is gained from the New Testament's, the Christian, religion of the doctrine of salvation for all times, rather than his knowledge of the historical development from the Old to the New Testament, is the reason for his basic distinction between the religions of the two Testaments.

Despite his agreement with the traditional Christian distinction of the different values of the two Testaments, Gabler keeps both together in his system of biblical theology. The Old Testament is an intrinsic part of his program. Its role in this program points to more than the facts that: (1) it belongs traditionally to the Christian Bible, (2) its authors, too, are "sacred" and inspired authors, (3) it, too,

---

especially refers to the substance of the Testaments, as in *formula fidei,* i.e., the formulaic expression of the substance of faith.

is authoritative, and (4) it also conveys the revelation of God. Its role in Gabler's *biblical* theology has to do with its necessary function of helping to verify the New Testament's doctrine of salvation for all times and places. The two stages of Gabler's program consist of a wide area including both Testaments and a narrower area within the wide. This narrower area is taken from within the New Testament itself. These two stages do not consist of an Old Testament theology in the first followed by a New Testament theology in the second stage. The two stages of Gabler's program must not be confused with the two stages of the Bible. Rather, the distinction between the two Testaments throughout Gabler's total program is a consequence of his decisive substance-critical vantage point for the method of this program. Similarly, the design of the method for separating the Testaments at the outset is a function of this vantage point.

1) In the *first part of the first stage* (140), each of the pertinent biblical ideas must be collected and classified and interpreted individually, for which the mentioned exegetical tools available at his time must be used (140-41). The assemblage is at the outset guided by the fact that each individual author expresses one principal idea. This idea is expressed repeatedly and diversely throughout the writings of the individual author, e.g., Paul. These many and diverse expressions of the principal idea in the book(s) of each author, or the "many opinions of the same author" which are "*typical* of each author" (emphasis mine) must be drawn out so that these many opinions may be reduced to "one idea and thing," or a "single principle of opinion"; in this way, the "many opinions of the same author" will actually show "the same meaning" (141). This "single principle" may be "expressly declared" or extrapolated from "the ideas that are stated." And as his discussion of Paul shows, the comparison of Paul's ideas happens with a set of heuristic questions by which one can recognize, above all other classifications, where he "proposes some opinion as a part of the Christian doctrine or some opinion that is shaped to the needs of the time" (141). "This process . . . requires considerable caution" (141). No wonder.

The isolation of each biblical book is easy. From then on, everything is very complicated. Gabler must know that it had already at his time become very difficult to decide which books, e.g., in the "Pauline" and "Johannine" literature of the New Testament, belonged to the same author; similarly, the issue of how many authors were involved in the same book or common block of books, e.g., in the Pentateuch, the by now so-called deuteronomistic history, or the book of Isaiah, had become complicated. If he ever aims at an exegetically based history of ideas in the sacred books, it remains mysterious how — in the context of the critical biblical exegesis of his time — he could say what he says. Before focusing on the ideas of the authors in their books he would have to say that one must first of all establish a history of the biblical literature — which he does not say.

Instead, he uses the authors and their books literary-historically uncritically as the distinguishable pools in order to focus in each pool on the system of each "author's" theology through — already in this part — the comparison of each author's ideas. The establishment of each system requires much more than only technical skills. Aided by these skills the interpreter must, by comparing the relevant (!, which already requires substance-critical decisions as to what is relevant and what not, and the criteria for such decisions) ideas in a "book," arrive at a systematized, i.e., stratified or hierarchized, typology of theological concepts. This systematization aims at recognizing the "one idea" or "single principle of opinion" which reveals "the same meaning" of all (141). Here it is necessary to add one point: if one idea does not show itself to be the most fundamental, one will have to decide which "one idea" is more fundamental than all others.

This total process requires substance-critical decisions from beginning to end. But it is decisively helped by the clearly expressed major criterion for what is most important, that which must be looked for and established: the distinction — already in the first part of the first stage of the program! — between ideas of "Christian doctrine" and others for "the needs of the time" (141). And being aware of what Gabler has already said, one has to add: Here Gabler refers to the Christian doctrine of salvation specifically, should there be a distinction between this specification and Christian doctrine in general within the New Testament.

Why is the theological system of each author subjected to this decisive criterion? Because Gabler wants to find out from the very beginning of the analytical and synthetic process which principal concept in each book represents potentially — if not actually — what is temporal, hence, human, and what is for all times, hence, divine.

Why does he focus on the ideas of the authors rather than on anything else? Because it is through the ideas that Gabler can at least start separating the human from the divine by separating the temporal from the eternal. He is laying the groundwork for the second part of his first stage. It is difficult to see how Gabler can be interpreted as having proposed historical analysis in the first stage and substance-critical theological synthesis only in the second stage of his method.

2) According to the *second part of the first stage* (141-42), "the various parts attributed to each Testament" must now be compared (141). The two Testaments have to be treated separately, which is a consequence of his previous statements about their difference. Within each Testament, then, the results — so one is led to interpret — of the previously analyzed and synthesized theological systems of the books of the individual authors must be compared. Although Gabler is not explicit, it must be inferred from his preceding guidelines that this comparison involves the major ideas if not the one principal concept of each book. At any rate, the process progresses toward a system of the systems of each Testament.

At this juncture, the "universal notions" or "universal ideas" (142) (*notiones universae,* 190) must be of help. To these universal notions "the individual principles . . . are to be subjected" (141-42) (*subiiciendae sunt . . . singulae sententiae notionibus universis,* 190), or "called back" (142) (*revocati,* 191).[21] A connection must be established between the (principal) opinions and the universal notions which are also recognizable in the Scriptures. But as soon as he demands this connection he emphatically warns against its misuse, which would cause "the worst damage to the truth" (142). He defines strict conditions for its application: Each idea must be "consistent with its own era [*aetas*], its own Testament [*religionis formula*], its own place of origin [*provincia*], and its own genius [*ingenium*]" (142, 190).

Gabler does not mean, of course, that the biblical ideas would be universalized through their connection with the universal notions, or abstracted through this connection from the reality of their historical context. Nor does he, notwithstanding two exceptions later, define the characteristics of those notions themselves. Why does he instead warn against the damage to the truth through a possibly inappropriate connection of the principal opinions with the universal notions? The universal notions apparently contribute something to the ideas in the work of each biblical author. This contribution must be kept from impairing the biblical ideas (142). Still, it is not clear whether or not these principal ideas themselves also reflect a commonly accepted notion of truth. Without being evaluated by the category of the universal notions, even the highest idea of an author might not be more than his own idea. The author's idea(s) must reflect a universal notion.

However, the contribution of the universal notions to the ideas is subject to the just-mentioned conditions, too, and very emphatically. They must remain tied to the concrete conditions of an author's work: era — a category of time; formula of religion — a category for religious distinction; *provincia* — a territorial category; and *ingenium* — a category of individuality. If these categories are ignored, truth is violated and "all the work which had been brought together in *diligently isolating*" (emphasis mine) "the opinions of each author" will be rendered "useless" and destroyed (142).

Hence, one must show that the authors' principal ideas reflect universal notions rather than only their personal opinions. At the same time, one must recognize that the commonly accepted universal notions reflect the characteristics of particular eras, types of religion, territories, and individual genius. Taken by themselves, they do not reflect timeless or eternal truth. They are era-specific. What

21. The translation of *sententia* as "principle" may be as problematic as its translation as "opinion." *Sententia* also means a "sentence." It is difficult to assume that Gabler intends a review of all sentences in the Bible in search of a universal notion. He seems to assume that the nature of the universal notions is known (i.e., as universally accepted ideas of what is universally valid), and that many of them "are expressly read in this or that place of the Holy Scriptures" (142). As they exist in scriptural passages and can be recognized as such, the already interpreted individual "opinions" *(sententiae)* must be called back, or subjected, to their controlling function. I prefer to read "principles" for *sententiae,* in semantic accordance with *principium sententiarum* (190), or "principle of opinion" (141).

must be established is that the principal concepts of the authors reflect (commonly accepted) ideas of what is universally valid, while at the same time it must be recognized that the universal validity of the authors' ideas is just as era-specific as their own ideas themselves.

Gabler's emphasis on the primary importance of the connection between the authors' ideas and the universal notions must be rooted in his basic interest in separating the temporal from the eternal in the Scriptures. With respect to this interest, the question arises of whether the universal character of the authors' ideas does not point to their quality of eternity and, hence, the pure divine revelation of the Christian religion. To this question, Gabler answers that the universal character of the authors' ideas or concepts belongs to the era-specific nature of those concepts and, therefore, does not indicate the eternal. The criterion for recognizing what is eternal, true for all times and places, lies somewhere else. By clarifying this distinction in the interpretative process, Gabler prepares for the second stage of his program in which he specifically focuses on the difference between the universal argument and Christian doctrine. Methodologically, Gabler needs the inclusion of the aspect of the universal notions in the interpretation of the authors' concepts in order to provide a clearly intelligible basis for the separation of the temporal from the eternal in the Bible.

When the total process expounded thus far is completed, the result will be a "system for biblical theology" (142). This system demands a high degree of both analytical and synthetic interpretation. The interpreters themselves must systematize the ideas of each individual biblical book into a system of ideas which is hierarchically ordered toward the discernment of the temporal and eternal. Based on these results, they must then compare the — principal — ideas of the books within each Testament, all the while keeping the two Testaments separate.

Gabler arrives at a system for biblical theology which consists of two juxtaposed theologies, an Old and a New Testament theology. The comparison takes place within each theology, whereas nothing is said about the comparison of the two. The comparison of the two is apparently not necessary, at least not explicitly as an additional step in a system of *biblical* theology, because Gabler already knows where the Christian religion for all times is documented and where it is not. The reason for the two separate theologies of the two Testaments as well as for passing up their comparison lies, once again, in Gabler's assumption of, and method for "discovering," the truth of the Christian religion in the New Testament. Nevertheless, the juxtaposition of the two theologies in one system of biblical theology means that the Old Testament, by virtue of not representing the essence of the Christian religion, contributes to proving the truth of this religion as documented in the New Testament. Gabler's concept of biblical theology reflects the traditional Christian understanding of the relationship of the two Testaments.

The comparison itself of the theologies within each Testament is limited to discerning wherein they "agree" or "differ" (142). More is not said, and more is not necessary at this juncture. Gabler might have said that the comparison of the agreements and especially the differences should lead to the recognition of their mutual relevance in an evaluative system. Instead, his method of comparison amounts to no more than a descriptive systematization in a phenomenology of religious ideas. This result represents a radical departure from his declared intention of establishing through biblical theology the evidence for the divine truth of the Christian religion in the Bible. Should Gabler have meant that this first biblical theology has its own independent purpose and that, therefore, biblical theology can henceforth be pursued without regard to the second stage (which *is* subservient to dogmatics), his concept for this system would fall short of his basic concern and goal, and his lecture would have to be considered a failure.

Instead, his first stage is — for him — sufficient for what it is. An additional step for the evaluation of the compared theologies is not necessary at this juncture because the evaluation focuses on and begins with the critical distinction between the temporal and eternal and, hence, the human and the divine. This distinction may dawn but does not yet fully appear in the first stage already, and only, presumably, as one described among all others and upon comparison registered as differing from all others. Its actual presence in the first stage prepares the way for its specific role in the second, "stricter" biblical theology. It becomes apparent that the phenomenologically oriented result of the first stage is not a sufficient end in itself. In the total biblical area, it is intended to represent the scientifically objectified basis for establishing the truth of the Christian religion in the Scriptures. It is, therefore, designed from that substance-critical vantage point and toward its proof.

Finally, Gabler singularly focuses on the ideas, especially the universal ideas. His first stage is a system of identified, arranged, and compared ideas. For this system, the recognition of era, religion, province, and ingenuity specificity of the ideas is indispensable. For what purpose? For producing a history of ideas, or for "diligently isolating" them from each other? Gabler emphasizes the era-specific nature of the ideas for distinguishing or isolating them from each other, with the objective of subsequently investigating each idea as to whether it is temporal or eternal. The fact that the organization of this investigation follows his — as everyone's — general knowledge of the historical sequence of the appearance of the ideas, a knowledge also resembling to some extent the historical sequence of the authors in the biblical books, does not mean that he is therefore aiming at a theological construct of their connectedness — in contrast to their isolated identity — in a history of ideas. Had he had such a construct in mind, his lecture would have had to express the connectedness of the ideas in a history of an ascending process of revelation. Also, his system would have to show how this process gradually evolves, not only how the mutually isolated ideas agree or differ. To whatever extent Gabler assumed such a process — and it is not unlikely that he did — he would, given his focus on the comparison of the ideas, still be confronted with this comparison as such, regardless of whether one idea is older or younger than another.

c. The second stage of the bipartite biblical theology

Gabler's discussion of the second stage of his biblical theology extends into his conclusion (142-44). As he increasingly speaks about the usefulness of this theology for dogmatic theology, one has to keep the following questions in mind. Does he now speak about some sort of double-faced function, intermediate position, or narrow linkage between the two wider fields of biblical and dogmatic theology? Is this second stage a "theology" that, by virtue of belonging halfway to the one and halfway to the other side, is, by the same token, neither a biblical nor a dogmatic theology? Or does he continue to speak about his "stricter" biblical theology, too, which is strict in the sense of a separate and independent concept for a biblical theology vis-à-vis dogmatics? The issue is whether the nature of this second stage is determined by its usefulness for dogmatics or by the essential independence of this stricter biblical theology from dogmatics, even as it is useful for dogmatics.

1) To address this issue, one must focus on what Gabler says about the second stage's biblical nature alone. This focus is directly suggested when he says, in the first sentence about this stage, that from now on not only may the question of the "dogmatic use" of the authors' "opinions" "then be profitably established," but "the *goals of both* biblical and dogmatic theology"[22] may also be "correctly assigned" (142, emphasis mine). Whether in terms of "goals" or "limits/boundaries," Gabler speaks in the second part of this main sentence about the separate arena for each theology.

"Under this heading" (142) *(quo nomine)* Gabler immediately announces the decisive "heuristic" question directing the investigation: "which opinions, then, refer to the constant formula of the Christian doctrine, and therefore pertain to us ourselves; and which ones are said only to the people of a certain era or formula" (142) (*quaenam sententiae spectent ad constantem doctrinae Christianae formulam, atque adeo ad nos ipsos pertineant; quaeque modo hominibus certi cuiusdam aeui aut formula dicta sint,* 191). And he explains:

> For among other things it is evident that the universal argument within the holy books is not designed for men of every sort; but the great part of these books is rather restricted by God's own intention to a particular time, place, and sort of men. (142)

Whence does he know that what he says here is "evident"?

If it has not already been done at the end of the first stage of his program, in the comparison of the principal ideas of the biblical books, the moment has now arrived when the authors' opinions, especially their universal ideas, must be separated into

22. The Latin word for "goals" *(fines)* may equally be translated by "limits" or "boundaries."

two basic classes: those referring to the constant substance of the Christian doctrine and those that were said only to the people of a restricted era or religious substance. Decisive for the separation is the difference between: (a) what is eternal, namely, the constancy of the substance of the Christian doctrine, with its "shape of the doctrine of salvation" (143) (*salutaris doctrinae typus,* 191), and (b) what is temporal, in the sense that its substance is restricted to a specific era.

Specifically, the Christian doctrine pertains to ourselves not because it is Christian, not even because it is the doctrine of salvation — such doctrines also belong to era-restricted religious forms! — but because it is eternal, for "all places and times" (138, 143) (*omnes loci et tempora* or *omnia tempora,* 185, 192). Thus what is Christian is not the ground for the doctrine of salvation for all times, but the doctrine of salvation for all times is the ground for what is fundamentally Christian. Here Gabler has arrived back where he started in his opening sentence about the "firm and certain hope of salvation" (134). Similarly, he has returned to his earlier reference to securing "happiness in this life and the life to come" (136). This phrase interprets the expression "all times" — and also "all places" — so as to include the time — and place — after death. "All places and times" means eternity.

Also, when contrasting the doctrine of eternal salvation with era-restricted doctrines, Gabler now focuses, with respect particularly to the era-restrictedness of certain universal notions, on forms of religion that are characteristic of specific eras. He does this not only with regard to the Old Testament but also with regard to the New Testament epoch. Subsequently he makes it clear: Not only were the Mosaic rites — which also were for salvation! — era-restricted, but also "Paul's advice about women veiling themselves in church" (142). For Paul's advice also reflects the religiosity of his era rather than his own personal whim. Gabler's focus on eras rather than on the individual authors enables him to formulate twice his general rule by which different authors, especially those of the early Christian era, too, can be grouped belonging together. Gabler demands that interpreters "must diligently investigate what in the books of the New Testament was said as an accommodation to the ideas or the needs of the first Christians and what was said in reference to the unchanging idea of the doctrine of salvation" (142-43). The result of this investigation will establish

> whether all the opinions of the Apostles, of every type and sort altogether, are truly divine, or rather whether some of them, which have no bearing on salvation, were left to their own ingenuity. (143)

It becomes very clear that the notion of the Christian doctrine of salvation for all places and times is the substance-critical vantage point for Gabler's distinctions. This notion reveals what is temporal and what is eternal and, hence, what is truly divine and what is merely human. It reveals that the *era-specific* universal notions themselves must be separated into those that are fundamentally *era-restricted* and those that, despite their era-specific articulations, express the doctrine of salvation for *all places and times.* He thereby acknowledges that the era-restricted doctrines were also restricted by "God's own intention" (142). This fact, however, is by no means a criterion for their eternal validity. On the contrary, it is relative to what is ultimately and therefore truly divine.

Furthermore, Gabler's concept of the era-restricted doctrines most importantly reveals that the New Testament itself is not identical with the doctrine of salvation for all times and places. The New Testament is not the criterion for the truth of that doctrine within it. Rather that doctrine in the New Testament is the substance-critical criterion for the legitimate reading of the New Testament. By this criterion the truths intended for the first Christians, like the era-restricted divine truths in the Old Testament, no longer apply because they do not represent that truth which is "truly divine."

Finally, the doctrine of salvation for all places and times is the criterion for the distinction and separation of this true form of religion from all other, nonbiblical as well as biblical, forms of "true" religion. Gabler's own category of religion itself is not a definitive criterion for the kinds and degrees of a religion's truth. At least from the perspective of Gabler's biblical theology of the Christian biblical religion, a religion's ultimate or relative truth depends on whether it represents the doctrine of eternal salvation or past, and surpassed, religious doctrines. Religion is not "truly divine" by virtue of being religion.

2) In his conclusion (143-44), Gabler arrives at what he set out to do in his introduction: to regain the Bible as "the one clear source" for "all true knowledge of the Christian religion" (134). In this process, the passages referring to the temporally restricted ideas are first of all to be separated from those that express or contain the constant ideas of what is eternal. Then one must distinguish through this separation what in the Bible is merely human, even if divinely ordained, from what is "truly divine." Finally,

> . . . those [passages] of the Sacred Scripture [are to] be selected [which are] perspicuous . . . [and] that pertain to the Christian religion of all times and exhibit in clear words the truly divine formula of faith: the *dicta classica* in the true sense of the word. . . . (143) (*erunt tandem illa S. S. selecta atque perspicua . . . quae ad religionem omnium temporum Christianam pertineant, exhibeantque claris verbis formulam fidei vere divinam, dicta veri nominis classica. . . .* (192)

These *dicta classica*

> can then be laid out as the fundamental basis for a more subtle dogmatic scrutiny. . . . For out of these [*dicta*][23] alone can those certain and undoubtful

23. Sandys-Wunsch and Eldredge interpret *Ex his* to mean "From these methods." However, in his preceding sentences and in this sentence, Gabler speaks about the function of the *dicta*

universal notions without doubt be ascertained which uniquely have a use in dogmatic theology. (143) (*Ex his enim solis erui possunt haud dubie certae illae et indubitate notiones universae, quae unice usum habent in theologia dogmatica,* 192)

Here, too, as throughout his lecture, Gabler casts everything he says about biblical theology in light of its function for dogmatics. Yet the question persists of what these statements say about biblical theology in its own right, apart from dogmatics.

First, his biblical interpretation, which certainly stands on its own grounds, leads to a selective reading of Scripture. This reading contains only passages which are *clear, scarcely of any doubt,* and taken from the New Testament. These selected passages culminate in the assemblage of the *dicta classica,* the classic expressions which show the truly divine formula of faith *unambiguously*. Gabler emphasizes the clarity, undoubtfulness, and unambiguity of this selection of biblical passages as the decisive epistemological criteria for his biblical theology in its own right. By these criteria, what one can and must know from the Bible with certainty becomes evident.

Secondly, what is meant by *dicta classica?* Five aspects are pertinent:

a) The *dicta classica,* which may be identical with the *dicta probantia,* are in function different from the *dicta probantia.* The *dicta probantia* are the biblical proof-texts for the already established dogmatic truth claims. Especially, they include more than only those references that express the doctrine of salvation for all places and times. The *dicta classica* are those classic passages in the Bible which represent the Bible's own expressions and opinions about the nature of the Christian religion of salvation for all times and places. Before serving as the proof for dogmatic statements, and apart from that function, they strictly belong to the biblical side of theology; they represent the pool for constructing biblical theology in the "stricter sense" of the term as a separate theology in its own right. Gabler's method clearly shows, regardless whether or not one agrees with the criteria for it, that the selection of the *dicta classica* is the result of a process of strictly inner-biblical investigation. After all, the claim has always been that these *dicta* themselves rather than dogmatics — again regardless of any different claims, especially by the Old Testament — represent the essence of the ultimate divine revelation. Whether this claim may be confirmed or contested, and on what grounds, depends before all else on the inner-biblical comparison of different claims. Therefore, this claim belongs to the discipline of the genuinely biblical theology, and not to any mixture of biblical and dogmatic theology.

b) The *dicta classica* are not more than a pool of passages collected from

---

classica for dogmatics. Hence, *ex his* ("from these") refers to the *dicta classica,* not to "method," let alone "methods."

different places in the various books of the New Testament. This pool does not yet represent a systematized doctrine. To be shaped into a doctrine, more is necessary than their mere assemblage and juxtaposition. They must be conceptually related so that, e.g., the relationship of Christology, soteriology, pneumatology, eschatology, and perhaps ecclesiology becomes clear. But again, for Gabler this systematization can and must be achieved on scriptural grounds themselves. Indeed, it is very often already explicitly done. It has nothing to do with dogmatic influence. Gabler's method for biblical theology makes it clear that systematization is intrinsic to its own execution. Systematization is neither a prerogative of dogmatics nor subservient to any dogmatic system.

c) Gabler's expression *formula fidei* ("formula of faith") is a technical expression used in Protestant, certainly in Lutheran dogmatics. However, his use of this expression for characterizing the essence of the biblical *dicta classica* does not a priori mean that he derives the definition of this essence from dogmatics. Whether or not this is the case depends on whether the definition of the essence of the *formula fidei* can be derived from the biblical passages alone, apart from dogmatics. Since this can be done — and nothing in Gabler's concept contradicts this conclusion — Gabler's use of this expression for his biblical theology only means that this formula is being used analogously with reference to the biblical subjects. It does not mean that such analogous use carries the dogmatic definitions with it into biblical theology.

d) Gabler says that the *dicta classica* can be "*sub*mitted" (emphasis mine) "to the place of the foundation for the more painstaking dogmatic observation" (143) (*possint fundamenti loco subtiliori observationi dogmaticae substerni,* 192). His Latin style, translated here literally, gives the impression that he wants to avoid the possibility of misunderstanding the *dicta classica* as anything but the basis for dogmatics. With respect to their relation to dogmatics, the *dicta classica* certainly have a function within the discipline of theology. But this function is defined as the *foundation* of dogmatics. This definition excludes the possibility of any combination with or dependence on dogmatics. His just-quoted formulation is crucial. For previously he mentioned the "bad mixture" of biblical and dogmatic theology (135), or the mixture of "completely diverse things" (137). Also, his lecture's title shows that the goal is their "proper" distinction. Hence, at the lecture's conclusion Gabler cannot possibly afford to be ambiguous about the proper separation of the two disciplines. Nor can he be ambiguous about their relationship by granting the *dicta classica* some sort of dual status between them.

e) Finally, the *dicta classica* also represent the separation of "universal notions" from "universal notions." After speaking about the unique use in dogmatics of those certain and undoubtful universal notions that can without doubt be ascertained out of the *dicta classica,*[24] he says:

24. For the translation, see above, 522-23.

> And if these universal notions are derived by a just interpretation from those *dicta classica,* and those notions that are derived are carefully compared, and those notions that are compared are suitably arranged, each in its own place, so that the proper connexion and provable order of doctrines that are truly divine may stand revealed; truly then the result is biblical theology in the stricter sense of the word. . . . (143-44)

Does Gabler speak about a biblical theology "in the stricter sense" which is based on a selection of specific universal notions and their separation from all other universal notions also assembled in the *dicta classica?* I think not. He certainly speaks about two separate kinds of universal notions. At what point in his method does their separation take place? Certainly it already takes place when he separates those that are era-restricted and human from those that are eternal and truly divine. Those identified as eternal and truly divine represent the pool of the *dicta classica.*

Does he speak of a further, second separation within the *dicta classica,* of those that would have no use for dogmatic theology from those useful for it? Such a step would come as more than a surprise. Nowhere in his lecture has he indicated that his biblical theology aims at more than the Christian doctrine of eternal salvation. Also, he frequently refers to biblical theology's use in dogmatics. Would he not have to have indicated that even when it comes to this Christian doctrine there is still a difference between — what? A general and a special eternal salvation? Would he not have had to say that the biblical *dicta classica* are as such not yet a sufficient basis for dogmatics?

But has he not said in the just-quoted statement that from the *dicta classica* alone can those universal notions be singled out which are uniquely useful in dogmatic theology? Which ones are "those"? Are they "singled out" from *among* the *dicta classica,* or are the *dicta classica* themselves the singled-out pool of those universal notions uniquely useful for dogmatics because they "certain[ly]" and "undoubtful[ly]" represent the passages expressive of the Christian doctrine of salvation? If the latter is not meant, why does Gabler not also speak of a biblical theology based on the *dicta classica* themselves, as long as he is interested in a separate biblical theology? Does he, from his all-encompassing first system of biblical theology, launch into a "stricter" one only for dogmatic theology? And does he thereby fail to develop the expected systematization of the *dicta classica* for a still strictly biblical theology, a systematization for which he evidently had established a basis?

Had Gabler understood his "stricter" biblical theology as extracted from *among* the *dicta classica,* it would only be an intermediate product at best, because it would indeed be determined from dogmatic criteria; his "stricter" biblical theology would scarcely deserve the name "biblical." For his total concept of biblical theology, including his intention to separate it from dogmatics, would be more than confused. It would collapse. It would collapse because his first system would evidently, and contrary to past interpretations, *not be a sufficient end in itself.*

Gabler's formulation[25] may be ambiguous, but it makes sense in the context and flow of his total argument. In light of his total argument, its understanding of a stricter theology selected from *among* the *dicta classica* creates great problems for that context and flow. His formulation means, therefore, that the *dicta classica* themselves contain those universal notions that have already been separated from the era-restricted notions through the second stage after the completion of his all-encompassing first stage. These notions are separately collected in the *dicta classica,* which, therefore, represent the clear *S. S.* ("Sacred Scripture"). They show: (1) "what in the sayings of the Apostles is truly divine" (143), (2) that "the formula of faith" is "truly divine" (143), (3) that this "stricter" theology represents the "provable order" of the "truly divine" doctrines (144), and (4) that dogmatics, too, built upon this order, is "divine" (144). The apostles' sayings, the formula of faith, and the provable order of doctrines are all equally truly divine. Dogmatics shares this quality almost equally by also being divine. More, Gabler does not say. These, and no other notions, are derived "by a just interpretation" from the *dicta classica,* and only from them because only the *dicta classica* shield the interpretation from an inner-biblical "bad mixture" of era-restricted notions with those about eternal salvation. Such a mixture would be the most serious of all causes for the "bad mixture" of biblical and dogmatic theology because it would happen within biblical theology itself.

One can see, now even more clearly than before, why the separation of temporal and eternal, the human and truly divine, has to be guided so decisively by the category of the universal notions and by Gabler's stern warning against their incorrect interpretation. The universal notions especially have lent themselves to being misunderstood, by virtue of being universal in contradistinction to what is not universal, as the yardstick for separating the divine or eternal from the human and passing. That misunderstanding is deadly for the unmistakably clear recognition of what is truly divine in contrast to what is also divine. It compromises, indeed destroys, the Bible as the source of the hope of eternal salvation by mixing general religious truth, even divinely revealed, with the specific truth of the Christian religion. The specific truth of the Christian religion is the sole yardstick for this separation.

In order to remove this dangerous misunderstanding, Gabler separates the era-restricted universal notions from those for all times by introducing the category of history into his biblical theology. This category makes it possible, not only for him but for his time, to recognize what in the universal notions is era-restricted. The fact that he uses the already generally accepted philosophy of historical relativity does not mean, however, that he uses it in order to establish a biblical theology

25. See above, 525.

of history. That he intends this is unlikely. It is at least a problem. It is only evident that he uses the category of history in the service of his different theological objective.

The *dicta classica* must be systematized into a "proper and provable connexion and order of truly divine doctrines" (144) (*commodus et probabilitis doctrinarum vere divinarum nexus ac ordo,* 192). Therefore, the *dicta classica* themselves are merely identified biblical passages about the pertinent universal notions found in the various books of the New Testament; they are neither doctrinal nor systematized. These passages must be shaped into doctrinal language of essentially formulaic nature — "by a just interpretation." The doctrinal formulations of the universal notions are "derived" from the *dicta classica,* and must be consonant with and remain controlled by them.

Once the doctrines are established, they all must be "compared"; then they must be "suitably arranged, each in its own place" (143-44). What must "come to the fore," or "become evident" *(ex[s]istere),* is the demonstrable order of their relations. The final result is a biblical theology which exists as a system of biblical doctrine containing the truly divine doctrines from the universal notions. This system is "firmly established," "provable," and always "the same" (144). It represents the essence of the Christian "religion" of all places and times. It is strictly biblical, not mixed with dogmatics. However, as long as dogmatic theology remains accountable to this system, it can be called "divine dogmatics" because it expounds the essence of this Christian religion, too.

B. Specific Items

1. Biblical and Dogmatic Theology

Gabler commits the main part of his lecture to the abolition of the inappropriate mixture of biblical and dogmatic work in theology. The reason why this mixture is "bad" can be recovered when one realizes its impact on the specific nature of the Christian religion, the source of which is the sacred Scriptures, especially the New Testament. Notwithstanding his intention, Gabler constantly speaks about the usefulness of biblical theology for dogmatics.

However, it is obvious that he says, apart from a few general formal and methodological statements, nothing about the full range and method of the dogmatic work. Indeed, his entire main part focuses on the method for biblical theology and the substantive aspects that generate the concept of this method. The reason for this focus is not that Gabler may have assumed that everything is clear in dogmatic work whereas nothing is clear in biblical work, and biblical work must therefore receive special attention. Rather, it lies in the acknowledged fact that the Scriptures are the foundation for dogmatics, not to be mixed with that derivative discipline let alone governed by it. If they are not the foundation exclusively, the work of both becomes unclear and the heart of theology is sick.[26] Gabler's focus on biblical theology is generated by the need for a firm theological understanding of the Scriptures which must therefore be based on a rational scientific theory, and not on — also legitimate — practical needs. At the same time, he can afford to presuppose what dogmatic theology does. Hence, he does not need to pay equal attention to the discipline of dogmatics in his lecture.

In his statements one has, then, to distinguish between his frequent references to the function of biblical theology for dogmatics — thereby noticing that for good reasons he never speaks about the function of dogmatics for biblical theology! — and what he says about biblical theology itself apart from its function in dogmatics. If this distinction were missed and his statements about biblical theology's function for dogmatics were taken as the essential vantage point and objective of his design for biblical theology, his actual and essential vantage point and objective would not be recognized. The actual concept of his program would remain out of focus, and his program would legitimately remain suspect of being nothing more than another variation of the bad mixture of the two.

However, his program shows the marks of a concept for biblical theology which as a whole is independent of dogmatics. His program can be done on the basis of the Scriptures alone, of what they themselves exhibit. And it can be developed into a systematic biblical theology which evolves from exegetical work but is generically distinct because it requires interpretative work. The interpreter must do what the Scriptures themselves have not done. One may question Gabler's decisive vantage point for his system; but one cannot deny that it is an inner-biblical system which does not depend on dogmatics, philosophy, or history. This system must be accounted for precisely because it cannot be executed by exegesis alone.

Gabler's vantage point is distinctly theological in nature. It is, therefore, neither coincidental nor an echo of traditional phraseology when he calls his biblical project "theology" rather than, e.g., a phenomenology of the Bible's religious ideas or a history of its religion or theologies.

Only one thing is out of focus. Instead of entitling his lecture "On the proper distinction of biblical and dogmatic theology" *(De iusto discrimine theologiae biblicae et dogmaticae . . .),* he could more accurately have said, "On the proper *separation* of biblical *from* dogmatic theology" *(De iusta* ***separatione*** *theologiae biblicae a theologia dogmatica)* because that is what he lectures on. Still, it remains affirmed that his separate biblical theology is useful in three ways. First, it is useful for dogmatic theology. Second, it provides the basis for the "common" person's

26. Gabler, himself extensively lecturing in dogmatic theology, left no doubt as to where he saw the basis for theological validity. He rejected the demand for binding submission even to the collection of the Lutheran Confessions as a "new papacy."

knowledge of the nature of the Christian religion. Third, it also provides the basis for the other theological disciplines.

2. The Universal Notions

The design of the first stage of Gabler's all-encompassing biblical theology shows that this system culminates in the use of universal ideas for the evaluation of the principal ideas of the biblical books. By strongly insisting, however, that the universal notions, too, must be evaluated for era-specific characteristics, Gabler implicitly triggers this question: Why is this step so decisive? The second stage of his program makes the answer clear. If the biblical ideas which are era-restricted are not discerned, those that are for all places and times cannot be recognized, and the distinction between the temporal and eternal and the human and divine cannot be drawn. It is clear that Gabler claims that the application of the universal notions serves the purpose of finally arriving at these distinctions. To this extent, they serve his theological goals, and it is doubtful whether he would have called for their application without these goals.

The universal notions are a philosophical category Gabler adopted from S. F. N. Morus (1736-1792), a classical philologist and philosopher (*habilitation* in philosophy, 1761) and New Testament scholar. One of Morus's preoccupations was to expound the critically exegeted doctrinal contents of the Scriptures in systematic form.[27] Gabler apparently presupposes that this category and the identifications of the individual notions are well known. Important in their adoption by Gabler is the fact that the roots for the development of this category do not lie in exegesis, at least not as exclusively as demanded by a claim to the total independence of biblical work from other disciplines. Does their adoption for his system of biblical theology therefore mean that Gabler's system is still mixed with other disciplines, by now with philosophy instead of dogmatics? It is, in the sense that the category of the universal notions does not appear, at least not in Gabler's system, to have been developed from within the biblical books. However, the undeniable fact that the notions are applied to serve his theological goal, which undoubtedly rests on discernible inner-biblical criteria, means that the question of whence they are adopted is of little significance. Had Gabler been prompted, from whatever discipline, to inquire into discernible universal notions also in the biblical books for distinguishing their era-specific characteristics, he could in no time have listed virtually all of them on the basis of nothing more than his knowledge of the biblical periods depicted in the Bible itself. Would that have been of greater help for his own goal? He would still be confronted with the question that governs his concept

27. Georg Müller Mangoldt, "Morus, Samuel Friedrich Nathanael," *Realencyklopädie für protestantische Theologie und Kirche,* vol. 13, ed. D. Albert Hauck (Leipzig: J. C. Hinrichs, 1903), 481-83.

of biblical theology: Why is the distinction of the era-specific universal notions from the notions for all times and places, and of the human from the divine, so decisively necessary?

More grave than his adoption of the universal notions from outside biblical studies is the inevitable conclusion that Gabler, whether he realizes it or not, by assigning them their function in his method, claims to use them as a means toward an unknown end. In fact he uses them for demonstrating the truth of his end, which he knows in advance and which is the reason and cause for adopting the universal notions in the first place. Unless proof exists to the contrary, Gabler's method does not escape the critical objection that it is caught not in a circular hermeneutic of separate disciplines but in a circular inner-biblical hermeneutic itself. The method of his system is less scientific than it claims, and more apologetic than he may want to admit. The case of the function of the universal notions in Gabler's method, along with possibly the methodological case of the same function of era-*specific* aspects within the Bible, for the purpose of separating the era-*restricted* from the *un*restricted universal notions, lastly affects his, and the, contention that the question of the ultimate biblical truth claim can be decided through historical-critical exegesis of the texts. Gabler's method does not prove, despite his explicit contention, that the ultimate biblical truth claim can be decided through historical-critical exegesis. On the contrary, critical analysis of his method proves that, in view of his a priori substance-critical decision, everything in the Bible that does not exhibit the essence of the Christian religion for all times and places and therefore for us is, at least with respect to this criterion, irrelevant theologically, regardless of any period, earlier or later, and of any history of the periods, as long as it is *era*-restricted, or historical. Nevertheless, the objection to the integrity of his method does not mean that Gabler could have used his a priori substance-critical vantage point for developing a method of biblical theology through which the biblical doctrines themselves are on *substantive* grounds adjudicated from that biblical vantage point. The predictable result would have been the same — as long as this vantage point is not contested from within the Scriptures. And as long as one accepts Gabler's vantage point, his theology has substantively more integrity without his method than with it.

Finally, it is striking that Gabler does not account for the fact that the Old Testament, too, exhibits at least some universal notions that are recognized by the New Testament as valid for all times and places and, hence, are also for Christians. Are they for this reason then not also truly divine, according to the logic of Gabler's method? Gabler may say that this is not the case, e.g., for the Ten Commandments. But can he deny that the doctrines, e.g., of creation and the fall are not also Christian doctrines for all places and times, and not relativized, or at least not contradicted, by the New Testament?

The question is not whether or not Gabler knows about these doctrines, but why he does not find it necessary to discuss this aspect, precisely because of his decisive focus on the eternal and truly divine. As far as his lecture reveals, one can arrive at only one answer: Even as the mentioned doctrines are also eternal and truly divine, and even as they, too, belong to the doctrine of the Christian religion, they are nevertheless not equal to those that are ultimately decisive, namely, the doctrine of the Christian religion of salvation. This very specific doctrine appears, lastly, as the criterion even for distinguishing between the eternal and truly divine on the one hand and between the eternal and truly divine on the other hand. It actually turns out to be the decisive criterion for separating — on theological grounds, despite his well-documented reverence also for the sacred Scriptures of the Old Testament — the totality of the Old Testament from the totality of the New Testament.

Certainly, Gabler calls for the separation of the Old and the New Testament's theologies in his method for the first stage of his biblical theology on the ground of the old and elementary compared to the newer and better Christian formula. However, the analysis earlier in this chapter has already shown that the reason for this separation is deeper and more specific than Gabler's comparative formulation indicates. It has claimed that the real reason is derived from the position of the Christian doctrine of salvation for all times, which is attested in the New Testament.[28]

By now, this deeper reason becomes even more evident when the question is answered why Gabler does not account for those Old Testament doctrines that are also acknowledged to be eternal and truly divine, even by the New Testament: They are true for all times and places, but not the doctrine of salvation for all times and places.

Last but not least, it becomes understandable what it means when Gabler complements his characterization of the Old Testament's old and elementary formula by referring to its characterization by Paul (Gal 4:9, in Paul's dispute with the Galatians about the absolutely decisive Christian criterion for salvation and freedom!). Gabler presupposes and adopts the specifically Pauline doctrine of salvation as the fundamental qualifier for the meaning of his own characterization of the Old Testament as old and elementary — even to the extent that he applies this qualifier to the entire Old Testament and, implicitly, all its doctrines, which Paul does not do in his discussions with the Galatians. No wonder, then, that Gabler does in effect distinguish between the eternal and truly divine on the one hand, and the eternal and truly divine on the other hand — without accounting for this de facto distinction.

28. See above, 513-14. See also Section II.B.3 (534-37).

Excursus: On Morus, a Profile of Morus Written by His Student Christian Friedrich Traugott Voigt[29]

The following is meant to highlight the specific aspects in Voigt's interesting description of Morus's life and work which are relevant for the further understanding of Gabler's lecture.

Gabler was indebted to Morus for much more than his entrée into the subject of the universal notions. His admiration for Morus, expressed in his lecture five years before the Leipzig professor's death in 1792, was certainly shared by his knowledgeable audience. Clearly, Gabler's lecture reflects the central concerns held in common by Morus as well as by Gabler and his audience. Gabler's own basic concern becomes even clearer when one reads Voigt's essay in memory of his teacher.

Voigt's essay reflects the spirit and concerns of the particular religious and theological community in and for which both Morus and Gabler lived and worked. This community was above all else faithful to the traditional doctrines of the Reformation, especially the Lutheran church. To be sure, its professors of theology, who were first and principle among all faculties of a university, were encyclopedically knowledgeable. Morus himself is said by Voigt to have possessed the most extensive knowledge in more than one field (. . . *dass Morus in mehr als einem Fache der Gelehrsamkeit die ausgebreitetsten Kenntnisse besass* . . . , 7). He was meteoric (*ein Meteor seiner Zeiten,* 7). However, in his Lutheran setting, Morus used his academic abilities to demonstrate the truths of the basic Christian doctrines, as well as to defend their reasonableness (5, 13). He personified the pleasure of their intellectual pursuit (6), and the happiness found in quiet piety (28), as opposed to those trends heralded by Enlightenment thought, which were seen in the pursuit of happiness for oneself in one's life on earth. Hence, Morus aimed at extricating the true values of Christianity from the vicissitudes of human knowledge. It is, therefore, no coincidence when the essential aspects in Voigt's essay are consonant with those in Gabler's lecture. The following points are noteworthy.

Morus is said to have educated the minds of his students toward the reality and fruits of eternity (*Ewigkeit,* 4-5). Eternity is specifically understood as the better, infinite world (6) of the life to come (31). That world is the better life (32), the blessed sphere, and the springtime morning (34). It consists of the rooms of peace (32) and the fields of light and eternal truth (34). It is the life of freedom in which one is eternally free from the darkness of life on earth (6, 31), as well as the knowledge and teaching of purity which are the source of happiness in this

29. Christian Friedrich Traugott Voigt, *Morus* (Leipzig: Wilhelm Gottlob Sommer, 1792), 3-34. A copy of this profile was provided for me by the library of the Johns Hopkins University, through the special efforts of Dr. K. C. Hanson, librarian at the School of Theology at Claremont. To the persons of both institutions I express my sincere gratitude.

mortal life (12). Here one is reminded of Gabler's concept of eternity in terms of all times and places, and his notions of happiness and hope in this life and the life to come.

Morus is said to have taught reverence for religion (17), by which he meant the religion of light (22) which is represented in the essential doctrine of the Christian religion (9). Voigt affirms that "Morus was a Christian" (20). When teaching dogmatics he defended the basic doctrines of Christianity (13). For this defense, he distinguished the doctrine in Scripture from its ecclesiastic specifications (13). Scholastic subtleties and hairsplitting were banned from his dogmatic school, and he mentioned the specific definitions added by the ancient and the new church only for the sake of the historical record (14). He impressed on his students the need for presenting the clarity of the doctrine of the Christian religion to the common people, and did so in his sermons (17).

It was important for him to demonstrate the consensus of the symbols of the evangelical church, especially the Augsburg Confession, with the doctrine of Scripture (14). And he was especially happy when he could show how the authors of these symbols and the Augsburg Confession had followed Scripture in perfect loyalty in their doctrinal statements. No wonder, then, that in his concern for teaching the eternal doctrines of the specifically Christian religion to the common people, Morus interpreted all books of the New Covenant (11), whereby his humanistic knowledge (9) helped him explain the individual occurrences out of the range of the whole history (11).

Voigt's profile of Morus shows that Morus had a comprehensive knowledge of history which he used in his discussion of the church's doctrines, as well as for his interpretation of Scripture, especially for explaining individual incidents in it in their total historical context. However, Morus was concerned with doctrinal religion, specifically with the Christian doctrines of eternity which represent the decisive core of the common person's knowledge of and reverence for religion. These doctrines are found in the New Testament — in which texts of the New Testament but those that contain the Christian doctrine of salvation for all times and places? In this concern, the concept of the universal notions — not mentioned by Voigt — was an important criterion for distinguishing between the truly divine and the passing human religious doctrines, whereby the question needs further clarification of whether Gabler's distinction between the era-restricted and the eternal universal notions represents his refinement of their understanding by Morus, or already Morus's own understanding.

That Morus was a defender of the essential Christian doctrines is also apparent through his strong interest in proving that the church's, especially his Lutheran, doctrines are in agreement with the doctrinal teaching of the New Testament. When compared with Morus's profile, one can see even more clearly what is already apparent in Gabler's lecture itself: Neither his distinction between biblical and dogmatic theology, nor his concept of the specifically Christian nature of religion, nor his thesis of the dependence of dogmatics on the essential Christian biblical doctrines, nor the relegation of the Old Testament in its entirety to secondary status were anything new. What was new, if anything, was Gabler's attempt to show by which method for biblical theology the specifically Christian doctrine of salvation contained in the New Testament could be firmly established independently of — as it wanted to be the foundation for — dogmatics. Lastly, then, the credibility of this attempt does not depend on its usefulness for dogmatics. Rather, it depends on the question of whether or not the method is designed to confirm a presumed substance-critical result, or to search for results as yet unknown in a truly heuristic process. This search involves above all else the comparison of the two Testaments.

3. The Relation of the Two Testaments

The question of the relation of the two Testaments must be distinguished from the question of the two stages of Gabler's biblical theology. His objective is to establish a theology that is "biblical." In his pursuit of this objective, the relation of the two Testaments plays an important role. This relation is, therefore, subservient to his total concept but nonetheless important in it.

For Gabler, all Scriptures are sacred and all their authors are inspired. They are witnesses to divine revelation, to God's own will and providence. However, these venerable facts are not sufficient for distinguishing between the truly divine and the divine in the merely human. Their validity is subordinate to the criterion for what is truly divine. Yet one should not simply conclude from their subordinate role that they are therefore irrelevant theologically. They are at least the major theological reason why Gabler speaks of "biblical" theology instead of only a theology of the Old and a theology of the New Testament. This theological reason amounts to more than his adherence to the togetherness of the two Testaments in the Christian tradition. The two Testaments belong together because both contribute to the clear recognition of the nature of the Christian religion for all places and times which is, therefore, also "for us." The way each of them fulfills this contribution, however, is different. While both are theologically important for "biblical" theology, the contribution of each to this theology is not the same. How, then, are their contributions to be distinguished?

It is clear, from Gabler's opening sentence on, that the New Testament is "especially" important for his theology. It is also clear that he speaks about their difference in historical perspective. He says that the New Testament is "newer" (139); he lines up the biblical authors, or books, with regard to those from the Old Testament, the Apocrypha, and the New Testament (140). He labels the total span of each Testament as a "period" (139) or "epoch" (140). And he says that history "teaches us that there is a chronology and a geography to theology itself" (137). Under each of these aspects the New Testament is, in distinction to the Old Testament, at the end of the historical lineage. It is "newer."

Is it for this reason also "better"? This is what Gabler also says (139). However, neither logic nor the total concept of Gabler's lecture indicates that the New Testament is better because it is newer. It is better for other, clearly stated reasons. Should Gabler imply that its qualitative superiority is also observable historically, he would do better to address the question why this is so. Whether he might then refer to the philosophical idea of a qualitatively ascending history or, e.g., to the letter to the Hebrews, makes little difference. In each case, the judgment that the final stage is better than the former stages depends on the comparison of *what* it is in the total development that is better than something else, rather than on the assumption that the end of this development is automatically and self-evidently better because it is its end. Indeed, what is better may very well be older, as Gabler himself knows from the development of the doctrine of the Christian religion after the New Testament epoch, even as he speaks about the fate of this doctrine in the history represented by Lutheran theologians (136), and in his current situation.

At any rate, whether Gabler implies a historically observable qualitative superiority or not, he does not discuss the questions of why and on what grounds this kind of superiority should — or should not — be observed. He would have to address and explain these questions especially if he assumes that the New Testament is better because it is newer. Gabler's lecture shows at several points that he passes up questions of which everyone is aware because they are not relevant for the advancement of his own argument. The fact that he does not discuss the obvious question resulting from his "newer and better" formula indicates that the question does not lie in the line of the argument which he pursues. The actual reason why Gabler calls the New Testament "newer and better" is not derived from a presumably necessary comparison of the qualitative and the chronological aspects. It is derived from his fundamental assumption of the nature of the Christian religion of salvation. This assumption causes him to distinguish not only between the two Testaments but also between the temporal and eternal religious aspects in the New Testament itself. Therefore, one cannot say that the criterion for Gabler's theological distinctions rests on nothing but his distinction of the two Testaments. The criterion for his basic distinction in the two Testaments is the separation of the era-restricted from the eternal and, hence, of the human from the divine. Under this criterion, parts of the New Testament are just as much not "for us" as the Old Testament. In this regard, parts of the New Testament belong theologically together with the Old Testament, which appears as a specific reason why the two Testaments belong together in a biblical theology.

What does it mean, however, that Gabler, when speaking about the two Testaments, differentiates between two parts within the New Testament while not applying the same kind of differentiation to the Old Testament? And what does it mean for his concept of "biblical" theology? A first, important, indication is given when he says that not all attest to "the same form of religion" (139) *(eadem religionis forma).* "Form," or "formula," of religion may also refer to era-restricted forms found in both Testaments. In immediate context, however, he applies the two terms, especially the term "form," to his basic distinction between the religions of the Old and the New Testament. Even as the New Testament contains the era-restricted form, too, there is still a basic difference: the New Testament is distinguished as a whole from the whole of the Old Testament because everything in the New Testament, including its era-restricted forms, reflects the Christian religion. This is not the case with the Old Testament. Although some notions in the New Testament are era-restricted and others eternal, both kinds are still Christian. Their difference means only that the Christian religion of salvation applies itself to concretization in historical, not repeatable, eras without, however, losing its character as the religion for all times and places. Even those concretizations that are not for all times emerge from, and are controlled by, the basic criterion for the Christian religion.

By contrast, the Old Testament's religious forms are not only altogether era-restricted — unless Gabler assumes exceptions for which he gives no indication — they are altogether non-Christian. They appear as more relativized. One cannot escape the conclusion that the distinction between what is and is not Christian in the sacred Scriptures is more fundamental for Gabler than his distinction between the divine and the human. At the very least, this conclusion is a basic consequence of his understanding of the nature of the Christian religion.

Gabler does not discuss the implications of what he says in his lecture about the relation of the two Testaments. This silence reflects the basically unresolved question of their relationship in the Christian tradition. This unresolved question has persisted since the rejection of Marcion's position, and the subsequent achievement of a consensus according to which the two Testaments belong together under the umbrella of the Christian Bible, without, however, a definitive explanation of the nature of their relationship. Gabler's explicit and implicit statements show that, precisely because of his biblical theology, this explanation is an urgent task. The question is, therefore, not whether or not he intended two separate theologies, one of the Old and one of the New Testament, but whether or not his concept of biblical theology leads to exactly this same unresolved consequence. A positive answer to this question can scarcely be denied. And the reason for it is not the historical perspective about the older Old Testament followed by the "newer" New Testament. It is intrinsically theological in nature. Nor are the two stages of his method, taken separately, a sufficient basis for two separate theologies of the two Testaments. Whereas an Old Testament theology could conceivably be executed on the basis of the first stage, but not also — without being prejudged by the Christian vantage point — on the basis of the second stage, a New Testament theology would require both stages of Gabler's method. But such a scenario would totally transform Gabler's concept and method. If anything, he proposes both stages for the study of both Testaments. In his "biblical" theology, whether intended or not, he uses the two Testaments inseparably in order to demonstrate, through the separate form of religion in the New Testament, the separate form of religion in the Old Testament. The fact that the method for his program does not lend itself to two separate theologies of the Bible does not change the conclusion that his concept consequently implies this separation, though under a different construct. Whether or not such separation, apart from Gabler's concept and apart from an appropriate construct for it, is advisable, is an entirely different question.

4. History and the Historical

Does Gabler's lecture show that his biblical theology, and the method for it, are designed as a history of biblical ideas? Or does it show, or ever prove, that it and the method for it are designed as a systematized typology of the biblical doctrines derived from historical-critical exegesis?

For the former assumption, evidence would have to be found for a system that describes and explains the continuities and discontinuities in a forward-moving historical process, be it a progress of ascending or a regress of declining ideas, or an alternation of both. The lecture would have to show a focus on questions such as: How and why are individual events, persons, ideas, eras, and periods or epochs linked in the transition from one to the other? And how can their total process be described and explained? It would have to focus on the linkages in the transitions of the individually described historical links. This methodological requirement presupposes the determination of each link but, rather than stopping when this task is completed, proceeds thence to describing and explaining their linkages, transitions, and trajectories.

In such a method, explicit attention would have to be paid not only to the movement of the total history of the eras and epochs under discussion, analogous to what Herder did a few years before Gabler's lecture, but also especially to a well-organized understanding of the historical succession of the biblical authors about whom and "their" books about which Gabler speaks so often. In order to establish a history of the biblical ideas found in the books, a history of the biblical literature would be required in Gabler's program itself, rather than as a direct offshoot from it after him. This requirement would be the obvious condition for developing the history of its ideas out of a history of the biblical literature. By contrast, a method designed to show only the distinctiveness of each link and its distinction from the others would not fulfill the required purpose. It would rather reveal the opposite; namely, the intention to determine the individual links for the purpose of comparing the ideas with each other directly, rather than in terms of their historical process. And attention to the chronological placement of the ideas in history would amount to the necessary determination of their historical specificity rather than, at least not by definition, to a chronologically based construction of their history.

If Gabler's biblical theology and the method for it were designed as a systematized typology of biblical ideas or doctrines derived by historical-critical exegesis, evidence would have to be found for a system that uses the determination of the historical distinctiveness of each idea. Its analysis would follow the presumed chronological order of their appearance, but its purpose would be to gather, arrange, and compare the particular concepts or doctrines themselves with the goal of establishing an either descriptively or evaluatively differentiating system of those ideas. This system is considered historical rather than being abstracted from history, and amounts to a typology of these ideas themselves rather than their historical process and development.

The so-called historical-critical method would be used to achieve this objective with respect to all conditions relevant for its objectified, differentiated, and distinct recognition. And while it may also be used for different objectives such as, e.g., the reconstruction of a history, or of history, or the history of the biblical ideas, its employment in no way means that its only function and objective are the reconstruction of history. If the categories of history and the work typical of historical investigation are collapsed into the same meaning, there truly is a "bad mixture" of both categories which prevents any clarification of *what* is to be achieved *with or through what* at the outset. A formulation interpreting Gabler's lecture by saying that he establishes biblical theology as a historical discipline is correct. But to conclude that he, by virtue of this fact, establishes it as a history of ideas is indefensible. Such a conclusion would have to be drawn from the subject and object under investigation, but not from the method for that investigation.

It is obvious that Gabler proposes neither a history of the biblical times nor a history of the biblical literature. He proposes a biblical theology. And he refers to the sacred authors in order to focus on their ideas. To whatever extent he might have meant a history, he could only have meant a history of — historical — ideas. The question is, then, if his lecture points to this meaning.

In his introduction, in which he defines the issues — the consensus of Christians and the four reasons for its collapse — the issue of history is not mentioned, neither as the particular aspect for the recognition of the Bible as the source of the Christian religion nor as one of the particular reasons for the collapse of "a solid understanding of divine matters" (134). Since this introduction sets up the framework and direction of his entire lecture, the question arises why he does not immediately highlight the category of history, if he sees the recovery of the Christian consensus from its malaise in a biblical theology of the history of the Bible's sacred ideas.

Nevertheless, Gabler indicates his awareness of history and speaks, however infrequently compared with whatever else he says, of history, chronology, and geography. And his references to the two epochs or periods, more than his references to restricted eras, demonstrate his clear picture of the order in their temporal sequence. His list of the biblical "patriarchs," too, followed by his reference to the "apocryphal books" — identified neither in terms of authors nor in terms of books, let alone in terms of their own historical sequence, but only as the category between the Old and New Testaments — concludes with the names of Jesus and the major assumed authors of the New Testament's doctrines. This total listing shows that it is not unrelated to Gabler's awareness of the place of these persons and the Apocrypha in general in the flow of history. The same must be assumed for his intention to determine the ideas of the individual authors and their books as specifically as possible, including the relation of the universal notions to them in accordance with their particular eras, testaments, places of origin, and personal genius.

All these references are exclusively found within his discussion of the first stage of his system of biblical theology, and not in the quite different discussions of his introduction, his second stage, and his conclusion. It is not surprising that the interpreters who view Gabler as separating biblical from dogmatic theology by proposing a history of the biblical ideas have referred to Gabler's first stage alone. What is surprising is that they ignore the *interpretation* of, rather than the mere repetition of, his introduction, and declare his second stage to be a mediating or double-faced thing between biblical and dogmatic theology, which has nothing to do with the independence of a historically based biblical theology. The isolation of this first stage from his total lecture is a decisive precondition for the possibility that Gabler might have proposed a system of theological history rather than, and despite all evidence to this alternative, a typologized system of the biblical ideas, concepts, and doctrines, also in this first stage itself.

One of the main causes, if not the main one, for saying that he proposes a history of ideas is the opening sentence to his discussion of the first stage:

> There is truly a biblical theology, of the historical genre, conveying what the holy writers thought about divine matters; by contrast, there is a dogmatic theology, of the didactic genre, teaching what each theologian philosophizes rationally about divine things, according to the measure of his ability or of the times, age, place, sect, school, and other similar factors. . . . (137) (*Est vero theologia biblica e genere historico, tradens, quid scriptores sacri de rebus divinis senserint; theologia contra dogmatica e genere didactico, docens, quid* . . . , 183-84)

Many have focused their interpretation of this statement on the expression of *genus historicum,* and that biblical theology of this *genus* has a "conveying" function. The consequence of this focus is to understand the *genus historicum* as conveying, i.e., transmitting, history. The particular subject this theology transmits is the history of the biblical ideas. This conclusion is drawn from Gabler's definition of the *genre* of biblical theology in complete disregard of what Gabler himself immediately defines as the subject — or the grammatical object — of what is conveyed through this genre of biblical theology: ". . . what the holy writers thought about divine matters." The subject is not what they thought about the *history* of the thoughts about these matters. According to Gabler, the biblical theology conveys through its historical genre the biblical authors' thoughts themselves — yes, they are humans — not something else about those thoughts, namely, their history.

Consequently, the term "conveying" *(tradens)* has been interpreted as referring to conveying the tradition history, or the history of the transmission of the ideas. But the fact of transmission or conveyance says nothing about the subject which — or grammatical object of what — is conveyed or transmitted. Again, Gabler defines this subject specifically, and his definition does not point to the history of the ideas. Had he had their history in mind, his programmatic definition would have missed this clearly necessary distinction at the outset. Yet unless there is proof that his definition represents an ill-considered formulation, the total definition cannot be taken as an implicit let alone self-evident sign for a proposal of a history of the biblical ideas. Indeed, his definition is well considered. It is in accord with his focus on a system of ideas themselves, or on a system of doctrines.

What, then, does Gabler's usage of the words *genus* ("genre"), *historicus* ("historical"), and *tradere* ("to transmit") mean? "Genre" refers to the — actually literary — kind of activity that is generally recognized as typical. A "historical genre" specifies the general type of this activity in the sense that it is involved in the interpretation of data which are historical in nature. The content of these data may be history or anything else, or the data may be investigated with respect to a matter of particular interest. Decisive is the fact that the investigation, in accordance with the historical genre, happens in accordance with the historical nature of the available data. It submits to these existing data and is bound to transmit or convey them as reliably as possible for what they say and reveal. To whatever extent it also teaches, it first of all teaches by conveying the information contained in the data. But neither the act of conveying nor the act of teaching can change the available source of information. That source is given, exists, and cannot be changed. The historical genre in which something is conveyed or transmitted is, therefore, that kind of activity which interprets data, or sources, with respect to their own unchangeable existence. The actual interpretations of these sources may have to change if they are insufficient, specifically because of the unchanging nature of the sources themselves. But the changes in interpretation do not change the sources for it; these sources are always the same and therefore fixed and stable.

In this sense, for Gabler the sacred Scriptures are given, fixed, stable, unchangeable, always the same, and in accordance with themselves. And the execution of biblical theology in accordance with the historical genre has to convey or transmit as reliably — and "cautiously" — as possible what can be gained from these always stable sources. Unless these sources are presumed to be always the same, the sacred books cannot possibly be the "one clear source" for the true recognition — not of a history of their ideas but — of the "Christian religion," "the only secure sanctuary in the face of the ambiguity and vicissitude of human knowledge," and of the aspiration "to a solid understanding of divine matters," as well as of the wish "to obtain a firm and certain hope of salvation" (134). For these reasons, biblical theology in all its stages must reflect, be congruous, or be complementary to the stability of the biblical books by being stable itself. And not coincidentally, Gabler says at the end of his lecture that biblical theology itself — and by now certainly including its second stage — "remains the same" and "is not made to accommodate our point of view" (144). In his concept, the two stages belong intrinsically together, the first being designed for the second, and the second presupposing the first. Both, not only the first, are subject to the historical genre. This genre is indispensable for his total program; indeed, it is especially indispensable for its second stage because this is where "the proper and provable connexion and order of doctrines that are truly divine" will have to stand out on the "firmly established foundations of biblical theology" (144). Lastly, it becomes clear why the historical genre is decisive for Gabler. It is not decisive because he, too, has learned a lot about historical-critical exegesis and the inevitability of attention to it if a person wanted to be a legitimate biblical scholar. It is decisive because it is *the* genre through which the truly divine nature of the Christian religion for all places and times could be recovered and solidly ascertained. The "historical genre" *(genus historicum)* has nothing to do with a "genre of history" *(genus historiae)*.

In order to check this interpretation against possible evidence in favor of a history of ideas concept, two important aspects from Gabler's lecture may be evaluated. One concerns his already-mentioned list of the biblical authors and books; the other concerns the function of his discussion of the eras.

Gabler's list of the biblical authors has been, and may be, taken as evidence for a program about the history of the biblical ideas: from Moses to David to Solomon to Isaiah to Jeremiah to Ezekiel to Daniel to Hosea to Zechariah to Haggai to Malachi "and the rest," and on via the Apocrypha to Jesus to Paul to Peter to John and to James (140). A history of ideas from Moses to James! Clearly, this list shows that he is aware of a chain in historical sequence in general. One also must grant that he had at his disposal no definitive knowledge of the historical sequence of the biblical "authors" or "books." However, if he ever intended to conceptualize his theology as a *history* of the biblical authors and their ideas under the strict exegetical conditions self-imposed for his program, he must have been perfectly familiar with some factors that everyone knew and especially with exegetical results which at his time had virtually become irrefutable, such as, e.g.:

a. that Hosea is placed after not only Daniel but also Jeremiah and Ezekiel. This place reflects the canonical sequence of the books, not the historical sequence of the authors.
b. that Zechariah and Haggai follow in Gabler's list neither the historical nor the canonical sequence.

Finally, he must have something other than history in mind when he refers to all other biblical authors as "the rest" (140).

The method for the order is different in his New Testament list; here he singles out Jesus, Paul, Peter, John, and James. The following must have been clear to Gabler:

a. Jesus is not the author of the books from Matthew to Luke. Also, Jesus is just as much the focal person in the Gospel of John as he is in these books. He comes first because his person and doctrine are the issue of the Synoptic Gospels.
b. The sequence "Paul, Peter, John, and James" does not reflect in principle the canonical sequence of "their" books. One might suspect that their sequence reflects Gabler's understanding of a historical sequence. Yet it is at least doubtful that he has a distinct opinion of the literary-historical sequence of their books. His conceptual basis for lining them up the way he does must be seen in something else, namely, in the differences between the doctrines of these books. His focus on their doctrines, not on their history, explains why Jesus comes first, Paul second (!), followed by Peter and John, and ending with James (!). Their order is arranged according to the main and different New Testament doctrines, in part even according to the order of their importance in the Lutheran tradition.

The focus on the doctrines also appears as the reason for his summary reference to the Apocrypha. They are useful but of little significance with respect to doctrine — so in the Protestant tradition.

If Gabler intends to establish a theology of the history of the biblical authors and books, he has — even without making an explicit point of this intention in his lecture — an outstanding opportunity to demonstrate his intention with the authors named in this very list. Yet if he has this intention, he does just about everything possible to conceal it in this list. And we have not even mentioned that Gabler, had he had this intention, had in his time to know that when talking about the five books of Moses and their author(s), he could no longer say nothing but "Moses." His list does not point to a history of the Bible's ideas. It points to their distinction from each other for the purpose of setting up their own comparison.

What is the function of Gabler's discussion of the eras? He nowhere indicates that he wants to identify them individually in order to use them as links for the construction of their linkage in a historically forward-moving chain of biblical ideas, for the construction of their own conveyance or transmission of ideas, from one stage to another. Had he had this function for them in mind, he would not only have had to say it; the conceptualization of his total program would have had to be very different. Of such a concept, nothing is in sight. There is good reason for the absence of such an intent: Gabler needs the individual determination of the ideas and their eras, including the universal ideas, in order to distinguish and lastly even separate them from each other according to their religious types so that these types may be compared. He does not need their isolation from each other in order to connect them into a history of ideas. *He wants to establish a biblical theology as a systematized typology of the religious ideas of the Bible, not abstracted from, but related to, their specific historical conditions, in order to establish through their substance-critical comparison, which is also served by the recognition of their historicity, the basis for the solid discernment of the Christian religion of salvation for all places and times in the sacred Scriptures.*

C. Assessment

For well-known reasons that have become ingrained in the Christian tradition of biblical theology, Gabler's name is remembered more than the name of any other theologian. These reasons, however, should be considered with differentiations. Gabler's program deserves neither to be wholly adopted as a basis for conceptualizing biblical theology, nor totally set aside, nor remembered solely because of our tendency to go back to the roots at the expense of the development following the roots. His program deserves to be considered as one among many. But its assessment depends on what it reveals to us rather than on whether it is the original one or is one among all others.

The assessment centers around four aspects: (1) The program's affirmation of the independence of biblical from dogmatic or systematic theology, (2) its aim as a system, (3) the role of the universal notions in it, and (4) the relation of the two testaments in such a biblical theology.

1. Independence from Dogmatic Theology

As a program for biblical theology which is independent of dogmatic or systematic theology, Gabler's program has integrity. This judgment is based on the evidence that it can be executed on the basis of what is observable in the biblical books alone, indeed what must not be ignored in them. The fact that the same theological judgments in the program also exist in dogmatic or systematic theology does not mean that the program is for that reason derived from those disciplines. Should the results of its interpretation in this study be sustainable, they also indicate that Gabler's program, while on occasion using categories from history and philosophy, and especially the method of both technical and substantive historical-critical exegesis, depends on inner-biblical theological aspects derived substance-critically rather than on the substance-critical presuppositions drawn from those categories or methods.

Gabler's use of historical-critical exegesis, the historical genre of investigation, stands clearly in the service of the theological vantage point and objective of his biblical theology. With respect to the question of which of these two factors depends on the other, if the integrity of either has to be considered compromised, it is the subservience of critical exegesis to theology rather than the subservience of the theological concept to critical exegesis. Gabler's contention that the final result of his biblical theology is the provable outcome from the employment of the particular procedure, for which the exegetical method — and not only this method — is used and which he so assuredly declares to be the clear and certain road toward that outcome, is indefensible.

Gabler's theological position also controls those aspects of history which he uses. There is no evidence that a certain concept of history predetermined his theological vantage point and objective. If he ever had a history of the biblical ideas in mind, his lecture not only reveals no explicit articulation of the requirements for such a program, the explicit presuppositions of his lecture would directly conflict with these requirements. His program would then be fundamentally self-contradictory. This, however, is not the case.

His adoption of the philosophical category of the universal notions is equally subject to his theological criterion. They are used for and serve that goal. Their application changes nothing about that criterion, neither its goal nor its result. This judgment has nothing to do with the question whether or not the universal notions are by themselves an appropriate philosophical or biblical category. In either case, for Gabler they are helpful because they serve his theological objective.

The integrity of Gabler's program rests on its inner-biblical foundation, a criterion that must be distinguished from the tradition of the maxim — especially in Protestant churches — that the Bible, if not separated from the church's doctrine, has nevertheless priority over it even to the extent that it is authoritative when contradicting that doctrine. With regard to this maxim in that tradition, Gabler says not only nothing new but he executes it, whereby the question whether he separates biblical theology more than he distinguishes it from dogmatics is relative, because he certainly does not want to replace dogmatics with biblical theology.

The criterion for Gabler's biblical theology must also be distinguished from the fact that it clearly stands on the shoulders of similar programs before his which had the same intention. The independence of his program is not valid or invalid, or more or less valid, because of that fact. The integrity of its own argument is just as separate from the programs of others as his biblical theology is separate from dogmatics.

Furthermore, the main reason why Gabler subsequently was considered as having established the independence of biblical theology was, ironically, a wrong one: because he conceptualized it as a theology of the history of biblical ideas in contrast to the focus on doctrines by dogmatics. Inasmuch as Gabler's lasting influence rests on this claim, his influence is groundless because the claim is groundless. The integrity of Gabler's program in its subsequent interpretation depends neither on its misunderstanding nor on its correct interpretation. It depends on what it reveals — in any adequate interpretation according to the historical genre — on its own terms.

Finally, the integrity of this program is unrelated to the question of how the relationship between biblical theology and church doctrine is understood. Whether certain churches consider the Bible as separate from church doctrine or as having priority over it, or whether other churches speak of Bible *and* (the) tradition (of the church's) doctrine, in neither case are both collapsed into one and the same. In each case, the two are distinguished, regardless how their relationship is determined. To this extent, the Bible and biblical theology are distinguishable from anything else.

2. *Aiming at a System*

Gabler aims at a system of biblical theology. The establishment of this system as a whole in its two stages rests on the unchangeability of the existing biblical sources — to which one will have to add: the unchangeability of whatever sources are in existence! — and, hence, on the stability of biblical theology inasmuch as it is required to interpret the sources in accordance with the rules that are commensurate with the controllable conveyance of these sources. Already in this respect, Gabler's biblical theology is systemic, and coherent.

Its systemic nature appears distinctly, however, where Gabler's method clearly distinguishes between the exegetical task and the task of systematizing the exegetical results. Exegesis conveys what the texts themselves say or presuppose. To gather, arrange, and compare these results amounts to the conveyance of more than only what the texts themselves say or convey. It amounts to a different kind of conveyance; namely, to the conveying work of the interpreter, which has not been done by the biblical writers. This work must be done, so to say, in the Bible's own interest, or the interpretation of the Scriptures is controlled by the predispositions of their readers alone and without the Scriptures' chance to reveal their own distinctions and priorities, or at least with their own part in the encounter between them and their readers. Yet indispensable as this work is, so that biblical theology serves the recognition of the "truly divine doctrine," a recognition not achievable by exegesis alone and which "is not made to accommodate our point of view" (144), this work of the interpreters is not only the extension of exegesis but is also controlled by the exegetical evidence — so Gabler. The fact that the exegetical process and evidence unquestionably confirm nothing but Gabler's result is, however, more than doubtful. And precisely the objection to his result on the basis of his own exegetical requirement for its achievement shows that the systematization of the exegetical results is not only necessary but that the demand for it is, in principle, also correct.

In any event, an objection to the necessity of systematization on the grounds that the interpreter should not do anything that has not been done in the Scriptures themselves fails to realize four important points: (a) Exegesis and biblical theology do not belong to the same genre. (b) Exegesis cannot replace but must lead to biblical theology. (c) Already the exegesis of texts itself indispensably involves the interpreter's own systematization of their meaning. (d) The reliability of both exegesis and biblical theology depends on whether or not interpretation reflects the Scriptures' own side in the encounter in a self-distantiated way, rather than whether or not the interpreter systematizes what the Scriptures themselves do not. Gabler was not the first, but he, too, knew what should still be known by everyone today. And the fact that the biblical texts and books are highly systematized compositions themselves has not even been emphasized.

In the history of biblical interpretation, especially in the history of the disciplines of biblical, Old, or New Testament theology, there has never been any publication that was not systematized in one way or another. One may question the conceptual shape of each of these systematizations but contestation of a theology's particular system proves neither the invalidity of systematization nor the sufficiency of exegesis — and exegetical commentaries — alone.

The inevitability of systematization also remains unaffected by the discussion whether — in terms of the understanding of Gabler's program — biblical theology would be conceived as a history of ideas or as a typology of historically related or even unrelated doctrines. Each of these concepts is systematized, or it would not be possible. Finally, systematized biblical theology is not invalid because dogmatic, or systematic, theology systematizes, too. The type of activity common to both has nothing to do with the different objects that must be systematized and certainly nothing to do with the intrusion of any ecclesiastic authority and its own hierarchized hermeneutic. If there is any unclarity about the role of systematization in the discipline of biblical theology, the clarity about it in Gabler's program alone is sufficient evidence for our inability to escape from it until today.

3. The Universal Notions

Gabler's focus on the universal notions might be seen as reflecting an understanding of the Bible in terms of doctrines abstracted from reality in general and from the existential human condition specifically. Such an understanding is scarcely appropriate. Doctrine is not necessarily abstract. For Gabler himself, the temporal doctrines to be identified must be embedded in the contingent or era-restricted realities of the biblical texts. They represent the thought systems of the texts, not abstractions from them. And his universal notions include the aspects of human individuality and existentiality. The doctrine of eternal salvation does not and never did mean that salvation aims at anything but the very existential condition of each human being. This condition is the condition from which universally each individual must be eternally saved.

It has been pointed out that Gabler's lecture is silent on the question of whether also the Old Testament contains universal notions which are not era-restricted, especially those that are also recognized by the New Testament as eternal. This silence compromises — at least in his lecture — the integrity of this category in his application of it to the Scriptures. But it has already been said that more is at stake.

The application of the universal notions by Gabler is irrelevant not because they cannot be taken as the indispensable criterion for deciding what is truly and what is not truly divine, but because they fail to clarify the relationship between univer*sality* and particu*larity* on the one hand and universa*lism* and particula*rism* on the other hand. All these aspects are found in the Scriptures. That "the universal notions" are a questionable category does not mean that the aspect of universality is irrelevant in biblical theology. In fact, it is one of the fundamental aspects of both Testaments. The only problem is whether this aspect is conceived universalistically or particularistically in the Scriptures. Universality that is subservient to particular interests, at the exclusion of the same validity universally, represents a particularistic ideology which, especially when adopted religiously and theologically, functions for the submission of what is universally valid to the legitimation of exclusive self-interests — be it by individuals, groups, nations, societies, churches, or other religions — and at the expense of the right of all others to the same interests. If universality is considered universal equally, it represents a legitimate universalistic stance which is precisely applicable to any particular condition because it is valid universally. By comparison, a particular condition is ideologized particularistically if it is considered at the exclusion of the same validity for all else. But it may be universalistic if it lends itself to being universalized by virtue of the fact that it is universally valid.

For instance, the long-standing and widespread argument by Christian, including biblical, theologians which says nothing else than that the Old Testament, in contrast to the New Testament, is based on the particularistic concept of Israel's election, people, and land, is, in light of what has just been said, beside the point. This argument ignores the distinction between particularism and particularity. True, the Old Testament is, though not everywhere — e.g., in much of the wisdom literature — particularly concerned with Israel's election, people, and land. However, where this concern reflects a particularistic paradigm for the exclusivity of Israel's election, at the expense of the election equally of all, and where it reflects a universalistic paradigm of Israel's election, as a sign of the equal election of all, is a question not yet addressed, let alone answered, by this long-standing and widespread Christian argument. The clarification of this question seriously affects the understanding of the relationship between God and the totality of the world in the Bible and theology.

As long as biblical exegesis and theology do not clarify, nor even clearly address, this question and do not operate with these distinctions, little matters.

However, when these distinctions are applied to the Scriptures, the result about what is theologically valid and invalid, or more valid than something else, will be very different from the result Gabler's lecture gains through the use of his "universal notions." His category fails, in this respect, to get to the heart of the problem, and must be abolished especially for this reason.

4. The Two Testaments and Biblical Theology

Gabler's lecture shows that he speaks of a biblical theology of both Testaments. It also shows why he considers the New Testament as a whole to be "better" than the whole of the Old Testament. The Old Testament's time not only consists of restricted eras, it is a restricted epoch in contrast to the epoch of the New Testament's time, which basically consists of the trans-historical Christian religion and its applicability to restricted eras. And, of course, the New Testament epoch is newer than that of the more elementary — an ambivalent term — epoch of the Old Testament. The lecture also shows that, in speaking of a "biblical" theology, he does not speak of two separate theologies, one for the Old and one for the New Testament.

For a variety of reasons, it is important that we distinguish between what is explicit in Gabler's lecture and what may or must be inferred by us about its own implications regardless whether Gabler saw these implications or not. We can only interpret what his lecture, not what Gabler himself, implies. As far as his lecture is concerned, it only shows that both Testaments belong, without discussion, to one biblical theology. Whether, as a consequence of his understanding of their difference, Gabler would have advocated two theologies of the separate Testaments or their correlation in one biblical theology, we do not know. In his lecture, this question does not exist. The fact that this question, rather than being advocated in one way or another, is nonexistent in the lecture — and one may for this reason say: for Gabler — means that the lecture implies consequences of what it says about the relationship of the two Testaments despite its silence about such consequences.

These consequences gravitate around the alternative between the transformation of the inherited Christian tradition of the combined Testaments into a united biblical theology which is conceptualized programmatically, and the transformation of that tradition into a programmatic separation of the Old and New Testament theologies. In either case, the question of the relationship of the two Testaments, which was not resolved by the inherited Christian tradition, must be addressed programmatically. This is precisely because the issue of the theology of the Christian Bible is programmatically addressed in Gabler's lecture, and because the lecture leaves no doubt as to how, by comparison, the Christian religion for all times in the New Testament as well as the religion of the Old Testament is to be understood.

What would the consequence be for the program of a united biblical theology?

Since Gabler's program for his biblical theology is derived from the theological criterion of the specific nature of the Christian religion, a first programmatic consequence would have to be that for such a theology, the relation of the two Testaments must be determined on the basis of his, or the lecture's, *theological* criterion rather than on the basis of the historical sequence of the two Testaments, even if that sequence were considered as a theological criterion itself. For such a theology, the historical sequence of the two Testaments could not be the criterion for determining their relationship theologically. Even if this historical sequence would be considered as the theological criterion itself it would, according to Gabler's lecture, still be subject to the substance-critical question of why the newer is better. The answer to this question lies in the specific substance of the doctrine of the Christian religion, which is the criterion for this historical religion itself as well as for the religion of the Old Testament, but not because of its "advanced," compared to the less advanced, place of the Old Testament in the process of history.

Gabler's program implies that the substance-critical aspect of the specific nature of the Christian religion is not only the criterion for determining the relationship of the two Testaments but also for saying that this relationship is not determined by the fact of the history of their religious development. This does not mean that a history of religion concept would not also be viable. But it does mean that such an approach would be subject to adjudication by the comparison of the different religious doctrines emerging during that history. Whether it is ironic or not, in the development following Gabler, and with Gabler as the crowning witness, the two Testaments have been kept united on the basis of the history of religion program at the cost of the subordination — to whatever extent it played a role at all — of Gabler's decisive criterion for his program. Gabler's lecture does not exclude the possibility of a religio-historical approach, but it would also focus on the criterion for recognizing the truth of the Christian religion in such an approach and, hence, on something different from the approach itself. The lecture does not address the question of the relationship between a biblical theology and a biblical history of religion. Rather, it focuses on the biblical doctrines which may be used to recognize the religious differences in the Bible. It is, in this sense, not only biblical theology but theology in the strict sense of the word. The insufficient attention to this focus in the discussion following Gabler is, then, most probably the major reason why the concept for an originally still united biblical theology could shift from Gabler's theological criterion to the history of the biblical religion approach as the criterion. Lastly, it is probably the reason why the theologies of the two Testaments were separated on the basis of their historical sequence.

Gabler's united biblical theology rests on different grounds, and the consequences to be drawn from those grounds amount to the conclusion that, theologically, the religion of the Old Testament belongs specifically to the Christian religion in the New Testament because it contributes to demonstrating that the New Testament as such is better and that, especially when confronted with the ultimate

Christian religion, its own religion is different. It demonstrates to Christians what is not "for us" and, hence, also what are not "the sacred Christian [things]" (134) (*Christiani sacri,* 180). Compared with the Christian religion, the Old Testament religion not only belongs to the past. It is passed.

This conclusion from Gabler's theological criterion for a united biblical theology — whether Gabler himself sees it or not — is not weakened by his own recognition of the divine revelation in past eras, however restricted this revelation was to those eras. It still means that it was valid for those eras only and is precisely for this reason no longer valid "for us." This theological criterion replaces the religio-historically based recognition of the validity of divine revelation germane to its historical eras. Bultmann, to mention the foremost representative of this position during the past generation, may or may not have thought about Gabler. He represents the position to which the consequence of Gabler's position leads.

One may object, saying that Gabler only speaks positively about the era-restricted doctrines of the Old Testament and does not say that they represent a religion alien to the Christian religion. However, this objection only shows that Gabler does not draw the full consequences from his biblical-theological stance. Had he said what this stance finally means, he would still have had to arrive at the conclusion which says that this religion is not "for us" because only the specific Christian religion of salvation for all times and places is "for us." It is precisely his *theological* criterion that makes this conclusion inevitable, and regardless whether one calls the Old Testament religion alien or not.

This conclusion is intensified by the fact that Gabler's biblical theology is actually what we call a biblical hermeneutic. By saying "for us," his method for an objectified construct of the biblical theology grounded in the Scriptures alone is, at the same time, intrinsically related to the relevance of the biblical truth for us. What is not relevant for us in terms of eternal salvation is passed up in biblical theology and, hence, functions in the Scriptures as a doctrine that demonstrates which divine revelations belong to the past. Consequently, the theological function of the Old Testament in Gabler's biblical theology can only be its role in this united theology as a testimony — in its own right! — about what the specific nature of the Christian religion is not, and to what "we" need not be pledged.

In light of this theological consequence from Gabler's concept, the question whether there should be a united biblical theology or two separate theologies of the two Testaments of the Christian Bible loses a programmatic urgency. As long as the two Testaments are considered as the two parts of the Christian Bible, and as long as their theological relationship is to be understood in light of the consequences of Gabler's program, the question is relative whether one executes a united biblical theology — which would not be united on the ground of the same doctrine — or two separate theologies for each of which, however, the substance-critical question of their relationship would have to be an a priori condition. As long as this condition would remain in focus and observed — and one cannot say that this is everywhere the case — the separation of the two theologies may be preferable because it would, for its theological rather than historical reason, signal that the substance-critical comparison of two essentially different theologies is at stake. Their separate existence would mean a warning against any understanding that a united biblical theology amounts to a, or the, unification or even harmonization of the Old and the New Testaments' doctrines.

One may for important reasons agree with some positions in Gabler's concept and disagree with others. However, unless one focuses on its decisive theological and hermeneutical presupposition, a critique of the relevance of this concept for the question of biblical theology is of little importance. When it comes to this focus, it is clear that the question of the theological determination of the relationship of the two Testaments receives center stage, and that in this question Gabler's position of the ultimate superiority of the specific doctrine of the Christian religion represents the criterion by which that relationship is predetermined. The critical problem, then, that must be addressed is whether or not the position of the ultimate superiority of the Christian doctrine of eternal salvation represents the decisive and sole criterion for the adjudication of the relationship of the two Testaments. The critical problem is not only whether this question is raised and answered by biblical interpreters but whether the answer to it in the New Testament is the sole and decisive answer. The problem of the relationship of the two Testaments, in terms of both Gabler's and the New Testament's position, has to confront the question whether or not the New Testament position determines their relationship exclusively.

In light of this definition of the problem, the virtually universally accepted nod to the demand that the Old Testament must have the right and freedom to speak out on its own terms must be scrutinized as to its integrity. Since this demand granted by Christian scholars — it is irrelevant for Jewish scholars anyway in the discussion about the Christian Bible — has never been made apart from the question of the relationship of the two Testaments, it has meant that the Old Testament must be free to determine its relationship to the New Testament itself. By assessing the Old Testament's religion from the standpoint of the Christian religion in the New Testament, Gabler's position by no means implies, let alone says, that the Old Testament is therefore not free to determine its own identity. On the contrary, that is exactly what — by correct method! — the Old Testament is asked to do. The only condition is that it must define itself in comparison with the specific agenda set by the Christian religion. What else could it do, then, but in its own right and in perfect freedom say that it does not represent that same agenda of salvation for all times and places and, of course, the christological condition for it and, hence, humbly declare itself as passed? As long as the self-definition of the Old Testament is controlled by the specific self-definition of the Christian religion in the New Testament, the Old Testament must in freedom give no different answer than the one also evolving from Gabler's program. It must give religious, theologically objectified witness, just as the Jewish people were expected to do, that its faith is inferior if not wrong because the Christian faith is right.

This situation changes when the formula changes under which the two Testaments define themselves without the self-definition of one of them being predicated by the formula of the other. Then, the question is what each means for the other, not only in terms of what it is lacking when compared with what the other does not lack, but also of what the other is lacking when compared with what is not lacking in it. This question amounts to the mutual encounter of the two Testaments on an open platform for their substance-critical comparison. On such a platform, the question will be raised whether the fact of salvation at all times and places, especially when considered in terms of the salvation of individual persons, is the sole decisive criterion for the recognition of the relationship between God and the world. Equally, the question will be raised whether the fact of the divine presence in this passing world and its eras is the sole criterion for recognizing the totality of all aspects involved with respect to the relationship of God and world. For this kind of question, Gabler's position provides no ground. Unless it can be shown that this question does not also spring forth from a systematization of the exegesis of both Testaments, Gabler's, and not only his, concept of biblical theology provides no foundation for a system of biblical theology, be it united or not.

Conclusion

Gabler's program for demarcating biblical from dogmatic theology is credible, especially in his own time. The same cannot be said for his design for biblical theology itself. The decisive reason for this negative conclusion lies in the irreconcilable conflict between his claim to total scholarly objectivity in the interpretation of all Scripture and his simultaneous a priori claim that the unique Christian doctrine of personal salvation expressed in the New Testament represents the decisive criterion for the evaluation of all other biblical doctrines. In the light of this doctrine, all other biblical doctrines, especially those of the whole Old Testament, appear to be passed, and not "for us." Any such a priori claim compromises and invalidates the claim of objective interpretation. But Gabler's lecture specifically reveals, especially regarding the Old Testament, that he sees no need for even mentioning, let alone comparing, important Old Testament doctrines vis-à-vis his decisive criterion. Yet these doctrines can by no means simply be passed. The same can also be said for the comparison of essential doctrines in the New Testament. The absence of such substantive discussion in this lecture is more than accidental or economical. It points to a preconceived judgment which is directly expressed in his statement about the two different epochs of religion. This judgment underlies the concept of his entire lecture. This judgment reflects the legacy of the total Christian tradition regarding the Old Testament from the time of the earliest Christian writings on. In this tradition, what was to become the Old Testament was, while acknowledged as sacred Scripture, never acknowledged as equal to what was to, and has, become the New Testament. Gabler is solidly imbedded within this legacy, and nothing in his scientific method shows that he has transcended it.

This legacy is also the basic reason why Gabler speaks about nothing more and nothing less than *biblical* theology, the theology of the total Christian Bible. Whereas we today, coming from a tradition of the separate theologies of the two Testaments, may and should move toward a biblical theology, Gabler does not propose a separation of the Old and the New Testaments' theologies apart from a biblical theology, let alone a specific Old Testament theology in its own right. He had no reason for such a proposal because of the legacy of the Christian tradition, in which the ultimacy of the revelation of Jesus Christ has been "proven" from its outset by contrasting it with — what therefore had to become — the penultimacy of the preceding revelations attested in the Hebrew Bible. Despite his clear distinction of the theologies of the two Testaments for the claimed scholarly reasons, Gabler keeps these theologies together in his biblical theology, for substance-critical reasons.

Gabler's approach to biblical theology, as any other, is fundamentally predetermined by the question of how the relationship of the two Testaments is conceptualized. As long as this approach remains prejudiced, as it has been for almost two millennia, by the unquestioned Christian claim that the criteria for theological ultimacy are contained in the New Testament, the Old Testament will always be a testimony to theological penultimacy at best. This will be so regardless of what it says in its own right, on its own terms, and regardless of the best exegetical scholarship with its theological systematization(s). In this case, we should correctly speak of a Christian biblical theology but no longer of a biblical theology. This Christian biblical theology may be intended for others as well as for Christians, even as it may and should for good reasons be advanced by Christians. Such a Christian biblical theology may be said to be sufficient for the confessional needs of Christians, but it cannot be granted the mark of scientific integrity as has been claimed before and after Gabler. Gabler's program belongs, together with virtually the total history of Christian interpretation of all Scripture and contrary to its claim to scientific objectivity, to the genre of apologetic theology. Basically the situation will only change when the two Testaments are interpreted independently of each other, with the goal of finding out, through substance-critical interpretation, what each contributes to the other critically as well as affirmatively. It stands to be argued that the findings from this basically different heuristic approach will lead to a very different, and new, understanding of the relationship of the two Testaments. It may well lead to new conceptualizations of the relationship between biblical concepts and to a systematizing biblical theology in which neither the Old nor the New Testament, neither the Jewish nor the Christian vantage point, is the criterion for the evaluation of the other, but in which the concepts and traditions of either are compared and in a critical synthesis transcended. It is this problem and the approach to it that lie, methodologically and in the various case studies, partly explicitly and partly implicitly, at the heart of the chapters in this volume.

Works Cited

Albrektson, B. *History and the Gods.* Coniectanea Biblica, OT Series 1. Lund: Gleerup, 1967.

Albertz, R., and C. Westermann. "רוח." *THAT* 2.726-53.

Altmann, A. "Articles of Faith." *Encyclopedia Judaica* 3 (1971): 654-60. New York: Macmillan.

Andersen, C. "Biographie." *Lexicon der Alten Welt,* 469-73. Zurich/Stuttgart: Artemis, 1965.

Anderson, B. *Creation versus Chaos.* New York: Association Press, 1967.

Andreasen, N. E. *The Old Testament Sabbath.* SBLDS, no. 7. Missoula, Mont.: University of Montana, 1972.

Baltzer, K. *Die Biographie der Propheten.* Neukirchen-Vluyn: Neukirchener Verlag, 1975.

Battenberg, F. *Das Europäische Zeitalter der Juden.* 2 vols. Darmstadt: Wissenschaftliche Buchgesellschaft, 1990.

Baumgärtel, F. "The Hermeneutical Problem of the Old Testament." In *EOTH,* ed. C. Westermann, 134-59. Richmond: John Knox, 1963.

———. *Verheissung.* Gütersloh: Bertelsmann, 1952.

Baumgarten, J. "Auf dem Weg zu grösserer wirtschaftlicher Gerechtigkeit. Der Beitrag des Neuen Testaments zur gegenwartigen wirtschaftsethischen Diskussion." *EvT* 53 (1993): 470-79.

Becker, J. *Gottesfurcht im Alten Testament.* AnBibl 25. Rome: Pontifical Biblical Institute, 1965.

Bergmann, J., and M. Ottosson. "ארץ." *TDOT* 1.388-405.

Bernhardt, K.-H. *Das Problem der altorientalischen Königsideologie im Alten Testament: unter besonderer Berücksightigung der Geschichte der Psalmenexegese dargestellt und kritisch gewürdigt.* VTSup 8. Leiden: E. J. Brill, 1961.

Bertholet, A. *Die Stellung der Israeliten und der Juden zu den Fremden.* Freiburg: J. C. B. Mohr, 1896.

Bertholet, A., et al. "Geist: 2. Geist und Geistesgaben im AT und Judentum." *Die Religion in Geschichte und Gegenwart.* Vol. 2. 2d ed. Tübingen: J. C. B. Mohr, 1928.

Bloch, E. *The Principle of Hope.* Trans. N. Plaice, S. Plaice, and P. Knight. Cambridge, Mass.: MIT Press, 1986. Originally published as *Das Prinzip Hoffnung* (Frankfurt am Main: Suhrkamp, 1959).

Blum, E. *Die Composition der Vätergeschichte.* WMANT 57. Neukirchen-Vluyn: Neukirchener Verlag, 1984.

———. *Studien zur Komposition des Pentateuch.* BZAW 189. Berlin: Walter de Gruyter, 1990.

Boers, H. *What Is New Testament Theology?* Guides to Biblical Scholarship: New Testament Series. Philadelphia: Fortress, 1979.

Boman, T. *Hebrew Thought Compared with Greek.* Trans. J. L. Moreau. Philadelphia: Westminster, 1960.

Boorer, S. *The Promise of the Land as Oath.* BZAW 205. Berlin: Walter de Gruyter, 1992.

Brueggeman, W. *The Land.* OBT 1. Philadelphia: Fortress, 1977.

Bultmann, R. "Prophecy and Fulfillment." In *EOTH,* ed. C. Westermann, 50-75. Richmond: John Knox, 1963.

———. "The Significance of the Old Testament for the Christian Faith." In *The Old Testament and the Christian Faith,* ed. B. Anderson, 8-35. New York: Harper & Row, 1963.

———. "δηλόω." *TDNT* 2.61-62.

———. "ἐλπίς." *TDNT* 2.517-23.

———, and D. Lührman. "φαίνω." *TDNT* 9.1-10.

Cazelles, H. "משה." *TWAT* 5.28-46.

Cazelles, H., A. Gelin et al. *Moïse, l'homme de l'alliance.* Paris: Desclée & Cie, 1955. Translated into German under the title *Moses in Schrift und Überlieferung.* Trans. F. Stier and E. Beck. Düsseldorf: Patmos, 1963.

Childs, B. S. *Biblical Theology in Crisis.* Philadelphia: Westminster, 1970.

———. *The Book of Exodus.* OTL. Philadelphia: Westminster, 1974.

———. *Introduction to the Old Testament as Scripture.* Philadelphia: Fortress, 1979.

———. *Myth and Reality in the Old Testament.* SBT 27. Naperville: A. R. Allenson, 1962.

———. "Some Reflections on the Search for a Biblical Theology." *HBT* 4 (June 1982): 1-12.

Clements, R. E. *God and Temple.* Philadelphia: Fortress, 1965.

———. *One Hundred Years of Old Testament Interpretation.* Philadelphia: Westminster, 1976.

Clifford, R. J. *The Cosmic Mountain in Canaan and the Old Testament.* Cambridge, Mass.: Harvard University Press, 1972.

Coats, G. W. Genesis: *With an Introduction to Narrative Literature.* FOTL 1. Grand Rapids: Eerdmans, 1983.

Cohn, R. L. *The Shape of Sacred Space: Four Biblical Studies.* Chico, Calif.: Scholars Press, 1981.

Conzelmann, H. *Die Mitte der Zeit.* BHT 17. Tübingen: J. C. B. Mohr, 1960.

Dahood, M. *Psalms I, 1–50.* AB. Garden City, N.Y.: Doubleday, 1966.

Dalman, G. *Arbeit und Sitte in Palästina.* 7 vols. Gütersloh: C. Bertelsmann, 1928-42.

Davies, W. D. *The Gospel and the Land.* Berkeley: University of California Press, 1974.

Dentan, R. C. *The Idea of History in the Ancient Near East.* 4th ed. New Haven: Yale University Press, 1967.

———, ed. *Preface to Old Testament Theology.* Rev. ed. New York: Seabury, 1963.

Descamps, A. "Réflexions sur la Méthode en Théologie Biblique." In *Sacra Pagina,* ed. J. Coppens et al., vol. 1, 132-57. BETL 12-13. Gembloux: J. Duculot, 1959.

Deschner, K. *Kriminal-Geschichte des Christentums.* Vols. 1-2. Hamburg: Rowohlt, 1986-89.

DeVries, S. J. *The Achievements of Biblical Religion: A Prolegomenon to Old Testament Theology.* Lanham, Md.: University Press of America, 1983.

Diepold, P. *Israels Land.* BWANT 95. Stuttgart: W. Kohlhammer, 1972.

Dunn, J. D. G. "Levels of Canonical Authority." *HBT* 4 (June 1982): 13-60.

Durham, J. *Exodus.* WBC 3. Waco, Tex.: Word Books, 1987.

Ebach, J. *Das Erbe der Gewalt: eine biblische Realität un ihre Wirkungsgeschichte.* Gütersloh: Gerd Mohn, 1980.

Eckert, W., N. P. Levinson, and M. Stöhr, eds. *Jüdisches Volk-gelobtes Land.* Abhandlungen zum christlich-jüdischen Dialog, vol. 3. Munich: Chr. Kaiser, 1970.

Eichrodt, W. *Theology of the Old Testament.* Trans. J. A. Baker. 2 vols. Philadelphia: Westminster, 1961.

Eliade, M. *Cosmos and History.* New York: Harper & Row, 1959.

———. *The Sacred and the Profane: The Nature of Religion.* Trans. W. R. Trask. New York: Harcourt, Brace & Co., 1959.

Fabry, H.-J. "לב." *TWAT* 4.413-51.

Frankfort, H., et al. *The Intellectual Adventure of Ancient Man.* Chicago: University of Chicago Press, 1946. Translated into German under the title *Frühlicht des Geistes.* Urban Bücher, no. 9. Stuttgart: W. Kohlhammer, 1954.

Freedman, D., and P. O'Connor. "יהוה." *TWAT* 3.533-54; *TDOT* 5.500-521.

Fries, H. "Die Offenbarung." Chap. 2 in *Mysterium Salutis: Grundriss heilsgeschichtlicher Dogmatik,* ed. J. Feiner and M. Löhrer, vol. 1. Zürich: Benziger, 1965.

Gabler, J. P. "De justo discrimine theologiae biblicae et dogmaticae regundisque recte ultriusque finibus." In *Kleinere Theologische Schriften,* vol. 2, 179-98. Ulm, 1831.

Gadamer, H.-G. *Truth and Method.* Trans. J. Weinshcheimer and D. G. Marshall. 2d ed. New York: Crossroad, 1990.

Gaston, L. "Abraham and the Righteousness of God." *HBT* 2 (1980): 39-68.

Gerleman, G. "Geist und Geistesgaben im AT." *Die Religion in Geschichte und Gegenwart,* vol. 2, 3rd ed. Tübingen: J. C. B. Mohr, 1958.

Gerstenberger, E. *Psalms, Part I: With an Introduction to Cultic Poetry.* FOTL 14. Grand Rapids: Eerdmans, 1988.

Goshen-Gottstein, M. H. "Christianity, Judaism, and Modern Bible Study." In *Congress Volume, Edinburgh, 1974,* 69-88. VTSup 28. Leiden: E. J. Brill, 1975.

———. "Jewish Biblical Theology and the Study of Biblical Religion." *Tarbiz* 50 (1980/81): 37-64.

Gottwald, N. K. *The Tribes of Yahweh.* New York: Orbis, 1979.

Gunkel, H. *Schöpfung und Chaos in Urzeit und Endzeit.* Göttingen: Vandenhoeck und Ruprecht, 1895.

Gunkel, H., and J. Begrich. *Einleitung in die Psalmen.* 4th ed. 1933. Reprint. Göttingen: Vandenhoeck und Ruprecht, 1984.

Guthrie, H., Jr. *God and History in the Old Testament.* Greenwich: Seabury, 1960.

Haacker, K., et al. *Biblische Theologie heute: Einführung-Beispiele-Kontroversen.* Biblisch-Theologische Studien 1. Neukirchen-Vluyn: Neukirchener Verlag, 1977.

Haag, H. " 'Offenbaren' in der hebräischen Bibel." *TZ* 16 (1960): 251-58.

Hanson, P. *Dynamic Transcendence.* Philadelphia: Fortress, 1978.

Haran, M. "The Divine Presence in the Israelite Cult and the Cultic Institutions." *Bib* 50 (1969): 251-67.

———. *Temples and Temple-Services in Ancient Israel.* Oxford: Clarendon, 1978.

Hasel, G. F. "Biblical Theology: Then, Now, and Tomorrow." *HBT* 4 (June 1982): 61-93.

———. *Old Testament Theology: Basic Issues in the Current Debate.* 4th ed. Grand Rapids: Eerdmans, 1991.

Hayes, J., and F. Prussner. *Old Testament Theology: Its History and Development.* Atlanta: John Knox, 1985.

Heiler, F. *Erscheinungsformen und Wesen der Religion.* Stuttgart: W. Kohlhammer, 1961.

Hermisson, H. J. *Sprache und Ritus im altisraelitischen Kult.* WMANT 19. Neukirchen-Vluyn: Neukirchener Verlag, 1965.

Herrmann, S. "Die Naturlehre des Schöpfungsberichtes." *TLZ* 86 (1961): 413-24.

Hesse, F. *Abschied von der Heilsgeschichte.* Theologische Studien 108. Zürich: Theologischer, 1971.

———. "The Evaluation and the Authority of Old Testament Texts." In *EOTH,* ed. C. Westermann, 285-313. Richmond: John Knox, 1963.

Hulst, A. R. "גוי/עם." *THAT* 2.321.

Jacob, E. *Theology of the Old Testament.* New York: Harper & Row, 1958.

Jenni, E. *Die Theologische Begründung des Sabbatgebotes im Alten Testament.* Theologische Studien 46. Zürich: Evangelischer, 1956.

———. "יהוה." *THAT* 1.701-7.

Jeremias, Jörg. *Theophanie.* WMANT 10. Neukirchen-Vluyn: Neukirchener Verlag, 1965.

Jewett, R. "Spirit." *IDBSup* 839-41.

Kaiser, O. *Introduction to the Old Testament.* Trans. John Sturdy. Minneapolis: Augsburg, 1975.

———. *Die Mythische Bedeutung des Meeres in Ägypten, Ugarit und Israel.* BZAW 78. Berlin: Töpelmann, 1962.

Keller, C. A. *Das Wort OTH als "Offenbarungszeichen Gottes": Eine philologisch-theologische Begriffsuntersuchung zum Alten Testament.* Basel: E. Hoenen, 1946.

Kellerman, D. "גר." *TDOT* 3.439-49.

Kelsey, D. *The Uses of Scripture in Recent Theology.* Philadelphia: Fortress, 1975.

Knierim, R. P. "Criticism of Literary Features, Form, Tradition, and Redaction." In *The Hebrew Bible and Its Modern Interpreters,* ed. D. Knight and G. Tucker, 123-65. Philadelphia: Fortress; Decatur: Scholars Press, 1985.

———. *Die Hauptbegriffe für Sünde im Alten Testament.* Gütersloh: Gerd Mohn, 1965.

———. *Text and Concept in Leviticus 1:1-9: A Case in Exegetical Method.* FAT 2. Tübingen: J. C. B. Mohr, 1992.

———, and G. Tucker, eds. The Forms of Old Testament Literature. 24 vols. Grand Rapids: Eerdmans, 1981-present.

Koch, K. "Wort und Einheit des Schöpfergottes in Memphis und Jerusalem." *ZThK* 62 (1965): 251-93.

Köhler, L. *Old Testament Theology.* Trans. A. S. Todd. Philadelphia: Westminster, 1957.

Kraus, H.-J. *Die Biblische Theologie: Ihre Geschichte und Problematik.* Neukirchen-Vluyn: Neukirchener Verlag, 1970.

———. *Psalms 1–59.* Trans. H. C. Oswald. Minneapolis: Augsburg, 1988.

———. *Psalms 60–150.* Trans. H. C. Oswald. Minneapolis: Augsburg, 1989.

———. "Schöpfung und Weltvollendung." *EvT* 24 (1964): 462-85. Reprinted in *Biblisch Theologische Aufsätze,* 151-78. Neukirchen-Vluyn: Neukirchener Verlag, 1972.

———. *The Theology of the Psalms.* Minneapolis: Augsburg, 1979.

Kühlewein, J. "קרב." *THAT* 2.674-81.

Kümmel, W. G. *The New Testament: The History of the Investigation of Its Prob-*

lems. Trans. S. McLean Gilmer and H. C. Kee. Nashville and New York: Abingdon, 1972. Originally published as *Das Neue Testament — Geschichte der Erforschung seiner Probleme.* 2d ed. (Freiburg and Munich: Karl Alber, 1970).

Lamberty, B. "Natural Cycles in Ancient Israel's View of Reality." Ph.D. diss., Claremont Graduate School, 1986.

Lang, B., and H. Ringgren. "נכרי." *TWAT* 5.454-63.

Leeuw, G. van der. *Phänomenologie der Religion.* Tübingen: J. C. B. Mohr, 1956.

———. *Sakramentales Denken.* Hassel: J. Standa, 1959.

Levine, B. A. "On the Presence of God in Biblical Religion." In *Religions in Antiquity: Essays in Memory of Erwin Ramsdell Goodenough,* ed. Jacob Neusner, 71-87. Studies in the History of Religions 14. Leiden: E. J. Brill, 1968.

Levy-Bruhl, L. *The Soul of the Primitive.* Trans. Lilian Clare. London: George Allen & Unwin, 1965.

Lind, M. *Yahweh Is a Warrior.* Scottdale, Pa.: Herald Press, 1980.

Lindblom, J. "Die Vorstellung vom Sprechen Jahwes zu den Menschen im Alten Testament." *ZAW* 75 (1963): 263-88.

Loretz, O. *Qohelet und der alte Orient.* Freiburg: Herder, 1964.

Luyster, R. "Wind and Water: Cosmogonic Symbolism in the Old Testament." *ZAW* 93 (1981): 1-10.

Maass. F. "אדם." *TWAT* 1.81-94 or *TDOT* 1.75-87.

Mangoldt, G. M. "Morus, Samuel Friedrich Nathanael." *Realencyklopädie für protestantische Theologie und Kirche,* vol. 13, ed. D. Albert Hauck. Leipzig: J. C. Hinrichs, 1903.

McCasland, S. V. "Spirit." *IDB* 4.432-34.

McKenzie, John L., S.J. *Myths and Realities: Studies in Biblical Theology.* Milwaukee: Bruce Publishing Co., 1963.

Meinhold, A. "Überlegungen zur Theologie des 19. Psalms." *ZTK* 80 (1983): 119-36.

Mendenhall, G. E. *The Tenth Generation.* Baltimore: Johns Hopkins University Press, 1973.

Merk, O. *Biblische Theologie des Neuen Testaments in ihrer Anfangszeit.* Marburger Theologische Studien, no. 9. Marburg: N. G. Elwert, 1972.

Milgrom, J. "קרב." *TWAT* 7.161-65.

Misch, G. *A History of Autobiography in Antiquity.* Trans. E. W. Dickes. Cambridge: Harvard University Press, 1951.

Moltmann, J. *Theology of Hope: On the Ground and the Implications of a Christian Eschatology.* Trans. J. W. Leitch. New York: Harper & Row, 1967. Originally published as *Theologie des Hoffnung.* 5th ed. (Munich: Chr. Kaiser, 1965).

Momigliano, A. *The Development of Greek Biography.* Cambridge: Harvard University Press, 1971.

Morenz, S. *Egyptian Religion.* Trans. Ann Keep. Ithaca: Cornell University Press, 1973.

Mowinckel, S. *Religion und Kultus.* Göttingen: Vandenhoeck und Ruprecht, 1953.

Müller, H.-P., and M. Krause. "חכם." *TWAT* 2.920-44 or *TDOT* 4.365-85.

Niebuhr, H. R. *The Meaning of Revelation.* New York: Macmillan, 1941.

Nordheim, E. K. von. "Der grosse Hymnus des Echnaton und Psalm 104. Gott und Mensch im Ägypten der Amarnazeit und in Israel." In *Theologie und Menschenbild,* 51-72. Frankfurt: Peter Lang, 1978.

Nötscher, F. *Das Angesicht Gottes schauen, nach biblischer und babylonischer Auffassung.* 2d ed. Darmstadt: Wissenschaftliche Buchgesellschaft, 1969.

Oepke, A. "καλύπτω." *TDNT* 3.556-92.

Ollenburger, B. C. "Biblical Theology: Situating the Discipline." In *Understanding the Word,* 37-62. JSOTSup 37. Sheffield: JSOT Press, 1985.

Ollenburger, B. C., E. A. Martens, and G. F. Hasel, eds. *The Flowering of Old Testament Theology.* Sources for Biblical and Theological Study, no. 1. Winona Lake, Ind.: Eisenbrauns, 1992.

Olson, D. *The Death of the Old and the Birth of the New: The Framework of the Book of Numbers and the Pentateuch.* Brown Judaic Studies 71. Chico, Calif.: Scholars Press, 1985.

Osswald, E. *Das Bild des Mose in der kritischen alttestamentlichen Wissenschaft seit Julius Wellhausen.* Theologische Arbeiten 18. Berlin: Evangelische Verlagsanstalt, 1962.

Otto, E. *Das Mazzotfest in Gilgal.* BWANT 107. Stuttgart: W. Kohlhammer, 1975.

Otto, E., and T. Schramm. *Festival and Joy.* Trans. J. Blevins. Nashville: Abingdon, 1980.

Pannenberg, W. *Christentum und Mythos.* Gütersloh: Gerd Mohn, 1972.

———. "Hermeneutic and Universal History." In *Basic Questions in Theology,* vol. 1, 96-136. Philadelphia: Fortress, 1971.

———. "Kerygma and History." In *Basic Questions in Theology,* vol. 1, 81-95. Philadelphia: Fortress, 1971.

———. "Redemptive Event and History." In *Basic Questions in Theology,* vol. 1, 15-80. Philadelphia: Fortress, 1971.

———. "Response to the Discussion." In *Theology as History,* trans. W. A. Beardslee, 221-76. NFT, ed. J. M. Robinson and J. B. Cobb, Jr., vol. 3. New York: Harper & Row, 1967.

Pedersen, J. *Israel: Its Life and Culture.* Trans. A. Möller. 2 vols. London: Oxford University Press, 1926.

Perlitt, L. "Die Verborgenheit Gottes." In *Probleme biblischer Theologie,* ed. H. W. Wolff, 376-82. Munich: Chr. Kaiser, 1971.

Ploeg, J. van der. "Une 'Théologie de l'Ancien Testament' est-elle possible?" *ETL* 38 (1963): 417-34.

Plöger, J. G. "אדמה." *TWAT* 1.95-105 or *TDOT* 1.88-98.

Poland, L. *Literary Criticism and Biblical Hermeneutics: A Critique of Formalist Approaches.* American Academy of Religion, Academy Series, no. 48. Chico, Calif.: Scholars Press, 1985.

Pokorny, P. "The Problem of Biblical Theology." *HBT* 15 (June 1993): 83-94.

Porteous, N. W. "Soul." *IDB* 4.428-29.

Pöschl, V. "Autobiographie." *Lexicon der Alten Welt,* 414-17. Zürich/Stuttgart: Artemis, 1965.

Preuss, H. D. "Alttestamentliche Weisheit in christlicher Theologie?" In *Questions Disputées d'Ancien Testament,* ed. C. Brekelsmans, 165-81. BETL 33. Leuven: Leuven University Press, 1974.

———. "Erwägungen zum theologischen Ort alttestamentlicher Weisheitsliteratur." *EvT* 30 (1970): 393-417.

Quell, G. *Wahre und falsche Propheten.* Part 1. BFCT, vol. 46. Gütersloh: Bertelsmann, 1952.

Rad, G. von. "Glaube und Welterkenntnis im alten Israel." In *Gesammelte Studien zum Alten Testament,* vol. 2, 255-66. Munich: Chr. Kaiser, 1973.

———. *Old Testament Theology.* Trans. D. M. G. Stalker. 2 vols. New York: Harper & Row, 1962-65.

———. "Some Aspects of the Old Testament World-View." In *The Problem of the Hexateuch,* trans. E. W. T. Dicken, 144-65. New York: McGraw-Hill, 1966.

———. *Wisdom in Israel.* Nashville: Abingdon, 1972.

———. "οὐρανός/שָׁמַיִם." *TDNT* 5.502-9.

Reed, S. A. *Food in the Psalms.* Ann Arbor, Mich.: University Microfilms International, 1986.

Reicke, B. "χρηματίζω." *TDNT* 9.480-82.

Rendtorff, R. "The Concept of Revelation in Ancient Israel." In *Revelation as History,* ed. W. Pannenberg, trans. D. Granskou, 25-53. New York: Macmillan, 1968.

———. "Geschichte und Wort im Alten Testament." *EvT* 22 (1962): 621-49.

———. *The Old Testament: An Introduction.* Trans. J. Bowden. Philadelphia: Fortress, 1986.

Rengstorf, K. H. "σημαίνω." *TDNT* 7.262-65.

Reventlow, H. G. *Hauptprobleme der alttestamentlichen Theologie im 20. Jahrhundert.* Darmstadt: Wissenschaftliche Buchgesellschaft, 1982.

Ringgren, H. "אלהים." *TWAT* 1.285-305 or *TDOT* 1.267-84.

Robinson, J. M. "The German Discussion of the Later Heidegger." In *The Later Heidegger and Theology,* 3-76. NFT, ed. J. M. Robinson and J. B. Cobb, Jr., vol. 1. New York: Harper & Row, 1963.

———. "The Jesus of the Sayings Gospel Q." Occasional Papers of the Institute for Antiquity and Christianity, no. 28. Claremont, Calif.: Institute for Antiquity and Christianity, 1993.

———. "Revelation as Word and as History." In *Theology as History,* 1-100. NFT, ed. J. M. Robinson and J. B. Cobb, Jr., vol. 3. New York: Harper & Row, 1967.

Rost, L. "Geist." *Biblisch-Historisches Handwörterbuch* 1 (1962): 534-36. Göttingen: Vandenhoeck & Ruprecht.

Sabourin, L. *The Psalms: Their Origin and Meaning*. New York: Alba House, 1974.

Saebø, M. "Johann Philipp Gablers Bedeutung für die Biblische Theologie." *ZAW* 99 (1987): 1-16.

———. "חכם." *THAT* 1.557-67.

Sanders, J. A. *Torah and Canon*. Philadelphia: Fortress, 1972.

Sandys-Wunsch, J., and L. Eldredge. "J. P. Gabler and the Distinction between Biblical and Dogmatic Theology: Translation, Commentary, and Discussion of His Originality." *SJT* 33 (1980): 133-58.

Sasse, H. "γῆ." *TDNT* 1.677-81.

Schmid, H. H. *Gerechtigkeit als Weltordnung*. BHT 40. Tübingen: J. C. B. Mohr, 1968.

———. "Schöpfung, Gerechtigkeit und Heil." *ZTK* 70 (1973): 1-19. Partially translated into English under the title "Creation, Righteousness, and Salvation." In *Creation in the Old Testament,* ed. B. Anderson, trans. B. Anderson and D. Johnson, 102-17. Philadelphia: Fortress, 1984.

———. "אדמה." *THAT* 1.57-60.

———. "ארץ." *THAT* 1.228-36.

Schmidt, H. *Die Psalmen*. HAT 15. Tübingen: J. C. B. Mohr, 1934.

Schmidt, W. H. *Exodus*. BKAT II/3. Neukirchen-Vluyn: Neukirchener Verlag, 1983.

———. "Geist/Heiliger Geist/Geistesgaben, I. Altes Testament." *TRE* 12.170-73.

———. *Die Schöpfungsgeschichte der Priesterschrift*. WMANT 17. Neukirchen-Vluyn: Neukirchener Verlag, 1964.

———. "אלהים." *THAT* 1.153.

Schmitt, G. *Du sollst keinen Frieden schliessen mit den Bewohnern des Landes*. BWANT 91. Stuttgart: W. Kohlhammer, 1970.

Schnutenhaus, F. "Das Kommen und Erscheinen Gottes im Alten Testament." *ZAW* 76 (1964): 1-22.

Schottroff, W. "ידע." *THAT* 1.682-701.

Seebass, H. "נפשׁ." *TWAT* 5.531-55.

Sheppard, G. *Wisdom as a Hermeneutical Construct*. BZAW 151. Berlin: Walter de Gruyter, 1980.

Smend, R. "Johan Philipp Gablers Begründung der biblischen Theologie." *EvT* 22 (July 1962): 345-57.

———. *Das Mosebild von Heinrich Ewald bis Martin Noth*. BGBE 3. Tübingen: J. C. B. Mohr, 1959.

———. "Universalismus und Partikularismus in der Alttestamentlichen Theologie des 19. Jahrhunderts." *EvT* 22 (1962): 169-79.

Snaith, N. "Time in the Old Testament." In *Promise and Fulfillment,* ed. F. F. Bruce, 175-86. Edinburgh: T. & T. Clark, 1963.

Snijders, L. A. "זר." *TDOT* 4.52-58.

Soggin, A. "שמים." *THAT* 2.965-70.

Stähli, H. P. "ירא." *THAT* 1.765-78.

Steck, O. H. *Der Schöpfungsbericht der Priesterschrift.* FRLANT, no. 115. Göttingen: Vandenhoeck und Ruprecht, 1975.

———. *World and Environment.* Biblical Encounter Series. Nashville: Abingdon, 1980.

Stendahl, K., and A. Dulles. "Method in the Study of Biblical Theology." In *The Bible in Modern Scholarship,* ed. J. P. Hyatt, 196-216. Nashville: Abingdon, 1965.

Stoltz, F. *Jahwes und Israels Kriege.* ATANT, vol. 60. Zürich: Theologischer, 1972.

———. "לב." *THAT* 1.861-67.

Sweeney, M. "Isaiah 1–4 and the Post-Exilic Understanding of the Isaianic Tradition." Ph.D. diss., Claremont Graduate School, 1983.

Tillich, P. "Offenbarung." *RGG*[2] 4:654-72 or *RGG*[3] 4:1597-1621.

———. *Religionsphilosophie.* Urban Bücher, no. 63. Stuttgart: W. Kohlhammer, 1962.

———. *Systematic Theology.* Vol. 1. Chicago: University of Chicago Press, 1951.

Utzschneider, H. *Das Heiligtum und das Gesetz.* Göttingen: Vandenhoeck und Ruprecht, 1988.

Van Seters, J. *In Search of History.* New Haven: Yale University Press, 1983.

Vaux, R. de. *Ancient Israel: Its Life and Institutions.* Trans. John McHugh. New York: McGraw Hill, 1961.

———. *The Early History of Israel.* Philadelphia: Westminster, 1978.

———. "Peut-on écrire une 'Theologie de l'Ancien Testament'?" In *Bible et Orient,* 59-71. Paris: du Cerf, 1967.

Vogt, C. F. T. *Morus.* Leipzig: Willhelm Gottlob Sommer, 1792.

Vriezen, Th. C. *Theologie des Alten Testaments in Grundzügen.* Wageningen, Holland: H. Veeman and Zonen, 1956. Translated under the title *An Outline of Old Testament Theology* (Oxford: Basil Blackwell, 1960).

Weiser, A. *The Psalms.* OTL. Trans. H. Hartwell. Philadelphia: Westminster, 1962.

———. "Zur Frage nach den Beziehungen der Psalmen zum Kult: Die Darstellung der Theophanie in den Psalmen und im Festkult." In *Festschrift Alfred Bertholet zum 80, Geburtstag,* ed. W. Baumgartner, O. Eissfeldt, K. Elliger, and L. Rost, 513-31. Tübingen: J. C. B. Mohr, 1950.

Wellhausen, J. *Die Composition des Hexateuchs und der historischen Bücher des Alten Testaments.* 4th ed. Berlin: Walter de Gruyter, 1963.

Westermann, C. *Beginning and End in the Bible.* Trans. K. Crim. Facet Books, Biblical Series 31. Philadelphia: Fortress, 1972.

———. *Blessing in the Bible and the Life of the Church.* Trans. K. Crim. Philadelphia: Fortress, 1978.
———. *Elements of Old Testament Theology.* Trans. D. W. Stott. Atlanta: John Knox, 1982.
———. *Genesis 1–11: A Commentary.* Trans. John J. Scullion. Minneapolis: Augsburg, 1984.
———. *Praise and Lament in the Psalms.* Trans. K. Crim and R. Soulen. Atlanta: John Knox, 1981.
———. "נפשׁ." *THAT* 2.71-96.
———. "אדם." *THAT* 1.41-57.
Widengren, Geo. *Religionphänomenologie.* Berlin: Walter de Gruyter, 1969.
Wolff, H. W. *Anthropology of the Old Testament.* Trans. M. Kohl. Philadelphia: Fortress, 1974.
———. "Das Kerygma des Jahwisten." *EvT* 24 (1964): 73-98. Reprinted in *Gesammelte Studien zum Alten Testament,* 345-47. München: Chr. Kaiser, 1964.
———. " 'Wissen um Gott' bei Hosea als Urform von Theologie." In *Gesammelte Studien zum Alten Testament,* 182-205. Munich: Chr. Kaiser, 1964.
Wolff, H. W., and W. Pannenberg. "Schwerter zu Pflugscharen — Missbrauch eines Propheten wortes?" *EvT* 44 (1984): 280-97.
Wright, G. E. *The Old Testament and Theology.* New York: Harper & Row, 1969.
Yeivin, Sh. *The Israelite Conquest of Canaan.* Istanbul: Nederlands Historisch-Archaeologisch Instituut, 1971.
Zimmerli, W. "Biblical Theology." Trans. U. Mauser. *HBT* 4 (June 1982): 95-130.
———. "I Am Yahweh." In *I Am Yahweh,* trans. D. W. Stott, 1-28. Atlanta: John Knox, 1982.
———. "Knowledge of God according to the Book of Ezekiel." In *I Am Yahweh,* trans. D. W. Stott, 29-98. Atlanta: John Knox, 1982.
———. " 'Offenbarung' im Alten Testament: Ein Gespräch mit R. Rendtorff." *EvT* 22 (1962): 15-31.
———. *Old Testament Theology in Outline.* Atlanta: John Knox, 1978.
———. "The Word of Divine Self-Manifestation (Proof-Saying): A Prophetic Genre." In *I Am Yahweh,* trans. D. W. Stott, 99-110. Atlanta: John Knox, 1982.

Index of Authors

Index of Subjects

Index of Scripture Passages

Old Testament

New Testament

Extrabiblical

Index of Hebrew and Greek Terms

Hebrew

Greek